THE BEHAVIORAL BASIS OF DESIGN

COMMUNITY DEVELOPMENT SERIES

Series Editor: Richard P. Dober, AIP

Volumes Published and in Preparation

CDS/28

THE BEHAVIORAL BASIS OF DESIGN Book 1 : Selected Papers

PETER SUEDFELD and JAMES A. RUSSELL

General Editors

Lawrence M. Ward, Stanley Coren,
Andrew Gruft, and John B. Collins

Book 1 Editors

Proceedings
of the
Seventh International Conference
of the
Environmental Design Research Association
Vancouver, British Columbia, Canada

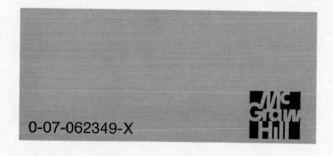

0-07-062349-X

EDRA AND THE SOCIAL IMPERATIVE

Don Conway, AIA
Chairperson, EDRA, Inc.

What a remarkable set of circumstances it was that brought Henry Sanoff, Ray Studer, Sid Cohn and a few other stray souls together in the late 1960's to create EDRA. Remarkable, it seems to me, because if one had attempted to chart the course of EDRA and the changes in American society from that date in the 1960's to today, with the intent of making the values of EDRA and Society join up in space/time, as it were, it would have seemed an impossible undertaking indeed. And yet, as I view things, this fragile meeting in time has taken place.

Consider, for a moment, some of the changes that have happened in Society at large. The decentralization of authority and decision making. The "back to the land movement" and the emigration from large urban centers to medium and small cities. The coming of the Second American Revolution, brought on perhaps by the Bicentennial, but with us today, nevertheless. The "anti-bigness movement" so eloquently espoused by E.F. Schumacher in his fast rising classic, SMALL IS BEAUTIFUL: ECONOMICS AS IF PEOPLE MATTERED. The rise of consumerism. Examples come to mind in a continous stream.

The point seems clear. The direction that society's values have taken has been nicely summarized by the prediction that, "The last third of the 20th Century - the post industrial revolution period - will see society concerning itself first and foremost with the welfare and well-being of the individual person. Nationalism, industrial empires, even religion will take a secondary position to this overwhelming concern for the individual."

And in the areas of design and the man-built environment isn't this same concern for the individual person the basic motivation behind environmental design research? Aren't the psycho-social consequences of good and bad design decisions in terms of the individual person what EDRA is really all about? I think so.

If the convergence of Society's values and EDRA's values that I am claiming has occurred is correct, then it is not too far fetched to say that a social imperative exists for environmental design research.

If this is the case, then it might be useful to think about the future for a bit and I can think of no better theme than the theme for the EDRA 7 conference - "BEYOND THE APPLICABILITY GAP: THE BEHAVIOURAL BASIS OF DESIGN".

What should EDRA's role be in the future - in the last third of the 20th Century, if you will? What posture should EDRA and its members assume to maintain the growing concern for the welfare of the individual in the built environment? How can EDRA and its members use their prime resource - knowledge - to bring about change in design decision making for the benefit of the individual person?

Several paths seem to be open. The first, and most obvious is for EDRA to simply do more of the same, which is to say to restrict itself to one conference a year and one set of proceedings, with the hope that somehow this will bring about change. To me, this just doesn't seem to be enough, particularly when I look back and try to see how change has been brought about in the built environment due to EDRA conferences and EDRA proceedings. Enough said, I think.

A second pathway open to EDRA and its members is to take on the role of educator. By this, I mean a series of out-reach efforts, in which EDRA members consciously undertake a series of activities (and the form isn't important, they can be workshops, lectures, TV spots or whatever) whose intent is to educate people outside of the research community on the issues addressed and knowledge gained through environment design research.

The third pathway I see for EDRA members is that of a resource. This role would have EDRA members aggressively making themselves known and available to design decision makers as a knowledge and skill resource to be applied to man-environment design problems. In effect, this would mean that some academicians would have to consciously divert their energies from research into practice.

Finally, I see a fourth pathway in the area of policy, regulation and the courts. In this role I see EDRA members zeroing in on policy and legislation at both the national and state levels and using the knowledge gained through man-environment research to shape, influence and change policy and legislation. In a similar fashion regulatory bodies such as the model building codes and zoning authorities could well benefit from EDRA knowledge. In the courts I see man-environment research coming to bear on issues such as jails (for which there is already some precedent), housing and mental health facilities -- probably in the form of class actions -- again with the intent of bringing about changes in these environments for the benefit of the individual person.

Whatever form the future roles of EDRA and its members may take to respond to the social imperative that I have claimed exists, one thing seems abundantly clear - the ball is in our court.

Society will not come looking for EDRA. Each of us must decide on a future course of action and then act upon our decision.

THE PUBLICATIONS OF EDRA-7

Françoise Szigeti
Gerald Davis

Publications Coordinators

EDRA Publications have had two main functions:

-Disseminate a selection of theoretical and research papers, and of reports on design applications; and,

-Record the actual content of the annual conferences of EDRA.

In some years, the conference chairmen have, in the publications, emphasized one or the other aspect, while a few chairmen have chosen to make explicit the two distinct, and different publication functions. EDRA-7 returns to the pattern used for EDRA-4, in which Book One contains mainly a selection of formal papers and Book Two records the Invited Papers, and the symposia and other participation sessions.

All of the formal papers in Book One have been approved by the refereeing committee and by the co-chairmen, both for publication prior to EDRA-7, and for discussion at specially scheduled sessions during EDRA-7. This Book One was sent to the publishers on February 17, 1976, so that the bound copies could be distributed to purchasers when they register at Vancouver on May 25. A few additional formal papers have been approved for publication, but were not available in camera-ready form when the material was assembled for the publisher; these additional papers will be included in Book Two, to be published some months after EDRA-7.

The symposia and other participation sessions, provide a survey of the "state of the art" in environmental design research, bridging and application at the time of the conference. The discussions, debates, and challenges, the sharing of experiences and development of new concensus occur during the conference. They cannot therefore be published in advance. We have included in this Book One only a brief summary of those sessions for which we had information at mid-February. Readers thus have a sense of what EDRA-7 is expected to discuss, and a listing of many of the participants scheduled in formal sessions. The conveners and participants in these sessions have been asked to prepare synthesis of the discussions, and of the main presentations, for inclusion in Book Two.

The co-chairmen of EDRA-7 have invited three distinguished speakers to address the conference, and have arranged for four theme symposia to discuss basic aspects of the conference theme. These sessions are described in Book One, and will be published in Book Two.

THE PUBLICATIONS OF PRIOR EDRA CONFERENCES

The publications of all prior EDRA conferences are now available for purchase. The Board of The Environmental Design Research Association, Inc., has arranged with Dowden, Hutchinson and Ross for the re-publication of the several volumes which had gone out-of-print. All except the publications of EDRA-3 may now be ordered from Dowden, Hutchinson and Ross at the following address:

Dowden, Hutchinson and Ross
Box 699
Stroudsburg, Pa., 18360
U.S.A.

Prior EDRA conference publications available through Dowden, Hutchinson and Ross include:

EDRA-1
H. Sanoff and S. Cohn, editors
pp 384. 1970

EDRA-2
J. Archea and C. Eastman, editors
pp 408. 1970

ENVIRONMENTAL DESIGN RESEARCH, Volume 1 and Volume II. EDRA-4
W.F.E. Preiser, Editor
pp 1120. 1973

MAN-ENVIRONMENT INTERACTIONS: Evaluations and Applications. EDRA-5
D.H. Carson, Editor
pp 1524. 1974

RESPONDING TO SOCIAL CHANGE. EDRA-6
B. Honikman, editor
pp 320. 1975

The publications of EDRA-3 were issued by the University of California, and may be obtained through:
Don Conway, AIA, Director of Research Programs
American Institute of Architects
1735 New York Avenue N.W.
Washington, D.C., 20006
U.S.A.
(Only a limited number of copies of this publication remain.)

ENVIRONMENTAL DESIGN: Research and Practice, Volume I and Volume II. EDRA-3
William J. Mitchell, editor
1972

EDRA-7 AND ITS FOCUS

Peter Suedfeld and James A. Russell
Co-Chairmen, EDRA-7

Environmental Psychology Programme
University of British Columbia

The seventh annual meeting of the Environmental Design Research Association, held in Vancouver, British Columbia, May 25-28, 1976, is simultaneously another step forward in a line established through a brief but vigorous tradition, and a novel departure from the past. For some years now, EDRA has combined a major focus on the design arts and sciences with a growing interest in the social and behavioural bases of design. In past conferences, there has been a growing emphasis on the need for architects and planners to incorporate relevant contributions from the social sciences in their work. Nevertheless, in EDRA as in the field as a whole, this synthesis has been more talked about than realized. While the number of papers by environmental psychologists, sociologists and economists has grown, the basic research in these fields has not been extensively translated into actual buildings or communities.

At first, this did not seem to matter much. The empirical data base was fairly small, the need for rapid decisions on the part of designers very great; and no one could complain if the latter did not perceive much usefulness in the former. A few years ago, the editor of an architectural journal wrote that there was usually no pressing reason why architects should not pay attention to the work of behavioural and social scientists. The very fact that this point of view was then a relatively enlightened one, and had to be stated specifically to the readership, tells us something about the relationship between the disciplines not too long ago. EDRA has done much to remedy this situation. It has brought together people from the two areas, and given them a chance to listen to and talk with each other. It has also emphasized the need for a broad integration of basic research and application. For example, the relevance of social research to the planning of environmental change was discussed in Basil Honikman's introductory comments to the EDRA 6 Proceedings.

The theme for EDRA 7 is thus a new but logical outgrowth of a relatively long-standing concern. "Beyond the Applicability Gap: The Behavioural Basis of Design" specifically identifies the position that the conference organizers wished to emphasize. That is, the issue is no longer whether the two lines of approach should be integrated, nor whether they can be integrated. We have even gone beyond the next question, how the integrations should be done. This conference was to focus on actual syntheses of behavioural and social science research on the one hand and the creative design and use of environments on the other.

In other ways, this conference has been a departure from previous ones. Quite appropriately in view of the theme, this is the first time that the conference is being sponsored and organized primarily by a group whose identification is with behavioural science rather than with design: the Environmental Psychology Programme in the Department of Psychology at the University of British Columbia.

Environmental psychology is a relatively new specialization, and represents the interaction between basic and applied work in the discipline. New concepts, such as human territoriality, developed from experimental research, become important considerations in the design of work and residential environments; real-life problems, such as those arising from crowding or from environmental monotomy, lead to laboratory work that increases the understanding of basic psychological processes and in turn feeds back into planning and architecture. Environmental psychology draws widely upon other areas within the discipline to answer a great variety of questions at many levels of control and abstraction. It is gratifying that EDRA has acknowledged its contributions by selecting us to be the host institution for the 1976 conference.

Not only is the environmental psychology programme at the University of British Columbia a new one, it is the first and so far the only one of its type in Canada. It is therefore particularly pleasing that, in another departure from tradition, we are able to welcome the first EDRA conference to be held outside the United States. There is a clear recognition that the concerns of EDRA are not restricted to any one nation, and that important work in environmental design and research is going on around the world. Vancouver's location has encouraged greater participation than had been possible in the past from workers in the Pacific rim countries as well as in the rest of North America.

The international nature of the endeavour is underscored by the fact that this conference is being held immediately prior to Habitat '76, the United Nations Conference on Human Settlements, which is also meeting in Vancouver. The opportunity for EDRA members to interact with people attending the larger United Nations meeting, and vice-versa, is an important extra attraction. In addition, the magnificent natural surroundings and the varied characteristics of the built environment of Vancouver and vicinity, are both enjoyable and professionally interesting to those attending the meetings.

Perhaps a reflection of the simultaneously
evolutionary and novel aspects of EDRA 7, we
received a very large number of submitted papers,
a high proportion of which were quite interesting
and well done. After a harrowing review procedure
(harrowing for both the authors and the Programme
Committee), those judged to be excellent both
methodologically and substantively, besides being
of wide interest within EDRA, were selected for
inclusion in the current volume. Many others are
being presented in informal sessions at the
conference itself, with the hope that they will
be disseminated through other publications or the
"invisible college".

ACKNOWLEDGEMENTS

As co-chairmen of the conference, we are grate-
ful to the Programme Committee and to the many
reviewers who contributed to the selection of
the papers included here.

CONTENTS

PART 1

Refereed Papers

This year, EDRA is able to present a highly selected and carefully reviewed set of papers for presentation and publication. Each paper submitted was reviewed by members of the Planning Committee and at least one outside, independent reviewer. Of the many fine papers submitted, less than one-third were finally selected in this way. The large number of paper submissions, which made this selection process possible, is a sign of the vigour of the environmental design research field. An even better sign, of course, is the excellence of the papers included here.

The papers are organized in four general sections. The first section, entitled "Bridging and Theory," sets the context for bridging the applicability gap between behavioural science and design implementation. These papers explore the theoretical basis for interaction between the spheres of research and application. They also discuss some of the problems encountered and those directions that seem to be most profitable.

The second section, entitled "Environmental Perception and Cognition," provides examples of behavioural research, its methodologies, and the data that it can provide. These papers deal with the most basic processes of man-environment interaction: perception of the molar environment, aesthetic responses, emotional responses, or, more generally, the way in which people process information from environmental settings.

The third section, entitled "Environment and Behaviour", explores the social and behavioural impact of various environmental interventions. Here we begin to see the complex interactions of the built and natural environment with the patterns of behaviour, social interaction, and quality of life, which are dependent on them.

The final section, entitled "Design Research and Evaluation" returns to the bridging theme with specific attempts at applying basic research to design problems. This section nicely demonstrates ways in which behavioural science theory, research, and methodology contribute to all the stages of the design process, and ways in which design and planning schemes can be evaluated by their effect on the quality of life and well-being of those individuals who are the ultimate users.

SECTION 1

Bridging and Theory

The EDRA-7 theme, "Beyond the Applicability Gap," stimulated a timely examination of the ways in which the behavioural and social sciences are now being and can be applied to design problems. In the first paper we present, Francescato, Weidermann, Anderson, and Chenoweth, argue that while it is useful to be optimistic about an eventual bridging of the gap between research and design, excessive optimism about progress already accomplished may be harmful. Before we can be beyond the gap, they argue, we need both more rigorous, relevant research and more systematic, accountable design. And, they correctly emphasize, we especially need a valid theoretical framework that links human behaviour to its environmental context. The remaining papers in this section consider specific theoretical issues, and thus implicitly support the thesis that theory plays a necessary role in bridging.

In the next paper, Wandersman proposes one such theoretical framework and discusses its implications for the phases of the design process: programming, design, construction, use, and evaluation. Any such broad theorizing is likely to arouse a good amount of controversy. Two of

Wandersman's more controversial proposals are that social science theory should be used to determine the goals or values for a design (and not merely the means to these ends), and that Carl Roger's humanism, B.F. Skinner's behaviourism, and Walter Mischel's social learning theory can be combined in a single framework.

Farbstein is also looking for a valid theoretical framework, but does so by making explicit the assumptions held by programmers. He then discusses how these assumptions can (and indeed must) be clarified, expanded, and empirically studied to yield such a theory, which, in turn, can be implemented in design.

Duffey-Armstrong and Kroll discuss research needs and implementation problems (i.e., the gap) in the specific area of aesthetics. Public agencies, they point out, often ignore the public's aesthetic concern--despite both the available techniques for evaluating the aesthetics of an environment and the important role that aesthetics play in personal and social well-being. Parenthetically, it has been argued elsewhere that designers' concern for aesthetic form conflicts with their concern for exerting a beneficial influence on the users' behaviour. In fact, behavioural science research suggests that there is no conflict, that the aesthetic quality of an environment is an important and beneficial influence on behavior.

In the next paper, Harman and Betak look not so much at the theory involved in bridging but at the type of data required. They describe three ways that a programmer may infer the "needs" of the user: first, by questioning the actual users; second, by observing the users' behaviour; and third, by inferring the needs from his own preconceptions or from social science theory, that is, without collecting any data from the actual users. Using the design of residential environments as an example, they detail some of the problems encountered when using the first method, specifically problems in translating users' verbal statements into design solutions.

Gruft and Gutstein do present a theoretical model, a model of urban development that concentrates on the decision-making process. Interestingly, of the papers in this section, theirs is the only one presenting a theory that deals with the effects of behaviour on environments, rather than environments on behaviour. They also discuss some methodological difficulties involved in modelling urban problems, such as including public discontent as a factor within the model and in using the case-study as a source of empirical data.

Relevant theoretical issues in psychology are examined in a final set of three papers. Cohen shows how stress research provides a useful theoretical framework for describing a large number of man-environment relations. Wiesenthal and Buchalter review studies of crowding, emphasizing environ-

mental mediators for social behaviour. And Hill discusses theoretical issues in the literature on human use of space. He criticizes the use of propinquity as an explanatory concept and concludes that designers should look to the social sciences for "insights" (ideas to be tried) rather than for precise formulations.

Are we beyond the applicability gap? The papers in this section imply that, indeed, there is no longer a need to discuss whether design and behavioural science can or even should be integrated. A question has been raised whether there now exists an adequate integration, but there is a general consensus on how the integration will come about: namely, an empirically validated theory that links environment to behaviour. These papers have begun the real task of building that theory by proposing and examining relevant concepts and the propositions that link those concepts. Of course, the designer is more concerned--and rightly so--with obtaining assistance on solutions to his current design problems than he is with developing a comprehensive theory. He can, as Hill points out, continue to view the behavioural sciences as a source of hypotheses to try out. But it is also important to appreciate the role that theory plays both within the behavioural sciences and in their implementation in design. For the behavioural scientist, a theory integrates diverse experimental findings and indicates which variables should be explored in further experiments, which variables must be controlled in these experiments, and which ones can be safely ignored. For the designer, a theory provides predictions for design problems that have not been the object of specific research. It is through theory that, for example, the designer can anticipate the impact of proposed novel designs before they are actually implemented.

IMPOSSIBLE DREAMS, UNREALIZABLE HOPES?

Guido Francescato, Sue Weidemann, James
Anderson, Richard Chenoweth

Housing Research and Development Program
University of Illinois
1204 W. Nevada
Urbana, IL 61801, U.S.A.

ABSTRACT

While it is useful to be optimistic about the
possibility of bridging the gap between research
and design, excessive optimism about progress
actually accomplished may be counterproductive.
Relevance and rigor in research and systematicity and accountability in design are postulated
as the preconditions for successful application
of research findings. The need and role of man-
environment theory in this process are also discussed.

There would not be an Environmental Design Research Association if we, its members, did not
believe that there is a need to generate design
relevant information through social and behavioral research. And in particular we would not
have EDRA 7 if we did not feel optimistic about
the prospects of meeting this need. Optimism
is welcome in any field of endeavor. Surely it
is most needed in the design field at the present
time when there is considerable doubt about the
degree to which designed environments fulfill
human needs and expectations (Norberg-Schulz,
1965). However, optimism must have its roots
firmly planted in the ground of the realistically possible; otherwise, it inevitably results
in rising expectations beyond the threshold of
what is obtainable.

What needs to be stressed is that if designers'
expectations are not met--and most surely they
will not be if unrealistically inflated--de-
signers will ignore research findings and will
fall back on uninformed judgment. The potential
contribution of the social and behavioral
sciences to the solution of environmental design
problems will have been thwarted. Disillusion-
ment of this kind would not be new. It occurred
in other fields as a result of overoptimistic
expectations about research coupled to unjusti-
fied depreciation of traditional practice (e.g.
Campbell and Stanley, 1969).

The design professions, and architecture in
particular, have a history of succumbing to the
temptation of employing slogans to describe
complex phenomena. A slogan is relatively
easily invented and remembered; it has a sufficient halo of ambiguity which permits it to mean
different things to different people; but above
all a slogan gives the impression that we have

grasped the essence of the phenomenon to which it
applies. In most cases, alas, this grasp is
illusory. So we have grown to mistrust such
utterances as "form follows function," "less is
more," "God is in the detail," etc. But just
when it seemed that we were ready to shun slogan-
ized oversimplifications, the "applicability
gap" appeared.

As long as this phrase is meant to remind us
that design is a practical activity, thus concerned with applicable knowledge, the "applicability gap" is not only a harmless slogan--it
may be useful. It gives researchers a target to
pursue and designers a criterion with which to
evaluate research results, albeit a target and a
criterion extremely ill defined. Recently, however, a tendency has been growing to single out
the "applicability gap" as the basic problem
facing environmental design research. Considerable amount of time was spent on the subject at
the last three EDRA conferences, and at other
similar gatherings. The Journal of Architectural
Research (1975) recently devoted an editorial to
this theme. Now EDRA 7 seems to invite us to
add unfounded optimism to oversimplification by
suggesting, via its official theme, not only that
there is an "applicability gap," but that we
have bridged this elusive chasm and are, in fact,
"beyond" it.

We submit that the adoption of this slogan ceases
to be harmless because it stands in the way of
the thoughtful discourse that is necessary among
designers and researchers, and between the two
groups, if expectations about environmental design research are ever to be fulfilled. These
expectations are high, and so are the difficulties inherent in attempting to meet them. The
discourse that we need is one that, without

falling into despair, will identify and define these difficulties and suggest realistic ways of overcoming them.

On the side of research we need a discourse based on the postulate that the road to applicability starts from the rigor with which a study was conducted. A rigorous study is one in which the problem to be investigated is sharply formulated, the research strategy is appropriate to the problem and its context, the measurement instruments yield reliable and valid data, the analytical procedures are adequate to uncover the relationships under study, and the conclusions are tested against alternative explanations and related to critical initial assumptions (Runkel and McGrath, 1972). It must be stressed that whereas it is possible to draw faulty inferences from rigorously collected and analyzed data it is highly improbable that valid inferences can be made on the basis of data which is inherently unreliable and invalid. Of conclusions based on such data one cannot even start asking questions of applicability, since the amount of confidence that can be placed on these conclusions is certainly as low, or lower, than that which can be placed on intuitive uninformed generalizations. To be sure, research rigor is a necessary but not sufficient condition for the applicability of research findings. Rigorous research can fail to advance our knowledge (and thus fail to be applicable), but in such cases the failure will be explicit and identifiable and the design practitioner therefore warned.

Rigorous research that produces findings on which confidence can be placed also produces new knowledge. Perhaps it is not widely perceived in the design field that knowledge is always applicable, though not necessarily always applied. A number of obstacles to the application of knowledge have been mentioned in the literature. Excessive and inappropriate use of impenetrable jargon in research reports has been criticized frequently (e.g. Deasy, 1975). Presentation of findings in a numerical/verbal, rather than visual/verbal, mode has been cited as a barrier thrown in the path of the presumably visually thinking designer (e.g. Dean, 1975). The organization of research in institutions such as universities, with restricted contacts with the world of practice is also seen as an obstacle between researcher and practitioner. A closer relationship of active cooperation between these two groups would perhaps enable them to approach problems from the same premises (e.g., Journal of Architectural Research, 1975).

No doubt these are all valid reasons for the lack of application of research findings. One should, however, approach with caution the suggestion that a great deal can be done to overcome such obstacles. For example, what is often regarded as jargon by designers may be seen as usefully precise and univocal terminology by researchers. Contrary to popular opinion, common English is not always the best choice when dealing with the communication of precise concepts and operations.

For instance, the concept of reliability, when it refers to measures and research strategies (as in this paper), has a specific meaning which is not quite the same as the meaning one finds in the dictionary. Likewise, progress can be made in presenting data and conclusions in a visual and easily comprehensible manner, but there is a limit to how far one can go in this direction before one loses the precision afforded by numerical values. Finally, there are known practical reasons of considerable weight for the organization of research in universities and similar institutions, reasons which will undoubtedly persist even though they may militate against closer contacts between researchers and practitioners.

On the side of design, we need a discourse which posits that application of research findings requires systematicity and accountability in the design process. This may be, at the present time, an unpopular position. After all it was Christopher Alexander who stood in front of a packed house at EDRA 6 (1975) to repeat the essence of his hand wringing statement of 1971 about design methods: "I would say forget it, forget the whole thing" (Alexander, 1971, p. 3). And it was Christopher Jones, whose book Design Methods (1970) bore the ambitious and dramatic subtitle "Seeds of human futures," who, in response to an EDRA 4 invitation, delivered an imaginary conversation between EDRA, Graham Stevens, Jung, Kant, and Walt Whitman, clearly meant to emphasize the confusing, puzzling, randomly conflicting--in one word, non-systematic --aspects of design.

Perhaps it was inevitable that, after the initial euphoria generated by the rosy promises of design methodology, the sober realization of the modest progress achieved thus far should precipitate this kind of reaction. Perhaps this backlash may even be useful if it serves to demonstrate the patent absurdity of modeling design as an algorithmic activity amenable to total explicitness and proceeding along orderly and completely predictable decision lines. The arguments brought against systematization of the design process seem to us, nevertheless, rather untenable.

One argument, of course, is the old spurious dichotomy between creativity, seen as an inalienable prerogative of the designer, and systematicity seen as a threat to that prerogative. Those who postulate this conflict, in our view, are simply covering up for the fact that they hold socially obsolete views of the designers as an artist unbound by the needs, requirements, and aspirations of those for whom he designs. As Don Conway has put it "architects have failed to explicitly and systematically address the issue of users response, and that is largely explained by architects' preoccupation with esthetics. Humanistic rhetoric notwithstanding, being an artist seems to come first, with everything else being secondary, at least for architects who regard themselves as primarily 'creative'" (Conway, 1975).

Another argument is that, so far, all attempts to design in a systematic manner have failed to produce buildings that are superior to those designed in a "traditional," or non-methodical, way (Alexander, 1971, p. 4; Hillier, et al., 1972). Apart from the fact that such statements, usually uttered without the benefits of supporting evidence, are debatable, they would fail to corroborate the argument even if correct. Systematicity and utilization of realible and valid information will never guarantee success in design. It has been affirmed that systematic design methods set out "to eliminate the risk involved in the relationship between an object and the value it holds" (Jones, 1975). But systematicity in design should not be aimed at this (unobtainable) objective. It would be quite a progress over the present state of affairs if we could only increase the likelihood of reducing the risk! In our view, the central problem of design systematization is a problem of prediction. Not only does the designer need to know how the various user groups "will comprehend and use the buildings he designs" (Hershberger and Cass, 1975), but he also needs to make predictions--as accurate as possible predictions-- about the actual, real-world performance of his design proposals. Which brings us back to the issue of research applicability since it is in the area of prediction where research--and particularly research on environments in use-- may be most helpful. (The operative word here is helpful, as opposed to more grandiose expectations of guaranteed success.)

Finally, a discourse about application of research to design must emphasize the role of theory in providing structure--and thus meaning --to the questions of practice and to the findings of research. It has lately become fashionable in some quarters to attribute to environmental design researchers naive paradigms of a positivistic hue. Thus we are warned against placing confidence in "case studies bursting with data" and against the "santification of research" (Robbins et al., 1975), against the "silly (but pervasive) idea that the outcome of research is 'knowledge'" [sic] (Hillier, et al., 1972), or against taking a "narrow view of what constitutes 'evidence'" (Sharples and Johnson, 1974).

While these authors seem to imply that they are the only one ever to have heard of Popper and Kuhn, and while their somewhat truculent prose seems slightly on the overkill side, nevertheless they do have a point to make. The point, of course, is that applications seldom, if ever, directly follow from data. Data, even reliable and valid data, is useful only inasmuch as it permits us to make inferences from it. In turn, inferences must be brought together in sets of hypotheses and the hypotheses must be organized in a theoretical framework before research findings can be applied in any meaningful way to real-world design situations.

Thus, for example, Hillier (1972) did not need

to explain the "deterioration in the acceptability of the designed product...in the UK...in spite of two decades of excellent [research] work, well disseminated in intelliglbe form" by reference to somewhat esoteric problems in philosophy of science. Apart from the fact that not all will agree with Hillier's positive evaluation of the quality of that research (e.g., Hole, 1974), a simpler question could have been asked: were the findings of these studies organized in a theoretical framework linking buildings to people and attempting to give a conceptual explanation for the behavior of this environment- people system? The answer, in our view, is clearly "no."

The fact is that whether one proceeds in an inductive mode, constructing usable guesses on the basis of data, or deductively, using empirical evidence to corroborate a set of hypotheses, the need for a conceptual frame of reference remains. Altman (1973) and Rapoport (1973) have discussed both the need for man/environment theory and the present state of its development. Even a cursory reading of these two papers would clearly demonstrate the complexity of the field as well as the magnitude of the task that remains to be accomplished. Any notion that we are "beyond" anything--whether "gap" or other problem--would be quickly dispelled at this point.

In conclusion, we have attempted to put forth the notion that the state of the art in environmental design research does not warrant the excessively optimistic assessment that we are "beyond the applicability gap." We have also postulated that competent research is relevant and rigorous and that competent design is systematic and accountable. Further, we have suggested that the bridge over the gap will be built mainly on theory.

It seems to us that considerable progress along these lines has indeed been accomplished since EDRA 1 and we feel that, by pursuing rigor, systematicity and theory, EDRA has an important role to play in the future if it accepts Kenneth Craik's (1970) remark that:

> the magnitude of the methodological and empirical groundwork that must be established as the basis for a mature branch of research makes it imperative to think in terms of decades rather than months or years, and makes it incumbent upon behavioral scientists to be humble in their advice and proclamations as well as incumbent upon environmental planners and designers to be patient in their expectations.

Otherwise, we may all collectively climb the ladder of impossible dreams and unrealizable hopes.

References

ALEXANDER, CHRISTOPHER. ["Interview with Max Jacobson"] DMG Newsletter, March 1971.

ALTMAN, IRWIN. "Some Perspectives on the Study of Man-Environment Phenomena" in Preiser, Wolfgang F. E. (ed.), Environmental Design Research, Stroudsburg, Penna., 1973, Vol. II, pp. 99-113.

CAMPBELL, DONALD T. and STANLEY, JULIAN C. Experimental and Quasi Experimental Designs for Research, Chicago, 1969.

CRAIK, KENNETH H. "The Comprehension of the Everyday Physical Environment," in Proshanski, Harold M., Ittelson, William H., and Rivlin, Leanne G., Environmental Psychology, New York, 1970.

CONWAY, DON, in Dean, Andrea O., "Examining the Nature and Values of the Endangered Species Architect," AIA Journal, 64, 3, Sept. 1975, p. 23.

DEAN, ANDREA O. "Examining the Nature and Values of the Endangered Species Architect," AIA Journal, 64, 3, Sept. 1975, p. 24.

DEASY, C. M. "Psychology and the Built Environment," AIA Journal, 64, 3, Sept. 1975, p.46.

EDITORIAL, Journal of Architectural Research, 4, 1, Feb. 1975, p. 3.

HERSHBERGER, ROBERT G. and CASS, ROBERT C. "Predicting User Responses to Buildings," in Carson, Daniel H. (ed.), Man-Environment Interactions: Evaluations and Applications, EDRA, Inc., 1974, part 4, p. 118.

HILLIER, BILL; MUSGROVE, JOHN; and O'SULLIVAN, PAT, "Knowledge and Design," in Mitchell, William J. (ed.), Environmental Design: Research and Practice, Univ. of California, 1972, Vol. II, p. 29-3-3.

HOLE, VERE. "Homes in High Flats: Some of the Human Problems Involved in Multi-storey Housing, by P. Tephcott," Journal of Architectural Research 3, 2, May '74, p. 57.

JONES, J. CHRISTOPHER, Design Methods, New York, 1970.

NORBERG-SCHULZ, CHRISTIAN. Intentions in Architecture, Cambridge, Mass., 1965.

RAPOPORT, AMOS. "An Approach to the Construction of Man-Environment Theory," in Preiser, Wolfgang F. E. (ed.), Environmental Design Research, Stroudsburg, Penna., 1973, Vol. II, p. 124-135.

ROBBINS, EDWARD; PYATOK, MICHAEL; THOMSON, THOMAS L.; and WEBER, HANNO. "Who Minds What Matters? An Epilogue," The

Application of Systematic Methods to Designing (Proceedings of DMG 3), Part 3, pp. 377-83, Berkely, California, 1975.

RUNKEL, PHILIP J. and MCGRATH, JOSEPH E. Research on Human Behavior, New York, 1972.

SHARPLES, S. and JOHNSON J. "A Critical Look at the Concept of User Requirements: The Example of a Scottish New Town," in The Impact of Research on the Built Environment, CIB 6th Congress, Budapest, 1974.

APPLYING HUMANISM, BEHAVIORISM, AND A BROADER SOCIAL DEVELOPMENTAL VIEW TO UNDERSTANDING AND RESEARCHING THE DESIGN PROCESS

ABRAHAM WANDERSMAN*

*Center for Community Studies
 George Peabody College
 Nashville, Tennessee 37203

ABSTRACT

This paper describes two gaps which have inhibited the development of building more habitable environments: the gap between planner and social scientist and the gap between planner and user. The perspectives of humanism, behaviorism, and a broader social developmental view (incorporating theory from life history, sociology, behavioral ecology, and social learning theory) are described and implications for what types of environments are best suited for people are drawn. These perspectives are then applied to the design process to suggest research in the areas of (1) goals of environmental designs, (2) planning processes, (3) construction, (4) use, and (5) evaluation, with the aim of narrowing the gaps.

1.0. INTRODUCTION

A major goal of the Environmental Design and Research Association (EDRA) is to bring together planners and social scientists who are interested in building more habitable environments for people. In the opening presentation to EDRA 6, Christopher Alexander, an architect, suggested that perhaps EDRA should disband, on the grounds that there had not been substantial progress toward the EDRA goal of building better environments. In this paper, I will briefly argue that there are two important gaps which inhibit the accomplishment of the primary goal of EDRA: "To help promote the creation of new and the preservation of existing habitable environments matched to the cultural tradition and equitable distribution and use of resources of a given population" (EDRA Goals)--the gap between planner and social scientist and the gap between planner and user. This paper will attempt to illustrate how social science theory and research can help narrow these gaps. The implications of humanistic, behavioristic, and broader social developmental models of the person will be applied to develop suggestions, hypotheses, and techniques about the criteria, planning process, construction, use, and evaluation of more habitable environments.

2.0. THE GAPS

2.1. The Gap Between Planner and Scientist

A gap between planners and social scientists in the area of environmental design is generally recognized. The theme of this conference is based on the premise that "much of environmental psychology has born a tenuous relationship to applied aspects of environmental design. There has been, in other words, an applicability gap between the theory and research carried out by the behavioral scientists and those who design and administer the environment" (from the application of the sponsors of this conference).

Altman (1975) describes several dimensions which are useful in understanding the gaps between practitioners and researchers. Practitioners usually are place-oriented; they are interested in how to design a specific room or home or building. Behavioral scientists are process-oriented; they are interested in phenomena such as privacy and crowding and are less concerned about a specific place. Practitioners are generally criterion-oriented, synthethizers, and doers; they must design an environment to attain a specific criterion using knowledge from many fields, e.g., architectural design, materials, psychology, and economics, and achieve an end product within a deadline. On the other hand, researchers are generally process-oriented, analyzers, and understanders. They are generally interested in what variables affect a certain behavior, analyzing the effects of specific variables on specific behaviors, and understanding the phenomena, often in a rather abstract and not directly applicable fashion.

2.2. The Gap Between Planner and User

A major contributing factor in environments that have become famous failures is a gap between planners and users. Several studies have shown that designers differ from laymen in their attitudes, beliefs, and perceptions about the environment (e.g., Hershberger, 1968; Petersen, Bishop, & Fitzgerald, 1969). Lansing and Marans (1969) found only a moderate correlation between residents and planners' evaluations of neighborhoods and suggest that perhaps this is due to a concentration by planners on aspects of the physical design (e.g., building set-back and land use characteristics) which may be less relevant to residents than upkeep of the neighborhood or noise level. Corbett (1973) found very favorable reactions by students to individual dome dormitories they had built. In contrast, various experts (university architects and architectural students) criticized the dorms as unesthetic and crude in design, and the county planning commission called them "unsightly igloos" which should not be encouraged. There is an apparent need for more research on users' needs and values, especially as they contrast with those of the designers.

Some planners argue that the gap between planners and users can be filled by user participation in decision making. The ensuing debate among planners that might be characterized as an "expert" vs "participatory planner" debate regarding the role of the user in decision making has been guided primarily by ideology. The need for and applicability of empirical research in this debate is discussed in more detail in a later section.

Obviously, I have only presented a brief sketch of the gaps between planner and scientist and planner and user. In the next section, the perspectives of humanism, behaviorism and a broader social developmental view are briefly discussed in order to provide background for (1) the implications of these perspectives of the person-environment relationship for the role and influence of planned environments (2) the application of these perspectives for conceptualizing and researching the design process.

3.0. HUMANISM, BEHAVIORISM, AND A BROADER SOCIAL DEVELOPMENTAL VIEW AS THEORETICAL PERSPECTIVES OF THE PERSON-ENVIRONMENT RELATIONSHIP AND THEIR IMPLICATIONS FOR WHAT TYPES OF ENVIRONMENTS ARE BEST SUITED FOR PEOPLE

In the course of planning an environment, a planner must have at least an implicit model of human nature, in terms of people's wants and needs, the relationship of behavior to environment, and the role and valence of planner, client, and user. However, most person-environment models are vague as to their implications for environmental design.

There is no dominant model of the person-environment relationship that is used in the designing of environments. Much of the research in environmental psychology has focused on the phenomena of personal space, crowding, territoriality, and privacy. The study of these phenomena do not suggest a clear person-environment model, rather, they, like the S-R behavioristic models of learning, develop principles that may apply across species. The physical determinism model that was common among planners (in which the environment acts on the person to produce a given mood or behavior) is gradually being replaced by broad reciprocal person-environment models (Ittleson, Proshansky, Rivlin, & Winkel, 1974; Altman, 1975), but so far they have had few specific suggestions that have been applied to the design process.

The perspectives of humanism, behaviorism, and a broader social developmental view as models of the person-environment relationship will be briefly discussed and then will be applied to the design process. It is beyond the scope of this paper to give a detailed description of humanism, behaviorism, and broader social developmental models (c.f. Wandersman, Poppen, & Ricks (in press) where these approaches are developed in detail).

3.1. Humanism

The humanistic perspective presents a human model,

distinct from models which account for animal or mechanical behavior, in which man is seen as a conscious agent with feelings, ideals, and intentions which affect his behavior. Humanistic thought is concerned with human growth, personal fulfillment, and self-actualization through increased self-responsibility, self-determinism, congruence between internal feelings and external expressions, and compassion as ends to be pursued. The physical and social environment may interfere with the expression of one's own inner potentialities and thus exert a major impact upon personality development and change. Jourard (in press) portrays the person as trying to obtain freedom from environmental forces, transcending aspects of "reality" which involves liberating oneself from dehumanizing forces in society to lead a life one has chosen independent from others.

Humanistic therapists have been characterized as passive catalysts, maintaining indirect control and being concerned with internal emotions, insight, and humanization. Humanistic ideas have been most influential in design in the "participatory planner" position.

3.2. Behaviorism

Behaviorism is commonly associated with the principles of learning theory, which may be common across species. Behaviorists are characterized by their use of experimental evidence and systematic, objective factual inquiry. Radical behaviorists such as Skinner eschew internalized constructs such as motives and needs, and concentrate on the behavior itself. In the Skinnerian perspective, the culture through parents, peers, and other socializing agents shapes the individual by reinforcing the behavior which it desires and punishing the behavior it does not desire, conditioning anxiety reactions to some situations but not to others, teaching norms of acceptable social behavior, and so forth. Genetic and cultural influences and the near environment are viewed as the shaping forces of the individual. The Skinnerian view is often seen as one of environmental determinism in which the environment influences behavior.

Behavior therapists attempt to replace maladaptive and/or stressful S-R relationships with more socially appropriate behavior taking an active role and maintaining direct control. Studer (1973) is a designer who uses a Skinnerian orientation to offer a strategy of environmental design which attempts to find connections between environmental contingencies and behavior.

3.3. A Broader Social Developmental View

A perspective is emerging which combines parts of humanism, behaviorism, social learning theory, life history, sociology, and behavioral ecology into *a broader social developmental view of the human being as an active organizer of his environment over time* (referred to as a broader social developmental view).

"A life history perspective on personality looks at human growth and decline over the whole life span, in the context of the entire social and physical environment (Ricks & Fleming, in press)."

In relation to environmental design, the life history perspective emphasizes the effects of the environment as they impact on a person's ongoing life, and suggests questions such as: What segments of the person's behavior does a specific environment engage? What are the short- and long-term consequences of a certain type of environment? What kinds of people live in what kinds of environments--for what kinds of people is it good, bad? What kinds of characteristics make a good planner? The sociological perspective reminds us that the person is a social being, as well as a biological and psychological entity, who is part of a society that needs a complex fabric of social roles and differentiation to fill the myriad needs of people. The behavioral ecology perspective studies the complex interdependencies between organisms and their environments over long periods of time. The behavioral ecology perspective raises many issues, including: good intentions of the designer or planner do not necessarily lead to improved habitability; the criteria of interventions must be picked with care and a longitudinal perspective even though they may have to contradict common sense, psychological theories, or social wisdom; and the complex interdependencies of systems including the physical environment, short-range behavior, and long-range outcome must be taken into account in evaluating interventions (Alexander, Dreher, & Willems, in press).

The broader social-developmental view encompasses the recent developments of social learning theory which describes the reciprocal person-environment relationship and places great importance on cognition, imitation, and self-reinforcement. Mischel suggests "a psychological approach which requires that we move from description of the climate, building, social settings, etc., in which we live--to the psychological mechanisms through which environmental conditions and people influence each other reciprocally" (in press). Mischel describes five types of cognitive social learning variables: (1) construction competencies--ability to construct particular cognitions and behaviors, (2) encoding strategies-- units and personal constructs for categorizing events and self-descriptions, (3) expectancies-- behavioral outcome and stimulus outcome expectancies in particular situations, (4) subjective stimulus values--motivating and arousing stimuli, incentives and aversions, (5) self-regulatory systems and plans--rules and self-reactions for performance and for the organization of complex behavior sequences. He suggests that these variables can conceptualize how the qualities

of the person influence the impact of stimuli (environments) and how each person generates distinctive, complex behavior patterns in interaction with the conditions of his life.

These brief sketches of the humanistic, behavioristic and broader social developmental models of the person indicate their very different conceptions of the person-environment relationship. In the humanistic view, the person strives to free himself of environmental constraints and to create unique environments for himself which can be congruent with his growth process. The radical behavioristic view pictures the person's behavior as determined by the environmental contingencies. In the broader social developmental view the person creates the environment, and the environment influences the behavior in a reciprocal process affected by the individual's own needs, perceptions, and abilities. The implications of such divergent models will be drawn in the next section.

3.4. Implications of Humanism, Behaviorism, and A Broader Social Developmental View for Designing More Habitable Environments

What types of environments are best suited for people? According to Alexander, Dreher, and Willems (in press)

". . . what we know about the habitability of environments is pitifully thin and leaves us with more questions than answers. We know what has not worked, retrospectively, and we can point to some existing conditions that create problems."

Humanism, behaviorism, and a broader social developmental view provide distinctly different implications for environmental design. This section provides an example of how a testable model of the person-environment relationship can be used to conceptualize the qualities of a habitable environment.

To some humanists, problems and distress are much of the basic stuff of life; to remove them completely would be absurd because the problem may be instrumental in providing more effective modes of living, and without problems an essential part of life is being denied. The humanistic perspective may suggest that planning be minimal in the sense of providing environments that are relatively unstructured, which allow freedom and opportunity for the growth of the individual. Radical behaviorists, on the other hand, argue for explicitly structured environments which build in positive reinforcement for appropriate behavior. Planning should be extensive by experts in behavior management who have empirically tested the most effective ways to control behavior. The broader social developmental view indicates that environmental planning needs to be specific to the environment and its ecological relations and to the person and what he brings to that environment. The implications of these models of the person-environment relationship can be illustrated as they apply to comprehensive environmental planning.

The developers of comprehensively planned new towns paint optimistic pictures about life in the new town as opposed to the random and chaotic planning that is common.

> "Picture a community where the homes touch on tree-lined walkways on which you can stroll or jog or bicycle in safety. This unique network of byways leads to shops, schools, parks, and community centers where people of all ages can find opportunities of many kinds. You are free to pick and choose and experience the good life as you envision it. Baseball, basketball, tennis, golf, swimming, boating and nearly all active pursuits are here to be enjoyed. So are the opportunities for participation in music, drama, dance, crafts, the visual arts, and special study courses. Then there are paths to explore, flowers to grow, shrubs to trim, and the good earth to feel flowing through your fingers.
> I invite you to discover for yourself what makes Riverton more than just a new place to live . . . what makes it *the way to live* (Simon in Riverton brochure, 1972).

At first glance this sounds like a humane environment designed to facilitate self-growth and positive reinforcement from the environment-- almost a perfect combination of humanism and behaviorism. However, behaviors of residents of new towns indicate that this view may be simplistic and that a fair number of problems exist (e.g., Rouse Co. In-House Report).

In fact, although there may be a large number of behavioral alternatives offered by this kind of New Town design, the range of kinds of behavior may all be limited to one style of life: "The way to live." The choice is not between different life styles, only between having fun swimming and having fun at art centers.

Studies of children in new towns in West Germany find that "amid soaring rectangular shapes of apartment houses with shaded walks, big lawns, and fenced-in play areas, the children for whom much of this had been designed apparently feel isolated, regimented, and bored." The children prefer playing by construction sites or hanging around shops. "The study finds that the children gauge their freedom not by the extent of open areas around them, but by the liberty they have to be among people and things that excite them and fire their imagination" (New York Times, May 9, 1971).

This is similar to the turned-off reaction most people have to Skinner's Walden Two. Skinner's society has most of the amenities of life but people find it unexciting and lacking in individuality.

From a humanistic viewpoint, the New Town environment may be "overplanned." There may be too many environmental constraints on the individual's life style (even though benign constraints) and too little opportunity to shape the environment. The environmental design may be humane, but from the humanistic perspective it is too static.

The broader social developmental view provides a refined conceptualization of the importance of behavioral alternatives. In the social learning framework, "freedom is defined in terms of the number of options available to people and the right to exercise them. The more behavioral alternatives and social perogatives people have, the greater is their freedom of action" (Bandura, 1974). While one implication of the humanistic position is that freedom increases with minimal planning and constraints, an implication of the social learning view is that we can plan to increase freedom by increasing the number of options available, increasing people's abilities to obtain options, and using social and legal contracts to insure the rights of individuals. From the broader social developmental perspective, it is not sufficient to provide many behavioral alternatives; alternatives need to be translated into meaningful choices by relating them to the needs, perceptions, abilities, and input of the individuals involved.

Thus the broader social developmental view of the human being as an active organizer of his environment over time provides a perspective from which to conceptualize the qualities of environments that are best suited for people. This view integrates parts of both humanism and behaviorism and then goes beyond them in specifying the important variables in the person-environment relationship. Behaviorism primarily emphasizes an environment which rewards appropriate behavior and humanism primarily emphasizes an open, noncoercive environment. The broader social developmental view specifies the conditions of these qualities: (1) what is a positively rewarding environment for each individual will depend on his behavioral repertoire, processing abilities, and needs and values, (2) the open, non-coercive environment needs to be related to these capacities of the individual in order for him to make use of them as real alternatives, (3) the environment needs to be open to change from the input and feedback of individuals as they select and create environments according to their own life space. Thus the broader social developmental view can provide a framework to conceptualize what qualities of environments are best suited for which people. In the next section, the implications of the broader social developmental view are applied to the design process, to explore how to achieve these more habitable environments.

4.0. APPLYING CONCEPTS AND RESEARCH FROM HUMANISM, BEHAVIORSIM, AND A BROADER SOCIAL DEVELOPMENTAL VIEW TO THE DESIGN PROCESS

Ziesel (1975) has formulated a five-step schema of the design process--programming, design, construction, use, and evaluation. This section argues that social science theory and research on the design process (specifically humanism, behaviorism, and a broader social developmental view) can be relevant to planners: (1) suggesting criteria for environmental designs based on a theoretical perspective, (2) suggesting options in types of planning processes available and types of planner-user relationships and how to investigate their effects, (3) discussing a user role in construction whose costs and benefits can be studied empirically, (4) discussing how we can study user adaptation and adjustment in different types of environments, (5) suggesting techniques to evaluate the design on a cost-benefit basis and suggesting how even the values of a designer can be empirically evaluated.

Most research on the design process has occurred at the evaluation stage--i.e., does the place meet user needs?, is it doing what it is supposed to do? (Altman, 1975). This section is aimed at suggesting that social science researchers need not be limited to working on the evaluation stage of the design process. Research relevant to the development of more habitable environments and also consonant with the values of researchers (Altman, 1975) is not only possible but necessary. Many of the issues raised here will not be new to planners. Many planners have become aware of problems in their designs and have used trial and error methods and imagination to develop innovative planning ideas. However, there is a dearth of systematic knowledge of the design process which could be helpful in planning better environments.

4.1. Identification of Design Criteria or The Goals of the Environment.

A hierarchy of goals based on a broader social developmental view ranging from simple basic requirements to maximal functioning has been formulated for therapeutic interventions (Ricks, Wandersman, & Poppen, in press). In this section, these goals will be extended to formulate criteria for environmental design interventions. The criteria are relatively doctrine-free. They can apply to all types of environments created by all types of approaches to design. They offer both the planner and social scientist a general framework for (a) establishing goals to aim for in planning an environment and (b) specific criteria to evaluate an environment. In order to illustrate the meaning of a criterion, examples will be described for each criterion in which either the criterion has been poorly met or the criterion is trying to be met.

4.1.1. *Criterion 1. Survival.* Expected survival rates can be calculated for a defined

group of designs. Environment can affect drug addiction, alcohol addiction, blood pressure, crime, and, therefore, death rates, for. example, Newman (1973) related the size of public housing units to deviant behavior and found a significant correlation between size and height of buildings to crime, including robbery (muggings), drug possession, rape, and murder. For example, crime rose from 2.6 per 1,000 for six-story buildings to 11.5 per 1,000 for buildings with 19 or more floors.

4.1.2. *Criterion 2. Effective Reproduction, Parenting, and Survival of the Culture or Subculture.* Effective reproduction and parenting is a general criterion for biological viability. One criterion of a well designed environment is that it enhances effective reproduction and competent mothering and fathering. The issue is not how many children are produced but whether people can have the children they want and rear them well. In the infamous high-rise project of Pruitt-Igoe, Yancy (1971) noted:

"In contrast to the slum, the architectural design of the project is such that as a child leaves an apartment he is out of his mother's sight and direct control . . . . As one mother explained: 'I find that I can't keep up with the children when they leave the house to play. When they go out, they play with just anybody, there are some people in the project who raise their children and some who don't. I want to have control over who they play with and when. So many people live in one place, you just can't choose your kids' playmates" (p. 8).

Survival of the culture is an important value for people as diverse as the psychoanalyst Freud, the psychologist Skinner, and the sociologist Devereux. Several studies have traced the effects of forced moving due to urban renewal. Young and Wilmott (1957) have found marked changes in the cultures. Young and Wilmott found strong, extended family networks with the "mum" as focus of social interaction and a pub culture in the city neighborhood of Bethnel Green. After the move to the suburb of Greenleigh, many of the aspects of the city culture changed, e.g., the focus was turned onto the nuclear family, and possessions and money began to matter much more.

4.1.3. *Decreased Vulnerability to Inner and Outer Sources of Stress.* Vulnerability is measureable in physiological indicators, like pulse rate, breathing rate, and in chemical changes in the blood, and in behavioral indicators, e.g., fear in leaving one's apartment. In a study cited by Michelson (1970), Fanning (1967) found that the morbidity rate of armed services' personnel living in apartments was 57% higher than those living in houses, although the groups were matched in occupational status and randomly assigned to their housing quarters. Differences were particularly high in neuroses

and respiratory infections. Newman's data (1973) indicate that those living in high-rise public housing projects are more vulnerable to crime than those living in low-rise housing projects.

4.1.4. *Increased Competence and "Good Fit" to One's Behavioral Niche in the Environment.* This criterion deals with people's feelings of competence and integration with or alienation from their environment. A study in Nigeria found a decrease in competence and fit with one's behavioral niche in the environment by many residents after urban renewal (Marris, 1962). According to one respondent,

> "And then, the condition of the houses at Suru Lere doesn't suit me. It's European style of building, there's no yard. They're just self-contained houses, and I'm used to communal living. When you come into a yard now, you see people coming and going, but out there there's just empty land" (p. 94).

Many of the women complained that it interferred with their role as women, part of which was to be a trader who would sell goods to government employees who commuted to the city. This could not be done when they moved to the suburbs.

4.1.5. *Feeling Better.* This criterion deals with increased enjoyment, greater feelings of satisfaction, well-being, and self-esteem. Wilner, et al. (1962) studied 300 families who had recently moved into new public housing and compared them with a control group of 300 who had remained in the slums. Among the positive changes they found were more personal satisfaction with life and higher self-esteem.

4.1.5. *Improved Social System Performance.* The ecological approach suggests that the consequences of an intervention for the social system must be evaluated. Baron (1975) describes the transformation in the functioning of several St. Louis public housing projects when they switched from private management to tenant management. In this program, tenants from the housing projects were trained to manage the housing project. They had the responsibility for hiring, firing, and supervising maintenance crews, admitting and evicting tenants, and preparing and controlling annual operating budgets.

> "In the field of soft management, the tenant corporations operate employment and social service programs, work closely with the public schools, and deal with residents' social problems. Their record to date shows that they have been successful both in improving the operating performance of their housing developments and in opening new opportunities for upward mobility of the residents" (p. 2).

In brief, there has been an improvement in the social system of the housing project.

4.1.7. *Designs are flexible to allow for change and growth.* The goals of humanism in a

sense are process-oriented; they are change- and growth-oriented, rather than ends-oriented. Studer (1973), who has a Skinnerian orientation, also perceives the inability of designs to change with changes in behavior as a central problem in designing environments. The following example describes a pilot project, under the auspices of the Canadian National Design Council (Warshaw, 1974), to increase options in housing. By allowing the user to play a major role in deciding upon the contents of the house and using contents that are movable and interchangeable, the house can be built to fit the user.

> "Perhaps the greatest advantage of an articulated system based on a conceptual/ physical separation of housing components, permitting a reduction of the initial housing content, is that it would allow the householder to define his own living spaces and modify them as his needs change, as well as the levels of quality and service that he requires in his physical surroundings. The housing production process would thus continue throughout the lifetime of the housing unit and the householder would be able to intervene in the process by becoming responsible for its outcomes once he occupies the basic shell" (p. 4-5).

This project may be an example of planning for freedom and growth that is consonant with humanistic and social learning implications for planning environments.

Ricks, Wandersman, and Poppen (in press) proposed an additional criterion of a reorganized personal world. This criterion does not appear to be a goal of most environmental designs—perhaps it is, perhaps it should be. Some planned environments either explicitly or implicitly do have a reorganized personal world as a goal, e.g., the New Town promises a new way to live.

The set of criteria presented are suggested by a broader social developmental view which concerns survival, behavior, satisfaction, system performance, and growth. The previous example of tenant participation in the St. Louis housing project illustrates that the criteria are interdependent. Although complete data are not available, informal reports suggest that the tenant participation project has worked well according to these criteria. Decreases in vandalism, vacancies, and traffic of hard drugs may be seen as leading to increased survival and decreased vulnerability to stress. Increased social interaction of the tenants also led to decreased vulnerability and greater sense of "fit" in the environment. All these changes, as well as direct services to facilitate parenting (e.g., day care) led to more effective parenting. Jobs and increased social interactions led to greater feelings of competence and efficacy. And all of these improvements contributed to a sense of residents feeling better. Continuing tenant participation enables management programs to change with changing needs. These criteria are not exhaustive and will not apply equally to all environmental designs. Any particular design might emphasize certain criteria, drop others, and modify those that they keep to fit their own particular user population. Planning can be seen in terms of interest groups, and the interest of the user was concentrated on in these criteria, which might not always coincide with the interests of the planners or paying clients. Planners may generate other criteria based on their own perspectives (e.g., esthetics, durability).

Wandersman and Becker (1975) have performed research which suggests that some of the criteria may be fulfilled or inhibited by the type of planning process, independent of the quality of the environment. The next section applies humanism, behaviorism, and a broader social developmental view to suggest theory and research for understanding and improving the planning process.

4.2. Planning Process--How we plan the environment to achieve goals.

What types of planning processes are available? What are the potential roles of the user in the planning process? What styles are available to the planner? What types of planning processes are most effective in fulfilling what types of goals?

There has been a debate in planning concerning the role of the user in the planning process, which may be described as an "expert" versus "participatory planner" debate. At one extreme of the participation debate is the "expert" or planning for others position, which has been adopted implicitly or explicitly by many experts in architecture, social planning, and cultural design (e.g., Skinner, 1953; Bazan, et al., 1973). This "expert" position argues that the expert, by virtue of his educational training and understanding of people, will design an environment that will make people happy and meet their needs. This approach argues that it is not necessary, and is often even undesirable, for the eventual users to participate in the planning of the environment, since they get in the way, do not have the necessary expertise, and resulting participatory committees make the project much more expensive and time-consuming. The "expert" position implies that the quality of the environment determines satisfaction, and that user participation is of little or no importance.

Many counterarguments are raised against the "expert" approach, including the ethics of control, interference with individual freedom, and the gap that exists between planner and user. In contrast to the "expert" approach, the argument of advocacy and participatory planners (e.g., Peattie, 1967; Coates, 1971; Tilley & Carr, 1975; and Lamb, 1975) and humanistic critics of cultural planners (e.g., Rogers in

Rogers & Skinner, 1956) is that people need to participate in planing their own environment to be satisfied. They argue that participation in planning gives users a feeling of control over their environment and is the only way users' needs and values can really be taken into account. Some advocates of this approach have suggested that the effects of participation may completely overshadow the effects of the "objective" quality of the environment produced--that is, ego involvement, dissonance, etc. may produce great pride and feelings of control and thereby overshadow the effects produced by the "objective" quality of the environment (Coates, personal communication). Other participatory planners have argued that user participation works because "it feels right" (Lamb, 1975).

Even the participatory planner approach does not solve all the problems of the gap between planner and user, and that there are important individual differences in users. Several professional planners and graduate students worked with a community group of parents, teachers, and students to develop a comprehensive recreational area incorporating playgrounds, ball fields, and an environmental education area.

"The planners expected the community to be very excited and enthusiastically participate in developing this facilty from design concepts through construction. They were disappointed that the community participants were unable to generate design concepts on their own, although they were willing to indicate the type of activities they wanted to engage in and the types of space and equipment they liked. It seemed that the design experts were not considering the community's willingness to tell them what kinds of activities they wanted to be able to do and equipment they liked as sufficient participation. For most designers, participation means the generation of design concepts and development of site plans, and not involvement in selecting from given alternatives or constructing equipment. Several community members had volunteered to help build the facilities, while others were interested in developing design concepts or supplying information about their preferences. The community seemed to define 'participation' in a more varied way than some of the professional planners" (Becker, personal communication).

While much of the "expert" vs "participatory planner" debate has been philosophical and subjective, Wandersman (in preparation) develops a conceptual framework for empirically investigating types of user participation and their effects. Involvement in the planning of an environment can involve different types of user participation, ranging from user feedback describing actual and desired activities, attitudes, and images, to the creation of forms and objects themselves, to the selection and arrangement of forms and objects that are provided, to a choice between alternative plans that are complete in themselves, to no choice at all. The latter three types of participation were investigated by Wandersman and Becker (1975) in a simulation of planning dormitory environments, keeping quality of environments approximately constant: (1) Self-planning--in which individuals generated alternative plans and chose a preferred one; (2) Choice--in which the individual selected a preferred room arrangement from alternatives generated by others; (3) No Participation--in which individuals simply rated a room arrangement provided for them (similar to the "expert" approach). In the framework of this study, there were few differences between Self-planning and Choice, and subjects preferred Self-planning and Choice to No Participation; they evaluated the room layouts more positively and reported feeling more control over the environment, a greater congruence between the environment and their needs and values, and better feelings about themselves (e.g., more helpful, responsible, and creative and less anonymous and alienated). These results are supportive of some of the views of the participatory planners and humanists. They suggest that user participation in the process facilitates matching the goals just outlined. Wandersman (in preparation) also found important individual differences in willingness to participate, which, the results suggest, are based more on the importance of the environment to the individual and his sense of competence in the area than to more global personality traits. This is in agreement with the broader social developmental view emphasis on the match between the environment and the individual's capacities, expectancies and values.

These issues and research regarding user participation raise questions about areas that have been virtually unexplored in regard to planning--What types of leadership roles are available to the planner? What styles of planner-user relationships are available? The humanistic and behavioristic and broader social developmental models of intervention offer methods to analyze the effect of current styles and offer suggestions for different styles of leadership. Research on style of leadership suggests that the effects of style of leadership are specific to the types of situations (e.g., planning a private house, planning an airport, planning a New Town); therefore, the results in organizational behavior and therapy can only suggest research hypotheses for the effects of leadership styles in planners. Below are some implications of leadership styles that require research: (1) in the "expert" approach where users are not consulted, the planner is active and in control of the strategy and details and should accept responsibility for his intervention. (Planners manipulate environments and therefore people.) (2) In a humanistically-oriented style, the planner acts as a passive catalyst while the user acts as a significant source of the ideas and strategies which can be realized through his interaction and relationship with the

planner. Thus, the responsibility of the planner is different. (3) Despite a planner's wishes to the contrary, he will always be viewed as an expert by the user, but the directness of his control may vary. Rychlak (1968) argues that there are several types of control, one is synonymous with "to have an effect on," e.g., positive reinforcement and persuasion; a second use of control is as a deliberate means of social influence. To control in this sense is to deliberately plan a set of procedures designed to have a certain effect upon a person--often without his foreknowledge. The many different types of user participation available allow the opportunity for different degrees of control by the planner and suggest many areas of research for the researcher.

4.3. Construction--Building the Project

Can the user play an important role in construction?

Wandersman and Becker (in preparation) distinguish several types of user participation, including participation in decision making (control, input or feedback) and participation in implementing the plans (implementation). The utilization of user effort in implementing plans appears to be increasing. The example of participatory planners and users cited on Page 7 (Becker, personal communication) illustrates that this was a type of participation preferred by many users. A role in construction may be very meaningful to users. It may fulfill needs of control over the environment, increase feelings of helpfulness and responsibility, and reduce feelings of alienation; it may be an important way to cut costs of projects. These are questions open to empirical study.

In the Canadian National Design Council Project for increasing options in housing, several levels of user roles in construction are discussed, e.g., the user hires professionals to carry out the plan, the user selects from available components and builds them himself, the user designs his own components and installs them. The report emphasizes the need to teach users about housing components, choice of sites, maintenance costs, etc., and the skills necessary to use tools. Behavioristic theory, social learning theory, and humanistic theory may suggest methods of teaching users.

4.4. Use--User Activities and Adaptations in The Designed Environment

How are people changed by their environments? How do people change their environments?

The observational methods of behavioral technology and behavioral ecology suggest techniques for studying the relationships between environment and behavior, or behavior-environment contingencies. Behavioral ecology (e.g., Alexander, Dreher, & Willems, in press) suggest how we may study the relationships among environmental systems, the use of those systems by people, and the emergence of behavioral problems. If we are to understand the relationship between behavior and environment, behavioral ecology points to the need of using systems concepts and studying complex dependencies, reciprocity, unanticipated consequences, and extended time-related cycles.

Mischel raises an issue that is relevant to the issue of planning and use of the environment--when are environments likely to exert powerful influences and when are person variables or the individual likely to be most influential? Mischel suggests that environments are powerful when they lead people to perceive them in the same way, induce uniform expectancies regarding the most appropriate behavior, and provide incentives for its performance, and require skills that everyone has to the same extent. Environments are weak when they are not perceived similarly, do not create uniform expectancies, do not offer sufficient incentive for performance of behaviors, or fail to provide the learning conditions required to perform behavior. Thus research can be performed relating types of environments to people's behavior.

A new environmental design provides a "new" environment to which people adapt (people change to suit their environment) and adjust (people modify the environment to suit their needs and values). Alexander, Dreher, and Willems suggest that behavioral/ecological systems follow rules of succession (stressing the importance of sequential phenomena) in which phases and changes of the system are of crucial importance. The perspective of a broader social developmental view suggests ways in which we can study how behavior develops over time in planned environments, how people are changed by environments, how they change environments to suit their needs and values, what types of people adapt and adjust, what types of environments are most coercive and force adaptation and what types are most flexible and encourage adjustment. (See Wandersman (1973) for more details on conceptualizing adaptation and adjustment and the development of behavior settings.)

4.5. Evaluation--Assessing Whether the Completed Design Meets the Criteria or Goals of the Design

How should we evaluate environments?

A broader social developmental view suggests the type of ecological approach that an ideal evaluation would include to take environmental complexities into account. The behavioral ecological approach stresses the importance of taking into account the complex interdependencies of systems, including the physical environment, short-range behaviors, unanticipated consequences, and long-range outcomes.

A sensitive description of the responsibility of the planner (which includes his role as an evaluator) is taken by Devereux (in press). Devereux argues that a responsible change agent (which should include environmental designers and planners):

". . . must necessarily take into account not only the best available knowledge about the empirical relationships among the realities he is dealing with, but also must work within an explicit sophisticated and empirically critiqued framework of values; he must be able, so far as possible, both to predict and to evaluate the consequences of whatever intervention he undertakes."

Devereux suggests three criteria for empirically critiquing values--effectiveness, efficiency, and functional adequacy. (1) Effectiveness--Instrumental values can be evaluated in terms of whether they fulfill their goal, (2) Efficiency--Building upon an ecological systems postulate of empirical interconnectedness in which a change in one variable will probably affect many other variables, then action taken in behalf of one value, whether or not it accomplishes its goal, may produce a number of side effects. These are secondary gains or costs and should be taken into account when evaluating the action.

"Responsible, rational intervention strategies must always follow some judgment about the relative efficiency of alternative strategies for the total set of values of the action. The minimum framework then involves some kind of cost-benefit calculus, in which an attempt is made to decide, on empirical grounds, which strategy promises the greatest net balance of gain for all the values which stand to be affected."

While the effectiveness criterion applies only to instrumental values, the efficiency criterion applies to means and final values, because action taken directly for final values also has costs or side effects. (3) Functional Adequacy --"This criterion is designed to critique the relevance of values and of action taken in their behalf, for the needs of various kinds of systems. Man is simultaneously a part of three orders of systems--biological, psychological, and social. Gains for one system may be at the cost to others." For example, while laissez-faire zoning may serve the psychological needs of some individuals, it might be dysfunctional to the social system, e.g., urban sprawl.

Devereux argues that psychological considerations are never by themselves sufficient criterion for any responsible intervention or reform because of the importance of social system needs which must be taken into account if the society is to survive and function well. Since man is destined to live in a social system, consequences to the social system must be predicted, taken into account, and evaluated.

5.0. SUMMARY AND CONCLUSIONS

The following hypothetical example briefly illustrates some of the major issues that have been developed in this paper. Different types of user participation are compared to demonstrate how research from a broader social developmental view can provide important data on the planning process. In this example, dormitory environments are built by four different planning processes and then inhabited by the users: (1) User Planning and Construction--users plan and build their own dome dormitories (e.g., Corbett, 1974); (2) Self-planning--users generate alternative plans from a pool of furniture and choose a preferred one; (3) Choice--users choose between two alternative environments planned by designers for students; (4) No Participation--users do not participate in the planning process and live in a room planned by a designer for students.

Identification of Criteria. We can discuss what criteria are relevant to a dormitory with clients and potential users. The criteria that seem most relevant from a broader social developmental view are suggested below: (their relevance to the client and potential user can be verified) Decrease vulnerability to inner and outer sources of stress (e.g., less conflict between roommates), increase competence and "good fit" to one's behavioral niche in the environment (e.g., development of skills, increase feelings of competence and responsibility, decrease feelings of alienation and anonymity); feeling better (e.g., feelings of satisfaction, self-esteem, and well-being); improve social system performance (e.g., students do well in school, little vandalism, student involvement and social interaction is high, the dormitories are filled so that the college can function);designs are flexible to allow for change and growth (e.g., rooms are modifiable so that they can fit new fashions, different styles of living, and new users).

Types of Planning Processes. The environments produced by different types of planning processes with different degrees of user participation will be studied. In each of the four processes the planner-user relationship varies. In user planning and building, the planner may act as a resource or consultant and may teach planning skills if necessary. The user has primary responsibility. In self-planning, the planner may develop the shell and infrastructure, choose the pool of alternative pieces of furniture and act as a design consultant. In choice, the planner acts as an "expert" and plans several rooms for users. In no participation, the planner acts as an "expert" and plans an environment for users. The user has no role with practically no opportunity for constructive feedback.

Construction. User planning and construction and self-planning allow for a user role in construction. The monetary consequences of a user role in construction can be evaluated.

Use. Are there differences in adjustment and adaptation to the different dormitories created by the different processes? How do such activities as social interaction and studying develop over time?

Evaluation. I feel that many arguments concerning the merits of participation have been unnecessarily confused and confounded because the debates used different conceptions of participation. Some have argued that user participation "feels good" and is better; others have argued that it is time consuming and often leads to poor designs. Still others have argued that it leads to enhanced designs and greater satisfaction with the environment. This suggests that user participation can be considered as a value rewarding in and of itself (e.g., participation is good because it is democratic and leads to feelings of control over the environment and a more favorable image of the self) or considered as a technique to design better environments. (Many participatory planners have the value of participation but argue for it by assuming its worth as a technique for providing enhanced environments.) The following example sketchily suggests that the worth of user participation as a technique can be empirically evaluated, and to some extent, its validity as a value can also be evaluated.

User Participation as a Technique for Designing more Habitable Environments.

Effectiveness--Do the different environments fulfill the criteria we have chosen?
Efficiency--Which environment fulfills the criteria best with the least cost in the short run (to build), and in the long run (to maintain, taking into account vandalism, vacancy, etc.)?
Functional Adequacy: In which dormitory environment does the system of dormitory and the larger system of the college work best?

User Participation as a Value.

In order to evaluate the effects of user participation as a value, we must vary types of user participation while keeping the quality of the environment constant. Thus a second experiment would be required in which quality of the environment would be held approximately constant. The reader may wish to read Wandersman (in preparation) or Wandersman and Becker (1975) for a discussion of confounds between user participation and quality of the environment and the need to separate them.
Effectiveness: Do the different processes fulfill the criteria we have chosen?
Efficiency: Which process fulfills the criteria best with the least cost in the short and long run?
Functional Adequacy: How does the process of participation affect other values, e.g., leisure, freedom, and health.

In this paper, I have suggested how applying the perspectives of humanism, behaviorism, and a broader social developmental view to the design process suggests concrete issues and hypotheses for research and suggestions for innovations in the design process, which the researcher can pursue that are in concert with his own needs and values as a researcher and the needs of planners. I also suggested ways in which theory and research can narrow the gap between planner and user. I believe we can go beyond the applicability gap if researchers perform research relevant to the needs of planners and planners use it; it is a dual responsibility.

References

ALEXANDER J., DREHER, G., and WILLEMS, E. Behavioral ecology and humanistic and behavioristic approaches to change. In A. Wandersman, P. Poppen, and D.Ricks (Eds.), Humanism and behaviorism: Dialogue and growth. New York: Pergamon, in press.

ALTMAN, I. The environment and social behavior. Monterey: Brooks/Cole, 1975.

BANDURA, A. Behavior theory and the models of man. American Psychological Association Presidential Address, 1974. Reprinted in A. Wandersman, P. Poppen, and D. Ricks (Eds.), Humanism and behaviorism: Dialogue and Growth. New York: Pergamon, in press.

BARON, R. Tenant management: A rationale for a national demonstration of management innovation. St. Louis: McCormack Associates, 1975.

BAZAN, G., et al. Wesley Town report. Unpublished manuscript, Pennsylvania State University, 1973.

COATES, G. Action research and community power: A prospectus for environmental change. Unpublished manuscript, Cornell University.

CORBETT, J. Student-built housing as an alternative to dormitories. Environment and Behavior, 1973, 5(4).

DEVEREUX, E. Models for man, value systems, and intervention strategies: A sociological critique of Wolpe and Jourard. In A. Wandersman, P. Poppen, and D. Ricks (Eds.), Humanism and behaviorism: Dialogue and growth. New York: Pergamon, in press.

HERSBERGER, R. A study of meaning and architecture. Man and His Environment Newsletter, 1968, 1, 6-7.

ITTLESON, W., PROSHANSKY, H., RIVLIN, L. and WINKEL, G. An introduction to environmental psychology. New York: Holt, Rinehart, and Winston, 1974.

JOURARD, S. Changing personal worlds: A human-istic perspective. In A. Wandersman, P. Poppen, and D. Ricks (Eds.), Humanism and behaviorism: Dialogue and growth. New York: Pergamon, in press.

LAMB, C. User design. Paper presented at EDRA 6, 1975.

LANSING, J. and MARANS, R. Evaluation of neighborhoods. Journal of the American Institute of Planners, 1969, 35, 195-199.

MICHELSON, W. Man and his urban environment. Reading: Addison-Wesley, 1970.

MISCHEL, W. The self as the person: A cognitive social learning view. In A. Wandersman, P. Poppen, and D. Ricks (Eds.), Humanism and behaviorism: Dialogue and growth. New York: Pergamon, in press.

NEWMAN, O. Defensible space. New York: Macmillan, 1973.

PEATTIE, L. Reflections on advocacy planning. Journal of the American Institute of Planners, March, 1967.

PETERSON, G., BISHOP, R., and FITZGERALD, R. The quality of visual residential environments: Perspectives and preferences. Man-Environment Systems, 1969, 5(13).

RICKS, D. and FLEMING, P. Humanistic and behavioral approaches from a life history perspective. In A. Wandersman, P. Poppen, and D. Ricks (Eds.), Humanism and behaviorism: Dialogue and growth. New York: Pergamon, in press.

RICKS, D., WANDERSMAN, A., and POPPEN, P. Humanism and behaviorism: Towards new syntheses. In A. Wandersman, P. Poppen, and D. Ricks (Eds.), Humanism and behaviorism: Dialogue and growth. New York: Pergamon, in press.

ROGERS, C. and SKINNER, B. F. Some issues concerning the control of human behavior: A symposium. Science, 1956, 1057-1066.

RYCHLAK, J. A philosophy of science for personality. Boston: Houghton & Mifflin, 1968.

SKINNER, B. F. Science of human behavior. New York: Mcmillan, 1953.

STUDER, R. Man-environment relations: Discovery or design. In W. Preiser (Ed.) Environmental Design Research, Volume II. Stroudsberg: Dowden, Hutchinson, & Ross Inc., 1973.

TILLEY, S. and CARR, S. Downtown Washington streets for people: User consultancy. Paper presented at EDRA 6.

WANDERSMAN, A. The development of adaptation

and adjustment: The New Town as a laboratory for understanding people and plans.
Unpublished manuscript, 1973.

WANDERSMAN, A. Psychology and planning residential environments: An exploration of
the roles of participation, quality of
design, and individual differences in
evaluating a designed environment.
in preparation.

WANDERSMAN, A., and BECKER, F. The effect of
type of participation in planning environments on user satisfaction. Paper presented at EDRA 6, 1975.

WANDERSMAN, A. and BECKER, F. Types of user
participation and their implications for
environmental design, in preparation.

WANDERSMAN, A., POPPEN, P., and RICKS, D. (Eds.)
Humanism and behaviorism: Dialogue and
growth. Elmsford: Pergamon, in press.

WARSHAW, L. Options in housing. Study for the
National Design Council of Canada, 1974.

WILNER, D., WALKEY, R., PINKERTON, T., and
TAYBACK, M. The housing environment and
family life. Baltimore: Johns Hopkins
Press, 1962.

YANCEY, W. Architecture, interaction, and
social control. Environment and Behavior,
1971, 3(1), 3-21.

YOUNG, M. and WILLMOTT, P. Family and kinship
in East London. New York: The Free Press,
1957.

ZEISEL, J. Sociology and architectural design.
New York: Russell Sage Foundation, 1975.

ACKNOWLEDGMENTS

I would like to thank Frank Becker,
Edward Devereux, J. R. Newbrough, and David
Ricks for their thoughtful comments. Special
thanks are owed to Lois Pall Wandersman for
her valuable conceptual and editorial aid.

ASSUMPTIONS IN ENVIRONMENTAL PROGRAMMING

Jay Farbstein, PhD

School of Architecture and Environmental Design
California Polytechnic State University
San Luis Obispo, CA 93407

ABSTRACT

Several environmental programming techniques are
examined and their assumptions regarding what we
know and what we need to know about client
requirements are pointed out. Assumptions
include: background premises and/or assumed
"facts" about person-environment relationships;
incomplete identification of users and their
objectives; bias in programming objectives and
logical errors of generalization or of the
treatment of part of a system as the whole.
Recommendations include: frankness about
assumptions; logical clarity and economy of
procedure; expansion of the theoretical and
empirical basis of programming; and program
implementation within a feed-back/feed-forward
framework.

1. INTRODUCTION

Environmental programming is one of the principal
areas in which behavioral science models and
methods are applied to environmental design.
Thus, it should form one of the bridges leading
across and "beyond the applicability gap".

There are, of course, a wide range of approaches
to programming. Despite the variety, certain
assumptions are quite common regarding what we
know, what we need to know, how we may find it
out and how it may be applied in the prescriptive
situations of planning and design. These
epistemological assumptions tend to limit the
power and validity of techniques in which they
are found. As in computer programming "garbage
in, garbage out", is held to apply. In order to
provide a sound behavioral basis for design,
limiting assumptions on environmental program
data must be understood and transcended. It is
hoped that pointing these assumptions out will
be a step in that direction.

2. ASSUMPTIONS

Several kinds of assumptions will be discussed.
Each will be illustrated by referring to one or
two approaches which best exemplify that
assumption. While many kinds of assumptions may
be found within any given approach, the
approaches themselves will not be exhaustively
or thoroughly analyzed. The present purpose is
not to criticize any particular technique, but
rather to enumerate the types of limiting
assumptions to which programs are prone.

2.1 Client Identification and Objectives

2.11 Who Is Involved?

The first set of assumptions considered are those
about who is to be involved in the programming
decision making process, and in what capacities
or roles. It is a very recent dictum that those
affected by an environmental intervention should
participate in its planning. This has thrown
programming open to the myriad demands to which
the proposed environment must, in fact, eventually
respond.   The selection of participants versus
representatives will be an index of the program's
breadth and inclusiveness. While some approaches
require information only from those higher up in
the hierarchy, others require representatives of
all major roles to participate (9,15,26), still
others seek to involve all users in programming,
design and even construction (1).

2.12 Client, User and Programmer Objectives

One frequent assumption is that users (and clients)
must agree upon values or goals in order for
programming and design to proceed. Thus William
Pena states that "any conflict between them must
be resolved" because "subsequent steps depend
notably on clear-cut, coordianted goals". (18,
p.17). While this is undoubtedly convenient, it
has not been proven as essential. It is perfectly
possible for various users to have (and retain)
conflicting viewpoints with regard to design
objectives. At least one technique is designed
specifically to accommodate this variety (25).
It is only among highly uniform populations

that, as Lawrence Halprin claims "by making them visible, differences then begin to fall away". (9)

Special problems develop when users do not conform to societal norms. Zeisel has pointed out three "Fundamental Values in Planning with the Non-Paying Client" (28): maximizing their freedom of choice in lifestyle; defining their needs in terms of the users' underlying social values rather than others' beliefs about them, and accommodating users' needs through the environment. Many examples can be marshalled where these values are ignored, especially in official planning and programmatic space standards. Maureen Taylor has pointed out the short-sighted and stereotyped view of women and the family which is taken by the British Department of Environment in their space recommendations/standards. Users who do not conform to official norms are poorly provided for and find few options for flexibility in use. (24)

Ergonomic studies, upon which these space standards are in part based, tend to define kitchen activities as belonging exclusively to women. These recommend working heights and layouts which are "optimal" for people of a particular size. The notion of satisfying requirements of taller or shorter women or men, or even the potential of men assuming domestic duties, seem to have been overlooked. Grandjean, for instance, while including male dimensions, claims that "studies of housewives' movement in the kitchen have indicated the best arrangement for equipment..." and "adequate space is especially important where a woman is dealing with cupboards, shelves and other storage." (10 p. 67, emphasis added).

Thus, the programmer's objectives for the program and for the performance of the system on which he or she is operating must be considered as background assumptions which will color and direct the entire process. Perhaps the most basic assumption may be that it will require a building to solve the clients' problems when some other means may be more effective (Michael Brill has often raised this point).

Great care must be taken that these assumptions do not render the program invalid or inapplicable.

2.2 Assumed "Facts"

So-called "facts" may be assumed which are entirely unproven. These may be of the nature of unstated premises about requirements of users or activities for particular environmental conditions when there is little empirical evidence establishing such a requirement. While the purpose of the program may be to establish the performance levels required of the environment, there is a general lack of empirical data to draw upon for specific situations (where data does exist its applicability may be questionable. See Section 2.5). Some methods, for example the Planning Aid Kit (17), invite users to specify

desired environmental performance characteristics. These state what the space must do to effectively accommodate its activities. While it may be as well to ask a user as a programmer, how they are to establish these characteristics and whether their desires will yield correct environmental performance levels are highly doubtful.

A related method (Moleski, 15) requires the programmer to make this "socio-physical specification". These are to form a theoretical link between a description of the likely behavior and the specification of physical system (building) characteristics. Twelve socio-physical characteristics are specified for no less than 22 aspects of activity for each "activity site". This specification is then translated into four categories (consisting of 22 particular) physical variables which may supposedly be manipulated to achieve the required performance levels. But the empirical basis for either the socio-physical performance specification or the physical-environmental specification must be questioned. How does the programmer know which socio-physical characteristics will support which activity and how does the designer know when an environmental configuration will yield the social performance specified, when relatively little evidence exists linking specific environmental characteristics to behavioral outcomes? (The related problem of specifying or manipulating parts of a whole system is discussed in Section 2.4.)

While certain unstated premises lurk behind these methods and cry out for empirical verification, at least the person-environment model which is seen to govern relationships and the desired level of performance are clearly stated. In the next section, more general unstated premises about the nature of this relationship are discussed.

2.3 Deterministic Models

Most person-environment researchers would seem to subscribe to the concept of a rather loose, non-deterministic relationship between environment and behavior perhaps within a dynamic, whole-system context (12, pp. 344-347). Some expend considerable energy destroying the deterministic viewpoint (14,19).

By contrast, programmers often seem to assume clear and consistent cause-effect determination, even if this is unsupported theoretically or empirically. The person-environment relationship expressed as a "requirement" or "need" makes it sound so absolute as to be unchallengeable. It seems to imply that an acceptable level of functional performance can only be achieved if the environmental requirement is met. That the need could be displaced from the environment to another portion of the system, say to increased reliance on interpersonal relations or economic reward, is not usually considered.

Even Michael Brill (who has shown elsewhere that

he knows better) has stated, with reference to the environmental characteristics discussed above, that "these are the qualities, or characteristics, which the environment must supply in order for the human user to perform the activity." (3, p. 317, emphasis added) He does not state that it should supply these character- istics, or that given levels of the characteristics correlate to given levels of activity performance, or with given costs or trade-offs; but rather that it must! And this 30-odd years after the Hawthorne studies (21).

2.4 The Part and the Whole

The notion of the person-environment system as a dynamically structured whole has been alluded to above. In programming, certain conceptual and practical problems develop from describing and specifying the environment in terms of particular and isolable variables or characteristics. The main limitation here is that the characteristics act in concert (or at least in context) to produce any effects they may have. Specifying them in isolation may not succeed in recreating the effect they had in ensemble. Rather little is known about how these whole systems operate or could be specified, but two examples are offered to clarify the situation. The first looks at the complexity of specifying "simple" areal requirements; the second at the limitations inherent in attempting to optimize an environment's performance on a single behavioral criterion.

Specifying areal requirements ought to be one of the more straightforward of programming tasks. Grandjean has summarized the best studies of space requirements for domestic activities from Europe and the US. His conclusion is highly equivocal: "Human space requirements from the standpoint of anatomy and physical needs are well understood. Even if many of the measurements are based on data that have not been fully verified, common sense usually allows the creation of useful recommendations and norms for the use of household fitments and furniture, and for passages, stairs and other building details. All these measurements, however, are partial measure- ments; that is, they concern only bits of the room. There are no practical criteria for assessing the total volume of a room, or its proportions, but in spite of this, minimum heights, areas and often volumes as well figure in the building regulations of many authorities." (10, p. 89)

Grandjean is particularly concerned with the limited knowledge about "psychological effects" of area and volume. But there are other aspects of the problem as well. In order to assess the areal requirements of an activity many factors must be taken into account including its context and relations to other activities, spaces and social and economic systems. Trade-offs between area and quality of finishes, time availability and alternation, the acceptability (for social or environmental reasons) of combining activities or individuals in the same space, the relationship between area and performance or satisfaction for that activity, and the cost of space at that or alternative locations are among the interdependent variables which may influence areal requirements.

Only at the extreme low end of the scale of provision will area itself become an absolute control on activity (no space, no activity). Above some threshold there will be many possible responses, e.g., sharing, displacement to another time or location, sub-optional performance, annoyance, conflict, etc. Even an overabundance of space may lead to economic or social costs (increased space costs, greater time-distances between locations, spatial isolation, etc.).

Looked at from another point of view, the systemic nature of the person-environment system means that any attempt to optimize for a single particular value or objective must be suspect. For example, programs have been developed which attempt to determine location for activities on the basis of required adjacencies or inter-accessibility. In these, some measure of the "association" or level of communications between persons and/or areas is used as an indication of the likely patterns of movement in a building. (23) Usually an attempt is made to minimize the total amount of time spent moving by locating persons with high association values as near as possible to one another. The methods used to estimate association are primitive and suffer from the same limitations of projection into the future as activity studies in general. The ends are also questionable in that they attempt to make the task-generated communication system most efficient. This treats movements as wholly instrumental, ignoring its value to relaxation, diversion, information gathering and in fostering informal contacts which have importance both socially and for the organization. (8) In addition, the single objective will often value certain actors' time over others (doctors, executives, etc.). Nor can efficiency in a single aspect create effectiveness overall.

Thus, the programmer must bear in mind that he or she is manipulating a complex system, and insure that single purpose objectives are not imposed on the entire system.

2.5 Generalization

Requirements, effects or relationships may be unjustifiably generalized from one context to another. This occurs when some ignored or unknown feature makes them incommensurable. The assumption is that an individual, activity, organization or building belongs to a type for which requirements have been established.

Categorization may be a prerequisite to description and analysis. However, the basis for categories will be weak if they derive from assumptions about classificatory features, simply represent socially legitimized categories (e.g., building types), or are not subjected to empirical validation.

One of the major applications of questionable categories such as occupancy or building type is in the codes and standards regulating space provision, construction type, access, etc. The assumption is that members of the class share certain requirements. How relevant (except as legal "facts") such standards may be to society or to individuals ascribed to that class is debatable. For example, studies of universities in Britain have found little relationship between University Grants Committee space standards (used as the basis for capital funding) and actual provision. (16)

When such standards ignore the unique requirements of the individual or organization or become the maximum feasible provision instead of the guaranteed minimum (as FHA or Parker-Morris standards have become) (7), then they are counter-productive.

Indeed, it may turn out that individually optimal environmental provision may be a precise balance of many factors which vary within extremely wide ranges--as has recently been shown to be the case for nutritional requirements ("biochemical individuality"). (27)

A second example of the limitations of generalization may be found in the pattern language. This is a collection of statements describing physical characteristics or arrangements which supposedly must be present under given circumstances in order to satisfy needs or solve problems thought to be defined by those circumstances.

The patterns are described as tentative and subject to rejection either as inapplicable to the context at hand or as lacking in empirical support. (2) However, there are additional philosophical problems which call into question their utility. Janet Daley has raised several issues with regard to an early formulation of the idea of the pattern (Alexander's "Atoms of Environmental Structures"). (6) She points out that Alexander incorrectly dismissed the value basis of judgements about the rightness or wrongness of a plan, and ignored the problem of undesirable or contradictory tendencies or needs. While recent developments may allow a degree of value judgement to be injected by the users, other limitations still hold.

Patterns are formulated as syllogisms: if (context or condition x), then (environmental characteristic y)...to solve problem (z). These are generalizations about all situations of a given type, suggesting that the problems (assumed to be present) will be solved by arranging the environment in a particular way. On what basis can it be decided whether a situation at hand conforms to that of the pattern? Can the pattern's prescription be expected to work in the situation to which it is being generalized? Finally, why the pseudo-scientific (if, then) formulation? The patterns may be full of good ideas. But if they are

to be useful they must be verified empirically and provided with a test for determining their applicability in a given context. In the meantime they should not be legitimized and universalized as other than interesting but untested generalizations.

2.6 Future Projections

One of the most difficult areas of programming is the necessity of making projections into the uncertain future. Problems of descriptions, relationships and generalizations are compounded when they concern future states of the client-environment relationship. In fact, very little is known about the spatial behavior or demand of client organizations over time. (5) There does not appear to be such consistent variation as to allow accurate predictions of growth or shrinkage in organization size, let alone changes in structure or behavior. The programmer may avoid responsibility for incorrect predictions by leaving it as the responsibility of the client.

However, to deal with this uncertainty, programmatic recommendations are often made for flexibility, adaptability or expansibility. Possible future reduction in operations is less frequently taken into account, perhaps because clients prefer not to consider it. Finally, the performance of buildings or building systems in providing various kinds of flexibility has hardly begun to be measured (4). The ability to predict spatial demand and relate it to building flexibility would seem to be a crucial area for the development of knowledge.

3. CONCLUSIONS AND RECOMMENDATIONS

It is only fair to point out that criticisms have been leveled here at the best programming techniques. It is probable that even more arbitrary and limiting assumptions are made in programming practices which remain unpublished.

Environmental programming is an emerging discipline, only about 10 to 15 years old. While the quality of programming at its best is probably improving, this process may be accelerated by adopting strategies which avoid the pitfalls involved in the above assumptions.

As a first step, programmers must be completely explicit about their objectives and their theoretical, "factual" and methodological assumptions. One problem in assessing programming documents is that they are frequently not explicit at all. While this can be understood in communications between professional and client, it cannot be accepted in published documents. Second, the logical and methodological fallacies described above must be repudiated and replaced with sounder approaches. Third, the theoretical and empirical basis of programming must be expanded beyond the mere gathering of "data" from which prescriptions magically appear. This will be achieved in part through the development of an expanded body of knowledge about the relationships between environment and behavior including its cross-contextual variability.

An additional strategy is to integrate programming (and design) into the research effort. A model of design-related activity suggested by Zeisel treats the prescriptive statements of programmers as hypotheses (which they may resemble) which are to be tested by evaluating the behavioral outcomes in the eventual building (29). This is a challenging notion, but fraught with difficulties. One of its major lacks is that it is clearly a-theoretical. An hypothesis (which one dictionary defines in part as a "groundless assumption") can never be definitively confirmed by comparing its predictions to empirical results, since other findings may always emerge to invalidate it. (On the other hand, any negative finding will immediately invalidate it.) Worse than this, so-called hypotheses concerning a particular building do not appear to grow out of any general theory, nor could they support or invalidate (i.e., test) a theory if they did. With their limitation to a specific and unique building context, the sample size (one) does not permit generalization.

Thus, only a body of theory and fact describing person-environment relations which is specific and cross-contextual (in order to be powerfully predictive) will provide a sound basis for programming. While this does not exist at present, promising approaches would include controlled experiments or the use of structured samples in the testing of hypotheses generated by particular theoretical contexts (20). In this situation, individual building programs can be combined into samples to test the generalizability of hypotheses and to identify the important dimensions of variation among organizations and contexts. Thus, the effectiveness of programming techniques can be evaluated along with the effectiveness of design solutions.

References

1. ALEXANDER, CHRISTOPHER, "An Early Summary of the Timeless Way of Building" in Lang, et. al., eds., Designing for Human Behavior, 1974, pp 52-59.

2. ALEXANDER, CHRISTOPHER, et. al., "A Pattern Language which generates multi-service centers", Center for Environmental Structure, Berkeley, 1968.

3. BRILL, MICHAEL, "Evaluating Buildings on a Performance Basis" in Lang, et. al., eds., Designing for Human Behavior, 1974, pp 316-319.

4. BUILDING PERFORMANCE RESEARCH UNIT, Building Performance, London, 1972.

5. COWAN, PETER, "Studies in the Growth, Change and Ageing of Buildings", Transactions of the Bartlett Society, V. 1, 1962-1963, pp 56 ff.

6. DALEY, JANET, "A Philosophical Critique of Behaviourism in Architectural Design", in Broadbent and Ward, eds., Design Methods in Architecture, London, 1969.

7. DECARLO, GIANCARLO, "Legitimizing Architecture" Forum (Dutch), XXIII, 1972, pp 8-20.

8. FARBSTEIN, JAY, "Organization, Space and Activity: The Relationship of Task and Status to the Allocation and Use of Space in Certain Organizations", PhD Thesis, University of London, 1975.

9. GOLDSTEIN, BARBARA, "Participation Workshops" (about Lawrence Halprin's Take Part Workshops), Architectural Design, 4/74, pp 207-212.

10. GRANDJEAN, ETIENNE, Ergonomics of the Home, Taylor and Francis, London, 1973.

11. HILLIER, W. R. G., "Psychology and the Subject Matter of Architectural Research", in David Canter, ed., Architectural Psychology, RIBA, 1970, pp 25-29.

12. ITTELSON, WILLIAM, HAROLD PROSHANSKY, LEANNE RIVLIN AND GARY WINKEL, An Introduction to Environmental Psychology, 1974.

13. LANG, JON AND CHARLES BURNETTE, "A Model of the Designing Process", in Lang, et. al., eds., Designing for Human Behavior, 1974, pp 43-52.

14. MICHELSON, WILLIAM, Man and His Urban Environment, Addison-Wesley, 1970.

15. MOLESKI, WALTER, "Behavioral Analysis and Environmental Programming for Offices", in Lang, et. al., eds., Design for Human Behavior, 1974, pp 302-315.

16. MUSGROVE, JOHN AND CHARLES DOIDGE, "Use of Space and Facilities by Universities", Report 6, Unit for Architectural Studies, University College London, 1968.

17. NIMH, Health Planning Aid Kit, (reprinted for the American Psychiatric Association Convention, San Francisco, CA, May 12, 1970).

18. PENA, WILLIAM AND JOHN FOCKE, Problem Seeking, Caudill Rowlett Scott, 1969.

19. RAPOPORT, AMOS, "Some Observations Concerning Man-Environment Studies", Architectural Research and Teaching (now Journal of Architectural Research), November 1971, pp 4-15.

20. ROBERTS, WILLIAM, "Physical Environment and Differential Influences on Sociocultural Development", PhD Thesis, University of Southern California, 1975.

21. ROTHLISBERGER, F. J. AND W. J. DICKSON, Management and the Worker, 1949.

22. SCICON CONSULTING SERVICES, "Layout Programs for Office Planning", London, 1970.

23. TABOR, PHILLIP, "Pedestrian Circulation in Offices", Working Papers 17-20, Land Use and Built Form Studies, Cambridge University, 1969-1970.

24. TAYLOR, MAUREEN, "The Official View of the Female User", Architectural Design, 8/1975, pp 471-472.

25. TZONIS, ALEXANDER AND OVIDIAH SALAMA, "Problems of Judgement in Programmatic Analysis in Architecture. The Synthesis of Partial Evaluations." Harvard University, Graduate School of Design (mimeo), 1974.

26. VERGER, MORRIS, "Interactive Planning System", Morris D. Verger, AIA; Los Angeles, no date (1972?)

27. WILLIAMS, ROGER J., Nutrition Against Disease: Environmental Prevention, Pitman, 1971.

28. ZEISEL, JOHN, "Fundamental Values in Planning with the Non-Paying Client", in Lang, et. al., eds., Designing for Human Behavior, 1974, pp 293-301.

29. ZEISEL, JOHN, Sociology and Architectural Design, Sage, 1975.

ENVIRONMENTAL AESTHETIC--THE GAP BETWEEN UNDERSTANDING AND APPLICATION FROM AN R&D PERSPECTIVE

Marilyn Duffey-Armstrong, Operations Analyst
Cynthia Ann Kroll, Urban Planning Analyst

Stanford Research Institute
333 Ravenswood Avenue
Menlo Park, California 94025

ABSTRACT

Recent development of various methodologies for evaluating aesthetic factors in the environment has not led to a general increase in consideration of aesthetic concerns by public agencies. While aesthetics has been broadly accepted as one factor to be considered in planning and project evaluation, interpretations of the concept and its value vary considerably in practice. Further research is needed on the role which aesthetic criteria can play in planning and action at different levels.

The term _aesthetics_ appears in many of the federal and local guidelines for project planning. Consequently, there is an increasing need for the planner to be able to make rational decisions in cases where the aesthetic factors must be considered concurrently with social, technical, economic, and ecological factors. The problem lies in the fact that the understanding and implementation of aesthetic considerations for planned activities are at different stages of development in the various local planning departments and corresponding federal agencies. Likewise, policies guiding the consideration of aesthetic factors differ. The result is not only lack of consistency but conflict. A common understanding of the term aesthetics and a comprehensive systematic method for including aesthetic factors in the project planning process are needed.

If we assume that aesthetic impacts are felt directly by individuals, then it is evident that not all individuals will react in the same manner and to the same extent to a given aesthetic stimulus. This arises from a variety of reasons, but the important implication is that different individuals will make different value judgments of the same aesthetic feature. This attitude is reflected in the cliche, "Beauty is in the eyes of the beholder." Ugliness, on the other hand, may be perceived and identified by diverse groups more easily. Junk lots, a high whining noise, a noxious odor are likely to receive more common disapproval.

Aesthetic effects do not stop with the individual, however. Because aesthetic properties affect an individual's sense of well-being, they will affect the manner in which he accomplishes his day-to-day interactions with other individuals. Accordingly, direct aesthetic impacts on individuals are transferred through these interactions into collective social effects. The behavioral manifestations of these social effects may not be uniquely related to aesthetic causes. For example, it will be difficult, if not impossible, to trace a high incidence of antisocial behavior to generally prevalent poor architectural (or other) design. However, the aesthetic character of the surroundings is likely to be cited by people as one factor affecting their satisfaction with their environment. The important thing is establishing a communicative link between project planners and the community intruded upon. An effort to make a structure pleasing to the surrounding community may carry a message that their value as people with feelings has been considered.

The rational implementation of a policy requires decisions based on a detailed knowledge of causal interactions, an explicit formulation of values, and criteria by which trade-offs can be made. We are just beginning to learn about causal interactions in the field of aesthetics, and to date the explicit formulation of values has been almost entirely in negative terms. Many methodologies for assessing aesthetic consequences concentrate on identifying levels of given aesthetic elements, without assessing comparative values of different elements. The development of criteria for trade-offs has been almost entirely economic until just recently, with the introduction of methods to quantify and measure aesthetic attributes in the environment.

A social policy can operate in several different modes: predictive, remedial, or interactive. Predictive policies reflect the planner's interpretation of how a desired goal can best be met in the process of new development. How a project should proceed is determined before the project begins. Remedial policies tend to be secondary attempts to satisfy needs which were overlooked in the initial planning and accomplishment of a project. Interactive policy incorporates procedures for ongoing review by concerned individuals and groups during the planning and implementation processes.

Because of the lack of information, predictive social policies concerning project aesthetics have been frequently unsuccessful, and sometimes spectacularly so. Such failures are often followed by remedial social policy. Remedial social policies (e.g., "plant morning glories") are better than nothing, but expensive. In the absence of sufficient information, the social policy most likely to be successful is the inter-active policy, which suffers from the disadvantage of being difficult to implement and apparently inefficient. (It is always quicker and easier to go ahead and get the job done as it ought to be done, until one reaches the point where it has been completed and is obviously a mistake.)

Some attempts have already been made to include aesthetic considerations in the decision process for all kinds of projects, from bridges and dams to urban redevelopment, and there is abundant evidence that public opinion demands much more.

Suburban sprawl and central city development rarely taken very seriously, before 1950, suddenly became a source of anxiety to both city and suburban administrators, spurring a growing army of professional planners to draft schemes for the orderly development of urban areas. Termi-nology for making aesthetic considerations became a part of the vocabulary of architects and urban planners everywhere. Terms such as "variety," "scale," "character," "uniqueness," "patterns," "texture," and many others were used to describe the aesthetic quality of an urban area.

Today, project planners face considerable pressure from private citizens on aesthetic issues. The purely functional cost-conscious engineering feats are no longer acceptable by communities adjacent to planned projects. A careful balancing of all aspects, including aesthetics, is now required in every planning activity. Passage of the National Environmental Policy Act (NEPA), 1969, placed further restrictions on planning activi-ties (at least publicly funded or licensed projects).

The objective of preserving aesthetic resources is clearly expressed in the NEPA where the Act requires the "Federal Government to use all prac-ticable means ... [to] ... assure for all Americans safe, healthful, productive, and aesthetically and culturally pleasing surroundings ... and to ... preserve important historic, cultural, and natural aspects of our national heritage, and maintain, wherever possible, an environment which supports diversity and variety of individual choice" (NEPA Sec. 101(b)(2,4)). To accomplish this, Federal agencies are directed to "utilize a systematic, interdisciplinary approach which will insure the integrated use of the natural and social sciences and the environmental design arts in planning and in decision making which may have an impact on man's environment" (NEPA Sec. 102(a)).

NEPA goes on to state that "all agencies of the Federal Government shall ... identify and develop methods and procedures, in consultation with the Council on Environmental Quality ..., which will insure that presently unquantified environmental amenities and values may be given appropriate

considerations" (NEPA Sec. 102(b)). It becomes obvious after reviewing Agency guidelines and planning procedures that the state-of-the-art for accomplishing this is at best in its infancy. Yet this section of the Act has no doubt encour-aged the continuing development at academic and research institutions of the methodologies for measuring and quantifying aesthetics.

Although the NEPA and CEQ recognize the necessity of considering aesthetic impact in environmental impact analysis there is indication of the kind of depth or investigation required for assessing aesthetic impacts. Guidance on how such impact should be considered and by whom is presently extremely vague.

A review of a few representative planning agencies demonstrates the wide range of responsibility assumed for aesthetics in environmental planning at various levels of planning activity. Though responsibilities are rarely clearly defined, it appears that Federal, state, regional, city and private agencies have begun to map out general areas of concern for aesthetics within their planning procedures. A number of generalized conclusions can be made about the state-of-the-art of aesthetics in the planning process. These are:

(1) Many agencies have institutionalized proce-dures for considering aesthetics which reflect the needs of the agency and its users. Such agencies, e.g., Federal Highway Administration, Park Services, U.S. Forest Service, have been concerned with the subject of aesthetics since long before the NEPA. Basic philosophical approaches that have developed over time demon-strate the diverse direction that each agency is taking. For instance, the primary objective of the Federal Highway Administration has centered around developing natural resources for the pur-pose of providing a pleasurable experience for highway users. Thus, highway beautification and aesthetics in general reflect an attitude of development, with considerable attention given to cost/benefit analysis and the idea of minimiz-ing, wherever possible visual impacts to the surrounding environment. This often means trying to camouflage the project (i.e., the "cosmetic attempt") or attempting to design visually attrac-tive facilities (e.g., retaining wall, clover leaf), nonetheless supporting the philosophy that man's desires (and the department's responsibili-ties) come first. The research funded by the highway administration supports this assumption by the very way it characterizes aesthetic factors and establishes criteria for evaluation of their importance. Aesthetic factors are identified by their usefulness to the driver and evaluated by their cost to the developer.

The National Park Service and (to some extent) the U.S. Forest Service appear to be more conservation-oriented, attempting to subjugate man's activi-ties to nature. Though the Park Service recently adopted a philosophy of "bold" design, their basic aesthetic consciousness is reflected in their preservation of natural resources rather than

development of them. Still, man's enjoyment is
of primary concern. The Forest Service emphasizes
the subordination of man's desires to the goal of
conserving natural resources. Visual amenities
have recently been included in their definition
of natural resources. Any activities planned or
reviewed by the Forest Service must be responsive
to the guidelines firmly established for visual
analysis of proposed projects. This often
results in costly, time consuming efforts on the
part of the planner, and in some cases, a total
re-evaluation of the need for the activity in
general.

There appears to be little, if any, attempt by any
Federal agency for establishing aesthetic criteria
at the national scale for resource development.
Problems of communication and coordination become
acute when more than one agency is involved in
development in a single area. Often the philosophical approach of either agency could apply,
but the coordination of two different sets of
values is difficult.

(2) There are no clear definitions of aesthetic
responsibilities at different levels of planning
activity. There seems to be no indication of
exactly who or what is involved in aesthetics
in environmental planning. The rather vague
generalized statements in Federal and state
guidelines as to the disciplines included under
"design arts" (they could be anyone from engineers
to potters) and the area of aesthetic concern
(i.e., what constitute aesthetic resources,
natural amenities, historical and unique areas)
offers little guidance to responding planning
agencies. Additionally, the lack of any established social policy for aesthetics leaves it
open for agency interpretation. As it stands,
aesthetic quality is often determined by an
elite few with very little public participation
or public feedback in the design process. The
tools that are used by planning agencies for
obtaining public opinion on proposed activities
are, at best, in their infancy.

The responsibilities for aesthetic or visual
quality have sifted down to the city and private
planners, who implement a large number of development projects. This places a tremendous responsibility on these individuals and local agencies
for protecting the aesthetic resources of an
entire nation. Other than a few very specific
acts (e.g., the Scenic Rivers Act, the Wilderness
Act, Highway Beautification Act, the NEPA), there
are no national controls for preserving aesthetic
quality in this country. The private sector and
city planning agencies, however, are beginning
to assume their responsibility for aesthetics
by investing both time and money in establishing
objectives for development and outlining appropriate aesthetic criteria. The problems encountered with this approach are reflected in the
fact that these agencies have a limited scope of
control (i.e., zoning, ordinances, building
codes) and are often dependent on the function
of planning activities from outside jurisdictions.
The need for coordinated planning is especially

strong at the regional level, where activities
(e.g., transportation) cross many geographic
boundaries. At the moment, this is one scale of
planning where impacts and responsibilities may
be mismatched, as implementation powers lie at
other government levels.

(3) Most progress in the use of aesthetic
assessment methodologies has occurred outside
of the public sector. There is very little
indication among agencies that any of the
aesthetic assessment methodologies available
for use are actually being tried. Most planners
either had never heard of the methods available
or found them useless for their work (a typical
complaint is that they are too subjective, too
time-consuming in data collection, not flexible
enough for diverse planning situations, and too
expensive). Only the private sector of planning
seems to consider aesthetics important enough to
spend the staff time and money to develop extensive assessment tools and seriously weigh aesthetic impacts in project evaluation. Perhaps public
pressure on the public image has initiated this
concern, but regardless, many lessons can be
learned from attempts that have been made recently
by private corporations in the area of aesthetics
in environmental planning.

In summary, we are only beginning to understand
the importance of the quality of our perceived
environment. Recent surveys show that the
Federal commitment to man-environment research
has grown considerably in the past few years.
However, much more is needed. All indications
point to the conclusion that research in the
area of aesthetics is proportionately less than
other areas of environmental concern (e.g., air
quality, land use planning, water quality) and
yet, aesthetics is as closely tied to the appreciation and acceptance of a project. The need
for variety, diversity, and freedom of individual
choice is important to the American way of life.
A growing population with diverse interests and
needs places unusually heavy demands on a world
of limited resources. In order to protect the
aesthetic rights of both present and future
generations we need to formulate social policy
for environmental aesthetics and define our goals.

The need for some nationally recognized criteria
for aesthetic considerations is apparent, particularly at the Federal agency level. Since
basic aesthetic philosophies differ among single-
purpose planning agencies, comprehensive planning
for large geographic areas is extremely difficult,
if not impossible. The following outline delineates
suggested areas for future research based on the
conclusions presented in this paper defining "where
we're at"--we now need to define "where we need to
go from here."

AN IMPROVED UNDERSTANDING OF AESTHETICS FOR
ENVIRONMENTAL QUALITY

The following research topics are proposed:

(1) At the micro-scale, research for defining man's <u>aesthetic needs</u> in his socio-physical environment:

- <u>Physicological needs</u>--Establish a range of human tolerance levels for environmental stimuli (air quality, noise, odor and other environmental factors). How do these affect man's ability for aesthetic experiences? Where is stress likely to occur?

- <u>Socio-psychological needs</u>--Define man's need for space, nature, variety, safety, tranquility, expression, belongingness, and so on. Relate to aesthetic conditions of environment. How do attitudes and values differ among individuals and identifiable subpopulations?

(2) At the macro-scale, research to define societal needs and influence of these on aesthetics:

- <u>Economic</u>--The effects of income and employment on aesthetic activities, i.e., leisure, recreation, consumerism, cultural events.

- <u>Political</u>--Social policy of agencies; predictive, interactive, or reactive. Special emphasis on environmental policy and laws.

- <u>Environmental</u> (physical)--Implications of limited resources, (open space, natural habitat, wilderness areas).

RESEARCH FOR APPLIED THEORY

The following research topics are suggested:

(1) Develop criteria for evaluating methodologies designed to assess aesthetic impacts--special emphasis on objectivity, secondary impacts, and aesthetics as an interrelated aspect of all environmental elements. Also should include aesthetics as perceived by all senses, not just visual.

(2) Increased emphasis on user preference studies for understanding individual attitudes and group values about aesthetic characteristics in the environment.

(3) Develop aesthetic quality indicators for different levels of concern (national, state-regional, community-local) and devise monitoring techniques.

(4) Develop tools for communicating aesthetic effects of changes resulting from planned activities--simulation labs for visual and auditory impacts.

(5) Develop an information system for source material on aesthetic research.

Research must proceed concurrently in each of the two general directions identified above. Our understanding of the problems must broaden, but at the same time we need to consider how this knowledge can be applied in the institutional setting.

THE NATURE OF THE APPLICABILITY GAP IN THE

DESIGN OF RESIDENTIAL ENVIRONMENTS

Elizabeth J. Harman

Policy Analyst,
Department of Regional Economic Expansion,
Government of Canada,
161 Laurier Avenue West,
Ottawa, Ontario,
Canada.   K1A OM4

John F. Betak

Assistant Director of Research,
Council for Advanced Transportation Studies,
University of Texas at Austin,
Austin, Texas, 78712,
U.S.A.

(This paper expresses the professional judgements of the authors. Points of view or opinions do not necessarily represent official policy of the institutions with which they are connected.)

ABSTRACT

The applicability gap is described as a set of unknown relationships between research on client needs in the social sciences and the search for design principles. In the belief that it is easier to bridge a gap when its dimensions are known, the paper explores the nature of the applicability gap using, as an example, the design of residential environments. A conceptual framework is outlined and identifies three basic inferences made by practising designers in interpreting the needs of their clients (users) in design terms. The most direct of these approaches is design based on needs inferred from client descriptions. Sources of difficulty which confuse even this approach are: the extent to which subjective housing concepts are verbalized; the precision of their definitions and association with other concepts; and reference or lack of reference to physical attributes of residential environments. Empirical evidence is introduced from a survey of 40 house searchers in Hamilton, Ontario, using personal construct and clustering procedures. Differences are examined between 25 classes of client-described needs in terms of likely problems in their translation into design. The intent is to indicate where, and why the applicability gap is being, and can be bridged to satisfy some housing needs more easily than others.

1.   INTRODUCTION

The EDRA Conferences were instituted seven years ago in the hope that they would provide an arena for the interdisciplinary sharing of ideas relating to environmental design. Most particularly, it was hoped that the conferences would help to bridge an "applicability gap" between research on client needs in the social sciences and the search for design principles. (In this paper the word "client" should be interpreted as the user.) The gap is evident, on the one hand, in the inability of researchers in environmental psychology and behaviour to apply their findings to design, and on the other hand, in the difficulty practising designers face in verifying that their designs are applicable to the major needs of clients, as these are identified by social scientists. The problem remains one of communication. The EDRA Conferences have largely failed to bridge the applicability gap, primarily because participants from both the client and the design realms rarely venture to communicate across the gap, but continue restricting their work to issues on either side of it.

It is easier to bridge a gap when its dimensions are known. This paper is, therefore, an exploration of the nature of the applicability gap, using as an example the design of residential environments. The first section introduces a conceptual framework. The second section reports on evidence for some aspects of the framework obtained from a sample survey of house searchers in Hamilton, Ontario.

2. THE APPLICABILITY GAP IN RESIDENTIAL DESIGN

Figure 1 depicts the major elements of the framework. The applicability gap is concerned with what is essentially an abstract concept, the actual housing needs of clients. (In this paper, the term "housing needs" is used as a general reference to cover the many requirements of people in residential environments, regardless of whether these are considered to be needs,

FIGURE 1: THE APPLICABILITY GAP IN THE DESIGN OF RESIDENTIAL ENVIRONMENTS

Realm	Element	Client-Designer Relationships
CLIENT REALM Focus of research by social scientists concerned with housing satisfaction and choice	CONTEXTUAL CHARACTERISTICS Family Status Cultural Context Socio-economic Status Environment Values and Behaviour (Life Style) Client-described Needs (Description of housing needs in terms of subjective concepts)	Design on the basis of needs inferred from client contextual characteristics. Design on the basis of needs inferred by designer from client behaviour in the residential environment.
APPLICABILITY GAP	Real Client Needs in Housing	
DESIGN REALM Focus of design research and activities of practising designers	Other Considerations (cost, technology) Physical Referents (Description of needs in terms of physical attributes) General Design Principles Elements of a Specific Design	Design on the basis of needs inferred from client descriptions.

wants, preferences, aspirations, expectations or constraints on choice and satisfaction.) Unknown functions relate the actual needs, to housing needs in the client realm where they are described in the form of subjective, verbalized concepts, and to their description in the design realm in terms of the physical attributes of residential environments.

2.1 The Client Realm

Although practising designers obviously relate to their clients, their major focus is design. Research on client needs is primarily done in analyses of the determinants of housing choice and satisfaction in marketing research and studies by environmental psychologists, sociologists, geographers and other social scientists. Housing needs are seen as determined by the values, behaviour and, therefore, the life style of the household. Values and behaviour are, in turn, a function of such contextual characteristics as stage in the family life cycle, culture, socio-economic status and past and present environmental conditions. (See reviews by Michelson, 1970; Moore, 1972; Sabagh et al 1969; and Simmons, 1968.)

Many of the more recent studies have adopted concepts and techniques from psychology, measuring attitudes to, and perceptions and preferences of people for residential environments. (Examples are papers by Flaschbart and Peterson, 1973; Flowerdew, 1973; Harman, 1975; Honikman, 1972; Johnston, 1971; Johnson, 1972; Leff and Deutsch, 1973; Michelson, 1966; Peterson, 1967; Redding, 1970; Sanoff, 1973 and Wolpert, 1965 and 1966.) In these studies residential

environments are described in the form of the subjective or mental concepts which people use to think about housing. The studies are generally limited to identifying those concepts which can be verbalized either by respondents or by the researcher. Concepts are labelled by respondents in tasks involving free response or construct elicitation, or by the researcher in designing structured questionnaires or interpreting the dimensions of factor analyses or scaling procedures. Subjective housing concepts range from references to design criteria (for example, a preferred number of rooms) to qualitative, psychological or life style requirements, including beauty, safety and privacy, for which the equivalent design criteria are often ambiguous.

In other studies relating to residential satisfaction and choice, housing attributes are defined in physical terms, or alternatively, it is not clear whether the descriptions are intended to represent subjective or objective referents. This is especially true of surveys based on structured questionnaires (for example, in the surveys of Butler et al, 1970; Hempel, 1970; and Lansing et al, 1964 and 1966), and in the theoretical models of housing and population distribution (for example, by Alonso, 1965; Herbert and Stevens, 1960; Kain, 1964 and Lowry, 1964). However, since the relationship between the subjective and physical descriptions of residential environments are as yet, undefined, and are, in fact, part of the applicability gap, much of this work only aggravates the problems of untangling the relationship at this stage. Hence, our best source of information about the requirements of people in residential environments remains their own subjective descriptions.

2.2 Design Realm

The housing needs of clients are a major factor, although not the only consideration, in the design of residential environments by architects, engineers, landscape designers and town planners. (Other concerns are, for example, cost, technical feasibility and conflict with other environmental uses.) In the process of design, client needs are interpreted in terms of elements and dimensions of the physical environment (e.g. lot size, shape and landscaping; dwelling size, style and materials; and type and location of area or building services).

2.3 Bridging the Applicability Gap for Design Purposes

Designers have traditionally interpreted the needs of people in residential environments and, therefore, bridged the applicability gap by intuitive means, although quantitative approaches are also being explored. (Cooke, 1975; Atkin, 1974 and 1975.) In the intuitive approach to design, three types of inference have been used to relate client needs to design corresponding to the three levels in the client realm (Figure 1).

First, client needs may be inferred from the contextual characteristics of prospective clients. This is the approach underlying most housing for special groups including the aged, handicapped, student, single parent and native clientele. It is also the method behind the design of housing estates by major developers who often also cater to a special group, the nuclear family with children at home. This approach is the least likely to satisfy the actual needs of individual households since it assumes knowledge of the several factors and unknown relationships which separate contextual characteristics from the physical environment in Figure 1.

The second method is design on the basis of needs inferred from values and behaviour. This is much less common in practice, although behaviour can be directly observed and design using behavioural observations is supported by some well-known studies including those of Kira (1966), Lynch (1960), and Sommer (1969). Time-space budgeting studies are also potentially useful in this respect (Stephens, 1975). This approach has a greater probability of satisfying the actual needs of clients than that derived from inferences related to contextual characteristics. In some cases, it may even be preferable to design based on the third approach, needs inferred from client descriptions.

Nonetheless, design on the basis of client-described needs remains a convenient and possibly the shortest inferential jump across the applicability gap. In this respect, the most effective means of obtaining information on needs may be in the one-to-one context of custom-built housing and by community involvement in planning where feedback between designer and clients is possible throughout the design process. However, custom-built housing is available to only a minority of higher-income home buyers and community involvement is successfully implemented very occasionally. The results of social science research on client-described needs and satisfaction, therefore, provide a useful additional source of information, particularly where a direct relationship between client and designer is impossible.

The remainder of this paper focusses on problems of bridging the applicability gap by the most direct route, i.e., design based on client-described needs. The problems of design based on behavioural observations and contextual characteristics is set aside for the present time.

Regardless of the means used to obtain information on client-described needs, their translation into a residential environment with a high probability of satisfying actual needs, depends on the ability of the designer to identify the equivalent physical referents for each subjective housing concept. Different degrees of difficulty, however, are involved since, even as it is intuitively understood, the nature and complexity of the relationship between subjective and physical attributes differs between individual concepts. Three major sources of difference based on the nature of subjective housing concepts, are discussed in this paper: (1) the degree to which concepts are verbalized, (2) the exactness of concept definition and, (3) reference to physical attributes, or the lack thereof.

To make an effective translation of actual needs into design, the designer relies on the ability of people, as clients or respondents, to verbalize their housing needs. At least some concepts, however, may not be expressed verbally. For example, a particular need may lie outside the context or domain of the discussion or experiment. (For an illuminating discussion of the nature of the doman, see Kelly, 1955.) In social science research, the extent to which the experiment relies on the ability of respondents to recall or recognize their needs, and the manner in which residential environments are displayed, are at least two factors implied in the methodology, which can greatly influence the needs which are elicited - hence, the arguments for multi-operational research designs, (Campbell and Fiske, 1959; Garner et al, 1956; and Webb, et al, 1966). Moreover, not all concepts occur in semantic or lexical codes. Preverbal and visual codes are discussed by Arnheim (1969) and Neisser (1966), among others.

The precision of concept definition is also important. The design process is facilitated by a precise, well-bounded definition of a housing concept and its one-to-one correspondence with design elements. However, there are at least two sources of concept imprecision. First, people differ in their ability to articulate their ideas, accurately. Secondly, the results of work on associative response provides evidence that concepts are interrelated, in the sense that the use of one unconsciously activates others. This has led coding theorists to the conclusion that concepts are organized into mental structures, including lists, schema, hierarchies and spaces, which must be identified if we are to understand the implications, connotations or meaning of a given concept. (See discussions in Kelly, 1955; Posner and Warren, 1972; Wickens, 1970.) A similar notion lies behind the concern with the measurement problems of "fuzzy sets" in behavioural research (Gale, 1972). The study by Peterson (1967) is, perhaps, the most well-known attempt to identify cognitive associations between concepts relating to residential environments. Identifying the design equivalent of an imprecise concept, or a complex cognitive structure, is much more problematic than for a simple, exact and relatively independent concept.

Finally, the design process may be simplified if clients can identify physical or design elements which they perceive as related to the satisfaction of a particular need. For example, a stated preference for 3 bedrooms to satisfy the space requirements of the household, contains an explicit design criteria. In contrast, a request for housing which allows privacy from neighbours has a more ambiguous meaning in design. The design requirements for external privacy have been extensively explored by architects such as Chermayeff and Alexander (1963) and Safdie (1961, 1966); yet, at least for some cultures, privacy may be a function more of behaviour than of the designed environment (Rapoport, 1969).

In the following section, the results of an empirical analysis of client-described housing needs are used to examine differences between subjective concepts in terms of their verbal description, precision of definition and association with other concepts, and reference to physical attributes of the residential environment. The intent is to indicate where and why the applicability gap is being, and can be bridged to satisfy some housing needs more easily than others.

3. SURVEY OF HOUSING NEEDS

3.1 Objectives, Sample and Research Design

A survey of 40 house searchers was conducted in Hamilton, Ontario, with the intent of eliciting the nature of the subjective concepts people use to evaluate and, hence, choose between alternative vacancies. The study was considered necessary despite the many previous studies with similar objectives simply because we still lack sufficient understanding of the nature of subjective housing concepts. This is manifest in the ambiguities relating to terms like "neighbourhood"; in the difficulties behavioural geographers face in operationalizing conceptual models of housing choice (Brown and Moore, 1970; Demko and Briggs, 1970; Gale, 1972, 1973), and by

no means least, in the existence of the applicability gap between social science research and design in residential environments.

An inductive, multi-operational design was considered most appropriate. Concepts used by respondents in their current search were obtained first, by free recall. The major data set, however, was elicited using Kelly's (1955) personal construct elicitation and repertory grid procedures. The terms "construct" and "concept" are used interchangeably in this paper. A photographic display of nine vacancies was utilized. The photographs were mounted on a map of the city and supplemented by additional, standard, real estate information on price, lot size and number of rooms and bedrooms.

The analysis involved first, identifying and classifying the total 438 elicited concepts on the basis of their semantic labels and secondly, a search for associations between concepts. The analysis of associations provided a test of the reliability of each class by establishing whether the concepts in a given class behaved consistently in their relationships with those in other classes. It simultaneously led to the identification of structures or clusters of associated descriptions. The initial labelling and classifying of concepts was achieved using a master code of over 200 words or phrases obtained from a preliminary content analysis. Concept associations were initially sought using a principal components analysis (INGRID; Slater, 1972), on the scores given to each vacancy on each construct in the 40 repertory grids. However, since this approach provided little insight into the relationships, a clustering procedure (Ward, 1963) was used to group concepts on the basis of their correlations and associated angular relations. (INGRID computes the angular distance (α) between two concepts, 1 and 2, as $\alpha_{12} = \cos^{-1} r_{12}$.)

The 438 concepts were classed into 25 broad categories listed in Table 1. The major associations between concepts of different classes are depicted in Table 2 and Figure 2, where the values refer to the mean angular distance between the designated concepts. A mean angle of less than 65° is arbitrarily taken as evidence that, at least in aggregate, concepts in the two classes are positively related, (P in Table 2). Conversely, angles near 90° indicate independence or a slight negative relationship between the two classes (I in Table 2). The associations identified in this manner were confirmed for the majority of individual grids by the pattern of correlations which were statistically significant and insignificant at the .05 level.

The non-verbalization of some important concepts - a situation which complicates the design process - did occur in the survey. Important concepts which do not appear are tenure and a concern for privacy in the dwelling. The need for internal privacy and its relationship to crowding and stress, particularly for lower-class households, is well recognized (see Schorr,

TABLE 1:   CONCEPT CLASSES AND FREQUENCY OF CONCEPT USE

Column A: Number of Respondents using Concepts of this Class
Column B: Total Frequency

Class No.	Description	A	B	Class No.	Description	A	B	Class No.	Description	A	B
1	dwelling size, internal space, no. of bedrooms	37	51	9	general appearance of house, cleanliness, and upkeep	9	9	16	trees, landscaping and topography	24	27
2	concerns about a basement	10	10	10	occupancy of dwelling, (single or multiple, attached or detached)	11	11	17	parking, garage and driveway	25	32
3	concerns about a dining room	6	6					18	other features of the lot	4	5
4	concerns about other rooms	2	3					19	neighbourhood considerations	19	34
5	concerns about room shape, location, versatility, redecoration and maintenance	5	5	11	no. of floors	12	12	20	accessibilities	18	32
				12	age of dwelling building material structure and maintenance concerns	28	40	21	urban downtown "in Hamilton"	5	5
6	concerns about windows	13	15					22	suburban, rural "out of Hamilton"	16	18
7	concerns about fireplace (s)	4	4	13	other aspects of house design	7	9	23	Place names:	12	12
				14	size & shape of lot	27	31	24	financial considerations	25	30
8	other aspects of dwelling interior	6	7	15	privacy of lot & dwelling, spacing from neighbours	23	27	25	uncoded	2	3
									TOTAL		438

FIGURE 2:   ASSOCIATIONS AMONG CONCEPTS BY TYPE

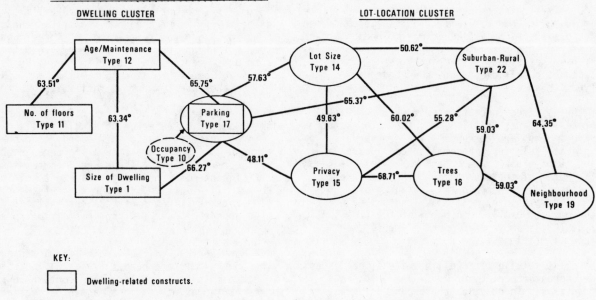

TABLE 2:   AVERAGE ANGULAR DISTANCE BETWEEN SELECTED CONCEPTS*

Concept Type	1	6	10	11	12	14	15	16	17	19	20	22
1	44.4 P	75.6	83.5	74.6	63.3	82.3	82.0	81.8	66.3	76.8	91.0	73.3
6		50.3 P	88.8	101.5	75.4	81.1	61.8	87.7	67.2	89.4	105.9	74.6
10			NA	109.7	85.1	67.8	73.7	86.5	64.7	90.8	77.0	67.0
11		I°	I°	NA	63.5	82.1	94.8	73.4	77.4	68.1	89.2	NA
12	P			P	49.8 P	80.3	77.3	70.1	65.7	69.7	88.8	75.3
14						70.0	49.4	60.0	57.6	74.5	83.8	50.6
15		P		I	P	P	42.8 P	68.7	48.1	76.0	98.3	55.3
16		I				P		46.2 p°	73.1	66.4	74.5	59.0
17			p°			P	P		56.1 p°	72.8	88.0	65.4
19		I°	I°							73.7	70.6 +	64.3
20	I	I		I°	I		I		I	+ P	53.5	86.9
22						P	P	P		P	I	42.9 P

P   positive relationship mean angularity < 65.00°   I   independence or a negative mean angularity > 85.00°

*   Angularities as computed by INGRID   o   Based on less than five cases

+   The average angularity between construct types 19 and 20 is biased by two respondents who use several constructs of both types. If these two are excluded the number of cases drops to 11, and the average angularity of these is 87.39°, with a standard deviation of 19.34.

1966). Its omission here may be explained if the sample, which was basically middle-class, assumed that privacy is satisfied in most Canadian urban homes. Alternatively, respondents unconsciously may have satisfied their privacy needs by acquiring a sufficient number of bedrooms (Type 1, Table 1).

Of the elicited concepts, those which are likely to present fewest difficulties for interpretation by designers, are concepts which are verbally explicit, relatively uncomplicated by associations with other concerns and refer to physical attributes of the environment. Major concept classes which may be in this category are: "Dwelling Size, Internal Space and Number of Bedrooms" (Type 1); "Occupancy of the Dwelling" (Type 10); "Number of Floors" (Type 11); and "Accessibilities" (Type 20).

The class relating to dwelling size (Type 1) has the highest frequency of use. The words and phrases used to describe these concepts are explicit references to physical dimensions including the size of the house, the number and size of rooms in general, and the number and size of bedrooms in particular. The dominant concern is for the number of bedrooms as opposed to other concerns such as the size and shape of rooms, arrangement of space or overall floor space. Very few respondents described their concern in general terms; e.g. "a large house". The content analysis indicated no association with other concepts although in Figure 2, dwelling size appears related to dwelling age and maintenance and to parking facilities.

Not unexpectedly, other straightforward concepts are those which referred to single family dwellings, apartments, condominiums and other shared structures (Type 10) and to a preferred number of floors (Type 11). There were too few instances of concepts mentioning a basement, dining room or fireplace to test for concept interrelationships, but from their content analysis, these also appear to pose few problems of interpretation.

More unexpected, is the straightforward nature of the accessibility concepts (Type 20). At first glance, this is a complex class containing references to a variety of local and non-local access concerns which could not be broken into separate classes, either in the content analysis or on the basis of concept interrelationships. However, while access, particularly within the neighbourhood, is seen as satisfying a number of higher psychological concerns such as anxiety about the safety of children, the descriptions of the concepts themselves are explicit, concrete references. Typical concerns are for local access in terms of distance to schools, public transportation, shopping, general services, open space and recreational areas. Access outside the neighbourhood, to work and the city centre, appears, but is not of major concern to this sample. Consistent with Redding's findings (Redding, 1970), locations which are both too near or too far from a given destination are seen as undesirable. Perhaps most interestingly, this set of concepts is one of the few to show a marked tendency to have a meaning and use independent of all other major classes (Table 2).

Designers face much greater problems in interpreting and, therefore, designing for such concepts as house appearance, cleanliness and upkeep (Type 9); dwelling age and related concerns (Type 12); external privacy (Type 15) and neighbourhood concerns (Type 19). Concepts in each of these classes are characterized by one or more of the problems of an ill-defined meaning, complex pattern of associations or lack of reference to the physical environment.

Concepts relating to the appearance of the dwelling have a strong intuitive meaning. Outside of their association in this sample, with a notion of cleanliness, however, the concepts are extremely difficult to pin down to a more precise definition, especially in physical terms. Words typically used to describe them are evaluative, e.g. "attractive", "acceptable", "ugly", "has character", "is interesting". The onus is, therefore, on the designer to suggest alternatives until one is recognized as acceptable or attractive.

The neighbourhood concepts (Type 17) also have a strong intuitive meaning but are equally difficult to interpret more precisely. In this case, the problem is not lack of references to the physical environment, but a multiplicity of labels for which it is impossible to distill a general concern. Respondents describe neighbourhoods using a variety of phrases including references to the social fabric, roads, sidewalks, traffic, housing and the built environment, services, amenities, vegetation and qualitative assessments of safety, beauty and noise levels. Moreover, this is the only major class of concepts which does not behave consistently in the associations between concepts within the class and with concepts of other classes. While these results confirm the elusive and multi-dimensional nature of neighbourhood which is widely discussed in social science research, it does not help the designer.

Concept classes Type 12 (age, materials, structure and maintenance concerns) and Type 15 (external privacy) pose a different problem. Both are complex concepts in that they have a number of distinct, but related connotations which, presumably, should be satisfied simultaneously in the physical environment for maximum effect. In

the case of the Type 12 concepts, the connotations are all contained within the class and relate to the dwelling age, the soundness of the dwelling structure, building materials and the possibility or necessity for maintenance and redecoration. They are grouped together because they frequently appear in different combinations in the same concept and in the test for class reliability based on inter-concept associations, Type 12 concepts do behave consistently.

In contrast, concepts relating to external privacy (Type 15) are complicated not only by the varied labels associated with privacy (Harman and Betak, 1974), but by a network of strong associations with other classes of concepts (Figure 2). These include associations with lot size (Type 14) and parking (Type 17), the desire for a rural-suburban location (Type 22) and, to a lesser extent, with concepts relating to trees and landscaping (Type 16). Note the similarity of this grouping and the one found by Peterson (1967) between open space, privacy and greenery. Presumably, the related concepts may contribute to the satisfaction of privacy concerns, which represent a higher-order need. However, the exact nature of the contributions is only intuitively understood at this stage, leaving designers with little substantive information on how to design with confidence for external privacy.

4. CONCLUSIONS

The nature of the applicability gap which separates social science research and the activities of practising designers is poorly understood and, therefore, difficult to bridge. This paper explores some aspects of the gap in the context of research and design for residential environments. Using a conceptual approach and some supporting data, the paper demonstrates some of the inferential problems which designers face in attempting to interpret and design for, the different housing needs of clients which are a major focus of much social science research. Concepts which are verbally explicit, non-complex and refer to the physical environment pose the fewest problems, and are, therefore, likely to be satisfied most often. Action is required to close the applicability gap, particularly for those housing needs which are still poorly articulated, complex and which are phrased only as abstract, psychological and life style requirements. This may require public education on the nature of design alternatives to encourage a clearer expression of client needs and a move to shift social scientists from their current preoccupation with subjective concepts to the nature of the relationship between the mental and physical world.

References

ALONSO, W. (1965) Location and Land Use: Toward A General Theory of Land Rent. Cambridge, Mass: Harvard University Press.

ARNHEIM, R. (1969) Visual Thinking. Los Angeles: University of California Press.

ATKIN, R.H. (1975) "An Approach to Structure and Urban Design". Series of three papers, Environment and Planning, 1974 and 1975.

BROWN, L.A. and E.G. MOORE (1970) "The Intra-Urban Migration Process: A Perspective", Geografiska Annaler, 52:B, 1-13.

BUTLER, E.W. et al (1969) Moving Behaviour and Residential Choice: A National Survey. Highway Research Record, National Cooperative Highway Research Report No. 81.

CAMPBELL, D. and D. FISKE (1959) "Convergent and Discriminant Validation by The Multitrait-Multimethod Matrix", Psychological Bulletin, 56, 81-105.

CHERMAYEFF, S. and C. ALEXANDER (1963) Community and Privacy. New York: Doubleday and Co. Inc.

COOKE, C. (1975) "Nikolai Krasil'nokov's Quantitative Approach to Architectural Design: An Early Example", Environment and Planning, B, 2:1, 3-21.

DEMKO, D. and R. BRIGGS (1970) "An Initial Conceptualisation and Operationalisation of Spatial Choice Behaviour: A Migration Example Using Multidimensional Unfolding", Proceedings of the Canadian Association of Geographers, 79-86

FLASCHBART, P.G. and G.L. PETERSON (1973) "Dynamics of Preferences for Visual Attributes of Housing Environments", in W.F.E. Preiser (ed.), Environmental Design Research, Volume I, Stroudsberg, P.A.: Dowden, Hutchinson and Ross, 98-106.

FLOWERDEW, R.N. (1973) "Preference Rankings on Several Attributes: Applications in Residential Site Selection", Environment and Planning, 5, 601-707

GALE, S. (1972) "Black Communities: A Program of Interdisciplinary Research", in H.M. Rose and H. McConnell (eds.), Perspectives in Geography 2: Geography of the Ghetto, Northern Illinois University Press, 53-86.

GALE, S. (1972) "Inexactness, Fuzzy Sets and the Foundations of Behavioural Geography", Geographical Analysis, 4, 337-349.

GALE, S. (1973) "Explanation Theory and Models of Migration", Economic Geography, 49, 257-275.

GARNER, W.R., H. HAKE and C.W. ERIKSEN (1956) "Operationism and the Concept of Perception", Psychological Review, 63, 149-159.

HARMAN, E.J. and J.F. BETAK (1974) "Some Preliminary Findings on the Cognitive Meaning of External Privacy in Housing", in G.H. Carson (ed.) Man-Environment Interactions: Evaluation and Applications, EDRA 5, 11. Cognition and Perception Basil Honikman (ed.) EDRA Inc. 41-55.

HARMAN, E.J. (1975) "A Behavioural Analysis of the Concepts Used in Housing Choice", Unpublished Ph.D. dissertation, Department of Geography, McMaster University, Hamilton, Ontario.

HEMPEL, D.J. (1970) "A Comparative Study of the Home Buying Process in Two Connecticut Housing Markets", Centre for Real Estate and Urban Economic Studies, Real Estate Report No. 10, University of Connecticut, Storrs, Connecticut.

HERBERT, J. and B.J. STEVENS (1960) "A Model for the Distribution of Residential Activities in Urban Areas", Journal of Regional Science, 2:2, 21-36.

HONIKMAN, B. (1972) "An Investigation of the Relationship Between Construeing of the Environment and its Physical Form", Proceedings of EDRA 3, University of California, Los Angeles, 6-5-1, to 6-5-11.

JOHNSTON, R.J. (1971) "Mental Maps of the City: Suburban Preference Patterns", Environment and Planning, 3, 63-72.

JOHNSON, R.M. (1972) "Trade-off Analysis: A Method for Quantifying Consumer Values", Market Facts Inc. mimeo.

KAIN, J.F. (1962) "The Journey-to-Work as a Determinant of Residential Location", Papers and Proceedings of the Regional Science Association, 9, 137-160.

KELLY, G.A. (1955) The Theory of Personality: The Psychology of Personal Constructs, New York: Norton.

KIRA, A. (1966) "Privacy and the Bathroom", reprinted in Proshansky et al, Environmental Psychology: Man and His Physical Setting, U.S.A.: Holt, Rinehart and Winston, 269-276.

LANSING, J.B. (1966) Residential Location and Urban Mobility: The Second Wave of Interviews. Ann Arbor: University of Michigan.

LANSING, J.B., E. MUELLER and N. BARTH (1964) "Residential Location and Urban Mobility, Institute for Social Research, The University of Michigan, Ann Arbor, Michigan.

LEFF, H.S. and P.S. DEUTSCH (1973) "Construeing the Physical Environment: Difference Between Environmental Professionals and Lay People", W.F.E. Preiser (ed.), Proceedings of EDRA 4. Stourdsberg, P.A.: Dowden, Hutchinson and Ross.

LOWRY, I. (1964) A Model of Metropolis Santa Monica: The Rand Corporation, RM-4035-RC.

LYNCH, K. (1960) The Image of the City, Cambridge, Mass: M.I.T.

MICHELSON, W. (1966) "An Empirical Analysis of Urban Environmental Preferences", Journal of the American Institute of Planners, 32, 355-360.

MICHELSON, W. (1970) Man and His Urban Environment: A Sociological Approach. Reading, Mass: Addison.

MOORE, E. (1972) "Residential Mobility in the City", Commission on College Geography, Resource Paper No. 13, Association of American Geographers, Washington, D.C.

NEISSER, U. (1966) Cognitive Psychology New York: Appleton-Century-Crofts.

PETERSON, G.L. (1967) "A Model of Preference: A Quantitative Analysis of the Visual Appearance of Residential Neighbourhoods", Journal of Regional Science, 7, 19-32.

POSNER, M.I. and R.E. WARREN (1972) "Traces, Concepts and Conscious Constructions", in A.W. Metton and E. Martin (eds.), Coding Processes in Human Memory, Washington: V.H. Winston and Sons, 25-43.

RAPOPORT, A. (1969) House Form and Culture Prentice-Hall, Toronto.

REDDING, M.J. (1970) "The Quality of Residential Environments: Preferences for Accessibility to Residential Opportunities", Published Ph.D. dissertation, Department of Civil Engineering, Northwestern University, Evanston, Illinois.

SABAGH, G., M.D. VAN ARSDOL, JR., E.W. BUTLER (1969) "Some Determinants of Intra-Metropolitan Residential Mobility: Conceptual Considerations, Social Forces, 48:1, 88-98.

SAFDIE, M. (1961) "Fallacies, Nostalgia and Reality", Habitat, 4:4, 2-7.

SAFDIE, M. (1966) "Habitat '67", Habitat, 8:5, 2-6.

SANOFF, H. (1973) "Youth's Perception and Categorization of Residential Cues", in W.F.E. Preiser, Proceedings of EDRA 4, Stroudsberg, P.A.: Dowden, Hutchinson and Ross. 84-97.

SCHORR, A.L. (1966) "Housing and its Effects", in Slums and Social Insecurity, U.S. Dept. of Health, Education and Welfare, Social Security Administration, Division of Research and Statistics, Research Report No. 1. 7-31.

SIMMONS, J.W. (1968) "Changing Residence in the City: A Review of Intra-Urban Mobility", Geographical Review, 58, 622-651.

SLATER, P. (1972) Notes on INGRID 72. London: Institute of Psychiatry.

SOMMER, R. (1969) Personal Space: The Behavioural Basis of Design, Englewood Cliffs, N.J.: Prentice-Hall.

STEPHENS, J.D. (1975) "Time-Space Paths and the Mechanics of Socio-Environmental Constraints" Paper read at the Annual Association of American Geographers, Milwaukee.

WEBB, E.J. et al (1966) Unobtrusive Measures: Nonreactive Research in the Social Sciences. Chicago: Rand McNally.

WICKENS, D.D. (1970) "Encoding Categories of Words: An Empirical Approach to Meaning", Psychological Review, 77, 1-15.

WOLPERT, J. (1965) "Behavioural Aspects of the Decision to Migrate", Papers and Proceedings of the Regional Science Association, 15, 159-169.

WOLPERT, J. (1966) "Migration as an Adjustment to Environmental Stress", Journal of Social Issues, 22, 92-102.

AUTHOR BIOGRAPHIES

Elizabeth J. Harman is presently a policy analyst employed by the Department of Regional Economic Expansion, Government of Canada, in Ottawa. She completed a Ph.D in Urban Geography from McMaster University in 1975, with a thesis entitled "A Behavioural Analysis of the Concepts Used in Housing Choice". Previous publications and papers which she has authored relate to housing, applications of multi-dimensional scaling and women.

John F. Betak is Assistant Director of Research at the Council of Advanced Transportation Studies, University of Texas at Austin. For the five years prior to 1975, he was Assistant Professor of Geography at McMaster University and holds a Ph.D in Geography from Northwestern University. He has eleven years of experience in professional planning as an agency planner and consultant on a variety of projects ranging from urban design through to transportation planning and environmental impact studies.

UNDERSTANDING URBAN DEVELOPMENT

Andrew Gruft and Donald Gutstein

School of Architecture
University of British Columbia
Vancouver, B.C., Canada
V6T 1W5

ABSTRACT

The past decade has seen a significant increase
in dissatisfaction with the urban environment,
and mounting citizen opposition to development
proposals throughout North America. Yet most
attempts at improvement have so far been
ineffectual.

This paper outlines the conceptual basis for the
construction of a simulation model of the urban
development process, describes the method by
which such a model can be built, and presents
a preliminary description of the model in order
to demonstrate both the feasibility and usefulness of the approach. It examines the methodological difficulties involved in (1) using so-
called urban problems and the public's discontent
(with the development of their cities) as a
focus for developing the model, and (2) the
case study method as the major source of
empirical data.

The study differs from other studies of urban
regions in one critical aspect. Other studies
model the interaction of demographic, economic
and physical processes of regions and test
various policy proposals on the simulation. The
consequences of implementation of these policies
are then presented to an elected decision maker
who is asked to make the appropriate decision.
This study, however, starts from a dissatisfaction
with the actions of present decision makers. It
hypothesizes that the major problems facing
our cities derive from the structure of decision
making, and the way in which citizens, and
information about their needs, are excluded
from the whole policy and planning process. It
therefore models the decision-making process
with the purpose of developing proposals for
improvement, and would test how these proposals
would fare at the hands of the decision makers
involved.

1.   THE CONTEXT

The past decade has seen a significant increase
in public dissatisfaction with the physical
development of our cities. Faced with
situations in which their wishes have been
ignored, citizens groups have opposed many
projects. Indeed there have been temporary
"victories". Unfortunately such projects reappear,
often in a different place or form, but with the
same objectionable characteristics as before.

This "brush fire" phenomenon cannot be allowed
to continue. Forced into a position where they
could only react negatively to decisions already
made, citizens groups tend to oppose almost all
development. Developers, in turn, further screen
their actions from the public. The result is a
totally polarized situation where all decision
making becomes suspect, and no citizen participation is possible. Given such a highly-charged,
volatile situation, the liklihood of making
good planning and development decisions is greatly
reduced.

Planners have very little real contact with the
public--the ultimate users of their projects.
They think of people in terms of market demands,
economic trends and age group distributions
rather than in terms of their values, goals and
activities. Given the profound impact of the
urban development process on all our lives, this
form of planning is inadequate. Every city
dweller requires the use of hundreds of physical
facilities as he goes about his daily rounds.
Therefore, it is essential that he have an
adequate voice in how these facilities are
conceived, planned and produced.

If the situation is to improve, our goal must be
the implementation of meaningful citizen participation in urban decision making, and realistic
planning based on comprehensive knowledge of
urban processes by both technically-trained
professionals and the lay public.

2.   THE PURPOSE OF THE STUDY

The first objective toward this long-range goal
must be a clear understanding of how urban
development actually occurs--what underlying
processes are at work to produce the urban
environment? If we could answer this question
--if we could identify the problem areas in the
urban development process, and appraise the
factors leading to these problems--we could
make realistic proposals for improving the whole
climate of decision making.

Because the urban development process is complex,
with many relationships between its parts, it is
most important that any study be comprehensive;
that it include all the subprocesses involved,
for any serious omissions would significantly
impair our understanding of how it functions.

One way of understanding such complex systems is
by simulating--building models of the system in
action--so that we may try out our proposals on
the model, and watch for unanticipated consequences of our actions.

This paper outlines the conceptual basis for the
construction of a simulation model of the urban

development process, describes the method by which the model can be built, and presents a preliminary description of the model in order to demonstrate both the feasibility and usefulness of the approach. It examines the methodological difficulties in using urban problems and public discontent with urban development as a focus for developing the model, and in using the case study method as a major source of empirical data.

The study differs from other studies of urban regions in one critical aspect. Other studies model the interaction of demographic, economic and physical processes of regions, and test various policy proposals on the simulation. The consequences of implementing policies are then presented to an elected decision maker who is asked to make the appropriate choice. Such studies pay little or no attention to the decision making process itself. For example, they ignore decisions that may be taken by other participants in the process, often with the express purpose of neutralizing the desired effect of the original intervention.

This study, however, started from a dissatisfaction with the actions of present decision makers. We hypothesized that the major problems facing Canadian cities derive mainly from the ways in which decisions were being made, and from the exclusion of citizens from the policy and planning process. We therefore examined the decision making process, and would test how proposals for improvement would proceed through the decision making maze. Empirical data was generated through a study of cases of decision making in the Greater Vancouver region.

3. SIMULATING COMPLEX SYSTEMS

There have been many partial studies of the urban development process--dealing with the construction industry, the housing market, real estate financing, land use planning, or the public economy. But rarely has there been a study of the "total process of preparing, producing, distributing and servicing the physical environment".[2] Yet, without comprehensiveness, understanding is inhibited: we require an overall framework which helps to relate the behavior of significant parts of the system.[3]

A significant characteristic of urban systems is that their component parts are related in very complex ways, so that it may be more important to study their interactions than to study any element in isolation.[4] Forrester pointed out that intuitive plans to solve complex urban problems often produce results opposite from those intended."[5]

Efforts to ameliorate the living conditions of the poor in one particular city attract more poor families to the city, eventually worsening the living conditions; or efforts to decrease automobile congestion by building freeways attract

more development, more cars and very soon, greater congestion than before. "In the complex system causes are usually found, not in prior events, but in the structure and policies of the system."[6]

Consequently, Forrester and others have concluded that a promising strategy for dealing with complex systems is to construct computer models, which by simulating the system's behavior, can reveal the dynamic characteristics of the system's structure and the relationships among its components. If the system's behavior could be simulated realistically, then an adequate basis would exist for suggesting ways for its improvement.[7]

Schwartz et al[8] have identified three situations in which it is both feasible and desirable to model decision processes. Consider the case where authority and power are fragmented. For the modelers of urban areas, "the task is to describe the system so that the consequences of different programs or policies can be better understood. The information is then presented to a decision maker to take appropriate actions."[9] But which decision maker? There are just too many organizations with overlapping jurisdictions, fragmented authorities and conflicting goals. To guide a policy proposal through the decision making maze may well be a more difficult task than to decide which policy should be implemented.

Second, they suggest that it may be appropriate to model decision processes if the modeler is outside the system.

Finally, decision processes may be modeled if the probable time to policy or structural change is short. This refers to the case in which there is a general desire for change by many groups, and a consequent likelihood of the changes actually occurring, but no clear idea as to which changes to make.

Schwartz et. al. cite the area of land use controls as being ideal for the modeling of decision processes because it meets all three criteria.

4. URBAN ENVIRONMENT PRODUCTION SYSTEM

The hypothesis which guided this project was that most urban difficulties stem from structural limitations in the system which produces our urban environment. To understand why citizens were excluded from participating in the development of their cities, attention would have to be focussed directly on the structural and instutional arrangements through which the system operated. The Midwest Research Institute's study recognized the centrality of this point: "There is...consensus that the present industry structure, given both internal and external constraints, cannot produce a radically different and better America, i.e., an environment much more responsive to human needs and values, unless fairly massive changes occur in structural relationships, operating styles, and the ways in which planning is accomplished."[10]

How had business and government coordinated their development efforts to their mutual advantage? How did the structure of city hall prevent any real contact between the planning department and the citizens being planned for? Why did plans for freeways keep reappearing even though citizens were dead set against them? Consideration of questions such as these led us to the hypothesis that inadequate decisions would continue to be made--and the urban environment would continue to deteriorate--unless major structural changes were made in the urban development process.

Decision-making situations never exist in a vacuum, but are dependent on many other decisions that may have been made previously, and others yet to be made in the future. When a group of decision-making situations interrelate strongly, they form a decision making system. In this study we were concerned with the system of decisions regarding the production of the urban environment, or the Urban Environment Production System.[11] This was defined as the complex set of processes which interact to transform money, land, material, labour and information into physical facilities--the roads, parks, buildings and other facilities which support human urban activities.

The structure of the system was then defined as the stable pattern of decision making behavior which had developed among the units to achieve the system's goals--within a variable environment and with the use of limited resources. It was seen to be hierarchical in nature; that is, the units themselves were composed of interrelated units.[12]

Eight groups of processes or subsystems were identified in our study:

A. Urban Policy Making
B. Allocation of Funds
C. The Urban Land Market
D. The Developer Processes
E. Municipal Assessment of Projects
F. Project Construction
G. Supply of Personnel
H. Distribution, Use and Assessment of Projects

We thought of each of these processes as a system of its own, with its own decision making structure among the units or subprocesses. For example, the Municipal Assessment of Projects was in itself a complex system with two of its basic units being Municipal Rezoning and Development Assessment which interacted in predictable ways.

3. LACK OF EMPIRICAL DATA

Although the building industry has been the subject of many studies and much data was available, most of this material was unsuitable for our purpose. To be useful, a study should be based on a comprehensive view of urban development; it should emphasize people as participants, not consumers; and it should focus on decision making. The bulk of the literature suffered from two additional flaws--each author viewed the urban situation through the spectacles of his own discipline, and, treated each problem separately, as an isolated piece. Consequently, the action which the author would suggest reflected his own attitude--financial, administrative, political, sociological, or aesthetic.

But more important, urban studies lack an empirical base. Referring to the recent uprising in concern about urban affairs, Lithwick concluded that an understanding of urban problems was based on inadequate evidence; that the evidence where provided was often meaningless or borrowed uncritically from the United States; and that solutions for the "urban crisis" (if indeed there was one) were based on fantasy and prejudices of the author.[13]

6. THE CASE STUDY METHOD

In order to consider the urban development process in depth we relied heavily upon the case study method--examining decision making situations by reconstructing the history of a project as a chronology of critical events.

Given the large number and great diversity of projects available for examination, three criteria were used to select representative examples: the presence of public opposition, indicating unsatisfactory decision making; project of large impact so that the most important developments in the city would be included; and a variety of types of development, so that most of the different modes of operation of the system might be uncovered.

The chronology of events was supplemented with more detailed studies of the participants in the project--development companies, financial institutions, government agencies and departments, and citizens groups who were involved or had some influence on the outcome.

The case study served many purposes: acting as a basic orientation to urban development issues, illustrating the system in action in a very concrete way and aiding in the identification of critical processes, key actors and organizations, major system outputs and in public dissatisfactions.

By abstracting the chronology of events, detailed descriptions of the cases were transformed into diagrams of the urban development process. The perils of such a method were fully recognized-- inadequate sample, unstandardized methods, difficulty in replicating results. Given our goals of comprehensiveness, generality and breadth of view, however, these were deemed acceptable.

7. THE CHRONOLOGY:

First, a chronology of events was prepared for each case from newspaper clipping files. Second, a detailed list of questions was prepared about the information obtained. What were the motives for the action? Why did the Mayor announce the plans at this time? Why did a certain lawyer keep reappearing?

Then all the available documents bearing on the case were collected: planning department reports, minutes of city council and other bodies; memos; letters on file. These documents provided many answers, but also generated another list of further questions.

The next step required interviews with the major participants and other persons knowledgeable about the case. Because a great deal was already known at this stage, specific questions could be asked. This was important, because people forgot, or they didn't want certain information known, or they had only a partial view of the situation. General questions such as "what acutally happened" gave next to useless results.

By the end of the interviews, and with the rearrangement of the material, the chronology was about as detailed and accurate as one was likely to get. The chronology thus prepared represented the basic data source.

8. ACTIONS:

The second phase of the work involved the extraction of actions from the chronology, and determination of the goals of the actions and the constraints operating on them. For example, regard the first item in Figure 1: "Mayor Alsbury approached William Zeckendorf, president of Webb and Knapp, responsible for the development of Brentwood Shopping Centre, to sponsor Vancouver's slum clearance program." What happened? Mayor Alsbury approached Zeckendorf. But if only role relationships were specified, and the particular people involved were ignored, the action reduced to: "promotion by Mayor towards developer". It could be seen that the unique event of Alsbury approaching Zeckendorf was in fact, only a typical case of a more general kind of event, and one that occurs frequently in many Canadian municipalities.

For each item in the chronology, then, a parallel action was designated and the actors determined. Although the action is an abstracted unit, it could be verified empirically. The number of promotions by mayors towards developers in various Canadian cities per year could be tabulated to learn if this is a standard behavior of the role. Presumably, there is a finite number of such actions, which in total, would make up the extent of the system's behavior of interest.

Below is a sample page from the Analysis of the Coal Harbour Development case study.

Figure 1. PRELIMINARY ANALYSIS OF COAL HARBOUR DEVELOPMENT PROPOSAL CASE STUDY.

DATE	ITEM FROM CHRONOLOGY	ACTION	CRITERIA (GOALS & CONSTRAINTS)
1961			
Aug 18	Mayor Alsbury approached W. Zeckendorf... to sponsor Vancouver's slum clearance program	Promotion by mayor towards developer	- need for urban renewal - desire to attract large scale development - mayor's desire to make name for himself
1961-1962	During the year Zeckendorf...all the land between Bidwell & Chilco	Land assembly by realty company for developer	- need to use local company - possibility of profitable development
1962			
Mar 29	Webb & Knapp announced plans for... and a marina of undisclosed size	Developer announces proposal to public	- publicity to attract funding and rentals - desire to create a good public image
1964			
Jun 24	Public meeting in Playhouse Theatre ... Rathie threatened to close down meeting	City Council holds public hearing with respect to zoning application	- required for zoning change by Charter - desire to neutralize opposition to scheme

9. CRITERIA

The next part of the analysis addressed itself to the "why" of the action. Why did the mayor approach the developer? Why did the city council hold a public hearing with respect to a rezoning application? It was assumed throughout that the action which occurred corresponded roughly to an underlying decision.

The research problem was to discover the set of criteria for each decision. These could be found in many sources. A whole set of criteria were set down in legal documents such as the Vancouver Charter, the Municipal Act, and Municipal Bylaws and Resolutions. Others could be found in operating manuals, organization and job descriptions, application forms, policy statements and a host of other documents, some public and some confidential. To date these sources have been scarcely tapped. A systematic and comprehensive effort will be required to give better results.

A group of criteria more difficult to investigate, and perhaps even more important, are the informal, unwritten ones, which exist in the minds and memories of the role players. Incumbents to a role undergo a period of socialization during which they learn the unwritten rules of office --the network of mutual expectations and power relationships that have evolved over the years as the normal way of "doing business". Because the mayor actively courted the developer in the first place, he had to become the developer's

advocate, forcing the development proposal through at any price. Therefore another goal may have been served in the holding of a public meeting: the desire to neutralize public opposition to the scheme, which could be achieved by a token hearing. This could be seen when council, in spite of massive opposition to the scheme, approved the rezoning the next day!

The area of informal goals and constraints was very difficult to map. In the present study, it was impossible to make any accurate descriptions. Gaming or other simulation techniques may be useful here. A game might be built in which knowledgeable persons played the roles of mayor, developer and planner, and were given situations in which they had to make decisions. Their perceptions of their own and the other players' motives could be used as a potential source of criteria, which would then be validated through other techniques, such as interviewing the real participants.

Figure 2.   MUNICIPAL REZONING PATTERN

CASE STUDY EXAMPLES					
COAL HARBOUR #1	COAL HARBOUR #2	COAL HARBOUR #3	ARBUTUS #1	ARBUTUS #2	REZONING PATTERN
Feb. 13, 1963: Meeting held between Mayor Rathie, John Oliver, the acting Planning Director, and Soden and Loftus of Webb and Knapp. Content not disclosed.	Aug.21, 1964: Mayor Rathie hails transfer of Coal Harbour property from Webb & Knapp to "local" consortium. Assures public new owners intend similar proposal.	May 1969: Prior to announcing their proposal, Four Seasons Hotels Ltd. obtained lease from Harbour Park Development Ltd. No documented discussions with city officials.	1966: Dominion Construction makes agreement for development of site at Arbutus and King Edward with CPR. Begins preliminary discussions with city.	1968: Soon after rumors of possible expropriation by city, Marathon Realty (CPR) announces "village square" scheme.	Developer initiates preliminary discussions with city officials.
March 30, 1963: Technical Planning Board refuse to approve the Webb and Knapp scheme until major changes made. Developers say changes would make scheme uneconomical and request review with council.	March 1965: Developers take 6 months to prepare proposal. During this time Planning Dept. policies in relation to the design are examined.	May 1969: Application did not spark immediate requests for changes (these occurred later).	June 1967: Between July '66 and June '67 Dominion conducts several studies at request of Director of Planning: market analysis and traffic studies for single dept. store shopping centre.	Documented requests occurred only after official application had been made.	City officials including the Director of Planning examine the proposal and make requests for additional information and/or alterations.
June 7, 1963: Webb & Knapp submit revised plans to Planning Dept. based on new set of zoning standards set down by council in May 1963.	March 16, 1965: Harbour Park Develop. Ltd. presents official application to council. New scheme includes 15 apt. blocks, large shopping centre, marina, restaurants.	May 6, 1969: Four Seasons Hotels Ltd. submit proposal to city.	Sept. 18, 1967: Dominion Construction submits proposal for two dept. store shopping centre.	April 24, 1969: Kiss & Harrison, architects for Marathon submit application for rezoning.	Developer submits official application for rezoning to city.
June 7, 1963: Brahm Weisman, ass't director of planning announces Planning Dept. will have to approve new plans and prepare case for public hearing.	April 1, 1965: Planning Dept. had processed application by this date.	August, 1969: Between May and August Planning Dept. assesses the proposal and notes several points contrary to planning policy.	Sept. 1967: Planning Dept. requests economic study of two dept. store shopping centre.	May 28, 1969: Marathon submits substantiating traffic study by Graham of Seattle.	Planning Depart. assesses proposal.
No input from the Design Panel noted in documentation of this case.	Design Panel not consulted until strong opposition encountered at public meeting in April.	No input from Design Panel noted in documentation of this case.	Dec. 14, 1967: Design Panel reviews application; unanimously agrees to refer scheme back for further study.	May 29 & June 5, 1969: Design Panel examines proposal. Question need for such centre and traffic implications.	Design Panel may assess proposal.
June 7, 1963: Ass't Director of Planning indicates publicly that Board of Administration will have to approve before any information released.	April 1, 1965: Technical Planning Board and Board of Administration had both dealt with application by this date.	April 22, 1969: Technical Planning Board demands changes, through-view and public areas adjacent to water. Their request incorporated the Board of Administration position.	Jan. 1968: Technical Planning Board receives report from Planning Dept. approving application with minor modifications.	July 4, 1969: Technical Planning Board recommend public hearing. Dir. of Planning approves scheme with minor modifications.	Technical Planning Board and Board of Administration assess proposal.
June 7, 1963: Town Planning Commission sets project committee back in motion to study final plans for presentation to public hearing.	April 1, 1965: Town Planning Commission had processed application on this date.	No input from Town Planning Commission noted in documentation of this case.	Jan. 12, 1969: Dir. of Planning presents proposal to Town Planning Com. After large public meeting protests the development, Com. voted against application Feb. 2, 1969.	Sept. 5, 1969: Town Planning Commission rejects new proposal 6-1.	Town Planning Commission assesses proposal.
June 24, 1963: Public Hearings attended by 600 people. Proposal generally opposed. Presentations limited to 10 minutes. Mayor Rathie threatens to evict noisy spectators.	April 26, 1965: Proposal meets strong opposition. Council decides to defer decision and refers plan to Design Panel.	Aug. 28, 1969: Public hearing indicates strong opposition.	Mar. 18, 1968: Over 1800 people attend hearing -- largely opposed.	Sept. 25, 1969: Approx. 1800 people attend hearing (24 briefs against, 8 for).	City Council holds public hearing.
June 27, 1963: Council approves application 10-1 with 10 pages of conditions.	June 1965: Council approves revised application and decides no further public hearings are required.	Aug. 29, 1969: Council approves development and requests $1m performance bond (reduced to $200,000 on Oct 22). Revised plans approved by council on Nov. 18, 1969.	Mar. 19, 1968: City Council rejects proposal 6-4.	Oct. 7, 1969: At coffee break 4 NPA council members agree to allow rezoning to CD-1 but to reject proposal. After heated debate motion was passed 7-4.	City Council votes on application.

10.   PATTERNS

Upon analysis of the actions it was seen that many events apparently occur in clusters, with a very definite order to them. In principle, each action should fit into at least one pattern, and perhaps more. There should be few unique events in the development process.

One important pattern--a municipal rezoning pattern--is tabulated on the previous page. The same pattern appeared in various case studies. In the Coal Harbour Development rezoning occurred three times over the ten year period, with each new developer's attempt to get a development underway. In the Arbutus Shopping Centre Proposal, rezoning occurred twice, as both Dominion Construction Ltd., and Marathon Realty Ltd. attempted and failed to build a large regional shopping centre in a middle class residential area.

Actions do recur in very definite patterns, and it was proposed to designate these as the basic subprocesses of the system--the structure of the system being the pattern of decision making behavior which has evolved through time. In principle, an analysis of a sufficient sample of cases should produce an exhaustive list of the basic decision points and subprocesses in the urban environment production system.

11.   URBAN PROBLEMS & PROCESSES

In spite of the shortcomings of work on urban problems, it seemed reasonable to assume that such reports, when taken together with numerous detailed studies of urban phenomena, covered a broad range of urban affairs. Such literature, when combined with a survey of citizens' views on urban problems, should produce an overview of the extent of the urban environment production system.

First, general works on urban problems were surveyed, such as Lithwick's study for the Federal Government, the Economic Council of Canada's survey of urban economic trends and a reader prepared for high school students and citizens groups.[14]

Next, specialized studies on each defined problem area were consulted. Each reference was noted for its analysis of the problem at hand. The major difficulty with this was that what one author considered to be a problem, the next author might consider to be the cause of another problem. One might consider land speculation to be a major cause of high housing costs, while another might believe high land costs to be a function of inflation, and speculation as a cause of something else--urban sprawl.

In order to avoid this confusion in the literature, we used the notion of the factor which led to the problem. With this notion, a middle course was

Figure 3.   FACTORS LEADING TO MAJOR URBAN
PROBLEMS

PROBLEM	FACTORS
1. Housing	
a. Cost of Money	-inadequate supply of mortgage funds -high interest rates inflation
b. Cost of Land	-inflation - speculation -land assembly procedures -proliferation of rules and regulations -multiplicity of jurisdictions -property taxation procedures -servicing requirements
c. Cost of Construction	-disorganized building industry -inadequate design and research -proliferation of rules and regulations
2. Urban Decay and Renewal	-lack of minimum standards -property taxation procedures -ageing of structures - slum landlords -lack of citizen participation -expropriation practices
3. Urban Sprawl	-uncoordinated development -inadequate planning procedures -property taxation procedures -land speculation -financing policies of senior governments -provincial government highway policy -zoning procedures -consumer preferences
4. Transportation	-lack of coordinated research -inadequate capital investment -consumer preferences - provincial highway construction policy -inadequacy of municipal financing and planning -lack of funds for mass transit - lack of regional transit and planning authority - favorable financial position of auto - increasing number of automobiles -pressure of auto, road-building and development industries
5. Pollution	-automobile design -consumer preference -highway and road design
6. Municipal financing	-inadequate provincial grants -unsatisfactory municipal provincial regulations -fragmented municipal authority -property taxation procedures - uncoordinated federal government policy

steered between a problem and its imputed "causes", the processes that produce it. For example, "inadequate supply of mortgage funds" and "high interest rates" were designated as factors affecting the problem of "high housing costs". They were not problems in themselves, yet they were not processes.

An assessment of the literature was made to produce a list of factors which were considered to be important in leading to each problem.

Figure 3 summarizes these problems and tabulates the factors which the literature considers significant in generating them. Many of these factors deal with political, administrative or business processes. Clearly it was essential that these processes be included within the system, if we were to generate the problems of interest to us.

With the set of factors determined, we then tried to visualize underlying processes which might generate these behaviors.

For example, if a proliferation of municipal rules and regulations governing development was thought to be a factor in adding to many urban problems, then we thought of a process which generates municipal rules and regulations, e.g. a municipal policy making process. Such a process would bear investigation, in order to isolate critical variables which might generate a surfeit of rules, bylaws, regulations, business laws and so on.

12. A PRELIMINARY MODEL OF THE URBAN DEVELOPMENT PROCESS

The final step in the study was to combine the unquantified processes identified through the literature, with the empirically-based patterns derived from the case studies. When all these processes were assembled, we had a first approximation of a model of the Urban Environment Production System.

Given limited time and resources, it has been possible to do this in a very crude and haphazard way, based partially on the methods outlined, and augmented by personal knowledge of the system's operation. Instead, the emphasis of the work has been on the conceptual framework and the method of investigation, rather than on the system content. Therefore no conclusions could be drawn about the Urban Environment Production System's behavior, and any speculation based on the work can only be tentative, and almost certainly unreliable.

The diagram that follows attempts to set out, in graphic form, the major processes or subsystems which interact to produce the urban environment. Each case study can be traced through the diagram generally from left to right, so that money, land, materials, labour and information appear as inputs from the left side and physical facilities as outputs on the right. Public reaction and use of facilities appear as a major feedback loop. At this stage of the work, 33 major processes have been identified.

Figure 4. URBAN ENVIRONMENT PRODUCTION SYSTEM: MAJOR PROCESSES

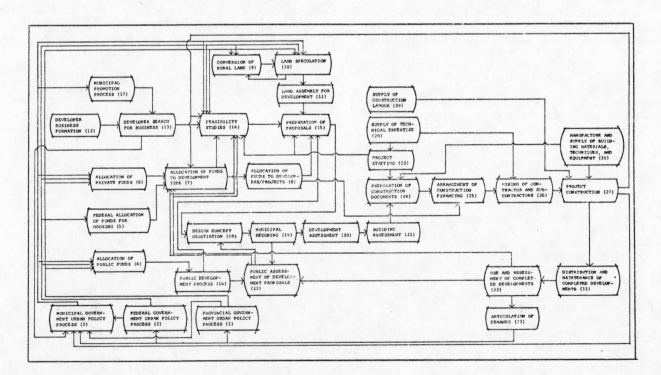

13.   FUTURE WORK

Three stages of work would be required to construct an operating model, although these need not be done sequentially.

The model must be made comprehensive. Public reaction to urban development, the outputs of the system and the organizations involved in the process, all require much further study. The literature must be reviewed to derive further potential processes and to examine other models which might be useful. More case studies must be undertaken so as to identify the different modes of operation of the system, and all discernable patterns of action. This should give an initial qualitative picture of the whole system.

Subsystem models must be constructed for each process. From lists of criteria, hypotheses would be proposed to explain the actions of each process. Then experiments would be performed where necessary and practicable. From the data collected quantitative values could be developed suitable to manipulation, and an operating submodel for each process produced.

For example, assuming that Municipal Rezoning is a critical process, the construction of its submodel might proceed by asking three general questions: Under what conditions are preliminary applications to rezone initiated? Under what conditions do such applications receive final approval? What is the impact of such rezoning approval on actual urban development practice and on further rezoning applications?

To answer such questions, a program of research would be undertaken into past rezoning applications. Note would be taken of such information as the location of land; existing and proposed uses; type of developer; estimated cost of development; date; organizations for and against the proposal; anticipated cost of services; approval or rejection of application at various stages; number of cars and people generated by the development; floor space ratio; and so on. With the identification of critical variables, quantitative values could again be developed.

The next step would be to link the submodels together in a model of the whole system in operation. Again the program would proceed by proposing hypotheses to explain the relationship between processes, such as between Municipal Rezoning and Land Speculation. These would then be tested, and finally the comprehensive simulation would be developed.

Once the model was running and had been calibrated, proposals for changing the system could be tested. The results could be observed and evaluated by citizens groups. Where results were considered desirable, citizens could effect appropriate action in order to implement the proposals. The model could also be used to compare the effectiveness of different courses of action in bringing about the desired changes.

Several years of work would be required to simulate realistically the behavior of a system as complex as the Urban Environment Production System. But this does not mean that nothing applicable will be produced until that time. By carefully choosing those portions of the work which seem to require action most urgently interim measures can be devised to provide more effective short term solutions to those urban problems which are most critical.

NOTES

1. Based on Research undertaken at the University of British Columbia with the aid of Canada Council Grant S70-0866. The study is fully reported in A. Gruft, D. Gutstein and D. Whetter, "The Urban Environment Production System", School of Architecture, University of British Columbia, April, 1973.

2. Midwest Research Institute, "The Building Industry: Concepts of Change (1920-2000)", in Creating the Human Environment, Urbana: University of Illinois Press, 1970, p. 157.

3. See M.A. Goldberg & C.S. Holling, "Systems Studies of Urban Regions". University of British Columbia, mimeographed, 1970.

4. The notion of organized complexity was first formulated by W. Weaver in "Science & Complexity", American Scientist, 36, 1948, pp. 536-544.

5. See Fortune Magazine February 1972, p. 137.

6. Jay W. Forrester, Urban Dynamics, Cambridge, Mass: M.I.T. Press, 1969, p. 9.

7. See Michael A. Goldberg & C.S. Holling, "The Vancouver Regional Inter-Institutional Policy Simulator", Vancouver: University of British Columbia, 1970; M.A. Goldberg, C.S. Holling, R.F. Kelly, "Vancouver Regional Simulation Study 1970-71", Vancouver, Resource Science Centre, University of British Columbia, 1971.

8. S. Schwartz, A. Sokolow & E. Rabin, "Decision Making", in N.R. Glass & D.E.F. Watt, "Land Use, Energy, Agriculture & Decision Making", A Report to the Natural Science Foundation, May 28, 1971.

9. Ibid., p. 204.

10. Midwest Research Institute, op. cit., p. 162.

11. System is used in the common sense of "a set of units with relationships among them... the state of each unit being constrained by, conditioned by, or dependent on the state of other units" (James G. Miller, "Living Systems Basic Concepts", Behavioral Science, 10, 1965, p. 200). It should be emphasized that a

system is a simplified abstraction; "an incomplete image of the real world" (Gordon
Pask, An Approach to Cybernetics, New York:
Harper & Bros., 1961.) Knowledge of the
system depends on several things: the
purposes of the observer, the observed
characteristics of the situation of interest
and the methods of both observing and recording those phenomena of interest. (Karl W.
Deutsch, The Nerves of Government, New York:
Free Press of Glencoe, 1966, pp. 5-6.)

12. Herbert A Simon, "On the Concept of Organizational Goal", Administrative Science
Quarterly, 1, June 1964, p. 2.

13. N.H. Lithwick, Urban Canada: Problems &
Prospects, Ottawa: Central Mortgage &
Housing Corporation, 1970, p. 13.

14. N.H. Lithwick, op. cit.; Economic Council of
Canada, The Canadian Economy from the 1960s
to the 1970s." Fourth Annual Review, Ottawa:
Queen's Printer, 1967. Ralph R. Krueger & R.
Charles Bryfogle (eds.), Urban Problems, A
Canadian Reader, Toronto: Holt, Rinehart &
Winston, 1971. For a general survey of Urban
problems, see also: N.H. Lithwick & G.
Pacquet (eds.), Urban Studies: A Canadian
Perspective, Toronto:Methuen, 1968; National
Commission on Urban Problems, Building the
American Economy. Washington, D.C.:
Government Printing Office, 1968; Editors of
Fortune, The Exploding Metropolis, Garden City,
N.J.: Doubleday-Anchor, 1958; H. Wentworth
Eldridge (ed.), Taming Megalopolis, Garden
City, N.J.: Doubleday-Anchor, 1967; Edward
Highbee, The Squeeze, Cities Without Space,
New York: Morrow, 1960; and A Question of
Priorities, New York: Morrow, 1970.

TOWARDS A COMPREHENSIVE MODEL OF HUMAN STRESS

Uriel Cohen

School of Architecture and Urban Planning
University of Wisconsin-Milwaukee
Milwaukee, Wisconsin 53201

ABSTRACT

The concepts of human stress and adaptation provide a useful framework for modeling some man-
environment relations, despite certain conceptual
and methodological limitations. A proposed
model emphasizes a holistic view and comprehensive analysis as an approach for further integration of fragmented, man-environment related,
traditional research. It is postulated that the
model is more operational for conditions of loss
and deprivation, in which the individual has to
cope with increased demands while personal resources and options are limited or decreasing,
e.g. illness and hospitalization. Imperative to
the understanding and interpretation of stress
research in these conditions are clearer definitions of "adaptive", "maladaptive" and the "cost
of stress", concepts that are central to any
eventual intervention by design.

INTRODUCTION

Human stress and adaptation are not new concepts,
nor are they underused theoretical frameworks,
as reflected in recent reviews (Lazarus, 1966;
Levine and Scotch, 1970; McGrath, 1970). What
follows is, then, not a development of a new
theory, but an attempt to build upon certain
aspects of recent and past work in human stress,
both in man-environment studies (MES) and in the
traditional disciplines. As Proshansky (1970)
notes, future development of theories unique to
the study of man-environment relations should be
preceded by "integrative phases": 1. concept
definition and elaboration, and 2. establishing
linkages between man-environment concepts and
ideas, research, and theory in various fields.

WHY STRESS AND ADAPTATION?

Of course there is no lack of plausible theoretical frameworks available to MES in allied
disciplines. In EDRA 4 proceedings, Rapoport
(1973) groups theories and conceptual frameworks
used in MES into twelve categories which are
based on a variety of contextual, methodological
and philosophical approaches. It demonstrates
not only the multi-disciplinary origin of these
theories, but also the search, in MES, for
broader theoretical orientation and models for
linking and integrating knowledge.

The concepts of stress, adaptation and performance are mentioned as one of Rapoport's
categories and take a prominant place in a later
collection, (Windley, et. al., 1975) of theories
in environment and aging. A review (Rapoport,
1975) of these selected contributions in gerontology has identified stress and adaptation as
one of the most frequently used and applied
concepts. I would argue that this is no coin-
cidence: situations in which the individual has
to cope with increased demands while personal
resources and options are limited or decreasing,
lend themselves more readily to theoretical
frameworks employing the concepts of stress,
adaptation and competence. Moreover, human
stress, being a process, is a coherent system of
relationships between environment and behavior.
It often deals with observable and measurable
variables, which make this framework less abstract and a better tool for description and
explanation of environment-behavior relations.

Conditions of loss and deprivation e.g., old age,
are not the only contexts in which the concept
of stress is being used: review of MES literature
yields assorted theoretical applications of
stress and adaptation. For example, Wohlwill
(1966; 1974) relates stimulation to equilibrium
and stress, and proposes the "optimization principle". Simmel (1959), Wirth (1938) and Milgram
(1970) talk about unusual sensory stimulation in
the urban context, and relate overload to coping

mechanisms of the city dweller. Stokols (1972 a; 1972 b) uses a stress model to distinguish between density and crowding, and Altman (1975) further explores crowding phenomena with reference to stress, its precipitating conditions, coping behaviors, and outcomes.

However, as the long list of research continues with an abundance of contextual and topical variations, it is also evident that narrower disciplinary perspectives of stress are prevailing.

THE LACK OF A COMPREHENSIVE STRESS MODEL

The different disciplines provide the basis for a converging multi-disciplinary view of the stress process, by supplying the information about the uniformities and regularities that constitute our knowledge base. Simultaneously, disciplinary perspectives usually hinder comprehensive understanding of human stress and adaptation by focusing on and amplifying selected parts of the process.

A clearer division between disciplinary approaches to stress is provided by the levels of measurement employed in research: although not the exclusive domain of the respective discipline, biology and physiology emphasize the physiological level, body functions, and organismic responses. Cognitive, emotional, and motivational functions are the focus at the psychological level; behavioral aspects of task-performance, social and interpersonal relations are the subject of the social sciences, and so on (McGrath, 1970).

While this disciplinary fragmentation is perfectly legitimate, as each discipline has its own goals and methodologies, it is an obstacle to integration. The complexity and difficulty of integration is also compounded by the semantic "jungle", the product of ever increasing disciplinary specialization and the resulting jargon.

THE NEED FOR A COMPREHENSIVE, SYSTEMATIC STRESS MODEL

Most of the available stress research comes from the traditional disciplines, with their methods and procedures, controlled laboratory studies, and experiments that can be characterized as mostly single variable, stimulus-response processes.

However, the analysis of primarily single variable research lacks the heuristic view of the complex real world phenomena. The stress process can be described as <u>dynamic system</u> with some non-constant probabilities that often handicap traditional research. Although classic science research ultimately facilitates most of the needed testing and generation of new information, it is the comprehensive model of the stress

process that would provide for better structuring of research as well as for more objective, balanced interpretation of its findings.

WHAT IS STRESS?

In order to facilitate the ensuing discussion, a general definition and description of "stress" is necessary, simplified and tentative as it may be.

As stress phenomena seem to have three main components-cause, process and outcome, some disciplinary theories and definitions are situation-based, others are process-related, and some emphasize stress responses (McGrath, 1970). Despite the different approaches, most present some image of the complete cycle; for example, Lazarus' view is that "stress is a generic term for the whole area of problems that includes the stimuli that produce stress reactions, the reactions themselves, and the various intervening processes" (Lazarus, 1966: 27). More specifically, human stress is conceived as a state evoked by many particular stimuli, or specified levels of a certain stimulus, called stressors. A characteristic of a stressor is its ability to trigger a coping process as a response to actual or perceived disequilibrium. The impact of stress is dependent mostly on the intensity of the stressor, the characteristics of the individual, and situational factors. The link between the perceived stimulus and physiological, psychological and behavioral responses, is through certain known nervous or hormonal pathways, or still unknown intermediaries. Through this process some resources are mobilized, and at times, depleted. Stress response is the activity and the outcome (both latent and manifest) of coping with the stressor.

TOWARDS GREATER INCLUSIVENESS

The focus of this presentation is the furthering of a convergence of stress-process models, a paradigm that is more inclusive, and yet possesses sufficient specificity. In order to make this model relevant to MES it should concern itself with external phenomena related to the physical environment; likewise, it should reflect, at the analytic level, spatial behavior as well as other responses (Rapoport, 1973). The purpose of the proposed model is also to simplify a complex process into a basic and generic taxonomy, and to increase its analytical and operational manageability. The model provides a clearer understanding of relationships between components of the process; it also enables one to deal with each component in isolation but with a perspective of the whole process. This, hopefully, will lead towards a future model of stress, that like the real-world phenomenon will transcend the arbitrary, narrower levels of analysis designated by biochemical, physiological, psychological or socio-cultural perspectives.

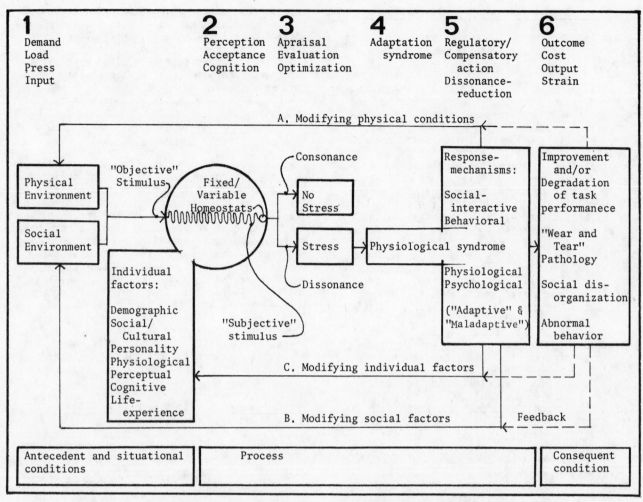

FIGURE 1:   THE PROCESS OF HUMAN STRESS: A PARADIGM FOR ENVIRONMENTAL ANALYSIS

A MODEL FOR THE STRESS PROCESS

The following model of stress--a schematic representation of a complex real life process--was
developed on the basis of various empirical
uniformities derived from a variety of sources.
As such, it represents a convergence of views
and approaches regarding the phenomenon of
stress. The groups of descriptors in the upper
portion of the diagram are the most common terms,
(often synonyms) for each phase, as encountered
in the literature.

The first stage of the process is the antecedent
and situational condition: the potential stressor
(the external stimulus) is generated by the physical and/or social environment; certain stimuli
are internally generated.

In the second stage, process, the stimulus is
appraised by the organism, and determined to be
stressor or non-stressor. This is the stage
where individual and situational differences
affect the way a stimulus is perceived.

These individual characteristics and the quantity and quality of the stressor also determine
the response mechanism that is being employed:
responses vary from physiological adaptation
syndromes to regulatory and compensatory actions
of various types. The boundary between these
categories is not clear-cut, as responses are
a result of interacting processes between physiological and psychological variables; some of
the responses are overt behaviors, others are
covert and many are not immediately detectable.
The consequent condition that follows is the net
outcome of the process, including long term
"costs" and other effects. Finally, the stress
process is indeed a dynamic one, and cyclic. As
suggested in the paradigm, certain reactions to
stress will change the realities surrounding the
individual, thus eliminating "old" stressors and
possibly creating new ones. Detailed description
of the model's components is beyond the scope of
this paper[1]. The following discussion is limited
to general description and some key aspects of
the process that have a bearing on later arguments.

Phase 1: Stress Inducing Stimuli-Stressors

Stress inducing stimuli are the forces of events that can cause stress by their excess, absence, or their special combination.

Potential stressors are most often traceable to an event or condition outside the organism, and thus the link of environment to behavior. Frequent stress-research topics are noise, temperature, radiation, pollution, pesticides, and other elements in the physical environment. Some potential stressors are physiological, e.g., physiological exertion, while others involve both physical and social-psychological elements, e.g., crowding, highway driving, isolation and confinement, perceptual overload, failure and social rejection, sensory deprivation, perceptual and social ambiguity, etc. Traditionally the main sources of stressors are grouped under the physical environment or the social environment—both also called external environment. Internal sources are classified as psychological or physiological. Interrelating and overlapping stimuli sometimes make identification and classification difficult. Situational factors such as goals, activities, duration, etc. also play a role in this phase: for example, if there is a social component in the situation, group structure, the individual's relation to the group and activity variables would be factors in stimulus configuration e.g., strangers vs. friends in high density space could be perceived as "crowding" vs. "no crowding", (Stokols, 1972 a).

Traditional conceptions of stress are often evolved around obvious and unequivocal extreme situations. Stress is, however, a continuum on which less severe instances are more difficult to identify and are subject to varying perception. Many of the above examples suggest that stress is evoked by changes in the environment that imply threat. However, stress reactions sometimes arise from continued interaction with an "objectively" unchanging environment. Moreover, as discussed later, some stressors are purposely sought after and are perceived as "positive".

Phase 2: Perception and Stimulus "Filtering"

As the still "objective" stimulus is being perceived and "filered" by the organism, several individual factors tend to discolor and affect its meaning. Whether a 90 db. sound is perceived as "music" or "noise", high density as "cozy" or "crowded" and so on, depends also on the properties of the individual. Different people perceive differently the social and physical environment, despite many basic characteristics that all human beings share. Cross cultural, sub-population and individual variations have their effect on human behavior and experience; these variations affect not only the perception of stimuli but also the selection of coping mechanisms and responses, once stress is encountered. "Variability factors" include life experiences; demographic variables such as age and sex; cultural variables such as ethnic and socio-economic background; personal-skill factors such as creativity and intelligence; physiological factors such as health, physical disorders, and motor skills; personality factors such as ego strength, need achievement and abnormality; perceptual capacity; cognitive capacity; and others.

Phase 3: Appraising the Stimulus

In this phase, the stimulus (by now subjectively perceived) is being appraised by the organism to determine if it is a stressor or non-stressor. This evaluation is performed through "fixed" or "variable" homeostats, monitoring and comparing actual vs. desired levels of stimulation. Steady state, homeostatic behaviors are related to the relatively stable and narrow human tolerance ranges e.g., change in internal body temperature. On the other hand, for some stimuli criteria of monitoring vary e.g., what is too much or too little changes with time and circumstances. This variability is termed "optimization level theory" by Wohlwill (1974). The evaluation of the stimuli involved in a situation, using some homeostatic criteria, determines if there is dissonance (or incongruity) i.e., stress, or consonance, i.e., no stress.

Phase 4: Coping with Stress/Physiological "Adaptation Syndrome"

The cognition of an actual or impending disequilibrium—stress—is followed by a series of coping responses. Termed by Selye (1956) as the General Adaptation Syndrome (GAS), coping is described as the adaptive or resistive process mobilized within the organism in response to stressors.

Activating this sequence of events are several neurophysiological and biochemical organismic systems including the autonomic nervous system reactions and the secretions of the adrenal glands, further divided into two categories: the adrenal cortical and the adrenal medullary activities. For example, perception of a situation as dangerous and fearful may instantly trigger mediation by adrenal medullary activity to produce several hormones; the better known ones are adrenaline and noradrenaline. Several acute physiological responses due primarily to adrenaline would follow: increased heart rate, blood pressure, blood sugar content and respiration rate, a shift of blood from the skin and viscera to the brain, and other alterations; these measures are designed for "fight or flight" responses, while other measures are designed for adaptation and "accommodation". The latter category include many homeostatic regulatory reactions, mostly autonomic, e.g. internal responses to over exposure.

It is important to note that as people have outgrown their prehistoric adaptation patterns of "fight or flight", many of the body's responses to modern times' stresses have become phylogenetically less efficient or inappropriate. This is due mostly to the lack of opportunity to complete natural biological cycles e.g., mobilization of energy, such as elevated hormonal levels, are often not discharged by action, and have to be internalized.

Knowledge and consideration of this GAS's aspect is central to the interpretation of "costs" and what is "adaptive".

Phase 5: Coping With Stress/Regulatory Action

In conjunction with internal responses and physiological regulatory action, other coping behaviors are potentially available to the individual. Their objectives are: 1. to deal with the stressor, eliminating or decreasing its stressful properties; and 2. preventing or decreasing the consequences of stress.

Courses of action available are schematically described as A. modifying the physical environment; B. modifying the social conditions; C. modifying individual factors on the physiological and psychological levels. For example, a situation of sensory overload such as a noisy party can be encountered by (A) retreat to a quieter environment, (B) social-interactive behavior aimed at reducing the noise, or (C) perceptual/cognitive "allocation of attention" to selected conversation.

The selection of particular "adaptation" action within the categories of coping behaviors is again influenced by individual and cultural factors.

Phase 6: The Outcome of Stress

The great capacity of people to adapt to environmental stresses under ordinary or even extraordinary conditions is often demonstrated (cf. Dubos, 1965).

However, while most frequently the process results in apparent resolution, each homeostatic activity performed by the individual to maintain its equilibrium has inherent cost in organismic resources. "Reasonable" demands result in "normal" wear and tear; excessive stress is followed by a more articulated physiological and/or mental pathology. The premise is that the coping responses in one body-system often have some pathological consequences for another body system (Levine and Scotch, 1970). Examples in the literature for "indirect" physiological outcomes range from fatigue to the "diseases of adaptation"; behavioral outcomes include depression and withdrawal, regression or aggression; changes in cognitive functioning affect information processing, and so on.

Finally, there are those "unresolved" stress situations with apparent "maladaptation" and consequent outcomes of performance degradation,

social disorganization, negative social-interactive behavior, in addition to the "costs" described earlier.

STRESS AND ADAPTATION: SOME ISSUES

The study of human stress and adaptation is not free of problems; some of the methodological and conceptual issues associated with this framework are indeed handicapping research. Some of the problems are: 1) perception and appraisal of stress are subject to great variability. 2) stress responses are also subject to the same variability. 3) usually only apparent costs of stress are considered. 4) stress can also be a positive force. 5) "adaptive/maladaptive" are subjectively and normatively interpretated.

We postulate that under certain conditions, defined as loss situations, much of these methodological and conceptual problems diminish, thus making the stress model a more effective and applicable tool.

Variability: The subject of individual-differential cognitive approaches in the appraisal of and reaction to stress was presented earlier. Especially with low stress levels, operational measures of the same presumed factor show disturbingly low relationships to one another (Lawton, 1975). If prediction is an important goal of the model, than perceptual variations should be controlled or become subsidiary components of the stress model.

Which Costs to Consider: Stress outcome is not always immediately manifested or directly related to the stress situation. The majority of stress research deals with overt, short term responses-- the apparent cost, but not necessarily the real or the only cost of stress. Covert, or even overt, long-term consequences of stress are rarely part of a research framework, with few notable exceptions e.g., Holmes (1971) who related life events and changes to health and morbidity.

What is Adaptive and What is Maladaptive?

The definition of "adaptive" turns out to be largely normative, subjective, and therefore, a complicated issue. The basic problem lies with the coping mechanisms that work in the short run but not in the long run; and those that work, but at a cost to the individual and his goals, either directly, or through secondary consequences.

Typically stress reaction determines the position regarding adaptation e.g., "good motor-cognitive performance" is "adaptive" while "post stress low frustration tolerance" is "maladaptive", (Glass and Singer, 1972). Clearly, the scope of events here is momentary, and the longer-term perspective as well as inclusion of variables other than task performance can change an apparent "adaptive" to "maladaptive".

Stress as a Positive Force: Stress research is mostly devoted to its "negative" aspects--the deleterious effects of stressful situations. However, under normal conditions, stress usually improves human performance for a relatively short period. Characteristically the performance curve would look like an inverted U, with improvement followed, after certain peak, by degradation and deterioration of performance. Milder or moderate stresses are noted as important requisites for normal human development of perceptual and cognitive functions, as well as for motivational processes. Nahemow and Lawton (1973) suggest that in the context of gerontology, for example, as individual competence decreases, the chance for maladaptive behavior and a negative effect increases. Small changes in environmental press in people of low competence may evoke positive change in the quality of affect or behavior; moderate stimulation is viewed here as a useful environmental intervention for therapeutic goals.

Cost vs. Benefit: Should all potentially stressful situations be controlled? Bertalanffy is one who views adaptation and homeostasis as outmoded notions for an organism which is not a passive recipient of stimuli:

"If life, after disturbance from the outside, had simply returned to the so-called homeostatic equilibrium, it would never have progressed beyond the amoeba which, after all, is the best adapted creature in the world--it has survived billions of years from the primeval ocean to the present day.
...Life is not comfortable settling down in pre-ordained grooves of being; at its best it is elan vital inexorably driven towards higher forms of existence." (Bertalanffy, 1968:192)

Indeed, there is no intent here to support the notion of ultimate control of all stresses for optimal human well being; it is well recognized that moderate disequilibrium, in the proper context, is an essential part of human growth and development.

It is beyond the scope of this study to examine the issue of stress from a cost-benefit view; it is not only extremely complex, in terms of information, but also involves the difficult question of personal and societal values. However, the control of stress should be exercised in many conditions when its impact is adverse, especially in situations of loss.

SITUATIONS OF LOSS AND DEPRIVATION

The title implies conditions that are lacking, to some degree, the opportunities, freedoms and flexibilities one normally expects in everyday life. Some examples of these situations are: forced relocation, particularly detrimental to sub-populations whose physical and related social environments are congruent with particular life style (Fried, 1963); living in an institu-

tional setting, with the attendent lack of freedom and autonomy. Restricted privacy and its effects is a common theme investigated frequently in psychiatric facilities (Ittelson, 1970), in prisons (Glaser, 1964) or college dormitories (Sommer, 1970); Human Physiological Deficiencies: Several sub-populations such as the physically handicapped, the elderly, etc., can be viewed as suffering from some loss and deficiencies, either developmental or associated with a sudden change; Environmental Deficiencies, e.g. Sensory Deprivation: Another set of deprivation situations are a variety of isolation conditions, from imprisonment and confined hospitalization to "exotic" environments--long term stay in submarines, space missions, antarctic and other remote stations, etc. Variables typical to these situations are:

1. Loss of supportive environment
2. Loss of physical mobility
3. Shrinking life-space
4. Loss of control and autonomy over space
5. Diminishing repertoire of potential responses and behaviors
6. Loss of information/stimulation inputs (sensory deprivation)
7. Abrupt environmental change

Although the emphasis here is on variables related to the physical environment, each encompasses also some social/psychological component. The degree of loss is variable, a point on a continuum from low to high; the condition's total loss-dimension is a cumulative sum of several loss variables. The following schematic diagram (Figure 2) illustrates hypothetical relationships between three selected loss situations and few loss variables.

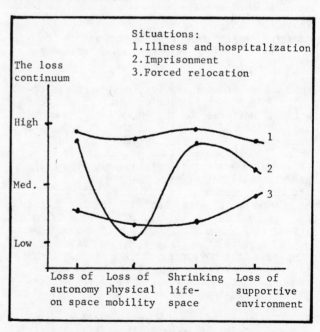

FIGURE 2: SCHEMATIC DIAGRAM OF SELECTED LOSS SITUATIONS, SOME RELATED LOSS VARIABLES AND THE LOSS CONTINUUM

While this illustration is hypothetical and schematic, it seems plausible to quantify loss situations on several pertinent dimensions, and determine case by case the extent of their relative "cumulative loss".

RELATIONS OF LOSS SITUATIONS TO THE STRESS PROCESS

As recalled from the stress model, active coping responses to various stressors are: A. modifying physical-environmental conditions, B. modifying social-interactive conditions, and C. modifying personal factors. Consider the example of a hospitalized patient: not only are some loss categories acting upon him as potential stressors (e.g., loss of valued interaction, privacy, supportive environment) but he has fewer options for response (due to loss of physical mobility, loss of control and autonomy over space, and shrinking life space). Modifying the physical environment, e.g., erecting, or removing barriers, is often virtually impossible as are changes in the social-interactive environment, e.g. seeking information and stimulation on personal demand, or leaving an "overloaded" situation. This leaves the patient with higher dependency on modifying his own individual factors (e.g., denial, changing behavior, etc.), since there are fewer opportunities to deal directly with the stressor. Finally, some stress coping mechanisms have the potential to create adverse consequences in illness and hospitalization, since their physiological and biological components might upset an organism already under physiological trauma. This might be especially critical in acute illness such as coronary conditions (Zohman, 1970).

THE EFFECTIVENESS OF THE MODEL IN LOSS SITUATIONS

The special aspects of stress in loss situations render the stress model more useful, since some of the methodological and conceptual problems discussed previously tend to diminish.

The higher level of stress considerably decreases response variability, and regulatory and compensatory options also decrease. The reduction in variability certainly reduces the complexity of the model.

In loss situations, homeostasis and congruence become more critical, as competence and options decrease. The higher criticality of the stress and its impact make the otherwise subjective, value laden issues of relative "costs" and "adaptation" easier to approach. Criticality also makes the long term perspective sometimes subsidiary to the momentary, basic survival.

CONCLUSION

A complete human ecological perspective, as attempted here, provides a broad and holistic view of the total stress process, its parts, their linkages and interdependencies. Although the directionality, the quantities and qualities of the relationships are only suggested in this paradigm, it should be valuable as a way of organizing, and thus conceptualizing, the set of relationships. This is important in times of increasing specialization and fragmentation of knowledge. The goal has been to provide a framework within which some integration of this knowledge could take place, leading to a more informed and balanced view of some man-environment relations.

Notes:

[1]For some representative, comprehensive disciplinary reviews and perspectives of stress see Levine and Scotch (1970); McGrath (1970); Appley and Trumbull (1976); Lazarus (1966); Selye (1956); Carson and Driver (1970).

References

ALTMAN, IRWIN, The Environment and Social Behavior, Monterey, California: Brooks/Cole, 1975

APPLEY, T. and TRUMBULL, R., Psychological Stress, New York: Appleton, Century and Crofts, 1967.

BERTALANFFY, LUDWIG, VON, General Systems Theory, New York: Braziller, 1968.

CANNON, W., The Wisdom of the Body, Norton, New York, 1932.

CARSON, DAN and B. DRIVER, An Environmental Approach to Human Stress and Well Being, Ann Arbor: University of Michigan, 1970.

DUBOS, RENE, Man Adapting, New Haven: Yale University Press, 1965.

FRIED, MARK, "Grieving for a Lost Home" in: Duhl, Leonard (ed.) The Urban Condition, New York, Basic Books, Inc., 1963, pp. 151-171.

GLASER, D., "Architectural Factors in Isolation Promotion in Persons" in: D. Glaser (ed.) The Effectiveness of a Prison and Parole System, New York: Bobbs-Merril, Inc., 1964.

GLASS, D.C. and SINGER, J.E., Urban Stress, New York: Academic Press, 1972

HOLMES, T.S., et. al., "Magnitude of Life Events and Seriousness of Illness" in: Psychosomatic Medicine, March 1971, Vol. 33, No. 2, pp. 115-122.

ITTELSON, W.H., PROSHANSKY, H.M., and RIVLIN, L., "The Environmental Psychology of the Psychiatric Ward" in: Proshansky, H.M. et.al. (eds.) Environmental Psychology, New York: Holt, Rinehart and Winston, Inc., 1970, pp. 419-39.

LAWTON, POWELL, "Competence, Environmental Press and the Adaptation of Older People: in: Windley, et.al. (eds.) Theory Development in Environment and Aging, Washington, D.C.: The Gerontological Society, 1975, pp. 13-84

LAZARUS, R.S., Psychological Stress and the Coping Process, New York: McGraw Hill, 1966.

LEVINE, SOL and NORMAN SCOTCH, Social Stress, Chicago: Aldine Publishing Co., 1970.

MCGRATH, JOSEPH, Social and Psychological Factors in Stress, New York: Holt, Rinehart, and Winston, 1970.

MILGRAM, S. "The Experience of Living in Cities", in: Science, 167:1461-1468, 1970.

NAMEMOW, L. and LAWTON, P., "Toward an Ecological Theory of Adaptation and Aging" in: W.F.E. Preiser, (ed.) Environmental Design Research, Stroudsburg, Penn: Dowden, Hutchinson and Ross, 1973, Vol. I, pp. 24-32.

PROSHANSKY, H.M., "Theoretical Issues in Environmental Psychology", in: Representative Research in Social Psychology, 4:1, 1973, pp. 93-109.

RAPOPORT, AMOS, "An Approach to the Construction of Man-Environment Theory", in: W.F. Preiser, (ed.) Environmental Research Design, Stroudsburg, Pennsylvania: Dowden, Hutchinson and Ross, 1973, pp. 124-135.

RAPOPORT, AMOS, "Aging-Environment Theory: A Summary", in: Windley, et. al. (eds.) Theory Development in Environment and Aging, Washington, D.C.: The Gerontological Society 1975, pp. 263-282.

SELYE, H., The Stress of Life, New York: McGraw-Hill, 1956.

SIMMEL, G., "The Metropolis and Mental Life" in: K. Wolff (ed.) The Sociology of George Simmel, New York: The Free Press, 1950.

SOMMER, R., "The Ecology of Study Areas", in: Environment and Behavior, 2:3, 1970 pp. 271-280.

STOKOLS, DANIEL, "On the Distinction Between Density and Crowding: Some Implications for Future Research" in: Psychological Review, 1972, 79 (3) 275-278 (b)

STOKOLS, DANIEL, "A Social-Psychological Model of Human Crowding Phenomena", in: AIP Journal, Vol. XXXVIII, No. 2, March 1972, pp. 72-83 (a).

WINDLEY, P, BYERTS, T. and ERNST, G, Theory Development In Environment and Aging, Washington, D.C.: The Gerontological Society, 1975.

WIRTH, L. "Urbanism as a Way of Life", in: American Journal of Sociology, 44:1-24, 1938.

WOHLWILL, J.F., "The Physical Environment: A Problem for Psychology of Stimulation" in: Journal of Social Issues, 22:4, 1968, pp. 29-38

WOHLWILL, J.F. "Human Adaptation to Levels of Environmental Stimulation", in: Human Ecology, 2:2, 1974, pp. 127-147.

ZOHMAN, L.R. and TOBIS, J.S., Cardiac Rehabilitation, New York: Grone and Straton, 1970.

RESEARCH AND THEORETICAL PROBLEMS IN THE STUDY OF HUMAN CROWDING[1]

David L. Wiesenthal[2] and Pepi Buchalter

Department of Psychology, York University,

4700 Keele Street, Downsview, Ontario

ABSTRACT

A discussion of the problems inherent in studies of crowding in abnormal populations indicated the problems arising from the interaction between diagnostic category and population density, confounded variables, and the difficulty of testing Esser's brain evolution model. The varying tasks and environmental manipulations employed makes interpretation of laboratory research difficult. Time of measurement, the operation of multiple stressors, and sex effects all need further clarification. The danger of overgeneralizing from ethological sources was seen to arise when the content of animal research rather than its methodology is uncritically applied to human behavior.

The importance of understanding environmental mediators for social behaviors was emphasized for the psychologist and for the planner.

Crowding as a topic of interest for social scientists and planners has greatly increased. This interest has been stimulated by recent concern with dwindling food and energy resources coupled with a rapidly increasing birthrate in many underdeveloped nations. Social psychologists have been especially interested in studying alterations of group process and structure for individuals interacting in groups with limited space. Crowding, or density, may be treated as an independent variable affecting dependent measures of aiding behavior, attitude change, and interpersonal attraction. For the clinician, crowding may serve to aggravate or mask disruptive behaviors by institutionalized populations. The urban planner, or the psychologist involved in community mental health, must acquire an understanding of the epidemiological studies of crowding related pathologies.

Problems With the Use of Abnormal Populations in Crowding Research

There are four basic problems encountered by crowding studies investigating abnormal populations. The first is the difficulty in obtaining phenomenological data. In crowding studies where subjects are drawn from the normal population, the experimenter is able to ask for subject validation of the crowding manipulation, but when dealing with the mentally retarded, or subjects with various personality disorders, it is often difficult to get an accurate response. It is not always known whether the subject indeed felt crowded, indicating that the density manipulation was successful. Since people vary in regard to spatial needs, this proves to be a handicap. In studies where abnormal populations are used, the level of crowding is defined solely by its population density per square foot. Researchers are not able to operate under a phenomenological model, but are forced back into the faulty density model.

The joint manipulation of social density and spatial density, confounds the results of many experiments. In most experiments conducted in institutions, density is varied by adding additional subjects to the experimental room. The social density, or number of people in the group, is varied simultaneously with the spatial density, or population density per square foot. This confounds the experiment by making it impossible to attribute behavioral change to either the lack of space or the additional people in the group. All effects are produced by a conjunction of the two conditions, whose interaction is currently unknown (Loo, 1973).

Studies done with abnormal populations often include many different types of dysfunctions in a single sample. This is due to the use of the ward, which often contains mixed dysfunctions. Past research (Hutt & Vaizey, 1966) has shown that crowding interacts with, or is affected by, the dysfunction. The mentally retarded become aggressive when crowded, whereas autistic children withdraw and face the wall. These differences appear in both the direction of the behavioral response and its intensity. This confounds the data and makes interpretation difficult when patients having different abnormalities are grouped together and serve as a single representative sample.

Experiments done with abnormal populations may have poor generalizability to normal populations.

[1] Portions of this paper were presented by the senior author at the Ontario Psychological Association Convention, Toronto, Ontario, Canada, 1975. This project was supported by grant number 9965-13 from the Defence Research Board (Canada). The authors wish to thank Professors Harold Proshansky, Norman S. Endler and Neil I. Wiener for their helpful comments.

[2] Reprint requests should be addressed to David L. Wiesenthal, Department of Psychology, York University, 4700 Keele Street, Downsview, Ontario M3J 1P3, Canada.

When experimenters observe patients and prisoners, they are dealing with captive groups, who are limited in their ability to vary or modify their environment. An analogous situation is evident in studying the behavior of caged animals rather than animals in their natural habitat (Hediger, 1950, 1955). Institutionalized subjects cannot leave the crowded condition temporarily to bring relief from stress, whereas in the normal population, behavioral changes to reduce stress are a common form of adaptation. If the building is too crowded we step outside for a few minutes, or if the radio is annoying, we turn the volume down. Often prisoners and patients do not have the ability or authority to do this. Also, patients have very limited and specialized ways of coping with stress. Typically their behavioral repertoire is either limited or not socially acceptable, so they are institutionalized. A comparison to the normal population, which has a rich and varied stock of adaptive resources and a large behavioral repertoire, may be narrow and invalid.

Since institutionalization itself may evoke certain behavior patterns (Goffman, 1961; Rosenhan, 1973; Zimbardo, Haney, Banks, & Jaffe, 1973) which have been demonstrated to be markedly different from behaviour in other situations, it is difficult to state how much of an effect each of these influences contributes in determining behavior of institutionalized people.

For these reasons, it is doubtful how much we can learn about the adaptation of normal people from observation on the institutionalized. However, the institutionalized are presently available for long term observation in crowded conditions, providing the researcher the opportunity to study adaptation to stress over months or years. It would be difficult to replicate these conditions outside the restrictive walls of the prison or mental hospital. Since information concerning long term adaptation is vital to the solution of the crowding problem that now occurs in most major cities, studies done with abnormal populations will continue to serve in a valuable capacity in the initial work of this field. Conclusions drawn from these groups may serve in a heuristic manner for later work with the normal population.

ISSUES IN THE STUDY OF HUMAN CROWDING

Cultural Value Judgments Made Regarding Crowding

In a recent review article, Lawrence (1974), criticized some existing prognoses of the dire "horrors" concerning crowding. The present authors would agree with this statement and underscore its importance relating to existing social policy. Newspapers, politicians and social science "experts" have made unfounded gloom and doom predictions concerning the harmful effects of apartment living on child development and family life (Cappon, 1971; Gregoire, 1971; Mitchell, 1971; Smith, 1971). It is important for the psychologist and planner to realize that there is little data to back up these statements, and generalizations from the existing literature may be tenuous. We must calmly eliminate some of the value judgments and begin to survey present knowledge before social policy can be intelligently constructed and implemented. Cross cultural and historical studies might be particularly useful (Draper, 1973; Hall, 1966; Mitchell, 1971; Schmitt, 1963, 1966) since they would illustrate that our problems may not be either recent or universal. Further attention will have to be given to important cultural differences since these issues may not be fruitfully studied unless we understand how the environment is interpreted by a specific culture. McLuhan (1974) has argued that North Americans go outside their homes to be alone, whereas Europeans go outside to be with people, and inside to be alone. North Americans go inside to be with people because the American home provides no privacy. McLuhan's statement that North Americans, unlike Europeans, use indoor areas for community, and public areas for privacy, may explain events like the Kitty Genovese incident. (A girl was murdered in a street below while 38 people observing the incident from their apartments, failed to intervene.) If this indicates that North Americans perceive public thoroughfares as being a no man's land, then efforts to change how public areas are perceived and used (Newman, 1972), are an important task for the environmental designer. The understanding of environmental mediators is crucial for the social psychologist's understanding of the processes involved in the individual's decision regarding intervention (Bickman, Teger, Gabriele, McLaughlin, Berger & Sunaday, 1973).

Role of Ethological Concepts in the Study

of Crowding

The overextension of ethological concepts seems to have occurred to some extent in the crowding literature. The recent work by Edney (1974) has indicated that many are aware of the dangers of this wholesale comparison and transposition of ethological concepts. When areas like territoriality, physiological processes and individual differences related to crowding stress are not yet well understood, it seems likely that overgeneralization will occur. We may perceive certain limitations in their use, but the fact that they are heuristic, provocative notions will enhance their usage.

Recent popular literature (Ardrey, 1966; Lorenz, 1966) has produced several attempts at an explanation of the effects of crowding stress on man through an animal analogy. In several cases there has been an overextension of ethological concepts which are dangerously misleading when they encompass wholesale comparison of men and animals (Edney, 1974). A leading ethologist, N. Tinbergen, commented on this trend: "Both Lorenz and Morris emphasize our knowledge rather than our ignorance (and, in addition, present as knowledge a set of statements which are after all no more than likely guesses) . . . *What we ethologists do not want, what we consider definitely wrong, is an uncritical application of our results to man.*" (Tinbergen, 1968 pp. 1411-1412, italics added for emphasis).

Ethology's misapplication in the case of crowding is threefold. Ethology's primary focus is to apply the methodology used for the study of animals to man rather than their results. Ethology's usefulness for the crowding theorist comes from its heuristic value in stimulating research rather than only content transferal. Ethology should tell the experimenter where to look rather than what he will find there. Furthermore, it is recognized that the phenomenological view found in the crowding literature (Stokols, 1972a; Milgram, 1970) is not applicable to the work on animals. For humans, crowding occurs when the level of stimulation is perceived as inappropriate for the situation (Baxter & Deanovich, 1970), while with animal samples, the experimenter has no way of testing whether the animal perceives itself as crowded, or feels his level of stimulation is appropriate. It is also to be noted that animals, in comparison to man, operate with lower levels of behavioral adaptation. Their behavioral repertoire is limited and stylized, making it difficult to use animal comparisons in explaining man's much greater adaptive power. René Dubos (1965) states that: "The readiness with which man adapts to potentially dangerous situations makes it unwise to apply directly to human life the results of experiments designed to test the acute effects of crowding in animals" (p. 108).

These limitations of the ethological viewpoint in crowding research do not extend to the use of ethological methodology in the explanation of man's behavior, nor do they deny the provocative and heuristic notions ethology can provide. They merely speak against wholesale acceptance of animal analogies put forth as knowledge of human behavior. Animals can be used to suggest hypotheses about man's behavior, but overgeneralization will occur if animal data is used exclusively to explain crowding in man.

Current State of Knowledge and Theory

Our knowledge of crowding is dependent upon an adequate understanding of related areas such as proxemics, nonverbal communication, privacy and individual difference variables (Lawrence, 1974). The available literature has been provided by anthropologists, biologists, physiologists, psychologists, urbanologists and psychiatrists, all of whom seem to be prisoners of their paradigms (Kuhn, 1970). An integrative explanatory

model is needed which links all these separate fact modules. This model, however, will have to wait until sufficient data are available for such sophisticated theorizing. Psychologists have shown that they have a healthy tolerance for ambiguity and vague theorizing (e.g., cognitive dissonance) and can produce meaningful data in (what is hoped to be) their temporary absence.

Generalizability of Laboratory Experimental Data

Another issue which continues to arise in psychology, is the issue of the external validity or generalizability of our data. Hovland (1959), in a classic paper, presented arguments why different relationships among attitude change variables were to be expected in the artificial environment of the laboratory, compared to the real world. Similar statements may be given for the few laboratory studies on human crowding. One central problem may be that for ethical reasons we are reluctant to experimentally vary environmental conditions simulating real world experiences of crowding with known deleterious effects. No sane psychologist would recreate the Black Hole of Calcutta or slave transport ships whose mortality effects have been well documented (see Biderman, Lovria, and Bacchus [1963] for a complete description of incidents of extreme crowding).

Another problem with laboratory research is that the time variable is necessarily quite limited. Experimental research on crowding has used the standard one half hour unit up to even longer periods of observation (e.g., the two four hour sessions employed by Freedman, Klevansky and Ehrlich, 1971) to a high of 12 hours (Skolnick, Moss, Salzgeber and Shaw, 1971). Stokols feels that any study of crowding will have to devote particular attention to the interaction of many variables and as well study the developmental sequence of these processes. Watts (1968) has pointed out that the time period, or times, at which phenomena are measured are often not considered in planning or interpreting psychological research and may constitute an important factor. Supporting this notion, Lawler, Koplin, Young and Fadem (1968) have demonstrated that quite opposite conclusions may be reached when the time of measurement is extended. Any investigation of crowding should therefore concern itself to studying changes over time in both individuals and groups experiencing crowding.

Another problem relating to generalizability concerns the notion of replicability of studies. While much of the laboratory research with regard to sex effects is replicated, many other findings are not. When one examines Freedman's research, one must wonder why the hypothesized effects were not obtained. Comparability between laboratory studies is difficult since different tasks, group sizes and density conditions are used by different investigators. Some of the studies employ phenomenological data to support their choice of experimental conditions, while others do not (Freedman et al., 1971) further complicating the issue. Additionally, the use of other stressors like heat (Griffitt & Veitch, 1971), makes it difficult to ascertain how much of an effect population density itself contributes to perceived crowding.

Very few studies have been performed in natural settings so that the ecological validity of much of the laboratory crowding literature is unknown. In one field experimental study, Stokols, Smith and Proster (in press), contrary to expectation, failed to find that increased partitioning of a motor-vehicle office would be perceived as less crowded. At the present time, little experimental research has been conducted which tests laboratory developed concepts in the field. Most field work has been either of an anecdotal or correlational variety. The personal space literature has been chiefly concerned with demonstrations of the phenomenon, rather than experimental tests of the interrelationships of variables producing crowding.

Behavioral Aftereffects of Crowding

The research cited earlier by Epstein and his associates, suggests that behavioral aftereffects of crowding are significant and have been overlooked by previous research. Sherrod's (1974) research on aftereffects of crowding demonstrated that although his crowding conditions had no effect on simple or complex task performance, significant negative behavioral aftereffects were observed for the crowded groups on a puzzle series constituting a frustration tolerance measure. Perceived control, operationalized as the subject's ability to leave the crowded room, ameliorated these negative aftereffects. However, unlike Glass and Singer (1972), Sherrod failed to find differences between his experimental conditions on a proofreading task administered to test postexperimental performance decrements. Animal research has recently indicated (Geockner, Greenough & Mead, 1973; Geockner, Greenough & Maier, 1974) that rats reared from weaning under high population density conditions were inferior in performance on learning tasks as compared to low density reared littermates. Possibly the same relationship may hold for man as is suggested by Marshall's (1972) finding that perceived crowding in childhood was related to privacy requirements in adulthood. All this points out the necessity for a longer time perspective when dealing with crowding.

Crowding and Related Stressors

One central problem in understanding the phenomena of crowding is to first gain an understanding of reactions to single stress agents operating in isolation. At the present time, the operation of single stress variables like noise (Glass & Singer, 1972) and elevated temperature (Baron, 1972; Griffitt & Veitch, 1971) on behavior are not that well understood. How then may psychologists begin to try to uncover their interactive relationships with density that produce crowding? Glass and Singer have demonstrated that noise is only a stressor when it is random and uncontrollable, rather than in its mere presence. Perhaps then, crowding is stressful or disruptive only when people perceive themselves helpless in their environment. This may be similar to the process of "learned helplessness" (Maier, Seligman & Solomon, 1969) where it has been observed that animals subjected to inescapable, uncontrolled electric shock are later found to be incapable or markedly retarded in learning to avoid the shocks (Goeckner et al., 1973; Geockner, et al., 1974).

Unexplained Sex Differences in Reaction

to Crowding

A consistent finding has been that males and females differ in their reactions to crowding. Generally the relationship is that males react more negatively to crowding than do females. Freedman, Levy, Buchanan and Price (1972) found that males were more competitive in small rooms and females were more competitive in larger rooms, while Epstein (in press) replicated this relationship only for the females. Epstein and Aiello (1974) found a nonsignificant trend across both crowded and control conditions for their male subjects to experience a higher level of physiological arousal. Epstein and Karlin (in press) found groups of men to be less cohesive and female groups more cohesive in crowded conditions. Epstein and Karlin also found that men were more competitive (although failing to reach conventional levels of significance) and women significantly less competitive under crowding. Their male subjects felt that the group discouraged displays of discomfort (p. < 10), while women significantly felt that the group encouraged such emotional displays. Of interest as well, was their finding that crowded men perceived each other as less similar while their crowded women perceived each other as more similar.

No satisfactory explanation of sex differences has yet been provided, especially considering the fact that these differences disappear in mixed sex groups. Men might find that the experience of being crowded with other men arouses homosexual fears, although this fear should also be reported for industrial and military groups working in close proximity. The notion of territoriality has also been extended to deal with this phenomenon. Since the ethological literature indicates that the male of the species is usually more involved in territorial matters, crowding should have more of an impact on males, for whom the salience and disconfirmation of territorial expectancies should be greater. Yet the literature cited indicates that the reported sex differences have been of opposing directionality rather than of intensity or degree.

Perhaps, since the present research is still in its early formative phases, we should be tolerant of some of these limitations. Since environmental psychology emphasizes concern with applied real world problems with a true Lewinian flavor, we may hope to see a closer integration between data derived from the laboratory and naturalistic sources. A trend also seems evident where ethological methodology, rather than its content, is employed in studying crowding in specialized institutional settings. Anthropological data suggests that cultures evolve specific adaptative mechanisms to deal with crowding as exemplified by the Chinese extended family living under the high density conditions of Hong Kong. Some cultures are also seen to derive satisfaction from crowding, whether they are Jacobs' (1961) urban dwellers of Greenwich Village, or the ! Kung Bushmen of the Kalahari desert. Current research can be profitably conducted in many settings, with differential sex effects and the construction of a generalized theory of stressors existing as challenging problems in search of a solution.

Sharper operational definitions and a choice of dependent measures that will allow for an explanation of why crowding elicits specific effects are also needed. This will require the talents of the social, clinical, and experimental psychologists, as well as related professionals. The traditional pleas for more research at the conclusion of a paper, will be expressed here as a call for more probing multidisciplinary research endeavors, validating hypotheses in both laboratory and field settings.

References

Ardrey, R. The territorial imperative: A personal inquiry into the origins of property and nations. New York: Atheneum, 1966.

Baron, R. A. Aggression as a function of ambient temperature and prior anger arousal. Journal of Personality and Social Psychology, 1972, 21, 183-189.

Baxter, J. C. and Deanovich, B. F. Anxiety arousing effects of inappropriate crowding. Journal of Consulting and Clinical Psychology, 1970, 35, 174-178.

Bickman, L., Teger, A., Gabriele, T., McLaughlin, C., Berger, M., & Sunaday, E. Dormitory density and helping behavior. Environment and Behavior, 1973, 5, 464-491.

Biderman, A. D., Lovria, M., & Bacchus, J. Historical incidents of extreme overcrowding. Washington, D.C.: Bureau of Social Science Research, 1963.

Cappon, D. Mental health in the high rise. Canadian Journal of Public Health, 1971, 62, 426-431.

Draper, P. Crowding among hunter-gatherers: The ! Kung bushmen. Science, 1973, 182, 301-303.

Dubos, R. J. Man Adapting, New Haven: Yale University Press, 1965.

Edney, J. J. Human territories: Comment on functional properties. Paper presented at the Convention of the American Psychological Association, New Orleans, 1974.

Epstein, Y. M., and Aiello, J. R. Effects of crowding on electrodermal activity. Paper presented at the Convention of the American Psychological Association, New Orleans, 1974.

Epstein, Y. M. and Karlin, R. A. Effects of acute experimental crowding. Journal of Social Psychology, in press.

Freedman, J. L., Klevansky, S. & Ehrlich, P. The effect of crowding on human task performance. Journal of Applied Social Psychology, 1971, 1, 7-25.

Freedman, J. L., Levy, A. S., Buchanan, R. W. & Price, J. Crowding and human aggressiveness. Journal of Experimental Social Psychology, 1972, 8, 528-548.

Glass, D. C. & Singer, J. L. Urban stress: Experiments on noise and social stressors. New York: Academic Press, 1972.

Goeckner, D. J., Greenough, Wm. T. & Maier, S. F. Escape learning deficit after overcrowded rearing in rats: Test of a helplessness hypothesis. Bulletin of the Psychonomic Society, 1974, 3 (1B), 54-56.

Goeckner, D. J., Greenough, W. T. & Mead, Wm. R. Deficits in learning tasks following chronic overcrowding in rats. Journal of Personality and Social Psychology, 1973, 28, 256-261.

Goffman, E. Asylums. Garden City, New York: Anchor Books, 1961.

Gregoire, M. The child in the high-rise. Ekistics, 1971, 186, 331-333.

Griffit, W., & Veitch, R. Hot and crowded: Influences of population density and temperature on interpersonal affective behavior. Journal of Personality and Social Psychology, 1971, 17, 92-98.

Hall, E. T. The hidden dimension, New York: Doubleday, 1966.

Hediger, H. Wild animals in captivity. London: Butterworth & Co., 1950.

Hediger, H. Studies of the psychology and behavior of captive animals in zoos and circuses. London: Butterworth & Co., 1955.

Hovland, C. I. Reconciling conflicting results derived from experimental and survey studies of attitude change. American Psychologist, 1959, 14, 8-17.

Hutt, C., and Vaizey, M. J. Differential effects of group density on social behavior. Nature, 1966, 209, 1371-1372.

Jacobs, J. The death and life of great American cities. New York: Random House, 1961.

Kuhn, T. S. The structure of scientific revolutions, (second edition), Chicago: University of Chicago Press, 1970.

Lawlor, E. E., Koplin, C. A., Young, T. E., & Fadem, J. A. Inequity reduction over time in an induced overpayment situation. Organizational Behavior and Human Performance, 1968, 3, 253-268.

Lawrence, J. E. S. Science and sentiment: Overview of research on crowding and human behavior. Psychological Bulletin, 1974, 81, 712-720.

Loo, C. Important issues in researching the effect of crowding on humans. Representative Research in Social Psychology, 1973, 4, 219-226.

Lorenz, K. On aggression. New York: Harcourt, Brace, & World, 1966.

Maier, S. F., Seligman, M. E. P., & Solomon, R. L. Pavlovian fear conditioning and learned helplessness: Effects on escape and avoidance behavior of (a) the CS-US contingency and (b) the independence of the US and voluntary responding. In B. A. Campbell and R. M. Church (Eds.) Punishment. New York: Appleton-Century-Crofts, 1969.

Marshall, N. J. Privacy and environment. Human Ecology, 1972, 1, 93-110.

McLuhan, M. Organized ignorance. Paper presented at Video 74, Stockholm, Sweden, 1974.

Milgram, S. The experience of living in cities. Science, 1970, 167, 1461-1468.

Mitchell, R. Some implications of high density housing. American Sociological Review, 1971, 36, 18-29.

Newman, O. Defensible space. New York: Macmillan, 1972.

Rosenhan, D. L. On being sane in insane places. Science, 1973, 179, 250-258.

Schmitt, R. C. Density, health, and social disorganization. Journal of the American Institute of Planners, 1966, 32, 38-40.

Schmitt, R. C. Implications of density in Hong Kong. Journal of the American Institute of Planners, 1963, 29, 210-217.

Sherrod, D. R. Crowding perceived control and behavioral aftereffects. Journal of Applied Social Psychology, 1974, 4, 171-186.

Skolnick, P., Moss, R., Salzgeber, R. & Shaw, J. I. The effects of population size and density on human behavior. Paper presented at the Western Psychological Association, 1971.

Smith, M. Despite Cadillac glamor, high-rises are no place to live. Excalibur, January 13, 1972.

Stokols, D. On the distinction between density and crowding: Some implications for future research. Psychological Review, 1972a, 79, 275-277.

Tinbergen, N. On war and peace in animals and man. Science, 160, 1968, 1411-1421.

Watts, W. A. Predictability and pleasure: Reactions to the disconfirmation of expectancies. In R. P. Abelson, et al. (Eds.) Theories of cognitive consistency: A sourcebook. Chicago: Rand McNally, 1968, 469-478.

Zimbardo, P. G., Haney, C., Banks, W. C., & Jaffe, D. The psychology of imprisonment: Privation, power and pathology. Unpublished manuscript, Stanford University, 1973.

SPATIAL PROPINQUITY AS AN APPLIED CONCEPT IN ENVIRONMENTAL RESEARCH AND DESIGN

Michael R. Hill

Department of Geography
University of Nebraska - Lincoln
Lincoln, Nebraska 68588

ABSTRACT

Application of the concept of spatial propinquity as an explanatory variable in social and environmental research has frequently masked the behavioral basis of human spatial behavior. This discussion concludes that designers should look to the social sciences for "insights" rather than for precise formulations or models of behavior based on deterministic views of space.

1. INTRODUCTION

Use of propinquity as an explanation for some forms of behavior, rather than as a descriptive measure of the spatial extent of that behavior within an environment, results in an unfounded spatial determinism. The obvious fact that human behavior has spatial properties cannot be logically inverted as an explanation for the existence of the spatial dimensions of behavior. A subtle confusion has developed in which the nature of the measurement instrument has been converted into an explanation of the observations.

Investigations concerned with relationships between built environments and human behavior form part of the rapidly expanding man-environment literature. Specific studies on propinquity as a factor within built environments have been contributed to this enterprise by researchers in several disciplines including: anthropology, economics, operations research, political science, psychology, social geography, and sociology. One of the more frequent themes in these studies concerns the supposed relationship between human interaction and spatial propinquity. The research often implies that if this relationship could be fully understood it would be possible to design environments and social arrangements which would either encourage or discourage social intercourse, as desired, on the basis of spatial configuration alone.

The explanatory view of propinquity has been pervasive, particularly in research from the not too distant past, research which has frequently found its way into many recent bibliographies of man-environment studies and environmental psychology. We should note with

some concern that only ten years ago Olsson (1965) was able to observe that practically all studies of the relationship between distance and human interaction considered distance as an independent, explanatory variable. Fortunately, this reified conception of spatial propinquity is beginning to crack, although not with equal force in all directions.

The position forwarded in this discussion suggests that considering propinquity or distance as a causal or explanatory variable is simply begging the question. It is maintained that once human behavior has been observed to have a spatial dimension, the relevant task facing the investigator is the search for the behavioral basis of the distribution of behavior along that dimension.

2. THE DESIGNER AND THE "SPATIAL" SCIENCES

The designer is a creator of spatial relationships within built environments. This fact, combined with the growing ties between design and social science research (as evidenced in EDRA), may tempt the designer to look with eager anticipation toward the results of "spatial" investigations within the social sciences in the hope that directly applicable discoveries and concepts may be found. Current fields of inquiry which may whet the designer's appetite include: crowding and human ecology, micromovement and social action space, consumer spatial behavior, environmental perception and cognitive mapping, neighborhood effects, and the spatial diffusion of innovations. This growing, interdisciplinary concern with the spatial aspects of human behavior adds a sorely needed perspective to our understanding of the realities of everyday life. It is also a perspective to which the designer as a manipulator of spatial relationships can easily relate, perhaps too easily.

As researchers turn from the artificiality of the experimental laboratory toward the everyday world as experienced by everyday people, they confront the complexities of behavior in an environment where the spatial dimension cannot be ignored. It becomes obvious, of course, that all social behavior occurs in a spatial context and has a spatial dimension.

Some researchers, however, have focused so narrowly upon "spatial relationships" that they have apparently lost sight of the original project. In the extreme case, the substance of their science (i.e., behavior) was replaced with a particular approach (i.e., spatial). A few of the more imaginative investigators even refer to their collective efforts as the "spatial sciences," an appellation which may lead the uninitiated to accept the proposition that there exists, within the social sciences, a subject of study which can be uniquely characterized as "spatial."

Many social scientists, building on notions borrowed from ecology, ethology, and operations research, are now giving human behavior the "spatial" treatment. The result of this work is a growing collection of spatial concepts, techniques, and generalizations which go a long way in describing behavior but provide little in the way of a conceptually satisfactory behavioral explanation of the human spatial patterns observed.

The relevance of this work for the designer becomes critical if he turns to a "spatial generalization" for application in a specific design problem without recognizing that the chosen generalization may not tell him anything about the behavioral basis of the observed pattern. If the object of design is prosthetic, then application of a generalization based on observed spatial regularities alone, rather than on the behavioral intentions and capabilities of the individuals for whom the design is executed, becomes problematic.

Spatial propinquity is discussed in this context with the aim of demonstrating that it is, by itself, an empty concept. Both the designer and the social scientist must go beyond the superficial attractiveness of spatial determinism if they are to understand the human basis of behavior within the built environment.

3. THE EXPLANATORY CONCEPTION OF PROPINQUITY

Most studies which address the "problem" of spatial propinquity treat distance as an independent variable with some form of social behavior as the dependent variable. This conceptualization is tantamount to asking what is the "role" of propinquity in relation to

human behavior. This question has been investigated at several scales within the built environment over a range of behaviors. Representative examples are indicated in Figure 1.

The results of these studies are frequently inconclusive, even contradictory in some cases, with regard to the influence of spatial propinquity on human behavior. Catton and Smircich (1964), for example, note that the empirical findings on the role of propinquity with regard to the selection of marriage partners ranged from those studies in which propinquity was not even mentioned, through those which viewed propinquity as a permissive factor, to those in which propinquity was seen to account for the relevant behavior. This wide range of results is not helpful to the designer who would like, if possible, for social science to provide him with some general principles to guide him in understanding the possible relationship between the spatial aspects of the environment and human behavior.

The picture becomes even more confused when the designer is confronted with suggested reasons why propinquity was not seen clearly as an important factor in those studies which report inconclusive or variable results on the "role" of propinquity. With regard to the literature on interpersonal relations, for example, Boalt and Janson (1956) list a number of "co-operating mechanisms" which are supposed to act in addition to the sheer geometry of distance including: the probability of intentional and unintentional social contacts, the degree of knowledge of opportunities, the homogeneity of groups and areas, and norms against gross deviations. Gans (1961) notes that the "effect" of propinquity may vary with age, sex, class, activity, and size of group. Keller (1968) adds other factors including: time, layout, ecological position, social similarity, and compatible moral and social standards. Timms (1971) also points to the importance of the nature of the population studied. The usual conclusion is that these factors modify the role of spatial propinquity. An alternative conclusion is that the problem lies within the conceptualization of propinquity as an explanatory variable. It is asserted here that there is much to be gained by considering distance as a dimension of behavior rather than as a cause of behavior.

4. THE DIMENSIONAL CONCEPTION OF PROPINQUITY

Propinquity in the general sense is an abstract concept referring to dimensional relationships. To speak of propinquity in the sense of a propinquitous relationship is to imply some measurable degree of nearness, closeness, or proximity between two or more elements in a system.

This view limits and redirects the kinds of

```
SCALE OF BUILT ENVIRONMENT
     Behavior Studied
          Representative Studies
     _____

UNIVERSITY HOUSING

     Communication
          Barnlund & Harland (1963)
     Friendships
          Priest & Sawyer (1967)
     Attitudes
          Bennett (1974)

MILITARY BARRACKS

     Choice of "Best Buddies"
          Blake, Rhead, Wedge & Mouton
               (1956)
          Loether (1960)

HOME FOR THE AGED

     Friendships
          Friedman (1966)

PUBLIC HOUSING PROJECTS

     Attitudes
          Wilner, Walkley & Cook (1952)
     Social Interaction
          Kriesberg (1968)
     Neighbor Relations
          Yancey (1971)

NEIGHBORHOODS, COMMUNITIES & SUBURBS

     Neighborhood Interaction
          Festinger, Schachter & Back
               (1950)
          Caplow & Forman (1950)
          Kuper (1953)
          Whyte (1956)
          Martin (1958)
          Gans (1961)
          Athanasiou & Yoshioka (1973)

CITIES

     Mate Selection for Marriage
          Bossard (1932)
          Katz & Hill (1958)
          Catton & Smircich (1964)
          Ramsoy (1966)

     Voting Behavior
          Reynolds (1969)

     Social Visits
          Wheeler & Stutz (1971)

     Micromovement
          Hurst (1974)
```

Figure 1

questions which can be meaningfully asked about propinquity. The question of what "degree" of nearness is required in order to say that a condition of propinquity exists, for example, is unanswerable. The question of what contribution propinquity makes as a factor in explaining human behavior in built environments becomes counterproductive.

Measurability and dimensionality are emphasized to caution against the conceptualization of propinquity per se as existing apart from its measurable dimension in specified units. For the purpose of illustration, consider Whyte's (1956) observation that, "There is just more downright propinquity in suburbia than in most places." Whyte's statement hints (as he undoubtedly understood) at something beyond a simple measure of nearness relationships, but the lack of a thorough explication of what actually was meant allows the possibility of attributing much more to what was said than may have been intended.

Conceptualizing propinquity in the way suggested here requires that the investigator be able to answer the following questions related to its use: (1) What are the bounds of the system? In Whyte's case this means asking what constitutes "suburbia" and what defines "most places." (2) What are the relevant elements in the system? Are they individuals, households or some other construct? (3) What is the dimension of measurement? Is it physical, psychological, or social space which is at issue?

Having answered these questions, the researcher is prepared to construct a measurement instrument and to make observations based on the concept of propinquity. When propinquity is conceptualized in physical terms, for example, measurements are made between identifiable elements in a bounded euclidean space. Spatial propinquity is merely the measured, physical distance between two specified elements. Nothing more can or should be attributed to it. For the distance involved to have "meaning," it must be interpreted in behaviorally relevant terms. The search for a meaningful interpretation should lead the researcher to the behavioral basis and significance of the magnitude of the observed measurement.

5.   THE BEHAVIORAL BASIS OF SPATIAL EXPRESSION

Two approaches to the modeling of spatial patterns have been developed. The first modifies spatial data and then uses it in a predictive model. The second substitutes a behaviorally relevant dimension, replacing physical distance data with observations from some other measurable dimension. The second approach leads away from a deterministic view of space to one in which physical space becomes the canvas for behavioral expression.

When it has been observed that spatial

propinquity is not highly explanatory in a direct sense, some researchers have found that the spatial data can be modified in a way which makes prediction of the dependent behavior more accurate. In the gravity model of human inter-action in space, for example, this has been accomplished by placing an exponent on the distance term so that the contribution of distance is appropriately adjusted (Carrothers, 1956; Olsson, 1970). Hence, spatial propinquity is still seen as a fundamental factor whose effect was merely distorted. Unfortunately, the "correction" of the distortion gives no clue to the behavioral significance of the distance data employed in the model.

However, it was also discovered that other dimensions could be substituted for the spatial dimension and that measurements made on these other dimensions were "better" predictors of the specific behavior under investigation. Examples of these other dimensions and their implications are outlined below.

5.1. Cost Dimensions

Nearness to an element can almost always be described in terms of how much it will cost to reach that element from a given starting point. The specific cost may be expressed in economic, temporal, physical, psychological or social terms. The designer in a world of considerable technological sophistication is able to reduce or increase many forms of interaction costs as desired. But, both the designer and the social scientist need to more fully appreciate that the behavioral relevance of these costs lies not in abstract space, but in the values and attitudes of the individuals who make use of a given environmental setting.

5.2. Probability Dimensions

Festinger, Schachter and Back (1950) introduced the notion of functional distance. It results from the nature and location of behavioral routeways: physical, visual and auditory. If, in a given social system, the probability of contact along a routeway is estimated, that probability represents the individual's functional distance from the larger community of potential contacts. Since the physical designer is frequently in a position to specify the length, permeability, and intersection of routeways, he has available some of the tools needed to satisfy his clients' desires for privacy or interaction. Again, the success of the design lies not in the physical manipulation of space alone, but in matching human values and attitudes with suitable physical arrangements.

5.3. Cognitive Dimensions

The solution to a given research or design problem may lie in the distance pereived to exist by the subject individuals. In suggesting the idea of "phenomenal" distance, for example, Priest and Sawyer (1967) observe that, "The way

the distance between two persons is perceived appears to depend upon the number of others who intervene." In other words, a neighbor five miles away in a rural area might be perceived as close, but a friend "on the other side of town" in a populous, urban area might be thought of as far away even though the intervening physical distance could actually be much less. Such research suggests that a qualitative understand-ing of the users' phenomenal world is required in addition to an understanding of his value system, since the relative importance of certain values may shift from one spatial setting to another.

5.4. Summated Dimensions

Obviously, no single substitution provides a full explanation of spatial distributions. Deutsch and Isard (1961) proposed the idea of "effective" distance which defines the distance between elements as a vector in n dimensional space. A similar, combined index is fundamental to Janson and Rudolfsson's (1965) notion of "ecological" distance. Both of these concepts point in the direction of multiple, interacting explanations for given spatial distributions of human behavior. The suggestion of summated dimensions goes beyond the deterministic view of propinquity in physical space as a cause or explanation of spatial behavior. Instead, summation consists of measurements in a conceptual space which sum up the many possible indicators of human values, intentions, and actions.

6. SUMMARY

The chief argument presented here is that models of spatial distributions which are powered by the same spatial data that they purport to explain are circular. Such models often have the appearance of precision, yet they are impoverished when it comes to behavioral explanation. Although some designers have looked to the social sciences for "exact" formulations, it is suggested here that the social sciences, perhaps surprisingly, are better suited to provide the designer with "insights" into the behavioral basis of human spatial activity rather than formulas with supposed universal application. To be useful, these insights must be interpreted by the designer in specific projects. When seen from this perspective, social science does not give the designer the "correct" answer. Rather, it points the designer in the direction of the right questions. This may seem a simple conclusion, but it is one drawn from many industrious and careful studies in which the concept of spatial propinquity has been applied, albeit sometimes unproductively, in environmental and social research.

reference

ATHANASIOU, R., & YOSHIOKA, G.A. The Spatial Character of Friendship Formation. Environment and Behavior, 1973, 5, 44-65.

BARNLUND, D.C., & HARLAND, C. Propinquity and Prestige as Determinants of Communication Networks. Sociometry, 1963, 26, 467-479.

BENNETT, D.C. Interracial Ratios and Proximity in Dormitories: Attitudes of University Students. Environment and Behavior, 1974, 6, 212-232.

BLAKE, R.R., RHEAD, C.C., WEDGE, B., & MOUTON, J.S. Housing Architecture and Social Interaction. Sociometry, 1956, 19, 133-139.

BOALT, G., & JANSON, C.-G. Distance and Social Relations. Acta Sociologica, 1956, 2, 73-97.

BOSSARD, J.H.S. Residential Propinquity as a Factor in Marriage Selection. American Journal of Sociology, 1932, 38, 219-224.

CAPLOW, T., & FORMAN, R. Neighborhood Interaction in a Homogeneous Community. American Sociological Review, 1950, 15, 357-366.

CARROTHERS, G.P. An Historical Review of the Gravity and Potential Concepts of Human Interaction. Journal of the American Institute of Planners, 1956, 22, 94-102.

CATTON, W.R., & SMIRCICH, R.J. A Comparison of Mathematical Models for the Effect of Residential Propinquity on Mate Selection. American Sociological Review, 1964, 29, 522-529.

DEUTSCH, K.W., & ISARD, W. A Note on a Generalized Concept of Effective Distance. Behavioral Science, 1961, 6, 308-310.

FESTINGER, L., SCHACHTER, S., & BACK, K. Social Pressures in Informal Groups: A Study of Human Factors in Housing. New York: Harper, 1950.

FRIEDMAN, E. Spatial Proximity and Social Interaction in a Home for the Aged. Journal of Gerontology, 1966, 21, 566-570.

GANS, H. Planning and Social Life: Friendship and Neighbor Relations in Suburban Communities. Journal of the American Institute of Planners, 1961, 27, 134-140.

HURST, M.E.E. Micromovements and the Urban Dweller. In M.E.E. Hurst (Ed.), Transportation Geography: Comments and Readings. New York: McGraw-Hill, 1974, 482-507.

JANSON, C.-G., & RUDOLFSSON, B. Ecological and Geographical Distances in Stockholm. Acta Sociologica, 1965, 8, 285-292.

KATZ, A.M., & HILL, R. Residential Propinquity and Marital Selection. Marriage and Family Living, 1958, 20, 27-34.

KELLER, S. The Urban Neighborhood. New York: Random House, 1968.

KRIESBERG, L. Neighborhood Setting and the Isolation of Public Housing Tenants. Journal of the American Institute of Planners, 1968, 34, 43-49.

KUPER, L. Living in Towns. London: Cresset, 1953.

LOETHER, H.J. Propinquity and Homogeneity as Factors in the Choice of Best Buddies in the Air Force. Pacific Sociological Review, 1960, 3, 18-22.

MARTIN, W.J. The Structuring of Social Relationships Engendered by Suburban Residence. In W.M. Dobriner (Ed.), The Suburban Community. New York: Putnam's Sons, 1958, pp 95-108.

OLSSON, G. Distance and Human Interaction: A Review and Bibliography. Philadelphia: Regional Science Research Institute, 1965.

OLSSON, G. Explanation, Prediction, and Meaning Variance: An Assessment of Distance Interaction Models. Economic Geography, 1970, 2, No. 2 (Supplement), 223-233.

PRIEST, R.F., & SAWYER, J. Proximity and Peership: Bases of Balance in Interpersonal Attraction. American Journal of Sociology, 1967, 72, 633-649.

RAMSOY, N.R. Assortive Mating and the Structure of Cities. American Sociological Review, 1966, 31, 773-786.

REYNOLDS, D.R. A Spatial Model for Analyzing Voting Behavior. Acta Sociologica, 1969, 12, 122-131.

TIMMS, D.W.G. The Urban Mosaic: Towards a Theory of Residential Differentiation. Cambridge: Cambridge University Press, 1971.

WHEELER, J.O., & STUTZ, F.P. Spatial Dimensions of Urban Social Travel. Annals of the Association of American Geographers, 1971, 61, 371-386.

WHYTE, W.H. The Organization Man. Garden City: Doubleday, 1956.

WILNER, D.M., WALKLEY, R., & COOK, S.W. Residential Proximity and Intergroup Relations in Public Housing Projects. Journal of Social Issues, 1952, 8, 45-69.

YANCEY, W.L. Architecture, Interaction and
    Social Control. Environment and Behavior,
    1971, 3, 3-21.

SECTION 2

Environmental Perception and Cognition

One broad, theoretical perspective on man-environment relations emphasizes the understanding of how the environment is perceived, how information from the environment is processed, and how, in turn, these basic processes mediate emotional and attitudinal responses to that environment. Papers in this section provide data to advance this formulation.

The first group of papers deals with cognitive mapping. A person's cognitive map may be defined as his beliefs about, or internal representations of, the relative location of objects, buildings, terrain features, cities, boundaries, or other features in the environment. The map is thus based on the person's perception and memory of his world. Rothwell, in the first paper, argues that cognitive mapping should be defined to include how such spatial information is acquired, coded, stored, decoded, and applied to the comprehension of the everyday physical environment.

The first three papers provide an interesting contrast in the size of the environmental unit studied, and thus together provide a more comprehensive picture of how persons cognize the whole environment. Rothwell's data are on the cognitive maps of homes. Kueffer is concerned with the perceptions (and behavioural patterns) of a city park. And Coren and Porac explore perceptions of the global environment: perceived sizes of and distances to major cities of the world. This last study also shows that cognitive mapping research can fruitfully use techniques other than hand-drawings of maps. By employing traditional psychophysical methods, Coren and Porac were able to obtain quantitiative data to validate certain hypotheses obtained from studies of drawn maps. But, they were also able to challenge another such hypothesis: that distortions in drawn maps show that people attribute less importance to far away places. By having subjects rate the importance of the cities, they showed that people actually attribute more importance to far than to close places. Cognitive mapping is thus beginning to employ a variety of methodologies to cross-validate its major findings, which is a good sign of progress in any research area.

In the next paper on mapping, Fehr and Fishbein report a test of the hypothesis that landmarks are helpful in the formation of spatial judgments. They found supporting evidence, especially with younger children. Taylor, Brower, and Stough examine a quite different component of our image of the environment: the social implications of certain visual features. They show, for example, that flower boxes and home ornaments imply the presence of people who care about their neighborhood.

The final group of papers in this section deals with emotional or aesthetic responses to environments. As in the mapping studies, these papers provide an interesting contrast in the size of environmental unit studied. Lewis deals with emotional and aesthetic experience of close, intimate contact with plants. McClelland and Auslander explore the perception of pleasantness and crowdedness evoked by settings that are visible from one location. One of their important results, incidently, is that crowded places are not necessarily unpleasant and, in some cases, may be quite pleasant. And finally, Banerjee and Gollub use an even larger unit of analysis--coastal regions--in their study of aesthetic responses. Their data show the importance of considering not only environmental characteristics but also characteristics of the responding individuals--age or income, for example--as determinants of aesthetic experience.

Many of the authors of these papers discuss the relevance of their individual study to the work of designers and planners. Yet, even the papers with no such immediate relevance contribute to an understanding of how the environment is perceived, remembered, experienced, or more generally responded to. Thus, in a broader sense, they are all relevant to our ultimate goal of a general theory of man-environment relations.

COGNITIVE MAPPING OF THE HOME ENVIRONMENT

David Rothwell
Department of Regional Economic Expansion
1135 - 161 Laurier Avenue West
Ottawa, Ontario
K1A 0M4

ABSTRACT

The paper describes an experiment in cognitive mapping. Cognitive mapping is the process by which spatial information is acquired, coded, stored, decoded and applied to the comprehension of the everyday physical environment. A cognitive map can also be a physical drawing, produced by hand to communicate the original map in the head. This paper uses the term, manual map, to distinguish the graphic hand drawn representation from the actual cognitive map. The experiment required adult household members to sketch a floor plan of their home, complete a spatial aptitude and graphic ability test and supply biographical, socio-economic, and attitudinal information. Children over the age of three also sketched a floor plan and completed an I.Q. test. All seventy sample households (222 respondents) lived in houses with identical floor plans.

A major finding of the experiment was that manual maps can be reliable and valid research instruments in the study of cognitive maps. Psychometric techniques were used in the data analysis to test for reliability and validity. Both spatial aptitude and graphic ability were found to be significantly related to the ability of individuals to communicate their cognitive maps. Persons with superior mental faculties have cognitive maps which more closely reflect reality. When psychophysical functions were examined, there appeared to be a linear relationship between subjective distance and area and real distance and area. Socio-economic variables, biographical data, and the subject's cognitive structure of the home as revealed through the semantic differential, did not produce significant correlations with the ability to communicate cognitive maps. Children's ability to produce a manual map which resembles reality is significantly related to age, spatial aptitude, and graphic ability. A child's manual map is a reflection of his general stage of mental development.

1.   INTRODUCTION

Cognitive mapping is the process by which spatial information is acquired, coded, stored, decoded, and applied to the comprehension of the everyday physical environment.

There is however, a paradox in the term cognitive map. It means both a map in the head and a map by the hand. In terms of making spatial decisions the cognitive map in the head is the only map available to the individual; the world for the individual is how he perceives the world to be. The actual communication of a cognitive map (in the head) may take many forms, one of which may be a graphic representation of the spatial arrangements of objects, commonly termed a "map". Distinction between the two concepts for purposes of the research presented here follows the convention of using cognitive map for the mental, in-head processes involved in assimilating, interpreting, and storing spatial information, and manual map for the graphic, hand drawn representations commonly used to communicate the original copy in the head.

For a number of years manual maps have been used as a research technique to examine spatial images. Kevin Lynch (1960) largely initiated the technique to study urban images and was copied by many others. Although most research of this type has concentrated on problems at the scale of the city, researchers have also used the manual map technique on a global scale, neighborhood scale, dwelling scale, and room scale.

The research reported in this paper examines some of the parameters of the manual map as a research technique.

The research had four main goals:

1.   Develop a valid and reliable quantitative method of analyzing manual maps. To this end the influence of both graphic ability and spatial aptitude were investigated to determine their affect on the individuals' manual map.

2.   Determine what form of psychophysical relationship exists between cognitive distance and real distance, as well as cognitive area and real area.

3.   Analyze the influence of biographical, socio-economic, and attitudinal variables in the individuals' manual map.

4.   Investigate the development of spatial cognition in children.

Even though the use of manual maps is widespread, the analysis of such data is almost invariably qualitative. The significance of the results depends upon the researcher's subjective interpretation of the "content" of the graphic representations. Because of this, the research is difficult to replicate and offers little opportunity to test the validity or reliability of the methodology. In response to these shortcomings, the research presented here is an attempt to develop a methodology by which manual maps can be analyzed quantitatively in addition to qualitatively.

2. RESEARCH DESIGN AND METHODOLOGY

The research setting devised to achieve the goals was to have people sketch a floor plan of their home. A unique feature of the experiment was that all homes had identical floor plans. The research setting ensured that subjects would be familiar with the environment to be mapped and allowed for easier measurement and definition.

Members of the family were divided into two groups - adults and children. The adults were asked to complete:

1. A free hand floor plan of their home.

2. A graphic ability test (Lurcat Test of Graphic Abilities).

3. A spatial aptitude test (Revised Minnesota Paper Board Test).

4. A questionnaire containing background information and socio-economic data as well as semantic differential designed to determine their attitude towards their home.

The children were asked to complete:

1. A free hand floor plan of their home.

2. The Goodenough-Harris Draw-a-Man-Test.

A sample of homes representing 222 persons from 70 families was obtained.

Central to the methodology is the manner in which the manual maps were analyzed. The basic concept of analysis was based on a psychological technique known as ratio estimation. In ratio estimation the subject is instructed to adjust a variable stimulus so that it appears subjectively equal to a certain fraction of a standard. In this experiment, the respondents supplied their own reference line in the form of the outside walls of the house. Ratio estimation is a standard technique used by both psychologists and geographers in studies of cognitive perception of geographic distance.

The ultimate task was to convert the free hand drawings to error measurements. This was accomplished by performing the following tasks (also see Figure 1):

1. Intersection Designation - The interesection of each wall with all others had to be marked and identified with a letter.

2. Digitize XY Coordinates - A Gradicon Digitizer was used to produce XY coordinates for all 24 wall intersections.

3. Calculate Distance and Area - 41 distances and 10 areas were calculated from the coordinates.

4A. Calculate Distance and Area Ratio Scales - The purpose of this calculation was to standardize the distances and areas so that all maps were equivalent to the same scale. The algorithm for calculating the geometric mean ratio was that of Ekman (1958). The ratio scales for 41 distances and 10 areas were calculated for all manual maps.

4B. Calculate Ratio Scales for Builder's Plan - In order to compare the true distance to the subjective distance the equivalent ratio scales for all walls and floor areas were calculated for the actual building plan.

5. Calculate Mean Ratio Scales - In order to compare individuals' manual maps to the group as a whole, the mean ratio scales for all walls and areas were calculated.

6A. Calculate Differences Between Individual Ratio Scales and Mean Ratio Scales - To determine the deviation between individuals and the norm, the absolute difference between individual and mean ratio scales was calculated to produce a Mean Ratio Error (MRE). The MRE was the sum of the absolute differences on each wall.

6B Calculate Differences Between Individual Ratio Scales and the True Ratio Scales - The same procedure was followed as in 6A. To produce True Ratio Error (TRE).

The MRE and TRE scores were then correlated against the other variables which were collected.

For the children it was not possible to digitize their manual maps. Instead, all the children's drawings were ranked independently by four separate judges. The judges were instructed to rank all of the children's maps into the order in which they depicted reality.

FIGURE 1: FLOW CHART OF MEAN RATIO
ERROR (MRE) AND TRUE RATIO
ERROR (TRE) CALCULATIONS

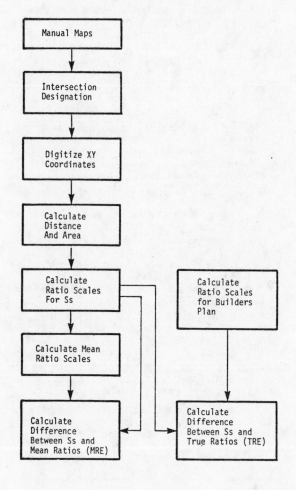

3. RESULTS

Reliability refers to the accuracy of the data
in terms of stability and repeatability. Various
tests of reliability including test-retest,
Crombacks Alpha, and internal consistency tests,
indicated that the manual map was indeed a
reliable test.

Validity refers to the extent to which a research
instrument actually measures what it is designed
to measure. Using the test of construct validity,
the manual map was shown to be a valid research
instrument. This was illustrated by the fact
that TRE=MRE for absolute error, that TRE=MRE = 0
for relative error, that there were exceptionally
high correlations between the subjects' ratio
scales and true ratio scales, and that the slope

of the curve between subjective and real distance
was 1. It was conclusively demonstrated that
the manual maps were a reliable and valid research
instrument.

Further correlation analysis demonstrated that
spatial aptitude and to a lesser extent graphic
ability are significantly related to an individual's
ability to communicate a cognitive map. This is
the first time that such variables have been
shown to be important in cognitive mapping.

Research also indicated that the researcher's
subjective assessment of "quality" of individual's
map was also highly related to error scores. This
indicated that a qualitative approach to the
analysis of manual mapping is also an acceptable
method of investigation.

There were no significant correlations between
error scores and socio-economic variables. This
appeared, however, to be due to the homogenous
nature of the sample. Almost all household heads
were of similar education, income and occupation.
Although the factor analysis of the semantic
differential produced a stable factor structure
there was no correlation between the individuals'
factor scores and error scores. It would,
therefore, appear that the attitudinal structure
of the home was not related to the spatial
cognitive structure of the home.

Standard methodology to test for the psychophysical
function, between subjective and real distance
revealed a linear relationship.

For the children it was found that the rank
given the manual maps, chronological age, I.Q.,
and graphic ability were all highly inter-related
(except for age and I.Q.). In other words,
a child's ability to produce a manual map which
resembles reality is significantly related to age,
spatial aptitude, and graphic ability. A child's
manual map is a reflection of his general stage
of mental development.

4. DISCUSSION

The research has shown that manual maps can be
a reliable and valid research instrument. This
lends credibility and support to previous
studies employing this research technique but
which have not dealt with the questions of
validity and reliability.

In addition to providing some validity for
other studies employing manual maps, evidence
is presented for the use of qualitative technique
of analysis. The research has illustrated that
a sense of "quality" of the manual map derived
from long study and appreciation could also
be a good predictor of error. This finding
should prove to be significant to those
researchers who are endeavouring to employ

subjective judgments of quality as data in other perception studies.

One of the more important results is that spatial aptitude and graphic ability appear to significantly influence an individual's cognitive and manual map. To date, these factors have been ignored. It would appear, however, that the quality of cognitive maps (and presumably the quality of spatial decisions an individual could make) is dependent upon the quality of the recording instrument, i.e. the human brain. Nevertheless, most studies in cognitive mapping have attempted to account for differences in manual maps through such variables as race, culture, role, socio-economic status, travel patterns, and sex. It is perhaps time that more effort was expended at the level of the individual to determine the psychological parameters of cognitive mapping.

The psychophysical function for distance and area perception proved to be linear. This supports the findings of both Cadwallader (1973) and Howard et al (1973) who also used ratio estimation as a research technique. The research, however, conflicts with results presented by others who contend that the psychophysical function for cognitive distance perception approximates Stevens Power Law. All experiments to date have used slightly different research designs and all use different geographic scales. Although Howard appears to have used the most rigorous research design, only replicative experiments using the same scale of distance will be able to settle the debate between linear and non-linear models.

This research generally supports the work conducted by Blaut et al (1970), and Hart and Moore (1971), in the study of spatial development and learning in young children. As the child develops and matures in his mental faculties, his perception also improve. The development of cognitive mapping closely approximates the development of mental maturity. Unlike other studies, however, significant difference could not be detected for sex or socio-economic status.

Although cultural variables are important in the development of cognitive maps, not enough attention has been given to the investigation of psychological and physiological variables. As Kaplan (1973) says "The ways we deal with the environment are largely dependent upon the sorts of mechanisms that have evolved for this purpose".

Reference

BLAUT, J.M., Mc Cleary, G.F., & Blant, A.S., 1970, Environmental Mapping in Young Children. Environment and Behavior, 3, 335-349.

CADWALLADER, M.T., 1973, An Analysis of Cognitive Distance and its Role in Consumer Spatial Behavior. Ph.D. Dissertation. Los Angeles: University of California.

EKMAN, G., 1958, Two Generalized Ratio Scaling Methods. The Journal of Psychology, 45, 287-295.

HART, R.A. & Moore, G.T., 1971, The Development of Spatial Cognition: A Review. Place Perception Reports. Report No. 7.

HOWARD, R.B., Chase, S.D., Rothman, M., 1973, An Analysis of Four Measures of Cognitive Maps. EDRA-4, 254-264.

KAPLAN, S., 1973, Cognitive Maps in Perception and Thought. In R.M. Downs and D. Stra (Eds.) Image and Environment Chicago: Aldine Publishing Co., 1973.

LYNCH, K., 1960, The Image of the City. Cambridge, Mass: M.I.T. Press

ROTHWELL, D.C., 1974, Cognitive Mapping of the Home Environment, Ph.D Dissertation, Vancouver: University of British Columbia.

BEHAVIOR AND USE PATTERNS IN A TUCSON PARK

William C. Kueffer
Graduate Student

Department of Landscape Architecture
School of Renewable Natural Resources
University of Arizona
Tucson, Arizona 85721

ABSTRACT

Basically, this study is to find out what the people's image of the park is and to provide some guidelines which would aid designers and planning officials in making valid decisions concerning park design and development. The methodology consisted of a series of questionnaires administered at the site and noninteractive observations. This particular work shall concern itself with three main objectives: (1) to provide an effective method for the assessment of public sentiment regarding park makeup, (2) to provide a meaningful process with which one could evaluate successful or disfunctional parks, and finally, (3) to demonstrate that behavioral research can be a useful tool in the design process.

1. INTRODUCTION

1.1. Background

In the past few decades, many studies have been conducted with reference to man's perception of his environment. Saarinen and Cooke (1971) studied the perception of environmental quality with marked success. Whitaker and Browne (1971) studied the need for parks and set forth many innovative suggestions as to their construction and design once it is decided what goes into the construction. deJonge (1967) makes reference to what different people want from a park and Lyle (1970) studies the behavior of people in parks throughout the world, much as Sommer (1969) did in his research. Wentworth and Wager (1974) studied Bryant Park in Manhattan.

1.2. Objectives

This particular study shall concern itself with three main objectives. The first is to provide an effective method for the assessment of public sentiment regarding park makeup. The results should show what the current park user or would-be user wants in his park. Secondly, it hopes to provide a meaningful process by which one could evaluate successfully functional or disfunctional urban parks. This would greatly aid concerned planners and designers with some form of empirical data. Finally, it would demonstrate that behavioral research is a useful tool that can be used to aid the design process.

1.3. Aims

With reference to the forementioned objectives, previous research and readings, this paper will have two major objectives:

1. It should demonstrate that the user public will respond willingly, that they will have strong views regarding the composition of parks, and that park users come from a cross section of society rather than a particular socio-economic status.

2. The site-administered questionnaire is a valid tool for providing designers and planners with empirical data aiding in park modification and future design.

2. METHODOLOGY

2.1. Interviews and Sample

The heart of this research is a personal interview conducted at Fort Lowell Park in Tucson, Arizona (Figure 1). The methods of study would be basically the same regardless of the park chosen. This study could serve as

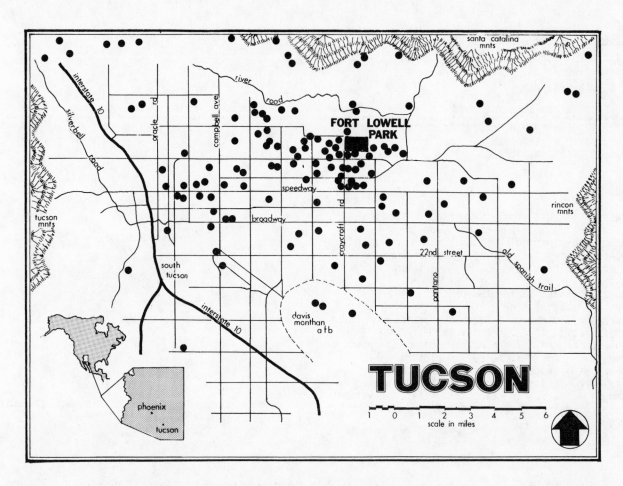

FIGURE 1: MAP OF TUCSON

a model for future studies in like parks, thus
giving the researcher a better cross reference
capability. The questionnaire will be
basically the same format used by Saarinen and
Cooke (1970). The interviews were conducted
at random while the interviewer walked a
specified transect course. The transect method
is simply picking a point in the relative center
of the park and walking a specified traverse
through the study area. (See Figure 2.) Seven
to eight interviews were taken each day. A
distinction was made between weekend and
weekday observation periods. Four major time
sequences of observation were selected to
lessen one season's dominance over the other
(winter, spring, summer, and fall). Within
each major time-period, a fourteen day-period
of observations was adhered to. The interviewer sampled every other day. A total of one
hundred and thirty interviews have been taken
thus far. The winter season remains to be
sampled.

2.2. Questionnaire

The questionnaire had twenty-one major questions
providing one hundred and one individual
responses per interview. Due to the length of
the questionnaire, it would be impossible to

reproduce it in its entirety within the space
limits of this paper. In short, the subject

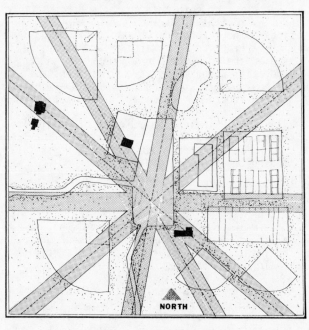

FIGURE 2: TRANSECT PATH

was asked such questions as: method of transportation, time of visits, activity preferences, and numerous other behavioral oriented questions regarding the park's physical make-up and unique character as viewed by the subject. The questionnaire was geared to the distinctive character of the southwestern park. The language of the questionnaire was kept as simple as possible to avoid confusing the subjects. The questionnaire data was supplemented by direct observation, thus providing another source of data for final tabulation.

2.3. Data Tabulation

Once the questionnaires were administered, the results were encoded on computer punch cards. The questionnaire itself was keyed into an existing program in the form of variables, variable labels and values. The Statistical Package for the Social Sciences (SPSS) program was used to tabulate the study. Thirty-eight separate cross-tabs were run to aid in answering the questions raised by this study.

3. LIMITATIONS

This study is merely a tool to be used with other tools in the construction of a more enlightened decision regarding park composition. It is not a panacea that will answer all design questions and allow concerned individuals to build one model park to satisfy all. The planner and designer must also temper popular ideas with sound judgment.

The size of the sampling (200) was small due to limited funding and the lack of qualified interviewers. The absence of a large sample tends to lead to grouping problems and completely eliminates doing valid cluster analysis. But there was only a 3.8% refusal rate, which was much lower than anticipated. Table 1 indicates the interviewer's appraisal of the interest and cooperativeness of the subjects. Park users are difficult to approach when engaged in some activity such as a baseball game or handball. The tendency of the interviewer is to approach individuals engaged in passive activities such as sunning and reading rather than someone engaged in athletics. However, this was overcome to some degree by direct observation methods. Prior to taking the first interview of the day, the interviewer annotated any large scale activities taking place in the park and the number of participants. For example: Sixteen people playing flag football in field across from crafts building. The transect method of sampling a site was applied in order to overcome the tendency to wander from one group of users to another or take an entire day's sampling from the same area. The accompanying map, Figure 2, shows the park and the sampling avenues. The main idea was to obtain as

diverse a sampling as possible, thus compensating for the relatively small number of interviews. I am confident that the results do reflect the user population's behavior patterns and perception of the park.

TABLE 1: INTERVIEWER RATING OF INTEREST AND COOPERATION

Degree of Interest	%	Cooperation	%
Very	60.0	Very	70.0
Somewhat	34.6	Somewhat	27.7
Uninterested	5.4	Uncooperative	2.3

TABLE 2: EDUCATIONAL LEVEL

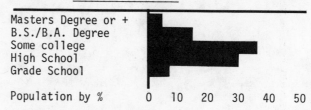

Masters Degree or +	
B.S./B.A. Degree	
Some college	
High School	
Grade School	
Population by %	0 10 20 30 40 50

4. RESULTS

4.1. User Profile

Surprisingly, 94.6% of the park users interviewed were Caucasian. Mexican Americans and other minorities constituted only 5.4% of the sample, although they constitute a higher proportion than this of the Tucson population according to the last state census. Perhaps the location of the park or lack of public transportation to the park inhibited their use of Fort Lowell Park (Figure 3) as a recreation site. (See Figure 1.) If one were to generalize, most of the Mexican American core neighborhoods are along the west side of the Santa Cruz River and south of Broadway. Furthermore, the users appeared to be rather well educated, as shown by Table 2 only 8.5% did not have at least a high school diploma. This might be attributed to the fact that students constituted the single largest body of park goers, as shown in Table 3. Most of the students interviewed were of college age; however, the mean age of park users was 35 years. That fact should dispel any notion that the interviewers, being of college age, subconsciously sought out their peers. The occupational table also reinforces the educational findings, since less than 4% of those interviewed were unemployed or chose not to answer. As might be expected in an auto-oriented city such as Tucson, most of the park users (77.7%) came to the park by autos. Adequate public transportation to the park would probably increase use by members of lower socio-economic groups. Only 14.6% walked to the park.

The grouping of users showed a wide range of possibilities; 33.8% came alone, 32.3% came with friends, and 30.0% were accompanied by

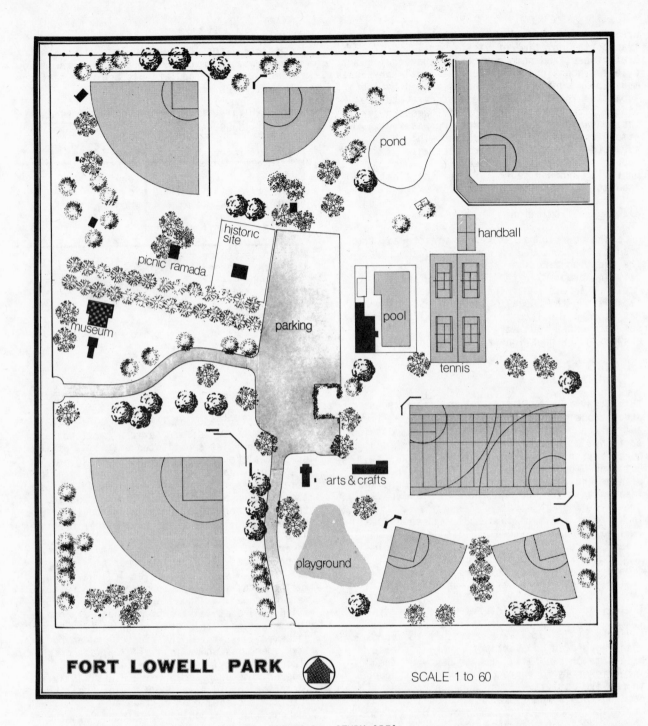

FIGURE 3: STUDY AREA

family members. Of course organized teams
dominated the park during their respective
seasons of play; i.e. Little League baseball,
football, and soccer teams. The length of
visit in the park, for the most part, was
limited to less than five hours but more than
one. The park catered to a wide range of users,
as seen from Table 5. There were a few
incidents of conflict observed between passive
and active groups. A group of individuals
sunning in the center of a field were forced off

by another group playing football. Fort Lowell
Park was never deserted. Some group was using
the park every minute it was open. This might
be taken as an indication of the park's success.

The park was used on a recurring basis by most
individuals; over half of those interviewed
visited the park two or more times a week.
There was a definite distinction between weekday and weekend users. Weekday users seemed to
engage in more passive or small group activities.

Weekend users tended to congregate in larger groups and participated in more team activities or picnics. Most park users came in the afternoon, with the exception of the summer period. The mean temperature for July is normally 86.6°F, however this year it was 4° higher than normal. A one-hundred-plus temperature puts the damper on most outside activities, including interviewing. The interview times for the summer had to be readjusted due to the absence of users from 1:00 PM to 3:00 PM. The only significant outside activity that took place during this hot period was swimming.

TABLE 3: OCCUPATION OF PARK USERS

Student
Housewife
Blue Collar
Retired
Professional
White Collar
Other

Population by % 0   5   10   15   20   25   30

4.2. Advantages and Disadvantages

By all indications, Fort Lowell Park is a successful park. Table 4 lists both the advantages and disadvantages of the park as perceived by the user. No predetermined categories were forced upon the subject. The answers were impromptu and classified later in the study. It should be noted that 46.2% felt that there were no disadvantages to the park. When questioned about the adequacy of the facilities, 78.5% stated that they were adequate; half felt facilities should be added. The majority of the needed facilities were playground equipment, courts, and more space. If the public had felt Fort Lowell Park was inadequate, undoubtedly more facilities would have been requested.

TABLE 4: PERCEIVED ADVANTAGES AND
          DISADVANTAGES OF PARK

Advantages	%	Disadvantages	%
Country-like	36.2	None	46.2
Pool	12.3	No shade	9.2
Pond	10.0	Crowded	7.7
Facilities	6.9	Fences	5.4
Playground	6.2	Leash law	3.8
Open Area	4.6	No equipment	3.8
Eat lunch in	3.8	Litter	3.1
Nice location	3.8	Few activities	2.3
Activities	3.1	Law breakers	2.3
Tennis Courts	3.1	Crowded	2.3
Close to home	2.3	Too much baseball	2.3
Ballfields	2.3	Too small	1.5
Historic	1.5	Dogs	1.5
All Others	3.9	All Others	8.6

4.3. Activities/Location

Fort Lowell Park was picked as a study area for three reasons. For its size it offers the broadest range of activities of any park in the city. All of the activities listed in Table 5 can be engaged in at the park. The park is centrally located and draws people from all over the city, as demonstrated by the demographic dots in Figure 1. The areas of high minority population are conspicuously missing. Its proximity to the University of Arizona facilitates easy access for study. The park is relatively compact, thus allowing an interviewer to make the most of a short observation period.

When asked, "Are there any other activities that have not been mentioned before that you do in this park?" the majority, 54.4%, responded "No". Others responded with numerous active and passive undertakings, as shown in Table 6.

4.4. Perception

Perhaps the most interesting portion of this study was the perceptual facet. The user was asked to indicate which words best described the park area. Two interesting points were made. (See Tables 7 and 8.) More than half of the individuals (55.4%) felt that the park was lush and green. By southwestern standards, the park is lush. Only one user commented that he viewed it as being natural desert (a tourist from Alberta, Canada). When asked if the park had too many or not enough trees, 50.9% who indicated the park was lush wanted more trees added. Apparently even more greenery would be desirable.

5. CONCLUSIONS

Park design is a multi-faceted undertaking. All too often parks are designed by individuals who consider only their own perception of what a park should be. Sampling of behavior patterns provides an adequate barometer by which to gauge a park's success and provide the designer with empirical data upon which to base future decisions.

The data collected indicated that Fort Lowell is, for the most part, a successful park. It has only one major flaw, which became evident after repeated observation and respondents comments. Too many activities have been put into too small an area. Fort Lowell Park could become over-developed and lose its tranquil atmosphere.

By sampling numerous parks in like geographic areas, one could build a data base upon which the desires of the users would become evident. For example, in the desert environment of Tucson most people would prefer even more greenery than was present in Fort Lowell Park. These desires, tempered with valid design and aesthetic considerations, would serve as a sound foundation upon which to build the parks of the future. Had Fort Lowell Park been a less successful park, this type of a study would have pinpointed the causes of its disfunctionality so that positive action could be taken to correct faulty design. It is anticipated that further analysis of the data should provide further insights useful for the design process.

TABLE 5: ACTIVITY FREQUENCY

Activity	Often %	Sometimes %	Never %
Picnicking	17.7	55.4	26.9
Sightseeing	17.7	48.5	33.8
Swimming	24.6	30.0	45.4
Walk for pleasure	40.8	36.2	23.1
Tennis	20.0	20.0	60.0
Handball	7.7	13.1	79.2
Baseball	5.4	26.9	67.7
Football	6.2	18.5	75.4
Soccer	3.1	3.1	93.8
Shuffleboard	2.3	7.7	90.0
Watching sport events	22.3	45.4	32.3
Bicycling	13.1	17.7	69.2
Attending outdoor concert/play	12.3	26.9	60.8
Arts and crafts	12.3	23.8	63.8
Visit museum/ historic site	13.9	55.4	30.8
Croquet	2.3	5.4	92.3
Badminton	2.3	10.8	86.9
Take child to playground	26.1	36.9	36.9
Walk a dog	17.0	18.5	64.6
Eat lunch	30.8	42.3	26.9

TABLE 6: OTHER ACTIVITIES

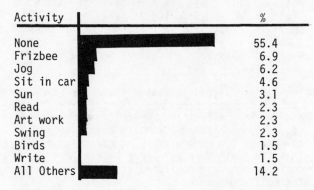

Activity	%
None	55.4
Frizbee	6.9
Jog	6.2
Sit in car	4.6
Sun	3.1
Read	2.3
Art work	2.3
Swing	2.3
Birds	1.5
Write	1.5
All Others	14.2

TABLE 7: VARIED PERCEPTION OF PARK

Shown by relative percentages

Flat land 77.7	Rolling 19.2	Hilly 3.1
Historic site 63.1	Point of interest 26.9	No historic value 10.0
Obviously planned 55.4	Somewhat planned 39.2	Not planned 5.4
Too many activities 10.0	Enough 82.3	Not enough 7.7
Crowded facilities 16.2	Somewhat crowded 40.8	Not crowded 43.1
Natural desert 0.8	Average vegetation 43.8	Lush green 55.4
Large 16.9	Medium 70.0	Small 13.1
Well maintained 83.1	Somewhat 16.9	Not maintained 0.0
Country setting 21.5	Suburb 60.8	City site 17.7
Not littered 60.8	Somewhat 30.8	Littered 8.5
Too many people 14.6	Not too many 77.7	Too few 7.7
Well patrolled 26.9	Somewhat 35.4	Not 37.7
Lots of parking 16.1	Enough 61.5	Not enough 22.3
Safe 63.1	Enough 31.5	Not safe 5.4

TABLE 8: VEGETATIVE PREFERENCE

Shown by relative percentages

	Too Many	Enough	Not Enough
Trees	0.8	56.9	42.3
Flowers	6.2	23.1	70.8
Grass	3.9	88.5	7.7
Shrubs	1.5	59.2	39.2
Paved areas	6.9	86.2	7.0

Reference:
DOWNS, ROGER M. and DAVID STEA. Image and the Environment, Chicago: Adline 1973
SAARINEN, T. F. and COOKE, R. U. Public Perception of Environmental Quality in Tucson, AZ, J.A.A.S., Vol.6 (1971)
SOMMER, ROBERT Personal Space. New Jersey: Prentice-Hall, 1969.

DISTANCE MAKES THE HEART GROW FONDER: ATTRIBUTES AND METRICS IN COGNITIVE MACROMAPS

Stanley Coren and Clare Porac

Department of Psychology, University of British Columbia, Vancouver, Canada

Department of Psychology, University of Victoria, Victoria, B.C., Canada

ABSTRACT

Direct psychophysical scaling was employed to obtain estimates of the perceived size, distance, and economic, political, and cultural importance of 52 cities distributed across the entire globe. The results indicate that apparent population and distance covary as a power function of actual population and direct distance measures. In addition, the empirically fitted equations reveal that the perceived cultural, political and economic importance of cities increases with increasing population and distance.

1.0 INTRODUCTION

Over the past two decades psychologists have become increasingly interested in the way in which perceptual representations of the surrounding environment may influence man's behavior. In order to study such percepts, many investigators have attempted to determine the spatial schemata or cognitive maps employed by observers (Downs and Stea, 1973; Lee, 1969; Stea, 1969). The importance of such schemata lies in the fact that they are ultimately reflected in aspects of human behavior which are distributed across the environment or spatially separated loci. For instance, since Zipi's (1949) pioneer study, it has been known that density of interaction decreases as a function of increasing geographical distance. In a similar vein, Ekman and Bratfisch (1965), Dornic (1967) and Bratfisch (1969) have shown that emotional involvement with events taking place in various cities decreases as a function of the observer's perceived distance from that particular city.

There are a number of limitations associated with available data concerning mental maps. To begin with, the majority of extant studies have used rather limited geographical areas, such as cities (Appleyard, 1970; Gulick, 1963), portions of cities (Saarinen, 1968), and neighborhoods (De Jonge, 1962; Ladd, 1970). Only recently have investigators turned to larger scale geographic distributions, such as continental Gould, 1973); transcontinental (Lundberg, 1973) or global (Saarinen, 1973). Such macromaps are useful in that they give the broadest range of geographical distribution possible within the

environment. Such increased range in distances should serve to accentuate relationships which might be expected to hold in smaller geographic units. In addition, with the exception of Lundberg and his associates, few of these studies have made use of modern psychophysical scaling techniques which have been so useful in the field of psychology.

The study reported below, utilizes such psychophysical procedures on a global scale in order to ascertain how attitudes and perceptions vary as a function of size and distance of urban centers. The research concerns 52 cities, distributed across the entire world. It is hoped that in addition to clarifying the interrelationship between spatial schemata and attitudes toward geographical loci, this research will serve to exemplify one form of quantitative scaling procedure which may be useful in studying other aspects of environmental perception.

2.0 METHOD

2.1 Target Cities

Fifty-two target cities were selected. One criterion for inclusion in the sample was that each particular city should be recognizeable or familiar to the majority of respondents. The cities ranged in size from just over 100,000 in population, to better than 11 million in population. Using Vancouver, B.C., Canada (where the study was to be run) as the origin, the cities ranged from approximately 200 miles to just over 12,000 miles in "as the crow flies" or "great circle" distance.

2.2 Subjects

Twenty-seven undergraduate volunteers from the University of British Columbia served as respondents. They were not aware of the purpose of the experiment, and were paid for their participation.

2.3 Procedure

Each subject received a list of 52 cities arranged in a different random order. For each city the respondent was required to estimate its direct distance from Vancouver in miles. In addition, respondents were required to estimate the population of the city.

Attitudes toward the specific cities were estimated using a rating scale patterned after that employed by Helson (1964). Respondents separately rated the cultural importance, political importance, and economic importance of each city on a nine point rating scale. The nine points were labeled extremely important, very important, important, moderately important, average importance, moderately unimportant, unimportant, very unimportant, extremely unimportant.

3.0 RESULTS AND DISCUSSION

In order to facilitate statistical analyses the cities were divided into groups. For the purpose of analyzing the effect of population, the cities were divided into five categories, each with an increasing mean population. The smallest population class contained cities with an average of approximately 400,000 population, while the largest had cities with a mean population of just over 7 million. A similar distribution was made by distance distribution. Five classes were determined, each with increasing distance from Vancouver. The closest group contained cities with an average distance of 1,500 miles from origin, while the farthest class averaged just over 10,000 miles from Vancouver. The purpose of dividing the cities into classifications according to these physical characteristics was to allow use of analysis of variance techniques in order to estimate statistical reliability of the findings. During the selection of target cities, the sample had been subjected to the restriction that the mean population in each distance grouping was approximately equal.

In order to describe the psychological relationship between these geographic and demographic variables and the rated attributes, power functions were fitted through the data via a computer program. All power function equations fitted the general format

$$y = ax^b$$

In this equation y represents the subjective estimate(such as rated importance or distance), x the physical parameter (such as actual distance or population), b the rate of change in the estimate as a function of variations in the physical parameter, and a is a constant. In addition, the coefficient of determination (r^2) which is a measure of goodness of fit, was computed for each obtained function. For ease of interpretation one may consider the square root of r^2 as analogous to a non linear correlation coefficient.

3.1 The Effect of Population Size

As might be expected, with increasing actual population, the estimated population increases ($F = 48.84$, df = 4/1373, p <0.001). The judged increase in population, however, is not linearly related to the true population. The resultant power function is

$$y = 7623x^{.39}$$

this means that population estimates increase more slowly than the actual population resulting in an underestimation of the size of larger cities ($r^2 = .95$). The estimated population size closely approximates the cube root of the actual value, times the constant 7623.

It might be expected, that the cultural, political, and economic importance of various cities, would vary as a function of the size of their population. Certainly larger urban centers would have a greater economic impact on their region, would carry greater political weight simply due to the increased number of voting or participant individuals, and would be better able to sustain cultural facilities, such as symphony orchestras or museums. It is thus not too surprising to find that all three of these sets of attributes co-vary with population. Cultural importance significantly increases with population ($F = 42.24$, df = 4/1373, p <.001), as does political importance ($F = 40.45$, df = 4/1373, p <.001) and economic importance ($F = 68.56$, df = 4/1373, p <.001). We may get some estimate as to the rate of increase in apparent importance of a city as a function of its population size by fitting the appropriate power functions through the obtained data. The size of the exponent serves as an indication of the rate of change. If the value of t-e exponent is 1, this would indicate that there is a linear relationship between attributed importance and population size. If the exponent is less than 1 it indicates that perceived importance is related to population size via a negatively accelerated function, wherein equivalent increases in population produce larger changes in apparent importance for smaller cities than for larger. The converse would be true if the exponent were greater than 1.

When we fit the power functions through these data, we find that the exponent for cultural importance plotted against population size is 0.11 ($r^2 = .90$), while the exponent for judged political importance is 0.12 ($r^2 = .95$) and the exponent for economic importance is 0.13 ($r^2 = .96$). It thus becomes clear that the relative importance in all three realms increases at a rate approximately equivalent to the eighth root of the population.

Another way of looking at the effects of population size on attributed importance is to build a composite index which would include cultural, political and economic factors. The simplest form of such an index simply consists of the sum of the three factors. A power function fitted through the relationship between population size and total importance produces an exponent of 0.12 ($r^2 = 0.95$). As might be expected, the relationship is somewhat stronger when estimated population size, rather than true population size is used in this equation. The functional relationship between total importance and estimated population size results in an exponent of 0.31 ($r^2 = 0.94$) which is reasonably close to a cube root relationship.

Thus it becomes clear that the relative importance of a city rises as its population size or estimated population size increases.

3.2 The Effects of Distance

The expectations relative to the effect of distances are somewhat less clear. To begin with, let us look at the relationship between the true distance and the distance estimates. As the distance increases, the distance estimate increases significantly ($F = 7166.52$, $df = 4/1373$, $p < 0.001$).

When we fit a power function between the true distance and the estimated distance, we find that the distance estimates co-vary much more closely with physical distance than the population estimates varied with true population. The obtained power function is

$$y = 20.2x^{.66}$$

with a coefficient of determination (r^2) equal to 0.99. This relationship is fairly close to linearity, falling between a direct relationship and a square root relationship. The implication is that variations in the relative distance of population centers are perceived fairly well, and relatively accurately.

When one turns to a consideration of the relationship between distance and perceived importance, the expectation on the basis of the available literature is that more distant cities would probably be adjudged to be less important. Work done by Zipf (1949) and work coming our of Lundberg's (1973) laboratory seem to indicate that emotional involvement, and amount of interaction decrease with increasing subjective distance. Such an analysis, however, ignores the fact that "emotional involvement" and "importance" refer to quite different psychological dimensions. The former assesses the degree of interaction, or intensity of feeling, evoked by a target stimulus, while the latter addresses itself to the polarity of a fairly static attitude. It is easy to imagine that one may feel that a given object is important, yet not have much emotional involvement with it. Thus if one is asked "How important is the Mona Lisa as a work of art?" it may well be possible to say that it is a very important piece of art, without necessarily indicating anything whatsoever as to the respondents emotional involvement, or for that matter, without giving any indication as to whether he likes it or dislikes it. One might have more emotional involvement with a piece of exotic art, yet not attribute to it much cultural or artistic importance. Thus when we measure importance, we are looking at a bipolar attribute scale rather than an index of emotional involvement, hence these dimensions might not produce similar psychological correlations with physical dimensions, such as distance.

When we begin to assess the relationship between distance and perceived importance, we find somewhat of a surprise. To begin with, the perceived cultural, political, and economic importance of urban centers seems to rise as a function of increasing distance ($F = 23.74$, $df = 4/1373$, $p < 0.001$; $F = 52.07$, $df = 4/1373$, $p < 0.001$; $F = 6.10$, $df = 4/1373$, $p < 0.001$ respectively).

When we fit the power functions through the rated importance of the cities as a function of increasing distance, we find a different pattern than that which appeared in the population equations. Whereas all three dimensions of importance increased uniformly with increasing population, there is significant asymmetry in the rate of change in perceived importance as a function of increasing distance for the three dimensions. A power function fitted through the cultural importance plotted against distance provides an exponent of 0.16 ($r^2 = .91$). This means that the perceived cultural importance of a city increases as a function of the sixth or seventh root of its distance from the rater.

The political importance of an urban center increases at a much faster rate than the cultural importance. The power function fitted through political importance and distance produces an exponent of 0.26 ($r^2 = 0.95$). This corresponds to a functional relationship between perceived political importance and physical distance somewhere between the third and fourth root of the distance.

The perceived economic importance shows the smallest rate of change as a function of increasing distance, producing an exponent of only 0.05 ($r^2 = 0.39$). This means that economic importance increases at approximately the twentieth root of the perceived distance.

At first blush these results appear to be quite difficult to interpret. However, they become clearer when one considers the type of communication which generally reaches an observer about distant cities. If the only information that an observer has about a given city is obtained predominantly through media channels, it is most likely that the events occurring in a city which he would encounter would be political events. Thus revolutions, wars, or assassinations tend to be most frequently reported. The next most frequent form of information which he would obtain would refer to the nature of cultural events within a center. These events would be reported in travelogues, or feature articles etc. Since such cultural features tend to manifest themselves in the media much less frequently than political events, they should produce a lower impact. News of economic relevance seldom enter distant media channels. Thus it is highly unlikely, that many individuals in North America can tell you much about the economic status of Zambia, or other such distant regions. Primarily, this occurs because so little coverage appears in any of the mass media providing such information, thus it is not surprising that the exponent is so low for economic importance. One might wonder as to why it is positive at all, given these suppositions. This suggests that there must be some additional variable operating in this situation.

Since we have already demonstrated that increasing population, or apparent population results in an increased apparent importance of a city, it would be interesting to know whether there was any relationship between distance and apparent population. There are logical reasons why we might expect such a relationship. Certainly, to the extent that one hears or reads about a given city, one is apt to attribute some size and impact to that geographical entity. In the absence of much information, such as would occur with more distant centers, it seems reasonable that the observer may be over-estimating the size of the urban unit. This would suggest a systematic relationship between estimated population and physical distance. In fact, such a relationship does appear, with more distant cities being judged as significantly larger (F = 9.14, df = 4/1373, p <0.001). The power function reveals an exponent of 0.28 (r^2 = 0.83). This exponent is sizeably larger than the exponent obtained for both rated economic importance and rated cultural importance. Thus it may well be the case that the positive slope obtained for these functions is simply due to the covariation of apparent urban center size with increasing distance.

3.3 Size, Distance, and Macromaps

These results point out some interesting features about the nature of global views. To begin with, although cognitive maps of a neighborhood or city may be affected by one's degree of interaction, or emotional involvement with these regions, within the macrospace of the world, we have little opportunity to come into direct contact with many geographical loci. The only information which we obtain about such centers comes through the written or spoken word, and usually through the mass media. Such media inputs tend to be biased toward exotic and more important events, presumably simply because it is rather expensive to send a reporter or journalist some distance from home, and only important events would warrant such an expenditure. Thus our picture of distant urban centers is composed of a concatenation of momentous events in its political history, or unusual cultural practices or spectacles which might catch a journalistic eye. Because of the operation of these factors more distant cities become more exotic, and more important.

In some respects it is hard to deconfound the effects of population size from that of perceived importance. There is a firm belief amongst many people that large urban centers are quite important. This manifests itself quite clearly in the obtained relationships between perceived importance and population size. However, estimated population may be inflated due to a secondary pressure. It is certainly possible that the correlation runs in the other

direction. If one perceives a population center as being important, one may be tempted to also perceive it as being large, perhaps in order to justify such impact. These two factors are quite difficult to separate. If we accept the causal flow suggested. These data make it quite clear that population, or perceived population size has a massive effect on our perceptions of the importance of cities, as does distance.

In addition to pointing out the importance of size and distance factors in cognitive maps of macrospace, these results also point out the difficulty of generalizing from one level of spatial inquiry to another. Most of the extant literature seems to imply that increasing distance results in less apparent importance or emotional impact. Yet in dealing with global attitudes and perceptions, due to the selectivity of the media, it is quite clear that this relationship reverses itself. Our perception of the world is quite different than our perception of our neighborhood. In the neighborhood things which are far away recede from our consciousness, thus bringing to mind the proverb "Out of sight out of mind". In the world the relationship is quite different. We might say that at the global or macromap level "Bigger is better" and "Distance makes the heart grow fonder".

ACKNOWLEDGEMENTS

We would like to acknowledge the assistance of Jeannie Garber and Joseph Porac in the scoring and analysis of these data. This research was supported in part by a grant from the National Research Council of Canada (A9783).

References

APPLEYARD, D. Styles and methods of structuring a city. Environment and Behavior, 1970, 2, 100-118.

BRATFISCH, O. A further study of the relation between subjective distance and emotional involvement. Acta Psychologica, 1969, 29, 244-255.

DE JONGE, D. Images of urban areas, their structures and psychological foundations. Journal of the American Institute of Planners, 1962, 28, 266-276.

DORNIC, S. Subjective distance and emotional involvement: A verification of the exponent in variance. Reports from the Psychological Laboratories, Stockholm, 1967, 237, 1-7.

DOWNS, R.M. and STEA, D. (Eds.) Image and environment: Cognitive mapping and spatial behavior, Chicago: Alidine, 1973.

EKMAN, G. and BRATFISCH, O.   Subjective distance
     and emotional involvement; a psychological
     mechanism. Acta Psychologica, 1965, 24,
     446-453.

GOULD, P.R.   On mental maps.   In Downs and Stea
     op. cit., 182-220.

GULICK, J.   Images of an Arab city. Journal of
     the American Institute of Planners, 1963,
     29, 179-198.

HELSON, H.   Adaptation-level Theory: An experi-
     mental and systematic approach to behavior.
     New York: Harper, 1969.

LADD, F.C.   Black youths view their Environment:
     Neighborhood maps. Environment and Beha-
     vior, 1970, 2, 64-79.

LEE, T.R.   The psychology of spatial orientation.
     Architectural Association Quarterly, 1969
     1, 11-15.

LUNDBERG, U.   Emotional and geographical pheno-
     mena in psychophysical research.   In Downs
     and Stea op. cit., 322-337.

SAARINEN, T.   Image of the Chicago loop. Uni-
     versity of Chicago: Unpublished paper,
     1968.

SAARINEN, T.   Student views of the world.   In
     Downs and Stea op. cit., 148-161.

STEA, D.   The measurement of mental maps: An ex-
     perimental model for studying conceptual
     spaces. In Cox, K.R. and Golledge, R.G.
     (Eds.) Behavioral problems in geography:
     A symposium. Evanston, Illinois: Northwes-
     tern University Press, 1969, 228-253.

ZIPF, G.K.   Human behavior and the principle of
     least effort. Cambridge, Mass.: Addison
     Wesley, 1949.

THE EFFECTS OF AN EXPLICIT LANDMARK ON SPATIAL JUDGMENTS

Lawrence A. Fehr and Harold D. Fishbein

Room 46 McMicken Hall, Department of Psychology

University of Cincinnati, Cincinnati, Ohio 45201

ABSTRACT

The present research was initiated to determine the effects of an explicit landmark on the development of spatial understanding. An experiment was conducted using as subjects 240 primary school children and 80 college students. Under various stimulus circumstances, groups of subjects were asked in each of 20 trials to rank order four maps on the basis of their similarity to a given array of objects. Data analysis indicated that the presence of an explicit landmark aided subjects in choosing correct maps. This was especially true for the two youngest age groups. On the other hand, the presence of an explicit landmark did not appear to have a significant effect on the consistency of the spatial judgments that were made by the subjects. The role that was played by an explicit landmark was also found to differ depending upon the task that was performed by the subjects. It played a more vital role in the performance of a difficult task referred to as Coordination of Perspectives than it did in a less difficult perceptual task.

INTRODUCTION

This study is concerned with the ability of an explicit landmark to effect the simple and complex judgments of subjects of various ages. The manner in which subjects, ranging in age from seven to adult, perform a Coordination of Perspectives task (complex) will be compared with their performance on a Frontal task (simple).

The concept of a landmark is one that has been studied in the framework of large-scale environments for a number of years. A landmark can be defined as a unique configuration of a perceptual pattern that identifies a specific geographical location (Siegel & White, in preparation). It is pointed out by Siegel and White that landmarks generally form a starting point for an individual's account of his spatial representations. Such places as the "church" and the "school" are the means by which people determine how they shall travel.

Perhaps the foremost study regarding the use of landmarks was performed by Lynch (1960). He concluded from his research based on adult populations in three American cities that one's image of his environment is at least in part dependent upon the number of and nature of the landmarks within his environment. Francescato and Mebane (1973) have in part verified the cross cultural applicability of Lynch's findings by obtaining similar results in a study that examined people's views of two Italian cities.

Landmarks are used not only to determine how we are to travel but also where we are located. Several recent studies (Acredolo, Pick, & Olsen, in press; Acredolo, 1975) have noted that landmarks are important in the determination of the frames of reference that are used by children. As the child develops, he appears to shift from an egocentric to a more fixed frame of reference using such cues as landmarks to coordinate his spatial perceptions.

The present research has sought to examine the question of whether the crucial role played by landmarks in macrospatial environments also exists in microspatial environments. The possibility that the manner in which landmarks are used in microspatial environments may at least in part be determined by the age of the individual observer must also be given due consideration. The present study deals with these issues under stimulus conditions of varying intellectual difficulty.

In order to understand the notion of stimulus difficulty as it pertains to the present study, the term Coordination of Perspectives must be introduced. In a typical Coordination of Perspectives task as originated by Piaget, a subject and an experimenter sitting opposite him look at a three dimensional array of objects and a set of two dimensional representations of those objects. It is the task of the subject (as related to the present study) to choose which one of four maps best approximates the arrangement of the array of three dimensional objects as seen by the experimenter. It necessitates that the subject remove himself from his own egocentric frame of reference in order to make an accurate judgment. It has been found in numerous studies (Piaget & Inhelder, 1956; Nigl & Fishbein, 1974) that a Coordination of Perspectives task is a more difficult task than a perceptual task in which the subject and experimenter view the array from the same position and where an egocentric frame of reference may be correctly used.

In the present study, 20 different types of maps were constructed, one of which was an accurate representation of the object array, and the remaining 19 were different systematic distortions of an accurate representation. One half of the subjects were presented with arrays of three objects and half with arrays of four objects. The fourth object represented the landmark and by definition, it was always represented in the correct place on all of the maps. The subjects were further subdivided by having half of the subjects perform a perceptual task in which the subject and experimenter had the same viewing position (called Frontal), and the other half perform a Coordination of Perspectives task.

Perhaps the most crucial issue that will be dealt with in this paper concerns the spatial factors that are used by the various subject groups in making their spatial judgments. It is hypothesized that the presence of an explicit landmark, the age of the subjects, and the difficulty of the task that is performed will effect the manner in which five hypothesized factors are used by the subjects in making their spatial judgments. Other hypotheses concern the contentions that the oldest subjects, those performing a frontal task, and those performing with the presence of a landmark will make fewer errors than their counterparts.

METHOD

Subjects

The subjects in this study were 240 middle class children from a suburban school in the Cincinnati area and 80 Introduction to Psychology students at the University of Cincinnati. The subjects were equally divided according to sex. The primary school children included 80 second graders with a mean age of approximately 7.5 years, 80 fourth graders with a mean age of approximately 9.5 years, and 80 sixth graders with a mean age of approximately 11.5 years.

The design of the experiment was such that there were 16 groups of 20 subjects. The subjects were grouped according to grade (2, 4, 6, college), task (Frontal, Coordination of Perspectives), and the presence of a landmark (landmark, non-landmark).

Apparatus

The stimuli consisted of three black blocks (cylinder, cube, triangle) and one red block (rectangle) which represented the explicit landmark. The cylinder had a diameter of 1.25 in., the cube was 1.25 in. square, the triangle had a base of 2 ins. and a height of 1 in., and the rectangle had a length of 3.25 in. and a width of 1.25 in. These objects were displayed on a 16 in. by 12 in. piece of white poster board and were arranged in the center of the board. There were four different initial arrangements of the blocks.

The two dimensional representations of the objects (maps) that were used as stimuli were constructed on a scale of .75 in relation to the actual three dimensional objects. There were a total of 80 maps with a landmark and 80 maps without a landmark. There were actually 20 different sets of relationships represented in each set of 80 maps. Each subset of 20 maps was grouped in accord with one of the four previously mentioned arrangements of the objects. Each

member of a particular subject group viewed a different random arrangement of the maps.

Procedure

Each subject was seated at a rectangular table and the three dimensional object display was located directly in front of him (or her). Each subject was introduced to the experimenter who then described the task that he was to perform. Each subject was presented with a series of five familiarization trials in which the relevant stimulus factors (to be described shortly) were brought to his attention.

Following the completion of the familiarization trials, each subject was presented with a series of 20 experimental trials in which four maps were shown. For each trial the subject first chose the map that he believed best approximated the appearance of the object array, then chose the second best map, and then the third best map. The best map was assigned the number 1, the second best map, the number 2, the third best map, the number three, and the last map, the number four. Since each map was seen exactly four times, the possible range of total scores per map was 4-16. Following the completion of a trial, the object array was rearranged in a predetermined manner. This procedure was followed for all 20 trials.

There were slight procedural differences between groups. During the perceptual task, the experimenter was seated in a chair to the right of the subject while in the Coordination of Perspectives task he was seated directly opposite the subject. The familiarization of the subject with his task was altered slightly between groups in order to point out task and stimulus differences. During the actual trials for the landmark groups, the landmark was arrayed in a series of four different positions that were established in conjunction with the four different arrangements of the other three objects (See Figure 1).

Scoring Procedure

Correctness ratings. An original configuration of the objects and the appropriate set of 20 maps (with landmark) appear in Figure 1. It can be noted that Map 16 is identical to the original object array. This is a veridical map. Each subject viewed four such veridical maps during his 20 trials. A percentage of correctness for a given subject group was determined by the number of times that this veridical map was picked as being the best map in a given trial.

Consistency ratings. During his 20 trials, each subject viewed 80 maps. A consistency rating for a given subject group represents the percentage of times that the subjects within that group had a consistent rating of any two maps in relation to one another. For example, if Maps One and Two were grouped together twice, a subject was consistent if he rated Map One as a better map than Map Two on both occasions, and he was inconsistent if he rated each map as the better map on one of the two occasions. There were 388 instances for each group of 20 subjects in which two maps were seen together exactly twice in 20 trials.

Stimulus factors. In order to better describe the manner in which subjects made their perceptual judgments, each map received a rating on each of five factors. The first factor is Relative Location. This refers to the number of objects (other than the landmark) that are located in the same position relative to one another on the maps as they are on the object array. A map may receive a rating of 0-3 on this factor. Referring to Figure One. Maps 15 and 16 received a rating of three on this factor because all three objects are in the correct relative location. Map 8 received a rating of two on this factor, Map 9 received a one, and Map 13 received a zero.

The second stimulus factor is called Displacement-1. This was determined by whether or not one object was far removed from the location of the other two on the map. If there was no displacement, a rating of one was given to the map e.g., Maps 3, 4, and 9. If there was a displacement, a rating of zero was given to that map e.g., Maps 1, 2, and 12.

The third stimulus factor is called Displacement-2. This was determined by whether or not two or more of the objects were located away from the center of the map. If there was no such displacement, a rating of one was given to that map e.g., Maps 16, 18, and 20. If such a displacement was present, a rating of zero was given to that map e.g., Maps 3, 10, and 15.

The fourth factor is called Horizontal. This was determined by whether or not the two objects which were horizontally arrayed were also represented in the map as being horizontally arrayed, and in the same plane as found in the array. If the two objects were properly arrayed a rating of one was given to that map e.g., Maps 4, 15, and 16. If they were improperly arrayed, a rating of zero was given to that map e.g., Maps 1, 2, and 3.

The final factor is called Vertical. This was determined in a way analogous to Horizontal. If the two objects were properly arrayed, a rating of one was given to that map e.g., Maps 7, 9, and 16. If they were improperly arrayed, a rating of zero was given to that map e.g., Map 11, 12, and 13.

Results

The percentage of correctness (the percentage of times Map 16 was judged as the best map) for each group representing each grade, task, and

stimulus circumstance appears in Table 1. Each cell represents a percentage of correct responses out of a possible total of 80 correct. The consistency ratings for each group also appear in Table 1.

It can be observed that as grade increases so does the percentage of correctness. Other trends that can be noted are that across stimulus circumstances and grades, subjects performing the Frontal task made fewer errors than subjects performing the Coordination of Perspectives task, and subjects in the conditions in which the explicit landmark was present made fewer errors than subjects in which it was absent. Regarding the consistency ratings, the major trend observed was that with increasing age, subjects became more consistent in their ratings of any two maps in relation to one another. Surprisingly, there were no clear-cut consistency patterns in relation to either the presence of an explicit landmark or the nature of the task that was performed (Frontal versus Coordination of Perspectives).

The final issues that need to be dealt with refer to the role of the stimulus factors that have been described previously. In order to determine the manner in which the five factors were used in making perceptual judgments, a multiple regression analysis was performed. The first result that was obtained pertains to the percentage of variance accounted for by all of the five hypothesized factors as well as for the two most salient factors for each subject group (percentage of variance accounted for refers to the ability of the set of factors to account for the perceptual judgments that were made by each subject group). These data appear in Table 2.

It can be noted in the table that in cases in which five factors were analyzed, about 90% of the variance has been accounted for. When only the two most important factors were analyzed (and they vary across age and condition), the percent of variance accounted for drops but less so for the second graders than the remaining groups. These findings indicate that our hypothesized factors were used by the subjects in making their judgments but they do not indicate the manner in which they were used.

In order to understand the weightings of the five factors within each subject group, beta weights must be examined. These values appear in Table 3. Each weight represents the partial regression attributable to a given factor within a subject group. In general, the higher the beta weighting, the more important is that factor in making spatial judgments, holding the influence of all other factors constant. Although obvious differences can and will be noted, Displacement-1, Relative Location, and Displacement-2 appear to be the most important factors. This matter will be given further consideration in the discussion section of this paper.

DISCUSSION AND CONCLUSIONS

The results that have been noted in this study indicate some interesting possibilities regarding the role that landmarks play in the formation of spatial judgments. Relative to the percentages of correctness that have been displayed in Table 1, landmarks were found to be especially helpful to primary school schildren on the Coordination of Perspectives task. The increase in the percentage of correctness on the Coordination of Perspectives task (as a result of the presence of a landmark) rose from 6.35% for sixth grade children to 17.4% for second grade children.

It would appear that landmarks are most helpful in making microspatial judgments in those cases where the inability to make accurate spatial judgments is most prominent. For the college students, whose performance was near asymptote, there was actually a slight decrease in the percentage of correctness on the Coordination of Perspectives task as a result of the presence of a landmark. The college students did not appear to need an explicit landmark to perform the Coordination of Perspectives task. However, they may have made use of such implicit landmarks as the edges of the maps. The relatively high percentages of correctness for older subjects and for those who performed the Frontal task were anticipated in light of previous findings (Nigl & Fishbein, 1974), however, the effects of the presence of an explicit landmark were somewhat unanticipated.

The effects of an explicit landmark on the consistency ratings was somewhat surprising. There appeared to be no significant differences in consistency as a result of the presence of a landmark on either the Frontal or the Coordination of Perspectives tasks. It would seem that the subjects adopt a particular strategy relative to the use of a landmark and they maintain that strategy throughout the majority of the 20 trials. The one expected trend that was found was that consistency increased with age (grade). The college students achieved consistency ratings that were up to ten percentage points higher than the primary school children. This finding was stable across tasks and stimulus conditions.

Perhaps the most interesting results that were obtained in this study pertain to the multiple regression analyses shown in Tables 2 and 3. Relative to the percentages of variance accounted for by all five hypothesized factors, three trends can be noted. The first trend is that a larger percentage of the variance was accounted for in the Frontal tasks than in the Coordination of Perspectives tasks (across grades and stimulus conditions). The second finding is that there was a larger percentage of the variance accounted for in Coordination of Perspectives with a landmark present than without a landmark. It can be inferred from this result that in the relatively difficult Coordination of Perspectives task, the presence of a landmark enabled subjects to better use the five hypothesized factors in making their spatial judgments. The one finding that was somewhat surprising was that on the Coordination of Perspectives task for the landmark groups, a larger percentage of the variance was accounted for with second grade subjects than the older subjects. The reasons for this apparent discrepancy will hopefully become clear in light of the remaining data that will be related from the multiple regression.

Relative to the percentage of the variance that was accounted for by the two most important factors for each subject group, two interesting trends can be noted. The first trend refers to the fact that on the Coordination of Perspectives task, the second grade subjects had a higher percentage of the variance accounted for than any of the older subjects. This actually indicates that on a relative basis, the second graders were unable to make proper use of all five hypothesized factors (this is supported by the fact that they made more errors with Map 16 than did the remaining groups). Two factors were able to account for almost as much of the variance as all five factors for the second grade groups, while this was not the case for the remaining groups.

The second trend is that for all groups, a larger percentage of the variance was accounted for by only two factors in the non-landmark than in the landmark conditions. This indicates that the presence of a landmark better enabled subjects to make comparable use of all five hypothesized factors. Fewer factors were used in the decision making process by the non-landmark groups.

The manner in which each particular subject group made their spatial judgments can best be inferred from the beta weights that appear in Table 3. It can be noted that most of the beta weights are negative. A negative beta weight is indicative of an inverse relationship between the mean scores of a given set of maps for a particular subject group and the ratings that the map received on the factor in question.

Several interesting trends can be noted in the beta weights. A comparison between the Coordination of Perspectives groups with and without a landmark indicates that the landmark did not alter the beta weights for the college students but that there were vast differences in relation to the primary school children.

It would be anticipated that if a subject was able to perform the judgmental task adequately, Relative Location would have a high negative beta weight. This would mean that as a greater number of objects were in their proper relative location, the judged similarity of the map in relation to the original object array would increase. Such was the case for all ages on the Frontal task and to a lesser extent for all ages on the Coordination of Perspectives task with a landmark. However, for the Coordination of Perspectives task without a landmark, this trend was only found to exist for college students.

The consistency of the manner in which the five hypothesized factors were used appears to increase with increasing age. The beta weights for the college students were the most consistent of all of the groups. The beta weights for the second grade subjects across experimental conditions appear to be very inconsistent in relation to the three key factors of Displacement-1, Relative Location, and Displacement-2.

Two other trends can be noted in relation to the beta weights. The first trend concerns the relationship between the use of a landmark and the Displacement-2 factor. The mean beta weights for this factor across tasks and grades (with a landmark) was -.60. For the non-landmark conditions it was -.28. This means that the displacement of two or more objects was a more important factor in the decision making process under the landmark than the non-landmark conditions. This finding may be attributed to the landmark accentuating the distance of the objects from their correct location in the center of the stimulus field.

The final trend that can be noted refers to the groups tested under non-landmark Coordination of Perspectives conditions. For the second and fourth graders, the mean beta weight for the Displacement-1 factor was -.71, while for the sixth graders and the college students it was -.30. This indicates that there may be a stage in development at which subjects can properly attend to the appropriate stimulus factors on a Coordination of Perspectives task. This finding supports the data reported by Nigl and Fishbein (1974).

It can be concluded from this study that landmarks are most helpful for young children performing a Coordination of Perspectives task. This can be observed in terms of the manner in which the five hypothesized factors were used as well as in terms of percentages of correctness. It can also be concluded that task and age are in themselves relevant factors in the adequacy of spatial judgments. The role of the five hypothesized factors was found to vary across age and task. Older subjects make more comparable use of all five factors than younger subjects. A final and most crucial finding is that older subjects attend to those factors that pertain to what is in the right place while younger subjects attend to those factors that pertain to what is in the wrong place. This is especially true for the

Coordination of Perspectives task without a landmark.

reference

ACREDOLO, L. P., Frames of reference used by children for orientation in unfamiliar spaces. In G. Moore & R. Golledge (Eds.), Environmental knowing. Stroudsburg, Pennsylvania: Dowden, Hutchinson & Ross, 1975, in press.

ACREDOLO, L. P., PICK, H. L., & OLSEN, M. G. Environmental differentiation and familiarity as determinants of children's memory for spatial location. Developmental Psychology, (In press).

FRANCESCATO, D., & MEBANE, W. How citizens view two great cities: Milan and Rome. In R. M. Downs, & D. Stea (Eds.), Image and environment. Chicago: Aldine Publishing Company, 1973.

LYNCH, K. The image of the city. Cambridge, Massachusetts: MIT Press, 1960.

NIGL, A., & FISHBEIN, H. Perception and conception in coordination of perspectives. Developmental Psychology, 1974, 10 (6), 858-866.

PIAGET, J. & INHELDER, B. The child's conception of space. London: Routledge and Kegan Paul, 1956.

SIEGEL, A. W., & WHITE, S. H. The development of spatial representations of large-scale environments. In preparation.

TABLE 1: <u>PERCENTAGES OF CORRECTNESS AND CONSISTENCY FOR ALL GROUPS</u>

	Second		Fourth		Sixth		College	
Stimulus Conditions	Cor	Con	Cor	Con	Cor	Con	Cor	Con
Landmark Frontal	78.7	67.0	96.3	75.0	96.3	77.3	98.8	77.3
Non-landmark Frontal	77.5	70.1	93.0	76.0	91.3	76.0	98.8	80.4
Landmark C. of P.	66.2	64.4	84.0	70.8	86.3	71.4	92.5	74.2
Non-landmark C. of P.	48.8	71.9	72.5	69.5	80.0	72.9	96.3	81.2
X̄	67.8	68.4	86.5	72.8	88.5	74.4	96.6	78.3

Cor=Correctness
Con=Consistency
C. of P.=Coordination of Perspectives

TABLE 2: <u>PERCENTAGES OF VARIANCE ACCOUNTED FOR BY ALL FIVE FACTORS AND THE TWO MOST IMPORTANT FACTORS FOR EACH GROUP</u>

	Second		Fourth		Sixth		College	
Stimulus Conditions	Two	Five	Two	Five	Two	Five	Two	Five
Landmark Frontal	77.5	91.3	64.4	94.9	69.6	93.8	67.5	91.8
Non-landmark Frontal	77.3	92.4	83.8	93.9	83.6	93.0	80.7	91.2
Landmark C. of P.	82.2	90.4	65.1	93.3	60.8	88.9	67.6	93.9
Non-landmark C. of P.	87.5	91.7	80.0	86.3	66.1	80.4	72.2	87.7
X̄	81.1	91.5	73.3	92.1	70.0	89.0	72.0	91.2

C. of P.=Coordination of perspectives

TABLE 3: <u>BETA WEIGHTS FOR ALL GROUPS BASED ON A MULTIPLE REGRESSION ANALYSIS</u>

Landmark Frontal

Grades

Factors	Second	Fourth	Sixth	College
Rel. Location	−.33	−.25	−.36	−.33
Displacement-1	−.25	−.40	−.38	−.34
Displacement-2	−.72	−.57	−.55	−.53
Horizontal	−.18	−.26	−.17	−.22
Vertical	−.23	−.27	−.26	−.29

Non-landmark Frontal

Grades

Factors	Second	Fourth	Sixth	College
Rel. Location	−.28	−.37	−.42	−.36
Displacement-1	−.50	−.45	−.40	−.40
Displacement-2	−.35	−.30	−.29	−.28
Horizontal	−.30	−.18	−.19	−.18
Vertical	−.17	−.30	−.27	−.35

Landmark Coordination of Perspectives

Grades

Factors	Second	Fourth	Sixth	College
Rel. Location	−.11	−.26	−.18	−.24
Displacement-1	−.38	−.32	−.36	−.28
Displacement-2	−.80	−.57	−.54	−.49
Horizontal	−.12	−.18	−.16	−.31
Vertical	−.17	−.42	−.47	−.41

Non-landmark Coordination of Perspectives

Grades

Factors	Second	Fourth	Sixth	College
Rel. Location	+.21	+.04	+.05	−.28
Displacement-1	−.78	−.64	−.32	−.28
Displacement-2	−.39	−.11	−.24	−.30
Horizontal	−.15	−.28	−.52	−.31
Vertical	−.25	−.35	−.44	−.40

FIGURE 1 : SKETCHES OF ARRAYS A,B,C,AND D AND THE APPROPRIATE SET OF 20 MAPS FOR ARRAY A

W = L___ l=Landmark   X = △   Y = O   Z = ▢

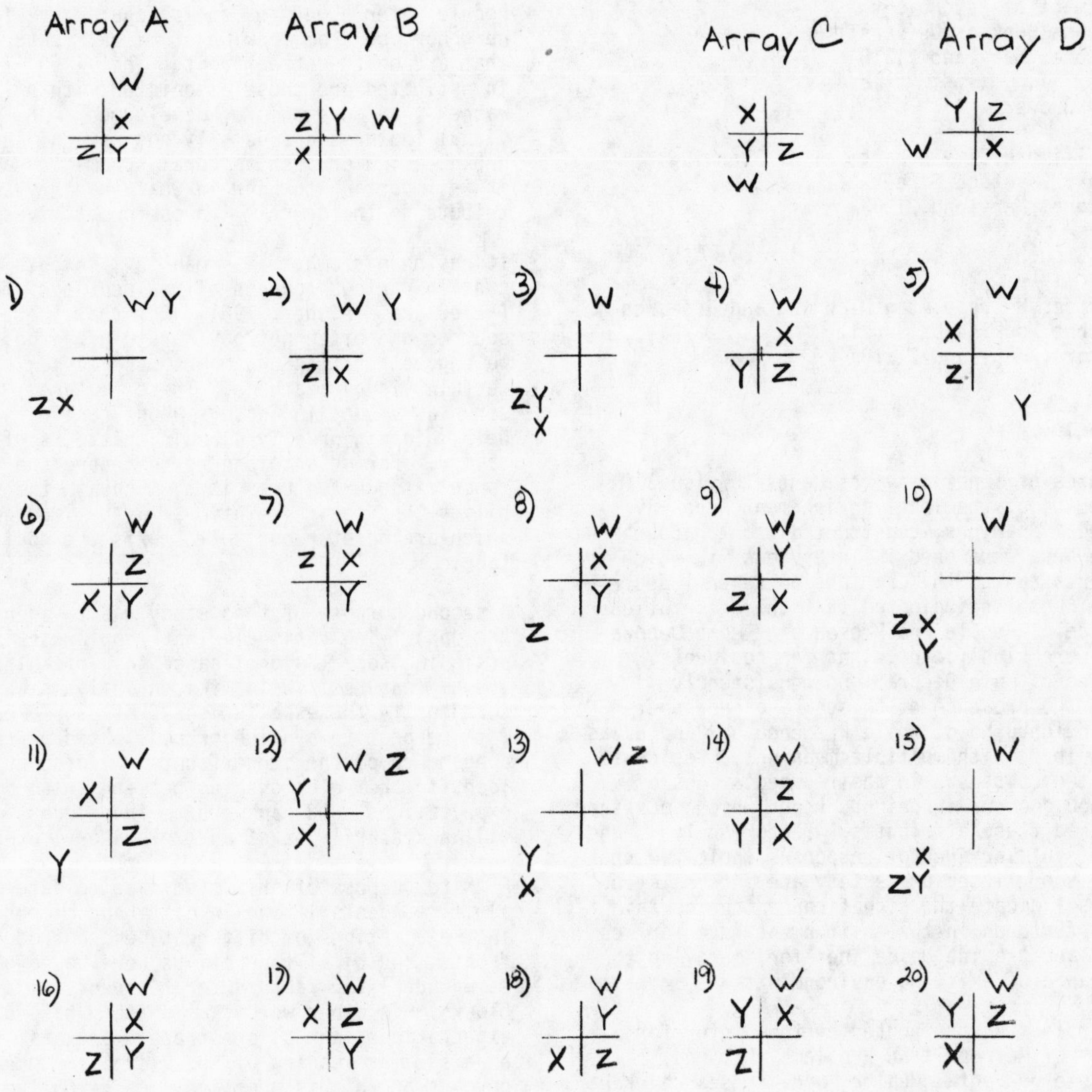

USER-GENERATED VISUAL FEATURES AS SIGNS IN THE

URBAN RESIDENTIAL ENVIRONMENT

Ralph B. Taylor

Department of Psychology
The Johns Hopkins University
Baltimore, Maryland 21218

Sidney Brower

The Baltimore City Department of Planning
222 East Saratoga Street
Baltimore, Maryland 21202

Roger Stough

Center for Metropolitan Planning and Research
The Johns Hopkins University
Baltimore, Maryland 21218

ABSTRACT

Responses of inner city residents to visual
attributes of the local environment were investigated. Drawings, constructed from photographs
of the area were used in interviews, in which
residents ranked the drawings on several descriptions. Results indicated that the descriptions
Presence of People and Presence of Home Decorations were significant signs for residents.
Presence of Home Decorations consistently sig-
nified the presence of those who cared about
their neighborhood, while Presence of People was
an attribute with multiple meanings. Residents
exhibited consensus in their expectations of
what would occur in neighborhoods which possessed
or lacked these attributes. Factor Analysis and
Analysis of Variance of responses indicated that
problems of litter and safety are interrelated.
Results indicate the significance that certain
visual features in the environment have for residents, and provide guidelines for improving the
appearance of existing environments.

This project was supported by the Center for
Studies of Metropolitan Problems, National
Institute of Mental Health, under research grant
#MH24047-01A1. Authors are indebted to LaVerne
Gray, Bernard Headley, Richard Gasparotti, and
Tom Land for their assistance in conducting the
interviews. The authors are also indebted to
Dr. Bert F. Green, Jr., for his advice in
experimental design.

A resident's cognitive map of local spaces reflects, among other things, his expectations
about how others will behave in certain physical
settings (Downs, 1970; Suttles, 1972; Downs and
Stea, 1973). Appleyard (1973) terms these expectations *inferential urban perceptions*, which are
a *generalizable system of environmental categories, concepts, and relationships which form

our coding system for the city (p. 110).

One purpose of this study was to examine the
relationship between the presence of resident-
generated visual features in neighborhoods, and
social expectations about people who live in
those neighborhoods. In other words, what do
people infer about the social character of a
neighborhood from looking at visual features
that are on the streetfront. The visual features
investigated are those associated with residency
rather than ownership or development. As these
visual features are usually not part of the
urban design or architectural scheme for a street,
it is important to know in what way they contribute to the overall impression it gives.

It has been shown that urban environments may
contain various sources of resident satisfaction
(Fried and Gleicher, 1961), and that these
sources are often not obvious to urban designers.
We suggest that an analogous case may exist for
certain visual features. These features may
serve as visual indicators about residents, and
help maintain orderly standing patterns of behavior. For urban planners to ignore the importance of such features is to increase the possibility that design solutions may be imposed
which are deleterious to the existing social
fabric.

A second purpose of this study was to identify
the underlying rationale that people use in
assigning social significance to particular
visual features. Using factor analysis we hoped
to identify the expectations that people have
with respect to a neighborhood, based on the
appearance of the streetfront. We also hoped to
identify the relationships between these different
expectations. Our answers to these questions
will necessarily be of an exploratory nature.

A third purpose of this study was to determine:
a) if residents living in different blocks agreed
in their ratings of different neighborhood street
fronts; and b) if the ratings were based on the
same underlying factors for residents of all
blocks. In other words: a) do they have similar
expectations; and b) are these expectations based
on a similar reading of the visual features. If
our answer to this question is affirmative, it
suggests that residents share elements of a common
language for "reading" the environment. It would
further suggest that these visual features function as signs, in the sense that they reliably
yield information about residents. The presence
of a common language made up of such signs has
important implications for urban designers.

1. METHODS

1.1 Subjects

Respondents were residents of the Harlem Park and
Upton areas in West Baltimore. The interviews
were conducted as part of an ongoing study of the
effects of open space on metropolitan community
life, in which the respondents were already

participating. Interviews were scheduled with the respondents by telephone. The interview was conducted in the respondent's home. Due to problems in contacting respondents and in scheduling, a total of 43 interviews were obtained. Thirty-eight interviews were completed successfully, and these thirty-eight are the data upon which the following analysis is conducted, except where otherwise noted. The number of respondents per study block ranged from four to seven. Respondents were paid for their participation.

1.2 Study Area

The Harlem Park and Upton neighborhoods consist largely of three-story row houses, almost all of which are over seventy years old. The area is predominantly residential. Population is over 99 percent Black, predominantly of low income. Sites in the study area consisted of six blocks, three in Harlem Park and three in Upton. Blocks were separated from each other by a distance of at least 2 blocks.

1.3 Stimulus Materials

Eight drawings, each 6½"x7", were used as stimuli. The drawings had all been photographically reproduced from a line drawing showing the facades of several houses. These had been traced from a photograph of a typical streetfront in the area. Each of the bare drawings was then altered to exhibit the following three visual features in varying combinations:

1. People. In four drawings figures were introduced. The figures suggested residents rather than passers-by; they were shown sitting out, playing ball, standing on the steps. Figures in each of the four drawings were identical. The other four drawings had no figures.

2. Decorations. In four drawings curtains were shown drawn, flowerboxes and ornaments were shown in the windows, and plants and furniture were shown at house entrances. Elements on each of the four drawings were identical. The other four drawings showed nothing on the sidewalk and drawn blinds in the windows.

3. Color and Tone of Facade. In four drawings there was variation in tone and color between individual houses on the streetfront. In the other four drawings the streetfront was shown with uniform color and tone. Varying tones of red, pink, and orange Zip-a-tone were used to color each drawing.

A total of eight drawings were thus constructed. The features on each picture are represented in Table 1.

The presence or absence of people was chosen as a visual feature because the presence of people is a characteristic of these neighborhoods. New housing units in the study area were making no provision to accommodate people sitting out in front. We wanted to know what significance residents attached to the presence of people sitting out front.

Embellishments of the kind shown on the drawings are seen in units scattered throughout the study area. Since they were not exhibited for "practical" purposes, it is likely that they have some symbolic significance for residents who are responsible for them. We wanted to know if their significance was generally recognized.

Painted housefronts of varying color are typical of the study area, but there are also streetfronts of uniform color. Designers generally set great value upon expression of individual units, and we wanted to know if residents shared this value.

1.4 Procedure

Respondents were allowed to familiarize themselves with the pictures. By asking questions, the interviewers verified that respondents actually perceived the three ways in which the eight pictures differed.

In addition to the eight picture stimuli, eight different neighborhood descriptions were developed. Five of these referred to the behavior of people in a neighborhood; two were general evaluations, and one involved a comparison with the study area.

Respondents were asked to rank order the pictures according to how well they fitted each of the eight neighborhood descriptions. The respondent was asked to pick the picture that best represented, for instance, a high class neighborhood, then to choose the picture that least represented a high class neighborhood, etc., until all pictures had been ranked according to the description, that is, high class neighborhood. Thus, in accordance with the principles of spatial paralogic (De Soto, London and Handel, 1965), the respondent constructed a linear ordering, building inwards from the two ends of the ordering. Respondents were also asked to give their reasons for their first four choices for each dimension, i.e., for the two best fits and the two poorest fits.

The eight different neighborhood descriptions according to which respondents ranked the pictures were: 1) best class of neighborhood/worst class of neighborhood; 2) neighborhood in which people are most likely to be signifiers/least likely to be signifiers (a signifier is one who minds others' business); 3) neighborhood most likely to be burglarized/least likely to be burglarized; 4) neighborhood most likely to be littered/least likely to be littered; 5) neighborhood that is most dangerous at night/safest at night; 6) neighborhood that has the most active community organization/least active community organization; 7) neighborhood that is most desirable as a place to live/least desirable as a place to live; 8) neighborhood that is most like where you live now/least like where you live now. Descriptions 1, 6, 7, and 8 were reflected such that for all descriptions a high score (bottom ranking of 8) represented the positive end of the description.

2. RESULTS

2.1 Ranks: Significance of Visual Features

The first task is to assess the significance, for the respondents, of the visual features which were varied in the pictures. The visual features possessed by each picture are indicated in Table 1. Aggregating across blocks, the ranking of each picture on each description is portrayed in Table 2.

TABLE 1: SPECIFIC VISUAL FEATURES POSSESSED BY EACH PICTURE

	Picture Number							
	1	2	3	4	5	6	7	8
Presence of People	+	+	+	+	0	0	0	0
Presence of Decorations	0	+	0	+	0	+	0	+
Varied Housefronts	0	0	+	+	0	0	+	+

TABLE 2: RANK ORDERING OF PICTURES ON EACH DESCRIPTION ACROSS ALL BLOCKS

Neighborhood Description

Ranking of Picture on Particular Descriptions	High Class	No Signifiers	No Burglars	No Litter	Safe	Comm. Org.	Desirable	You Live Now
1	6	5	4	6	2	2	6	3
2	8	7	2	8	4	4	8	4
3	2	6	3	5	8	8	2	1
4	4	8	1	7	6	6	4	2
5	1	3	8	3	1	3	1	7
6	5	1	6	1	3	1	5	6
7	7	2	7	2	7	5	7	8
8	3	4	5	4	5	7	3	5

NOTE: A ranking of 1 means that that particular picture ranked highest on that particular description. The numbers in the matrix are numbers identifying particular pictures.

The rankings suggest the following:

The presence of people (residents) on the streetfront is seen as typical of the study area, a deterrent to burglars, but they are associated with littering and signifying;

The presence of decoration is a sign of a desirable, high class neighborhood, safe at night, with a strong community organization. The addition of residents means greater safety at night and a stronger community organization, but it makes the neighborhood somewhat less desirable;

The presence of individually colored row houses did not appear important to the respondents for the descriptions being considered here. No clear pattern emerged concerning this visual feature.

2.2 Reasons: Interpretation of Visual Features

In order to better understand why particular visual features were significant for rating particular pictures on a specific description, we examine the reasons offered by respondents for their first picture choice on a description. These reasons are shown in Table 3. The particular visual feature of the picture is noted, and also the interpretation, for the respondent, of that visual feature, is noted. Although many respondents were unable to verbalize the "meaning" of a particular visual feature, in cases where respondents were able to verbalize, a pattern is indicated. With the exception of Description 3, it appears that the presence of decorations has a consistent agreed-upon significance: the presence of decorations indicates residents who care about their neighborhood.

TABLE 3: INTERPRETATION OF VISUAL FEATURES - REASONS

Neighborhood Description	Visual Feature Mentioned When Asked "Why This Picture?"	Interpretation of Visual Feature by Respondent (Significance)
1. Class	(21) presence of decorations	(8) like flowers (4) people care
2. Signifiers	(22) presence of people	(8) inside people snoop around (5) outside people mind others' business
3. Likely to be burglarized	(23) no people (8) decorations	(7) indicates there is something to take
4. Litter	(22) presence of people	(14) people throw litter
5. Safe	(20) presence of people (7) decorations	(14) people help out if there is trouble
6. Active Community Organization	(8) decorations	(4) people care
7. Desirable	(15) decorations (8) presence of people	(5) people care (5) people help if trouble

TABLE 3 (continued)

8. Where you   (11) no deco-
live now   rations
                (14) people

NOTE: Numbers in parentheses indicate number of
people who offered that feature or that interpretation. Missing data are due to respondents who
were unable to offer interpretations, or whose
interpretation was not clearly related to a
visual feature.

In contrast, the presence of people has many
different implications. The presence of people
has negative implications in that people throw
litter and mind other people's business. The
presence of people has positive implications in
that they keep burglars away, and may help out
if there is trouble.

For some descriptions, both the visual features
people and decorations are mentioned by a number
of respondents; for example, on the Safety description and the Desirable description. This
suggests that the implications of the presence
of people may be partially dependent on the
presence or absence of decorations. People in
a decorated neighborhood are people who will
help out if there's trouble; people in an undecorated neighborhood may be less likely to
help out if there's trouble.

No respondents mentioned the visual feature
color of housefronts as a reason for their first
picture choice on a description, suggesting that
this feature was relatively unimportant in
evaluating the streetfronts on the descriptions
given.

It is noteworthy that the verbalized interpretations of the visual features are consistent
with the rank order data.

2.3 Structure of Expectations: Underlying Factors

The matrix of original rankings of all subjects
across blocks was transformed by correlational
analysis into a descriptions x descriptions
matrix, 7x7. (Description 6, active community
organization, was excluded from this matrix due
to a large proportion of missing data.) The
resulting correlation matrix was subjected to a
principal axis factor analysis with iterations,
using a varimax rotation, to a simple orthogonal
structure.

The purpose of this analysis was: 1) to determine the interrelationships between the neighborhood descriptions on which respondents had
rated pictures of streetfronts; and 2) to describe the factors underlying these various
judgments.

Our findings based on the factor analysis can
only be considered exploratory given the following limitations which obtained to the study.
1) A select nonrandom subset of possible
streetfront types was used. It is uncertain

how and to what extent the results of the factor
analysis would be changed had a different subset
of streetfront types been used. 2) The dimensions x dimensions correlation matrix is constructed from ordinal level data, i.e., ranks.
A certain amount of inaccuracy is inherent in
the matrix constructed from this data. 3) The
descriptions on which respondents rated pictures
of streetfronts were chosen on the basis of
prior interviews with local residents, which
indicated these descriptions as important and
relevant for the evaluation of neighborhood
streetfronts. However, the addition of new
dimensions may alter the resulting factor structure.

The factor loadings for the two factor solution,
aggregating across all blocks, are shown in
Table 4.

TABLE 4:   FACTOR LOADINGS OF NEIGHBORHOOD
           DESCRIPTIONS: TWO FACTOR SOLUTION

Neighborhood Description	Factor I	Factor II	Commu- nality
High Class	(.06)	.73	.53
No Signifiers	-.54	(.22)	.34
No Burglars	(.36)	(.03)	.12
No Litter	-.66	(.29)	.52
Safe	.62	.42	.56
Desirable	(-.12)	.75	.58
Where you live now	.50	(.08)	.26
Lambda	1.53	1.40	
% Variance Accounted For	30.2	26.6	Total 56.8

NOTE: Factor loadings of less than .40 are
shown in parentheses.

Factor I is essentially a description of where
respondents presently live; the neighborhood
streetfronts are characterized by the presence
of safety, signifiers, and litter. Factor II
appears to be essentially a description of what
would make a desirable neighborhood streetfront:
a high class neighborhood that is fairly safe.

By examining Table 2, and observing the particular pictures that are high on the descriptions that comprise the factor structure, the
following is indicated: pictures at one end of
Factor I (safety, where you live now) are pictures with people and decorations (pictures 2
and 4) while at the other end of Factor I (no
signifiers, no litter) are pictures with decoration and no people (pictures 6 and 8), and those
with no decorations and no people (pictures 5
and 7); pictures at one end of Factor II (desirable, high class) are those with decorations
and no people (pictures 6 and 8) and pictures at
the other end of this factor are essentially
pictures with no decorations (pictures 5, 7,
and 3).

These results indicate that where residents live

is characterized by the presence of people. The presence of people ensures the safety of the streetfront, but at the same time brings with it problems such as litter and people minding others' business.

Thus it seems that a neighborhood which is desirable and high class is characterized by the presence of decorations and people. Decorations indicate residents who care about a neighborhood, making such a place desirable. The presence of people ensures safety: they will watch out for children playing and help out if there's trouble. Residents in such a high class neighborhood would probably not be signifiers or litter throwers.

2.4 Repeated Measures Analysis of Variance: A Closer Examination of Visual Features

Inspection of the picture rankings and respondents' interpretations of the visual features has suggested that two of these features, decorations and people sitting out, are user-generated signs: they are considered to be reliable indicators of the social characteristics of the residents, and the factor analysis has suggested a structure underlying respondents' rankings of the pictures on the different neighborhood descriptions.

Color of housefront does not appear to be a reliable indicator. This may be due to the fact that in an area where home ownership is less than 30 percent, exterior decoration of this kind is likely to reflect upon a non-resident landlord rather than upon the occupant.

While the rankings were concerned with the pictures themselves and the factor analysis was concerned with the relationship between the different neighborhood descriptions, the ANOVA (Analysis of Variance) allows a closer inspection of the effects of the specific visual features. (See Appendix.)

In an effort to clarify the preceding results, a repeated measures analysis of variance was performed on the picture rankings. The ANOVA was performed only on pictures 1,2,5, and 6, for the following reasons:
Factor analysis of the pictures x pictures matrix collapsed the rankings into four clusters of two pictures each (1+3, 2+4, 5+7, 6+8). This indicated that color and tone of housefront was not significant;
Respondents, in their interpretations of pictures, made no mention of housefront color as a reason for a first choice on a description;
In the rank order data, housefront color appeared unimportant.
The color of housefronts was not tested. The design was a 2x2x7 factorial (Persons x Decorations x Neighborhood Description). The analysis was performed on the responses of the twenty-five respondents who did not have any missing data in their interviews.

On the basis of the factor analysis (Table 4) and analysis of respondents' interpretations of

features, the following hypotheses were formulated.

1. Inasmuch as the presence or absence of people has a variety of implications, depending on the description asked for, we do not expect a main effect for People.

1a. We do expect a significant People x Neighborhood Description interaction effect, since the significance of the presence or absence of people depends upon the description being asked for.

2. We expect a main effect for Decorating, since the presence of Decorations has one fairly consistent implication across various neighborhood descriptions;

3. We expect a significant People x Decorations interaction, since it appears that the implication of people depends upon the context in which they are seen.

No predictions were made concerning the three-way interaction.

New data were not collected to test these hypotheses; we are using the same data to test the hypotheses as were used to generate the hypotheses. Nonetheless, the analysis of variance is useful since it can give us a rough idea of the correctness of the conclusions drawn from the factor analysis, the rankings, and respondents' interpretations of reasons.

Hypothesis 1 is confirmed. There is no significant main effect for people (F<1). Hypothesis 1a. is confirmed by the results. The People x Neighborhood Description interaction (AxC) is significant (F = 12.92, $df_1/df_2 = 6/144$, p<.001). The interaction is portrayed graphically in Figure 1.

FIGURE 1: PEOPLE x NEIGHBORHOOD DESCRIPTION INTERACTION (AxC)

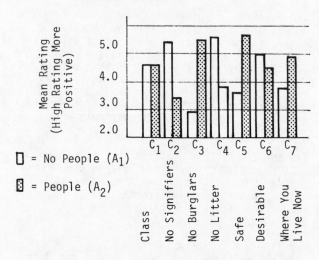

☐ = No People (A$_1$)

▨ = People (A$_2$)

The presence of people is most important for descriptions concerning signifiers, burglars, litter, safety, and where you live now; somewhat important for descriptions concerning desirable neighborhoods; and not at all important for descriptions concerning class.

Hypothesis 2 is confirmed: a significant main effect for Decorations is observed (F = 22.95, df_1/df_2=1/24, p<.001). Pictures with decorations are rated more positively on all descriptions, with the exception of the No Burglars description.

An unexpected Decorations x Descriptions (BxC) interaction is observed (F = 7.51, df_1/df_2= 6/144, p<.001). This interaction is displayed graphically in Figure 2. Inspection of Figure 2 suggests that it is <u>not</u> the case that the presence of decorations has different meanings. Rather, it suggests that decorations are important for some descriptions (class, safe, desirable) and relatively unimportant for others (no signifiers, no litter).

FIGURE 2:   DECORATIONS x DESCRIPTION
            INTERACTION

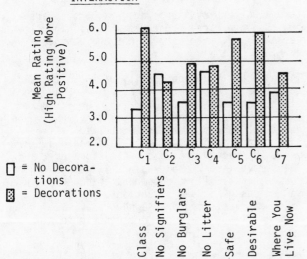

☐ = No Decorations

▨ = Decorations

Hypothesis 3 is confirmed: the People x Decorations (AxB) interaction is significant (F = 78.94, df_1/df_2=1/24, p<.001). This interaction is portrayed graphically in Figure 3. Inspection indicates that pictures with no decoration are rated more positively in the presence of people than in the absence of people.

There is a significant three-way interaction (People x Decorations x Descriptions), but since it accounts for such a small portion of the variance (6%) we are relieved of the burden of trying to interpret it.

Thus, our interpretation of the results, which is based on the rank data, the interpretations given by respondents, and on the exploratory factor analysis, has been further supported by the analysis of variance.

2.5   The Question of Consensus Across Blocks

Another question is to what extent do the

FIGURE 3:   PEOPLE x DECORATIONS INTERACTION

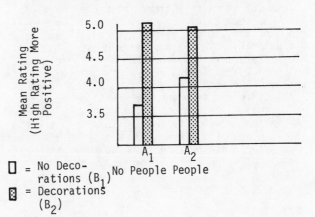

☐ = No Decorations (B_1)

▨ = Decorations (B_2)

residents of the different blocks agree on their interpretation of the specific visual features which appear in the pictures. To what extent is there consensus, across blocks, on the ranking of the pictures.

In order to answer this question, the pictures were ranked, for each block, aggregating across all descriptions. Treating each block as an individual, the picture rankings of each block were compared to each other block, using a Spearman rank order correlation coefficient. The pattern of inter-block agreement on picture rankings is presented in Table 5.

TABLE 5:   INTER-BLOCK AGREEMENT ON PICTURE
           RANKINGS

Block Reference Number

	001	016	022	032	038	039
001		.64*	.64*	.17	.88****	.71**
016			.83***	.55	.62	.91****
022				.24	.62	.79**
032					.29	.62
038						.83***
039						

**** p<.01
*** p<.02
** p<.05
* p<.1

It appear that residents on the different blocks are, by and large, in agreement on the picture rankings, with the exception of block 032. This agreement suggests that residents on these different blocks do share a consensus on the interpretation of visual features of neighborhood streetfronts.

The interpretative image of the residents of block 032 seems at variance with the image of the respondents of the other blocks. Physically and socially, block 032 is also anomalous. The structures there are two story houses, and it is a smaller, more compact block than the others, with backyards facing each other across a narrow alley. The neighboring pattern on the block is also different from the pattern in other blocks. Residents in this block are more likely to know the neighbor who lives behind them than are the residents on the other study blocks. Thus it is not surprising that the residents of this block have a different interpretative image of street-fronts.

3. DISCUSSION

Our results suggest that expectations about the character of neighborhood residents are derived from the presence or absence of specific resi-dent-generated visual features on the sidewalk. These visual features serve as signs to others. Furthermore, residents share a consensus on the interpretation of these signs, even when the signs have multiple meanings.

The presence of decorations unequivocally sig-nifies that residents care about their neighbor-hood. The facts underlying the social implica-tion of this physical sign are probably the following: decorations such as flowers require a fair amount of attention and work. Flowers serve no practical purpose. A person only works to make his front attractive if he cares about, and has pride in, his neighborhood. If resi-dents feel this way about their neighborhood, it must be a fairly desirable place to live.

Such an interpretation suggests that mainte-nance and beautification of other aspects of the residential environment, such as block parks, will also indicate to other residents that the people living there have pride in their immedi-ate neighborhood, if the visual features are clearly resident-generated.

Most likely the absence of decorations does not unequivocally indicate residents unconcerned about their neighborhood. It is possible that residents are concerned about beautifying their streetfront, but, due to continued vandalism, have given up their beautification projects.

The presence of people has several different meanings, depending on the question asked, and the presence or absence of decorations. The people portrayed in the particular pictures were of no particular status or race, except insofar as the pictures did suggest that the people were residents. People were rated more positively when they appeared in conjunction with decorations, probably because respondents assumed them to be higher-class residents. Given that residents are capable of a wide variety of activities, the multiple signifi-cance of the presence of people is not

surprising.

The physical attribute of housefront color was insignificant to respondents for the neighbor-hood descriptions used in this interview. This may be, as was suggested earlier, because exte-rior decoration of this type is more likely to be associated with a landlord's maintenance than with a resident's care, and that it does not provide, therefore, a reliable clue to the social identity of the building occupant. The fact that varied housefronts did not score high on either the desirability or class scales suggests, however, that this kind of individual self-expression may be less sought after by residents of the study area than it is by most profes-sional designers.

The factor analysis used in this study suggests that two factors are underlying residents' expectations concerning activities on neighbor-hood streetfronts. The first factor, a Present Situation Factor, assesses how much the street-front resembles the respondent's present living situation: how many people are hanging around, how much litter is there, etc. The second fac-tor, a Desirable Neighborhood Factor, assesses how much the streetfront resembles a high class neighborhood, with decorations and residents who care.

The generality and centrality of these two fac-tors remain to be determined. We can have con-fidence in these two factors insofar as there are no contradictions to this interpretation in our data. The factors are supported by the ANOVA and respondents' verbalized reasons. How-ever, the factor analysis was exploratory, and the sample interviewed was not large. Further-more, the stimuli were somewhat reduced repre-sentations of actual situations. A confirmatory factor analysis could be conducted, using either more complex stimuli or more descriptions.

However, two results of the factor analysis seem quite clearcut. First, two major problems for residents of the study area, namely safety and litter, are intimately interrelated. A safe situation, where there are a lot of resi-dents out on the street or who have eyes on the street usually means that there will also be a lot of trash around, because people generate litter. (An exception to this rule is high class neighborhoods, where the residents care enough not to throw trash.) If you keep the people away to get rid of the litter, then you have an unsafe situation. There is no one to help you out if you get into trouble, no one to watch out for your children or watch your house while you are gone. Secondly, social and phys-ical attributes are in dynamic interaction. This interaction is evidenced by such findings as: decorations (physical) indicate people who care (social); and the presence of people (social) is rated more positively in the pres-ence of decorations (physical).

Social and physical visual features are inter-dependent. From these features, the charac-teristics of the streetfront are inferred: how safe is it, how desirable is it, what is the social class of the residents, etc. These visual features, which are often construed as inconsequential by designers and architects, are important for the maintenance of an existing social order.

Planners and designers are urged to consider the significance of such features for residents. By ignoring these features they run the risk of imposing design solutions which may be deleterious to the existing social fabric.

APPENDIX

RESULTS OF REPEATED MEASURE ANALYSIS OF VARIANCE

Source of Variance	SS	df	MS	F	eta
A (People)	7.2	1	7.2	<1	
B (Decorations)	285.44	1	285.44	22.95***	.421
C (Dimension)	22.73	6	3.79	2.51*	.046
AxB	15.75	1	15.75	78.94***	.212
AxC	491.05	6	81.84	12.92***	.310
BxC	253.25	6	42.21	7.51***	.196
AxBxC	27.42	6	4.57	2.98**	.060
S(w/i Ss)	52.34	34			
AS	258.53	24	10.77		
BS	298.66	24	12.44		
CS	217.48	144	1.51		
ABS	4.78	24	.19		
ACS	912.31	144	6.33		
BCS	809.74	144	6.62		
ABCS	221.11	144	1.54		
TOTAL	3877.8	699			

*** $p < .001$
** $p < .01$
* $p < .05$

Reference

APPLEYARD, DONALD. Notes on urban perception and knowledge. In R. Downs and D. Stea (eds.), Image and Environment, (Chicago: Aldine Publishing Company, 1973).

DE SOTO, C.B., LONDON, M., AND HANDEL, S. Social Reasoning and spatial paralogic. Journal of Personality and Social Psychology, 2, 1965:513-521.

DOWNS, ROGER M. Geographic space perception, past approaches and future prospects. In C. Board, R.J. Chorley, P. Hoggeth, and D.R. Stoddart (eds.), Progress in Geography, (New York: Saint Martin's Press, 1970).

DOWNS, ROGER M. AND STEA, DAVID. Cognitive maps and spatial behavior: process and products. In R.M. Downs and D. Stea (eds.), Image and Environment, (Chicago: Aldine Publishing Company, 1973).

FRIED, M., AND GLEICHER, P. Some sources of residential satisfaction in an urban slum. Journal of the American Institute of Planners, 27, 1961.

SUTTLES, GERALD D. The Social Construction of Communities. (Chicago: University of Chicago Press, 1972).

PEOPLE/PLANT PROXEMICS: A CONCEPT FOR HUMANE DESIGN

Charles A. Lewis, Horticulturist

The Morton Arboretum
Lisle, Illinois 60532

ABSTRACT

Expected qualitative differences in responses to vegetation are discussed in terms of subject vantage point; distant observational as in perception studies, or intimate participatory as in gardening. Gardening, from a behavioral viewpoint, is an intimate human experience with vegetation, productive of its own distinct responses. Observations of gardening programs in low income housing in three cities over a twelve year period reveal gardening as a user activity which enhances quality of life as evidenced in reduction of vandalism, resident improvement of buildings, and improved social contacts among residents. Anecdotal evidence indicates that strong feelings of pride and self-esteem are generated by the gardening process. Intrinsic qualities of plants and plant processes which encourage improved behavioral attitudes are examined. These same qualities are basic to the effectiveness of gardening as a therapeutic and rehabilitative technique in a wide array of settings. People/plant proxemics is suggested as a concept which includes all aspects of human association with plants. The process of gardening provides designers with an intimate view of a user-generated and user-maintained system that helps adapt the built environment to user needs. Designers are challenged to consider gardening as a readily implemented technique for easing stress, developing beneficial attitudes and enhanced social patterns in existing and yet to be built human environments.

1. INTRODUCTION

The role of primitive environments in shaping biological and psychological responses has been a source of endless inquiry. The survival of early man depended to a large degree upon his ability to respond and accommodate to the natural world around him. Patterns acquired in response to those early experiences remain submerged, yet active, within our psyche and biology. The past is ever with us and our primitively patterned selves still walk with us in our cities. Occasionally, reexamination of familiar contemporary cultural patterns will expose unexpected, longstanding, subtle relationships between man and his environment. For example, the accepted use of flowers and plants to convey sympathy, concern, and joy at times of death, illness, or celebration, can be traced back as far as Neanderthal man, who buried his dead with garlands of flowers (Solecki, 1971).

Researchers are now giving serious thought to the evolutionary role of vegetation in shaping man's biological and cultural needs (Iltis, Loucks, Andrews, 1970). They raise questions as to whether or not the urban environment frustrates certain human needs acquired through evolutionary development. To what degree can man adapt, and to what degree must primitive needs be accommodated to produce a satisfying human environment? Behavioral responses to environment are being gathered through examining people's attitudes toward and perception of vegetation in sites ranging from wild forest to urban environment. In these studies the subject, as a passive observer, is shown a wide array of photographed scenes depicting wild nature, parks, campgrounds, cityscapes, etc., and his responses are recorded. Analysis and interpretation of responses help to reveal personal attitudes toward the scenes viewed.

Another area of human response to vegetation is found in gardening, long considered solely for its aesthetic or cosmetic value. Reexamination of gardening from a behavioral viewpoint identifies it as a human experience with vegetation at a closer physical and psychological distance than that recognized in perception studies. In gardening, the individual is an active participant in nature processes rather than a passive observer of nature. His responses to intimate participation with vegetation are of a different order than those examined at the more distant observation level. The situation might be compared with Hall's (1966) delineation of distance in terms of proxemic effect. Using differences in psychological meanings of space as a measure, he was able to differentiate intimate distance, personal distance, social distance, and public distance. Similarly, an examination of man's response to plants at a participatory intimate distance provides psychological and cultural insights not revealed through studies at an observational remote distance.

A need for the two modes of plant perception, observational and participatory, has been recognized, particularly for urban areas. "City dwellers need not only parks in which to walk and picnic...they (also) need places where they can actually create parks and plant trees." (Sommer, 1972, p. 59)

There have been almost no investigations of behavioral responses to vegetation at the intimate participatory level. Initial studies into kinds of satisfaction found in gardening (Kaplan, 1973), and effect of plants on patient behavior and staff attitude (Talbott, Stern, Ross and Gillen, 1975), however, demonstrate the potential for behavioral research in this area.

Gardening and horticulture are usually considered in terms of their end products: trees, flowers, vegetables and plants. However, human responses to gardening delineate the process of horticulture which includes all the thoughts, actions, and responses taking place from the time the gardening activity is first contemplated, through planting, and growth of seed to mature plant. The process is deliberate with the person performing a series of acts to provide conditions favorable to plant growth. Behavioral benefits gained might be seen as by-products of this process.

2. GARDENING IN LOW INCOME AREAS

In New York, Philadelphia and Chicago, residents of low income areas involved in gardening contests produced results far beyond the aesthetic or cosmetic effect expected from the gardening act itself (Lewis, 1972, 1973, 1975). While documentation is largely observational and anecdotal, the similarity of the pattern of results in the three different cities cannot be ignored. These programs are particularly appropriate for designer consideration in that they demonstrate what the user has done to make his situation more livable.

2.1. New York City

The New York City Housing Authority Tenant Garden Contest, conceived in 1963 as a device for promoting better communication between tenant and management, annually exceeds expectations set for it. Tenants wishing to garden apply to the Authority, which provides them with a garden site on the grounds of their project, manpower to turn over the ground, thirty-five dollars for the purchase of seeds, plants, tools, and fertilizer, plus a gardening manual and other instructional materials for each participating group. All phases of design, planting, and maintenance are the responsibility of the sponsoring group -- a full summer's activity.

The participating groups represent formal organizations such as Boy Scouts, senior citizen clubs, or casual associations of neighbors participating together in their garden. Gardeners include a wide range of ages, and all ethnic elements of the population. The group requirement for garden sponsorship assures new opportunities for social interaction.

The gardens are judged in August, followed by

a prize-awards ceremony in September. On the surface, the garden contest appears to be a simple amenity, bringing beautification to depressed areas. Flowers in the ghetto are the obvious result, but deeper meanings are revealed in new attitudes and social patterns resulting from the gardening.

With vandalism rife, the large number of gardens remaining intact for judging attests to the ingenuity of sponsoring groups. Inquiry reveals several methods used to outwit vandals. One group said they invited the troublemakers to join in the gardening and assigned them the job of guarding the gardens. Result: no more vandalism. Other protection systems included scheduling tenants as lookouts in high-rise buildings, or setting up regularly assigned patrols of neighbors to sit and guard the gardens. No one asked for police protection. It is important to note that the groups, through knowledge of their social milieu, were able to devise cooperative ways of protecting their communal work. When gardens were vandalized, immediate replanting of the flowers was the best antidote to further depredations (Robbins, 1969, Chap. 12).

Other expressions of social involvement are revealed in the evolution of the garden as a special place where graduation and wedding pictures are taken and where one meets to talk with friends. Gardeners' personal expressions, either verbal or written, reveal their individual involvement in the garden. A gentle woman with a Spanish accent stood by her garden, and when asked why she grew it, said simply, "They told me you couldn't grow flowers on Avenue D, but I wanted to try. Now you should see the old folks come out every day to enjoy the flowers." Another contestant said, "This is the first creative thing I have done in my life," and added that she had gone to the library to study books on gardening. Similar expressions of personal response are revealed in letters received by the Housing Authority, "...what is more important is everyone getting to know each other, everyone smiles and discusses our garden. They worry over too much rain, they're all so pleased that the children are interested in caring, not destroying. From early morning till late at night you can see neighbors leaning over the garden fence. It has become the center spot of our court where everyone is a friend."

Underlying these expressions is a deep pride of accomplishment by the gardening group. At judging, residents and gardeners usually try to convince the judges that their garden should win a prize. Where there are gardens, vandalism is reduced outside and often inside the buildings. Less debris litters the lawn and tenants urge groundsmen to provide superior maintenance to the surrounding area. Where landscape plantings installed by the Authority were previously destroyed, after several years of the garden contest, tenant groups requested that they be allowed to assist in landscaping the buildings. Tenant groups collected money among themselves to plant spring flowering gardens which would bloom in advance of the summer contest gardens. They formed garden clubs and requested a winter contest for windowsill plants.

A meaningful insight was gained while judging a Japanese-inspired garden, complete with pond, bridge, stones, and walks constructed of bricks, cinder blocks, and scrap lumber. It was the entry of a teenage group, members of a street gang who were guided into the contest by a social worker. He said that the boys had worked diligently, bringing building materials from across the city to construct the paths and edge the beds. Maintenance was meticulous and their pride was obvious. Each of these boys had a police record.

2.2. Philadelphia

Effectiveness of the gardening technique is not dependent on physical urban structure. A Philadelphia window box program in neighborhoods of privately owned row-houses clearly demonstrates human response to plants. Sponsored by the Neighborhood Garden Association, the program makes window boxes and plants available to any block in which eighty-five percent of the residents sign up. The only requirement is that they maintain their window box gardens for two years. The window boxes spark spontaneous activities by residents of the block. Streets are cleaned; curbs, tree trunks, and door steps are whitewashed; houses are cleaned and painted; curtains are hung in windows; debris-laden lots are cleared and replaced with playgrounds or gardens. None of these activities are prescribed in contest rules. This program, started in 1953 by Louise Bush-Brown, is now carried out annually in five hundred blocks (Bush-Brown, 1969).

Comments by gardeners again underscore the human involvement: "Before it was just a house, now it looks like a home." "I've lived on this block for fifteen years. It's so nice to come to know the names as well as the faces of the other people on the block. I never knew them before." "This was the most dumpified place I had ever seen. Now it even smells good." "I guess I'll wash my windows now."

2.3. Chicago

The Chicago Housing Authority sponsors a garden contest patterned on the New York program. Here too, the gardens act as a catalyst for social and behavioral responses. Gardeners develop similar cooperative methods for preventing vandalism. Their verbal expressions reveal great pride and sense of accomplishment. They speak of friendship and closeness between participants. One commented, "We shared our produce and ourselves." In many projects the vegetable harvest is shared at communal dinners

for all residents of the building.

The gardens inspire clean-up activities on the part of residents. At one of the Robert Taylor Homes' tall impersonal highrise structures, a red and white garden was the inspiration for painting entrance pillars, benches, and chains along walks in matching colors. Very quickly other buildings were decorated too, reaching a peak of expression with the appearance of large painted murals. These were exceedingly well designed and executed at the entrances of most of the buildings in this project. Notwithstanding regulations prohibiting personal decoration of exteriors of these structures, murals even appeared on buildings without gardens. The anonymous paintings served to individualize sterile facades. The gardener, having gained self-identity through his garden, also sought to create a personal identification for the building in which he lived.

Social and behavioral benefits of gardening are found not only in housing, but in other urban situations. The number of broken windows at the Benjamin Raymond School in Chicago has decreased yearly since establishment of a student-maintained garden. The garden has also led to the appointment of a full-time naturalist on the staff and varied gardening projects in the classroom (Beatty, 1974).

Displays at the Chicago Flower Show, sponsored by inner-city schools, reveal the interaction of child with environment. The "Scentuous Garden" displayed by Austin High School in 1973 featured an artful sculpture, "Pollution in Bloom," which was constructed of mufflers, tailpipes, coil springs, and hub caps interlaced with hanging pots of plants and flowers. A gazebo sitting area in their garden was fashioned from the body of a junked Volkswagen, which they cleaned and painted. Its hood and engine areas, now planters, bore a profusion of flowering plants. Other flower show displays featured terraria, bottle gardens, dried flower arrangements, and many more representations of classroom projects. The people-plant activities aided in the expression of a wealth of creativity by inner-city children.

3. BEHAVIORAL RESPONSES TO GARDENING

How might gardening generate these extra-horticultural benefits? Lacking data from precise investigations, it has been suggested that enhancement of self-esteem may play a central role (Lewis, 1975). Stainbrook (1973) cites the need for self-esteem in maintaining emotional health: "An environment of ugliness, dilapidation, dirtiness, over-built space, and lack of natural surroundings confirms the negative self-appraisal a person may have developed through other contacts with society. Self-esteem is the keystone to emotional well being; a poor self-appraisal, among other

factors, determines how one treats his surroundings and how destructive he will be toward
himself and others. These factors set up a
vicious circle that is difficult to break."

How can gardening enhance self-esteem? The
garden plot is a physical entity, in public
view, the site of individual activity outside
of the building. For the inner-city resident,
cut off from adequate means for self-
identification and self-expression, the garden
becomes a highly visible representation of
himself. Whatever happens on the garden plot
is a reflection of the gardener involved.
Through his nurturing activities, the gardener
gains a sense of responsibility for the well
being of his plants. Daily increases in
plant growth provide him with continuous
evidence of his success. One can see that,
with the high degree of personal involvement,
the blooming garden or productive vegetable
plot represents a personal triumph for the
gardener. This triumph is achieved in a public
space, and is viewed by everyone passing by --
indisputable evidence of the gardener's
success and ability to effect a change. Thus
encouraged, he goes on to effect other changes
around him: streets are cleaned, curbs painted,
buildings repaired and painted, vacant lots
cleaned and turned into gardens and playgrounds. The pride found through gardening
is thus expressed in physical improvement of
his environment.

Through gardening, which is often a group
effort, he comes to know his neighbors and
gains a sense of community. Together they
plan, care for, and protect their effort.
Comments of gardeners underscore their evident
pride -- not only in gardens, but in the
neighborhood and newly found friends. These
spontaneous activities show gardening as a
catalyst for improved behavioral and social
responses.

Gardens enhance a proprietary sense of
territoriality, providing residents of public
housing an opportunity for a private statement
on public grounds. Newman (1972), in his study
of crime in public housing, states that any
activity which brings residents out onto the
grounds and extends the sense of private
community to public areas will establish a
sense of territoriality which helps to safe-
guard the building. Activity areas where
people sit and talk, repair their autos, or
wash and dry their clothes are under casual
surveillance by concerned family members and
thus establish a sense of territoriality. The
garden is visible evidence of personal activity.
It proclaims a sense of private domain, even
when no one is present caring for it. Though
Newman's study was conducted at the projects
of the New York City Housing Authority, he did
not investigate the effect of the tenant
gardening contest in establishing a sense of
territoriality.

Matthew Dumont is cited (Lieberman, 1970) as
identifying three distinct needs underlying
mental health of cities: (1) stimulation, to
break the monotony of daily life; (2) a sense
of community, which arises not because people
are forced to live together, but from some
spontaneous action; (3) a sense of mastery of
the environment, reassuring the individual that
he has a degree of control over what happens
around him and is not a helpless cog in the
overwhelming machinery of living. Inner-city
gardening speaks to all of these needs.

Would it be helpful to conceptualize the
varied human responses to plants for the comprehension and study of these phenomena?
Patrick Horsbrugh (1972) suggests people/plant
proxemics, meaning "the continual association
of man with plants, not only respecting (their
effect on his) air and food, but particularly
those contacts which feed the eye, employ the
hand, and sustain the soul....that proximity
which is both aesthetic, sensual and
psychological."

4. LIFE-ENHANCING QUALITIES OF PLANTS

What inherent qualities of living plants
encourage these responses? Plants are non-
threatening and non-discriminating in a world
that is constantly judgmental. Plants respond
to care -- not the race, intellect, age,
affluence, or physical capacity of the gardener.
The garden is a benevolent setting in which
an individual with all his real and imagined
handicaps can take a first step toward
confidence. A gardener, accepting responsibility for the well-being of his plants, tries
to supply plant needs through repeated acts of
watering, fertilizing and cultivating. He
receives his reward in new leaves, shoots and
flowers.

Plants offer time-clues to longer rhythms than
those in which man races. They respond visibly
to the sun in its daily course and signal the
change of the seasons. It takes time for a
cutting to grow roots, a seed to germinate, a
leaf to open. These plant-intrinsic rhythms
were set in the genes of the plant by the same
forces that set man's biological clock. The
feel of soil between the fingers is something
very basic, connecting one with all earth, even
from a twenty-fifth floor apartment, a hospital
ward, or a concrete-asphalt world. Through
plants we are put in touch with surroundings
that we may not even know. They provide a
sense of natural place in non-natural surroundings. They tell us in an infinite variety of
ways that beauty has not gone out of the world.

Plants are alive and communicate life qualities
to those who tend them. Since no living thing
is static but is always changing, plants speak
of a dynamic stability achieved through continuous change. The phases of growth are
predictable, following a stable, orderly

progression from seedling to mature flowering plant. How different are the erratic and often bizarre patterns of our technological society, where the flow of life is constricted by regulation, changes course as it responds rapidly to fads and other distractions, and is subject to constant threat by new man-made terrors.

Plants take away some of the anxiety and tension of the immediate Now by showing us that there are long, enduring patterns in life. There is a certainty in knowing that an oak tree has looked like an oak tree for thousands of years, and a rose is a rose is indeed a rose...at all times and in all places.

The life-enhancing qualities of plants are also effective in mental hospitals, physical rehabilitation institutions, geriatric centers, schools for exceptional children, drug and alcohol rehabilitation centers, and correctional institutions where horticulture is employed as an adjunct to diagnosis and treatment. Horticultural therapy joins human responses to plants with directed medical guidance to ease psychological problems and direct the retraining of muscle and spirit. Gardening techniques help patients regain confidence in themselves, express hidden emotions, and gain social confidence in group activities. At physical rehabilitation institutions, simple tasks such as placing broken shards in the bottom of a pot, transplanting seedlings, or rooting cuttings are utilized as diagnostic tests of a patient's progress or as activities to strengthen weak muscles.

Three universities have four-year undergraduate curricula in horticultural therapy, and one offers a graduate program. Serving as a communication focus for all activities in this field is the National Council for Therapy and Rehabilitation Through Horticulture, Mt. Vernon, Virginia, established in 1973.

5. HORTICULTURE - A PROCESS FOR DESIGN

Horsbrugh (1974) calls for the extension of horticultural therapy to city design and planning, "Can therapeutic practices that are applied to the person be applied to place also? ....the application of therapeutic treatment seems to be confined to the individual only, and never applied to the physical environment for achievement of social benefits....If this (horticultural) concept of individual benefit is sound, it applies, also, on the scale of society in general, and to environmental conditions in total. There may be some analogy of providing treatment for a patient while ignoring the state of the bed, the filth of the room, the hygienic degradation of the house....The cities are no less ailing, sick, disabled, retarded in their development than their inhabitants.... distress of person as a result of distress of

place...is one interactive condition, providing one inevitable dislocation that afflicts our cities, almost without exception. The remedy lies...in the appreciation of the natural synecosystems and applying them to urban planning as a basic design principle....It is essential for any designer to regard 'person' and 'place' as one ecosystem....Habitat and inhabitant are of one substance, in life even as they are in death."

In their studies of the visual environment, Kaplan and Wendt (1972) say, "If indeed man is likely to go out of his mind before he runs out of any of the traditional basic requirements of life, then a close look at the conditions and environments that are sanity-preserving and even satisfaction-enhancing seems essential. One facet of this issue is simply that of what man likes and why." On the basis of empirical evidence presented, the process of horticulture can indeed be sanity-preserving and satisfaction-enhancing. Will this man-environment relationship be understood and utilized for prevention as well as alleviation of human stress?

The theme of EDRA-7, "Behavioral Basis of Design - Beyond the Applicability Gap," implies a need for behavior-enhancing techniques that are applicable to design problems. The cited behavioral responses to gardening are happening today in the real world of low-income housing, mental institutions, rehabilitation centers. They delineate a user-generated and user-maintained system that enhances the quality of life.

The techniques of gardening are known and easily put into practice. The positive behavioral and social responses engendered reach far beyond horticulture. The people/plant proxemic viewpoint provides a window for viewing people in the microcosm of their immediate environment, giving the designer user input at this personal scale. Human benefits gained through the process of gardening help to ameliorate existing situations and can, through design and planning implementation, become beneficial forces in environments yet to be built -- environments which will encourage rather than thwart the pursuit of a rewarding and happy life.

A humane environment is one in which the user "able to create, to mold, to change his surroundings, to leave his personal imprint on the world, and affect other people" (Sommer, 1972, p. 13). The process of gardening is accomplishing these ends today in the real world. It has been brought this far by horticulture. Its future role in easing human stress will depend on imaginative implementation by designer and planner.

"To be fully human, man needs to create as well as choose, to make things beautiful as well as admire beauty." (Sommer, 1972, p. 59)

6. NOTE

This work was supported in part through a grant from Mrs. Enid A. Haupt to the American Horticultural Society People/Plant Program.

reference

BEATTY, V. L. Highrise horticulture. *American Horticulturist*, 1974, 53(2), 42-46.

BUSH-BROWN, L. *Garden blocks for urban America.* New York: Scribners, 1972.

HALL, E. T. *The hidden dimension.* Garden City: Doubleday, 1966.

HORSBRUGH, P. Human-plant proximities: A psychological imperative. *Indiana Nursery News*, 1972, 33(4).

HORSBRUGH, P. *Urban horti-psychotherapy.* Talk presented at meeting of National Council for Therapy and Rehabilitation Through Horticulture, 1974, Mt. Vernon, Virginia.

ILTIS, H. H., LOUCKS, O. L. & ANDREWS, P. Criteria for an optimum human environment. *Bulletin of the Atomic Scientists*, 1970, 26(1), 2-6.

KAPLAN, R. Some psychological benefits of gardening. *Environment and Behavior*, 1973, 5(2), 145-161.

KAPLAN, S. & WENDT, J. S. Preference and the visual environment: Complexity and some alternatives. *Proceedings of EDRA3/AR8*, 1972.

LEWIS, C. A. Public housing gardens -- landscapes for the soul. *Landscapes for living, U.S.D.A. yearbook of agriculture*, 1972, 277-282.

LEWIS, C. A. People-plant interaction: A new horticultural perspective. *American Horticulturist*, 1973, 52(2), 18-25.

LEWIS, C. A. American Horticultural Society people/plant program: Human perspectives in horticulture. *Proceedings of symposium on children, nature and the urban environment*, U.S.D.A. Forest Service, 1976 (in press).

LIEBERMAN, M. Parks and urban mental health. *Park Practice Trends*, 1970, 7(3), 30-32.

ROBBINS, I. Tenant's gardens in public housing. *Small urban spaces* (Ed. Seymour, Jr.), New York: New York University Press, 1969, 139-147.

SOMMER, R. *Design awareness.* Corte Madera, California: Rinehart Press, 1972.

STAINBROOK, E. Man's psychic need for nature. *National Parks and Conservation Magazine*, 1973, 47(9), 22-23.

TALBOTT, J., STERN, D., ROSS, J. & GILLEN, C. Flowering plants as a therapeutic/ environmental agent in a psychiatric hospital. Manuscript submitted for publication, 1975.

DETERMINANTS OF PERCEIVED CROWDING AND
PLEASANTNESS IN PUBLIC SETTINGS

Lou McClelland and Nathan Auslander

Department of Psychology
University of Colorado
Boulder, Colorado 80302

ABSTRACT

68 subjects viewed 144 slides of public settings
(restaurants, stores, sports events, airports,
libraries, etc.) in the Denver area, and rated
each slide on crowdedness and pleasantness. The
slides varied, and were rated by experts, on
several dimensions thought to be important in
determining perceptions of crowding: number of
people, amount of space, lighting, type of
activity, social factors, and others. These
dimensions were used to predict the crowding and
pleasantness ratings in stepwise multiple regression. Scenes are rated as more crowded if they
picture more people in less space with smaller
interpersonal distances, if the scene is more
complex and disorderly with fewer visual escapes,
and if the people are working rather than
playing. Crowding predicts pleasantness very
well (r=-.63); other significant factors are
work-play, joint activity, light level, orderliness, number of people and activities, and
standing in lines. The correlation between
crowding and pleasantness is negative except
for settings in which the presence and observation
of others is an integral part of the activity (a
professional basketball game, a dark and noisy
restaurant, etc). Advantages and disadvantages
of the methods are also discussed.

1.0 INTRODUCTION

Two issues have dominated the study of crowding
in humans in recent years: the physical and
social factors determining crowding, and the
affective evaluation of crowding. The study
described here is addressed to both these issues.

Although early research (Freedman, Klevansky, &
Ehrlich, 1971; Griffitt & Veitch, 1971) explicitly
or implicitly defined crowding in terms of space
per person, more recent work (Stokols, 1972;
Valins & Baum, 1973) has stressed the essentially
subjective nature of the concept and has focused
on "perceived crowding" and even on "perceived
density" (Rapoport, 1975). Determinants of
perceived crowding demonstrated empirically or
hypothesized include not only number of people
and amount of space, but also architectural
features, type of activity, intergroup relations,
personal factors, and others. An extensive list
of possible determinants of perceived density,
applicable both to indoor and outdoor environments, is included in a theoretical article on
the "redefinition of density" by Rapoport (1975).

Views on the affective impact of crowding and
density have also changed with continued
research. While high density has generally
been found to lead to feelings of dissatisfaction
and unpleasantness, this relationship is now
recognized to be mediated by characteristics of
the individual such as cultural background and
sex, characteristics of the group such as degree
of prior acquaintnace and homogeneity, and
characteristics of the activity such as amount of
competition and hierarchical structuring.
Freedman (1975) has proposed that density and
crowding are not unpleasant in themselves, but
rather intensify the already prevailing affect;
a crowded party is better than an uncrowded one,
but the converse is true of a subway ride. In
Rapoport's (1975) view, perceived density is
compared to that expected or desired, with
discrepancies in either direction judged
unpleasant. Thus, pleasantness may be a function
of crowding or density, at least partially, but
the form of the function is probably not as
simple and monotonic as initially hypothesized.

Past research has addressed the issues of crowding
determinants and the crowding-pleasantness
relationship by two basic methods: (a) the
experimental method, including both laboratory
and field studies, with experimenter control
and/or measurement of a few factors hypothesized
to determine crowding; (b) the survey method, in
which a larger number of factors can be assessed,
but the direction of causality cannot be assured.
In virtually all studies to date except that of
Desor (1972), subjects have experienced
directly--that is, been in--the environments
they reacted to.

The methods of the present study differ from
those described above in several ways. First,
subjects were presented with representations
of environments--color slides--rather than
placed within them. Second, a large number of
factors were purposely varied; these factors,
henceforth called "cues," are listed in the
methods section below. Third, the cues were
not varied orthogonally as in an experimental
design; rather, an attempt was made to match
in the slides their pattern of joint occurrence
in real life, in an attempt to increase the
generalizability of the results (see Brunswick,
1956, for an account of the logic of this
approach). Finally, each subject reacted to
all the environmental representations, rather
than only experiencing one set of cue levels.

2.0 METHOD

Subjects rated a series of slides on crowding
and pleasantness scales; the slides were also
rated by "experts" on several dimensions
thought to be important in determining crowding.

2.1 Subjects

Seventy-eight University of Colorado introductory psychology students served as subjects
to fulfill course requirements.

2.2 Slides

The stimuli were 144 35 mm color slides. The
slides are all of public or semi-public (e.g.
an office) spaces in the Boulder-Denver area;
they depict restaurants, classrooms, airport
waiting areas, sports events, supermarkets and
other stores, libraries, and a few outdoor
settings, with from 1 to 20 slides showing any
given setting. Each slide shows at least one
person; all were taken with a 35 mm lens using
existing light (filters were used to correct
for light source). An attempt was made to
include slides showing some crowded and some
uncrowded settings, and to obtain at least some
variance on the several hypothesized dimensions.

2.3 Procedure

Subjects, in groups of 40, were presented the
slides at a rate of about four per minute. They
rated (by placing a check on a 6 cm line) each
slide on crowding ("How crowded does the scene
seem to you? That is, if you were in the situation pictured, would you feel crowded?") and on
pleasantness ("How pleasant is the situation for
the people in it?") Of the first 65 slides, 15
were presented a second time, at the end, so that
each subject made 159 pairs of ratings. After
that, they filled out demographic, background
experience, and personality questionnaires; the
data from these are not presented here.

2.4 Expert Ratings

Three student research assistants ("experts")

rated each slide on the following dimensions:
number of people; number of visual escapes
(windows, doors, etc.); amount of space (a 1-7
scale); average interpersonal distance in feet;
number of different ongoing activities,
orderliness, and complexity (1-7 scales);
moving/still; standing/sitting; people
acquainted/not; low/high light level; light/
dark color; cooperative/competitive situation;
work/play; independent/joint activity; and
in/out-of-doors. The ratings were made by
each expert independently, then combined (using
the modal rating on dichotomies, median on
continuous scales) to obtain one rating on each
of the 16 dimensions for each slide.

2.5 Data Filtering

The subjects' check-mark ratings were converted
to 1-9 ratings by dividing the line into 9
equal segments. Examination of rating distributions for individual slides and of the
replication correlations (correlation of time
1 ratings with time 2 ratings over the 15 slides
presented twice) for individual subjects
revealed obvious instances of inattention,
confusion, or carelessness by some subjects.
Therefore, the data were filtered in two
ways: (a) 10 subjects with low (under .40)
replication correlations and/or a high number
(4 or more) of deviant ($z \geq 3$) responses were
removed, and (b) all ratings with $z \geq 3$ were
removed; these were primarily ratings of 1 or
9 given by a few subjects for slides rated
at the opposite end of the scale by the large
majority of subjects. This procedure deleted
about 100 of the over 10,000 possible data
points. The replication correlations, after
filtering, are significant for every slide and
for every subject for both crowding and
pleasantness.

FIGURE 1: PERCENTAGE DISTRIBUTIONS OF CONTINUOUS CUE DIMENSIONS OVER ALL SLIDES

People	number	1	2-5	6-10	11-20	21-60	61-100	≥200
	%	4	21	22	26	20	4	3
Amount of Space	rating	1	2	3	4	5	6	7
	%	5	13	17	18	19	14	14
Average Inter-Personal Distance	feet	1	2	3	4	5	6-10	11-20
	%	23	18	18	16	18	14	3
Visual Escapes	number	0	1	2	3	4	5	≥9*
	%	33	35	16	7	0	2	7
Number of Activities	rating	1	2	3	4	5	6	7
	%	38	42	17	0	2	0	1
Orderliness	rating	1	2	3	4	5	6	7
	%	6	12	12	9	25	29	7
Complexity	rating	1	2	3	4	5	6	7
	%	11	21	19	16	17	13	3

on all ratings, 1 = low, 7 = high
*outdoor slides

FIGURE 2: <u>CUE INTERCORRELATIONS, WITH PERCENTAGE DISTRIBUTIONS OF DICHOTOMOUS CUES</u>

	No. of People	Space	Distance	Escapes	Activities	Orderliness	Complexity	Movement	Standing/Sitting	Light	Color	Acquainted/Not	Competition	Indepen./Joint	Work/Play
Amount of Space	.37														
Interpersonal Distance	-.32	.06													
No. of Visual Escapes	.24	.47	.20												
No. of Activities	.28	.36	-.27	.01											
Orderliness	-.27	-.09	.24	-.04	-.46										
Complexity	.31	.28	-.30	.00	.53	-.65									
Still(82%)/Moving(18%)	-.12	.20	.24	.19	.30	-.21	.12								
Standing(59%)/Sitting(41%)	.12	-.16	-.04	-.09	-.28	.43	-.39	-.40							
Low(20%)/High(80%) Light	-.09	-.02	-.01	.01	.02	.14	-.10	.07	.04						
Dark(44%)/Light(56%) Color	-.25	-.19	.17	.09	-.22	.23	-.25	-.02	-.04	.56					
Acquainted(39%)/Not(61%)	-.35	-.09	.15	-.10	-.05	.02	.00	.11	-.13	.11	.05				
Competition(5%)/Coop.(95%)	.08	-.05	-.02	.06	-.07	.09	-.14	.01	.11	-.11	-.05	.05			
Indepen.(80%)/Joint(20%)	.12	.03	-.10	.17	-.04	-.12	.09	-.07	-.04	-.12	-.02	-.55	-.17		
Work(47%)/Play(53%)	.05	.19	.10	.07	.21	-.08	-.01	.27	-.18	-.10	-.13	-.22	-.06	.26	
Out(7%)/Indoors(93%)	-.24	-.40	-.21	-.82	.06	.06	.07	-.19	.11	.02	-.06	.16	-.06	-.17	-.14

correlations of .18 or more significant with $p \leq .05$; of .24 or more significant with $p \leq .01$

3.0 RESULTS

The results are discussed in three sections: relationships among the dimensions or cues, the crowding-pleasantness relationship, and relative importance of the cues in predicting crowding and pleasantness.

3.1 <u>Cues</u> <u>and</u> <u>Their</u> <u>Relations</u>

Figure 1 shows the distribution over slides of the 7 continuous cues. Figure 2 shows both the distributions of the 9 dichotomous cues and the intercorrelations of all cues. These data, then, simply describe more precisely the nature of the sample of slides. A moderate amount of variance was achieved for most dimensions; the 8 outdoor scenes were included in the sample only for exploratory purposes.

3.2 <u>The</u> <u>Crowding-Pleasantness</u> <u>Relationship</u>

There is in general a negative relationship between crowding and pleasantness, yielding a correlation of -.63 (N=144, $p \leq .01$) over slides. Of the 68 subjects, 54 have significant negative correlations between their crowding and pleasantness ratings, ranging up to -.96; 14 have nonsignificant correlations, ranging to +.16. In Figure 3 is shown the scattergram of crowding versus pleasantness over slides; the regression line (pleasantness = 6.94 - .39 X crowding) is drawn in. Circles have been drawn around two groups of slides: 8 slides for which the predicted pleasantness value is at least 1.50

less than the actual value, and 11 slides for which the predicted pleasantness value is at least 1.50 greater than the actual value. The first group--those less pleasant than would be expected--is composed entirely of slides showing lines or severe congestion and waiting in shopping situations at the campus bookstore and a supermarket. (About 3/4 of all "waiting" slides are in this group.) As can be seen in Figure 3, all these slides have mean crowding ratings of 7.5 or greater, and mean pleasantness ratings of 2.5 or less. This indicates that the large distance from the regression line may be a result of ceilings on the scales (that is, subjects might have rated these slides more extremely if it had been possible to do so), rather than any actual difference in the crowding-pleasantness relationship.

The second group of slides--those more pleasant than expected on the basis of their crowding ratings--includes all 6 spectator sports scenes (4 slides of a professional basketball game with about 10,000 spectators; 2 of a gymnastics meet with 200 spectators), all 3 slides showing dark, "atmospheric" restaurants, and the only participant sports slide, of two men playing racquetball. Neither the crowding nor pleasantness ratings are extreme for this group of slides, and the crowding ratings range from 3.8 (racquetball) to 8.5 (basketball game).

An examination of Figure 3 shows that while the mean pleasantness ratings for the uncrowded scenes cluster between 4.5 and 7.0 (neutral to moderately

FIGURE 3: PLOT OF MEAN CROWDING VERSUS PLEASANTNESS FOR 144 SLIDES

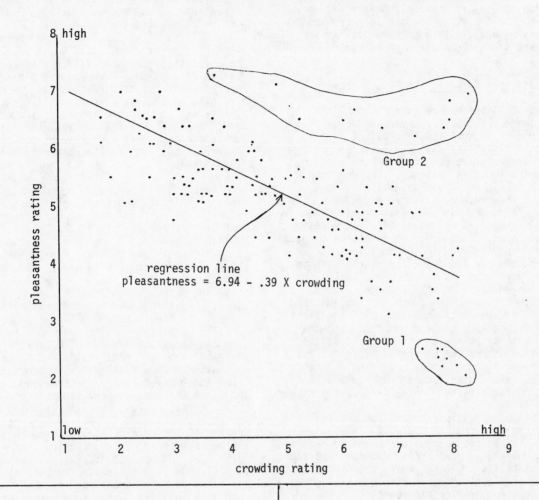

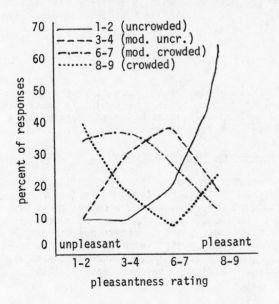

FIGURE 4: DISTRIBUTION OF PLEASANTNESS RESPONSES FOR EACH CROWDING LEVEL

pleasant), those for the crowded slides range from 2.0 to 7.0, a much broader spread. The variance in mean pleasantness ratings for the 21 slides with mean crowding ratings of 3.0 or less (very uncrowded) is .41; the variance in mean pleasantness ratings for the 20 slides with mean crowding ratings of 7.5 or more (very crowded) is 4.26. This difference in variances is significant (F-max test, $p \leq .01$).

An analysis of the individual ratings confirms the view that unpleasant ratings are a function of crowding, but pleasant ratings come from both crowded and uncrowded slides. Figure 4 shows the distribution of individual pleasantness ratings for each level of crowding ratings (no "5" ratings are included in the graph, because evidence indicates the use of this rating as both a neutral rating and a category of indifference or inattention). The very unpleasant (1-2) ratings are more likely to accompany very crowded (8-9) than moderately crowded (6-7) than uncrowded (1-4) ratings, as would be expected from the negative correlation. However, very <u>pleasant</u> ratings (8-9) are more likely to accompany very crowded (8-9) ratings than either moderately crowded (6-7) or moderately uncrowded (3-4) ratings. Viewed another way, the curve representing very uncrowded scenes is unimodal, peaking at very pleasant, but the curve for the very crowded slides is bimodal, with a primary peak at very unpleasant and a secondary peak at very pleasant.

3.3 Predicting Crowding and Pleasantness

The several dimensions or cues rated by the experts were selected for their possible importance in determining perceptions of crowding and pleasantness. To test the overall and relative abilities of the cues to predict the subjects' ratings, the technique of stepwise multiple regression analysis was used. In this method, a single dependent variable (i.e. crowding or pleasantness) and several independent variables (i.e. the cues) are designated. Zero-order correlations between the dependent and each independent variable are computed, and the independent variable with the highest correlation is selected to "enter" the regression equation first. Then the partial correlations between the dependent variable and remaining independent variables, with the first-entered cue controlled, are computed, and the independent variable with the highest partial correlation enters the equation. This process continues until none of the remaining independent variables make a significant contribution to accounting for variance in the dependent variable.

The result of a multiple regression analysis is a regression or prediction equation which specifies how the scores on the independent variables can be combined to predict the dependent variable. The R^2 statistic indicates what percentage of the variance in the dependent variable is accounted for by that combination of predictors. The independent variables are called predictors because, if they do enter the regression equation, this indicates that one can predict the dependent variable better given knowledge of the independent variable than without such knowledge. If the independent variables are related to each other (as they are in this study; see Figure 2), the entry of one predictor (such as joint/independent activity) may greatly diminish the probability of entry of another, related predictor (such as acquainted/not). Thus independent variables not entered into the equation cannot be said to be unimportant--only unimportant given the presence of the variables already entered into the equation.

Since the various cues occur in real situations in conjunction with each other rather than independently, all cues were used as predictors in the regression analyses. The following changes were made in the sample of slides: (a) outdoor scenes were deleted because they were so few in number, seemed to be qualitatively different in atmosphere, and varied radically from the other slides on the dimensions of escapes and amount of space; (b) scenes showing only one

person were deleted for similar reasons; (c) slides of the professional basketball game were deleted--they showed over 10,000 people, with no other slides showing over 200; (d) the first 23 slides, considered practice for the subjects, were not rated by the experts. These deletions left 105 slides with ratings on all dimensions; mean crowding and pleasantness ratings (averaged over 68 subjects) were then predicted by the set of cues. All cues described in Figures 1 and 2 were included as predictors, except in/outdoors. In addition, the log of number of people was used rather than the raw number, to correct for the extremely skewed distribution.

In Figure 5 are summarized the results of the stepwise multiple regression on mean crowding ratings. Slides are rated as more crowded if they picture more people in less space with smaller interpersonal distances, if the scene is more complex and disorderly with fewer visual escapes, and if the people are working rather than playing. The multiple R^2 is .80, indicating that these cues, taken together, do a rather good job of predicting mean crowding ratings for the slides. No other cues were significant.

Figure 6 shows the results of a parallel analysis on pleasantness ratings. Since subjects made the pleasantness ratings immediately after making the crowding ratings, and since the focus of the study is crowding, not general pleasantness, the mean crowding rating was entered as an additional predictor; it entered the regression first. Factors predicting more pleasant ratings are playing (not working), joint (not independent) activity, low light levels, orderliness, greater numbers of people and activities, movement, and sitting (rather than standing). No other cues were significant. The final two factors, movement and sitting, at first seem contradictory since one cannot both move and sit simultaneously; however, one can both stand and be still simultaneously, and one does this when in a line; lines are rated as quite unpleasant. The multiple R^2 in this analysis is .82, again quite high.

4.0 DISCUSSION

The implications of the results presented above fall into three areas: determinants of crowding, the relationship of crowding to pleasantness, and methods for future research.

4.1 Determinants of Crowding

The results of the multiple regression confirm the view that several types of factors are important determinants of perceived crowding: physical factors such as number of people, amount of space, and interpersonal distance; informational factors such as complexity, order, and escapes; social factors such as the type of ongoing activity. They also speak, albeit

FIGURE 5: SUMMARY OF STEPWISE MULTIPLE
          REGRESSION ON CROWDING RATINGS

Step	Variable	R^2	b
	Constant		5.95
1	Log No. of People (low/<u>high</u>)	.52	.99
2	Amount of Space (<u>low</u>/high)	.65	-.30
3	Complexity (low/<u>high</u>)	.73	.20
4	Interpers Distance (<u>low</u>/high)	.75	-.10
5	No. of Visual Escapes (<u>lo</u>/hi)	.77	-.28
6	Orderliness (<u>low</u>/high)	.78	-.21
7	<u>Working</u>/Playing	.80	-.48

All entries are significant with p ≤ .01
Cues predicting more crowding are underlined
b coefficients are not standardized
R^2s computed at the end of each step

FIGURE 6: SUMMARY OF STEPWISE MULTIPLE
          REGRESSION ON PLEASANTNESS RATINGS

Step	Variable	R^2	b
	Constant		5.50
1	Crowding (<u>low</u>/high)	.55	-.55
2	Working/<u>Playing</u>	.64	.45
3	Log No. of People (low/<u>high</u>)	.72	.33
4	<u>Joint</u>/Independent Activity	.76	-.74
5	Standing/<u>Sitting</u>	.78	.37
6	<u>Moving</u>/Still	.79	-.40
7	<u>Low</u>/High Light	.80	-.42
8	Orderliness (low/<u>high</u>)	.81	.11
9	No. of Activities (low/<u>high</u>)	.82	.19

All entries are significant with p ≤ .03
Cues predicting more pleasantness are underlined
b coefficients are not standardized
R^2s computed at the end of each step

indirectly, to the issue of the importance of
density and the effects of increasing numbers
of people versus decreasing amounts of space.
The zero-order correlations of the relevant cues
with mean crowding ratings are as follows (N=144):
number of people, .51; log number, .74; space
(a 1-7 scale), .07; average interpersonal
distance, -.53. The partial correlation between
space and crowding with log number controlled
is -.52. Thus for this sample, number of people
is directly related to perceptions of crowding,
while amount of space is not; however, when
number is controlled, space becomes highly
important. Note also that interpersonal
distance enters the regression after the effects
of number of people and amount of space have
been entered, indicating that the distribution
of people in space, not just the amount of
space per person, is important in determining
perceived crowding. Finally, note that the
correlation between crowding and log number of
people (.74) is significantly higher than that
between crowding and unadjusted number (r=.51,
z=2.93, p ≤ .01). This is probably due partly to
reduced skewness in the distribution, but may
also reflect a tendency of subjects to make
(unconsciously) log transformations of the number
of people themselves, so that equal differences
in number are perceived as more important in
small groups of people than in large groups.

4.2 The Crowding-Pleasantness Relationship

Although perceived crowding accounts for more
than half the variance in the pleasantness
ratings (R^2=.55), a simple negative linear
function does not adequately describe the
relationship between the two variables. While
the scenes judged most unpleasant are almost

invariably crowded, those judged most pleasant
are sometimes uncrowded, sometimes very crowded,
as is shown in the stylized diagram in Figure 7.

FIGURE 7: DIAGRAM OF THE CROWDING-
          PLEASANTNESS RELATIONSHIP

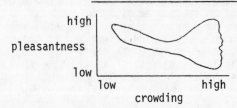

The nature of the pleasant-but-crowded
scenes--spectator and participant sports, dark
convivial restaurants--especially when
contrasted to the scenes judged least pleasant
and most crowded (waiting in line), suggests
that both information overload (c.f. Rapoport,
1975) and constricted freedom of movement
are important factors in making crowding
unpleasant. Further, situations which one
enters to achieve a particular goal (e.g.
make a purchase, listen to a lecture), in
contrast to those in which the situation
itself is the goal (a sports event, a party)
will be more likely to be judged unpleasant
when crowded. This distinction is probably
heightened when the presence and observation
of other people is an integral part of the
situation-as-goal; a basketball game with 100
spectators is simply not the same event as
one with 10,000. For more personal or private
activities--hiking, daydreaming, visiting
an art gallery--the distinction may not be
true; the current sample of slides is
inadequate to answer this question.

4.3 Methods and Future Research

The method used in this study has several advantages over more usual experimental and survey methods: (a) the sample of situations can be much larger, allowing variation on many dimensions; (b) this sample is totally identifiable, can easily be transported over time and space, and can be altered in specific ways to include or delete types of situations and dimensions; (c) successful analysis does not depend on orthogonality of the dimensions, thus allowing a high degree of "mundane realism" of the stimuli; (d) a large number of subjects can be run in a short time, with no deception; and (e) virtually every analysis can be done on individual subjects as well as on the group data, thus allowing exploration of individual differences (such analyses have not been reported here). Basically, the method allows the use of large numbers of stimuli and subjects, both varying on numerous dimensions, without large experdlure of time, space, or money.

Of course, the general method and its specific use here also have disadvantages: (a) seeing a slide is not the same as entering a setting; certain dimensions (e.g. temperature, smell, noise level) are eliminated altogether, and others are certainly distorted. (It could be argued, however, that seeing a slide of a real place is more "real" than entering an 8x10' room constructed of panels in the psychology lab.) Use of the general technique could be extended to include exposure of subjects to actual places rather than to representations, or to more elaborate representations; this, of course, would increase the costs. (b) Judgements obtained from subjects (in this case, crowding and pleasantness) are not independent, thus making the estimate of their relationship inflated. In future studies each dependent and independent dimension will be judged by separate groups of subjects to circumvent this problem; then, however, individual analyses of relations among the dependent variables will not be possible. (c) Because of confounding of the dimensions, regression analysis does not yield a clear-cut list of important and unimportant cues; related dimensions (such as acquainted/not and independent/joint activity in the present analysis) may "stand in" for one another in the analysis.

The current study suggests several avenues for future research: expansion of the sample to include many outdoor settings; restriction of the sample to include only one type of setting, such as libraries; investigation of individual differences in response; separation of perceived density and crowding; use of actual settings rather than representations; more systematic testing of dimensions of particular theoretical or practical interest.

References

BRUNSWICK, E. Perception and the Representative Design of Psychological Experiments (2nd edition). Berkeley and Los Angeles: University of California Press, 1956.

DESOR, J. Toward a Psychological Theory of Crowding. Journal of Personality and Social Psychology, 1972, 21, 79-83.

FREEDMAN, J. Crowding and Behavior. San Francisco: W. H. Freeman & Co., 1975.

FREEDMAN, J., KLEVANSKY, S., & EHRLICH, P. The Effect of Crowding on Human Task Performance. Journal of Applied Social Psychology, 1971, 1, 7-25.

GRIFFITT, W. & VEITCH, R. Hot and Crowded: Influences of Population Density and Temperature on Interpersonal Affective Behavior. Journal of Personality and Social Psychology, 1971, 17, 92-98.

RAPOPORT, A. Toward a Redefinition of Density. Environment and Behavior, 1975, 7, 133-158.

STOKOLS, D. A Social-Psychological Model of Human Crowding Phenomena. Journal of the American Institute of Planners, 1972, 58, 72-83.

VALINS, S. & BAUM, A. Residential Group Size, Social Interaction, and Crowding. Environment and Behavior, 1973, 5, 421-439.

THE PUBLIC VIEW OF THE COAST: TOWARD AESTHETIC INDICATORS FOR COASTAL PLANNING AND MANAGEMENT

Tridib Banerjee and James Gollub

School of Urban and Regional Planning
University of Southern California
University Park
Los Angeles, California 90007

ABSTRACT

This paper is based on the preliminary findings of a research project attempting to identify critical indicators of the visual quality of the coastal landscape derived from user perceptions and evaluations. Four two minute long 16mm films were made of four different locations on the Los Angeles area coastline recording a 360° view and ambient sounds. These films were shown at the Hollywood Preview House for audience response. The audience (n=377) was given a questionnaire after each film segment was shown and asked to evaluate the environments represented in the film. A subset of this audience (n=150) was required to register their immediate reactions while watching the films by turning a dial attached to the armrests. The device is known as Instantaneous Response Profile (I.R.P.) recorder. Other demographic, behavioral and attitudinal data were obtained via a second questionnaire. This paper will report on the findings based on the data obtained from the I.R.P. recorder for only one of the four film segments. This particular film segment was taken in a location in the city of Long Beach. The findings suggest important differences among age-groups in perceptions of aesthetic quality; they also suggest that most of the environmental elements identified in this study may be valid indicators of aesthetic quality.

1. INTRODUCTION

This paper presents some of the preliminary findings of a user response study designed to identify and establish the validity of a set of environmental quality indicators that can be utilized to assess the overall esthetic quality of the coastal landscapes. The study is based on the premise that a fundamental step in the development of an objective assessment methodology is the identification of components or indicators of the environmental quality being assessed. The measures and aggregation schemes can only follow once the indicators are established.

While there are many different ways of establishing environmental quality of indicators, as a recent state-of-the-art review of literature (EPA, 1973) suggests, most of them are arbitrarily chosen, or at best, based on judgments of experts or technical staff of agencies usually responsible for managing the quality of our environment. The proclaimed objectivity of such procedures are often suspect, and untenable particularly when such intangible environmental qualities as aesthetics are involved. Hence, this study was designed to identify the indicators of aesthetic quality on the basis of responses of a cross-section of users of the environment.

1.1. Background

The interest in this study grew out of one of the authors' involvement in the development of the "Appearance and Design" element of the South Coast Regional Plan of the California Coastal Zone Conservation Commission. The commission was established by a popular initiative known as "Proposition 20", introduced in the ballots of the November 1972 elections in California. The initiative mandated the preparation of a coastal zone plan for the entire State by 1976, and specifically called for restoration, enhancement and preservation of scenic resources of the California coastline.

It became apparent during the process of preparing the plan, that there were very few known mechanisms to assess the scenic qualities of the coastal landscape. It was believed that such mechanisms would be particularly necessary to evaluate the effects of the appearance and design policies, once the plan is implemented at the state, regional and local levels. The broad objective of this study was thus seen as one of developing a set of aesthetic indicators. It was expected that they could serve many useful purposes in coastal planning and management: identifying areas of the coast that are in the need of preservation, restoration and enhancement; assessing esthetic impacts of future developments; monitoring changes in aesthetic quality over time; and so on.

2. THE METHOD

2.1. Determination of an Environmental Display Mode

In searching for a suitable method of assessing environmental preferences the authors first examined the Process Model for the Comprehension of Environmental Displays (Craik, 1968) and the Taxonomy of Classification Techniques for Measurement and Analysis of Behavioral and Physical Design Parameters (Lozar, 1973). It appeared, from the review of these materials, that some version of a visual display of different types of coastal setting may be an effective way of eliciting responses from the subjects of this study. Further consideration of visual medium suggested that motion pictures would offer a greater versatility in representing a wider range of the ambient qualities and activities of an environmental setting. Through the use of a movie camera it is possible to capture a 360°

panoramic view of a setting. Furthermore, in
addition to capturing the dynamic qualities of
the environment it is feasible to record the
ambient sounds, therby making a more sensitive
and complete simulation of the setting than
would be otherwise possible.

Four locations on the Los Angeles area coastline
(from the northern boundary of Orange County)
were chosen as test environments for the study.
These settings represented some of the broad
categories[1] of coastal development ranging from
low intensity natural settings to high intensity
urbanized settings. In addition to representing
the broad categories of coastal development
these settings also manifested a wide variety of
activities, structures, natural features and
activity settings.

The films were taken with a 16mm camera, using a
variable length lens, on a tripod; the sounds
were recorded separately with a tape recorder
and a sound boom. The sound was later merged
with the film as an optical sound track.

A standard system of photography was developed
for filming the settings, to minimize any "journalistic" biases of the researchers or the cam-
eraman. The level of the tripod was kept constant, and an uniform clockwise "panning" sequence was used for all four settings. The panning sequence involved rotating the camera in a
slow pan for about 45 degrees, then holding it
steady for seven or eight seconds;[2] the "pan"
and "hold" sequences were alternated eight times
to complete a full circle of the camera movement.

According to this system a 360[0] panorama could
be completed in less than 2½ minutes, a length
of time regarded as adequate for conveying the
sense of the environment.

The filming always began with a randomly selected focal point of each setting. The sound
boom was also moved and held steady following
the camera rotation pattern. After each film
sequence was completed, the crew set up still
photography equipment and, using a "panorama
head" adopter, took color transparencies and
black and white photographs for later use in
analyzing audience response to the films.

---

[1] The choice of these locations was based on the
analysis of coastal development pattern done as
part of the "Appearance and Design" element.
See South Coast Regional Commission, Appearance
and Design, (adopted September 30, 1974).

[2] This "hold-pan-hold-pan..." sequence was
chosen over a continuous "pan" sequence to avoid
excessive "strobing" effect (caused by shutter
motion in the camera), which might have caused
a loss of bearing, confusion, if not dizziness,
among the viewers.

2.2. The Response Format

Once developed, a content analysis of the films
was done using instant recall of several different groups of viewers. These viewers, totaling
50, came from different backgrounds, ranging
from students and secretaries to professors and
the professional staff of a regional planning
organization. Each group was instructed to view
the film paying close attention to the content.
Following each film the reviewers were asked to
write down everything they remembered seeing in
the film, and their impressions of what they
saw. The free recall responses proved quite
useful, for they represented an exhaustive range
of elements perceived to exist in those films.
The responses could be generally classified
under the following categories: Beach Activities, Water-based Activities, Beach Objects,
Water Objects, Land Objects, Distant View,
Sounds and Qualities. However, from the sum of
the open recall responses it was possible to
extract 44 specific elements or element categories that seemed to provide a reasonably exhaustive checklist to describe the contents of all
four film segments. This checklist was used as
part of the larger audience evaluation of the
film segments.

Each item on the check list had a "beautiful -
ugly" rating option, so that a respondent could
not only check what he/she saw in the film but
he/she could also evaluate the element he/she
checked as beautiful or ugly. In addition to
the aesthetic judgment regarding each of the
elements four other broad evaluative judgments
were solicited on the questionnaire. These pertained to a respondent's perception of the total
environment. On five-point rating scales the
respondents were required to rate the environment. On five-point rating scales the respondents were required to rate the environments in
terms of development (intensely urban - rural),
beauty (extremely beautiful - extremely ugly),
complexity (extremely complex - extremely simple), and interest (extremely interesting - extremely dull).

To assess the relevance of demographic and locational characteristics of the sample population
on their responses to the environmental display,
the authors designed a demographics questionnaire and a supplemental questionnaire inquiring
about the time required for the respondent to
get to the Pacific Coast, frequency, length and
purpose of visits to the coast, preferred recreation location (wilderness, coastal areas, moun-
tains, cities, etc.) and a coastal area activity
check list consisting of 40 items. A final
question asks if the respondent voted on Proposition 20, and if they did whether it was pro
or con.

2.3. The Testing Facility

In trying to optimize the costs of doing a statistically valid study the authors utilized the services of A.S.I. Market Research, Inc. This organization operates a market study complex known as the "Preview House" in Hollywood. This somewhat unique service (the company operates similar facilities in Florida and Japan) is primarily utilized by the television networks and television commercial studios to obtain independent and advance rating of their productions. The majority of television shows and commericals are audience tested in the Hollywood Preview House.

The Preview House processes over 3/4 of a million respondents through its theatre yearly. It has a skilled staff of demographers, data analysts experiment designers and engineers. Every night two or three clients pay to use a block of the 2 hour testing time with over 400 respondents in the theatre. The respondents that comprise the audience are recruited in the Los Angeles area by trained interviewers, who initially select the sample in the field by means of quota samples, based on desired characteristics of sex, age, or in certain cases a group selected by a client.

Statistically, the sample is not totally representative of the population of the Los Angeles Metropolitan area; it is usually biased toward younger age group, higher median income and higher education level. Nevertheless, the sample has proved reasonable reliable to make predictions about television commercials and shows not just regionally, but nationally. In general, however, the sample represents a reasonable cross section of the metropolitan population.

Prior to the beginning of the evenings testing each respondent fills out a comprehensive demographics questionnaire. The data from this questionnaire is provided to all the clients, in addition to their own test results. These negated the need for the authors to provide their own demographics questionnaire.

The Preview House also has additional response measurement tools, one of which is the Instantaneous Reaction Profile (IRP) Recorder. In this study the authors made use of the IRP Recorder (also called the Instantaneous Interest Measure). To use this tool a specially selected sub-sample of 150 persons is assigned to seats in the theatre which are equipped with dials for the Instantaneous Reaction Profile Recorder attached to the armrests. These respondents are instructed to manipulate their dials during each of the film sequences and to register their opinions of what they liked and disliked in each film. This represents somewhat of an adaptation of the device, which was intended to measure interest; however the principal of reaction is the same. Prior to the screening of the films the dial respondents

were shown a control film cartoon of Mr. Magoo, which has been used with every sample to establish a baseline response from the dials. As the films were shown during the experiment the IRP Recorder integrated and recorded the audience's instantaneous reactions to the film content in the form of profile curves.

The profile curves are measured on a scale ranging from 0 to 1000 with the normal position on the dial corresponding to the numerical value 500. The height of the resulting profile curve above or below this normal line is the measure of positive or negative response by the film. Readings are taken from the graph every five seconds, giving a more general description of the trends. The authors broke the sub-sample respondents into four groups; Total audience, male-female, under 25, 25 to 49, 50 plus and income over 1,250 dollars per month and below 1,250 dollars per month.

2.4. The Testing Process

The audience was informed that they were participating in a study being conducted by one of the larger local universities. Then the respondents were asked to fill out the preliminary location-activity-attitude questionnaire. These were then collected and everyone was asked to watch the following short films about the coastal area, and following the film to respond to the first questionnaire (Check-list and ratings). The dial-respondents were also asked to respond during the film and to respond to the questionnaire. This procedure was repeated for four films. The entire elapsed time for the adminstration of the four films, the instructions and the completion of responses was thirty minutes.

In order to analyze this IRP profile against specific contents of the films, a videotape of the film segments was made. Using a color video play back unit, and several stop watches, the authors timed the films on a linear montage of the panoramic photographs taken at each site noting the exact timing of the camera holds and panning sequences for each film, as well as the five second intervals from the commencement of each film. Transfering the data from the IRP Chart onto the graph below the panorama provided an indication of the vicinity in which the IRP responses were generated. (see Figure 1). The graphed responses to the film provide a comparison to the recall protocal and ratings for each film, suggesting possible relationships between immediate and retrospective evaluation of environmental characteristics.

3. FINDINGS

The findings presented in this paper are based on preliminary analysis of the output obtained from the Instantaneous Reaction Profile Recorder and the checklist and rating questionnaires

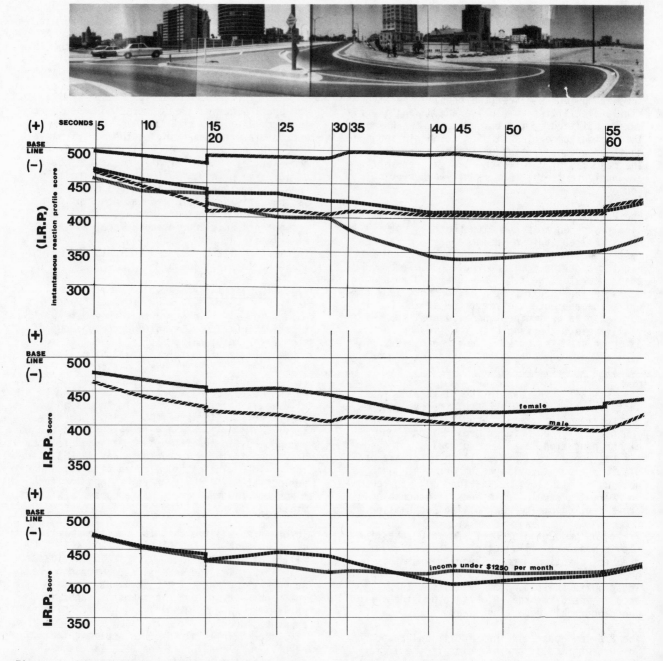

Figure 1. INSTANTANEOUS REACTION PROFILE SCORES BY SEX, AGE AND INCOME

provided after the showing of each film segment. Furthermore, this analysis will be limited to the audience reaction to the film segment taken in the Long Beach setting only.

The Long Beach film segment portrays a highly urbanized coastline, with a number of highrise apartment, office and hotel complexes. The remaining skyline consists of almost a solid wall of medium-rise buildings, which are mostly residential. The film was taken at a point where a recently finished coastal highway meets Ocean Avenue, one of the major thoroughfares

in the city. The film segment also includes views of a number of offshore oil islands, (cleverly camouflaged to look like landscaped parks with modern structures), vast expanses of sandy beach, parking lost, and some vacant areas. The celebrated oceanliner Queen Mary, (now permanently anchored in the Long Beach harbor) can also be seen in this film segment along with the derricks and cranes of the dock area, and the civic auditorium which looks like a giant oil storage tank. These elements can be recognized in the 360° panoramic view shown in Figure 2.

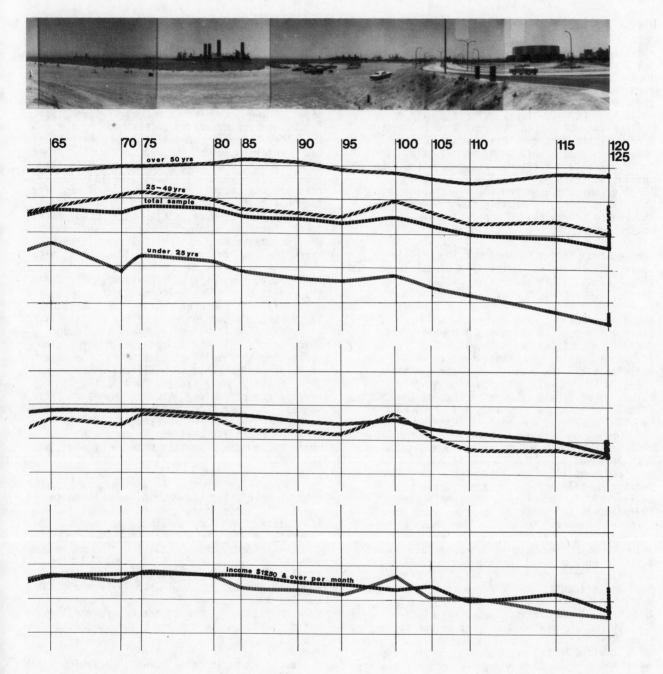

The three sets of graphs below the panoramic view of the Long Beach setting are based on instantaneous reaction profile scores for the audience broken down by age, sex and income respectively. Vertical lines represent intervals of 5 seconds; when two numbers appear on the same line, it means that the camera was held steady at that point for over 5 seconds. The fact that the vertical lines appear at uneven intervals merely reflects the fact that the camera movement was uneven, and that it was not always possible to strictly adhere to seven to eight seconds holding time, as planned orig-

inally. These variations are to be expected, since the camera movement was manually controlled.

The horizontal lines represent only a segment of the entire scale of instantaneous profile scores (which range from zero to 1000) within which the scores for this film segment were limited. These scores represent a normalized aggregate for the particular group of audience one is interested in. A score of 500 represents a neutral position, and always the time zero position, when all the dials are set at the middle location. If everyone in the audience turned their dial to the extreme left (negative reaction) the cumulative normalized score for the whole audience would be zero; if everyone in the audience turned their dial to the extreme right position (positive reaction) the cumulative normalized score for the whole audience would be 1000. Similarly, if every male member of the audience turned their dial to the extreme left position, the cumulative score for that population group would be 0, if all males turn their dials to the extreme right position, the cumulative score would be 1000, and so on. In these graphs the high profile score never went over 510 and the low profile score never under 250 (Hence it was not necessary to show the entire range of score in the diagram).

Some general trends in the reaction profile can be identified fairly easily from visual inspection. First, it is clear that as the film progressed, the negative reactions increased for the audience as a whole, and all other demographic groupings, with the exception of the older age group (50 and over). However, the decline in positive reaction was not uniform. It appears that as the water, water related activities and the beach become first visible there is an upturn in the reaction profile curve. However with the appearance of the islands, and parked cars in the foreground the negative reactions continue to increase. Second, the view of the water makes a sharp rise and that of the islands a sharp drop among the youth. The appearance of Queen Mary seems to have a sharp rise among audience who are between 25 and 49 years old, male and income are under 1250 dollars per month. Third, and significantly, there appears no major difference among those with income over 1250 dollars and those under 1250 dollars, in terms of overall reaction profile. Fourth, the male respondents seem to be a little more critical of the environment than the female respondents. Finally, and perhaps most significantly, the difference between the three age groups is quite dramatic. The youth appear to be most critical, and the old least critical (infact, almost indifferent, since their profile curve hovered around the 500 line throughout), while the middle age group seemed to lie in-between and similar to the overall audience profile. This difference seems to indicate that perhaps

there is a "generation gap" in critical attitudes and levels of tolerance toward high intensity development in the coastal area. We don't know the extent to which this may reflect difference in fundamental value orientations of the younger age group in contrast to the older age group. Perhaps the environmental movement that began in the late sixties and early seventies -- including such events as celebration of the Earth Day in college and school campuses -- has had greater impact on the youth more than other age groups. Perhaps this merely reflects the fact that the youth of Southern California treasure the coast more dearly than others, for they are most actively involved in the enjoyment of this resource, and so on. At any event, the difference in tolerance level toward manmade adaptations of the coastal zone certainly makes the task of indicator building difficult.

Admittedly, the descriptive interpretation of the reaction profiles in terms of the contents of the film is somewhat speculative, particularly since we did not know if the reaction time (i.e. the time it takes a subject to see something in the film and to register his reaction by turning the dial) was substantial. However, it is our belief that the collective reaction time probably never exceeded one or two seconds and did not effect our interpretations of broad scenes. For our interpretation seems to be independently confirmed by the data obtained brom the checklist part of the questionnaire which was handed out after showing of each film segment.

It will be recalled that in the checklist type questionnaire, the respondents were asked to check only those items they saw in the film and indicate whether they thought they were ugly or beautiful by marking the appropriate blanks. Thus, in effect, the checklist served at once a recall and an evaluative instrument. Tables I and II show the ranking of the elements that were checked as beautiful or ugly by the total sample, and various age groups. For brevity's sake only those elements checked by more than a third of the sample group are included in the Tables.

A close examination of Figure 1 and Tables I and II will reveal the consistency in responses

TABLE I. ELEMENTS OF COASTAL LANDSCAPE SEEN AS "BEAUTIFUL" (Rank ordered by frequency of mention) BY AGE GROUP 1

Total Sample (N=377)	Under 25 years (N=137)	25-49 years (N=152)	Over 50 years (N=88)
Water (65.8)	Water (64.2)	Water (65.8)	Water (68.2)
People in Beach (55.4)	People in Beach (63.5)	People in Beach (52.6)	Ships (51.1)
Beach/Sand/Dunes (48.5)	Beach/Sand/Dunes (56.9)	Ships (45.4)	People in Beach (47.7)
Ships (45.9)	Ships (43.1)	Beach/Sand/Dunes (43.4)	Beach/Sand/Dunes (44.3)
Distant View (36.6)	People in Water (42.3)		Large Structures (40.9)
People in Water (36.6)	Distant View (38.7)		Distant View (39.8)
	Islands (38.0)		Highrise Buildings (38.6)
	Sound of Waves (35.8)		Sound of Waves (34.1)

1 Figures within parentheses reflect percentages.

TABLE II: <u>ELEMENTS OF COASTAL LANDSCAPE SEEN AS "UGLY"</u> (<u>Rank ordered by frequency of mention</u>)
BY AGE GROUP 1

Total Sample (N=377)	Under 25 years (N=137)	25-49 years (N=152)	Over 50 years (N=88)
Sound of Traffic (54.9)	Sound of Traffic (65.7)	Parked Vehicles (55.3)	Oil Equipment (45.5)
Oil Equipment (52.8)	Highways (63.5)	Sould of Traffic (54.0)	Industrial Structs. (44.3)
Industrial Structs. (50.9)	Industrial Structs. (62.8)	Oil Equipment (50.7)	Sound of Traffic (39.8)
Parked Vehicles (49.1)	Oil Equipment (59.9)	Vacant Lots (50.7)	Vacant Lots (36.7)
Vacant Lots (47.0)	Large Structs. (56.9)	Parking Lots (49.3)	
Parking Losts (46.7)	Parking Lots (55.5)	Large Structs. (48.0)	
Large Structs. (46.4)	Parked Vehicles (54.0)	Industrial Structs. (44.1)	
Highways (45.1)	Street Fixtures (52.6)	Traffic (42.1)	
Traffic (41.6)	Utility Lines (51.8)	Highways (41.5)	
Construction (40.6)	Traffic (51.1)	Construction (40.8)	
Street Fixtures (37.9)	Vacant Lots (49.6)	Highrise Bldgs. (36.8)	
Highrise Bldgs. (37.9)	Construction (48.9)	Roads (34.2)	
Utility Lines (36.1)	Highrise Bldgs. (47.5)		
Roads (35.8)	Roads (46.0)		
	Offices (38.7)		

1 Figures within parentheses reflect percentages.

obtained through the dials and the checklist. For example, "water", "people in the beach", "beach/sand/dune" are three elements that appeared consistently at the top of the list of "beautiful" elements for all age groups. At the same time Figure 1 shows an upswing in the reaction profile curve for all age groups as soon as those elements become first visible around 55-60 seconds time period. The element "ship" appears consistently in this list also; again in Figure 1 we can see a sharp rise in the profile after Queen Mary, the only ship in the scene, appears in the film.

Similarly the decline of the reaction profile curve generally follows the list of "ugly" elements. For the sample as a whole, and for all other categories of respondents except for the older age group, the sharpest decline in the reaction profile curve takes place in the first 40 seconds which shows most of the elements that appear at the top of the "ugly" list: highways, parking lots, sound of traffic large structures, vacant lots, street fixtures, and so on.

An interesting discrepancy in Tables I and II are worth noting. While the "oil equipments" rate high in the "ugly" list among the under 25 age group, the "islands" appear in the "beautiful" list. In the Long Beach scene the "islands" (which are man-made) are also the oil derricks. We do not know how many of our respondents are aware of this fact. It will be our guess that most residents of the Southern California region are familiar with this fact from their everyday learning about the region from friends, media, and so forth. However, for a non-resident or a relatively newcomer this may not be immediately apparent. For, unlike the offshore oil platforms in the Santa Barbara channel, or Gulf of Mexico, there is nothing the Long Beach oil platforms that resembles the all familiar oil drilling equipments, because everything is so carefully camouflaged. We suspect

that the respondents (38.0 per cent of the under 25 age group) who checked the islands as beautiful responded to the architectural forms and landscaped appearance of the islands without knowing that they are actually oil platforms; on the other hand, those who recognized them as oil platforms probably checked them as "ugly" (59.9 percent of the under 25 age group).

Despite occasional upswings, it must be noted, the overall reaction profile managed to remain in the negative zone (under 500) for the total sample and most other categories of respondents with the exception of the over 50 age group. This negative evaluation is generally confirmed. by Table III which shows the overall evaluation of that particular film segment obtained by means of the separate questionnaire handed out after the showing of the film.

4. SOME OBSERVATIONS

In this paper we have reported the data obtained from the instantaneous interest measurement instrument for only one film segment. We would of course expect different patterns of overall responses for the other three film segments which present completely different types of coastal settings; an undeveloped natural setting; a marina that shows residential and recreational uses; an industrial site on the coastline. If similar differences among groups persist, our speculation about generational differences in attitudes and perceptions will be strengthened substantially. Reactions to specific elements in the setting will also be noted to see if similar elements consistently evoke positive or negative reactions. If such consistent patterns can be found, a case for identifying those elements as the key aesthetic indicators can be made with some degree of confidence.

TABLE III.   OVERALL EVALUATION OF THE LONG BEACH SEGMENT BY SEX, AGE AND INCOME

AUDIENCE STUDIES
ENVIRONMENTAL FILM   L5-5901 11   IN-THEATER   07/30/75
MARINA/LEO CARILLO/LONG BEACH/SCATTER

	TOTAL AUDIENCE	MALES	FEMALES	TOT AUD UNDER 25	TOT AUD 25-49	TOT AUD 50&OVER	INCOME $1250 OR MORE	INCOME UNDER $1250
	(01)	(02)	(03)	(04)	(05)	(06)	(07)	(08)

"LONG BEACH"

DESCRIBE LOCATION   **

	TOTAL AUDIENCE	MALES	FEMALES	TOT AUD UNDER 25	TOT AUD 25-49	TOT AUD 50&OVER	INCOME $1250 OR MORE	INCOME UNDER $1250
EXTREMELY BEAUTIFUL	13 3.45%	3 2.00%	10 4.41%	4 2.92%	4 2.63%	5 5.68%	4 2.65%	9 4.19%
SOMEWHAT BEAUTIFUL	68 18.04%	24 16.00%	44 19.38%	12 8.76%	29 19.08%	27 30.68%	30 19.87%	35 16.28%
NEITHER BEAUTIFUL NOR UGLY	102 27.06%	45 30.00%	57 25.11%	46 33.58%	34 22.37%	22 25.00%	35 23.18%	63 29.30%
SOMEWHAT UGLY	111 29.44%	45 30.00%	66 29.07%	45 32.85%	54 35.53%	12 13.64%	52 34.44%	58 26.98%
EXTREMELY UGLY	34 9.02%	12 8.00%	22 9.69%	16 11.68%	15 9.87%	3 3.41%	15 9.93%	19 8.84%
NO ANSWER	49 13.00%	21 14.00%	28 12.33%	14 10.22%	16 10.53%	19 21.59%	15 9.93%	31 14.42%
* TOTAL RESPONDENTS	328 87.00%	129 86.00%	199 87.67%	123 89.78%	136 89.47%	69 78.41%	136 90.07%	184 85.58%

Aside from substantive findings of this study pertaining to our search for aesthetic indicators of coastal environments, we are quite encouraged by the potentials of audience response format in future studies dealing with direct user responses to environmental displays. It is now generally agreed that survey research is becoming an extremely expensive tool for research, particularly if no compromise in sampling design is allowed. We might add parenthetically however that very few studies can maintain that degree of rigor. At any event, the cost of collecting 377 interviews would have been exorbitantly high if we had to do it by means of survey research. While we were not able to obtain a true representative sample of the region, we did have a sample that had some empirical credibility based on past experiences of the Preview House. Since we could not have undertaken a full-fledged survey research within the resources we had, we feel that the trade-off has been worthwhile.

Authors' Note: The research upon which this paper is based was supported by the National Oceanic and Atmosphoric Administration of the United States Department of Commerce, Grant No. 04-3-158-36.

references

CRAIK, KENNETH H., The Comprehension of the Everyday Physical Environment. Journal of the American Institute of Planners, Vol. 34, No. 1, January 1968.

LOZAR, CHARLES C., Measurement Techniques Toward A Measurement Technology. Daniel H. Carson (ed.) Man-Environment Interactions: Evaluations and Applications, Stroudsburg, Pa: Dowden, Hutchinson and Ross, 1975.

OFFICE OF RESEARCH AND DEVELOPMENT, United States Environmental Protection Agency. Aesthetics in Environmental Planning, EPA-600/5-73-009, Washington, D.C., November 1973.

SECTION 3

Environment and Behavior

Papers in this section represent a different theoretical perspective than those in the last section. Here, the concern is with linking environments directly to important overt behaviours (and thus bypassing any concern with intervening perceptual or cognitive process). Behavior is defined in a broad sense to include a range of human activities from momentary feelings to relatively stable social patterns or life styles. These papers cut across traditional disciplinary lines in a way that has become characteristic of behavioural science efforts concerned with environmental problems. In addition, many of them contain cogent discussions of the potential uses and misuses of behavioural data and conclusions in the design process.

The first four papers present field studies concerned with the effects on behaviour of various aspects of restricted, institutional environments. The papers by Stokols and Marrero and by Rosenbloom provide new examples of the effects of local architectural features on patterns of social behaviour. In a fine example of field research, Stokols and Marrero examine racial polarization in a youth training school. They

found an interesting mixture of positive and negative effects of a change to a more sociopetal furniture arrangement in the school's day room. Rosenbloom studied the effects of sociopetal versus sociofugal furniture arrangements, as did Stokols and Marrero, but also studied the use of portable barriers to create open or enclosed spaces within a college student lounge. Enclosing the space resulted in the formation of groups that were smaller, stayed longer, and interacted with each other less, than groups in the open space.

Presthold, Taylor, and Shannon observed inmates and staff of a women's prison as they moved from an old, crowded, dilapidated facility to an elaborate, new complex--with somewhat discouraging results. The design of the "ideal" modern prison resulted in fewer contacts between staff and inmates and in this way probably hindered the rehabilitative ability of the institution. Finally, Sims used a more exploratory interview technique to study environmental effects on the effectiveness of a halfway house for parolled prisoners. He suggests that, indeed, privacy, appearance, noise, and other building and site features are important influences on both the programme and its relationship to the surrounding neighborhood.

The next seven papers are concerned with the influence of larger units of the environment-- units ranging from neighbourhoods to regions within a state. Fish compares neighbourhoods that differ in the degree to which the residents were homogeneous or heterogeneous in socioeconomic status. She reports that heterogeneity relates to satisfaction with place of residence and to a variety of social behaviour patterns.

Grabow and Salkind, in investigating the "hidden structure" of childrens' play, show that children not only know their urban neighborhood in some detail, but also use its elements creatively in play, often ignoring the more conventional play structures provided. Taylor and Hall discuss the effect of various aspects of community design on subjective noise ratings. They provide interesting data on the apparent inability of residents to adapt to freeway traffic noise and on the inadequacy of building design alone to reduce noise impact.

Passino and Lounsbury report some fairly dramatic sex differences in responses to a proposed community-wide environmental change: a nuclear power plant. In a somewhat more qualitative study of a neglected type of planned community, Alanen traces the evolution of a planned company town over a period of 60 years. Current residents show great satisfaction with, and a sensitive awareness of, the design elements originally used in planning the town. A similar type of social-evolutionary study of a small, no-growth, industrial city is reported by Greenbie, who then suggests an ethological model, with suggested policies for the city's future growth that preserve the positive, stable aspects of its present social and environmental situation. In the final paper of this group, Jobes discusses the problems of implementing planned resource development on a regional level and reports a survey of residents' attitudes towards land use and development.

The last three papers of this section are concerned with methods of obtaining data needed for input to design decisions. Reischl and Reischl discuss a radio-telemetry system for the simultaneous collection of information about both environmental parameters and a variety of physiological measures of human functioning. Stahl describes the development and preliminary evaluation of a simulation model of human behaviour in high-rise building fires. His paper has broad implications for the usefulness of such methodologies in other areas as well, and may provide the means to avoid some costly design mistakes. And in the final paper of this section, Biel describes his very interesting Journey to Work Game, in which players examine their own choices among transportation modes and routes along their journey to work. In this way, players observe the effects of transportation policy and urban location on commuting behaviour.

THE EFFECTS OF AN ENVIRONMENTAL INTERVENTION ON RACIAL POLARIZATION IN A YOUTH TRAINING SCHOOL[1]

Daniel Stokols and David G. Marrero
Program in Social Ecology
University of California, Irvine

ABSTRACT

The effects of a shift from sociofugal to sociopetal (Osmond, 1957) furniture arrangements on racial polarization in a youth training school were assessed through a quasi field-experiment. The occupants of a control and an experimental dayroom were observed over repeated measurement periods for one month before and one month after the furniture rearrangement. Results provided partial support for the major hypotheses, indicating that within the experimental dayroom, levels of positive interracial contact and favorable evaluations of staff increased while, at the same time, disruptive behavior increased and levels of overt aggression, racial polarization (spatial), ratings of general satisfaction and of fellow inmates remained unchanged. The implications of these findings for future interventions in correctional settings are discussed.

There appears to be growing sentiment among members of the criminal justice professions that traditional and time-worn modes of correctional rehabilitation have been monumentally ineffective. This increasingly self-critical sentiment is reflected in the recent writings of both prison officials and researchers in the field of criminology.

Martinson (1974) reviews the findings from 231 studies that evaluated correctional treatment methods during 1945-1967 and concludes that none provides any evidence for the effectiveness of educational and counseling programs in reducing recidivism rates among juvenile and adult offenders. Sykes (1958) contends that the correctional environment poses a continual threat to the inmate's identity and self-concept. Wright (1973) portrays prisons in America as fortresses of racial prejudice and violence. And, while critics such as Sykes and Wright have focused upon the appalling social conditions existing within contemporary prisons, Nagel (1973) presents a comprehensive critique of the dilapidated and dysfunctional physical conditions existing within the majority of correctional facilities built since the Nineteenth Century.

The present research coincides with a burgeoning interest in the field of corrections concerning the impact of physical and social conditions in prisons on the health and behavior of inmates. Specifically, the effects of an architectural intervention on patterns of racial polarization are examined within a youth detention facility.

Previous research on correctional treatment has not examined the effects of prison design on racial polarization. Yet, despite the lack of scientific data concerning the specific relationship between prison architecture and inmate behavior, an increasing amount of research on environment and behavior is being implemented in non-correctional settings. The findings from this research provide a potential basis on which to develop and test correctional interventions designed to reduce behavioral and psychological problems among prison inmates.

Increased awareness of ecological problems throughout the world contributed to the emergence in 1970 of environmental psychology, or the systematic study of the ways in which physical and social dimensions of the environment affect individual and group behavior (Craik, 1970; Proshansky, Ittelson, and Rivlin, 1970; Wohlwill, 1970). Environmental-psychological research places a strong emphasis on the use of naturalistic, longitudinal methods of observation as a means of examining the longterm behavioral effects of natural and man-made environments.

Among the issues investigated by environmental psychologists are the effects of noise, crowding, and architectural features on human task performance and social interaction. One of the most extensively studied problems in the field is the manner in which architectural arrangements affect patterns of social behavior. Three programs of research are particularly relevant to this concern: Sommer's (1969, 1972, 1974) research on the interior arrangements of institutional facilities, the work of Festinger, Schachter, and Back (1950) on the relationship between residential proximity, friendship formation, and attitude change, and the research of Deutsch and Collins (1956) on the reduction of racial prejudice through desegregation of housing projects.

Sommer has conducted numerous studies concerning the effects of furniture arrangements in a variety of settings including hospital wards, airport lounges, and health-care facilities for the aged. Much of this research has been based upon Osmond's (1957, 1959) distinction between "sociopetal" and "sociofugal" environments. The arrangement of the former environments (e.g., dormitory lounges) tends to encourage social interaction whereas that of the latter settings (e.g., libraries) operate to limit interpersonal encounters. The general pattern of findings from Sommer's research is that levels of group cohesion and invdividual well-being can be heightened in institutional settings by shifting from linear, sociofugal arrangements of furniture to clustered, sociopetal designs. The basic explanation for such findings is that sociopetal environments foster eye contact, increase the likelihood of conversation, and thereby contribute to the development of sustained interaction patterns among occupants of the setting.

The research conducted by Festinger, Schachter, and Back focused on the dimension of residential proximity as an antecedent of friendship formation and attitude change. The study was carried out on the campus of the Massachusetts Institute of Technology. Residents of a married-student housing complex were interviewed to determine whether their closest friends were in fact those neighbors whose apartments were nearest to their own. The results of the study revealed a strong association between the distances separating the front doors of various apartments and the friendship choices reported among residents of the housing complex. Moreover, residential proximity was found to be highly correlated with attitude similarity among the residents.

The research of Deutsch and Collins explored the effects of racial desegregation in New York and Newark apartment buildings on the prejudicial attitudes of white residents. The study compared the attitudes of residents living in both segregated and integrated buildings and found that the latter group displayed a reduction in racial prejudice following the desegregation of their apartment complex. These results were explained in terms of "equal-status contact theory." It was reasoned by the authors that proximity with same-status members of a previously-devalued group provided the prejudiced person with an opportunity to observe outsiders in activities which were similar to his/her own routine (e.g., engagement in parental roles). Such experiences enabled individuals to view others as more similar to themselves and, therefore, less deserving of scorn.

All of the above studies emphasize the positive value of interpersonal proximity in promoting prosocial behavior and suggest at least one type of architectural intervention that might be applied in correctional settings as a means of decreasing racial polarization: namely, the substitution of sociopetal furniture arrangements in recreational areas for those that are socio-fugal in nature. This type of environmental change was employed as the experimental intervention in the present study. In line with earlier research, the major experimental hypotheses were as follows:

Subsequent to a shift from sociofugal to socio-petal furniture arrangement, the users of the sociopetal area will display (H1) less aggression, (H2) more positive interracial contact and reduced racial polarization, and (H3) more favorable ratings of satisfaction with the institution in general and, more specifically, with staff and peers, than those occupants of a comparable area in which sociopetal arrangements have not been implemented.

METHOD

Setting

The present research was conducted at the

California Youth Training School (YTS) in Chino, California. The residents of YTS are incarcerated for charges ranging from minor offenses (e.g., incorrigibility) to major crimes (e.g., armed robbery, assault with a deadly weapon, and murder).

The school consists of three living units, each housing 400 persons. Each unit is divided into four teams, a team being comprised of two companies with 50 residents apiece. Each team is characterized by the particular orientation of its program, for example, drug rehabilitation, intensive treatment, security (protective custody), and college program.

Individual companies are assigned to their own dayrooms which are equipped with such facilities as a television set, ping-pong table, tables, chairs and water fountain. Each team also has access to an outdoor recreational yard with a volleyball net, punching bags and weight lifting equipment. Data from the present study were gathered during the evening hours when the majority of residents from each of two companies occupied the dayrooms assigned to their team.

Subjects

Subjects for this study were chosen from Companies C and D of Living Unit I. Residents of C company comprised the experimental population and those of D company, the control population. Companies C and D were selected as the research groups due to their similarities on a number of dimensions. First, most of the residents from these companies were involved in the YTS college program. Second, the physical arrangements of the dayrooms for these companies and the staff policies regarding inmates' usage of these areas were identical. And, third, the ages of the inmates in Companies C and D were comparable (between 18 and 24) and the membership of both companies represented a cross-section of four racial or ethnic groups, i.e., Blacks, Mexican-American, Caucasian and Oriental. Each company reflected approximately the same ethnic ratio, which, while subject to fluctuation, displayed consistency throughout the study. The average ethnic composition of company C, for example, was 24 Blacks, 14 Mexican-Americans, 8 Caucasians and 4 Orientals. D company's composition was nearly identical.

Despite these similarities, Companies C and D were unavoidably different in certain respects. Most notably, the frequency of aggressive inter-racial encounters had been higher in Company C than in Company D, for several months prior to the initiation of this research. This difference, in fact, was the basis on which Company C was designated as the experimental group, and Company D as the control.

Independent variables

The study incorporated a single between-groups factor, furniture rearrangement, and one within-group factor, time. The experimental group received a restructuring of the semifixed features in the room designed to encourage positive interracial interaction and reduce racial polarity (See Figures 1 and 2). The experimental intervention was based upon both theoretical considerations (i.e., the distinction between sociofugal vs. sociopetal architecture) and (2) patterns of racial territoriality observed in the dayrooms during a period of baseline data collection.

Specifically, it seemed clear from our initial observations that the dayrooms for Companies C and D were divided into ethnic and racial territories. For example, in both dayrooms, Blacks typically occupied the rows of chairs directly in front of the T.V., whereas the Caucasians, Mexican-Americans and Orientals generally claimed separate groupings of chairs

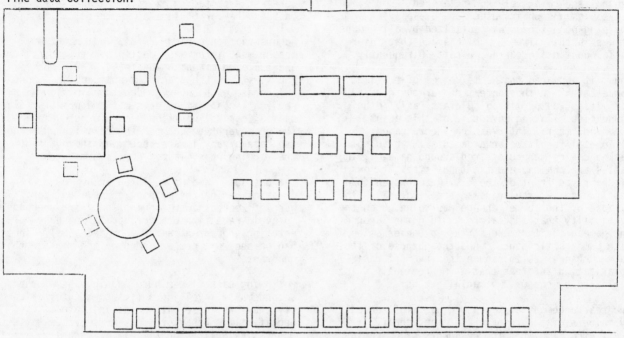

FIGURE 1: SOCIOFUGAL ARRANGEMENT OF THE DAYROOM (DIAGRAM DEPICTS THE ARRANGEMENT OF DAYROOM C PRIOR TO THE INTERVENTION, AND OF DAYROOM D THROUGHOUT THE STUDY)

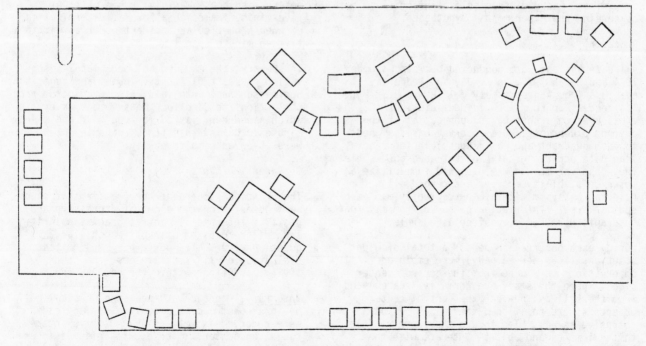

FIGURE 2: SOCIOPETAL ARRANGMENT OF FURNITURE IMPLEMENTED IN EXPERIMENTAL DAYROOM C

lined up against the rear wall of the room
(See Figure 1). It was further evident that
such racial territories were consistently maintained and that territorial violations were infrequent.

At the same time, however, it was noted that
certain areas of the dayroom were racially
neutral and relatively non-polarized. For example,
the tables and chairs used for game-playing and
the ping-pong tables were utilized by all groups.
It was in this "free", public space that interracial contacts occurred, albeit infrequently.

Thus, it appeared that some degree of "relaxed
competition" in the context of various game
activities was permitted to cross racial/ethnic
boundaries. Taking advantage of this point,
the experimental intervention incorporated
sociopetal furniture arrangements in which soft-
backed chairs were clustered around game-playing
tables and chairs, and the three straight rows
of chairs in front of the T.V. were broken down
into two semi-circular rows (See Figure 2). The
purpose of the former change was to heighten the
possibility that spectators would gather around
the game activities and strike up conversation
with game participants. And the purpose of the
latter change was to reduce the level of racial
polarization in areas that were previously
dominated by one or two racial groups.

The rearrangement of Dayroom C was implemented
by members of the research team and the YTS
staff at a time when the residents of Companies
C and D were attending classes, and their respective dayrooms were unoccupied. It should be
noted that at no time were the dayroom staff in
Companies C and D given specific information
concerning the experimental hypotheses.

Procedure

All observations were conducted between November
1974 and March 1975, on Monday and Wednesday
evenings from approximately 7:15 PM to 9:30 PM.
The recreation room was divided into four
equal-area quadrants based upon copies of the
dayroom blueprints. One observer was assigned
to each quadrant and was responsible for recording data occurring only in that quadrant. This
four-observer method was designed to maximize an
observer's ability to view and record all
relevant behavior within a perceptually-manageable
spatial area. Information gathered from all four
quadrants was then composited as a whole.

During each observation period a total of eight
observers (four per company) were employed. All
observations were done from the control center
(i.e., where the staff are normally located) and
from the hallways nearest the control center.
Observers were positioned there to be as unobtrusive as possible, though they were visible
to the inmates and able to interact with them.
Inquiries from the inmates concerning the purpose
of this research were answered by observers with
the response that they were architecture students

studying the use of furniture and activities in
the dayroom in order to facilitate the design
of better recreational rooms in the future. At
no time were the inmates given specific information
about the experimental hypotheses. While the
presence of visible observers may have resulted
in Hawthorne effects, these effects seemed equally
likely to occur in Dayrooms C and D and thus,
were not expected to exert differential effects
on the behavior of inmates in these two rooms.

An observation period was divided into four
measurement intervals (designated t_1, t_2, t_3,
and t_4) each of which consisted of two phases.
The first was the spatial mapping phase. During
this phase each observer drew upon a floor-plan
replication any fixed or semifixed objects (e.g.,
tables, chairs) positioned in his/her quadrant.
The observer then charted the relative position
and race of any inmate occupying the quadrant.
The mapping phase lasted for five minutes.

Because some inmates would enter or leave the
quadrant during the mapping phase, the maps
were "fixed" at four minutes and thirty-seconds
to avoid repeating or overlapping measures. Those
entering a quadrant after four and a half-minutes
had passed were not recorded on the map for that
quadrant.

Following each five-minute mapping phase, the
second phase involving a fifteen-minute period
of behavioral observation was initiated.
Specifically, behaviors that were judged to be
aggressive, either physically or verbally, were
recorded as were any positive interracial contacts. Both rates of incidence and racial composition were recorded. Each fifteen-minute
observation phase was divided into three
five-minute frames to allow for determination
of when a particular incident occurred within a
fifteen minute span.

In summary, the mapping and behavioral observation phases took twenty minutes and constituted
one measurement interval. Each evening of data
collection included four measurement intervals
which, together, lasted for one hour and twenty
minutes. During this time, Companies C and D
were observed simultaneously.

Dependent Measures

The principal dependent measures in this study
were observational indices of aggressive and
positive interracial contact, racial polarity,
archival records of disruptive behavior, and
questionnaire scales pertaining to inmates
evaluation of YTS staff, peers, and general
living conditions within the institution.

Interracial contact. Verbal and physical behaviors construed as unequivocably aggressive
were recorded as well as any positive interracial encounters. Three categories of interracial contact were charted: verbal interaction
between inmates and staff, verbal interaction
between inmates, and physical encounters between

inmates.

Within each behavioral category, the number and ethnicity of the interactants were recorded as well as the quality of the interaction. Thus, a notation of "-2B1W" under category "Phys-In" indicated that two Black inmates and one White inmate were engaged in an aggressive physical encounter.

Aggressive acts were defined as those which were blatantly hostile in tone, e.g., one inmate physically assaulting another in a clearly non-joking manner; or a verbal assault with raised voice (yelling) and expressive body gestures (clenched fists, extreme proximity, etc.). Positive interracial contacts were defined as any non-aggressive interaction between the members of two or more racial groups.

All aggressive encounters were charted, regardless of racial composition. Positive interactions, both verbal and physical, were recorded only if they occurred interracially. Among the kinds of positive interaction recorded were extended conversations (tabulated as one incident per time interval), game-playing activities, and friendly backslapping.

The levels of aggressive and non-aggressive interaction were analyzed separately. Within each observation period, the number of negative and positive contact occurring in each quadrant of the dayroom were summed to yield interaction total-scores for t_1, t_2, t_3, and t_4 These scores were utilized as the main units of data analysis regarding interracial contact.

Racial Polarity. Racial polarization was defined as the spatial clustering and separation of ethnic groups within the dayroom.

The index of polarity for each dayroom quadrant was derived by calculating the extent to which the percentages of Blacks, Mexican-American, Caucasians, and Orientals found in the quadrant deviated from the actual ratio of these groups reflected among the total number of inmates occupying the dayroom during the observation period. Thus, if the membership of a particular quad was 90% Black and 10% Oriental, whereas the composition of the dayroom was 40% Black, 30% Mexican-American, 20% Caucasian, and 10% Oriental, the polarity index for the quad would be 100 (i.e., the total absolute value of all deviation scores: B-B, M-M, C-C, and O-O).

For each of the four mapping phases within an observation period, a polarity score for each quadrant of the dayroom was derived. The four quadrant scores within each fifteen-minute interval were averaged to yield a mean index of racial polarity at t_1, t_2, t_3, and t_4. These mean-scores served as the primary units of analysis in assessing patterns of racial polarization within the dayrooms.

Disruptive behavior. All forms of disruptive behavior occurring within Companies C and D before and after the experimental intervention were counted from available institutional records. These records were compiled by staff, who, in connection with their regular duties, formally reported the occurrence of unusually disruptive events. Among the behaviors listed as disruptive were assaults on staff or inmates, possession of weapons, stealing, attempted escape, bribery, malingering, and failure to follow safety or sanitation rules.

Questionnaire data. The fourth set of dependent measures employed in this study included separate clusters of seven-point semantic differential scales. These scales pertained to inmates'overall satisfaction with living conditions at YTS as compared to the conditions at similar correctional facilities; their feelings toward the staff; and their evaluations of fellow inmates. A supplementary set of open-ended items probed residents' opinions about the best and worst features of their living situation, and the types of design changes they would like to have implemented in their dayroom settings.

The questionnaire scales were administered individually to randomly selected samples of residents in Companies C and D both prior and subsequent to the experimental intervention.[3] The open-ended items were administered only after the intervention had been implemented. The semantic-differential data were tabulated as follows: For each person, item responses were averaged within clusters to yield separate summary scores on the dimensions of residential satisfaction, staff ratings, and evaluation of peers. Subsequently, individuals' summary scares within each racial group were averaged to yield four group means (Black, Mexican-American, Caucasian, Oriental) on each dimension of response. These group summary-scores served as the major units of data analysis.

Research Schedule

Prior to the commencement of the research, observers attended a series of instructional sessions designed to acquaint them with the observational protocols. Subsequently, a preliminary series of observations was conducted in the dayroom settings to assess the statistical reliability of the behavioral measures used in the study. Reliability data was collected during five observational sessions conducted during November, 1974.

The collection of baseline data commenced during late January, 1975 and extended through February, 1975. The experimental intervention was implemented in Dayroom C on March 3, 1975. Observational recordings were made during four pre-intervention and four post-intervention sessions. It should be noted that in Dayroom C, the experimental rearrangement of furniture remained relatively constant throughout the four-week period of post-intervention observations.

Questionnaires and structured interviews were administered on February 26th, 1975 (pre) and on March 19, 1975 (post).

RESULTS

All behavioral and questionnaire data were analyzed in terms of repeated-measures multivariate analysis of variance (MANOVA) with one between-groups factor, furniture arrangement.

An assumption underlying the use of MANOVA procedures was that all summary scores within each experimental group and within each time frame were statistically independent. To assess the degree of statistical dependence among data cases within each cell of the design, specific control procedures were employed in analyzing both the behavioral and questionnaire data.

In the analysis of the behavioral data, a preliminary repeated-measures MANOVA (measurement intervals X furniture arrangement) was performed to determine whether the four summary scores obtained during each evening of observation (t_1, t_2, t_3 and t_4) were confounded by temporal trends. The results of this analysis indicated the absence of linear, quadratic, or cubic effects on the data, as well as any interaction effects involving these temporal components and the between-groups factor. Subsequently, the summary scores derived within each of the original, eight observation periods were collapsed into four assessment phases for the primary repeated-measures analysis (phase X furniture arrangement) involving an assessment of inmates' pre- and post-intervention behavior (Phases I and II being comprised of pre-intervention data from periods 1-4, and Phases III and IV of post-intervention data from periods 5-8). This procedure insured that data collected during at least two different evenings were included within each time frame of analysis.

In the analyses of the questionnaire data, summary mean-scores for four ethnic groups (Black, Mexican-American, Caucasian, and Oriental) were computed on the basis of data collected from individual inmates in Companies C and D both before and after the experimental intervention. The ethnic mean-scores then were analyzed in terms of a three-way (ethnicity X furniture arrangement X time) repeated-measures MANOVA. No main effects or interaction effects involving the ethnicity factor were obtained. On the basis of this analysis, the ethnic group summary-scores were treated as independent data cases within each time frame and treatment group. The primary analysis of the data, thus, involved a two-way (furniture arrangement X time) repeated-measures MANOVA[5].

Analyses of Behavioral Data

Reliability of behavioral measures. To assess interobserver reliability on measures of racial polarization and interracial contact, two independent observers were assigned to the same dayroom quadrant[6]. The degree of correlation between the observers' recordings of aggression, positive interaction, and polarization during each measurement interval was computed. Correlation coefficients for each measure during each interval were averaged to yield summary reliability scores for each observational period. The mean reliability scores obtained during each of the five observation periods then were averaged to yield overall reliability coefficients for each measure.

The reliability coefficients for the summated index of verbal and physical aggression were 1.00, .95, .99, 1.00, and .98 yielding an overall reliability coefficient of .98. For the measure of positive interracial encounters, the coefficients were .77, .90, .91, .86, and .92 yielding on average reliability coefficient of .87. And, for the index of racial polarization, individual reliability scores were .90, .89, .93, .85, and .84 with an overall reliability coefficient of .90.

Reliability data for the disruptive-behavior measure were not available.

Verbal and physical aggression. According to the first experimental hypothesis, levels of aggression in Dayroom C would exhibit a post-intervention decrease and, in Dayroom D, would remain at the same level during the pre- and post-intervention phases. Contrary to expectation, the occurrence of overt aggression was quite infrequent and not noticeably different in the two dayrooms. In Dayroom C, one aggressive incident occurred during Phase I, two during Phase II, and two during Phase III. In Dayroom D, only one such incident was observed during Phase I, and one during Phase IV. The minimal occurrence of aggressive behavior contributed to an elevated coefficient of reliability (.98) on the summary index of aggression, but precluded statistical analysis of the data.

Positive interracial contact and racial polarization. The second experimental hypothesis predicted that within Dayroom C, the frequency of positive interracial encounters following the experimental intervention. The levels of interaction and polarization in Dayroom D, however, were expected to remain unchanged subsequent to the intervention. In MANOVA terms, a significant treatment X linear-trend interaction effect was expected on the two measures.

The mean levels of positive interracial contact and racial polarization during all observation periods of the study are presented in Tables 1 and 2, respectively. The collapsed mean scores for the two measures during Phases I, II, III, and IV of the investigation are shown in Figures 3 and 4.

TABLE 1: <u>MEAN LEVELS OF POSITIVE INTERRACIAL CONTACT IN DAYROOMS C AND D DURING PRE-INTERVENTION AND POST-INTERVENTION PHASES OF THE INVESTIGATION</u>[a]

Dayroom	Observation Period							
	Pre-1	Pre-2	Pre-3	Pre-4	Post-1	Post-2	Post-3	Post-4
C	8.25	8.00	2.75	12.75	9.00	5.50	11.75	6.75
D	1.25	1.75	.75	0.00	6.75	9.00	3.00	3.25

a. Larger means indicate higher levels of positive interaction.

TABLE 2: <u>MEAN LEVELS OF RACIAL POLARIZATION IN DAYROOMS C AND D DURING PRE-INTERVENTION AND POST-INTERVENTION PHASES OF THE INVESTIGATION</u>[a]

Dayroom	Observation Period							
	Pre-1	Pre-2	Pre-3	Pre-4	Post-1	Post-2	Post-3	Post-4
C	68.10	75.30	106.20	69.00	94.10	85.70	59.80	46.90
D	73.50	87.40	127.60	101.60	101.30	85.60	82.80	68.60

a. Larger means indicate higher levels of racial polarization.

These data suggest that the levels of interracial contact and racial polarization were markedly different within Dayrooms C and D both before and after the experimental intervention.

Evidence for the significance of between groups differences on measures of interaction and polarization is presented in Table 3 (multivariate $F_{(2,13)}$ = 63.28, p < .001). Significantly higher levels of positive interracial contact ($F_{(1,14)}$ = 135.85, p < .001) and lower levels of racial polarization ($F_{(1,14)}$ = p < .007) were exhibited by the occupants of Dayroom C than by those of Dayroom D.

The above findings do not indicate whether the behavioral differences observed among members of Dayrooms C and D were attributable to experimental or non-experimental sources of variation. Results from the within-groups analyses, though, provide a more specific assessment of the effects of the experimental intervention (see Table 3).

The within-groups analyses revealed a significant, multivariate linear trend indicating that levels of interracial contact increased while those of racial polarization decreased throughout all phases of the research ($F_{(2,13)}$ = 8.12, p < .005). Significant univariate linear trends were evident for interracial contact ($F_{(1,14)}$ = 4.94, p < .043) and racial polarization ($F_{(1,14)}$ = 7.81, p < .014).

The observed linear trends were qualified by a significant quadratic trend (multivariate $F_{(2,11)}$ = 6.50, p < .014) and a marginally-significant treatment X quadratic interaction effect (multivariate $F_{(2,11)}$ = 3.14, p < .08). Inspection of the univariate results revealed a significant quadratic trend on the index of polarization, such that levels of polarization in Dayrooms C and D increased prior to the experimental intervention and decreased subsequent to it ($F_{(1,13)}$ = 17.06, p < .001). Moreover, a significant treatment X quadratic interaction effect on levels of interracial contact was found, indicating that a gradual rise in interaction levels occurred in Dayroom C whereas an initial rise and subsequent decline in levels of interaction occurred in Dayroom D ($F_{(1,13)}$ = 7.18, p < .019).

The interactive effect of the furniture-arrangement factor and the quadratic component provides some evidence that the between-groups differences between Dayroom C and D were attributable in part, at least, to experimental sources of variance.

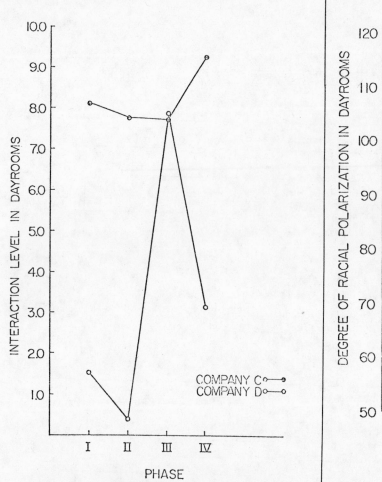

FIGURE 3: MEAN LEVELS OF POSITIVE INTERRACIAL CONTACT DURING EACH PHASE OF THE INVESTIGATION

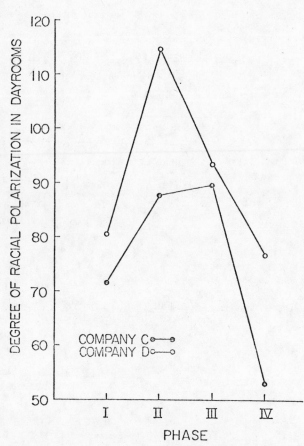

FIGURE 4: MEAN LEVELS OF RACIAL POLARIZATION DURING EACH PHASE OF THE INVESTIGATION

TABLE 3: MULTIVARIATE ANALYSIS OF VARIANCE ON REPEATED MEASURES OF POSITIVE INTERRACIAL CONTACT AND RACIAL POLARIZATION OVER PHASES I, II, III, AND IV OF THE STUDY

Source	Uni-variate df	Positive Contact		Polarization		Multivariate F
		MS	F	MS	F	
Between Groups						
Exptl. Treatment (E)	1	95.06	135.85****	987.21	9.80***	63.28****
Error Between	14	.70		100.76		
Within Groups a						
Linear Component (L)	1	930.25	4.94**	29523.64	7.81**	8.12***
E x L	1	360.99	1.92	2.23	<1.00	<1.00
Error Within (Linear)	14	188.35		3778.07		
Quadratic Component (Q)	1	63.67	1.97	21758.48	17.06****	6.50**
E x Q	1	231.53	7.18**	2.23	<1.00	3.14*
Error Within (Quadratic)	13 b	32.26		1275.26		

a. Tests of cubic component and related interactions yielded statistically insignificant results.

b. Tests of quadratic component and related interactions performed using the linear score as a covariate.

        * p < .10   ** p < .05   *** p < .01   **** p < .001

Disruptive behavior. Since the reliability of this measure was indeterminate, no statistical analyses were performed on the related data. Nonetheless, because of its unobtrusiveness, the disruptive-behavior index was viewed as a useful supplement to the observational measures used in this research.

The total numbers of recorded disruptive behaviors occurring within Companies C and D before the experimental intervention (between January 30-March 2, 1975) were 37 and 38, respectively. Subsequent to the intervention (between March 3-April 5, 1975), 48 disruptive events were recorded in Company C and 35 in Company D. These data suggest that the rearrangement of furniture within Dayroom C led to a rise in the incidence of disruptive behavior among members of Company C.

Interestingly, the magnitude of change in disruptive behavior between pre- and post-intervention periods was quite different for the Black, Mexican-American, Caucasian, and Oriental groups. Within Company C, the amounts of change in disruptive behavior between pre and post assessment periods were +15, -5, +1 and 0 for the above groups respectively. Within Company D, the

corresponding change scores were 2, -4, -3, and 0. Thus, the post-intervention rise in disruptive behavior was greatest among the Black members of Company C.

Analyses of questionnaire Data

The third experimental hypothesis predicted that within Company C, levels of inmates' general satisfaction with their living situation, ratings of staff, and ratings of fellow inmates would rise subsequent to the experimental intervention. Elevations in these behavioral levels were not expected to occur within Company D. Thus, a significant treatment X linear-trend interaction effect was expected on the three questionnaire measures.

The mean levels of satisfaction, ratings of staff, and evaluation of peers, before and after the experimental intervention, are presented in Table 4. These data indicate that within Company C, ratings of satisfaction and staff increased while ratings of peers decreased following the intervention. Among the residents of Dayroom D, however, ratings of satisfaction and staff declined while evaluation of peers increased.

TABLE 4: MEANS ON QUESTIONNAIRE ITEMS PERTAINING TO INMATES' SATISFACTION WITH THEIR LIVING SITUATION, RATINGS OF STAFF, AND RATINGS OF PEERS DURING PRE- AND POST-INTERVENTION PHASES OF THE INVESTIGATION

Questionnaire Scale	Company			
	C		D	
	Pre (N=18)	Post (N=15)	Pre (N=18)	Post (N=13)
Satisfaction with YTS Relative to Other Correctional Facilities	2.52	3.70	3.86	2.57
Ratings of Staff on Companies C and D	3.72	4.20	4.49	3.83
Ratings of Fellow Inmates Companies C and D	4.57	4.12	4.45	4.66

a. Larger means indicate higher ratings on the attributes listed.

TABLE 5: MULTIVARIATE ANALYSIS OF VARIANCE ON REPEATED MEASURES OF INMATE SATISFACTION, RATINGS OF STAFF AND OF FELLOW INMATES DURING PRE- AND POST-INTERVENTION PHASES OF THE INVESTIGATION

Source	Uni-variate df	Inmates' Satisfaction		Inmates' Rating of Staff		Inmates' Rating of Fellow Inmates		Multivariate F
		MS	F	MS	F	MS	F	
Between Groups								
Exptl. Treatment (E)	1	.04	<1.00	.08	2.00	.09	<1.00	<1.00
Error Between	6	.31		.04		.16		
Within Groups								
Linear Component(L)	1	.30	<1.00	.06	<1.00	.12	<1.00	<1.00
E x L	1	7.90	2.76	2.62	9.28*	.88	2.17	3.87
Error Within (Linear)	6	2.86		.28		.41		

* p<.05

The significance of the above trends were assessed through a repeated-measures MANOVA, the results of which are presented in Table 5. No main effects of the experimental treatment on the subjective-report measures were found. The within-groups analyses, though, revealed a significant treatment X linear-trend interaction effect on inmates' ratings of staff (F (1,6) = 9.28, p .023), such that ratings of staff increased significantly within Company C and decreased significantly within Company D.

This finding should be interpreted with caution in view of the non-significance (p .112) of the multivariate F for the treatment X linear interaction effect. It should be noted, however, that the statistical tests of these effects were somewhat conservative in that ethnic-group means rather than individual scores served as the units of analysis (thereby yielding a marked reduction in degrees of freedom for error).

DISCUSSION

The results of this study indicate that rates of verbal and physical aggression remained unexpectedly low and were virtually unaffected by the experimental intervention. The low incidence of aggression in Dayrooms C and D may have been due to the overly restrictive nature of the observational criteria (hence, weak to moderate forms of aggression may have gone unnoticed), or to the fact that acts of overt aggression were simply uncommon in Companies C and D. In the latter case, it is possible that inmates restrained their aggression either temporarily while outside observers were present or more permanently due to the negative consequences of participating in aggressive incidents (e.g., withdrawal of recreational privileges).

Unobtrusive measures obtained from institutional records, however, suggest that various forms of disruptive behavior increased in Company C following the experimental intervention.

Additional evidence for the behavioral impact of furniture rearrangement is reflected in the significant linear-trend and treatment X quadratic-trend interaction effect on levels of positive interracial contact. Occupants of Dayroom C displayed elevated levels of interracial contact following the intervention whereas those of Dayroom D exhibited a post-intervention reduction of interracial contact. Together, the archival and observational data suggests that the shift from sociofugal to sociopetal arrangements was accompanied by greater frequencies of both disruptive as well as prosocial, interracial behavior.

The abrupt elevation of interracial contact within Dayroom D at Phase III was initially quite puzzling. A subsequent perusal of institutional records pertaining to disruptive events during the research period revealed that on the day of observation period 6, an attempted escape from YTS occurred. This incident, which was of mutual interest to members of all ethnic groups, may have provided a basis for interracial conversation which ordinarily would not have occurred. The effects of the incident on interracial contact would not have been as pronounced in Dayroom C where levels of interracial contact were characteristically higher (hence, the significant between-groups main effect on this data).

An alternative explanation is that the abrupt rise in interracial contact within Dayroom D at Phase III was attributable to a "grapevine" effect of the experimental intervention. That is, information concerning the rearrangement of Dayroom C may have prompted increased levels of interracial conversation among the members of Company D concerning the alleged purposes of this intervention. Increased levels of conversation about the restructuring of Dayroom C would have been most pronounced while this change was still novel (i.e., at Phase III rather than at Phase IV).

Turning to the racial polarization data, levels of polarity were significantly higher in Dayroom D than in Dayroom C and, in both companies, levels of polarization decreased significantly subsequent to the experimental intervention. It is unclear from these findings whether the significant treatment-control difference and the quadratic trend reflected in the polarization data are attributable to experimental or non-experimental sources of variance. It is possible that the reduction of polarity in Dayroom C resulted from the furniture rearrangement there, and that the decreased polarity in Dayroom D resulted from a grapevine effect whereby information about the changes in Dayroom C provided the inmates in Dayroom D with a basis for increased conversation and interracial contact. It seems more likely, however, that the parallel reduction of polarization in Dayroom C and D following the intervention was the result of non-experimental, coincidental factors in view of the nearly identical rates of change reflected in Figure 4.

Finally, the semantic differential data provide evidence that the shift from a sociofugal to a sociopetal arrangement of furniture in Dayroom C prompted more favorable ratings of the staff by members of Company C and less favorable staff evaluations by residents of Company D. This pattern of results may be due to the fact that inmates perceived the environmental intervention as a sign of the staff's interest in the quality of their living situation, whereas the absence of physical changes in Dayroom D may have provided the basis for attributing negligence and lack of concern to the staff by members of Company D. Such attributions would have been especially likely to the extent that inmates in Company D felt relatively deprived vis-a-vis the members of Company C.

Overall, the results of this study provide only partial support for the experimental hypotheses. On the one hand, levels of aggression, racial polarization, and subjective ratings of general satisfaction and fellow inmates were not affected by the experimental manipulation. On the other hand, levels of positive interracial contact and ratings of the staff reflected the influence of the furniture rearrangement.

There are a number of factors which might explain the above pattern of results. Reasons for the infrequency of observable aggression were mentioned earlier. The persistence of racial polarization subsequent to the experimental intervention may be related to the existence of strong, clearly-defined social norms concerning ethnic territoriality. Earlier studies have documented the strength and pervasiveness of territorial norms within correctional settings (cf., Esser, 1973: Polsky, 1962; Sundstrom and Altman, 1974; Wright, 1973). In such settings, ethnic territoriality apparently serves as a mechanism for reducing intergroup conflict, avoiding intragroup conflict, avoiding intragroup peer pressure, and establishing self-identity in relation to one's referent group. The racially-polarized structure of the dayroom, then, would have been of high

functional utility to the inmates and, therefore, relatively unchangeable through a sociopetal furniture arrangement. Consistent with this reasoning, the post-intervention rise in disruptive behavior, particularly among the most dominant subgroup of the experimental population, may have reflected the social strains arising from an arbitrarily imposed threat to the existing and highly-stabilized territorial system.

By contrast, levels of positive interracial contact would have been less resistant to the influence of the experimental intervention since the major proportion of casual interaction among different ethnic groups occurred within the "transition areas", or non-polarized sections of the dayrooms, (e.g., areas around the game tables). The sociopetal furniture arrangement implemented in Dayroom C was designed specifically to increase the size of transition areas within the room for it was assumed that in such areas, social norms dictating ethnic territoriality would be least salient to the occupants. Thus, although it was unlikely that clustering the chairs in front of the T.V. would encourage Whites to enter a previously all-Black territory, the addition of extra chairs within existing transition areas may have increased the likelihood of interracial conversation there.

The questionnaire data, as well as the behavioral results, suggest that the environmental intervention employed in this study was too limited in scope to effect major changes along attitudinal and spatial dimensions of racial polarization. While inmates' ratings of the staff seemed to improve as a function of the experimental intervention, their general satisfaction with living conditions at YTS and their feelings toward peers remained unaffected by the environmental change.

Inmates' responses to open-ended questions administered at the conclusion of the research may help to explain the generally low levels of reported satisfaction, and the absence of increased satisfaction following the intervention. Two of the open-ended items asked respondents to list the least-liked features of their dayroom, and the kinds of changes in the dayroom they would prefer most. The most frequently cited problems among members of Companies C and D were (1) excessive noise in the dayroom, (2) inadequate ventilation in the dayroom, and (3) the uninteresting, bland appearance of the dayroom. As for the preferred changes, the following were cited most often: (1) installation of curtains and carpeting, (2) replacement of old furniture with new pieces, and (3) separation of active and quiet activities so as to reduce the noise problem. In general, these data suggest that the rearrangement of furniture failed to ameliorate several important environmental problems, all of which contributed to low levels of satisfaction among the wards.

The lack of treatment effects on the peer-evaluation and racial polarization data, and the rise in disruptive behavior during the course

Page 136

of this study, further suggest that the impact
of the present intervention was limited by its
failure to address the social and psychological
bases of racial prejudice. While the provision
of increased opportunities for eye contact and
conversation among inmates apparently promotes
heightened levels of positive interracial contact,
it presumably does not ensure the reduction of
prior prejudice, present polarization, and future
violence. To achieve the latter goals, in the
present setting at least, it may be necessary to
implement an intervention incorporating both
physical and social components (c.f., Kohlberg,
Kauffman, Scharf, and Hickey, 1974; Sherif and
Sherif, 1953). A follow-up study currently
is planned which will investigate the separate
and combined effects of architectural and social-
structural changes designed to reduce racial
polarization in a correctional facility.

References

COLE, J., and GRIZZLE, J. Applications of muti-
variate analysis of variance to repeated
measurement experiments. Biometrics, 1966,
810-828.

CRAIK, K. Environmental psychology. In K.
Craik, B. Kleinmuntz, R. Rosnow, R. Rosenthal,
J. Cheyne and R. Walters, Eds., New directions
in psychology, Volume IV. New York: Holt,
Rinehart, and Winston, 1970.

DEUTSCH, M., and COLLINS, M. Interracial housing.
In W. Peterson, Ed., American social patterns.
Garden City, N. Y.: Doubleday and Co., 1965.

ESSER, A. Cottage fourteen: Dominance and
territoriality in a group of institutionalized
boys. Small Group Behavior, 1973, 4, 131-146.

FESTINGER, L., SCHACHTER, S., and BACK, K. Social
pressures in informal groups. Stanford, Ca.:
Stanford University Press, 1950.

KOHLBERG, L., KAUFFMAN, K., SCHARF, P., and
HICKEY, J. The just community approach to
corrections: A manual, Part I. Cambridge,
Massachusetts: Harvard University School
of Education, 1974.

MARTINSON, R. What works? - Questions and
answers about prison reform. Public Interest,
1974, 35, 22-54.

NAGEL, W. The new red barn. New York: Walker
and Co., 1973.

OSMOND, H. Function as the basis of psychiatric
ward design. Mental Hospitals, 1957, 8,
23-30.

OSMOND, H. The relationship between architect
and psychiatrist. In C. Goshen, Ed.,
Psychiatric architecture. Washington, D.C.:
American Psychiatric Association, 1959.

POLSKY, H. Cottage six: The social system of
delinquent boys in residential treatment.
New York: Russell Sage Foundation, 1962.

PROSHANSKY, H., ITTELSON, W., and RIVLIN, L.,
Eds. Environmental psychology. New York:
Holt, Rinehart, and Winston, 1970.

SHERIF, M., and SHERIF, C. Groups in harmony and
tension. New York: Harper and Brothers,
1953.

SOMMER, R. Personal space. Englewood Cliffs,
N.J.: Prentice-Hall, 1969.

SOMMER, R. Design awareness. San Francisco:
Rinehart Press, 1972.

SOMMER, R. Tight spaces. Englewood Cliffs,
N.J.: Prentice-Hall, 1974.

SUNDSTROM, E., and ALTMAN, I. Field study of
territorial behavior and dominance.
Journal of Personality and Social Psychology,
1974, 30, 115-124.

SYKES, G. The society of captives. Princeton,
N.J.: Princeton University Press, 1958.

WRIGHT, E. Politics of punishment. New York:
Harper and Row, 1973.

WOHLWILL, J. The emerging discipline of environmental psychology. American Psychologist,
1970, 25, 303-312.

FOOTNOTES

[1] The present reserach was supported by a grant to
the first author from the California Youth
Authority Division. The authors wish to express
their appreciation to Jim Xarhis, Bill Zannella,
Lloyd Wolfe, Gene Wagoner, Bob Rudin, Mike
Oskins, and Don Reetz, staff members, and
R. L. McKibben, Superintendent, of the California
Youth Training School in Chino, California, who
facilitated the conduct of this study. Also,
thanks go to Ed Andrus, Ed Arvizo, Bonnie Condict,
Tom Grabowski, Carol Iacano, Matt Lynes, John
Ormond, Bill Parham, Walter Rohwedder, Alice
Schmidt, and Bill Wright who assisted in the
collection and coding of data.

[2] Requests for reprints should be sent to Daniel
Stokols, Program in Social Ecology, University
of California, Irvine, Irvine, California 92717.

[3] Random selection of wards for the interview
sessions was accomplished by assigning all
residents within each company a number and
drawing a pre-determined quantity of numbered
slips of paper from a container. Those inmates
whose numbers matched the ones appearing on the
selected slips of paper were interviewed.

^{4}To test the statistical significance of temporal
trends within observation periods, group summary
scores on each behavioral measure at t_1, t_2, t_3,
and t_4 were transformed into weighted linear,
quadratic, and cubic scores (using the polynomial
coefficients, -3, -1, 1, 3; 1, -1, 1, -1; and
-1, 3, -3, 1 respectively). A within-subjects
MANOVA then was performed on the transformed
scores (cf., Cole and Grizzle, 1966). In the
primary repeated-measures analyses, transformed
scores were derived from the group means on
each measure at Phases I, II, III, and IV to
assess temporal trends before and after the
experimental intervention.

^{5}In the analyses of the questionnaire data,
only linear trends were assessed.

^{6}A different quadrant was utilized to provide
reliability data during each of the five preliminary observation sessions. Three of these
quadrants were drawn from the dayroom of Company
C and two from that of Company D.

OPENNESS-ENCLOSURE AND SEATING ARRANGEMENTS AS SPATIAL DETERMINANTS IN LOUNGE DESIGN

Steven Rosenbloom

Department of Psychology
Vanier College
Montreal, Quebec

ABSTRACT

A field experiment was undertaken in a college lounge environment to determine the effects of the openness-enclosure dimension (barriers surrounding the area vs no barriers) and seating arrangements (sociofugal vs sociopetal) on a number of behavioural indices of typical lounge behavior. Student researchers, employing behavioral mapping and questionnaire procedures, monitored behaviors of lounge users for 3 mornings per experimental condition of a 2 x 2 factorial design. Three hypotheses were generated in the present study: (1) That an enclosed lounge would tend to have a smaller but longer staying population than an open lounge due to increased privacy; (2) That enclosed lounges would support more non-interactive (study) behavior than open lounges; (3) That seating arrangements would summate with openness-enclosure to produce different extremes in socializing behavior. The data confirmed Hypothesis I and II and partially confirmed Hypothesis III. The results of the present study are discussed in terms of a model in which lounges are seen as multi-activity centers, which should be designed to support a number of different behaviors.

1   INTRODUCTION

In recent years architects and designers have become increasingly concerned with the relationship between physical designs and their ecological consequences. Models such as the behavior contingent design approach (Studer, 1970) have emphasized the importance of fitting the physical system to the requisite behaviors occurring in a proposed environment. In a recent textbook on environmental psychology (Ittelson et al, 1974) noted the need for "proper environmental supports" to maintain equilibrium in a frequently changing behavior-contingent system.

The realization of such a human-structure interface depends to a certain extent upon experimentally determined relationships between design factors and their social-environmental consequences. An important consideration in this regard is the study of architectural effects by a systematic alteration of physical settings in real-life environments. Recent investigations by Cohen (1974) in prison, public school and laboratory settings and Brady et al (1974) which focused on experimentally

controlled work and living quarters are good examples of progress in this direction. However, Baum (1974) has commented on the paucity of research relating architectural variables and behavior. The experiment presented here is an attempt to study the effects of manipulating design variables on natural behaviors occurring in a student lounge setting.

The design of student lounges has received little attention in the environmental design literature. Sommer (1974) mentions that these areas, which can potentially serve as multi-activity centers of university life, are often poorly located in social center type campus buildings and are consequently underused. Sommer also points out that academic buildings of universities lack such lounge spaces, resulting in little social interaction within these structures.

The present study arises out of a practical need on the part of the college at which the principal investigator is employed, to design attractive areas on the upper floors of the Campus building so as to increase the usage of these floors. A vacated open area, which is located in a busy section of a classroom floor, was chosen as an experimental field station where sociopetal-sociofugal seating arrangements and openness-enclosure dimensions of the space were manipulated in an attempt to determine the behavioral correlates of the different design configurations. The present paper is composed of (a) a review of the relevant literature on the independent variables, (b) the field experiment.

1.1   Openness-Enclosure

Because of the nature of the chosen field station (an unbounded rectangular space), it was decided to vary the openness-enclosure dimension of the area. A number of authors (Lynch 1971, Simonds 1961, Spreiregen 1965) seem to agree that the organization and characteristics of vertical elements (e.g. walls, colonnades, trees) distinguish an undifferentiated open area from a confined articulated, enclosed area.

Hayward and Franklin (1974) using one-point perspective drawings as stimuli have shown that perceived openness-enclosure of a space is a function of a ratio between the height of the boundary around the area and the distance of the observer from the boundary. (H/D ratio)

In another vein, research on the effects of partitions and barriers in different situations show that these enclosures provide a number of spatial advantages for persons within the enclosed area. For example, Newman (1973) has found that hedges and low walls act as "symbolic barriers" which delimits the territory of an apartment building as being a semi-private area. Sommer (1966) has noted that barriers in study situations provide privacy for persons in libraries and study halls. Similarly, Desor (1972) demonstrated that persons feel less crowded in partitioned than fully open rooms. Finally, Baum (1974) showed that persons protected by a small barrier (an enclosure around a water fountain), are more likely to resist spatial intrusions and can more easily protect their personal spaces. What might be construed as a disadvantage of a partitioned environment is the finding in office situations (Gullhorn, 1952) and army residences (Blake et al, 1956), that while social interaction increases within the enclosed area, it decreases as far as the larger social group is concerned.

1.2 Sociopetal-Sociofugal Seating Arrangements

Sommer (1969) has described sociofugal seating designs as discouraging interaction and concentrating activity towards the periphery of a room, while sociopetal designs encourage interaction and concentrate activity towards the centre of a room. Sommer demonstrated in a geriatric ward of a hospital, that sociopetal designs were more effective than sociofugal seating arrangements in increasing social interaction between patients.

2 METHOD

The present study, which was field-experimental in nature, employed a 2 x 2 factorial design in which furniture arrangements (sociopetal and sociofugal) and openness-enclosure (barriers versus no barriers) were the independent variables. Both variables were counterbalanced so that no seating or enclosure situation was duplicated from one condition to the next.

The field station was a 22' x 17' open carpeted space located near an intersection of two main corridors on the third floor of the Ste.Croix campus building of Vanier College. The designated lounge area was around the corner from a bank of classrooms and faced a heavily trafficed stairwell. Previous to the present study, the area was vacant and had not been used for any activities before the previous semester. A variety of lounge furniture (2 and 3 seater vinyl-covered couches, single seat vinyl chairs, a coffee table, a study table and four hard-backed chairs were placed in the lounge such that there was seating capacity for 19 persons at any given time. Barriers utilized during the enclosure conditions were constructed out of fibre-board with plywood frames and consisted of 5 - 8' x 4' sliding panels which could be moved easily (see Figure 1 for photograph of barriers). As previous research (Hayward and Franklin, 1974) has shown that perceived enclosure is a function of the height of the barrier, the present barriers were devised so as to maximize experienced enclosure as well as to provide maximum visual and to some extent auditory privacy. Lighting for the lounge was provided by standard overhead fluorescent panels which are common to academic buildings.

3 PROCEDURE

Two methodologies, behavioral mapping (Ittelson et al, 1970) and a user satisfaction questionnaire were employed in this study. Prior to commencement of actual experimental conditions, four student researchers were trained to accurately observe and note behaviors on a combined floor plan and check list, which had been devised in a pilot study (Rosenbloom, Barmish and Zelecovic, 1974). This training procedure which was carried out immediately after the lounge furniture was haphazardly placed in the lounge, took two weeks and was continued until inter-rater reliability between any two researchers was .90. In order to determine the feasibility of starting a coffee cart service in the college lounges, it was decided that one task of the researchers was to sell freshly perked coffee during the experimental sessions. This procedure, which helped to make the observers less obtrusive, also served to delimit the length of observation periods and make students aware of the existence of the lounge. An advertisement was placed in the Daily Newsletter to the effect that freshly perked coffee would be sold in the third floor lounge every Tuesday, Wednesday and Thursday between 10:45 a.m. and noon.

The actual experiment was carried out during the aforementioned times and days for a period of 4 weeks (3 days per experimental condition x 4 conditions). During an experimental session, the 4 student researchers were stationed strategically in the lounge such that each researcher was able to keep a complete behavior record on each user entering his "territory". Experimenters alternated as coffee salesmen during the observation period. Any person who (a) entered the lounge and stood in the area 1 full minute (b) took a seat, was classified as a user and a complete record of the individual's activities was kept. This record included the sex, physical location (seated, standing, sitting on floor), activities engaged in (socializing, studying, drinking coffee, etc), the number of persons the indivi-

Figure 1: EXPERIMENTAL LOUNGE DURING BARRIER CONDITIONS

dual came in and left with, and whether or not the user moved the furniture arrangement. Copies of a user satisfaction questionnaire which dealt with perceptions which lounge frequenters had of the seating arrangements social activities and general atmosphere in the area, were handed to each user who purchased coffee and were left on the coffee table to be answered at the discretion of the users. During the sociopetal conditions couches and chairs were placed close together at 90 degree angles to one another in such a manner to facilitate eye contact (see Figure II a), whereas in the sociofugal conditions the same furniture was arranged either at 180 degree angles and far apart, or back to back so as to discourage interaction (see Figure II b). At the start of each experimental session furniture was arranged according to a pre-set floor-plan in exactly the same locations. During barrier conditions, the enclosures were placed around the periphery of the lounge and remained there throughout the experimental condition (3 days).

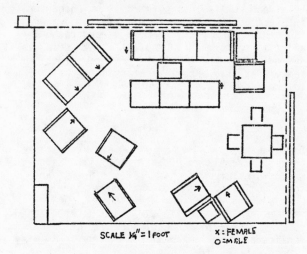

SCALE ½" = 1 FOOT   X = FEMALE
                           O = MALE

Figure IIa SOCIOPETAL SEATING ARRANGEMENT

4   HYPOTHESES

The literature suggests several hypotheses worth investigating in the present context.

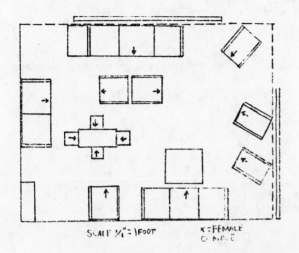

Figure IIb SOCIOFUGAL SEATING ARRANGEMENT

Hypothesis 1

Physical enclosure of a previously unbounded lounge area results in a more private territory less prone to spatial invasion. Consequently, barrier conditions should produce a smaller but longer staying population than the no barrier conditions. This hypothesis is based partially upon the finding of Newman (1973) that a symbolic barrier is likely to keep outsiders away from an enclosed territory.

Hypothesis 2

Physical enclosure of a lounge area creates more visual privacy for the individual within. It is hypothesized that barrier conditions should support more non-interactive behaviors (studying) than "no barrier" conditions.

Hypothesis 3

The effects of "sociopetal" seating arrangements should summate with "no barrier" conditions to produce the highest rate of socializing while "sociofugal" seating arrangements should summate with "barrier" conditions to produce the lowest rate of socializing.

5 RESULTS

Evidence from the present study lends support to the notion that enclosure of a previously unbounded lounge area tends to create a more private and less populated space. Z-tests (Edwards, 1960) of the significance of the difference between proportions reveal that the population of the lounge was significantly

larger in the "no barrier" versus "barrier" conditions ($z=2.83$, $p < .005$, one-tailed test), but that population size differences attributable to "sociofugal" versus "sociopetal" seating arrangements were not significant (see Table I).

TABLE I: NUMBER OF PERSONS USING LOUNGE IN EACH EXPERIMENTAL CONDITION

	SOCIOFUGAL	SOCIOPETAL
BARRIER	92	77
NO BARRIER	111*	111

Barrier versus no barrier condition significant at .005 level

Table II shows the number of persons staying in the lounge for differing time intervals as well as the median amount of time spent by each group.

TABLE II: FREQUENCY DISTRIBUTION AND MEDIANS FOR AMOUNT OF TIME SPENT IN LOUNGE BY USERS IN DIFFERENT EXPERIMENTAL CONDITIONS

	SOCIO-PETAL	SOCIO-PETAL +BARRIER	SOCIO-FUGAL	SOCIO-FUGAL +BARRIER
1- 5 min.	49	13	23	8
5-10 min.	23	17	23	12
11-15 min.	15	11	7	15
15-30 min.	15	22	22	39
> 30 min.	9	14	6	18
TOTAL	111	77	81	92
MEDIAN	6.5 min.	14.8 min	8.9 min.	19.3m.

Table III provides a breakdown in terms of the number of persons staying in the area less than 5 minutes versus the number of those remaining in the lounge more than 5 minutes. Support for Hypothesis I is provided by the finding that significantly more persons stayed longer periods in the "barrier" than "no barrier" conditions ($z=5.43$, $p < .0005$, one-tailed test), a result which is confirmed by the considerably larger medians in the "barrier" conditions.

* Only data on total number of subjects is available for the last day of "sociofugal no barrier" condition. Therefore other tables only include data on 81 subjects for this condition.

Page 142

TABLE III: NUMBER OF PERSONS STAYING IN THE
LOUNGE < 5 MINUTES VERSUS THE
NUMBER OF PERSONS STAYING IN THE
LOUNGE > 5 MINUTES IN ALL EXPERI-
MENTAL CONDITIONS

	SOCIOPETAL NO BARRIER	SOCIOPETAL +BARRIER	SOCIOFUGAL NO BARRIER	SOCIOFUGAL +BARRIER
<5	49	13	23	8
>5	62	64	58	84

Added evidence for the notion that physical
enclosures create a more private milieu comes
from the findings that more individuals came
to the lounge with others in the "no barrier"
conditions than in the "barrier" conditions
($z=3.00$, $p <.01$), and questionnaire data to
the effect that lounge users met more friends
on "no barrier" days than on days when the
lounge was enclosed ($z=2.45$, $p <.01$). In
addition to the above results, there was the
unexpected but interesting finding that
significantly more users stayed shorter periods
in the "sociopetal" than in "sociofugal"
conditions ($z=3.26$, $p <.01$).

Table IV shows the number of lounge-users
observed studying in each of the four
experimental conditions. Z-tests revealed
that significantly more persons were observed
studying in the "barrier" as opposed to the
"no barrier conditions" ($z=5.58$, $p<.0005$, one-
tailed test), whereas differences between
seating arrangements on this variable were not
significant ($z=1.00$, N.S.). It would appear
from the above findings, that physical
enclosures provide a milieu which encourages
non-interactive activities such as studying.

TABLE IV: NUMBER AND PERCENTAGE OF LOUNGE
USERS STUDYING IN EACH EXPERIMENTAL
CONDITION

	SOCIOPETAL NO BARRIER	SOCIOPETAL +BARRIER	SOCIOFUGAL NO BARRIER	SOCIOFUGAL +BARRIER
STUDYING	47 (42.3%)	48 (62.3%)	29 (35.8%)	68 (73.9%)
NOT STUDYING	64	29	52	24

Table V shows the number and percentage of
percentage of persons observed socializing in
each of the experimental conditions.

TABLE V: NUMBER AND PERCENTAGE OF USERS
SOCIALIZING IN EACH EXPERIMENTAL
CONDITION

	SOCIOPETAL NO BARRIER	SOCIOPETAL +BARRIER	SOCIOFUGAL NO BARRIER	SOCIOFUGAL +BARRIER
SOCIALIZING	85 (76%)	58 (75%)	73 (90%)	60 (65%)
NOT SOCIALIZING	26	21	9	32

This data only partially substantiates
Hypothesis III in that the lowest rate of
socializing occurred in the "sociofugal plus
barrier group." The fact that this same condition supported the most studying (90%) adds
credence to the above finding. The result
showing that the "sociofugal - no barrier" group
had the highest number of persons socializing
is both unexpected and difficult to explain.
One factor which may explain this result is the
amount of furniture movement occurring in the
different seating conditions. It was found
that there was significantly more instances of
furniture movement in the sociofugal than in
the sociopetal conditions ($z=3.59$, $p < .001$,
two-tailed). It is conceivably possible that
users might have created their own sociopetal
situation during our sociofugal experimental
period, thus contaminating these results.

6   DISCUSSION

The present study substantiates the commonly
accepted notion among architects and designers
that the delineation of a space by the use of
boundaries helps to contain activities within
that space by lending "definition" to the area.
The experimenters who monitored our lounge
noticed a sharp transition in behavior within
the space from a more "social activities"
oriented area when the space was unbounded to
a "study center" concept during the barrier
conditions. The data indicates that persons
in an unbounded lounge area stay shorter
periods of time, meet their friends more often,
come in groups more often and study less than
persons in lounge delineated by barriers.
Another finding which adds weight to the notion
that an unbounded lounge served more the function of a social center was the result that
more users bought coffee in the "no barrier"
than in the "barrier" conditions ($z=2.41$,
$p. <.01$) and in significantly larger quantities
(number of cups) ($z=4.03$, $p <.001$). Zajonc
(1965) has discussed the concept of "social
facilitation", wherein individuals both human
and infrahuman will engage in more consummatory
behavior even when satiated when in the presence
of others and in a conducive social atmosphere.
The smaller population, longer lounge visits
and greater amount of studying observed in the
barrier conditions suggest a complex of
variables operating to produce this situation.

Contributing to the better fit of the bounded lounge as a "study center" is the fact that our barriers tended to create the "symbolic barrier" mentioned by Newman. As the data suggests, persons were reluctant to enter this space in groups and observations by experimenters confirm the fact that potential users hesitated more frequently before entering the enclosed lounge. That both "no barrier"and sociopetal conditions resulted in shorter lounge visits may be explained in several ways. Rappaport (1975), in a recent article has introduced the concept of "perceived density" by which an individual evaluates the density of space by a number of criteria including the presence or absence of boundaries, etc. It is possible that an unbounded easily traversed area might have a greater perceived density by users than the same space with boundaries. Hence, individual anticipations of crowded conditions, spatial invasions, etc. may have resulted in more persons leaving the lounge earlier. Certainly "no barrier" conditions and seating arrangement designed to increase interaction would most likely be prone to such interpretations. The fact that users preferred the"barrier"to no"barrier"conditions comes out in questionnaire data, and attempts by users to replace the barriers during the no barrier conditions. What might equally serve as an explanatory device for the above findings is the very nature of behavior in lounge settings. Beck and Rosenbloom (1975) have noted that student lounges serve as multi-activity centers (i.e. a given individual will utilize the space for a number of different activities during the same time period). However, should a given area fail to fit the activity in question, the individual will move on. In the case of the unbounded lounge, while socializing activities were adequately served, studying needs were not; hence the flight of some users to greener study pastures.

At present, the principal investigator is engaged in a study involving the design, monitoring, and evaluation of lounge spaces in a college setting. An effort is being made to determine among other things,the effects of having claim to a traditionally public space (a study carrel, or lounge area) on the behavior of individuals who are given this privilege. Similarly, some lounges are being bounded by lockers with the intention of determining whether these multi-activity clusters are "colonized". The main aim of the present study, as well as proposed future research, is to utilize environmental psychological tools in an attempt to maximize man-environment fit.

references

BAUM A. et al (1974) Architectural variants of reaction to spatial invasion Environment and Behavior 6,1 (March): 91-100.

BECK R. and S. ROSENBLOOM (1975) User Generated Program of Socio-Physical Design Requirements for Non-classroom Space, Vanier College.

BLAKE R. et al (1956) Housing architecture and social interaction Sociometry, 1956, 19, 133-139.

BRADY, J.V. et al (1974) Design of a programmed environment for the experimental analysis of social behavior in R.A. Chase (ed) Environmental Design Research: EDRA 5 Vol. 7 Stroudsberg, P.A.: Dowden, Hutchinson & Ross.

COHEN, H.L. Designs for learning: case/space studies in a university, a prison, a laboratory and a public school in R.A. Chase (ed) Environmental Design Research: EDRA 5 Vol. 7, Stroudsberg, P.A.: Dowden, Hutchinson & Ross.

DESOR, J. (1972) Towards a psychological theory of crowding. I of Personality and Social Psychology 21: 79-83.

EDWARDS, A. (1960) Experimental Design in Psychological Research. New York: Holt, Rinehart & Winston.

GULLHORN, T. (1952) Distance and friendship as factors in the gross interaction matrix. Sociometry, 1952, 15, 123-134.

HAYWARD, G. and G. FRANKLIN (1974) Perceived openness-enclosure of architectural space Environment and Behavior, 6, (March) 37-52.

ITTELSON,W.H. L.G. RIVLIN, H.M. PROSHANSKY, G.H. WINKEL An Introduction to Environmental Psychology, New York, Holt, Rinehart and Winston.

ITTELSON,W.et al (1970) The use of behavioral maps in environmental psychology pp. 658-668 in H.M. Proshansky, W.H. Ittelson L.G. Riolin (eds) Environmental Psychology: Man and His Physical Setting. New York, Holt, Rinehart & Winston

LYNCH, K. (1971) Site Planning Cambridge: M.IT. Press.

NEWMAN, O. (1972) Defensible Space New York. Macmillan & Co.

RAPOPORT, A. (1975) Toward a redefinition of density. Environment and Behavior 7, (June) 1975.

ROSENBLOOM, S. S. BARMISH & A. ZELECOIVIC (1974) Unpublished mimeo, Vanier College.

SIMONDS, J.O. (1961) Landscape Architecture New York: F.W. Dodge.

SOMMER, R. (1966) The ecology of privacy
      The Library Quarterly 36, 243-238.

SOMMER, R. (1969) Personal Space Englewood
      Cliffs, N.J.: Prentice-Hall.

SOMMER, R. (1974) Tight Spaces Englewood
      Cliffs, N.J.: Prentice-Hall.

SPREIREGEN, P.D. (1965) Urban Design: The
      Architecture of Towns and Cities New York:
      McGraw-Hill.

STUDER, R.G. (1970) The dynamics of behavior-
      contingent physical systems in H.M.
      Proshansky, W.H. Ittelson & L.G. Rivlin
      (eds) Environmental Psychology: Man and
      His Physical Setting.

ZAJONC, R. (1965) Social facilitation Science,
      149, 260-274, 826.

THE CORRECTIONAL ENVIRONMENT AND HUMAN BEHAVIOR:

A COMPARATIVE STUDY OF TWO PRISONS FOR WOMEN

Perry H. Prestholdt
Robert R. Taylor
William T. Shannon

Department of Psychology
Louisiana State University
Baton Rouge, Louisiana, USA, 70803

ABSTRACT

This study deals with a dramatic environmental
change experienced by the inmates and staff of
a correctional institute for women. They moved
from an old, crowded, dilapidated facility to
an elaborate new complex, from open-bay barracks
to private rooms; from a "Girl Scout camp" to a
prison. The environmental change provided a
unique opportunity to conduct a comparative
study of the effect of architectural design on
human behavior and attitudes. At both
facilities the researchers administered
environmental evaluation instruments, checklists,
and questionnaires, as well as collecting
behavioral mapping data. The study resulted in
sufficient evidence to conclude that the
architectural design of prisons does influence
the behavior patterns, attitudes, and social
relations of inmates and correctional personnel.
Although generally evaluated more positively
than the old facility, the new facility had a
negative effect on the social atmosphere and on
staff-inmate relations.

1.   INTRODUCTION

The staff and inmates of a women's correctional
institution have recently experienced a
dramatic environmental change. They moved from
a crowded, dilapidated, century-old facility
into an elaborate new prison. The old facility
presented a very simple open design; several low
buildings and a fence-enclosed, grassy compound.
Because of its physical condition, open layout,
wooden structures, and social atmosphere, it was
described aptly by its residents as a Girl Scout
camp.

In contrast, the complex layout of the new
facility resembled a multi-building campus
surrounded by a tall chain-link and barbed wire
fence. Situated within this fence were six
glass, brick, and steel buildings linked
together with a covered walkway. These
contemporary institutional structures housed
work facilities, a chapel, classrooms,
recreational space, cafeteria, infirmary, and
administrative offices. The entire complex was
dominated by a two-story Y-shaped dormitory.
All buildings were air-conditioned.

The contrast between the architectural features
of these two institutions was most apparent in
their dormitory structures. At the old facility
the residents occupied two large open-bay
barracks which lacked air-conditioning and
adequate heating. Each dorm contained sleeping
space for about 50 residents, a small TV room,
and shower and toilet facilities. Beds were
lined up in rows the length of the open barracks.
Each resident had a small upright locker for
their belongings and a nightstand for a hot
plate and radio. The openness, the arrangement
of furniture, and the absence of barred windows
gave these dorms the appearance of military or
camp barracks.

Obviously, this open type of design didn't offer
the occupants much opportunity or space for
privacy. However, it did allow for easy
surveillance by the correctional staff. A
single correctional officer standing at the door
could easily and unobtrusively observe everyone
in the dorm.

At the new facility, the residents were housed
in a single large two-story structure. The plan

of the dorm formed a Y and each arm of Y was a separate dormitory unit. At the intersection of these arms was an open circular control area. In the center of this area was a circular counter which contained the television surveillance monitors and the equipment consoles that controlled the security and communication systems. Heavy barred doors separated the control area from the dorm units. In order for the residents to exit from this building they had to pass through these barred gates and the control area.

Each of the three dorm units contained a living room and a glass-enclosed TV room bordered by the private rooms of each resident. Each resident occupied a separate room which was furnished with a toilet and sink, a bed, a free-standing closet and a small desk. Narrow floor-to-ceiling windows provided natural lighting for the private rooms but the living rooms and TV rooms were without windows. The fact that each resident was assigned to a private room greatly enhanced the opportunities for privacy at the new facility. However, although the living room and TV room were visible from the control area, the size and arrangement of spaces made surveillance difficult and seldom unobtrusive.

A similar contrast in design features existed for the outdoor spaces of each facility. The compound at the old facility simply consisted of two large adjacent open yards unobscured by buildings. Because these yards contained benches and playing fields, they served as areas for recreation, relaxation, and socializing. In contrast, the design of the new facility produced several distinct and visually separated outdoor areas. The central area was a mall or courtyard formed by the cluster of buildings. But tucked behind and between these buildings were numerous large and small outdoor spaces which were hidden from view. Also, unlike the old facility, there were no benches or specific areas which facilitated social interaction. The only area appropriate for outdoor games was located behind the dormitory.

Overall, the emphasis on security was much more apparent at the new facility than at the old facility. Perhaps because it was designed with the advice and supervision of the U. S. Department of Justice, the new facility bristled with some of the latest in correctional technology: huge electronically-controlled barred gates, surveillance television, and elaborate communication systems. In contrast to the informal camp-like appearance of the old facility, the new institution definitely was a prison. Thus, in spite of its dirty and dilapidated condition, the old facility represented what Robert Sommer (1974) might describe as soft architecture, while the cleaner and more comfortable new facility could be described as hard architecture.

Because of the obvious contrasts in designs of these facilities, it was reasonable to expect that the two environments would have divergent effects on the behavior and attitudes of the inhabitants. Thus, the transfer of the entire inmate and staff population from one environment to the other provided several unique educational and research opportunities.

From a research perspective, the move offered an ideal showcase for an applied behavioral study of the effect of architectural design on human behavior, attitudes, and emotions. Specifically, the transfer presented a rare opportunity to conduct a comparative study of the effect of these two contrasting environments on the behavior of the same group of individuals.

The relocation of the prison population occurred while the senior author was teaching a seminar in Environmental Psychology. Thus, an opportunity became available here for architecture and psychology students to observe first-hand the behavioral impact of these different architectural designs. It was hoped that this experience would increase the student's awareness of how specific design decisions affect human conduct. In addition, this research project provided these students with experience in designing, conducting, and interpreting empirical research. To enhance their appreciation of the empirical method and the usefulness of empirical research, the students themselves were involved in all phases of the study.

2. METHOD

For purposes of this study a battery of seven self-report instruments was assembled. This battery included an activity questionnaire which was designed to determine the location and frequency of the residents' activities and a job checklist which assessed their attitudes toward their work assignments and work environment. The battery also contained a hostility scale and an emotions checklist. These instruments were used to assess the moods and hostile feelings of the residents. Another instrument, the correctional officer checklist, was developed to measure the residents' attitude toward and relationship with the correctional staff. To determine their perception of the built environment, the residents were given a lengthy environmental evaluation questionnaire consisting of 20 bi-polar adjectives. Separate environmental evaluations were obtained for the residents' living area (dorm or private room) and the entire prison complex. The last instrument in the battery was a general questionnaire which assessed the residents' opinions and knowledge on a variety of topics. For example, questions were directed at the residents' feelings about privacy, their attitudes toward the rules and regulations of the institution, their personal relations with correctional officers, and the frequency with which they observed or participated in certain types of activities such as fighting and homosexual acts.

The entire battery of instruments was administered to 40 inmates and the entire staff at the old facility approximately one month before the move. A few days later behavioral mapping data was collected. Every half hour from 7 A.M. until 8 P.M. observers recorded the location and activity of all residents and staff at the prison. Approximately one month after the relocation of the prison population, the same battery of questionnaires was administered to 40 inmates at the new facility. Half of these respondents had completed the questionnaires while at the old facility. The other half had never seen these instruments before. Also, one month after the transfer observers used the same procedure to collect behavioral mapping data at the new facility.

In addition to the quantifiable data obtained from the questionnaires and the mapping, the researchers informally interviewed many of the residents and recorded their own observations on the activities of the occupants and architectural features of both facilities.

All quantifiable data were analyzed using a multiple analysis of variance design. The three factors used in this analysis were site (old facility versus the new facility), classification of inmate (first offender versus multiple offender), and the race of the inmate.

3. RESULTS

This study produced a voluminous amount of data and no attempt will be made here to describe all of the findings. Instead, emphasis is placed on the effect of these built environments on the residents' evaluation of the environment, their use of space, social interactions, and their relationships with the correctional staff.

The data from the environmental evaluation questionnaires provided information on the inmates' perceptions and evaluations of the two environments. As expected, when individuals move from a dirty, old structure into modern new surroundings, the evaluations of the new facility were consistently more positive than evaluations of the old facility. The new complex was seen as fancier, cleaner, less crowded, friendlier, roomier, and more pleasant, beautiful, and peaceful. Comparisons between the living spaces of the respective facilities revealed similar results. The private rooms were considered to be more friendly, interesting, comfortable, private, etc., than the barracks of the old facility. However, significant inter- actions indicated that these differences were most pronounced for first offenders. They evaluated the old facility much more negatively and the new facility much more positively than

did the multiple offenders. Similarly, the first offenders had a more positive regard for the private rooms than for the barracks, while the multiple offenders tended to prefer the barracks over the private rooms. The change in environments definitely had a positive effect on the first offenders' evaluations but had little impact on the multiple offenders'.

This result may have been due to the multiple offenders' additional experience with the old facility or with prisons in general. A number of them indicated that they felt comfortable with the open-bay barracks and expressed concern about the confining effects of the private rooms at the new facility. In fact, it was found that the living area of the new facility was perceived by all residents to be more confining than the living area in the old facility. This perception may have resulted from the presence of the barred gates, the separation of the dorm units, the small size of the private rooms, and the generally more prison-like design of the new facility.

Multiple offenders and first offenders, however, did agree that the private rooms were the most positive space in the new facility. They saw the individual rooms as cleaner, less crowded, and more peaceful, comfortable, and private than any other space. But the private rooms were seen as cramped, small, and confining. Also, it was found that the residents were very satisfied with the privacy of their sleeping and toilet areas in the new facility, while they had been totally dissatisfied with the privacy of the old facility. In general, the residents liked the private rooms and the privacy they provided.

Turning to the relationship between architectural design and the use of space, it was discovered that the change in environment had an interesting effect on the location and pattern of inmate behavior. At the old facility, residents tended to congregate in the outdoor area between the two dorms where the major pathways merged. This area apparently served as a public space or common ground where the occupants of both dorms could socialize, play cards, dance, or simply observe the activities of others. The mapping data indicated a high frequency of inmates and staff congregated in this area while talking to others, playing games, watching activities, or sitting alone. Following the relocation to the new facility, the residents attempted to establish a similar common area for social interaction by moving furniture from the separate living rooms into the control area. For a short while, this indoor area served the same function as the old dorm yard. However, because the control consoles and security equipment were located in this space, the correctional staff had to prohibit the inmates' use of the control area. As a result, no single area of the new facility ever really developed into a common ground or congregation area. Instead, these kinds of social activities occurred at several scattered locations throughout the new facility. Rather than finding a large concentration of inmates in one area, it was more typical to observe numerous small groups in several separate areas. This dispersion of inmates was accompanied by a slight decrease in social interactions and a definite decrease in the spontaneous social activities, such as games and dancing, which had been typical of the old facility.

However, there were two indoor areas where inmates were more frequently observed in the new facility than the old facility. These areas were the TV room and the dining room. Both the mapping data and the inmates' self-reports indicated that more time was spent watching TV in the new facility than in the old facility. Similarly, the frequency of inmates observed socializing in the dining room was greater in the new facility. Since the dining area was the only indoor space where residents from the separate dorm units could congregate, it did, to some extent, replace the old dorm yards as a common ground for social interaction.

The change in environments also affected the frequency and location of outdoor activities. All outdoor social and recreational activities, including watching activities as spectators, occurred less frequently at the new facility. Obviously, the fact that the new structures were air-conditioned was important, but design features also contributed to this reduction in outdoor activities. For example, at the old facility the open arrangement of the yards and the direct access to the yards from the dorms facilitated outdoor activities. In the new facility, outdoor areas were not directly accessible from the living areas and the areas large enough for athletic activities were hidden behind the dorm. This layout not only impeded the occurrence of spontaneous games, but necessitated the presence of a matron. However, because the overall size and complexity of the new facility demanded so much more surveillance everywhere than did the old facility a correctional officer was seldom available to supervise athletic activities. A reduction in this type of activity was the result.

The existence of the private rooms had very little impact on the behavior patterns at the new facility. One would expect that the decrease in social interaction and outdoor activities was related to inmates retreating to the solitude of their personal territory. But this was not the case. In spite of their positive evaluations of the rooms, the residents seldom used them except to sleep. In fact, the time spent in their private rooms was considerably less than the amount of time they had spent on their beds or in their dorms at the old facility. Apparently, these inhabitants preferred the public spaces where social interaction was possible.

Perhaps the most dramatic and disturbing effect of the environmental change was its impact on the behavior of the staff and their relations with the residents. The layout of the old facility made supervision of inmates an easy and unobtrusive task. Correctional officers were typically observed sitting on a bench, standing in a dorm, or strolling around. They had ample opportunities to talk with inmates, supervise games, etc., without neglecting their security responsibilities. Because of the openness and simplicity of the facility the inmates' activities and movements were seldom restricted. The prevailing atmosphere was permissive and friendly.

In contrast, the size, complexity, unobservable spaces, and exposed control consoles precipitated serious security and surveillance problems at the new facility. The new facility required greater control over the activities, location, and movement of residents. Thus, new rules were instituted and the barred doors were closed. Certain areas, both indoors and outdoors, became off-limits unless supervision was available. The inmates' reaction to this change was understandably negative. While they had felt that the rules at the old facility were just right, they indicated that the new facility had too many rules and was too restrictive. So, instead of the friendly, informal Girl Scout camp atmosphere of the old facility, the atmosphere which evolved at the new facility resembled an authoritarian, regimented military camp.

The procedural changes precipitated by the new environment directly affected the matron's behavior and her contact with inmates. Rather than freely moving about the complex, correctional officers were posted at certain control points. The TV equipment, also, allowed matrons to maintain surveillance without leaving the control area. As a result, the presence of matrons in inmate living areas and their contact with inmates dramatically decreased. For example, while correctional officers were frequently observed in the old barracks, they were never observed in the living areas of the new facility. The staff-inmate interactions that were observed tended to occur in the inhospitable control area, while interactions were observed with equal frequency throughout the old facility. Apparently the complexity of spaces and the specific control points resulted in a physical and social separation of the staff and inmates.

The reduction in staff-inmate contacts, the restrictive rules, and the tighter control clearly affected the nature of the relationship between the correctional personnel and the inmates. The informal, friendly, and equitable relationship which had existed at the old facility changed to a formal, inequitable, and role-specific relationship. One subtle indication of the increase in role differentiation was the spontaneous appearance of uniforms on staff members shortly after the move. But the mapping and questionnaire data more directly revealed the transformation in staff-inmate relations produced by the environmental change. The informal social interactions between staff and inmates so typical of the old facility occurred much less frequently at the new facility. Staff activities, such as standing and talking or sitting and talking to inmates, occurred five times more frequently at the old facility. The residents themselves reported that the matrons were less accessible, that they spent less time talking to matrons, and that they less frequently talked to matrons about their problems at the new facility than at the old facility. Also, they felt that, at the new facility, correctional officers did not watch them closely enough. So at the new facility, the correctional officers interacted less with inmates; they weren't around as much, and the security of their presence was missed by the inmates.

Similarly, the move to the new facility had a negative effect on the residents' attitude toward the staff. But this effect was largely due to the attitude change of white inmates. These inmates viewed correctional officers somewhat positively at the old facility, but adopted a negative attitude at the new facility. However, the original negative opinion of the staff held by black inmates remained essentially the same after the move. Apparently, the environmental change and the subsequent change in staff-inmate relations had the greatest negative impact on white inmates.

4. CONCLUSION

There seems to be sufficient evidence in this research to conclude that architectural design does influence the behavior of inmates and staff. In general, the size, complexity, and additional air-conditioned space of the new facility resulted in a decrease in outdoor recreational and social activities and an increase in indoor and semi-social activities, especially watching television. Correspondingly, the location of the activities shifted from large concentrations of inmates and staff at a central point in the old facility to a diffusion of smaller groups throughout the new facility and from spending time outdoors or around their home territories to spending more time in the TV and dining rooms.

In spite of the generally more positive evaluations of the new facility than the old facility, the negative effect of the new facility on staff-inmate relations was disturbing to the inhabitants. Likewise, the fact that the design of this "ideal" moderate security prison resulted in greater separation and less interpersonal contact between inmates and correctional personnel should be unsettling to correctional officials and designers. The

reason is that a positive relationship between inmate and correctional officer is essential in rehabilitative efforts. The matron is the most influential figure in an inmate's life and has the greatest potential as a change agent. Correctional researchers (Glaser, 1964) have discovered that real changes in inmate behavior are related to close interpersonal relations with correctional officers. Yet, this new, large, complex facility with its emphasis on control and security has actually decreased genuine staff-inmate communication while increasing the social distance and superior-inferior distinction between staff and inmates. Staff-inmate contacts occur less frequently and are more indirect and impersonal. Unfortunately, compared to the old facility, the design of the new facility has not promoted, and possibly has hindered the rehabilitative efforts of the institution.

references

GLASER, DANIEL, The Effectiveness of a Prison and Parole System. Indianapolis: Bobbs-Merrill, 1964.

SOMMER, ROBERT, Tight Spaces. Engelwood Cliffs, N.J.: Prentice-Hall, 1974.

Page 150

THE HALFWAY HOUSE: A DIAGNOSTIC AND PRESCRIPTIVE EVALUATION (1)

William R. Sims

Department of City and Regional Planning and
Program for the Study of Crime and Delinquency
The Ohio State University
Columbus, Ohio 43210
Phone (614) 422-2257

ABSTRACT

This paper describes a post-occupancy evaluation
of a fairly typical half-way house program. The
consequences of a number of building, site, and
locational attributes on program effectiveness
are examined. The study employs a holistic,
qualitative research approach. Results indicate
that a number of environmental factors do contribute to or detract from program effectiveness.
Policy implications are developed from the
findings.

1. INTRODUCTION

The physical setting in which any innovative
social program must operate is usually a neglected factor--both in its initial development and
subsequent evaluation and refinement. It is
usually assumed that this setting is merely a
passive container, having little or no effect on
the programmatic environment. The "halfway-
house," in its various forms, is an example of
just such an innovative program. It has become
widely accepted as a means of ameliorating the
adaptation problems arising from the sudden
transition between life in various caretaker
institutions and the outside world. The physical
facilities, location, and resources of these
programs share a number of typical features.
Because of small budgets and their innovative,
often temporary character, they are typically
located in large-older residences which are
generally shabby and rundown. Because of time
pressures and low budgets these residences
usually receive minimal renovations to meet
programmatic needs. Because of community resistance, the typical halfway house is located
in the most socially disorganized, and consequently, the most behaviorally open milieu
of the city. What are the consequences of these
factors on program effectiveness as far as in
achieving their goals of facilitating transition
from institution to outside, and of reinforcing
behavioral and other changes attempted by the
institution? This question was examined in our
recent (1973) evaluation of the Ohio Adult
Parole Authorities' program of Community Reintegration Centers. (2)

The Community Reintegration Center is an experimental halfway house program, developed to
reduce parole violators within Ohio's correctional system. At the time of this evaluation, the
program consisted of Centers located in each of
Ohio's three largest cities: Columbus, Cleveland
and Cincinnati.

While there were purposeful variations in the
content and form of the programs at each of the
Centers (which I won't detail here), they
basically consisted of a short-term (2-3 months)
residence in the Center, and participation in
several types of treatment. These programs were
designed to improve the parolee's self-image;
ability to obtain and hold employment; communicative skills including oral, written and
listening abilities; handling of personal finances
including budgeting, credit and priorities;
handling of interpersonal activities including
recreation, drinking, sex and other crisis-pro-
ducing situations. The programs consisted of
programmed learning packages, counselling, group
therapy, job counselling and placement, etc. In
addition, the Centers are used to generally
cushion the strains of re-entry, by providing a
place to stay, some money, personal grooming
supplies, clothing and someone to talk to.

This report covers the portion of the evaluation
study which dealt with the effects of two
different aspects of the physical setting of the
Centers. First, we examined the immediate environment, the building itself and its immediate
grounds. Secondly, we looked at the effects of
the surrounding neighborhood and general locational attributes, such as accessibility to
employment, services, and for visitors.

2. METHOD

The study employed a holistic, qualitative
research approach. Two general means of collecting data were utilized - a site inspection and
in-depth interviews of a small sample of staff
and residents. The site inspection consisted
of tours of the building, ground and immediate
neighborhood during which obvious malfunctions
and successes were noted. No a priori data collection stategy or instrument (such as a
checklist) was used. We then interviewed three
staff members and three residents chosen at
random from each Center. (3) These interviews,
administered in the Centers, generally ran from
forty-five minutes to an hour and a half. Some
occasionally required over two hours. The
interview schedule was structured so that it
began with very general open-ended questions,
aimed at obtaining responses which were as un-
directed as possible. Then the questions were

gradually focused and responses were directed to specific areas of interest. Extensive use of non-directive probes like "can you tell me more about that" was made throughout the interview. The responses were then qualitatively analysed as follows. First, the responses were transcribed and duplicated. Then after several readings, those portions dealing with a particular theme were cut out and placed in a pile. Responses which dealt with multiple themes were placed in each of the appropriate categories. For example, a response such as "my room is too small and not very private" would be placed in the categories pertaining to size, rooms, and privacy. After the initial categorization process, each of the piles was sorted according to sub-themes and for relationship to other themes. No formal quantification was attempted, rather we went directly from the categorized and related data to our conceptualizations.

This method was chosen for several reasons. First, much of the treatment program involved highly structured programmed learning packages with continuous testing. Because of this, we felt that another highly structured experience, such as a self-administered questionnaire, might alienate the residents. Secondly, and more importantly from a research perspective, we simply did not know enough in advance to formulate a structured questionnaire. And finally, because most people are unaccustomed to explicitly formulating their attitudes and feelings toward their environment and to considering how it affects their actions, we chose to interview a few residents and staff members in considerable depth. We chose this rather than the more conventional route of interviewing many respondents superficially because we felt that this would allow us to explore the attitudes and feelings of these respondents more thoroughly, and would in turn allow the respondents to formulate their responses at length. At the same time it is possible that they are not representative of the staff and residents of the Centers. Further, it should be noted that although we believe the Reintegration Centers to be a fairly representative halfway house type program, it does at the same time have a number of unique qualities which might limit the generality of our findings.

We would also like to note that the emphasis of study was on action or policy rather than science. By this we mean that we were more interested in assisting the Adult Parole Authority in their task of guiding the program than in answering questions of academic interest. This had two effects on our research. First, it controlled the direction of our inquiry, channelling it toward questions or variables that were at least potentially actionable. Secondly, it forced us to assume a stance which seems exceedingly incautious to a scientist. But to paraphrase Abraham Kaplan, "we were in a taxi and the meter was running." (4) Given the commitment to re-evaluation, re-assessment

and continuous refinement characteristic of most social programs (5), we believe this research orientation to be more contributive to rational policy formulation than is the traditional scholarly posture of rigor and caution.

3. FINDINGS

This section discusses the major findings derived from both our observations and from the interviews. The first section focuses on the building and immediate grounds, and the second examines the surrounding environment of the Centers.

3.1 The Immediate Environment

The building and its immediate grounds probably constitute the most important environment of the Center, in terms of the extent to which the program and people within it are forced to interact with physical artifacts, and have their interpersonal interactions shaped by a physical container. This discussion examines the perceptions of both staff and residents regarding the way the environment of the Center affects their ability to function in the program.

3.1.1 Appearance

Staff and residents alike appreciated the residential character of the buildings. They felt that this quality was useful in maintaining a non-institutional atmosphere. At the same time, however, many of the same respondents believed that the drab and dingy appearance of the Centers often increased the stereotypically negative response of outsiders to a program dealing with ex-convicts. They further noted that this drab-dingy environment did not provide a good working atmosphere, and tended to act as a depressant to the morale of both the staff and residents.

Also important was the report by staff that their efforts to improve the external appearance of buildings and grounds had been the major factor in lessening community opposition to the Centers. They emphasized that this had been more effective than a fairly extensive traditional community relations effort.

3.1.2 Privacy

Next we sought to ascertain whether the buildings afforded reasonable opportunities for both staff and residents to have control over their interactions with others. We asked them whether there were places where they could conduct a private conversation without fear of being overheard or interrupted, or simply where they could get away from others when they needed to relax or concentrate.

Both residents and staff at the Cleveland and Cincinnati Centers, which are the largest of the three Centers, responded that there were plenty of places to hold a private conversation without fear of being overheard under most circumstances. Both groups at the Columbus Center, however, noted that there were few places where such conditions of privacy prevailed. It was noted that the counseling room, which is divided into two sections by a low partition, affords no privacy. Residents expresses a reluctance to speak frankly about their problems under such circumstances. Staff members reported frequent occurrences where staff conversations regarding individuals were overheard and communicated to the individual concerned.

Residents at all three Centers reported that there was insufficient privacy for receiving visitors. This was attributed to a uniform policy restricting visitors from the resident's rooms. Although several of the residents we interviewed reported that they had received no visitors, they all believed this policy to be overly restrictive. Those who had received visitors reported that it was often a difficult and stressful time, which was exacerbated because they were restricted to areas used as recreation spaces by other residents, and consequently their visits were always subject to interruptions and scrutiny by others.

All the residents interviewed were appreciative of the private rooms and emphasized the importance of this feature. All stated that this was one of the most valued attributes of the Centers and one which most distinquish the Centers from the institutions. They all emhasized that it was very important to be able to get away from others at times, and that this was a critical factor in their management of tensions and hostilities.

We observed that most of the treatment coordinators shared office space. Although no staff member reported this as being a problem of concern, we did observe that their activities were frequently disturbed or interrupted.

3.1.3 Supervision

In response to a general question aimed at eliciting perceptions of problems caused by the building and grounds, the staff most frequently mentioned a problem centered on the question of supervision. Staff members in all three Centers mentioned that it was difficult to provide what they believed to be adequate supervision of the behavior of residents because of the size and configuration of the buildings. One staff member said he believed a kind of unobtrusive supervision was necessary, wherein the staff would know what was goind on and have a sense of being in control, without this being obvious to the residents.

A subsequent question specifically addressed to this dimension revealed the following consider-

ations. Because the facilities were not designed with this problem in mind, all have several exits which are not observable from any one point. This, along with the fact that during certain periods only one or two staff persons are on duty, makes any attempt at unobtrusive control impossible. As a consequence, several problems emerge. First is the problem of contraband. Because it is possible for a resident to leave and re-enter unobserved via one of the many exits, occasionally alcohol, drugs, and other contraband have been brought into the Centers. Further, it is easy to hide contraband in some of the Centers. The Columbus Center is a notable exception to this latter problem, since it is the smallest of the three Centers, and all its spaces are used, stashes of contraband are almost immediately discovered. Staff at all three Centers emphasized that this was not a severe problem, and infractions of this nature happened infrequently.

A second related problem arising from the size and complexity of the three buildings had to do with supervising the behaviors of the residents while in the Center. It is possible for residents to engage in prohibited activities such as drinking or gambling without the knowledge of the staff. Given the present configuration of the building, it is impossible to prevent or discourage these kinds of activities short of overt actions, such as periodic room checks or shakedowns which violate the open atmosphere of the Centers.

A third less serious but frequently mentioned problem arising out of the complexity of the layout was noted by staff members at all three Centers. It is simply difficult to locate a person in the Center. Mention was made at all the Centers of the need for a public address system to solve this problem.

3.1.4 Noise

Most residents and staff thought the buildings were exceptionally quiet. There was little mention of problems caused by internal noise transmission, partly due to rules governing the use of radios, stereos, etc. Residents mentioned that this, along with the private rooms, was one of the most valued features of the Centers, and one which most distinguished it from the constant din of noise in the "joint."

3.1.5 Interior Finishing and Furniture

Both staff and residents at all three Centers mentioned the need for painting, particularly, bright colors to "cheer the place up". They all felt the Centers to be drab and dingy, and many expressed a willingness to do the painting themselves. Staff members of the Columbus and Cleveland Centers mentioned the desirability of newer and brighter furniture and draperies. One staff member discussed at some length the detrimental effects of the prevalant dingy colors on morale.

3.1.6 Recreation

Inadequate space for outdoor recreation was the problem most frequently cited by both staff and residents. While the three facilities vary greatly in the size of their grounds, all of the staff members interviewed, and many of the residents, emphasized the need for more on-site recreation space which would accommodate physically vigorous games like baseball, football or basketball. These activities were mentioned by both groups as being especially important in relieving boredom and tension. It should be noted that the original concept of reintegration into the community involved making use of existing community facilities. However, staff members at all three facilities mentioned that attempts had been made to use community facilities but, because of staff shortages and current scheduling practices, there were fewest staff available when residents have the most free time to engage in recreational activities, on evenings and weekends. Consequently, recreational trips are few despite good intentions and an awareness on the part of staff members, that getting out regularly is an important means of alleviating residents penned up feelings. It is not surprising, therefore, that boredom was the most frequent complaint of the residents.

Both staff and residents at the Columbus Center cited their facility as having inadequate indoor recreation space as well. This Center does not have sufficient space to utilize the indoor equipment provided the program by the State.

3.1.7 Size-Capacity

Staff and residents at both the Cleveland and Cincinnati Centers emphasized that their facilities had some excess capacity and could easily accommodate more men. Residents cited certain advantages accruing from this condition, emphasizing the comfortable, uncrowded, relaxed atmosphere, and noting that it eliminated the cramped, locked-up feeling they were familiar with in the institutions. They pointed out that this led to a resultant lessening of tension and conflict, which can be caused by over-stimulation and lack of privacy.

Staff members mentioned that this excess capacity enabled them to easily accommodate new residents, or new functions or activities. It was further noted that this made possible the separation of residents so those with similar problems did not engage in mutually reinforcing each other in negative directions.

The Columbus Center was operating at less than theoretical capacity and had sufficient individual rooms to accommodate up to 15 residents, but the support facilities appeared to be too small to accommodate that many residents comfortably. The staff here cited the need for more space of various kinds, ranging from inside recreation space to office space, more counseling and treatment space, more lounge areas, etc. While the staff emphasized that these were not critical problems, our observations and the frequency with which these inadequacies were cited led us to conclude that until more support space can be provided this Center should probably remain at its present population level, or perhaps be decreased slightly.

3.1.8 Adaptability

One measure of the suitability of a building for an experimental program is the extent to which it will quickly and easily accommodate changes in the program. It is desirable to be able to add or delete activities with a minimum of renovation to the building and its concomitant delay and expense. The staff at the three Centers were queried as to whether the building had posed any limitations in this regard.

The Cleveland and Cincinnati Centers reported plenty of excess capacity in their facilities which would allow them to accommodate almost any new activity they desired. Further, the spaces and arrangements typical of these older residences seemed quite well suited to the types of additional activities which grew out of program modifications.

The smaller residence housing the Columbus Center posed a different situation however. Because it was operating at near "theoretical capacity," any new program required either new space, temporal or scheduling changes, or renovations of existing space. All of these were expensive, slow and disruptive. Consequently, fewer program innovations were possible.

3.1.9 Resident Rooms

The importance of private rooms, a place they could call their own, was stressed by residents at all three Centers. They felt that this was their own place which they could decorate, and control their surroundings to some extent. They also felt that the privacy which these rooms afforded was very important to their personal efforts at tension management. They all mentioned the importance of being able to "get away from others" and to relax out of the eyes of others. They believed this to be another highly valued difference from the "joint".

One of the staff members noted that some residents do not like to be in individual rooms, and although we did not receive any such comments, it would seem both desirable and possible that a few rooms be maintained which could serve both double or single occupancy.

Some of the residents at the Cleveland Center mentioned that some of the larger rooms felt awkward when occupied by only one or two men. They emphasized, however, that they did not mean that more residents should be accommodated in them but rather that the rooms should be subdivided.

3.1.10 Bathroom and Toilet Facilities

Aside from complaints about old plumbing and leaks at all three of the Centers, few references were made to these facilities. Residents mentioned that their program of regular cleaning kept these facilities in acceptable condition.

3.1.11 Maintenance

All three Centers utilized residents to clean and maintain the building and grounds. Each resident was responsible for cleaning his own room and one or two sections of the public areas of the building. Both staff and residents at the three Centers reported this system worked well, although the buildings were old, very large, and required a good deal of continuous work to keep clean and operating.

Staff members noted that they placed a good deal of emphasis on cleanliness, and they believed that the heavier repair-type maintenance was especially beneficial to residents, since it taught them basic skills and a sense of self-reliance/sufficiency which they expected would make them less vulnerable to expensive repair bills once released.

The most severe problems, mentioned about equally by staff from all three Centers, stemmed from the age of the buildings. These had to do with frequent plumbing leaks, cracked plaster and the need for extensive repainting to brighten up the "gloomy, dingy atmosphere" of the Centers.

3.1.12 Smells

The presence and transmission of odors does not appear to be a problem of any significance at any of the Centers. None of the staff or residents of the Cleveland or Cincinnati Centers reported any problems in this regard. Members of the Columbus Center noted that smells from the kitchen were transmitted throughout the house but this was not felt to be a problem. One member of the staff observed that a generally musty odor pervaded the Columbus Center.

3.1.13 Lighting

From the staff's point of view, all three of the Centers have lighting problems. Inadequately lighted hallways and offices were cited as moderate problems. It is interesting to note that residents mentioned no areas which they believed to be poorly lighted.

3.1.14 Counseling and Treatment Facilities

Cleveland and Cincinnati reported that their counseling ang treatment facilities were adequate. At Columbus, however, the counseling rooms lacked adequate privacy. The treatment room was reported to be too small and awkwardly shaped, and in need of certain ancillary facilities, such as a closed circuit video taping system which could be used in the group therapy programs. It was also mentioned that it might be desirable to have more than one treatment room, so that different treatment programs could be run at the same time without interference.

Staff members at the Columbus Center also mentioned that while their treatment room was supposed to function also as a T.V. room in the evenings, it was seldom used as such. They hypothesized that this was due to association of the place with the group therapy sessions which were often quite painful for the residents.

3.2 The Surrounding Environment

The second portion of the interview consisted of a number of questions which explored problems related to the location of the reintegration Centers.

According to staff members at the three Centers, a sizeable proportion of their residents had alcohol-related problems. They mentioned that one especially recurrent problem stemmed from the nearby location of bars or other places where residents could purchase alcohol. They felt that the presence of these facilities posed a constant temptation in times of boredom or stress. Thus, the location of the Centers near these facilities coupled with the ease with which residents can leave and re-enter without being seen, results in a situation which is somewhat conducive to a return to previous behavior patterns. A staff member from the Cincinnati Center described this situation: *"Very near here is one of the worst areas in the city. A collection of bars at an intersection which are frequented by criminals of all kinds. This raises the potential for residents to become involved in illegal activities and constitutes a constant temptation for those with alcohol problems. This intersection is located such that residents must pass by it on their way to the drugstore."*

Temptation, for want of a better word, was as common theme running through the response of the residents as well. They mentioned that constant exposure to people and habitats where illegal activities are encouraged: *"...makes it hard to go straight. People know you and proposition you. Take these air conditioners here...if a guy wanted to sell one to buy a bottle of wine it wouldn't be hard to find a buyer here. Guys are always coming by with wine, and prostitutes come around."*

This problem seemed to be most severe at the Cleveland and Cincinnati Centers, which are located in high crime areas and somewhat less so at Columbus, although the latter area does have a nearby bar which is apparently a local criminal hangout.

A second common theme in the responses of residents at the Cleveland and Cincinnati Centers had to do with problems caused by the location of centers, which were composed of a predominantly white population, in areas which were almost totally black. Several problems seemed to flow from this condition. Any notions of participation in community affairs on the part of residents were quickly discouraged. For example, at one of the centers, residents reportedly tried to attend the local chapter of Alcoholics Anonymous and were rebuffed. In addition, fear was a common theme, especially at the Cleveland Center. All the residents interviewed cited examples of people from the center being assaulted or intimidated in the immediate neighborhood. From the responses of the residents, it was clear that they believed these incidents to be racially motivated. They believed themselves to be a highly visible and highly vulnerable minority in a hostile territory.

3.2.1 Accessibility

All three centers are located in close proximity to most of the requisite commercial and community facilities and no residents or staff mentioned problems in this regard with the exception of recreational facilities, discussed earlier. All centers are located on major transit lines which, according to the adequacy of the system, provide at least some level of accessibility to all areas of the city and to jobs. It should be noted, however, that residents at both the Cleveland and Cincinnati Centers reported that most of the major employment areas were located on the opposite side of town, often requiring a one-way bus ride of over an hour.

An additional problem mentioned by many of the residents stemmed from the fact that they were not "from" the city where the center was located, and that they wanted to return home once released from the program. At the same time, because the program had placed most of them in jobs which they were reluctant to quit, they were faced with a conflict of some magnitude.

Finally, as a result of the same locational decision, many residents mentioned that the centers were sufficiently far from their home communities as to discourage visits from family and friends.

4. POLICY IMPLICATIONS

Many of the problems discussed in the previous section, as well as some of the successful aspects of the physical settings of the centers, lead to suggestions for alterations to those facilities, or suggestions regarding appropriate criteria for the selection of future facilities. While these grew out of our evaluation of one particular program, it is our belief that many have general applicability to other halfway-

house type programs. (6)

4.1 Privacy

All residents should be provided the option of a private room. All counseling rooms should be adequately soundproofed and located away from the major activity centers of the building. Staff offices should be adequately soundproofed and if it is necessary for staff to share offices, they should have immediate access to a private counseling space. Private visiting rooms should be provided so that a resident can be assured of a distraction-free visit during this often stressful period.

4.2 Size

Where possible, some degree of excess capacity should be maintained so as to facilitate implementation of new programs and activities.

To the extent that resources permit, the current size of resident populations (15-20) should be maintained. This will enable the centers to keep their relaxed non-institutional character, which is highly valued by residents and staff alike.

4.3 Recreation

Wherever possible, on-site recreational facilities which would accommodate informal basketball, baseball, volleyball or football games should be provided. This should be supplemented with scheduled off-site visits to surrounding facilities. In addition, adequate indoor facilities should be provided.

4.4 Supervision

To the extent possible, all entrances should be visible from some point commonly used by staff. This would allow for the unobtrusive control desired by the staff. It might further help to segregate activity areas according to their temporal patterning. This would allow for the consolidation of activities into one area on one floor which could be more easily watched by one or two staff.

4.5 Lighting

Adequate lighting should be provided to prevent a dark-dingy atmosphere.

4.6 Appearance

Considerable stress should be placed on the outside appearance of the building and grounds as a means of maintaining good relations with the community. Interior finishes and furnishings should employ bright, cheerful colors rather than the drab institutional colors currently prevalent. Where possible, residences, rather than "institutional" type structures, should continue to be used.

4.7 Location

Our findings suggest that the current policy of locating centers according to the availability of relatively inexpensive space and lack of community resistance is one which should be re-examined. Areas of any city vary greatly in the kinds of behavior which are permissible within them and the extent to which residents and other users will conform to and enforce that implicit social contract. The sites selected for two of the existing Reintegration Centers are located in the most behaviorally open milieus of their respective cities. These areas are habitats where criminal and other deviant behavior patterns are often the norm, or in any case, are seldom prohibited or discouraged. Consequently, Reintegration Center residents are not exposed to areas where the accepted rules of behavior are congruent with those advocated in the treatment programs. Rather they are immersed in a community in which the accepted and normal behavior pattern is much closer to that for which they were originally institutionalized.

If the purpose of the Reintegration Centers is "reintegration back into a community" then some care should be given as to which community that is to be. In our view, the program is much more likely to succeed in its goals of changing values and behavior patterns of residents, if it changes their environment as well to one which is more congruent with the purpose of the program.

To the extent possible, any expansion in the program should be accommodated by additional centers located in other regions of the state, so as to increase the ability of residents to reintegrate back into their home community if they desire, and maintain the employment secured while at the center. This ability to increase locational stability should be a major factor in reducing adaptation stresses on residents. A somewhat more decentralized locational policy should facilitate visiting and family contact as well.

4.8 Racial Composition

So long as the program continues to attract a predominately white population, centers should be located in areas which have a similar racial composition. To do otherwise makes the residents a highly visible minority, easily identifiable as ex-cons and therefore vulnerable to discriminatory actions and to solicitations aimed at re-involving them with criminal activity.

4.9 Access

Access to employment should be considered in the selection of a site for a center. While it is not possible to predict a specific location where any individual is likely to find employment, it should be possible to identify the major employment areas in the city in question, which are likely to offer employment opportunities to residents, and in addition, to identify the major public transportation routes serving those areas, and then to select a location which is easily accessible to the employment areas. A reasonable criterion would be one-way commuting of no more than 45 minutes, with no more than one transfer required. Access to other required services should be considered as well.

5. CONCLUSIONS

In general, this evaluation has shown that the typical pattern of facility selection used by halfway-houses seems to be a good one. The large, old residences are well suited in general to their needs. At the same time, however, our findings show rather conclusively that the companion policy of locating halfway-house type programs so as to minimize community resistance is one which should be re-examind.

6. NOTES

(1) This report was funded in part by a grant (3860-00-J3-72) from the Administration of Justice Division of the Ohio Department of Economic and Community Development. Such funding does not necessarily indicate concurrence with the findings or recommendations within. I am also indebted to Ms. Marcia Cohen for editorial assistance, and to Ms. Ellen Wallace for typing of this report.

(2) It should be noted that this study was only a small portion of a comprehensive program evaluation conducted by the Program for the Study of Crime and Delinquency at the Ohio State University.

(3) It should be noted that this was not a random sample in the strict sense of the word, rather staff and residents were interviewed on the basis of availability. No formal process of random selection was employed.

(4) Abraham Kaplan, "Some Consideration for a Planning Program for Puerto Rico," unpublished paper delivered at the Conference of the American Institute of Planners, 1959.

(5) To be fair, this commitment is also a product of the new Federal guidelines which mandate periodic evaluation.

(6) It should be noted that a number of specific policy suggestions for the three centers examined have been omitted from this report. Only those which we believed to have some general application are included.

THE EFFECT OF HETEROGENEITY ON NEIGHBORHOOD SOCIAL BEHAVIOR

Gertrude S. Fish, Ph.D.

College of Human Ecology
University of Maryland
College Park, Maryland   20742

ABSTRACT

Builders and government policy makers need more information about socioeconomic residential mixing. A random sample of 19 hamlets in Tioga County, New York State yielded 229 interviews of wives and female heads of households. The hamlets were divided into homogeneous and heterogeneous groups by adding the standard deviations for education of the husband, occupation rank of the husband, income per capita of the household, and amenity level of the house. Households were divided into high income and low income at the $9,000 level. Path analysis yielded the variables having an effect significant at the five percent level on satisfaction with the house, satisfaction with the neighborhood, and propensity to move. The data support the following statements: 1) low income households have a higher propensity to move than do high income households regardless of the socioeconomic heterogeneity of the neighborhood, 2) low income families in heterogeneous neighborhoods have a lower percent of their total visits from relatives than do low income families in homogeneous neighborhoods, 3) heterogeneity has a positive influence on organizational attendance for low income families, 4) organizational attendance for low income households in homogeneous neighborhoods has a positive influence on propensity to move, 5) more status oriented variables influence satisfaction in heterogeneous neighborhoods. The methods employed in analyzing the data, namely, using the standard deviations to measure heterogeneity and path analysis to demonstrate that a different ambience influenced satisfaction under contrasting degrees of heterogeneity, were found to be effective.

Recent legislation supports socioeconomic mixing of households in residential settings. The Housing Act of 1974 encouraged builders to designate 20% of the units in new buildings for low income households by increasing the number of Section 8 units set aside for subsidy to the builder. A scattersite housing policy is being urged upon upper and middle income communities in the name of justice and equality, and the Housing Allowance program would allow lower income families to rent units priced for higher income level households.

Builders of new towns and other large scale residential developments must make decisions about the range of rents or selling prices of the dwelling units to be built. The range chosen may prohibit poorer families from living there and determine the attractiveness of the area for high income families. Furthermore, large developments, once built, pre-empt the range of choice that piecemeal development might afford as to price and amenity of housing. As a result, the socioeconomic mix of residents and the social composition of the residential environment is partially predetermined by the builder. By removing free market choice, large scale developers incur an added burden of responsibility to make informed decisions.

However, the government and large scale builders do not have much information on which to base their decisions. The need for more information about socioeconomic mixing of residents has recently been documented by the report to HUD entitled Freedom of Choice in Housing: Opportunities and Constraints (Report of the Social Science Panel, p.63) which said;

> A more adequate knowledge base is needed in order to determine the feasibility of socioeconomic residential mixing. More information is needed about why people live where they do.

Gans (p.163, 1968) suggests that

> The proper solution is a moderate degree of homogeneity, although at this point no one knows how to define this degree operationally or how to develop planning guides for it.

Government and builders keep on operating with or without an adequate knowledge base. That's nothing new. What is new and distinctly encouraging is the man-environment research that EDRA members are doing, and I am happy to be here today to tell you about the results of my research on the effect of heterogeneity on social behavior in residential neighborhoods. Our task as man-environment researchers is to expand the information available to builders and government policy makers about why people live where they do and to develop planning guides for socioeconomic mixing of households.

If we want to talk about the effect of the characteristics of groups on the behavior of individuals in the group, what kinds of behaviors can we measure? In other words, what are some researchable questions? One question that I asked of my data was whether there was a difference in social interaction patterns in homogeneous as compared to heterogeneous residential neighborhoods. When I talk about heterogeneity I am talking about socioeconomic heterogeneity as opposed to religious, racial, or age heterogeneity. Do people behave differently in homogeneous neighborhoods than in heterogeneous neighborhoods? Does their satisfaction with the house and neighborhood depend on the same kinds of variables in both contexts?

My research indicates that there is a difference in social behavior between residential areas with different degrees of heterogeneity. The social behavior that was measured was number of visits during the week preceding the interview, the percent of those visits that were from relatives, and whether the effect of the visiting was positive or negative on the family's satisfaction with the house, satisfaction with the neighborhood, and increased or decreased the household's propensity to move. Comparing social interaction patterns in homogeneous and heterogeneous neighborhoods included measures of attendance at formal organization meetings. Do people living in homogeneous neighborhoods exhibit a different level of organizational attendance, and is the effect of that social behavior on their propensity to move the same in all cases?

My sample* consisted of 229 wives and female heads of household who lived in rural neighborhoods in Tioga County in New York State (just south of Cornell University). Actually, they were residents of hamlets, and as such, their neighborhoods were clusters of houses surrounded by uninhabited land. A random sample of hamlets was drawn, and all households were interviewed. The sample was divided on the basis of income into those households having an annual income of $9,000 or more and those having $8,999 or less; the sample was also divided into homogeneous hamlets and heterogeneous hamlets on the basis of the sum of standard deviations of socioeconomic status measures. These divisions allowed me to compare the determinants of residential satisfaction in approximately equal-sized groups in the following contexts:

1) high income households in homogeneous neighborhoods
2) high income households in heterogeneous neighborhoods
3) low income households in homogeneous neighborhoods
4) low income households in heterogeneous neighborhoods

---

*The collection of the data was supported by funds from the New York State Agricultural Experiment Station, Cornell University, Ithaca, New York. The analysis of the data was supported by a grant from the New York State Urban Development Corporation, Avenue of Americas, New York City. The findings from the path analyses are limited by the size of the sample.

Three groups of variables measured status-oriented, person-oriented and voluntary contract behavior. If the significant effects on residential satisfaction came from the amenity level of the house, the education level of the wife, or ownership of the house I interpreted the data to indicate that the households' satisfaction was derived from measures of social status. If the significant effects on residential satisfaction come from measures of using leisure time in the same ways as the other residents and visiting I interpreted the data to indicate that the households' satisfaction was derived from measures of person-orientedness. Attendance at formal organization meeting was also measured, and is related to what Esser terms "voluntary contract," a group staying together for individual (cultural) reasons (p.2 in Smith, 1971).

The strategy in general was to analyze the relationships among the variables by using path analysis. The three sets of variables (status-oriented, person-oriented, and voluntary contract) are all in the regressions for each group, but the path diagram shows only the variables that have an effect significant at the 5 percent level on satisfaction with the house and neighborhood and propensity to move. Each diagram then represents a finding, for each one illustrates for that particular subsample the variables from the basic set that have statistically significant effects on the measures of satisfaction. If the determinants of satisfaction for low income households in heterogeneous neighborhood are different that the determinants of satisfaction for low income households in homogeneous neighborhoods, then we may conclude that the degree of heterogeneity is causing the difference. The variables that are in the path diagram for each subsample indicate behavior in a context specifying income level and socioeconomic heterogeneity.

The data indicated that:

Low income households have a higher propensity to move than high income households. The difference between the mean propensity to move for all high income households (0.85) and the mean for all low income households (1.25) was significant at the 5 percent level. Thus it was concluded that level of income has a significant effect on propensity to move regardless of the socioeconomic heterogeneity of the neighborhood (Fish, 1973).

The path diagram for high income households in homogeneous neighborhoods indicates that ownership of the home (OWNER) and attendance at formal organization meetings (ORGATT) have a negative influence on propensity to move (MOVE) (see Figure 1). Organizational attendance increases satisfaction with the house (HOUSAT); satisfaction with the house increases satisfaction with the neighborhood (NHDSAT). Visiting (VISITS) however, increases the propensity to move and decreases satisfaction with the neighborhood. This model explains 32 percent of the variance in propensity to move, 19 percent of the variance in satisfaction with the neighborhood and 6 percent of the variance in satisfaction with the house [the residuals (.68, .81, and .94) measure the variance not explained by the model but attributed to all other influences not accounted for]. Households with incomes of $9,000 or more and living in homogeneous neighborhoods showed the lowest mean propensity to move of any of the subsamples the highest mean satisfaction with the neighborhood, and the highest mean satisfaction with the house.

FIGURE 1. MODEL FOR RESIDENTIAL SATISFACTION FOR HOUSEHOLDS WITH INCOMES OF $9,000 OR MORE LIVING IN HOMOGENEOUS NEIGHBORHOODS. (n=55)

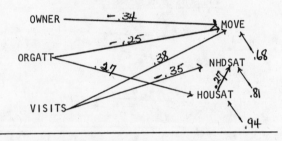

The desire for privacy for the nuclear family is documented in Whyte's Organization Man (Chapter XXV). The wives struggled with conflicting forces, one the desire to be a member of the neighborhood group, the other to preserve privacy for a separate family life. We could speculate from the path model that formal organization meetings place the interaction away from the family circle thus preserving its privacy.

The model for high income households in heterogeneous neighborhoods shows only variables indicating status-oriented behavior (ownership of the house and amenity level of the house) and voluntary contract behavior (organizational attendance). Notice that satisfaction with the house does not affect the propensity to move (MOVE), but that satisfaction with the neighborhood (NHDSAT) has a strong influence (see Figure 2). The negative effect of attendance at organizational meetings on satisfaction with the house is difficult to explain.

FIGURE 2. MODEL FOR RESIDENTIAL SATISFACTION FOR HOUSEHOLDS WITH INCOMES OF $9,000 OR MORE IN HETEROGENEOUS NEIGHBORHOODS. (n=62)

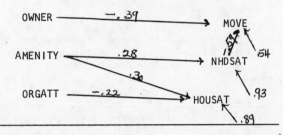

Though the findings were not significant, the direction of the means in Table 1 suggests that satisfaction with the neighborhood is higher in homogeneous neighborhoods.

TABLE 1. RELATIONSHIP BETWEEN VISITS FROM NEIGHBORS AND SATISFACTION WITH THE NEIGHBORHOOD (N).

Group (HH=Household)	Standardized Beta	NHDSAT
High income HH/homog. Ns	-.35	4.06
All HH/homogeneous Ns	-.15	3.92
All high income HH	-.11	3.91
Low income HH/homog. Ns	-.05	3.81
High income HH/hetero. Ns	.09	3.79
Low income HH/hetero. Ns	.20	3.70

The mean number of neighborhood visits received by the household during the week preceding the interview was not different for all households in homogeneous neighborhoods than the mean for all households in heterogeneous neighborhoods, i.e., the homogeneity of the neighborhood was not affecting the number of neighborhood visits in the sample. However, the number of visits had a significant negative effect on neighborhood satisfaction for high income households in homogeneous neighborhoods with a standardized beta of -.35. The beta for all households in homogeneous areas was -.15 and had an effect significant at the 10 percent level. Though the effects were not significant, the direction of the betas shows a pattern of negative influence in homogeneous areas and positive influence in heterogeneous areas (see Table 1). This pattern indicates that visiting is indeed disturbing privacy in homogeneous neighborhoods even though there is not a significant difference between the mean number of visits for any two subsamples, i.e., the same level of neighborhood visiting is disturbing in a homogeneous setting but not in a heterogeneous setting.

Notice that the means for neighborhood satisfaction run in the opposite direction. Is this
again an illustration of the tension at the
interface of privacy and belonging?

One explanation for the positive influence of
visiting on satisfaction may be found in the
percent of the household's total visits that
were from relatives. It had been hypothesized
that low income households would have a higher
percentage of visits from relatives than high
income households. The data did not support
this hypothesis. Table 2 shows that low income
households living in homogeneous neighborhoods
had a mean percent of total visits from relatives of 0.40 while low income households in
heterogeneous neighborhoods had a mean of 0.30
(see Table 2). The households of the same income level (low income) but in different degrees
of socioeconomic heterogeneity have means that
are significantly different at the 5 percent
level for percent of visits by relatives. This
would support an interpretation that the contextual quality of socioeconomic heterogeneity
has a significant effect on patterns of social
interaction for low income households. Therefore, the positive effect of neighborhood visiting for low income households in heterogeneous
neighborhoods may have depended partly on the
fact that the visitors were relatives.

TABLE 2. PERCENT VISITS FROM RELATIVES BY
          HOUSEHOLD INCOME AND NEIGHBORHOOD
          TYPE.

	Homogeneous	Heterogeneous	All N's
Low income	.404	.300	.359
High income	.371	.349	.360
All households	.388	.327	.359

Even though the mean for organizational attendance for all low income households living in
homogeneous neighborhoods is low in comparison
to the other groups (see Table 3), organizational attendance for low income households in
homogeneous neighborhoods had a significant
positive effect on propensity to move (see
Figure 3).

TABLE 3. AVERAGE ORGANIZATIONAL ATTENDANCE
          PER YEAR BY HOUSEHOLD AND NEIGHBOR-
          HOOD TYPE.

	Homogeneous	Heterogeneous	All N's
Low Income	27.78	43.27	34.42
High income	35.00	47.15	41.44
All	31.12	45.46	38.00

The difference between the means for number of
meetings attended for all households in homogeneous neighborhoods and all households in
heterogeneous neighborhoods was significant at

the 5 percent level indicating that heterogeneity has a significant positive effect on
organizational attendance.

FIGURE 3. MODEL FOR RESIDENTIAL SATISFACTION
           FOR HOUSEHOLDS WITH INCOMES OF
           $8,999 OR LESS LIVING IN HOMOGENEOUS
           NEIGHBORHOODS. (n=64)

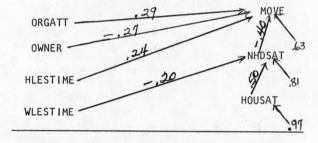

FIGURE 4. MODEL FOR RESIDENTIAL SATISFACTION
           FOR LOW INCOME HOUSEHOLDS IN HETERO-
           GENEOUS NEIGHBORHOODS. (n=48)

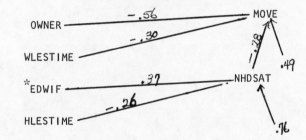

*education of wife

Figure 4, the model for low income households in
heterogeneous neighborhoods, explains more of
the variance in propensity to move than any of
the other models (.49 percent is unexplained and
attributed to all other causes not accounted
for). Figure 4 also has the lowest residual for
neighborhood satisfaction (.76) and is therefore our "best" model. The model for high income households in heterogeneous neighborhoods
explains the next highest percentage of the
variance in propensity to move (54 percent is
not explained). Ownership of the dwelling unit
had a negative influence on propensity to move
in all circumstances, though its influence was
stronger in heterogeneous neighborhoods than in
homogeneous neighborhoods after controlling for
income level (compare the betas on OWNER → MOVE
in Figures 1 thru 4).

Differences in the use of leisure time influenced
the satisfaction of lower income households.
Differences in the use of leisure time for
husbands in low income households in heterogeneous neighborhoods had a negative influence on
satisfaction with the neighborhood; in homogeneous neighborhoods differences in the
husbands' use of leisure time had a positive

influence on propensity to move. Both effects indicate dissatisfaction. The effect of differences in the use of leisure time for wives in low income households in homogeneous neighborhoods also has a negative influence on neighborhood satisfaction. These influences indicate person-oriented behavior.

In Figure 4, however, differences in the use of wives' leisure time had a negative influence on propensity to move (a positive effect on satisfaction). In this diagram the education of the wife (EDWIF) had a significant positive effect on neighborhood satisfaction. One might interpret the data as supporting a statement that wives from low income households who had more than eleven years (the mean) of formal education would have a higher level of satisfaction in a heterogeneous neighborhood than wives with less than that level of education. The wives in this group demonstrate a desire for privacy or autonomous behavior while the husbands indicate dissatisfaction with the neighborhood when their use of leisure time differs from that of the other husbands.

To summarize, low income families in heterogeneous neighborhoods had a significantly lower percent of their total visits from relatives than low income families in homogeneous neighborhoods; heterogeneity had a significant positive effect on organizational attendance for low income households; organizational attendance for low income households in homogeneous neighborhoods had a significant positive effect on propensity to move; more status-oriented variables influenced satisfaction in heterogeneous neighborhoods.

Does any pattern emerge from these findings? Homogeneity and heterogeneity both seem to call forth desirable behaviors. Heterogeneity, in general, seems to encourage what Robert Ardrey calls voluntary contract behavior.

> Our social contracts, as Robert Ardrey phrases it, are voluntary contracts in contrast to those of the animal which as to abide by the involuntary contract of communal blood and soil, where the group stays together for biological reasons. But with man the posibility arose that a group stay together for individual (cultural) reasons (Esser, p.2).

Voluntary contract behaviors would seem to involve people in the mainstream of society. Person-oriented behaviors would seem more akin to the emotional part of the brain, "crystallizations of our social life which are based on shared experiences", and further,

> It implies that you value where you are born and to whom you are born, that you know and like your territory and your friends, that the

unknown outside is hostile and all outsiders are strangers (Esser).

Are both kinds of behavior necessary to healthy social functioning of neighborhoods? Let's refer to the literature, to case studies of neighborhoods. Gan's study of The Urban Villagers was about a group of people who were bound together on the basis of kinship and territory. Their lack of involvement in organizations outside their immediate neighborhood doomed them to be demolished by urban renewal. Marc Fried caught the essence of their emotions in "Grieving for a Lost Home" showing their attachment to a particular territory. In Tally's Corner, the study of negro street corner men by Elliot Liebow, the men were not able to sustain kinship and family roles and were reduced to an existence in which only the street corner had meaning for them--only a territory reassured them of their individual existence. Elizabeth Bott found that couples with tight knit kin groups had less interaction between husband and wife. They kept in contact with their own friends and kin, and there was little communication or joint activity between husband and wife. This condition is similar to the wives' behavior in the families in Tally's Corner where survival demanded that the female ties in the extended family be strong. The result is that there is less invested in the family relationships and the endurance and stability of the family is undermined. Emotional investment seems to coincide with economic dependence, prompted by the instinct to survive perhaps. Young and Willmott's study of London slum families moved to a new housing estate demonstrates again that there are groups of people in modern society at the lower end of the economic scale who are not able to negotiate voluntary contracts, who still live by the "involuntary contract of communal blood and soil" (Ardrey and Esser).

When the families moved to a new housing estate they changed from a people-centered to a house-centered existence and lived in social isolation. Young and Willmott observed that:

> their need for respect is just as strong as it ever was, but instead of being able to find satisfaction in actual living relationships, through the personal respect that accompanies almost any steady human interaction, they have to turn to the other kind of respect that is awarded, by some strange sort of common understanding, for the quantity and quality of possessions with which the person surrounds himself.

Liebow, Bott, Gans, and Young and Willmott document patterns of interaction that separate families of lower socioeconomic status from the mainstream of society. The case studies cited here were about neighborhoods which had all of the benefits of homogeneity but one of the benefits of heterogeneity. The data from my research showed that heterogeneity had a significant positive effect on organizational attendance, and that low income households in homogeneous neighborhoods who attended organization meetings had a higher propensity to move. These findings might be interpreted to mean that those who can negotiate voluntary contracts feel impelled to leave a group who cannot to join the mainstream of society.

The benefits of homogeneity are demonstrated by the literature also. Small differences, or homogeneity, would create a social environment that would encourage communication and social involvement. In Social Pressures in Informal Groups: A Study of Human Factors in Housing, Festinger, Schacter, and Back found that:

> ...social groupings create channels
> of communication for the flow of
> information and opinions. Standards
> for attitudes and behavior relevant
> to the functioning of the social
> group develop, with resulting uni-
> formity among the members of the
> group. Pressures toward conformity
> to these standards may result in the
> exclusion of deviates from the
> social group.

Festinger, Schacter, and Back's study was done on an extremely homogeneous group, returned war veterans in married student housing at MIT.

Eleanor Maccoby's study of "Community Integration and The Social Control of Juvenile Delinquency" offered evidence that socialization from such informal neighborhood pressures was effective for constraining the behavior of youth.

Other studies document the effect of social environment on political effectiveness, the rates of divorce, admission to mental institutions, and favorable treatment outcomes for mental patients (Wechsler and Pugh, Jaco, Moos). If, as the data indicates, satisfaction with the house is highest in homogeneous neighborhoods and satisfaction with the neighborhood is highest in homogeneous neighborhoods, the logical conclusion is that there is a greater degree of social organization in homogeneous neighborhoods that is supporting and constraining the behavior of the residents and preserving their control of the environment.

We may conclude that we have in essence tested Gan's statement on Page 1 and found that the "proper solution is (indeed) a moderate degree of homogeneity"; by measuring socioeconomic heterogeneity by the standard deviation method we have offered an operational definition that seems to work; and we have added a few bits and pieces of information that may help determine the feasibility of socioeconomic residential

mixing. Path analysis of the data is helpful when seeking determinants of satisfaction when the researcher expects those determinants to shift from one set of variables to another.

A larger sample would be required to validate the findings of the investigation reported here, but the methods used have characteristics which recommend them to social area analysis. Planning guides could come from repeating this study on a large urban sample.

reference

ELIZABETH BOTT, Family and Social Network. (London: Tavistock Publications, 1957).

ARISTEDE H. ESSER, "Strategies for Research in Man-Environment Systems", in Smith, W. M. (Ed.), Ecology of Human Living Environments. (Green Bay, Wis.: The University of Wisconsin-Green Bay, 1971).

LEON FESTINGER, STANLEY SCHACTER, AND KURT BACK, Social Pressures in Informal Groups: A Study of the Human Factors in Housing. (Stanford: Stanford University Press, 1950).

GERTRUDE S. FISH, The Effect of Socioeconomic Level and Heterogeneity on the Determinants of Residential Satisfaction and Residential Mobility: A Relational and Contextual Analysis, dissertation, Cornell University, Ithaca, New York, 1973.

MARC FRIED, "Grieving for a Lost Home", in Leonard Duhl, (Ed.), The Urban Condition. (New York: Basic Books, Inc., 1963).

HERBERT J. GANS, The Urban Villagers. (New York: The Free Press, 1962).

HERBERT J. GANS, "Planning and Social Life: Friendship and Neighbor Relations", in People and Plans (New York: Basic Books, 1968), p.163.

J. HENRY, Culture Against Man. (New York: Random House, 1963).

E. GARTLY JACO, "Social Stress and Mental Illness in the Community", in Community Structure and Analysis, Marvin Sussman, Ed. (New York: Thomas Cromwell, 1959).

ELEANOR MACCOBY, "Community Integration and the Social Control of Juvenile Delinquency". Journal of Social Issues, 14, 1958, pp.38-41.

RUDOLPH MOOS, "Assessment of the Psychosocial Environments of Cummunity-Oriented Psychiatric Treatment Programs", in Rudolph Moos and Paul Insel (Eds.), Issues in Social Ecology. (National Press Books: Palo Alto, Calif., 1974).

Social Science Panel Report, <u>Freedom of Choice in Housing: Opportunities and Constraints</u>. National Academy of Sciences-National Academy of Engineering, Washington, D.C., 1972.

HENRY WECHSLER AND THOMAS F. PUGH, "Fit of Individual and Community Characteristics and Rates of Psychiatric Hospitalization", <u>American Journal of Sociology</u>, 73 (November, 1967).

WILLIAM H. WHYTE, JR., <u>The Organization Man</u>. (New York: Doubleday and Company, Inc., 1956). Chapter XXV

MICHAEL YOUNG AND PETER WILLMOTT, <u>Family and Kinship in East London</u>. (London: Routledge and Kegan Paul, 1957).

THE HIDDEN STRUCTURE OF CHILDREN'S PLAY IN AN URBAN ENVIRONMENT*

Stephen Grabow, Ph.D.
School of Architecture and Urban Design
University of Kansas

Neil J. Salkind, Ph.D.
Department of Educational Psychology
University of Kansas

ABSTRACT

Although play has been investigated from a variety of perspectives, the way in which the child in an urban setting interacts with the environment is relatively unexplored. The primary objective of the project was to determine the location and extent of use of provided play areas (parks, open spaces, playgrounds, etc.) utilized by a sample of urban elementary school children, and to compare these findings with the actual or observed locations of use. The results yielded a spatial image of children's play in the city and strongly suggest that a "hidden" structure does exist. That is, children do not place as much importance on structures provided by conventional agencies as they do on elements they create themselves. Further analysis in cognitive mapping indicated a spatial or sequential adaptation to the city, evidencing a maturity and a grasp of the intricacies offered by the urban environment.

1. INTRODUCTION

Play is one of the most powerful and fascinating themes within the province of human development. Whether seen as an end in itself, or as the release of surplus energy, play has recently become a focal point of investigation for social and behavioral scientists, although even the Greek philosophers engaged in speculation on the topic.

Plato felt that play must be voluntary and that regimentation of any form was counter to its nature. Aristotle, on the other hand, stressed that play must be moderated and tempered to fit the needs of the individual. Jean Piaget (1962), the noted Swiss developmental psychologist, assumes that play, as the main basis of civilization, is unique in that it is a pure activity and remarkably alike for all people. Huizinga (1967) also comments extensively on the importance of play as a distinct and integral factor in the cultural life of society. He observes that civilization arises and develops as play progresses. His theoretical orientation is reminiscent of G. Stanley Hall's (1916) notion that an organism "recapitulates" the history of its development as part of a species.

*This research was supported by a grant from The National Endowment for the Arts, Washington, D.C.

These classical notions of play are congruent with the beliefs postulated by contemporary developmental psychologists who stress the importance of personal experience and adaptive processes in human growth.

1.1. Review of the Literature

Ellis (1973) presents the most comprehensive summary of approaches to date, dividing theories of play into three sets: classical, modern, and recent. The classical theories focus on surplus energy, instinctual needs, preparation for later life, recapitulation, and relaxation to allow for participation. Modern theories seems to focus more on the importance of experience than on any inherited or pre-existing tendencies in the individual. These theories have become popular since the turn of the century. The last set discussed by Ellis consists of recent theories of play, formulated during the last ten years, where theory and methods in other fields have contributed substantially to a better understanding of the topic.

In seeking a broad spectrum of experiences to satisfy developmental needs, such as autonomy and independence, children strive to maximize their interaction with the world outside of their own immediate life space (Erickson, 1972). Almost twenty years ago, R.W. White (1959) offered the thesis that the motivational concept of competence can be introduced to further the process of effective interaction with the environment. Millar (1968) has advanced the hypothesis of the importance of play as a catalyst which forces the child to interact with various environmental components. While the direct purpose of play may not be identifiable in these views, there is nonetheless an insistence of the belief in some intrinsic need to deal with the environment.

Ellis and others generally believe that play is motivated by a need to raise the level of arousal towards the optimal. The basic theme of this definition provides a foundation upon which the hypothesis of the present study is based. Specifically, that children seek out experiences and environments that maximize their total growth.

1.2. The Problem

The substance or content of play itself has been extensively researched, including the context within which it takes place. A major weakness of many of these studies, however, is the use of methods where the researcher investigates "individual constancies" (under the designated conditions) but disregards "individual variants" (under different conditions). A behavior as complex and significant as play must be studied under a variety of conditions and seen as dependent upon the context within which it occurs. A few descriptive studies do exist for both suburban and inner city contexts (Aiello et al., 1974; Coates and Bussard, 1974; Coates and Sanoff, 1973; Cooper, 1974; Rothenberg et al., 1974), and they provide a useful comparative foundation for the present study.

Although the importance of play as a component of healthy psychological development is undisputed, few studies have addressed the broad issue of how effectively children use and are served by the play environments available to them. This question is necessary if one is concerned with the applicability of research in the area of children's play.

Most social institutions (including cities) attempt to satisfy children's needs by providing a structured pattern of recreational and open spaces such as playgrounds, parks, and schoolyards. This traditional pattern, incorporated into many city charters, is based on the early 20th century idea of the "urban neighborhood" (Keller, 1968). It is becoming increasingly clear, however, that this pattern of play and learning spaces for children in urban settings is inadequate and a major factor in the rapid growth of supposedly child-oriented suburbs (Jacobs, 1960).

Recent findings suggest that despite convenient access, good maintenance, and organized recreational "programs," neighborhood parks are grossly underused (Gold, 1972). The problem of the non-use of existing facilities appears to be a symptom of the fact that only recently have children's needs been understood to be an important factor in environmental design (Moore, 1970). The recent growth of research activity in the behavioral sciences related to early childhood development has created a demand for alternative and innovative approaches to the design of play environments (Gramza, 1971).

Although some alternatives to the traditional pattern of play environments have been proposed (Dattner, 1969; Cooper, 1970; Carr and Lynch, 1968; Friedberg and Berkeley, 1970), it is still quite clear, however, that little systematic knowledge has been accumulated regarding the way urban environments actually function in relation to children's play behavior (Derman, 1974). Not only must the content of play be described, but the context as well, including the children's own representational schemes of "their" environment. Similarly the child's desires and conceptions of play spaces must be more clearly understood before application of research can be achieved. The present study, for example, suggests that some of the critical assumptions about the utility of the traditional pattern of play spaces need re-evaluation when examined in terms of childhood play behaviors.

1.3. Objectives

The primary objective of this study was to determine the locations, extent of use, and activity patterns of "provided" play areas (municipal properties, playgrounds, parks, open spaces, etc.) utilized by urban elementary school children, and compare these findings to the observed or actual locations used by the children. The four sub-objectives included (a) to determine the normative type play behaviors surrounding a selected urban elementary school; (b) to compare the location of play activities to the location of provided facilities in the target neighborhood; (c) to examine

the relationship between the structure of play and the structure of the environment in which the play activities take place; and (c) to describe spatially the hidden structure of play from both the child's frame of reference as well as that of the planner or designer.

1.4. Description of the Site

The area selected for study was a residential neighborhood adjacent to the central business district of Kansas City, Missouri. The inner city population of this neighborhood of about 7,500 persons is predominantly low-income and racially mixed (white, black, and Mexican-American). The neighborhood itself is well-defined by railroad tracks and freeways and conforms nicely to Keller's (1968) model of "urban neighborhood."

The housing is a mixture of single-family bungalow, multi-family walkup, and public project-type units. The overall density is relatively low, with an abundance of small parks and vacant lots, typical of midwestern cities. Recreational facilities for the approximately 1,000 elementary school age children consist of a school playground, four public parks, a landscaped park area along the principal through street, two tot-lots, and a vest-pocket park. The elementary and junior high school are central.

1.5. Survey Sample

The sample population consisted of 45 elementary school children between 9 and 11 years old. This range was chosen because of research findings which indicate that the greatest amount of out-of-house play of any group of children is characteristic of this age group (Smart and Smart, 1972). The racial mix was representative of the neighborhood as a whole (33% black, 36% white, and 31% Mexican-American).

2. INSTRUMENT DEVELOPMENT AND ADMINISTRATION

A series of interviews, inventories, and diaries were employed to determine the locations, extent of use, and activity patterns of play areas utilized by the children. In addition, "cognitive maps" were drawn by each child.

2.1. Pre-mapping Interviews

Each child was taken from the classroom to a small interview room provided by the school. The child was introduced to the research team and asked questions about neighborhood play (e.g. favorite games, favorite places, etc.) These interviews were taped and transcribed for later analysis.

2.2. Cognitive Mapping

Following the interview, each child was asked to draw maps of their neighborhood environment. (Earlier exercises in mapping were conducted with the cooperation of the art teacher.) The utility of user-drawn maps in eliciting information about the environment was first demonstrated by Lynch

(1960) in his study of urban imagery in three American cities. In the past decade, "cognitive mapping" has emerged as a powerful research tool in environmental design (Honikman, 1974; Lee, 1975) and has been useful in descriptive studies of children's environments (Blaut and McCleary, 1970).

The essence of the Lynch model is that people form images of their environment in terms of five basic elements: nodes, or high concentrations of activity; districts, or large areas identified by some thematic concentration, such as land-use; paths, or connections between high-use places; edges, or boundaries between elements; and landmarks, or points of orientation and identity in the overall pattern. Lynch found that people in diverse urban environments tend to structure their images of these environments in terms of these basic elements and that they learn to do this in childhood (Lynch and Lukashok, 1956).

Analysis of maps in this study revealed that children in this age group (9-11 years) cognitively structure their environment in terms of nodes, landmarks, and paths and that districts and edges receive marginal (if any) articulation. Their maps

correspond to what in human geography is called the "home range" (Anderson and Tindall, 1972; Andrews, 1973). In the case of children, the home range is the series of territorial linkages and settings voluntarily traversed by the child, alone or in groups. Collectively, the home range of a representative sample of children in a community is a reliable indication of the structure of their environment. In addition to the home itself, it is the world in which they spend most of their time.

During the mapping sessions each child was asked to show how he or she went from school to home and then from home to play, identifying distinctive elements, favorite places, etc. Each session was taped and the transcribed summaries were used together with the maps and verbal interviews for detailed analysis.

A composite map was drawn from the calculation of path lengths, path frequencies, the collective list of principal elements (with a 10% cutoff), and an intuitive impression of the child's world which comes from studying their maps, field observation, and familiarity with the Lynch model (see FIGURE 1). This map represents a collective image of the child's environment with particular

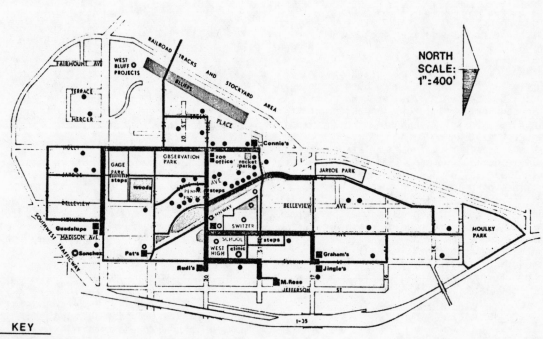

KEY

● Child's Home
■ Node
▢ Open Space
○ Landmark
▬ Major Path
— Minor Path

COMPOSITE MAP
PLAYSCAPE

FIGURE 1

emphasis on play spaces for 9-11 year olds. It gives a fairly accurate picture of the important features of the environment from the child's point of view and indicates the hidden structure of play within a detailed part of the city. These principal elements were later analyzed as "play settings" in terms of activity and environment "type" from the transcriptions of the diaries and from detailed field observations.

The individual maps were analyzed by structural type according to Appleyard's (1970) classification scheme. He found that respondent's maps fell into two broad structural categories: <u>sequentially</u> dominant (emphasizing paths and landmarks) or <u>spatially</u> dominant (emphasizing districts and nodes). Each category of map type in Appleyard's study consisted of four subtypes representing a gradation of increasing complexity and sophistication. (Examples of both categories of maps are illustrated in FIGURES 2 and 3, which are reductions of actual maps drawn by children.

SPATIAL MAP TYPES

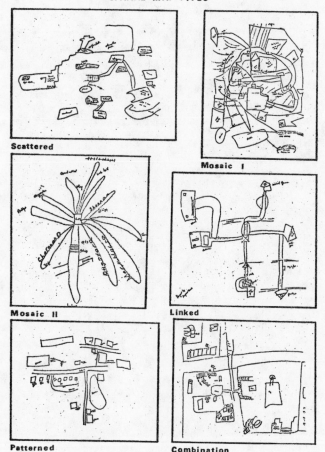

Scattered

Mosaic I

Mosaic II

Linked

Patterned

Combination

FIGURE 3

SEQUENTIAL MAP TYPES

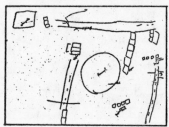

Fragmented

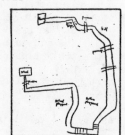

Chain

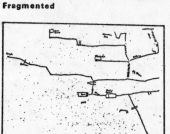

Branch

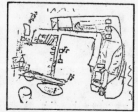

Branch and Loop

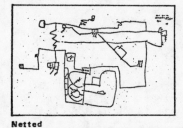

Netted

Combination

FIGURE 2

2.3. Inventories

A set of inventories was developed and each child was asked to complete a "<u>Where</u> Do I Play?" and a "<u>When</u> Do I Play?" itemized description of his or

her activities. A total of 118 "games" or activities were elicited from neighborhood children during off-school hours. Later, each child was given the "Where Do I Play?" and the "When Do I Play?" inventory to complete during free time at school or at home, with the help of older siblings or parents. The categories for "When?" and "Where?" were generated by the research staff based on the interviews and subsequent field observations.

2.4. Diaries

One group of 25 children was asked to keep diaries (called "daily journals") of their activities on the way to school, after school, and after dinner. For each of these time periods they kept track of the following information: What did I do? Where did I go? and How long did I do it? The diaries were used to supplement the inventories described above and were the primary source of information (in addition to field observation) used to develop the classification scheme described below.

3. ACTIVITY/ENVIRONMENT INTERACTIONS

A classification scheme was developed to integrate the nature of the activity with the environment in which these behaviors occurred:

ACTIVITY

structured   unstructured

3.1. Structured Activity/Structured Environment (SA/SE)

The type of activity/environment interactions that are classified in Cell I are scheduled events which take place at some fixed or constant time of the day (on a daily or weekly basis), and occur in an easily identifiable setting. Examples of such activities might be church-going (on Sunday at Guadalupe Church, for example) or watching a specific television program. The activities are both time and space bound, and included any activity sponsored and supervised by outside agencies such as Boys Clubs, etc.

3.2. Unstructured Activity/Structured Environment (UA/SE)

The type of activity/environment interactions that are classified in Cell II are spontaneous behaviors (non-regulated by time and space) taking place in a setting which does not dictate what activity should take place, but is essential for the activity to occur. Such activities are not commonly observable events, since (1) they are "hidden" due to their unpredictable spontaneity, and (2) they are "hidden" since such behaviors are more frequently than not unrecognizable as play to the outsider. Examples of such activities might be fence climbing, bicycle "cruisin" and garage roof jumping. These environments make these activities produce an "intent" or direction of use, but not a use of the environment solely for the intended purpose that the environment was created.

3.3. Structured Activity/Unstructured Environment (SA/UE)

The type of activity/environment interactions that are classified in Cell III are "preplanned"

or structured (rule governed) activities that take place in an environment not necessarily designed for the intended use for which it is being utilized. Such an unstructured environment is not a "static" entity, but one that is as flexible as the demands placed on it. Examples of such activities might be playing football in the street, basketball using a hoop nailed to a utility pole, or a variety of "ball games" such as "Russia," or stickball requiring a minimally structured play space. To an outside observer, such activities are easily recognizable, but the environment might be less influential in determining the behavior of the child than entries in Cell I. An unstructured environment, then, is one that does not dictate what activity is to take place within that environment.

3.4. Unstructured Activity/Unstructured Environment (UA/UE)

The type of activity/environment interactions that are classified in Cell IV are behaviors which have a designated format (such as running) but yet are spontaneous in nature, and are not location-bound. Examples of such activities might be aggressive behaviors (such as fighting), chasing dogs, snowball fights, etc. Like those activities classified in Cell III, it is difficult to observe spontaneous behaviors through any systematic procedure.

An important component to the understanding of any activity and its interrelationship with the environment is the joint effects of structuredness and unstructuredness. That is, an activity classified as "structured" taking place in an unstructured setting is viewed differently than if it were taking place in a structured setting. All activities, then, just as all environments, cannot be evaluated independently of their counterpart dimension. Those structured activities taking place in a structured environment are most akin to those activities referred to as "supervised play." On the other extreme, those activities that are relatively unstructured in format, content, and setting, are most recognizable as "pure play" as it might traditionally be known. This type of play is one that seeks an end in itself.

4. RESULTS AND DISCUSSION

The percentage of children who mentioned the listed activities as either a node, landmark, or path was computed. It is interesting to observe that for both landmarks and nodes a large number of frequently mentioned elements are commercial in supposed (or designed) function (e.g. Jingle's Market, Connie's Store, Rudi's and Graham's Drugstore). Other elements occupying the upper ranks are parks (Observation Park, Gage Park, Jarboe Park) and the housing "projects." These findings support the notion that these children see as important those elements which vary along a variety of dimensions such as function and location.

Interestingly, the average percentage across all elements mentioned as landmarks or nodes is higher for non-provided than for provided facilities. For example, provided elements were mentioned as landmarks, on the average, by 14% of the children while landmarks that are not provided facilities were mentioned, on the average, by 21% of the children, a significant increase of almost 50 percent.

A summary of classification of maps (according to Appleyard) broken down by sex, race, and zone of residence for maps drawn describing school-to-home activities is presented in Table 1(a). The larger percentage of maps drawn (58%) were spatial in format, while the remaining 42% were sequential. Interestingly, when the total frequency for home-to-play maps classified by map type is examined, 43% of the children's maps were classified as the more sophisticated of the spatial type, the opposite of the results reported in Table 1. According to these results, it appears that while school-to-home maps are primarily sequential, home-to-play maps are primarily spatial. Furthermore, for both school-to-home, and home-to-play maps, sequential and spatial maps respectively appear to be distributed in a non-random fashion (indicating more sophisticated spatial maps being drawn for home-to-play and less sophisticated sequential maps being drawn for school-to-home).

of the growing autonomy and self-development discussed earlier.

Each of the four types of activity/environment interaction are illustrated by map type in Table 2. One of the primary uses of the diaries and interviews was to determine the character of the activity/environment interaction. As might be expected, the largest number of entries were S/S across both categories of maps, and the smallest were U/S. It appears then that the determining factor in most instances is whether or not the activity was structured or unstructured, not the environment. The high incidence of activities in the S/S cell across both sequential and spatial map types is due to a disproportionate number of activities like television watching and other indoor play.

Total Frequency of Diary Entries by Map Type and Activity/Environment Interaction

| | MAP TYPE | | |
	Sequential	Spatial	Total
S/S	181	135	316
U/S	19	3	22
S/U	54	36	90
U/U	41	25	65
Total	295	199	494

TABLE 2

CLASSIFICATION OF MAPS BY SEX, RACE, AND ZONE OF RESIDENCE

(a) School-to-Home (b) Home-to-Play

| | SEQUENTIAL | | | | | | | | SPATIAL | | | | | | | | | |
	Fragmented (a) (b)		Chained (a) (b)		Branched (a) (b)		Netted (a) (b)		Scattered (a) (b)		Mosaic (a) (b)		Linked (a) (b)		Patterned (a) (b)		Total (a) (b)	
Male	3	2	7	2	2	3	1	2	1	2	1	1	4	6	1	2	20	20
Female	8	3	4	2	1	3	2	2	3	2	3	3	3	7	1	3	25	25
Mexican	0	2	4	1	1	1	2	2	3	1	1	1	5	7	0	1	16	16
Black	6	1	3	2	1	1	0	1	1	1	1	2	0	2	2	4	14	14
White	5	2	4	1	1	4	1	1	0	2	2	1	2	4	0	0	15	15
Zone 1	0	1	2	1	1	1	1	1	1	0	0	0	2	4	0	0	7	8
Zone 2	7	3	8	2	1	4	1	1	2	3	2	2	5	8	2	5	28	28
Zone 3	4	1	1	1	1	1	1	2	1	1	2	2	0	1	0	0	10	9
Total	11	5	11	4	3	6	3	4	4	4	4	4	7	13	2	5	45	45

TABLE 1

If one examines the characteristics of a spatial or sequential type map this result is not surprising and does support a theoretical orientation regarding child/environment interaction. Quite simply, the school-to-home map reflects a path taken by the child to reach a direct goal, while the home-to-play map reflects an increasingly large set of choices for the child and in many ways is an indication of his successful adaptation to the environment. It is not coincidental that those maps best describing play behavior were spatial in format, more sophisticated, and consequently characteristic

5. SUMMARY AND CONCLUSIONS

At the same time that the fabric of cities is continuously built and rebuilt in a kind of "disjointed incrementalism" through urban planning and design, our knowledge of its underlying structure and form has changed significantly. The earliest conceptual models of the city were devised from reading the plans of historical settlements. Since then, demography, social structure, activity patterns, communication flows, and cognition have succeeded in articulating a finer and finer grain while making the totality more elusive than ever. The attempt to describe urban spatial structure in terms of human behavior and development is an excellent example of this duality.

Nonetheless, a single theme persists--a progressive _internalization_ of the concept of the environment--a persistence which appears to result in a new attitude toward cities and toward their planning and design.

This internalization may be characterized by an increasing tendency to conceptualize the environment experientially and by a decreasing tendency to conceptualize it objectively, as external phenomena, in Cartesian terms. By seeing the environment as an extension of self, and collectively, as an extension of society, we inevitably form new and different criteria for its care and maintenance.

This study has examined the city as a supportive environment (and in particular, supportive of the satisfaction of developmental needs in elementary school children). We have asked how well the city performs this role by looking at how children interact with their everyday urban environment and assessing the extent to which the environment encourages adaptive behavior.

The four sub-objectives presented earlier in the introduction of this report outlined a systematic attempt to determine how the child who lives in an urban environment conceptualizes and uses the elements in that environment.

It is naive to conclude that, based on the findings reported herein, children who reside in urban settings do not use the facilities provided for them in their daily activity/environment interaction. It is also naive, however, to conclude that these same children do not create their own "hidden structure" of play (both as individuals as well as in groups) in an effort to master their environment. The results reported have shown that children do not place as much importance on structures provided by conventional agencies as they place on elements they create themselves. Cognitive maps indicating a spatial and sequential adaption to the city (depending upon the content of the map) also evidence a maturity and a surprising grasp of the intricacies that an urban setting offers. In fact, the maps drawn by the children are not unlike those drawn by adults and reported in the literature.

Although a "hidden structure" does exist, some interesting and profound questions remain unanswered. For example, what implications do these findings have for the planner/architect in terms of creating an interesting and facilitative environment for the young child? Can this hidden structure be artificially created by setting the stage--by making old tenements and alleys "safe," by expanding the area around corner drugstores and candy stores, or by

purposefully creating such structures to enhance interaction with the environment? How do children outside of urban centers conceptualize their surroundings, and what elements (paths, landmarks, etc.) do they use to create a potentially masterful setting?

Much of the research in the behavioral sciences, particularly developmental psychology, has elaborated the concept that children maximize their growth when presented stimuli somewhat discrepant from already existing schema. The lack of familiarity that the inner-city child has with the suburban environment is clearly expressed by the child's withdrawal and effort to find something to establish a tie to "old things" in that alien setting. The child who is placed or places him or herself in a similar, yet different setting (discrepant but not novel) adapts, thrives, and grows if the setting demands it.

References

AIELLO, J.F., GORDON, B. and FARRELL, T.J. "Description of Children's Outdoor Activities in a Suburban Residential Area," in D. Carson (ed.) EDRA 5, 6:12 (1974).

ANDERSON, J. and TINDALL, M. "The Concept of Home-Range," in W. Mitchell (ed.), EDRA 3, 1.1 (1972).

ANDREWS, H.F., "Home-Range and Urban Knowledge of School-Age Children," Environment and Behavior, 5:1 (March, 1973).

APPLEYARD, D. "Styles and Methods of Structuring a City," Environment and Behavior, 2:1 (June, 1970).

BLAUT, J.M. and McCLEARY, G.S. "Environmental Mapping in Young Children," Environment and Behavior, 2 (1970)

CARR, S. and LYNCH, K. "Where Learning Happens," Daedalus (Fall, 1968).

COATES, G. and BUSSARD, E. "Patterns of Children's Spatial Behavior in a Moderate-Density Housing Development," in D. Carson (ed.), EDRA 5, 6:12 (1974).

COATES, G. and SANOFF, H. "Behavioral Mapping: The Ecology of Child Behavior in a Planned Residential Setting," in W. Mitchell (ed.), EDRA 3, 13.2 (1972).

COOPER, C. "Children's Play Behavior in a Low-Rise Inner City Housing Development," in D. Carson (ed.), EDRA 5, 6:12 (1974).

DATTNER, R. Design for Play (Van Nostrand, 1969).

DERMAN, A. "Children's Play: Design Approaches and Theoretical Issues," in G. Coates (ed.), Alternative Learning Environments (Dowden, Hutchinson, and Ross, 1974).

ELLIS, M.J. Why People Play (Prentice-Hall, 1973).

ERIKSON, E. "Play and Activity," in M.W. Piers (ed.), Play and Development (Norton, 1972).

FRIEDBERG, P. and BERKELEY, E.P. Play and Interplay (Macmillan, 1970).

GOLD, S. "Non-Use of Neighborhood Parks," Journal of the American Institute of Planners, 38:6 (November, 1972).

GRAMZA, A.F. Unpublished report. Motor Performance and Play Research Laboratory, Children's Research Center, University of Illinois, 1970.

HALL, G.S. Adolescence: Its Psychology and Its Relation to Physiology, Anthropology, Sociology, Sex, Crime, Religion, and Education, Vol. 1 (Appleton, 1916).

HONIKMAN, B. "Environmental Cognition: Its Potential for Enhancing Design and Policy Formulation," in D. Carson (ed.), EDRA 5, 6:11 (1974).

HUIZINGA, J. Homo Ludens: A Study of the Play Element in Culture (Routledge and Kegan Paul, 1949).

JACOBS, J. The Death and Life of Great American Cities (Penguin, 1960).

KELLER, S. The Urban Neighborhood (Oxford University, 1968).

LEE, S.A. "Cognitive Mapping Research," in B. Honikman (ed.), Responding to Social Change (Dowden, Hutchinson and Ross, 1975).

LYNCH, K. The Image of the City (MIT, 1960).

LYNCH, K. and LUKASHOK, A. "Some Childhood Memories of the City," Journal of the American Institute of Planners (Summer, 1956).

MILLAR, S. The Psychology of Play (Penguin, 1968).

MOORE, R. "Landscape of Childhood," Way, 26:7 (September 1970).

PIAGET, J. Play, Dreams, and Imitation in Childhood (Norton, 1962).

ROTHENBERG, M., HAYWARD, D.G. and BEASLEY, R.R. "Playgrounds: For Whom?" in D. Carson (ed.), EDRA 5, 6:12 (1974).

SMART, H. and SMART, R. Children (Macmillan, 1972).

WHITE, R.W. "Motivation Reconsidered: The Concept of Competence," Psychological Review, 1959, 66, 297-333.

RESIDENTIAL PLANNING IMPLICATIONS OF SUBJECTIVE

RESPONSE TO NOISE: SOME EMPIRICAL FINDINGS

S. Martin Taylor

Department of Geography, McMaster University,
Hamilton, Ontario

Fred L. Hall

Department of Geography and Department of Civil
Engineering, McMaster University, Hamilton,
Ontario

ABSTRACT

Noise constitutes an immediate problem in many
urban residential areas close to major transportation routes. A more complete understanding
of subjective response to noise is needed as a
basis for evaluating approaches to noise impact
reduction. Using data collected in a recent
study in the Hamilton-Toronto area of Southern
Ontario, this paper tests two sets of hypotheses
which have a direct bearing on the evaluation of
noise impact reduction approaches. The first
set relates to residents' ability to adapt to
transportation noise and the second to the
effect of various aspects of community design on
subjective noise ratings. The main conclusions
are that in general residents are unable to
adapt to road traffic noise; that building design
alone is insufficient to reduce noise impact; and
that disturbance due to train noise appears to be
less of a problem than noise from road, and
particularly freeway traffic.

1. INTRODUCTION

A recent government investigation revealed that
noise levels in a newly constructed, but still
to be occupied, residential development in a
suburb of Toronto are up to 25 dBA higher than
limits regarded as acceptable by the U.S. Housing
and Urban Development Department. Comparable
standards have yet to be established in Canada
with the result that there is little control
imposed on housing developments in areas subject
to high levels of noise exposure. In the Toronto
case, the source of the noise is an adjacent freeway and the methods suggested to reduce the discomfort to residents due to noise include the
construction of a solid barrier to separate the
homes from the freeway and the installation of
air conditioning and double glazing. Even so,
government researchers are skeptical about the
effectiveness of such measures and conclude that:
"On occupation of the dwelling units as proposed
at present, complaints due to sleep interruptions
and activity interference will be very likely.
In our view, this existing development is
adversely affected by high noise levels from the
ever increasing traffic volume on the adjacent
highway and is unsuitable for residential land
use in such an undesirable living environment"
(Toronto Star, September, 1975).

This is but one of several similar cases that
could be quoted to illustrate a serious outcome
of the imbalance of supply and demand for
residential land in existing major urban centres;
namely, that areas previously avoided by
residential developers because of their proximity
to major noise sources, particularly transportation arteries, are now being seriously considered as potential housing sites because of the
scarcity of land elsewhere within city or metropolitan boundaries. The problem has been further
compounded in areas adjacent to major highways by
the increased volume of traffic and particularly
trucks and other heavy vehicles which are
commonly the cause of higher noise levels.

Despite the immediate importance of this problem
there is a lack of systematic research to direct
the choice of policy alternatives. In particular,
our knowledge of subjective response to noise
under real-world conditions is very limited.
While it is true that previous research has
examined the relationship between physical
measures of noise and the intensity of personal
disturbance or annoyance (Griffiths and Langdon,
1968; Robinson, 1971; Johnston and Carothers,
1974; Hall and Allen, 1975), the findings have
not been conclusive. Furthermore, there has
been little advance from this diagnostic stage
toward research having a prescriptive emphasis,
aimed at identifying means of reducing the impact
of noise in residential areas.

Reflecting this latter concern, the purpose of
this paper is to consider alternative approaches
to noise impact reduction by means of exploring
empirically some fundamental aspects of subjective
response to neighbourhood noise. Such an investigation is regarded as a necessary precursor of
effective policy formulation and evaluation. A
number of hypotheses related to the intensity of
personal reaction to general and specific noise
sources are stated and tested using data collected
in a study recently conducted in the Hamilton-
Toronto area of southern Ontario.

The paper is divided into the following sections: a brief outline of possible approaches to reducing noise impact in residential areas; a statement of hypotheses; a description of the data base used in the empirical analysis; a description and discussion of the results of testing the hypotheses; and finally a concluding statement emphasizing the relevance of the present findings for residential planning.

2. REDUCING NOISE IMPACT IN RESIDENTIAL AREAS

Several possible approaches to reducing noise impact in residential areas have been suggested and to varying degrees have been tested. In this section, attention will be confined to surface transportation noise since this forms the focus of empirical inquiry in this paper. Three broad approaches appear possible. The first is to ignore the problem and assume that the impacted residents will discover means of adapting to their noise environment. These adaptations may take the form of a passive response--simply "getting used to it". They may be of a more active kind, involving adjustments in behaviour-- for example, always keeping the windows closed or never using the backyard for recreational and leisure purposes. Finally, the adaptations may involve modifications and additions to the home such as the installation of air conditioning, double-glazing or extra insulation. While the assumption that residents adapt to noise in any or all of these ways is largely unsubstantiated, this approach does accurately describe the status quo in many urban areas in Canada, where, as indicated earlier, acceptable noise standards have yet to be established. Given this situation, it is important that the validity of the assumption regarding the resident's capacity to adapt be tested and, if unsubstantiated, that measures aimed at reducing noise impact be considered and implemented.

Two basic approaches exist. The first is to reduce the noise at source. With respect to surface transportation, noise reduction measures can concentrate on vehicle design, (e.g., car, truck or train), routeway design (i.e., road or rail) or both. This is in many ways the most attractive approach since it attacks the root of the problem, but it has the disadvantage that the necessary technology is costly to an extent frequently regarded as prohibitive.

The second approach to noise reduction relates to various aspects of community design. One option here involves land use control which itself may take various forms. Suggested measures include: the retention of an open buffer zone separating the source and the residential area; and restricting the land adjoining the source to noise insensitive structures (e.g., warehouses, industrial premises or closely-spaced, sound-treated hi-rises which could function as shielding for the residential area at a greater distance from the source). These alternatives have the disadvantage of being extremely costly to implement,

especially in existing communities where extensive expropriation and/or reconstruction would be necessary. The open buffer zone also has the disadvantage that it is relatively ineffective in attenuating noise while at the same time exhaustive of land. For these reasons it is basically unfeasible in most urban areas.

Two other community approaches which are probably more realistic at least in the short-term are to improve noise insulation in existing buildings and to construct noise barriers. The effectiveness of the first of these is limited to internal spaces while the second should serve to reduce noise exposure levels both inside and outside. In addition, berms, though perhaps aesthetically displeasing, do have the supposed advantage of providing a visual barrier between the resident and the source. Again the relative costs and benefits of these alternatives have to be considered as a basis for a policy decision in a particular situation.

The subsequent sections of this paper describe and discuss some empirical findings which relate directly to an effective evaluation of the approaches outlined above. In no sense do these findings comprehensively deal with all of the critical issues, rather they cast partial light on a selected number.

The research questions relating to the first approach, that of ignoring the problem, are designed to test the validity of the assumption that residents adapt to noise over time. The analysis focusses largely on the relationship between disturbance levels and length of residence as an index of adaptation. Concern for the type of adaptation is limited to an examination of the noises respondents reported having "got used to".

No attempt is made to cast light on the second approach which concerns noise reduction at source. This was outside the scope of the research project from which the data used in this paper are drawn.

The third approach is that of noise reduction by means of community design in the form of land use control, building insulation, and the construction of noise barriers. In the case of land use control, an attempt is made to determine whether a certain type of dwelling is more insensitive to noise by examining the relationship between residents' ratings of noise and their dwelling type. Two questions related to building insulation are considered: whether in-home air conditioning reduces disturbance levels and the more general yet very relevant question of whether residents are more frequently disturbed indoors or outdoors. With respect to noise barriers, the effect of different types of shielding on residents' ratings of noise is examined.

These various research questions can be stated more specifically as the following hypotheses which form the basis of the empirical analysis reported in this paper:

1. Hypotheses related to residents' adaptation to noise.
   1.1 Level of disturbance decreases with length of residence.
   1.2 Adaptation differs significantly by noise source.
   1.3 The proportion of residents who get used to noise differs significantly by noise source.

2. Hypotheses related to the community design approach to noise impact reduction.
   2.1 Level of disturbance differs significantly by type of dwelling.
   2.2 Level of disturbance is lower when air conditioning is present.
   2.3 Residents report being disturbed by transportation noise more often outdoors than indoors.
   2.4 Level of disturbance is lower when shielding is present.

Before proceeding to a description of the empirical results, it is important to outline the structure of the study from which the data are drawn.

3. DESCRIPTION OF THE STUDY

The data base for the analysis reported in this paper is drawn from a recent study of community response to noise in the Hamilton-Toronto area of southern Ontario. This study had the following two broad objectives:

1. To assess the impact of noise on residents in selected neighbourhoods within the Hamilton-Toronto Corridor.

2. To relate measures of social impact to physical measurements of noise.

To fulfill these objectives two types of information were sought: household questionnaire data and physical measures of noise. A carefully constructed and pretested questionnaire was completed by 837 respondents--approximately 30 from each of 28 sites. A comprehensive set of questions was asked to determine various aspects of residents' attitudes and behavioural responses to noise. A determined effort was made to go beyond the somewhat superficial data collected in many previous studies. This is evidenced for example by the measurement of responses to specific noise sources rather than relying on a general neighbourhood rating of noise as has been common in community studies hitherto (City of Toronto, 1973; Foreman, et al., 1974).

A further distinguishing feature of the questionnaire design was the use of a bipolar rating scale for measuring the intensity of respondent reactions to specific and general noise levels. Previously, the practice has generally been to employ unipolar disturbance or annoyance scales. This procedure was not followed in the present

study because it precludes the respondent from indicating a positive response to noise. In the pre-test when a unipolar disturbance scale was used the interviewers noted that in many instances a positive response occurred particularly in rating the general level of neighbourhood noise, hence supporting the adoption of a bipolar scale in the major data collection phase. A nine-point scale was employed ranging from extremely agreeable to extremely disagreeable with a neutral mid-point. The study therefore did not proceed on a definition of noise as unwanted sound as most previous studies have done because pretest responses indicated the questionable validity of doing so.

The 28 neighbourhoods used in this study were selected to provide a number of sites within each of seven noise environment categories. The primary criterion for site selection was the dominant non-residential noise source, with particular emphasis on transportation facilities. An attempt was made to include sites in which a single source acted in isolation, and others in which two or more sources were combined. An additional concern was to vary the degree and type of shielding present at each site. The major types of sites were as follows:

Freeway Sites   (N=8, Respondents=237)
Arterial Sites   (N=6, Respondents=165)
Main Rail Sites   (N=4, Respondents=122)
Secondary Rail Sites   (N=3, Respondents= 90)
Freeway/Main Rail Sites   (N=2, Respondents= 58)
Industrial/Commercial Sites   (N=2, Respondents= 60)
Control Sites   (N=3, Respondents=105).

A deliberate effort was made to vary the socio-economic characteristics of the respondents among the sites, and to obtain a representative set of respondents within each site.

Tabulating the personal data shows that the sample approximates a representative cross-section of the general population with respect to the age, education level, and income of the respondents. There is a bias towards female respondents who comprise 75 percent of the sample and an associated bias towards housewives. This can be defended on the grounds that it is women at home who experience the most exposure to neighbourhood noise and hence are the most appropriate respondents.

Sampling across this range of site types ensured the desired variance in the exposure of residents within the sample of transportation noises, while, at the same time, yielding a sufficient number of responses from each site type to make aggregate comparisons reliable.

The collection and analysis of physical measurements of the noise at each site is an on-going task. Because of the incompleteness of that data set, this paper relies primarily on the questionnaire responses.

4. RESULTS OF HYPOTHESIS TESTING

Hypothesis 1.1: Level of disturbance decreases with length of residence.

An obvious and reasonable measure of adaptation to noise is the direction and strength of the relationship between level of disturbance and length of residence. This relationship was determined by calculating rank-order correlations (Kendall's Tau) between measures of subjective response to general and specific noise sources-- based on the nine point bipolar scale described previously--and length of residence. Kendall's Tau was preferred over Pearson's product moment coefficient on the basis of the cautious assumption that the subjective response scale possessed no more than ordinal properties. Separate sets of coefficients were calculated for each of seven noise environments in seeking to exert a reasonable control in the type and level of noise exposure. These environments were as follows: shielded and unshielded freeway sites; shielded and unshielded arterial sites; shielded and unshielded rail sites; and control sites.

Five measures of subjective response were used in calculating the coefficients. The overall neighbourhood noise rating was a relevant measure in each case; the source specific ratings used differed with the type of environment. Ratings of freeway traffic noise and truck noise were relevant for freeway sites; ratings of arterial traffic and trucks for arterial sites; and ratings of trains for rail sites. The coefficients obtained are shown in Table 1. To confirm the hypothesis as stated would require that the coefficients be both negative and statistically significant. In all but one case this condition is not satisfied; indeed ten of the seventeen coefficients are positive and significant beyond the

.05 level. Overall therefore the results provide a convincing rejection of the original hypothesis and furthermore indicate that in the majority of noise environments studied there existed a direct relationship between level of disturbance and length of residence.

It is interesting to note that Borsky (1961) also reports a positive relationship between level of disturbance and length of residence in a study of community responses to noise in the vicinities of military airfields in the United States. He found that, following an initial period of adaptation, the longer a person lived in a given neighbourhood, the more he was bothered by noise. This conclusion suggests that the relationship between disturbance and length of residence may be non-linear. Attempts to fit a non-linear function to the data in the present study failed however to increase the values of the correlation coefficients.

Returning to the question which gave rise to the hypothesis, the results certainly do not validate the assumption that residents are able to adapt to neighbourhood noise levels over time. One possible explanation is that in recent years there has almost certainly been a steady increase in noise levels at each of the residential sites included in the study. Such an increase is typical of urban residential areas generally and the probable result is that the adaptive capacities of the residents have been exceeded. The existence of a significant positive relationship between general level of disturbance and length of residence even at the control sites supports this explanation.

TABLE 1
Correlations of Level of Disturbance and Length of Residence

Noise Environment	Noise Source Rating Scales									
	Neighbourhood		Freeway Traffic		Trucks		Arterial Traffic		Trains	
	no shield	shield	no shield	shield	no shield	shield	no shield	shield	no shield	shield
Freeway	.2329 ***（87)	.2047 ***（144)	.1481 *（71)	.2373 ***（103)	.1258 NS（59)	.3191 ***（48)				
Arterial	.1303 *（128)	.0390 NS（35)			.0506 NS（45)	.5205 *（9)	-.0138 NS（78)	-.0344 NS（13)		
Rail	.1277 *（100)	.1451 *（73)							-.1005 NS（85)	-.3307 ***（50)
Control	.1788 **（101)									

*** significant at .001 level   * significant at .05 level
** significant at .01 level   NS not significant

Figures in parentheses indicate the number of observations on which the coefficients are based.

Hypothesis 1.2: Adaptation over time differs by noise source.

The correlations between level of disturbance and length of residence reported in Table 1 also provide a basis for testing this second hypothesis. In this case confirmation of the hypothesis requires that the strength and/or direction of the correlations differ across types of noise environment. On the basis of the correlations between the overall neighbourhood rating and length of residence, the hypothesis is clearly rejected since all the coefficients are significant and positive. However, when the correlations between source specific ratings and length of residence are considered a marked discrepancy emerges in the response to trains. For both shielded and unshielded sites, the coefficients are negative and in the latter case the relationship is significant beyond the .001 level.

This finding is consistent with the hypothesis as stated and suggests that the ability of residents to adapt to trains is greater than that associated with other transportation noise sources. The result indicates that in general longer term residents at rail sites reported lower disturbance levels with respect to trains than did more recent arrivals. A plausible explanation of the contrasting responses to road traffic and train noise is that the latter is characteristically intermittent while the former is relatively continuous, particularly at freeway sites. Comments volunteered by the respondents suggest that this aspect of noise is almost certainly an important factor contributing to the observed variation in adaptation to the different sources.

Hypothesis 1.3: The proportion of residents who get used to noise differs significantly by noise source.

This hypothesis is obviously closely related to the previous one; it is distinguished by being based on responses to a different question. Respondents were asked whether there were any noises which had disturbed them in the past but no longer did. Where this was the case, a reason was requested and one possible response was "got used to it". In order to test the hypothesis, the number of respondents who indicated having got used to three specific noise sources--freeway traffic, trucks and trains--were compared with the number of respondents who indicated being currently disturbed by those same three sources. The resulting figures are shown in Table 2. A chi-square test was conducted to test for significant differences in responses to the different sources. The statistic obtained was significant beyond the .001 level reflecting the differing abilities of residents to get used to the different types of noise.

It is clear from the entries in Table 2 that the major factor contributing to the highly significant chi-square value is the marked difference in response to train noise as compared with freeway traffic and truck noise. But it is also

TABLE 2
Numbers of Respondents Indicating Being Disturbed
by or Getting Used to
Specific Transportation Noises

Subjective Response	Noise Source		
	Freeway	Trucks	Trains
Disturbed	124	133	61
Got Used To	17	5	28
	141	138	89

Chi Square = 36 (significant at .001 level; df=2)

important to note that the difference in responses to freeway traffic and trucks is in itself statistically significant. The result therefore is consistent with that related to hypothesis 1.2, and serves to strengthen the conclusion that ease of adaptation does vary significantly by noise source, and in particular that residents find it easier to adapt to noise from trains than to noise from road traffic.

Hypothesis 2.1: Level of disturbance differs significantly by type of dwelling.

Type of dwelling was dichotomized to distinguish between single family and multiple family dwelling units. The relationships between general and specific noise ratings and dwelling type were calculated for each of the seven noise environments specified with respect to the previous hypotheses. The significant relationships are summarized in Table 3.

TABLE 3
Hypotheses 2.1 and 2.2: Summary of Significant
Relationships

Community Design Factor	Noise Rating Scale	Noise Environment	N	Chi Square
Dwelling	neighbour-hood	freeway unshielded	89	20.15**
Dwelling	neighbour-hood	freeway shielded	145	27.02***
Dwelling	freeway traffic	freeway shielded	103	21.29***
Dwelling	trucks	freeway shielded	48	14.16*
Dwelling	neighbour-hood	control	103	17.05*
Air Conditioning	Trucks	Arterial Unshielded	46	11.30*

*** significant at .001 level
** significant at .01 level
* significant at .05 level

The hypothesis was strongly confirmed in the case of freeway sites. In each of the four instances where significant relationships emerged, the distribution of responses indicated an appreciably higher level of disturbance among residents in single family dwellings. A significant difference also occurred in ratings of overall neighbourhood noise at control sites and here again residents in multiple family dwellings reported lower levels of disturbance. These results however have to be interpreted in light of the high degree of overlap between type of dwelling and type of tenure within the data. Further research is necessary to clarify whether the differences are a function of dwelling type, tenure base or, as seems most plausible a combination of the two.

Hypothesis 2.2: Level of disturbance is lower when air conditioning is present.

The results failed to support this hypothesis as stated. In only one instance was the relationship between noise ratings and air conditioning significant (see Table 3) and in that case the distribution of responses was contrary to expectation. Higher rather than lower levels of disturbance due to truck noise at arterial sites were reported by respondents with air conditioning in their homes. Caution should be applied in interpreting these results however, since the number of respondents having in-home air conditioning was generally small with the result that the contingency tests performed were on the margins of statistical validity in several cases.

Hypothesis 2.3: Residents report being disturbed by transportation noise more often outdoors than indoors.

The question of where people are when disturbed by transportation noise has immediate implications for the types of measures needed to alleviate the problem. For each source of noise rated as disturbing, respondents were asked whether they were inside, in their yard or elsewhere when the disturbance occurred. Table 4 shows the frequency of mentions of inside and outside for three major transportation noise sources--freeway traffic, trucks and trains.

TABLE 4

Hypothesis 2.3: Frequency of Responses Indicating Disturbance Inside and Outside the Home

Location	Freeway Traffic	Trucks	Trains	Total
Inside	79	105	55	239
Outside	106	125	64	295
	185	230	119	534

Unfortunately there were insufficient sample points to permit the performance of a difference of means test. It is nonetheless clear that for each of the three sources, mentions of outdoor disturbance exceed those for indoors. A chi square test was performed to determine whether a significant difference existed between sources in the distribution of responses. The resulting

chi square value was very low and not statistically significant. The results indicate that disturbance outdoors is probably the more frequent problem which seems intuitively plausible since the walls of the home can be expected to attenuate the noise to a varying degree dependent on the structural characteristics and on the types of insulation present. The fact that the interviews were conducted during the summer when people were likely to be involved in back yard activities should not be overlooked as a possible factor affecting the number of mentions of disturbance outdoors. It is intended in a future study to conduct interviews during the winter to see whether the same pattern of responses emerges. The results shown here certainly suggest that interior design factors may be insufficient in alleviating disturbance due to major transportation noise sources and that some exterior barrier may be needed to reduce the noise levels experienced outdoors.

Hypothesis 2.4: Level of disturbance is lower when shielding is present.

A specific criterion in the site selection procedure was the presence or absence of shielding at a macro scale. For each type of noise environment both shielded and unshielded sites were included. The shielding was in the form of housing, light industry or woodland separating the site from the source. Tests for significant differences in general and specific noise ratings at shielded and unshielded sites were performed for freeway, arterial and rail sites. Two of the nine relationships tested were significant and both supported the hypothesis that level of disturbance is lower when shielding is present (see Table 5). At freeway sites, the improvement in the overall neighbourhood noise rating associated with shielding was highly significant, but no differences emerged in the specific ratings of freeway traffic and trucks. This result is important because it indicates that, although specific sources remain intrusive, the overall neighbourhood noise levels are more acceptable. The implication therefore is that shielding achieves the desired effect.

The presence of shielding on individual housing lots in the form of fences, trees, hedges and shrubbery separating the source and the respondent was recorded on the questionnaires. While such landscape features do little to attenuate the noise levels, they may nevertheless have a positive psychological effect by reducing the visual intrusion of the noise source. In many cases, testing for relationships between noise ratings and the presence or absence of these types of shielding was precluded by insufficient sample sizes. Where valid tests were possible, the results were inconclusive. The distribution of responses neither consistently confirmed nor rejected the hypothesis that disturbance levels are lower when landscape features are present. This outcome perhaps indicates that because the effect of landscaping is largely psychological it tends to be individualistic and hence difficult to assess across a sample group.

TABLE 5

Hypothesis 2.4: Summary of Significant
Relationships

Community Design Factor	Noise Rating Scale	Noise Environment	N	Chi Square
Shielding	neighbour-hood	freeway	234	33.16***
Shielding	trucks	arterial	55	15.10*

*** significant beyond .001 level
  * significant beyond .05 level

5. CONCLUSIONS

This paper has examined several aspects of subjective response to transportation noise each of which has an important bearing on the selection of residential planning and design alternatives. The first question examined was whether residents demonstrate an ability to adapt to noise over time. The results provided a strong rejection of this supposition based on the relationships between length of residence and the ratings of overall neighbourhood noise, freeway traffic noise and truck noise. The relationships were consistently positive and significant indicating that over time level of disturbance tended to increase rather than decrease. The hypothesis was however supported in the case of train noise in which case the relationship with length of residence was negative and significant. The differences in adaptation to different noise sources were underlined by examining the frequency with which residents indicated getting used to a particular noise source. It was again clear from the results that adaptation was more likely to occur in response to train noise than to road traffic noise.

Two important conclusions can be drawn from this set of results. First, there is no empirical evidence to support the assumption that people in residential areas impacted by road traffic noise are able to adapt to noise over time. Hence, the policy of doing little or nothing to reduce noise impact in these areas appears untenable. Second, the apparent ability of residents to adapt much more successfully to train noise than to road traffic noise suggests that the existence of a rail line near to a potential residential site is not necessarily an obstacle to development. Certainly it would appear to be far less of an obstacle with respect to noise than is an adjacent freeway. More research is clearly needed to clarify the relationship between adaptive abilities and frequency of train movements. The findings reported here are based on low to medium frequency movements only.

Conclusions to be drawn from the testing of the second set of hypotheses relating to the effect

of community design factors on response to noise are necessarily tentative given the limitations of the data set. Residents in multiple family dwellings commonly reported lower disturbance levels than single family residents. At freeway sites in particular, residents in multiple family dwellings reported significantly lower disturbance levels. While this result may in part be a function of the sites included in the study, there does appear to be some empirical support for the argument that single family residents are more disturbed by noise levels in their neighbourhood. It was not clear whether this was a function of type of tenure or type of dwelling per se since in most cases the two were synonymous.

The findings indicated that measures designed to reduce transportation noise levels need to be effective both indoors and outdoors. This questions the adequacy of simply providing extra insulation, double-glazing or air conditioning whereby noise reduction is limited to indoors. It is necessary to place greater emphasis on the provision of shielding (ie. intervening land-uses or noise barriers) to achieve a significant reduction in both indoor and outdoor noise levels. The data showed that the existence of shielding in the form of intervening land-uses can significantly reduce disturbance levels at freeway and arterial sites. It seems likely that this reduction effect would have emerged more consistently had the number of sites been greater.

In summary, the main conclusions from the data used in this paper are firstly that in general residents are not able to adapt to road transportation noise; secondly, that building design alone is insufficient to reduce noise impact and therefore some form of external shielding is necessary; and thirdly, that the problem of disturbance due to noise does not appear to be as great at rail sites.

Reference

BORSKY, P.N. (1961) Community Reactions to Air Force Noise. National Opinion Research Centre, University of Chicago.

CITY OF TORONTO (1973) Noise Control Study, Technical Report, vol. 2.

FOREMAN, J., EMMERSON, M. and DICKINSON, S. (1974) "Noise Level and Attitudinal Surveys of London and Woodstock, Ontario". Sound and Vibration, 8, 16-22.

GRIFFITHS, I.D. and LANGDON, F.J. (1968) "Subjective Response to Road Traffic Noise". Journal of Sound and Vibration, 8, 16-32.

HALL, F.L. and ALLEN, B.L. (1975) "Toward a Community Impact Measure for Assessment of Transportation Noise". Paper presented at Transportation Research Board Meeting, Washington, D.C.

JOHNSTON, G.W. and CAROTHERS, R. (1974) Urban
    Traffic Noise Annoyance Measurements and
    Derived Indices, University of Toronto -
    York University Joint Program in Transport-
    ation Research, Report No. 24.

ROBINSON, D.W. (1971) "Towards a Unified System
    of Noise Assessment", Journal of Sound and
    Vibration, 14, 279-298.

TORONTO STAR (1975) "Homes Built Too Close to
    the 401: Noise Study". Article Appearing
    in September 4th edition.

SEX DIFFERENCES IN OPPOSITION TO AND SUPPORT FOR CONSTRUCTION OF A PROPOSED NUCLEAR POWER PLANT

Emily M. Passino and John W. Lounsbury

Organizational Psychology
408 Stokely Management Center
University of Tennessee
Knoxville, Tennessee 37916 USA

ABSTRACT

The current study investigated sex differences in views toward a proposed nuclear power plant for a rural Tennessee County. Results from a simple random survey of adults (171 males and 179 females) revealed that females more frequently than males opposed the plant ($t=-3.29$, 330 df, $p < .001$). Ratings of the likelihood of occurrence of 24 possible outcomes associated with the construction and operation of the plant were factor analyzed. Five factors emerged--labelled Hazards, Economic Growth, Social Disruption, Lower Costs, and Community Visibility. Males and females were compared on the five factor scores. Again, sex differences emerged, with females viewing as more likely the Hazards factor and as less likely the Economic Growth and Community Visibility factors. While the differences in expectations formed a logical explanation for the observed differences in support, they also raised further questions. These were discussed, along with implications for policy decisions and future social impact assessments.

1. INTRODUCTION

The purpose of this paper is to report on preliminary findings from a social impact assessment project for a proposed nuclear power plant in a rural Tennessee community (Schuller; et al., 1975).[1] A survey of adult residents revealed a sex difference associated both with views on permitting construction of the plant and with expectations regarding its potential impacts.

As with other biographic indicators, the sex of a person is often a shorthand summary of a whole lifetime of qualitatively different experiences. As such, the classification has served as a basis for interpreting and predicting certain attitudes, cognitions, and behaviors.

---

[1]This report is part of a larger generic study conducted by the Social Impacts Assessment Group of the Oak Ridge National Laboratory's Energy Division, and sponsored by the Division of Biomedical and Environmental Research of the U.S. Energy Research and Development Administration.

For example, studies of political participation have found females to be more politically conservative (Gruberg, 1968; Levitt, 1967), less coherent in their overall political outlook (Rambo, Jones and Finney, 1974; Smith, 1972), and less likely to become active political participants (Berelson, Lazarsfeld, and McPhee, 1954: Milbrath, 1965). In fact, the psychology of sex differences is rapidly evolving as an independent area of theory building and empirical research (cf., Maccoby and Jacklin, 1974; Mednick and Weissman, 1975).

However, there is a dearth of analysis and research on sex differences in the field of social impact assessment. In the case of large scale environmental projects which affect whole communities, it seems reasonable to ask whether the social impacts are perceived to be the same or different for males and females. If social impacts are perceived to be different, what are the bases for these differences? Under what conditions are such differences attenuated? The study of social impacts associated with the construction of a proposed nuclear power plant in a small community afforded us the opportunity to examine these questions.

2. METHOD

2.1 Setting

The site chosen for the study was Hartsville, Tennessee, and the surrounding area of Trousdale County, a rural county 40 miles northeast of Nashville, where the Tennessee Valley Authority (TVA) has proposed to locate a 4-unit, nuclear power plant. For almost a century, the county has maintained a relatively stable population of about 5000 residents. The proposed plant, which would occupy approximately 1900 acres of what is presently prime farmland, would require a 5000 person work force during its projected eight year construction period and would cost in the neighborhood of $2.15 billion. Approximately 350 people would be employed thereafter to operate the plant (U.S. Nuclear Regulatory Commission, 1975). At the time of the first survey (January-February, 1975), the licensing process was underway, with public hearings scheduled for September, but a construction permit had not been issued. The object of some controversy, the proposed plant was already receiving considerable attention in the local and area news media.

2.2 Prodecure

A simple random sampling technique was used to select 350 adult respondents (171 male; 179 female) from the approximately 3600 adults living in Trousdale County. Each was interviewed by a locally hired, trained interviewer for approximately one hour, for which each received $5. Included among the 28 subscales on the survey were standard demographic items, such as age, marital status, educational level, and number of years lived in the county. Another item asked, "If it were up to you, would you permit construction of the TVA power plant here in Hartsville?" A five-point response choice format ranged from "definitely yes" to "definitely no." Respondents were also asked to indicate on a five-point scale ranging from "very likely" to "very unlikely," the likelihood of occurrence of 24 outcomes potentially associated with the construction and operation of the plant. Included were such items as radiation hazards, cheaper electricity, crowding in recreation areas, and more jobs.

A t-test was used to test for differences in the "permit plant" variable, comparing males and females in general as well as with controls for differences in demographic variables. Perceived likelihood scores for the 24 potential outcomes were constructed by factor analysis and unit-weighted simple sums; these were tested for sex differences as well.

3. RESULTS

Nearly two-thirds of the total sample indicated that they would permit construction of the plant if it were up to them. However, males and females differed in their support of the plant: 73% of the males versus 57% of the females answered either "definitely yes" or "probably yes" to the question of permitting construction. Using the full five-point scale, with the lower scores indicating more positive responses, the mean response level for this item was 2.05 for males and 2.59 for females. A t-test indicated (t=-3.29, 330 df) that this difference was significant at a two-tailed probability level of p<.001.

There was, however, a significant difference between males and females on some of the demographic variables, and there were marginally significant correlations between some of the demographic variables and the "permit plant" variable. Accordingly, median splits were performed on the age, length of county residence, and education variables, and t-tests were run comparing males and females on the permit construction variable for each of the six control conditions.

The results indicated that females were more opposed to construction of the plant than males regardless of whether the respondents were above or below the median age (46 years) and educational level (12 years), or above the median level for number of years lived in the county (30). For respondents who had lived in the county less than 30 years, males and females did not differ significantly (t=-1.53, 167 df, p=.13). For the employment variable, since only 18 males were unemployed (compared to 65 females), we only compared the means of employed males versus employed females. Here the sex difference was attenuated (t=-1.81, 246 df, p=.07).

As can be seen in Table 1, nearly all of the outcomes were classified by most respondents as either undesirable (e.g., 92% of the sample did not want air pollution to occur from the plant) or desirable (e.g., only 2% said they would not like to see lower taxes occur). There was, however, substantial variation between persons on the perceived likelihood of the outcomes, with a majority of the items having a standard deviation of 1.0 or more.

To reduce the dimensionality of the full set of outcome measures, a principal components analysis using varimax rotation was performed. Five factors emerged which were labelled: Hazards, Economic Growth, Social Disruption, Lower Costs, and Community Visibility. These factors and the loadings of items in the factors are also displayed in Table 1.

Unit-weighted simple sum factor scores were formed for the five factors. While there were no differences between males and females on the desirability of individual items in these factors, the use of t-tests revealed that the sexes differed significantly in their assessment of the likelihood of occurrence of three of the factors (Table 2). Specifically, males viewed the economic growth and community visibility factors as more likely to occur than did females, and they viewed the hazards factor as less likely to occur. For females only, permitting construction of the plant correlated significantly with the community visibility, economic growth, and hazards variables; for males only and for the total sample of respondents, only the latter two variables correlated significantly with permitting construction.

4. DISCUSSION

This study found less support among females than among males for construction of a proposed nuclear power plant in their community. In fact, the different levels of support found among Hartsville men and women (73% vs. 57% permitting construction) mirror almost exactly

TABLE 1. SUMMARY OF DESCRIPTIVE STATISTICS AND FACTOR ANALYSIS FOR PERCEIVED OUTCOME LIKELIHOODS

Outcome	Factor Loadings					Percent Not Favoring Outcome	Percent Estimating Likely or Very Likely
	I	II	III	IV	V		
Factor I - Hazards (26% of variance)							
Radiation hazard	.80	-.10	-.08	.24	-.03	92	27
Accidents/Sabotage	.78	-.13	-.04	.00	.05	95	33
Air pollution	.73	-.14	-.08	.20	-.08	94	38
Water pollution	.69	-.07	-.14	.24	-.18	92	39
Factor II - Economic Growth (12% of variance)							
More jobs	-.13	.74	.08	-.08	.11	2	84
Better pay	-.27	.65	.26	-.07	.16	1	62
Increased business	-.09	.61	-.13	-.08	.02	2	89
Industrial development	-.13	.60	.31	.03	.11	3	65
More public entertainment	-.06	.59	.31	-.13	.24	3	52
Dating with workers	.01	.52	-.18	.28	-.07	24	58
Factor III - Lower Costs (7% of variance)							
Community stays same	-.19	-.08	.74	-.14	.04	11	21
Lower taxes	-.01	.23	.77	-.10	-.05	2	9
Cheap electricity	-.24	.39	.55	-.10	-.14	1	23
Factor IV - Social Disruption (5% of variance)							
Traffic congestion	.15	-.02	-.04	.80	.01	79	71
Crowding/shopping areas	.07	.03	-.02	.70	.14	55	68
Overcrowding/schools	.32	-.18	-.12	.62	.14	88	81
Increased crime	.40	-.23	-.20	.57	.07	96	57
Crowding/recreation areas	.26	.29	-.15	.54	-.27	59	58
Factor V - Community Visibility (5% of variance)							
Public recognition	-.18	.20	-.03	.02	.66	4	86
More taverns and bars	.10	-.04	-.24	.38	.59	71	69
More tourists	-.01	.33	.26	.07	.50	11	71
Other outcomes							
Opportunity to meet people	-.09	.45	-.01	-.11	.43	2	93
Increased noise	.49	-.09	-.10	.40	-.02	84	59
Drug problems/schools	.42	-.28	-.23	.42	.42	97	67

TABLE 2. SEX DIFFERENCES IN PERCEIVED LIKELIHOOD SCORES

Variable	Possible range of response		Means		Degrees of freedom	t-value	Exact 2-tailed probability
	Very unlikely	Very likely	Male	Female			
Hazards	4	- 20	11.39	12.86	291	-3.47	0.001
Economic Growth	6	- 30	23.25	22.35	312	2.10	0.036
Lower Costs	3	- 15	4.41	4.61	319	-1.04	0.299
Social Disruption	5	- 25	19.14	19.07	244	0.17	0.868
Community Visibility	3	- 15	12.16	11.56	325	2.99	0.003

the results of a national Harris poll, where 73% of the men, versus 54% of the women favored the building of more nuclear power plants in the United States (Harris and Associates, Inc., 1975). This suggests that the finding for Hartsville is not atypical.

The different levels of support may be explained, at least partially, by differences on the perceived likelihood scores for the economic growth, community visibility, and hazards factors. Two of these three factors correlated significantly with the variable of permitting construction of the plant. Since females perceived economic growth and increased visibility for the Hartsville community as less likely than did males but viewed the threat of a group of hazardous outcomes as more likely, there appears to be some justification for the lower level of support for the plant found among female respondents. However, the reason for the male/female differences in perceived likelihoods for these three factors is not at all clear. For example, why would males perceive "more jobs" to be a more likely event than females? Conversely, why would females view radiation hazards as more likely to happen than males?

One could argue that the different subjective estimates of likelihood were a function of different levels of information conceivably arising from sex-segregated communication patterns. Thus, in line with their social roles, males might logically be expected to have more prior information about job openings associated with the proposed plant. However, in a community the size of Hartsville, where people report knowing virtually everyone else, it would seem likely that information about such a salient issue would become public knowledge fairly rapidly, particularly when 80% are married and could be expected to share such information with their spouses.

A more productive approach may lie with theories of attitude formation which explain different levels of information as a function of selective exposure and/or selective retention of information (cf. Campbell, 1950). Thus, it is suggested that individuals selectively expose themselves to new information and selectively retain information which is consistent with their initial position. Or, the observed differences between men and women in our sample may also reflect differences in general values. Perhaps what is being tapped here is a difference in basic values--such as a difference in economic and aesthetic values, to use two of the values in Allport, Vernon and Lindzey's (1951) sixfold classification of values. It is interesting to note that Allport, et al. (ibid) did in fact find that men obtained higher average scores for economic values than women, but lower average scores for aesthetic values.

Along these lines, the present findings for the economic growth and hazards factors are consist-

ent with those reported by Lansing (1971) and Levitt (1967) who observed that the voting behavior of women appears to be less motivated by economic self-interest and more by humanitarian considerations. If one accepts the argument that women, because of their channelled socialization are less comfortable with technology (cf. Bem and Bem, 1971), it could follow that they are less likely to be convinced of the adequacy of safety and ecological precautions. Thus, when weighing the trade-off between a short term economic gain on the one hand, versus possible long-range harmful effects to the community on the other, they would tend to be more mindful of the latter.

Given these differences observed from our survey results, this still leaves open the question of the conditions under which such differences might be attenuated. For example, we don't know whether the differential levels of support will persist over time given that the plant is constructed and put into operation. If a construction license is granted, we are planning to monitor this and other issues in later stages of a long-range panel study of the same persons. There is also the question of whether these differences are specific to a rural Southern community. It has been observed that when women's roles are more nearly equal to that of the male role, sex differences in attitudes appear to decline (Lansing, 1971; Levitt, 1967; and Milbrath, 1965). We saw this trend in our comparisons among employed males and employed females, where the difference between men and women on the "permit plant" variable was reduced. Intriguingly, the sex difference on the economic growth factor among employed respondents completely disappeared (t=.07, 258 df, p=.946), but the difference on the hazards factor remained sharp (t=-2.95, 258 df, p=.003). Replications elsewhere are needed to more completely address this question.

Finally, the issue of how others might view the sex differences found here should be addressed. Supporters of the plant might attempt to influence or persuade the minority to adopt the majority viewpoint. This could lead to a strategy of trying to bring the women into alignment with the males' opinions. Although it is not within the scope of this study to take a stand on this issue, we would merely point out that a dissenting viewpoint can also prove useful in the role of watchdog on such issues as pollution, radiation hazards, or disruption of the community. In fact, there is evidence (U.S. Nuclear Regulatory Commission, 1975) that TVA is already planning amelioration strategies in the Hartsville area which are intended to minimize the negative outcomes associated with construction and operation of the plant.

There is at least one direct implication of the present findings for future studies in social impact assessments for large-scale environmental change projects. An impact analysis which consulted only males, or a disproportionate number of males, to obtain data may produce an overly optimistic picture of the outcomes, just as oversampling females might produce unduly pessimistic findings for estimates of a total population.

The problem of positing a theoretical construct to underly the sex difference found in our study in views toward the proposed nuclear power plant presents many possibilities, which may prove extremely difficult to untangle. Only through careful conceptualization and measurement will future research be able to provide some answers. Further, studies such as the one reported here not only help extend our present knowledge of sex differences, but also generate new knowledge regarding the views of citizens in general toward such large-scale construction projects.

Reference

ALLPORT, G. W., VERNON, P. E., and LINDZEY, G. Study of values. Boston: Hougton-Mifflin, 1951.

BEM, S. L. and BEM, D. J. Case study of a non-conscious ideology: training the woman to know her place. In D. J. BEM, Beliefs, attitudes and human affairs. Belmont, Calif.: Brooks/Cole, 1970.

BERELSON, B. R., LAZARSFELD, P. F. and MC PHEE, W. N. Voting. Chicago: University of Chicago Press, 1954.

CAMPBELL, D. T. The indirect assessment of social attitudes. Psychological Bulletin, 1950, 47, 145-158.

GRUBERG, M. Women in American politics. Oshkosh, Wisc.: Academic Press, 1968.

HARRISand Associates, Inc. A survey of public and leadership attitudes toward nuclear power development in the United States. Study number 2515, conducted for Ebasco Services, Inc., August, 1975.

LANSING, M. L. Sex differences in voting and activism. Paper presented to American Political Science Annual Meeting, Chicago, September, 1971.

LEVITT, M. The political role of American women. Journal of Human Relations, 1967, 15(1), 23-35.

MACCOBY, E. E. and JACKLIN, C. N. The psychology of sex differences. Stanford, Calif.: Stanford University Press, 1974.

MEDNICK, M. T. and WEISSMAN, H. J. The psychology of women — selected topics. Annual review of psychology, 1975, 26, 1-18.

MILBRATH, L. W. Political participation. Chicago: Rand McNally, 1965.

RAMBO, W. W., JONES, W. H. and FINNEY, P. D Some correlates of the level of constraint in a system of social attitudes. Journal of Psychology, 1973, 83, 89-94.

SCHULLER, C. R., FOWLER, J. R., MATTINGLY, T. J., JR., SUNDSTROM, E., LOUNSBURY, J. W., PASSINO, E. M., DOWELL, D. A. and HUTTON, B. J. Citizens' views about the proposed Hartsville nuclear power plant. Technical report, ORNL-RUS-3, Oak Ridge National Laboratory, Oak Ridge, Tenn., 1975.

SMITH, D. D. Sex, reference others, and the affective-cognitive consistency of opinions on social issues. Social Science Quarterly, 1972, 53, 145-154.

U.S. NUCLEAR REGULATORY COMMISSION. Mitigation of socioeconomic impacts. Final environmental statement related to construction of Hartsville nuclear plants of the Tennessee Valley Authority. NUREG-75/039, Office of Nuclear Reactor Regulation, June, 1975.

SIXTY YEARS OF TRANSITION IN A PLANNED COMPANY

TOWN, WITH A PORTRAYAL OF CURRENT RESIDENT

EVALUATIONS[1]

Arnold R. Alanen

Department of Landscape Architecture
University of Wisconsin, Madison

ABSTRACT

Most company towns in the United States, because
of their paternalistic overtones and rather
minimal design standards, receive scant attention in reviews of previous new town and new
community development efforts. At the same
time, however, it has been noted that certain
similarities exist between these previous cor-
porate-sponsored entites and many contemporary
planned communities. In an effort to consider
the processes that one of these older developments has experienced over a span of sixty
years, this paper traces the evolution of Morgan
Park, Minnesota, one of the few company towns
which has received favorable attention for certain design and planning-related criteria. The
partial results of a recent resident survey are
also discussed so as to determine the extent to
which some of these initial inputs are still
recognized and appreciated by present day inhabitants.

1. INTRODUCTION

Imperfect though they may be, new towns and
planned communities continue to attract attention as one, albeit partial, alternative to contemporary urban development patterns. Until
recently, however, relatively little empirical
evidence has been available which provides insight to actual levels of resident satisfaction
within such environments. It is only during
this decade that several research efforts have
begun to explore a host of issues ranging from
evaluations of specific design components to
analyses of community planning and governance
mechanisms (e.g., Lansing, et al., 1970; Zehner,
1971; Godschalk, 1973; Keller, 1973; Marans &
Rodgers, 1973; Burby, 1974).

A major factor underlying many of these research
endeavors involves the amount of control a
developer can or should exert in the process of
creating a new community. Proponents of strong
developer rights contend that centralized controls are necessary if certain innovations are
to be realized and standards maintained;

[1]Research support for this paper was provided
by the Graduate School of the University of
Wisconsin.

on the other hand, opponents of this view argue
that new communities should truly be democratic
and serve as vehicles for the engendering of
greater public participation and involvement
(Burby, 1974). In essence, the questions are
somewhat similar to those posed decades ago when
various industrial enterprises were establishing
company towns in the United States. Certainly
the degree of paternalism within America's former company towns was much greater than in
today's planned communities; but yet, parallels
exist between the two situations, even as evidenced by the use of the term "company town" to
describe certain contemporary suburban developments (Brooks, 1971; Godschalk, 1973).

Given this evidence, it would appear that the
actions, procedures and results relating to the
transition from corporate to individual ownership might provide some insights to design,
planning and management decisions for today's
planned community situations. For example, did
the character of the socioeconomic and physical
environment in these company towns change
noticeably after corporate (i.e. developer)
controls were terminated; and was the transition
period a traumatic one, or did it occur with
relatively little difficulty? Of even greater
interest are questions relating to perceptions
and evaluations of the current community milieu.
In other words, are the features of a planned
environment still evident and/or appreciated by
residents after such a community has existed for
many decades and has already achieved maturity?

1.1. Approach and Procedure

The following discussion and analysis will seek
to address the above questions by focusing upon
the planned company town of Morgan Park,
Minnesota. During its initial quarter century
of existence as a U.S. Steel Corporation company
town and subsequent three decades as a non-cor-
porate entity, the community has undergone
several transitional phases which range from
changes in management and ownership practices to
problems of local economic stability. Although
a study which deals with a single community may
appear overly idiographic, Morgan Park is one of
the few company towns in the United States which
has received positive evaluations from several
observers (e.g., Magnusson, 1918; Reps, 1965;
Glaab & Brown, 1967). Since Radburn, the

Greenbelt towns, Columbia, Reston and a few
other similar examples often serve as case
studies for the analysis of different planned
community eras in the United States, it can be
argued that Morgan Park stands out as a company
town model which merits further inquiry.

The ensuing study begins with a description of
the community through its company and post-
company town phases, and follows with a brief
discussion of events which recently led to the
closing of the adjacent steel manufacturing complex. (Ironically, this same industrial facility was responsible for the initial development
of the community during the early part of the
century.) The latter portion of the paper is
devoted to an analysis of community evaluations
and perceptions as expressed by Morgan Park's
current residents; these results, in turn, are
compared to findings derived from studies of
more recently built communities.

1.2. An American Company Town Context

Whereas relatively few company towns are built
in the United States today, their development
was a relatively commonplace occurrence during
the 19th and early 20th centuries.[2] Such communities generally emerged in remote, resource
oriented areas of the country where normal
housing supply channels could or would not
satisfy local needs and requirements. Unfortunately, however, the company town story in the
United States is hardly an attractive one. As
Porteous (1974) has stated: "Physical planning
in company towns has often been conspicuous by
its absence; entrepreneurs are characteristically oriented toward production and profit,
rather than the onerous task of housing their
employees." Although there have been any number
of such developments in the United States, one
of the classic negative examples is provided by
Gary, Indiana, a city once characterized as
"...a complete example of what not to do in
future developments" (Comey & Wehrly, 1939). In
other cases where planning was tightly structured, as at Pullman, Illinois, the resulting
social controls were so strict that dissension
and conflict eventually erupted (Buder, 1971).

Between these two poles, characterized by
Pullman's highly regulated situation on the one
hand and Gary's haphazardly planned environment
on the other, were some company towns which appeared to provide a relatively humane milieu

_____
[2]More recent manifestations of the company
town theme can be found in Canada, especially
along the nation's northern resource frontier.
There also is the possibility that company towns
may once again emerge within the U.S. if large-
scale exploitation of coal and other energy
resources in the Great Plains and Rocky Mountain
regions should occur.

for resident-worker existence. To determine if
this indeed was or is the case, the following
discussion will focus upon the sixty year evolution of one such community.

2. MORGAN PARK: PAST TO PRESENT

2.1. Community Origins

Unlike many company town endeavors where the
rapid exploitation of a resource meant that
housing for laborers was built quickly (and
often poorly), Morgan Park's development took
place quite slowly. The major reason behind
this languor was the hesitency of U.S. Steel
even to become involved with steel production
operations in Northeastern Minnesota. In fact,
it was not until the State of Minnesota, during
1907, threatened to impose a tonnage tax on
U.S. Steel's vast iron ore holdings that the
corporation reluctantly agreed to establish a
steel production unit proximate to the city of
Duluth (White & Primmer, 1937). Various manifestations of this arrangement, entered into by
America's first billion dollar corporation and
a state with enormous, but nonetheless finite
mineral wealth, would continue to mark the
course of events that affected the community
during ensuing decades.

When U.S. Steel officials first announced their
plans to construct a steel production unit in
Minnesota, it also was stated that the corporation would not build homes for employees, but
would leave this task "to others" (Duluth News
Tribune, 1907). By 1910, however, plans were
being made to develop a company town which would
"...include strictly modern homes, beautiful as
to architecture and commodious of arrangement,
business houses, paved streets, a perfect sewer
and lighting system, and halls for public
meetings and places of amusement" (Duluth News
Tribune, 1910). Apparently the major thrust
behind this change in plans was the corporation's perception of Northeastern Minnesota's
labor situation. Since most employment opportunities in the region were highly seasonal, a
large portion of the labor force was quite foot-
loose; hence, it was surmised that a dependable
work force could be provided only if certain
inducements were used. In the case of Morgan
Park the major inducement was the provision of
housing and services qualitatively better than
that offered in the surrounding area (Iron Age,
1913).

By 1918, a national architectural journal was
reporting that Morgan Park's planning and
development "...had been along systematic and
orderly lines, correct principles of town
planning have been followed and the educational
and recreative elements necessary in a development of this character have been provided in a
most modern and satisfactory manner" (American
Architect, 1918). When compared to the monotonous grid pattern of most company towns, Morgan

Park does stand out as a rather positive contrast. A curvilinear street pattern was utilized, not so much for novelty's sake, but especially to enhance the relationship with the adjacent wooded terrain, lake shore and ravines. All wires were placed underground and efforts made to preserve as many trees as possible. The housing, largely constructed during the 1915-18 interim, provided accommodations for about 20 percent of the local work force (Magnusson, 1918). Since the residences were built of concrete, the units proved to be durable but somewhat drab; however, the "bomb shelter" appearance of the exteriors was mitigated by various architectural features such as gables, eaves and pitched roofs. The interiors of the residences were likewise designed to provide each house with a simple but unified appearance. "Family areas flowed into each other, eliminating dark, wasteful hallways and small isolated rooms" (Scott, 1974).

While the vistas, broad streets and rather dominant public and commercial buildings provided Morgan Park with some modest properties of the City Beautiful, it was the attempt to promote social policies through physical design which brought most attention to the community. Morgan Park, as noted by one U.S. Department of Labor analyst, was both a physical and social planning experiment (Magnusson, 1918). Although some of these efforts displayed evidence of social enlightenment, others were no more than paternalistic gestures couched in seemingly altruistic terms.

Much of the corporation's social planning was referred to as "welfare work." As noted by one local observer, the corporation was interested in its employees "...not only during their hours of labor, but (also) during their hours of rest," and was likewise concerned with "...questions of how the employees live; how they obtain their recreation; how they spend their money; and how their children are educated" (McCarthy, 1916). The same observer, however, pointed out that such practices were related to sound business principles; and another spokesman claimed that the corporation's welfare work was not "sociological meddling," but only an attempt to increase worker efficiency through better living conditions (Stowell, 1918).

Within the community some homes were provided for all socioeconomic levels, ranging in scope from multiple and row houses for lower income laborers to large substantial residences for managers. Whereas residents generally were selected in order of application, other considerations also were used: the character of the applicants' services, his general desirability as a tenant and the likelihood of his becoming a permanent employee (Magnusson, 1918). Nevertheless, a certain amount of "weeding" apparently occurred in the process of selecting applicants. One observer stated that while housing was available in adjoining, less attractive townsites, it was "the skilled workmen and the families of

their high grade, permanent class (who) have the privilege of Morgan Park homes" (The Zenith, 1915).

Although there never have been large numbers of blacks living in the Duluth region, those employed in steel plant operations were excluded from the Morgan Park residential community. Likewise, certain facilities and events based within Morgan Park but which had a constituency larger than the community itself, were limited to white participants alone. Such practices were defended by stating that separate events could be held for non-whites at some later date; or that the large number of general community events simply utilized all available facility time and could not be used by smaller (i.e., minority) groups (Good Fellowship Club, 1920 and 1923). Perhaps these were isolated examples, but they do nonetheless point to the ease with which social, economic and racial homogeneity could be maintained within most company towns.

The employment-residence relationship, which often made employee completely subservient to employer, always has been a consistent criticism of company town life. When coupled with their usual monotony and lack of services and amenities, it is no wonder that company towns came to be regarded as no more than utilitarian living environments at best. On the other hand, in towns such as Morgan Park where the full force of corporate planning and sponsorship was applied to the community setting, a myriad of local organizations and activities were developed for and by workers and their families. By 1919, for example, some 36 organizations, most of them housed in a central facility donated to the community by the corporation, had emerged in Morgan Park. The amount of direct company involvement in Morgan Park never even approached that of Pullman, but it is quite obvious that with the provision of so many free-time opportunities in the community, outside (and perhaps antagonistic) influences could be held to a minimum.

Finally, it would be remiss if one very specific regulation were not mentioned: the complete ban on the sale of any alcoholic beverages within Morgan Park. This form of prohibition, which only served to move the dispensing establishments outside the town limits, was practiced in several company towns throughout the country. Hence, not only were there company stores and company housing in towns such as Morgan Park--there also were "company morals."

2.2. From Company to Private Ownership

During the 1920's and most of the 1930's, Morgan Park's status as a company town remained unchanged. Interestingly enough, however, it was the corporation and not the residents that initiated action to bring company ownership to an end. During 1938, the company announced that the residents could buy their homes if they were interested (MacDonald, 1942). This action at the

local level reflected a broader U.S. Steel decision to sell much of its property throughout
the country. The reasons behind this plan were
listed as increasing taxes, plant relocations,
operating and selling charges, unused land and
depleted mining properties (Iron Age, 1938).
Other reports, however, stated that the company
actually was concerned with the relationship between corporate paternalism and labor conflicts
(Architectural Forum, 1951).

Overt paternalism did not appear to be of ex-
ceeding concern to Morgan Park residents since
only two individuals purchased their homes between 1938 and 1942. The company, during 1942,
then announced that because of the hesitancy
displayed by residents, a real estate sales approach would be adopted. Acknowledging that
the steel corporation was not equipped to engage
in such activities, the company proceeded to
make plans to sell its residential holdings to
a nationally-based realty firm. Although it was
stated that the firm would sell or rent the
dwelling units to occupants who wished to remain
in Morgan Park (MacDonald, 1942), a group of
residents responded by protesting that "turning
us over to the tender mercies of a real estate
outfit doesn't eactly appeal to us" (Morgan Park
Community Club, 1942). Nevertheless, the transaction was completed by the end of 1942, and
the disposal of individual properties began
thereafter.

For several years the relationship between the
realty firm and Morgan Park residents was rather
strained. Since the operation and maintenance
of the community had formerly been undertaken
by a subsidiary arm of the steel corporation,
the sale brought many services to an immediate
end. This transition caused considerable consternation within the community. Several residents, for example, expressed dismay when the
realtor discontinued heating and lighting within
the large community garages, and some inhabitants were rankled when certain services such
as sidewalk snow removal were terminated
(Morgan Park Community Club, 1945). It was not
until a larger number of residences had been
sold to individual owners that such administrative and management problems were finally
resolved.

2.3. The Community Today

Because of their solid construction, residences
in Morgan Park have consistently ranked higher
than neighboring areas relative to value, condition and number of facilities (U.S. Census of
Population and Housing, 1940, 1950, 1960, 1970).
Apparently because of the community's residential attributes, Morgan Park, during the 1960's,
was the only older area of Duluth to display a
total population gain[3] and experience very

---

[3]Nevertheless, Morgan Park's 1970 population
was only 2,461 residents--334 more than in
1919.

little decline in the number of younger family
residents (City of Duluth, 1969).

By the early 1970's, however, the relative
tranquility of Morgan Park was once again interrupted. Because of the pollution emissions discharged by an increasingly antiquated manufacturing plant, environmentalists began to focus
their attentions upon the steel production unit.
Although the State of Minnesota, during 1970,
gave U.S. Steel three years to determine its
future plans for the plant and two additional
years to meet pollution standards, the corporation proceeded to shut down the blast furnaces
during late 1971 and early 1972. (The fabri-
cation mill was closed two years later.)

U.S. Steel's actions obviously created a new
set of conditions that had to be faced by many
community residents. Even though the plant had
never been much more than a marginal facility
within the U.S. Steel production framework, its
relatively minor national role did not reduce
the actual local impact of the closing. A
number of employees transferred to various U.S.
Steel operations in Minnesota and the United
States, others were able to retire or qualify
for pensions, and the remainder either pursued
altogether different employment options or attempted to cope in some alternative manner.
Whatever the case, one fact was indisputable:
Morgan Park was a steel town no more.

3. RESIDENT SURVEY

Whereas some observers expected that Morgan Park
would turn into a ghost town overnight, the community appeared to retain its relative stability. Given this observation, an effort was made
to assess resident attitudes and perceptions
some three years after the initial plant
closing. To undertake the study, a telephone
survey was made of 341 Morgan Park households
(45 percent of the community) during June 1975.[4]
Questions asked related to current perceptions
and evaluations of the local community environment, actions following the steel plant closing,
attitudes toward U.S. Steel and its procedures,
and normal demographic information. Only the
results which have greatest relevance for this
study are discussed in the following section.

3.1. Resident Turnover Rates

Whereas there were no exact data available which
indicated how many residents actually left
Morgan Park because of the steel plant closing,
it was possible to derive some idea from the
resident survey. Just over 12 percent of the
respondents had moved into the community during
the three and one-half year period following
U.S. Steel's phasing-out operations. By way of
comparison, the turnover rates during the two
three-year periods preceding the steel plant

---

[4]Assistance was provided by the Wisconsin
Survey Research Laboratory.

closing were 8.3 and 8.5 percent respectively. Thus, there undoubtedly was an increase in resident turnover following the closing, but it was not as inordinately high as might have been expected. (A later part of this discussion will focus upon former steel workers who decided to remain in Morgan Park.) As far as future residential stability was concerned, 69 percent of the respondents stated that they intended to remain in the community for at least ten years or more.

3.2. Morgan Park: A Planned Community?

To determine if present day residents were even cognizant of the community's rather unique genesis, respondents were asked whether Morgan Park could be considered a "planned" community or not. About 82 percent answered affirmatively, four percent said no, and the remainder stated that they did not know. Hence, it appeared that at least an image, if not definite knowledge, of the community's origins still persisted among a large majority of Morgan Park's residents some 60 years after initial development efforts began.

3.3. Community Features

Table 1 depicts the evaluations of certain community features made by Morgan Park residents when asked to compare their community to other nearby neighborhoods. The only feature considered to be roughly equivalent in both Morgan Park and adjoining areas was the amount of useable outdoor space. (The somewhat higher housing densities in Morgan Park probably contributed to these perceptions.) More than one-half of the residents considered Morgan Park's community facilities to be superior to adjacent areas, but 12 percent of the respondents, when asked to name the community's most serious shortcoming, listed the inadequacy of such facilities. (Over the 60 year period, few facilities had been added to the initial array provided by U.S. Steel: a community building, two churches, a school and a small commercial center.) Finally, local community maintenance was perceived as being superior to other neighborhoods by 57 percent of the respondents. However, a much larger proportion considered maintenance to be at least satisfactory. (Only three percent listed maintenance shortcomings as a major problem.) This is a rather important factor since other studies have noted the strong relationship that exists between neighborhood maintenance and resident contentment (Lansing, et al., 1970; Marans & Rodgers, 1973).

3.4. Community Evaluations By Length of Residence and Age of Respondent

Cross tabulations were made to determine if length of residence within Morgan Park or age of respondent were related to community evaluations. As indicated by Table 2, tenure within Morgan Park was accompanied by progressive increases in favorable perceptions of the local environment.

TABLE 1: COMPARISON OF SELECTED MORGAN PARK CHARACTERISTICS WITH NEARBY NEIGHBORHOODS, AS EVALUATED BY MORGAN PARK RESIDENTS

Characteristic	Better in M.P. %	Same in M.P. %	Worse in M.P. %	Total %	n*
Quality of Housing	74.5	25.2	.3	100	330
Presence of Landscaping	70.4	27.7	1.9	100	358
Community Facilities	58.5	40.1	1.4	100	354
Community Maintenance	57.4	41.5	1.1	100	352
Useable Outdoor Space	46.2	48.7	5.1	100	351

*Total figures vary since all responses were not useable.

Similar findings were also revealed when the age of respondent was considered. Although the table with the cross tabulations has not been included here, over 76 percent of the 18 to 25 year old residents preferred Morgan Park to any other area of Duluth, while 94 percent of the group over 64 years of age evaluated the community in a similar manner. These findings are similar to those of Marans & Rodgers (1973), who determined that younger persons are generally least satisfied with their local environment, while older, retired individuals are the most contented.

TABLE 2: PREFERENCE FOR MORGAN PARK AS A PLACE TO LIVE, BY LENGTH OF RESIDENCE IN COMMUNITY

Length of Residence in M.P.	Prefer to Live in M.P. Rather Than Any Other Area of Duluth			
	Yes %	No %	Total %	n
0 - 3 years	55.6	44.4	100	45
4 - 10 years	78.1	21.9	100	73
11 - 20 years	90.1	9.9	100	81
Over 20 years	94.4	5.6	100	162
Total	85.3	14.7	100	361

Chi-Sq. = 47.14 with 3 DF; Prob. = .001

3.5. Housing Quality By Socioeconomic Background

Table 1 indicated that a sizeable proportion of local residents considered Morgan Park's housing to be of higher quality than that found in adjacent neighborhoods. In an effort to offer further insight to such findings, a cross tabulation (Table 3) was made between the socioeconomic backgrounds of respondents and evaluations of housing quality. As with the community environment, the retired persons (86 percent) were most likely to consider Morgan Park housing to be of superior quality.

TABLE 3: MORGAN PARK HOUSING QUALITY COMPARED TO
ADJOINING NEIGHBORHOODS, BY SOCIOECONOMIC BACK-
GROUND OF MORGAN PARK RESIDENTS

Socioeconomic Group	Better in M.P. %	Same in M.P. %	Worse in M.P. %	Total %	n
White collar	71.3	27.7	1.0	100	94
Blue collar	72.5	27.5	-	100	109
Retired	86.2	13.8	-	100	94
Other	57.6	42.4	-	100	33
Total	74.5	25.2	.3	100	330

Chi-Sq. = 10.82 with 6 DF; Prob. = .094

Over 70 percent of the blue and white collar
residents also expressed the belief that the
housing was of a higher standard, but only 58
percent of the "other" group (comprised primarily
of students and women not working outside the
home) held similar opinions. Since the socio-
economic breakdown was derived from considering the
occupation of the major wage earner in each
household, financial constraints might have
relegated many members of this group to the community's poorest housing. While these responses
likely were conditioned by personal involvement
with the lower end of the community's housing
continuum, it is important to note that none of
these respondents expressed the belief that
Morgan Park's housing was of poorer quality than
that found in other neighborhoods.

3.6. Residential Desirability and Former U.S.
      Steel Employees

The final tabulation was limited to former U.S.
Steel employees who had decided to stay in
Morgan Park even after the steel plant closed.
The members of this group were asked if the
desirability of Morgan Park as a place to live
had influenced their decision to remain in the
community. Although the cell sizes in Table 4
are somewhat small, it is interesting to note
that 87 percent of the respondents indicated
that Morgan Park's positive attributes had influenced their decision to stay either very
much or somewhat. Even the blue collar workers,
whose outlook might have been expected to be
conditioned more strongly by job-related criteria, displayed a rather decided affinity for
the community.

4. CONCLUSION

Keller (1973) has stated that meaningful advances
in residential design will be possible only if
"post-mortem" studies are done on planned communities and other similar environments. Such
studies, she argues, are necessary before the
success and actual outcome of initial planning
and design proposals--especially in the eyes of
residents and users--can be determined. Likewise, the national surveys of planned environments conducted by Marans and Rodgers (1973)
and others provide a broad data base to which

TABLE 4: RESIDENTIAL DESIRABILITY OF MORGAN
PARK, AS EXPRESSED BY FORMER U.S. STEEL EMPLOYEES
STILL RESIDING WITHIN THE COMMUNITY

Socio-economic Group	Extent to Which Desireability of M.P. Influenced Decision to Remain in Community After Steel Plant Closing				
	Very Much %	Some-what %	Not at all %	Total %	n
White collar	77.8	-	22.2	100	9
Blue collar	60.0	34.3	5.7	100	35
Retired	80.0	-	20.0	100	15
Other	75.0	-	25.0	100	4
Total	68.2	19.1	12.7	100	63

Chi-Sq. = 7.96 with 6 DF; Prob. = .241

findings in specific communities can be compared.
This study of Morgan Park, a planned company town
in Northeastern Minnesota, was undertaken so as
to trace the temporal evolution of one such community, and to determine resident evaluations of
the local environment some 60 years after initial
planning and design proposals had been initiated.

In looking at Morgan Park's early history, the
reviewer is struct by an immediate dichotomy:
the praiseworthy qualities of the physical plan
and related facilities on the one hand, and the
paternalistic character of the community on the
other. Perhaps it might be argued that corporate
ownership and guidance ensured the perpetuation
of many attractive features within the community;
but such paternalism, benevolent though it might
have been, undoubtedly influenced the lives and
actions of residents in both direct and subtle
manners. Social and racial homogeneity were
ensured, and the close linkage between home and
steel hearth was a constant reminder to any
worker who might have questioned or challenged
certain corporate practices.

Nevertheless, when company ownership of the community did come to an end in 1942, it was the
residents and employees who expressed greatest
dismay. Of special concern to the community's
inhabitants were: 1) the procedures that were
followed in selling all residential properties
to an intermediate agent who then resold the
dwelling units to individual buyers, and 2) the
ensuing actions of the agent in phasing out and
downgrading many community services. This period
of instability and difficulty, however, is indicative of the problems faced by many past and
present communitarian ventures: i.e., the question of how to make the transition from singular
ownership and management "...to a thriving and
democratic polity" (Brooks, 1971).

While the issue of paternalism is a matter of past history in Morgan Park[5], a more immediate question involves the community evaluations made by residents currently living in such a "mature" planned development. The findings of the resident survey described in the previous section indicated that most inhabitants still appreciated the legacy of physical features, structures and facilities originally provided by the U.S. Steel Corporation. Overall satisfaction with the community was quite high, with most residents placing greatest stress upon Morgan Park's housing qualities. While such evaluations of housing and related maintenance attributes conform to studies undertaken elsewhere in the United States, it also has been pointed out that the local social setting is an additional and important factor in determining overall levels of satisfaction with one's immediate environment (Marans & Rodgers, 1973). Once again, Morgan Park's citizenry appeared to be quite satisfied: When asked to name the single most attractive feature of the community, the greatest number of respondents (30 percent of the total) listed the positive qualities of their neighbors and fellow residents. Only two percent indicated that the presence of "undesirable" residents constituted a major community problem.

The above findings are more interesting when it is recognized that Morgan Park consists of an almost equal proportion of blue collar, white collar and retired residents (see Table 3). Although the older residents gave Morgan Park the highest overall ratings, a majority of members in the other groups were also quite satisfied with their community. Hence, it would appear that not only can many of the physical qualities of a planned environment be perpetuated over a span of several decades; but that such communities, at least at a limited scale, can also provide a framework which nurtures social heterogeneity and diversity. Granted Morgan Park is but a small example, but it might offer some indication of what today's emerging developments can be like a half century from now. If this is the case, perhaps we should not render final judgments on planned communities until they have achieved maturity.

references

American Architect, 113, June 1918, pp. 743-758 & 761.

Architectural Forum, 95, November 1951, pp. 136-143.

BROOKS, RICHARD. Social Planning in Columbia. Journal, American Institute of Planners, XXXVII, November 1971, pp. 373-379.

BUDER, STANLEY. Pullman: An Experiment in Industrial Order and Community Planning, 1840-1930. New York: Oxford University Press, 1967.

BURBY, RAYMOND J. Environmental Amenities and New Community Governance: Results of a Nationwide Study. In Proceedings, EDRA 5, ed. by Daniel H. Carson. Kansas City: Environmental Design Research Association, Inc., 1974.

City of Duluth, Department of Research and Planning. Community Renewal Program: Population Profile. Duluth: Department of Research and Planning, 1969.

COMEY, ARTHUR C. & WEHRLY, MAX S. Planned Communities. In Urban Planning and Land Policies, Vol. II of the Supplementary Report of the Urbanism Committee to the National Resources Committee. Washington, D.C.: U.S. Government Printing Office, 1939.

Duluth (Minn.) News Tribune, April 2, 1907, pp. 1 & 5; and March 24, 1910, p. 10.

GLAAB, CHARLES N. & BROWN, A. THEODORE. A History of Urban America. New York: The Macmillan Company. 1967.

GODSCHALK, DAVID R. New Communities or Company Towns? An Analysis of Resident Participation in New Towns. In New Towns: Why--And for Whom?, ed. by Harvey Perloff & Neil C. Sanders. New York: Praeger Publishers, 1973.

Good Fellowship Club (Morgan Park). Minute Book, August 6, 1920 and November 13, 1923.

Iron Age, 92, September 18, 1913, pp. 603-605; and 142, November 3, 1938, pp. 162 & 163.

KELLER, SUZANNE. Friends and Neighbors in a Planned Community. In Frontiers of Planned Unit Development: A Synthesis of Expert Opinion, ed. by Robert W. Burchell. New Brunswick, N.J.: Center for Urban Policy Research, Rutgers University, 1973.

LANSING, JOHN B., MARANS, ROBERT W., AND ZEHNER, ROBERT B. Planned Residential Environments. Ann Arbor: Survey Research Center, Institute for Social Research, University of Michigan, 1970.

MACDONALD, J. G. Letter to Morgan Park Good Fellowship Club, August 10, 1942.

MAGNUSSON, LEIFFUR. A Modern Industrial Suburb. Monthly Review of the U.S. Bureau of Labor Statistics, 6, April 1918, pp. 729-753.

[5]It might be argued that Morgan Park's single industry orientation, which continued until the 1970's, constituted a form of economic paternalism. Discussion of such a point, however, is beyond the scope of this paper.

MARANS, ROBERT W. & RODGERS, WILLARD. Evaluating Resident Satisfaction in Established and New Communities. In Frontiers of Planned Unit Development: A Synthesis of Expert Opinion, ed. by Robert W. Burchell. New Brunswick, N.J.: Center for Urban Policy Research, Rutgers University, 1973.

MCCARTHY, GEORGE D. Morgan Park--A New Type of Industrial Community. The American City, XIV, February 1916, pp. 150-153.

Morgan Park Community Club. Minute Book, August 29, 1942, and January 16 & 20, 1945.

PORTEOUS, J. DOUGLAS. Social Class in Atacama Company Towns. Annals, Association of American Geographers, 64, September 1974, pp. 409-417.

REPS, JOHN. The Making of Urban America: A History of City Planning in the United States. Princeton, N.J.: Princeton University Press, 1965.

SCOTT, JAMES A. Duluth's Legacy: Architecture. Duluth: Department of Research and Planning, 1974.

STOWELL, C.R. Industrial City of the Steel Workers of Duluth. Realty, 4, March 1918, pp. 27 & 28.

U.S. Census of Population and Housing. Washington, D.C.: Government Printing Office, 1940, 1950, 1960, 1970.

WHITE, LANGDON & PRIMMER, GEORGE. The Iron and Steel Industry of Duluth: A Study in Locational Maladjustment. Geographical Review, 27, January 1937, pp. 82-91.

ZEHNER, ROBERT B. Neighborhood and Community Satisfaction in New Towns and Less Planned Suburbs. Journal, American Institute of Planners, XXXVI, November 1971, pp. 379-385.

Zenith, The (Duluth, Minn.), November 1915, pp. 25-63 & 113-143.

AN ETHOLOGICAL PROFILE OF A SMALL
NO-GROWTH INDUSTRIAL CITY

Barrie B. Greenbie

Department of Landscape Architecture
and Regional Planning
University of Massachusetts, Amherst

ABSTRACT

The population of 40,000 is comprised of two
major and some minor ethnic groups. An ethological model is applied as part of a program
to reverse a depressed economy and decaying
business district. It is hypothesized that
cultural and social differences will be expressed
spatially. Findings are that the model does not
fit the city at present, though it probably did
in the past. Culturally and spatially the city
is remarkably homogeneous. This is attributed
to lack of significant in-migration for more
than two generations. City policies to upgrade
the area may change this, and the model, in combination with a Garden City model, is proposed
for the future.

1. INTRODUCTION

The report presented in the following pages is
the result of a pilot project sponsored by the
City of Jamestown, New York, and the University of
Massachusetts Agricultural Experiment Station
in the summer of 1975. It was part of an
"human parameters" componant of an Innovative
Community Development proposal initiated by
Research Director Julian Naetzker with the
encouragement of Mayor Stanley Lundine. The
study was conducted by the author and research
assistants, Elliott Chase, Gregory McGinty, and
Douglas North, over a period of six weeks in
the field.

The theoretical framework is a modification of
the anthropological thrust of the initial program. It includes a spatially oriented ethological model formulated by the author (Greenbie
1974, 1975a, 1975b), which calls for observing
behavior of a population without participating
very actively, confining observations to public
areas. In this respect it resembles somewhat
the "ecological psychology" of Roger Barker,
but makes no pretense of following Barker's
exhaustive detail (Barker 1968). Confining observations to public behavior is also a principle
of E. T. Hall (1966, 1974), who has called the
use of space as a cultural communication system
proxemics.

The spatial requirements of the public end of
the social spectrum are those which normally most
interest political leaders, municipal officials
and administrators. To deal with pluralistic
public spaces, the concept of distemics was
formulated by the author (1975a, b) which is
combined with Hall's proxemics. Stated simply,
the theory is that in any human community which
is not a culturally homogeneous village there
will be sub-cultures with special interests,
needs, and ways of using space, based on ethnic
identity, social class, or other group differences
(proxemics). On the other hand there will be
spatial requirements which one or more of these
groups share, the purpose of which is to provide
opportunities for cross-cultural exchange
(distemics). Satisfactory urban design in this
concept thus has a dual purpose, to provide and
protect adequate space for all sub-cultural
interests in a community and at the same time
facilitate maximum communication and cooperation
between those interest groups.

2. THE STUDY AREA

The main focus of this study is the municipality
of Jamestown and its environs, the area around
Lake Chautauqua at the western end of New York
State. It is an industrial city of 40,000
straddling a u-shaped bend in the Chadakoin
River, where it drains that attractive lake.

Chautauqua County reaches to the shores of Lake
Erie and includes the cities of Dunkirk-Fredonia,
which are well within the Buffalo Metropolitan
influence. However, the central and southwestern
part of the country surrounding Lake Chautauqua
are separated from the Lake Erie area by a steep

watershed. Thus isolated, Jamestown has not become a satellite in a larger metropolitan region, but rather is a regional center in itself.

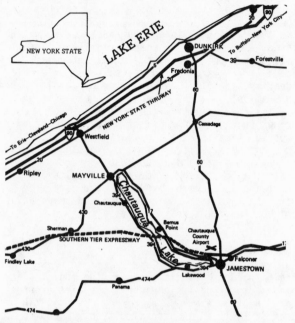

The first settlers were English or Scotch-Irish moving west from New England, followed by skilled Swedish carpenters who increasingly made up the workforce of its emerging furniture industry. The Swedes eventually became the dominant portion of Jamestown's population. Italian settlers began arriving in 1887, and by the turn of the century a sizeable Italian community had developed. Many were skilled artisans in their home country, but they appear to have had more difficulty than the Swedes in initially finding a use for their skills in Jamestown's industry, and often took laboring jobs. In terms of public image, the Swedes and Italians remain the major ethnic divisions in the city.

Jamestown's steel furniture eventually became as well known as its wood furniture had been earlier, and to it was added tool making and other kinds of manufacturing. Most factories remain so-called job shops, requiring a skilled workforce.

Both economically and in terms of population growth, the high point in Jamestown's history came in the 1920's. Since the depression of the thirties the population had declined slightly and more or less continuously from its peak of 45,000 in 1930 to just under forty thousand in 1970. The nature of employment has shifted somewhat from manufacturing to service jobs, with a decline in the number of skilled craftsmen. However, Jamestown does not seem to have suffered as much as many other manufacturing cities in the current recession. This may be attributed not only to the diversity of its

industry, but also to the efforts of the present City administration, through a widely recognized labor-management program, to upgrade both the quantity and quality of work.

Physically the city is a low-rise, low-key urban community on the relatively steep slopes of hills bordering the Chadakoin River Valley. Red brick mills line the river valley in the center and east, with the central business district rising up from the riverfront on the north side within the arc of the river bend. Visually the environment is enhanced by a great many red-brick streets which extend the warm, if dusty, color of the mills and chimneys into the residential areas lined with healthy trees, oaks and maples. A new city hall and an expanding landscaped street mall have enhanced the upper levels of the CBD, but a still uncompleted urban renewal project at the river level leaves a rather bleak hole below it, somewhat intensifying the feeling that mills are not flourishing. A dam constructed many years ago for industrial purposes raised the level of the river so that a marshy lowland separates the city from the lake. The Parks Department is about to begin construction of a large park on a former dump site along the flood plain in this area.

The industrial district along the river bisects the city and includes a railroad. There is a fairly uniform spread of lower-to-upper class houses on both hillsides, with both sides containing some dilapidated areas toward the bottom and more affluent residential blocks towards the heights. On the southeast quadrant the upland is called Swede Hill, the only area in the city with an ethnic name. As is usual, multi-family housing is concentrated near the city center, but with the exception of some converted hotels and one new building for the elderly, most of this consists of converted private houses. Housing in Jamestown is almost equally divided between single family and two-family homes; these two types together account for well over ninety-percent. Eighty-four percent of the total housing stock was built before 1939. Only about five percent has been built in the past decade. Well over half the houses are owner occupied, but this proportion too has declined slightly since 1960. The sense of small town "middle America," even in areas of highest density close to the business district, is pervasive. One consequence is that the crime rate, comparatively speaking, is very low.

Jamestown is at the center of an area comprised of a number of smaller, mostly rural, townships, surrounding Lake Chautauqua on the west and reaching to the Pennsylvania line to the south. In the late 1960's, eight of these towns and a number of villages joined in forming a Southern Chautauqua Regional Planning program, identified as the Chautauqua Lake Region. The Region, like the city of Jamestown, has generally lost population since 1930; however, there seems to be a greater probability than in Jamestown that the trend may shift upwards in the future. Boundaries between city and country are fairly sharp and clear. A number of factories are now located outside the city, and a large Shopping Mall has presented stiff competition to attempts to upgrade Jamestown's business district. In its vicinity a suburban pattern has begun to emerge, but otherwise there is little urban sprawl. Despite an extremely attractive recreational environment, the Chautauqua Lake Region as a whole has not, as of yet, felt the second home impact that has struck so many areas of similar quality. For many decades the lake has been a summer resort, and the shore front is now almost entirely in private ownerships, with a very limited number of public access points. There are a number of impressive and expensive summer homes, but there are also a great many small, owner-built camps. Many of these summer places on all economic levels have become year around homes. The Chautauqua Institute is world famous, but its general atmosphere and clientele have remained quite conservative, not to say nostalgic, in taste, if not in spirit.

Like Jamestown itself, the atmosphere of the Lake Region is very low-key. This may be explained by the same factor that has kept Jamestown itself free of some of the explosive pressures that have affected so many Metropolitan regions in the past generation: the relative geographical isolation of the area. Good railroad service has enabled local industry to serve its markets, but, at least partly because of the topography, the region has been off the beaten track of the Upstate New York and Great Lakes connurbations. However, this situation could change suddenly. The region is in fact the center of a triangle formed by the Cities of Buffalo, Cleveland and Pittsburgh within a 2 to 3 hours drive of each city, which may be considerably shortened by completion of a new Southern Tier Expressway. A condominium complex has already appeared on the northwest shore of Lake Chautauqua. A major new industry has moved into the region near Jamestown. A new sewer system may force out smaller and more marginal summer camps, and thus change the socio-economic pattern around the lake.

3. THE STUDY HYPOTHESIS

Early discussions with city officials and various citizens led to a clear impression that Jamestown is very diverse culturally and socially. We were told that its citizens were preoccupied with national origins, especially the two major ethnic constellations, Swedes and Italians, which are also expressed in the two major religions in the city, Lutheran and Catholic. Plans for various Italian festivities in the study year, and for Swedish ones the following year, which include a visit from the King of Sweden, seemed to support this conclu-

sion. Strong social class divisions were also assumed, based on the history of labor unrest and some reported continuing problems being faced by the Labor-Management Committee, despite its relatively spectacular successes.

We took as our first objective determining to what extent, if any, these might influence attitudes of the citizenry to such recently completed projects as the new City Hall, a Downtown pedestrian mall, an urban renewal project, as well as projects for the near future, such as a recently funded Chadakoin Park, expansion of the mall, and public housing. It early became apparent that our initial hypothesis would not be sustained. Jamestown emerged as remarkably homogeneous, physically, culturally, and to a surprising extent, socially. Much of our efforts after the first week of field work were directed at exploring the reasons for this apparent contradiction between self-image and behavior and its significance for decision-making by the city government and the future development of the city and region.

4. STUDY METHODS

The initial strategy involved stationing observers in those areas of the city which inspection showed to be activity centers. It was assumed that in addition to obvious public areas, such as the City Hall plaza, the downtown pedestrian mall, and the major parks, which are considered "distemic" in the model used here, there would appear a number of local public areas which might represent neighborhood centers of the type considered "proxemic," that is, used by a particular sub-group of the population, whether defined by ethnic origin, by class, or by age. We were also interested to what extent, if any, use of the more obvious distemic centers was preferred by any one particular group.

The strategy proved not to be productive, because, except for some special events and a certain amount of ordinary movement along streets and in shopping centers, there was relatively little public activity in the city. There also appeared to be no reliable distinguishing characteristics in dress, manner or behavior that could be attributed to any particular ethnic group. We thereafter adopted a modified interview-observer technique. We approached people on the street or sitting on their porches and engaged them in casual conversation. In order to avoid intimidation, we did not take notes or refer to written questions, but memorized a general set of questions, including possible names and locations of a neighborhoods, location of shopping and social activities, and attitudes toward parks, downtown development, and provision of services. Initially we also asked the respondents to draw cognitive maps of their neighborhoods.

We found relatively few people on the streets, except in a mixed commercial section which will be called Washington. People sitting on porches often vanished into their houses as we approached. One observer gives a vivid image of empty chairs still rocking as he came up the steps. When a man and a woman were on the porch, if one remained it was likely to be the woman. However, with the opportunity to compare opinions between males and females, no significant differences were found. The reluctance to meet us was attributed by one respondent to frequent visits by recruiters for religious organizations. During this and other phases of the project, all observers introduced themselves frankly as urban planners doing a study for the city government. We found that once we were able to make contact and introduce ourselves, people were friendly, responsive, and quite willing to talk, showing considerable interest in the affairs of the city. This remained true throughout the study.

The cognitive mapping experiment was interesting, but it appeared only to corroborate verbal information. As the process was too time-consuming for a short pilot project, it was abandoned after a few days. The combination of direct observation and informal interviews or conversations as the opportunity presented itself remained the basic technique throughout the project. It was used at various public gatherings downtown and in major parks as well as in the neighborhoods. Observation periods varied, but the most favorable were in the late afternoons and early evenings and Saturdays. Summer weekends in Jamestown, appeared remarkably quiet. We made it a practice to patronize various restaurants and taverns, both downtown and in outlying zones, engaging people in conversation. The taverns proved to be a most rewarding source of information (see LeMasters, 1975).

As a final phase of the field work, a structured survey was pretested by the observers with a stratified sample of residents, selected according to accepted statistical techniques. At the end of the structured interviews, we engaged the respondents in less formal conversation to continue the approach adopted at the outset. A mail survey, revised according to the pre-test, followed the interviews survey.

We made comparative observations of the use of the downtown pedestrian mall and the competing enclosed Chautauqua Mall in the adjacent village of Lakewood. In addition to noting the kind and types of people, we kept count for selected half-hour periods at various times of the number of persons carrying packages, on the theory that this would help distinguish those who were actively shopping from those who were window-shopping or otherwise enjoying themselves in a public place. We also made an intensive windshield survey of the Chautauqua Lake Region, including the lakefront and surrounding towns, with on-foot "participant-observation" and some informal interviewing in key activity centers.

5. RESULTS AND CONCLUSIONS

5.1. Ethnic and Social Structure

Nowhere in the city, with the possible exception of the area we are calling Washington, did we find evidence of traditional neighborhoods. The general attitude of residents of Jamestown on this question is well summed up by an elderly lady who said, "This street is my neighborhood, and, beyond that, Jamestown is my neighborhood."

An overview of the physical city suggests rather a series of social-architectural gradients, ranging from quite elegant, large, well landscaped homes at one end of the scale, through large sections of modest frame houses with well kept yards, to some unevenly maintained wooded structures on narrow lots. In comparison with a great many U.S. cities today, the visible range between poverty and affluence in Jamestown is not extreme in either direction. Certain differences in style, based on period of development, do appear in various sections of the city, but nothing we found suggests that they reflect important social or cultural dichotomies. More or less the same sort of people are to be found in all of them. The 1970 census data supports this.

The lower sections along the Chadakoin River valley are where the original Italian settlements occurred. The 1970 census data suggest that there is some tendency for Italians to remain in these areas. Census data for "Swede Hill," show few recent arrivals from Italy, but a modest number from Sweden. However, the data also show a fairly even distribution of both groups across the city. The mail interview survey confirmed this pattern. The Italian population of Jamestown goes back three and four generations and the Swedish population more than that. Both Italians and Swedes in Jamestown seem to maintain a clear national self-identity no matter how long they have also been Americans, but this seems to conform to Milton Gordon's theory of "the sense of peoplehood" rather than ethnic cultural behavior (Gordon, 1964). There is little visible expression of cultural differences in these areas, certainly nothing comparable to the "Little Italy" of many of our cities, such as Boston's North End or the East Side of Manhattan.

Apparently at one time there did exist a strong Italian neighborhood in an area around a Catholic Church on the South Side of the River, which was demolished in an urban renewal program. The younger generations of Italians seem to have spread out through the community. The parish of the still largely Italian Catholic Church is growing, but according to its priest, 90% of marriages are now interfaith. The name Swede Hill strongly suggests that there originally was an equivalent Swedish sub-community in the city, and the fact that it was on the hill above the Italian one reinforces the conclusion that the Swedes, being the more established settlers at the time of the original Italian immigration, held more status in the larger city. Conversations with residents in both areas lead to the conclusion that Italians, Swedes and others now live together in Swede Hill, and we have been unable to find anyone who can give us a clear firm boundary for that area.

If there is anything resembling a neighborhood at all, it is the relatively low-income, racially mixed area which will be called Washington. Housing in Washington ranges from modest, but neat, well kept single family homes with landscaped lawns to extremely dilapidated single and multi-family houses. Here again we find the general level of maintenance and apparent affluence increasing as the land rises. There have been sewer problems on the low area near the flood plain; a number of houses here have been condemned for Chadakoin Park. We found no evidence of anyone being dissatisfied with relocation. Washington Street itself is heavily traveled, and zoned for business. Commercial development, like housing, tends to be marginal. Washington Street does not appear to divide the community, but rather seems to be the center of whatever spatial identity exists.

Although we saw more people on the streets here than elsewhere, discussions with residents indicate that the main focus of social life is on home and family, as elsewhere in Jamestown, but that homes and yards are less adequate for this purpose than elsewhere in the city. We frequently heard references to "the black community," but we saw no streets without some white people. Whatever sense of community may exist is apparently one of social identity based on poverty rather than race, but even that is relative and not uniform. A young Italian woman gave us the impression that her family was industrious, ambitious, and felt hard pressed by life, but not poverty stricken. She expressed considerable dislike for the neighborhood because it was noisy and the neighbors did not maintain their property, but did not express any racial prejudice toward the mostly black families on her block. Of the blacks we interviewed, some did seem to feel discriminated against in jobs and even in athletics. They appeared to distrust the city government and politicians in general, but none of us found expressions of hostility toward white neighbors on the part of blacks or vice versa, and certainly none toward ourselves as white people. By contrast, in an area on the eastern end of the Central Business District, we did encounter overt hostility to a small number of Puerto Ricans who are relatively recent

arrivals. One old man, interviewed in his yard, declared the area had become a "gotto." He seemed to feel the city in general was going to the dogs, and expressed hostility also to the Immanuel Lutheran Church nearby. But a public meeting with Puerto Ricans indicates that they like Jamestown. A small area in the northern part of Washington has a number of black families, who along with their neighbors appear to be well-off, even affluent. Discussions with people there predictably found more satisfaction with life and a more positive attitude toward the city government.

The cognitive maps that were drawn by residents in the first phase of the study never exceeded five blocks in area, and in many cases showed only the respondent's own street and the nearest intersections. Generally, the respondents' houses were located precisely, with the maps terminating at some significant activity point, most often a school, sometimes a store. This suggests an open ended social range, rather than an enclosed neighborhood.

5.2. Social Life and Recreation

The impression we have of Jamestown's social life is very similar to that of its physical environment: -- low-key, small scale, home and family oriented. Our visual observations and our discussions with residents suggest that there is a great deal of small group socializing in homes and on porches, card parties and general visiting, probably much of it among relatives. This is confirmed by the interviews and mail surveys. There seemed to be a considerable amount of yard work going on; gardening, painting, etc. Most social needs that are not met by home and family are provided by various clubs and organizations. Some are national clubs -- the Vikings and the Vaasa for the Swedes, the Gaeta for the Italians. These seem to have less appeal for younger people than for their elders. Many of these clubs provide substantial physical facilities for meetings and recreation; some, especially the Swedish organizations, have extensive summer facilities on Lake Chautauqua Churches also provide an important center for social life as well as ethnic identity for Jamestown citizens, and they seem relatively active and well attended. Traditional sports such as baseball and bowling are engaged in, both by organization and family groups, in one or another of the city parks and the school yards. A nine-hole golf course is a major feature of the new Chadakoin Park. There is mixed evidence as to whether this is desired by the people in Washington.

There are a large number of taverns, and a good deal of socializing, both on a neighborhood and city wide basis, seems to occur in them; this too is supported by the survey. There also are a number of restaurants, both in the downtown and in the outlying areas; some seem to be primarily working class, and others primarily middle class. As elsewhere in the country, the chains are popular with teenagers. A large chain restaurant which recently opened in the Brooklyn Square urban renewal area, serving modestly priced meals twenty-four hours a day, appears to be popular with all classes and ages. Apparently a large number of people of all ages, including family groups, drive out to the Chautauqua Shopping Mall in Lakewood and walk around just to socialize, without intent to buy anything. Even the proprietor of a leading downtown store said he did this with his family! Chautauqua Lake is a main focus for Jamestown's recreational life during the summer. A number of people we talked to had cottages on the lake, or had relatives or friends with cottages. Those not so fortunate reported knowing many others who were. As with other blue-collar populations (LeMasters 1975), among Jamestown men in particular, hunting and fishing seemed to be major interests. Weekly band concerts in one of the larger parks seemed to draw from all over the city, but were not well attended at times we were there, again possibly because of the greater attractions of Lake Chautauqua. There are a number of movie theatres, two old ones downtown, two new ones at Chautauqua Mall, all now owned by the same chain. There are also two drive-ins on the outskirts of the city.

Chautauqua Institute is only half an hour by car from downtown. For more than a century it has been providing entertainment of an inspirational and intellectual nature for the people of Jamestown and the surrounding region, as well as from all over the country, especially the Midwest. Most people we talked to seemed aware of it and reasonably proud of its juxtaposition to Jamestown. Institute events are well published at Jamestown Community College, and regular bus runs from there are scheduled. Adolescent young people in general seemed to feel that the town was dull, that there "is nothing to do," but this is an attitude quite commonly found in small cities and towns, and suburbs. We have no reason to suspect the problem is any worse in Jamestown than in most other communities of its size and type, and it may, if anything, be somewhat less serious in Jamestown than many other places. Jamestown young people seem very preoccupied with automobiles. There appears to be a lot of random cruising around and burning of rubber in souped up and reconstructed cars, some of them absurdly elegant as such cars can be.

5.3. Shopping

Most people we talked to liked the suburban Chautauqua Mall, and indicated that they went there for the fun of it as well as for shopping. Attitudes to the downtown pedestrian mall fell into three categories; those who liked the street improvements and were proud of the changes because they felt they were revitalizing the

city; those who seemed to like the improvements but felt there were more important things to spend city funds on; and those who were very hostile to the project and felt it was a waste of money. Generally speaking these followed socio-economic lines, with people in the better kept residential areas expressing approval.

Our counts of people passing a given point who had packages as compared with those who did not, at various times and various days, suggest that in both shopping areas a large number of people have non-shopping objectives. The ratio downtown varied from one with packages to three without on a Saturday afternoon, to one-to-four on a weekday morning. At Chautauqua Mall, where there are fewer non-commercial activity centers, the ratio was one-to-two on a Saturday afternoon and on-to-three on a weekday. These ratios suggest that on Saturday afternoons, when there is not much going on other than shopping and socilizing, half the people at Chautauqua Mall and two-thirds of the people downtown may have been out for socializing alone and not "window shopping."

5.4. Housing

Our impression of Jamestown preferences in regard to housing is overwhelmingly in favor of single-family homes with private yards. Only among the very elderly was there any interest in apartment living as such. However, the moderately high-rise new Senior Citizen housing and some hotels converted for that purpose downtown seemed to be satisfactory to their inhabitants and sought after by others. There is apparently a real need for such units. With the preponderance of older houses, porches are much more common in Jamestown than in newer suburban communities. People seemed to use front porches extensively, and but we cannot say for certain if this apparent pattern of socializing was simply a response to conditions as they were found or represented a desired form of proxemic life-style.

5.5. Regional Relationships

We found little evidence in the surrounding region of city-country or city-county antagonisms. Except for those who work in Jamestown, people we talked to around the Lake seem more or less indifferent to the city. Jamestown people look upon the Lake as a recreational asset. We found no complaints about lack of public access, which is nevertheless very limited probably because so many Jamestonians have shore lots or friends and relatives who have. One fireman whom we met on "Fireman's Day" at a lakefront community told us he had moved out there from Jamestown and was "glad to get out of the city," but expressed neither affection nor dislike for his former home.

6. DISCUSSION

I strongly suspect that the absence of major population changes for more than two generations accounts for the social homogeneity of Jamestown. It has apparently changed from a community that must have corresponded to my proxemic-distemic hierarchy model quite well before World War II to the large single "neighborhood" we find today. The entire city appears to be a large small town. In this sense, Jamestown fits very well the American image of the melting-pot, and quite justifies the title awarded it, "All-American City." While this image fits "all" America much better as myth than as reality, undoubtedly there are a great many communities like Jamestown where the myth describes actuality. I suspect they will almost all be found outside of the major metropolitan regions. A new hypothesis that has come from this study is that social stability of this sort in a human community requires at last two generations of common experience in a common space, and that this is more critical than size in defining one.

The Chatauqua Lake Region at present seems to follow the same culturally homogeneous pattern. But a number of factors exist which may make this homeostatic situation very vulnerable. The city administration has taken very bold and imaginative steps to reverse economic stagnation on several fronts, although the Mayor and his staff seem to be intuitively aware that whatever changes take place in Jamestown must take place with appropriate character and scale. Imminent completion of the Southern Tier Expressway may have the consequences that such highways have had on numerous other rural and small urban areas in the past two decades (Greenbie 1970), bringing explosive commercial strip development, highway oriented industry, and an influx of new populations, both as commutors and as vacationers. The relatively unspoiled environment of the lake region makes it not only a likely target for massive second home developments, but also for industry seeking to attract high quality personnel with inducements of "the good life."

Any or all of the above factors may result in a relatively sudden migration into the Jamestown area. The people who are likely to come will probably have urban, suburban, or exurban values and aspirations which in important respects may conflict with those of present Jamestonians. Some in Jamestown will undoubtedly welcome such changes; others may resist or resent them, in which case unity of outlook in the city is not likely to be improved. The amount of old housing in the city and the general old-fashioned ambience may lead Jamestown's middle class to joining them in sprawling suburbs as it has in so many American cities, reducing the interest in upgrading the city environment. Jamestown as one large "neighborhood" could become demographically and physically a blighted area, as so many once viable neighborhoods in larger cities

have in recent years. In this connection the rather consistent preference of Jamestown people for Chautauqua Mall should not be dismissed lightly.

While my proxemic-distemic hierarchy does not fit Jamestown at present, I believe it may be useful as a model for the future which will accommodate growth without destroying assets. In this approach, municipal Jamestown should be considered the primary proxemic sub-center, or "neighborhood," relative to the Chautauqua Lake Region. Its physical boundaries, its general urban form, its existing social and cultural centers, and its overall life style should be preserved and enhanced insofar as possible, insofar as this is meaningful and desirable for any significant portion of the population. In addition, the political independence, the self-image and the spatial integrity of surrounding communities should be maintained. Each of these should be viewed as proxemic territories within the larger Chautauqua Lake Region.

The region in this model, should also preserve and enhance its centers, with Chautauqua Institute and the revitalized CBD especially serving as important distemic nodes. Our experience in this study suggests that the downtown will retain only limited appeal to the working people of the city. Its appeal to them should be heightened by special attention to their interests, but it also should be balanced by more effort to make it appeal to the city's middle class and to visitors to the Lake area.

So long as current economic and physical revitalization programs do not result in very large in-migrations, and can manage to retain or recapture the most dynamic portions of the younger generation in both city and environs, there seems little to recommend except continuation of present policies. However, preparation for at least the possibility of significant changes in the population as a result of continued success in these policies is very much in order. This can best be achieved, in my opinion, by locating new residential populations in one or more new centers of their own, bounded by greenbelts from the older ones, as in the classic Garden City model. Such centers should be built around some of the existing small towns, if the towns so desire and will cooperate.

References:

BARKER, ROGER G. 1968. Ecological Psychology: Concepts and Methods for Studying the Environment of Human Behavior, Stanford, California, Stanford University Press.
GORDON, MILTON M. 1964. Assimilation in American Life: The Role of Race, Religion and National Origins, New York, Oxford University Press.
GREENBIE, BARRIE B. 1975b. Design for Diversity: Planning for Natural Man in the Neo-Technic Environment. Elsevier Scientific Publishing Company.
_____. 1975a. "Design for a Socio-Spatial Continuum." Workshop on Communality

and Privacy, EDRA-6, Lawrence, Kansas. To
be published by M-E.S. Focus, Orangeburg,
New York.

GREENBIE, BARRIE B. 1970. "Interchange Planning
in a Rural Area." Traffic Quarterly,
24:2:265-277.

_____. 1974. "Social Territory,
Community Health, and Urban Planning."
Journal of the American Institute of Plan-
ners, 40:2:74-82.

HALL, EDWARD T. 1974. The Handbook of Proxemic
Research. Washington, D.C., Society of the
Anthropology of Visual Communication.

_____. 1966. The Hidden Dimension.
New York, Doubleday.

LEMASTERS, E.E. 1975. Blue-Collar Aristocrats:
Life-Styles at a Working-Class Tavern.
Madison, Wisconsin, University of Wisconsin
Press.

THE RIGHT TO PARTICIPATE: ATTITUDES REGARDING LAND USE AND DEVELOPMENT IN SOUTHEASTERN MONTANA[1]

Patrick C. Jobes

Associate Professor
Department of Sociology
Montana State University
Bozeman, Montana 59715

ABSTRACT

The National Environmental Protection Act and similar legislation provide legal mechanisms for facilitating warranted resource exploitation. This paper describes and illustrates problems associated with the implementation of these pieces of legislation because of their failure to specify alterations in social systems. Policy implications of these problems are mentioned.

INTRODUCTION

The development of land and energy resources has been subject to public scrutiny since private ownership of real estate became possible for most persons. Although the form of most development has been largely determined by free market principles, such principles have gradually become mediated through legislation intended to serve the commonweal. Recent important examples of legislation intended to optimize the benefits and costs of land use and resource development include the National Environmental Protection Act (NEPA) and the Montana Environmental Protection Act (MEPA). These and similar pieces of legislation were written with the intent of providing legal mechanism for facilitating warranted exploitation of land and natural resources while protecting the interests of all relevant parties.

Despite an earnest attempt to direct implementors of legislation in the mechanisms of implementation, much legislation often falls short of its goal. In part, omissions are the result of failure to anticipate all potential uses or requirements of the legislation. No one is born with a crystal ball. In order to avoid unnecessarily long or restrictively precise documents, persons drafting MEPA and NEPA opted for documents of considerable

breadth and depth which retained sufficient flexibility to respond to specific problems encountered with the legislation.

The object of this paper is to describe and illustrate one set of problems associated with the implementation of these pieces of legislation. That is, social impact statements are now required by law before developments having potentially significant social impacts may be carried out.

The Declaration of Policy for the act reads, "It is the purpose of this act to produce an understanding of the Nation's natural resources and the environmental forces affecting them, to promote and foster means and measures which will prevent or effectively reduce any adverse effects on the quality of the environment in the management and development of the Nation's natural resources, and to create national policy and conditions under which man and nature can exist in productive harmony and fulfill the social, economic, and other requirements of present and future generations of Americans through a comprehensive and continuance program of study, research, review, and coordination." (7)

A first and most immediate problem centers around what constitutes a significant change. Second, and perhaps more difficult question emerges around what defines the appropriateness or adequacy of information determining potential social impacts. These issues are addressed in each policy act.

"To document and define changes in the natural environment."(7)

"To initiate and utilize ecological information in the planning and development of resource-oriented projects."(7)

"Representative samples of important natural environmental systems, including natural areas for observation and for manipulation."(7)

Directs that an EIS must cover "Environmental Impacts, primary and secondary, beneficial and adverse."(5)

And, "Relationship between local short-term uses of the environment and maintenance and enhancement of long-term productivity."(5)

A third question relates to how such information is to be used by decision makers determining the fate of the development. This paper will focus upon the last two questions by drawing upon materials collected in the Fort Union Coal region.

Data analysis in this project proceeded through several phases. Upon completion of keypunching and verifying, information was transferred to disks. Information was then processed through data cleaning programs to eliminate any errors

[1]Data reported here were collected under a grant administered through the Montana Energy Advisory Council.

yet undetected. Summaries of responses and descriptive statistics (mean, median, mode percentage, standard deviation, variance, etc.) were then run for responses to each question. Response categories were then recoded where appropriate in order to assure valid categories as well as sufficient cases per category to perform subsequent statistics.

Since information was collected from a population, rather a sample of population, the decision was made to compute measures of association rather than tests of significance.(1) That is, the statistics reported are statements of the strength of relationship between particular variables rather than statements expressing the probability of that respondents reliably reflect the rest of persons in the area.(2) The primary measure of association utilized for this purpose is gamma (γ), an ordinal statistic which has the characteristic of permitting a proportional reduction of error interpretation.(3) The higher the statistic, the stronger the association between the variables being analyzed.

Generalizations concerning population attitudes are usually rather difficult to make. In the case of Decker-Birney area residents, however, generalizations regarding satisfaction with the area easily can be summarized. Most persons in the Decker-Birney area appear to be satisfied with the area (c.83%) and with their life quality in the area (c.80%). As a population, they are strongly opposed to coal strip mining (c.83%) and attendant coal development (c.65%). Still, their feelings regarding planning and development are much more diverse and complicated than are their feelings of satisfaction. Acknowledging poor quality of such items as local roads and medical facilities, most respondents favored the improvement of many facilities, services, and opportunities but strongly opposed coal as a means toward bringing them to the area. Most persons (c.62%) were ignorant of any area-wide planning attempts. Moreover, a minority (c.27%) favor the principle of an areawide plan with most others (c.54%) taking a wait-and-see position. If a plan was developed, respondents feel local persons should develop it (c.71%), although only a few (18.4%) feel the local residents will develop a plan.

Generalizations by themselves are often misleading and certainly not entirely revealing. Distinct differences occur when different sub-categories are considered. In fact, some differences in feelings about development and planning occur between all sub-categories. For purposes of brevity only, the strongest categorical differences which emerged from the research will be presented here.

The three most important characteristics in the Decker-Birney area were number of years resided in the area, occupation and where respondents lived, i.e., rural versus town. The differences occurring among respondents in different

categories are reported in the following section.

Where Respondents Currently Reside

During the process of interviewing one of the most evident differences among respondents was where they lived, i.e., in the rural area or in Ashland. The most obvious socio-demographic differences were in their occupations. Rural dwellers were most likely to be ranchers (83.3%) whereas townspeople were almost equally divided among the private section (33.7%) operators and construction (32.7%) and the public sector (28.6%) (γ = .35). Differences also were evident in the sex respondents. Forty percent of town respondents were men whereas 41% of rural respondents were women (γ = -.37).

Recent arrivals (γ = .53), younger persons also seemed more frequent in town than in the country. The data indicate 26.8% of town dwellers and 15.7% of rural dwellers are in the youngest age group (17-29). In the country 28.3% of the respondents are over sixty years old compared to 15.5% in town (γ = .24).

In spite of considerable attachment to the Decker-Birney area, townspeople, as a category, are relatively less embedded than are rural persons. Nearly every measure of attachment - amount of time lived in the area, being a native of the area, having rural and Montana heritage, plans against moving - indicate rural dwellers tend to have greater attachment and more permanent involvement than do townspeople. Certainly, Ashland is among the most remote type of town envisioned by most urban dwellers. Still, residents of Ashland in many ways are different in how they see themselves, and are seen by rural residents. Townspeople, however attached to their town, are probably less threatened by social change than are country dwellers, especially in an area so remote as the Decker-Birney area. After all, as was repeatedly pointed out by ranchers, there are many towns to live in and most persons choose to live in them. But, there are relatively few good undeveloped ranch areas left and the Decker-Birney area is one of them. They conveyed a sense of impending loss which was less frequent among townspeople. These impressions, reflecting the inclusive nature of involvement of rural dwellers with the area are continually demonstrated through their responses.

Rural residents are less likely to see changes in the area as improvements (γ = -.29). In congruence with their opposition to change, rural dwellers also express suspicion of potential agents of change. They more frequently feel industrial interests in the area are too powerful (γ = .46) and would like a moratorium to be placed on leasing of state and federal coal lands (γ = .25). They also more strongly favor a moratorium on power plants (γ = .30), new strip mines (γ = .35) and transmission lines (γ = .38). They feel industrialization within the area will upset the community (γ = .53).

For example, over one-half of the rural respondents have noticed a shift in power from ranchers to the coal industry ($\gamma = .24$). Townspeople, on the other hand, see a shift in power from themselves to ranchers ($\gamma = .50$).

Despite their opposition to development, rural dwellers also oppose potential advice from federal planners ($\gamma = -.92$). Moreover, they more strongly (67.7%) support the right of land owners to develop resources if they wish ($\gamma = .37$). They (67.8%) generally do not favor professional planners in the area ($\gamma = -.49$) and they more frequently feel their friends ($\gamma = -.34$) feel the same way. More of them (22.4%) would sign a petition opposing a comprehensive plan, though many more respondents, rural and town alike, are uncertain how they would respond ($\gamma = -.33$). 91.3% of rural dwellers feel the people living in the study area need a strong voice ($\gamma = .34$).

Nearly 70 percent of rural residents feel local residents should decide the adequacy of any plan and only 11.8% feel state or federal governments should decide ($\gamma = .28$). Personal benefit does not seem to be the key factor involved in feeling toward planning. In fact, relatively few rural residents (26.7%) feel they would be harmed by a comprehensive plan.

Rural dwellers resist coal development from a wide variety of perspectives. They do not feel Montana coal should be mined merely because the federal government says it is necessary to meet energy needs ($\gamma = .27$). While most respondents (71.4%) feel the nation needs Montana coal, rural dwellers disagree it should be developed ($\gamma = .41$). Most rural dwellers fear development will mean dammed rivers ($\gamma = .24$) and most feel there are already enough strip mines in Montana ($\gamma = .23$). They most heavily favor no more mining and rarely favor local generating plants ($\gamma = .30$). Only few (6.8%) feel an obligation to generate electricity ($\gamma = .48$) or to develop more industry for Montana ($\gamma = .55$).

Some of the opposition to coal development expressed by rural persons may rest with a greater apprehension regarding outsiders. More of them feel miners do not adapt like the local residents ($\gamma = .23$). They (76.4%) feel, even more frequently than townspeople (67.3%) that clean air can not be sacrificed in order to create industrial jobs. They more frequently report that construction workers have different values from local residents ($\gamma = .37$). Moreover, rural dwellers are less likely to want to move in spite of opposition to coal ($\gamma = .34$) even though they expect coal development and population influx to affect their family ties ($\gamma = .50$) and area residents ($\gamma = .49$). In fact, a majority, especially strong among rural dwellers (83.2%), agree development will benefit outsiders more than themselves ($\gamma = .48$).

Most persons in the study area are concerned with coal development and planning for their futures. Rural persons are more likely to have learned of planning efforts from personal contacts or written media (77.3%) while townspeople more frequently learned through radio, television or some other source (63.2%). Most respondents, but especially rural dwellers (77.0%) feel outsiders (to the study area) are poorly informed about coal development ($\gamma = .22$), although a minority of residents, especially townspeople had not heard that as many as seven generating plants had been proposed for the area ($\gamma = .54$).

In spite of considerable opposition to planning by state and federal representatives, local residents do have guidelines they would like to use for the future. Most (75%) respondents feel Montana agricultural experts should decide when reclamation has been achieved. Though 14.4% of rural dwellers would prefer land restored to original form and productivity, they (90.7%) feel decisions regarding development should be based on "people reasons" rather than economic ones ($\gamma = .38$). However, they (73.9%) agree that current coal company policies are dictated more by law than by feelings for people ($\gamma = -.22$). Although most favor equal voting abilities for everyone, a few (6.8%) disagree ($\gamma = .23$). They more frequently agree social costs must be considered for any development ($\gamma = .31$) and that people like themselves should influence the coal decisions ($\gamma = .52$). Most feel strip mining is incompatible with good land use practice ($\gamma = -.37$) 67.1% fear crop water will be lost and springs dry up ($\gamma = .59$) if mining occurs ($\gamma = .33$). They (70.2%) feel area residents will not be better off if strip mining occurs ($\gamma = .52$). They strongly disagree that strip mines will be the best things for Montana ($\gamma = .45$). They (87%) see the agricultural productivity of Decker-Birney land as too high to exchange for strip mining ($\gamma = .67$) even though they recognize the low sulphur content of the coal ($\gamma = .20$). They also strongly disagree (77.6%) that our timber is so poor as to warrant strip mining ($\gamma = .33$).

Occupation

Among variables associated with position in the social system probably none is more important nor more frequently studied than occupation. The occupational structure reflects the character of the entire social structure. The Decker-Birney Area clearly exemplifies this relationship. Agricultural occupations, for the most part ranchers and kindred workers, comprise over one-half (53.7%) of the occupations for household heads in the Decker-Birney area. Persons holding positions in the public sector, businessmen, professional and managers contribute 17.0% followed closely by heads of households in construction and in the public sector, teachers, Bureau of Land Management, Forest Service, (14.7% each).

Agricultural and public sector persons are more likely to express concern more frequently than construction or public sector persons when many matters are considered. The agriculture and public sectors more frequently feel that industrial interests are too powerful in the area ($\gamma = -.28$), that a moratorium on leasing state and federal lands should be extended ($\gamma = -.21$), that more power plants should not be built in the area ($\gamma = -.30$), that more strip mines should not be developed in the area ($\gamma = -.34$), that no rail or power lines should be built in the area ($\gamma = -.24$), and that the area should not be the site of generating plants ($\gamma = -.29$).

Some of the reasons for this opposition to industrial development more frequently expressed by agricultural and public sectors are: that population influx might negatively influence family ties ($\gamma = -.27$), industrialization may upset local decision making ($\gamma = .20$) and the community ($\gamma = -.31$), that neither the nation ($\gamma = .20$) nor the Federal administration needs Montana coal ($\gamma = .32$), that local residents have the right to interfere with coal development ($\gamma = .36$), that residents have no duty to generate electricity ($\gamma = .21$) or to develop Montana industry ($\gamma = .31$), that they should not have to move if area coal develops ($\gamma = .26$), that coal decisions are based more on economic than human reasons ($\gamma = .43$), that coal companies respond only to the law rather than that the power companies are not really concerned with the environment ($\gamma = .21$), that development should not occur just because power companies claim a need for more electricity ($\gamma = .23$), for compassion for the people ($\gamma = -.23$), that rivers will be dammed following industrialization ($\gamma = -.23$), that the area is good timber land ($\gamma = .35$), agricultural land should not be strip mined ($\gamma = .46$), that power plants would use water for crops ($\gamma = .27$), that springs would dry up ($\gamma = -.47$) following strip mining, that strip mining is incompatible with other land uses ($\gamma = .38$), that deep mining is more desirable for Eastern Montana ($\gamma = -.20$), that recreation land can not be sacrificed for coal development ($\gamma = .29$), that claims for reclamation are unbelievable ($\gamma = .28$), that ranch operations will be effected by power plants ($\gamma = .41$), that area residents would not be better off if strip mines are developed ($\gamma = .39$), that strip mines would not be the best for the area ($\gamma = .26$) or for Montana ($\gamma = .46$), that no more coal development is needed for Montana ($\gamma = -.28$), that miners would not adapt like local residents ($\gamma = .31$), that social costs have not been considered ($\gamma = -.23$). Rather, they see outside areas benefitting from coal development ($\gamma = .21$).

In consequence to the general satisfaction expressed regarding the area as it is and general opposition to further development, especially of an industrial nature, persons in the agricultural and public sectors tend to know more and participate more regarding planning than do persons in the private sector and, especially, in construction. Agricultural and Public sector persons more frequently stated that they were aware of efforts for planning in the local area ($\gamma = -.29$), found out about these efforts through formal contacts and unspecific means than through friends ($\gamma = .21$). However, they had not heard of planning quite as early as had the other sectors ($\gamma = -.27$). They feel they should influence coal decisions ($\gamma = .31$) although they do not feel they influence development decision making ($\gamma = .26$) and do not feel they currently have too much power ($\gamma = .20$). Only a majority of the public sector feels that progress can be stopped, heavily influencing the association ($\gamma = .27$) along this dimension.

Number of Years Lived in Study Area

The number of years a respondent has lived in the Decker-Birney area is one of the most important indicators of attachment to the area. The decision to remain in the area is an implicit approval of the location in comparison to other locations. That decision involves more than mere attachment to the physical characteristics of the area. Rather, the environment provides the arena in which family attachments are established, business is transacted, education is obtained and other meaningful activities in life are experienced. (4) Sentiments attached to these activities become associated with place in such a way that a place takes on value to persons beyond the desirability of its earth, air and water. And, the more of these activities and sentiments which are associated with a place, the greater is the extent of social control on that person. Consequently, a strong association is found between years in area, as a measure of social control, and feelings related to planning and development of the area.

The broadly based satisfaction expressed by persons who have spent many years in the Decker-Birney area at times seem to obscure a sensitivity to changes within the area although they are more likely to have noticed changes ($\gamma = .48$). Persons who have arrived more recently often seem more aware and feel more strongly about changes than do old timers although old timers feel changes generally had been for the worse ($\gamma = .28$). For example, recent arrivals are more likely to feel scenic resources are being destroyed ($\gamma = -.24$), that population growth in the area is problematic ($\gamma = -.45$). Recent arrivals also more frequently support establishing wilderness areas ($\gamma = -.26$) and requiring builders to set aside acreage for public use ($\gamma = -.36$).

Consequently, new arrivals express willingness to shut down generating plants polluting beyond acceptable standards ($\gamma = -.21$). Over ninety percent of new arrivals feel development decisions should be based on non-economic reasons, a feeling considerably stronger than the 81% among old timers (γ = -.22). Still newcomers are less suspicious of land reclamation efforts. They (21.8%) feel coal companies have compassion for the land in contrast to the 8.3% of old timers who feel that way (γ = .20). Newcomers more frequently prefer deep mining to strip mining (γ = .21). They also are far less likely to perceive a serious energy crisis (γ = .25). Old timers also feel less in control of inflation (γ = -.28) but more satisfied with life (γ = .29).

Old timers generally appear less likely to acknowledge or to seek to halt changes. Though most (77%) feel scientific knowledge should be used to deal with problems, they are less likely to feel this way than recent arrivals (γ = -.20). Old timers are less favorable toward using state (γ = -.36) or federal planners (γ = -.47) in Montana. They feel more strongly that privately owned resources should be controlled by their owners, (γ = -.21) and that the rate of coal development should be controlled by persons like themselves (γ = -.22). Despite a strong majority (85.4%) supporting the notion of "one man one vote", fewer old timers feel this way than recent arrivals (γ = .37). They further believe that ranch owners are continuing to hold political power more frequently than do the newer arrivals (γ = -.23) although they (81.3%) agree with the way power is distributed (γ = .25).

Feelings expressed regarding planning generally are not associated with years spent in the area. Knowledge regarding plans and sources for that knowledge are essentially the same for all categories by tenure. However, old timers are less likely to have heard of effects of planning (γ = -.48). They also are much more suspicious of planners coming into the area (γ = -.36). And, they feel their close friends (γ = -.25) feel similarly suspicious. Old timers state they would more likely sign petitions to oppose (γ = -.22) and less likely vote for a comprehensive plan (γ = -.31). This suspicion of control is especially directed to outsiders. 76.6% of old timers feel local residents or officials should decide on land use in comparison to 59.3% of recent arrivals who feel that way (γ = .23). Old timers also feel residents should decide reclamation of stripped lands instead of outsiders (γ = .20).

The antipathy expressed by long timers is perceived by them to be in their own self interest. They are less likely to feel potential benefit from a plan (γ = .30). They strongly agree, (83.3%), however, that Decker-Birney area is good agricultural land and should not be strip-mined (γ = -.27). A small majority (58.3%) of old timers than newcomers (76.9%) feel the national forest in the area are well managed (γ = .24).

The general profiles of respondents according to the number of years residency differ considerably. On the one hand are the more

recent arrivals who tend to be more urban and less agricultural than old timers. Newcomers are generally more receptive to planning, especially through implementation of outside authorities. Their feelings tend to reflect greater sensitivity to currently publicized issues of land use planning and environmental policy.

On the other hand are the old timers, many of whom have become integral parts of the social system in the area. They know the persons and love the area. They cherish the control of the area by the persons who reside there. Their greatest concern seems to center around who will make decisions and how those decisions will be made rather than with what decision is made. They are wary of outsiders and wary of controls, even if outsiders and controls might help to protect aspects of the area which they personally value. More than any other category, old timers in the Decker-Birney area conform to the ethic of individualism so evident in the area. This conformity, expressive of attachment to a particular life style, clearly demonstrates some of the paradoxes associated with values which ultimately prove to be mutually exclusive.

The conclusions to be reached from this data are complex and cannot be fully explored in this brief paper. However, certain summary statements are appropriate. The more time persons have spent in the study area, residing in town and being employed in the private sector and construction are consistently associated with lower opposition coal development than agricultural employment, rural residence and having spent relatively less time in the area. Consistent with this finding is that comprehensive planning is more opposed by the same categories with the exception of agricultural workers who are opposed to planning. However, what controls comprehensive planning differs from this otherwise consistent pattern. Similarly, agricultural workers and persons in construction favor local development of any plan more frequently than do other occupational sectors. This position also is taken by persons who have spent more years in the area and who reside in the country.

Reasons for the relatively low support for planning in spite of general opposition to development presents a paradox. On the one hand most persons report being against development and its negative effects while at the same time express antipathy toward support of a mechanism which might minimize impacts. In part, this paradox may be explained as a failure of many local residents to fully appreciate the potential implications of either development or planning.

CONCLUSION AND RECOMMENDATIONS

Returning to the original issue described at

the onset of this paper, it is again necessary to ask, what information is adequate and appropriate for meeting the needs of an environmental impact review? The author maintains that the positions taken on development by the local populace are of critical importance. The distinction between man and environment is largely an artificial simplification. In reality men form part of the environment along with the "natural" factors of flora and other fauna. The unique characters of inhabited places, in large part, reflect the imprint of their inhabitants. Although imprints are most evident in technologically advanced areas they also are evident in sparsely settled spaces inhabited by technologies as primitive as slash and burn agriculture. Mountain climbers report that such remote and uninhabited areas as Mount McKinley even show the residual effects of humanity. More obtusely, such remote places show minimal human induced effects largely because of man-made decisions. That is, even remote areas in national parks retain pristine qualities because of decisions to create and administer such places. In short, the commonly made distinction between man and environment is not founded.

We conclude, therefore, that the human effects within a geographical area form an integral part of the environment. The cultural system exhibited by the inhabitants: their technology for exploiting the geography, their style of life experienced, their rules for living, and all other values, attitudes and behavior, form part of the environment. Certainly this human characteristic must be considered as viable as social patterns among prairie dogs or elk. Moreover, there may be reason to believe that humans may object to having their social world altered or destroyed at least as much as do other inhabitants in the environment. This logic, it seems, is probably that which has led the administration of the Montana Environmental Protection Act to stress the importance of social factors in environmental impact assessment. The author wishes to emphasize that social impacts involve more than the socio-economic and socio-demographic alterations upon the indigenous population. Alterations in the way of life, interaction systems, i.e., social factors reflecting choice, may constitute the most profound impacts upon the social environment.

The other major issue described in the introduction involves how decision makers are to use information provided them through impact assessment reports. Assuming that the information in the report has some utility, exactly how decision makers will utilize the information is rather unclear. Many decision makers are not familiar with the information presented in reports by specialists in other fields. Correcting communication inadequacies through the use of available specialists, however, still does not eliminate the problems of what to do with the information.

Traditionally, decision makers have decided to develop resources given sufficient common need. One planning text succinctly states, "should local interests conflict with national interests, national interests will need to take precedence." If the existence of the nation is threatened, sacrifices must be made. However, it is questionable whether genuine threats occur as frequently as do sacrifices. Although few persons would disagree with the logic behind the statement, matters of the extent and timing of exploitation are not addressed. The author suggests, therefore, that local sentiments take precedence over other factors unless crisis is imminent. And, to the extent that crisis is foreseeable, planning should notify and prepare local opposition for inevitable development. A reasonable period of preparation might be the length of a generation--roughly twenty-five years. Given a time of this length, local inhabitants would be able to prepare for change. Adults would be permitted to live out life in the style they had grown to expect. The young, on the other hand, would grow with the knowledge that they can no longer take the style of life for granted if they remain in the potential impact area. They would know that the area would change according to national needs.

Such a lengthy time period, of course, demands a well developed plan. And, given the extensive resources in the United States, not only is such a plan necessary but sufficient delay time is possible. This approach would assure two goals consonant with the desires of most citizens and with the environmental protection acts of both the Federal and the Montana state governments. The protection and prudent use of the resources could occur while protecting the quality of the social and physical environments.

Reference

ANDERSON, THEODORE R. and MORRIS ZELDITCH
    1969   A Basic Course in Statistics.   New York: Rinehart and Winston.

BLAYLOCK, HUBERT M.
    1960   Social Statistics.   New York: McGraw-Hill.

COSTNER, HERBERT L.
    1965   "Criteria for Measures of Association." American Sociological Review (June): Pp. 341-353.

HOBBS, DONALD A. and STUART J. BLANK
    1975 Sociology and the Human Experience. New York: John Wiley and Sons, Inc.

MONTANA ENVIRONMENTAL PROTECTION ACT.

NATIONAL ENVIRONMENTAL PROTECTION ACT.

"Resources, Conservation and Environmental Quality Act of 1969." United States Government Printing Office. Washington: 1969.

MONITORING SYSTEM FOR REMOTE SENSING OF
ENVRIONMENTAL STRESSES AND PHYSIOLOGICAL
RESPONSES

Uwe Reischl, Ph.D.
Peter Reischl, Ph.D.

Program in Social Ecology
University of California
Irvine, California 92664
U.S.A.

ABSTRACT

This paper describes a radio telemetry system
used for obtaining environmental and physiological data under stressful environmental conditions. The system provides seven data
channels simultaneously and has the signifi
cant advantage of telemetering data in real
time. The back-pack telemetry system has been
designed to be compatible with most types of
transducers.

I. INTRODUCTION

To make advanced multidisciplinary research in
the field of environmental health possible at
the University of California, Irvine, a prototype environmental monitoring system has been
developed which is capable of simultaneously
monitoring thermal stresses and physiological
responses of persons working and resting in
occupational environments. The monitoring
system will be used by health specialists,
engineers, architects, and psychologists in
cooperative research to quantitatively assess
selected physical environmental stresses
affecting persons working in modern urban
environments. The research will focus on
environmental stresses in industry, office
buildings, and public mass transportation
systems.

2. DESCRIPTION

Presently the environmental monitoring system
(EMS) is capable of detecting, transmitting
and recording information about environmental
stresses such as air temperature, humidity,
and heat radiation surrounding a person at
work or at rest. Furthermore, physiological
responses such as pulse rate, deep-body
temperature and skin temperature are also
continuously monitored and recorded.

The system is based on multi-channel radio
telemetry. Seven data channels are utilized
in this system and can readily be adapted to
transmit also several other kinds of information such as environmental noise, vibration,
air velocity, and also bioelectric signals,
strain-gauge respirometry and plethysmography,

direct or indirect blood pressure manometry,
basal skin resistance, and galvanic skin
response, to name but a few.

The EMS consists of a light-weight "back-pack"
case with a transmitter system and a transducer
rack. All data are obtained by a small light-
weight portable receiver. Dials are connected
to the receiver for direct read-out. Strip-
chart recorders may be interfaced whenever
desired.

The transmitter system, multiplexer, signal
conditioner and batteries are mounted into a
chasis 11" x 6" x 2" which is then placed into
the back-pack case with the sensor rack
attached to the top. The total weight of the
back-pack unit is 7 pounds. It has an operating time of four hours and a range of one
mile. The back-pack is shown in Figure 1.

The light-weight receiver unit measures 6" x
4" x 2" and weighs 1/2 pound. The dials are
attached for direct data read-out. The receiver unit is shown with the back-pack in
Figure 2.

3. SYSTEM DESIGN

Various commercial radio telemetry transmitters
are available on the market. In selecting the
appropriate transmitter, channel capacity,
telemetering range, and power requirements were
considered. Seven data channels were thought
to be sufficient in conjunction with a transmission range of about one mile.

Since environmental and physiological changes
are frequently slow and small in magnitude, a
very stable system was required which could
maintain a high degree of accuracy over the
radio frequency link. A sub-system was
selected that utilizes bridge type transducers
with pulse width modulation. Such a sub-
system can maintain a high degree of accuracy
with low power consumption. Also, the sub-
system selected uses time division multiplex
where all seven data channels are transmitted
by a common radio frequency carrier.

The overall system was designed such that the
transducer bridge networks couple the environmental and physiological signals to the signal
conditioner. The signal conditioners are low
noise, broad band, high-gain differential amplifiers which provide signals of the proper level
to the multiplexer. The function of the multiplexer is to combine the different signals from
the amplifiers into a time serial stream which
modulates the transmitter. The transmitter
sends environmental and physiological information to the distant receiving station 50 times
each second for each of the 7 data channels.
The transducers control the width of the pulse

going to the transmitter. As the environment or physiology changes, the width of the pulses associated with each transducer changes and carries the new intelligence. The transmitter sends a burst of radio frequency energy every time a pulse from the pulse duration multiplexer is present. Thus the environmental and physiological information is encoded in the pulse width of the transmitted signal.

The receiver picks up the signal, amplifies and detects it, and then shapes the pulses and converts the serial train of pulses into separate pulses whose width corresponds to the environmental or physiological information on each channel. These pulses are then passed to the servo amplifiers and used to position an output device in response to the transmitter input signal.

The seven data channel monitoring system is diagrammatically illustrated in Figure 3.

4. DISCUSSION

There are numerous technical reports in literature about the development of telemetry systems, but few which deal specifically with measurement of environmental stresses using commercially available equipment. One telemetry system useful for measuring environmental stress conditions is described by Bergey, et.al.,(1968). This multi-channel transmitting system is worne in a quick-donning garment. It was developed by the U.S. Navy. Its transmitting range is limited to 200 feet. Other multi-channel radio telemetry systems designed and constructed for the monitoring of subjects during work while exposed to environmental stress are described by Murray, et.al., (1968), Cupal, et.al., (1968), Nagasaka, et.al. (1966), Watson, et.al., (1968), and Bodenlos (1966). All their systems were built specifically for their own research purposes and none is commercially available.

No complete environmental monitoring radio telemetry system was commercially available to the Program in Social Ecology. A system was designed and developed in Social Ecology which uses a commercially available transmitter-receiver sub-system. A useful subsystem was available through Kraft Systems Inc. which included transmitter and receiver decoder and output devices. The sub-system did not come with an environmental transducer interface but was modified and incorporated into the overall environmental monitoring system (EMS) in Social Ecology.

The environmental monitoring system in its present condition will be useful for worldwide data acquisition. By using a data phone it will be possible to transmit data over the standard telephone system. Currently this method is used in several biomedical applications (Bennett, et.al., 1970 and Hanley, et.al., 1969). The data phone converts the signals from the radio frequency receiver into a form that can be sent over regular telephone lines. Data phone sets are light-weight and portable and are easily interfaced with the Social Ecology environmental monitoring system (EMS).

The concept of a personal environmental monitoring system has been realized with the EMS. Application of this system to Social Ecology research will successfully generate new information about environmental stresses affecting individuals' health and well being within a wide range of urban environments.

References

BERGEY, GEORGE E., SIPPLE, W.C., HAMILTON, W.A. and SQUIRES, R.D.: Personal FM/AM Biotelemtry. Aerospace Medicine, May 1968, pp. 488-492.

BODENLOS, LEONARD J.: Transmitter Back-Pack for Free-Roaming Animals. Laboratory Animal Care, Vol. II, No. 5, 1966, pp. 454-458.

CUPAL, JERRY J., WARD, A.L., and WEEKS, R.W.: A Repeater Type Biotelemetry System for Use on Wild Big Game Animals. I.S.A.B.M. 74329, 1974, pp. 142-152.

MURRAY, R.H., MARKO, A., KISSEN, A.T., and McGUIRE, D.W.: A New, Miniatured, Mutlichannel, Personal Radiotelemetry System. Journal of Applied Physiology. Vol. 24, No. 4, April 1968, pp. 588-592.

NAGASAKA, TETSUO, AUDO, S., TAKAI, T. and TAKAGI, K.: A Radio Telemetering System and the Changes of EKG and Heart Rate of Subjects Engaging in Mountaineering at Great Altitudes. Nagoya Journal of Medical Science, Vol. 29, 1966, pp. 93-103.

WATSON, NOLAN W., FRANKLIN, D.L., and VAN CITTERS, R.L.: Back-Pack for Free-Ranging Primates. Journal of Applied Physiology, Vol. 24, No. 2, February 1968, pp. 252-253.

FIGURE 2: RECEIVER SYSTEM AND DIALS SHOWN WITH "BACK-PACK" UNIT

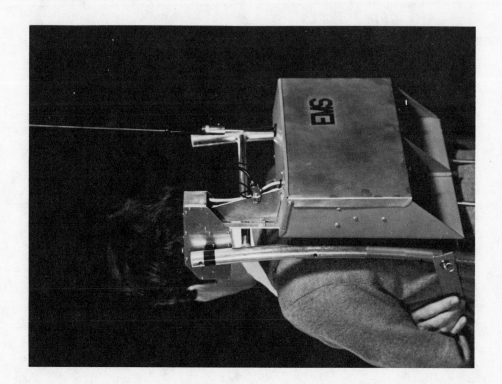

FIGURE 1: "BACK-PACK" UNIT IN CARRYING POSITION

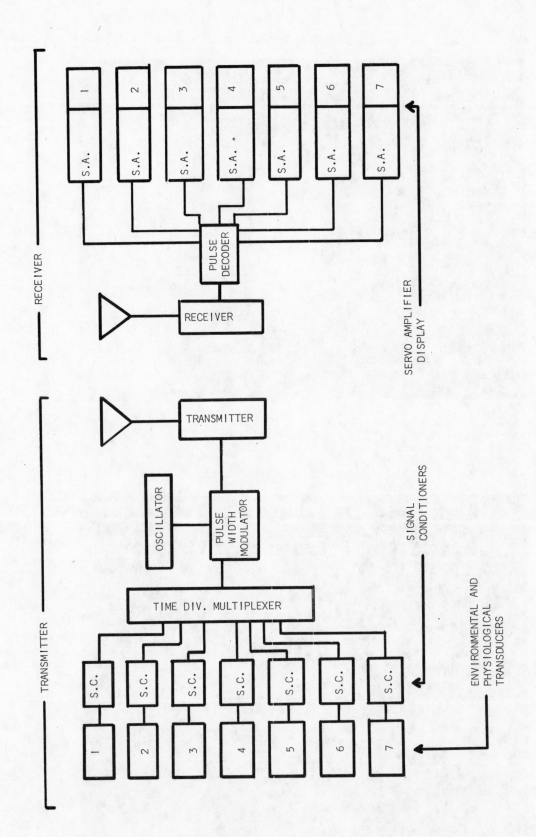

FIGURE 3: DIAGRAMMATIC ILLUSTRATION OF 7 CHANNEL MONITORING SYSTEM

SOME PROSPECTS FOR SIMULATING HUMAN BEHAVIOR IN

HIGH-RISE BUILDING FIRES: A PILOT DEMONSTRATION

Fred I. Stahl, M.Arch.
Environmental Psychology Program
The City University of New York
33 West 42nd Street
New York, New York 10036

ABSTRACT

The development of adequate fire safety
provisions for buildings is seen to depend upon
a valid formulation of a total building fire
system, in which human-behavioral and physical
phenomena interact. In an effort to comprehend
and model such a system, predict human responses
in building fires, and assess the usefulness of
safety code provisions, a simulation-modeling
methodology was evaluated for the case of high-
rise office buildings. The model investigated
generates human movement decision making
behavior under conditions of stress and
uncertainty, and is based on the probabilistic
Markov process. The internal validity of the
present model is examined, by (a) assessing the
extent to which variance in the dependent
variable (safe egress from the danger zone) is
accounted for by predictor variables measured
during actual simulation runs, and (b)
determining whether the model is capable of
distinguishing between diverse spatial designs.
Simulation runs were conducted for two different
office arrangements, and there were five
replications for each arrangement. It was found
that (a) Depending on the configuration of
predictor variables, up to 88% of the variance
in the criterion could be accounted for, and
that up to 93.3% of the actual results of
simulation runs were predictable by knowledge
of these predictors. (b) The present model was
incapable of distinguishing between "open-office"
versus "compartmentized" designs on the basis of
occupants' final egress status, time spent by
occupants in threat-invaded zones, or time
required by evacuees to reach safety zones.
Implications of the findings, and areas for
further investigation, are explored.

1. INTRODUCTION

The utility of various life safety policies and
building design regulations becomes suspect, once
considered in light of the casual assumptions
about emergency behavior upon which actual
decisions are based. The development of adequate
and useful safety provisions is seen to depend,
therefore, upon a valid formulation of the
building fire system, in which factors describing
the threat, human responses, environmental
structures and other contingencies continuously
interact. Moreover, various experimental or

quasi-experimental techniques involving field
observations appear - at least at the present
time - incapable of providing data sufficiently
useful for developing either a valid model of
the building fire system, or a predictive tool
for designers and policy makers (note 7 and 9,
for extensive reviews of the literature on
human behavior in building fires).

The objective of the present study has therefore
been to develop an alternative approach through
which to comprehend and model the building fire
system, predict human responses in building

fires, and thereby evaluate the "life safety potential" of various building designs, and assess the usefulness of specific safety policies and code requirements. The current report proceeds with the presentation of a simulation methodology, reviews data derived from an illustrative experiment designed to assess the method's usefulness, and points to research tasks necessary for continued progress in this area.

Throughout the course of the project, emphasis has been placed upon the study of fires in high-rise office buildings. Several factors contribute to this emphasis, notably: (a) In recent years, many cities have experienced disasters or near-disasters resulting from fires in tall buildings. (b) There appears to be growing public resistance to the idea of tall buildings. (c) Tall buildings appear most likely to pose severe physical limitations to emergency egress. (d) Tall buildings are generally considered to pose certain limitations on the control and extinguishment of the fire-threat itself. The author wishes to stress, however, that the basic techniques discussed within the scope of the paper are expected to be applicable to a considerably wider range of building types and user groups.

2. APPLICATION OF SIMULATION-MODELING TECHNIQUES TO THE FIRE PROBLEM

2.1 Rationale

With prospects for testing hypotheses about emergency behavior through field experimentation in actual settings considerably dimmed, the exploration of simulation-modeling techniques emerges as a viable alternative approach. The long-range practical benefits of experimenting with simulation models are expected to derive from opportunities for evaluating safety policies and code provisions, and for examining the life safety potential of design alternatives while still on the drawing board.

In the short run, moreover, the heuristic utility of the technique must be carefully considered as well. In particular, treatment of the building fire problem through simulation methods (whether via machine, game, or combination modes) is expected to yield immediate benefits in terms of our evolving understanding of the total building fire system. Simulation studies in which such variables as flame and smoke migration, building design and spatial organization, and occupant preparedness (to name just a few) are experimentally manipulated shall elucidate interrelationships among the many complex factors inolved; continually demanding that researchers define their concepts and clarify their conceptualizations as explicitly as possible. The application of simulation-modeling techniques to the building fire problem carries the further potential, then, of displaying

theoretical structures underlying the building fire system, as such structures are brought to the surface over time. The heuristic value of simulation methodologies has been considered at length (note, e.g., 6, 8, 11).

2.2 A testable model of human behavior in a tall-building fire

Several attempts by various investigators to simulate human movement behavior in spatial contexts, and under a variety of conditions, have appeared recently (e.g., 1, 4, 12, 14). Clearly, these studies have been enormously useful as research tools, identifying parameters, assumptions and special difficulties, and demonstrating the potential value of a variety of simulation strategies.

One somewhat flagrant problem, however, has been a reliance upon deterministic explanations of human choice behavior and spatial movement strategy construction. Deterministic approaches implicitly assume that within some tightly bounded system, responses to stimuli or events are completely predictable by the model at hand. Accordingly, any additional variables not identified by the researcher, nor included within his or her definition of the system, are not accommodated by the overall analytical scheme. When comparisons between real-world findings and data derived from simulation experiments yield wide discrepancies, it is never really clear whether the difficulty lies in the structural design of the model in question, or in the possibity that some combination of unidentified variables is operating to contribute a sizable proportion of the total variance.

By contrast, the behavioral model upon which the current simulation study is based is essentially a stochastic process, which permits only the prediction of some range of outcomes, given a particular stimulus environment. Such a probabilistic paradigm recognizes that, indeed, some variables may have been overlooked or even purposefully excluded from the model, and that in their place some element of "chance" shall operate systematically.

A model so developed as been suggested primarily as a point of departure for more intensive simulation research into the nature of the building fire system. As shall become evident from the data presented here, the model was designed to describe human movement behavior in response to life threatening stimuli, within the boundaries of a single floor in a high-rise office building. Within a hypothetical environment so bounded, the model simulates individual and group movement decision making in a spatial field which contains information about a fire-threat advancing in real-time, as well as potentially mal-adaptive responses to sudden interruptions in goal directed behavior (10).

Accordingly, the building fire system is thought to be approximated by a Markov process (note 2, 3). Transition of this stochastic process from state to state is believed to be directly analogous to incremental changes in the fire system as it proceeds through real-time. For example, the system at time t may be described in terms of specific locations of individuals, flame and smoke products, numbers of individuals clustered into various groups, and the range of movement alternatives from those locations (etc.). At time $t+1$, the system has advanced to the next state: people have relocated to new spatial positions, flames and smoke have advanced (or retreated, etc.), and so on. Incremental changes in state-defining parameters are assumed to occur probabilistically, on the basis of parameter values for the most recent state only.

The current simulation-model is outlined in FIGURE 1. Note that each iteration of the routine represents a single transition of the building fire system between any two points in time, t and t+1. Specific details outlining the model's actual structure may be obtained from the author.

3. AN EXPLORATORY INVESTIGATION OF THE MODEL'S VALIDITY: DESIGN

3.1 The issue of validity in simulation-modeling

Two forms of validity may be considered in the present context. Internal validity refers to the logical consistency of the model's structure. One would expected, for example, that an internally valid model is relatively free of contamination from the confounding effects of uncontrolled variables, those dealt with accounting for a very substantial proportion of the system's total variance.

In addition, external validity generally concerns the degree of verisimilitude demonstrated by the model. One would consider a simulation externally valid if it produced data highly similar to those obtained from the real-world, with significant consistency. Ordinarily, an investigation of external validity would presuppose either the availability of reliable historical data, or the facility to conduct on-going or ad-hoc experiments in the real-world, against which to compare simulation data and thereby evaluate its verisimilitude. But in the case of the building fire system, neither opportunity is likely to be afforded the simulation researcher.

Under such circumstances, an alternative approach to examining external validity is offered through a variation of Turing's test (13). Such a procedure would basically require that data from both simulation runs and real-world experiences be presented to a "panel of experts" (the sources of data concealed), and

that the experts attempt to distinguish between them. If, in a significant number of trials, the experts are in fact unable to distinguish those data generated from the simulation, then (according to Turing) one might be justified in considering the model externally valid. In connection with the current problem, experts might include fire victims, fire fighters, building code officials and architects.

One means of conducting Turing's test focuses on the administration of questionnaires to chosen experts. These instruments would include various statements about occupant behavior in building fires, to include (a) statements culled from interviews and actual reports by fire victims, etc., and (b) statements contrived by the researcher, designed to reflect behavioral patterns of ficticious "victims" of simulated building fires. In developing the original objectives for the investigation, it was hoped that such a test could in fact be affected, and that an initial effort toward ascertaining the model's external validity could be made. As the modeling and simulation strategies evolved over the course of the study, however, it became quite obvious that an attempt to apply such methods as Turing's test would lie well outside the intended scope of work. This belief stems from the facts that, (a) simulation-based statements for inclusion in the test could be generated only after sufficient data from simulation experiments had actually been obtained and evaluated, and (b) the whole issue of external validity itself only becomes salient once the model's internal consistency has already been largely verified.

But, Turing's test aside, these requirements themselves suggest somewhat formidable tasks. In light of the project's intended scope, then, the specific purposes of the current paper are to present: (a) a detailed discussion of the methods actually utilized to generate data describing a simulated building fire system, (b) an analysis of such data relevant to a discussion of the model's internal validity, and (c) indications of research tasks immediately useful in connection with the refinement of techniques and concepts initiated here.

3.2 The simulation model

The process of generating simulation data first required that the component routines of the model - conceptually expressed as schematic configurations - be developed into lists of logically executable statements. Such a statement listing has several distinct purposes, including (a) as an operational program for use in manually run "machine" simulation experiments, (b) as detailed guidelines for developing computer programs necessary for running high-speed complex machine simulations, and (c) as a framework for running the model as a simulation-game.

For the present validation study, the data resulted from manually operated "Monte Carlo" simulation runs. These involved the use of a desk calculator and random number table for computing probability functions and executing probabilistic steps. The locations of fire and smoke products, and of the simulated occupants, as well as other characteristics of each were graphically recorded by means of a pencil-and-paper technique, in which a single illustration represents the state of the building fire system at a given point in time, t. The default value for simulated time was preset (arbitrarily) at 12 units. At that point, any occupant in the run which had neither successfully exited nor been consumed by fire or smoke, was considered to have been still alive, but "trapped" within the danger zone.

The issue of calibration has been largely omitted from the present, illustrative study. Accordingly, it is not possible to assess exactly how much "real-time" is being represented by a simulated discrete unit of simulated time; and by extension, it is difficult to reflect just how quickly events would in fact occur in a real fire (e.g. flame/smoke movement, viz. occupants' own rates of movement). Accordingly, one cannot say just how far into the threat period the simulation penetrates in the course of 12 units of time.

The "operations sequence" (statement listing) is organized into a series of subroutines designed to accommodate the steps comprising the model. The subroutines, therefore, perform a variety of complex tasks, including: (a) Initilizing the simulation run (i.e., probabilistically presetting the threat-mode to operate during the run, the number and initial locations of simulated occupants, as well as certain individual characteristics of the "occupants"); (b) Flame and smoke migration over time; (c) Environment evaluation, probabilistic "interruption" prompting and execution, movement probability adjustment, spatial relocation of occupants (movement), and move evaluation, for each simulated occupant in each unit of simulated time; and (d) Updating all data records at the completion of each discrete time unit. The detailed operations sequence is available from the author.

3.3 Several assumptions underlying the current procedure

In evaluating data generated by the model, the reader should keep the following assumptions and caveats in mind:

1. Injuries incurred by "occupants" may be physical, resulting from fallen structural materials (for instance), or psychological, either resulting in permanent immobility for the remainder of the simulated time period.

2. At the start of a simulation run (time = 0), fire may have already done extensive damage elsewhere in the building, weakening its structure and increasing the likelihood that an occupant's path of choice be blocked by fallen materials (etc.), or that he/she even be injured by such materials.

3. Occupants who work in the building have participated in evacuation drills, and are already familiar with egress routes.

4. Secondary and tertiary fire ignition points (and concommitant migration patterns) have not been incorporated into the current model.

5. The model generates a constant fire/smoke migration pattern, which ignores the action of such external forces as air currents or extinguishment efforts.

6. The model does not simulate "helping behaviors" by occupants who confront injured individuals (note, for instance, 5).

7. The model does not generate auditory stimuli (e.g. "crashing" sounds, screams, public address messages, and so on), nor does it simulate human responses to either verbal or sign cues.

3.4 The simulation and validation experiment

This section outlines the structure of the experiment, while the findings themselves are summarized in part 4, below. The objective of the validation study, as mentioned, was to generate the behavior of a simulated building fire system (viz. a single floor of a high-rise office building), and to evaluate this behavior in such a manner as to shed light on the internal validity of the simulation model with which we are presently concerned. The specific problems addressed by the experiment were to determine (a) the degree to which "occupants'" successful egress from the danger zone is predictable from knowledge of other variables accommodated within the model, and (b) whether the model is capable of distinguishing between building plans which differ in spatial design (a presumably valuable function). Concerning the later issue, it was hypothesized that more "occupants" would escape safely from open-plan (versus compartmentized) spatial layouts - since these are presumed to offer a greater number of movement alternatives at any point in time, and to provide fewer corners and other opportunities for trapping individuals. It was also hypothesized that occupants of the open-office arrangement (viz. compartmentized space inhabitants) would spend fewer time units in locations already occupied by combustion products. Moreover, it was expected that occupants having escaped safety will have done so in fewer time units in the case of the open-office design (again, since there were presumed to be fewer barriers to goal directed movement behavior).

Method: "Occupants'" goal directed movement behavior was recorded in each of two simulated environments (open-plan versus compartmentized), in which a radially expanding fire-threat was simulated. Each of the environments (note FIGURES 2 and 3) was based on the same fundamental arrangement, viz. area, shape, and location of safety-egress zones (i.e. fire stairs). The two layouts - each representing ordinary "office" functions - differed only in terms of spatial articulation: one utilizing a relatively barrier-free arrangement, the other a cluster of enclosed office areas.

The expanding fire threat progressed radially from a predetermined point in the spatial field, and equal number of distance units per time unit. The model treats the movement behavior of occupants and combustion products independently, each in conjuction with its own rate of spatial displacement (adjustable by the researcher). The present configuration of the model operates under the assumption that flame and smoke migration are both slower and considerably more predictable than the movement of people. Accordingly, (a) a distance increment for flame/smoke migration is only a small fraction the size of a person-movement distance unit, and (b) the threat-migration subroutine in the simulation operations sequence generates flame and smoke expansion in a simple radial pattern.

The threat-migration subroutine, moreover, permits the simulation experimenter an opportunity to simulate various contingencies, viz. differential expansion and contraction of the separate entities, or phenomena produced by different types of fires, air-handling systems, etc. In the simulation experiment discussed here, smoke was further assumed to expand three distance units to every one unit of flame migration, per unit time. These rates were held constant over all simulation runs, for each of the test environments.

Simulated occupants, and the initial locations of each within the spatial layout, were randomly selected prior to any actual simulation runs. It was felt that a sufficiently rich array of illustrative behaviors could be observed (considering the size of the environments) by including six "occupants" in each run. Individuals were sampled on the basis of "their" (a) occupant status (i.e., "regular occupants" presumed to be familiar with egress routes, or "visitors"), and (b) interruption tolerance level, a factor utilized by the model in processing an individual's response to any sudden interruptions to his/her goal directed behavior that may occur. Once six individuals were selected, and their initial locations randomly assigned, they remained constant across all runs conducted for each of the test environments. Accordingly, the only parameter to vary between test environments was spatial layout. By controlling for flame/smoke migration patterns, individual "occupant characteristics", and occupants' locations viz. the fire ignition point and safety zones at the start of the run, it was expected that variations in the number of

occupants to exit safety from each environment could be attributed to differences in physical design.

Procedure: The actual simulation experiment was conducted in a straightforward manner, as follows: After occupant characteristics and locations, and the threat-migration mode were predetermined, five replications were conducted for each test environment. This resulted in 30 occupants having "experienced" each environment. Although only six unique combinations of occupant status and interruption tolerance level characterized these 30 individuals, the stochastic model generated a unique building fire experience for each. Each replication was conducted in accordance with "rules" prescribed by the operations sequence. Occupants' move probabilities were adjusted by means of simple numeric functions, and movement decisions were made on the basis of random numbers drawn from a table.

The probability that an occupant would be suddenly interrupted by an external stimulus or cognitive association at any point in time was arbitrarily preset (for want of empirical evidence) at p=.50. The model permits this value to be varied, enabling it to reflect findings from empirical studies, or any other objective. Four illustrative examples of movement interruptions were actually incorporated into the current experiment, including: (a) a fear reaction resulting in temporary immobility of the occupant, (b) recollection of some recent item, event, or stimulus, or other cognitive association, precipitating "back-tracking" behavior, (c) physical or mental disability resulting in an occupant's total immobility, and (d) a physical blockage of an egress route, causing the occupant to re-evaluate alternative move possibilities. In the current experiment, each of these interruption modes was assigned (again, arbitrarily) an occurrence probability of p=.25. Again, it should be noted that these values can be manipulated by the experimenter (or designer) to reflect either empirical evidence which may become available, or special research or design objectives. In the present study, selected p-values are intended to be illustrative, and somewhat reflective of the lack of useful field data at the present time. Copies of simulated-occupant movement records resulting from typical runs may be obtained from the author.

Finally, a simulated-occupant was considered to have been consumed by fire (burned to death) or smoke (asphixiated) if s(he) (a) remained in a threat-occupied zone for more than three consecutive time units, (b) remained in a zone completely saturated by flame and smoke, for at least one time unit, or (c) entered into a completely saturated zone.

4. FINDINGS AND DISCUSSION

4.1 Predicting successful egress from the danger zone

It was expected that the parameters manipulated within the model would account for a substantial proportion of the variance in the dependent measure: the final status of simulated occupants. TABLE 1 displays means generated by five simulation runs for each of two environments. Data was provided by the model in the following categories: (a) occupants' final status, i.e. safely-exited, trapped within, or consumed; (b) occupants' original locations viz. egress zones; (c) occupants' original locations viz. the flame/smoke ignition point; (d) occupants' interruption tolerance levels; (e) total number of interruptions experienced by occupants in relation to their total numbers of active time units during a run; and (f) the total numbers of time units occupants spent in threat-occupied zones.

Matrices of correlations among these variables are provided in TABLE 2, for each of the experimental environments. Several intuitive expectations have been born out by these findings. The correlation coefficients reported here are for the compartmentized and open-office designs, respectively. For example, occupants located closer to egress zones at the time of threat ignition tended to escape more often than individuals located at greater distances from these zones ($r=-.54, -.43$; $p=.05$). Moreover, occupants located at greater distances from the ignition point tend to escape more often than those more closely situated, at the start of a simulation run ($r=.49, .36$; $p=.05$). In addition, it was found that occupants who evacuated the danger area spent relatively few time units in threat-occupied zones ($r=-.77, -.84$; $p=.01$).

Multiple regression analyses were conducted to assess the extent to which the criterion (whether or not a simulated occupant exited safely) could be predicted from knowledge of other parameters. The findings are summarized below:

Compartmentized office layout: It was found that knowledge of predictors (b)-(d) and (f) above accounted for 64% of the variance in the criterion ($R=.80$). In the instance where all five predictors were utilized, it was found that $R=.84$, with some 71% of the variance accounted for. The increase in R is significant at the .05 level ($F=4.89$, $df=1,24$).

In the case of an actual project in fire safety planning, however, a designer may only have approximations of parameters (b) and (c) viz. the hypothetical locations of work stations in relation to fire stairs, and estimations of potential ignition points. Even knowledge of these two variables yielded $R=.54$ (although only 29% of the variance is accounted for.

All R values reported above are significant at the .01 level. Where all five predictors are utilized, the following multiple regression equation was derived:

$$Xa'=.40Xb+1.08Xc-.09Xd-2.00Xe-.71Xf+2.22$$

Open-office layout: In this instance, knowledge of all five predictors accounted for 88% of the variance in final occupant status ($R=.94$). This was significantly greater than predictions on the basis of measures (b)-(d) and (f) ($R=.88$, $F=19.96$, $df=1,24$), or (b), (c) and (f), ($R=.87$, $F=10.16$, $df=2,24$). These R values and F ratios are all signficant beyond the .01 level.

Using the locational parameters (b) and (c), estimates of which might be derivable by architects, a great deal more error is introduced, as only 21% of the total variance in the criterion is accounted for ($R=.46$, $p=.05$). The following equation was constructed on the basis of all five predictors:

$$Xa'=-1.21Xb-2.84Xc-.70Xd-2.00Xe-.97Xf+15.39$$

4.2 Detecting differences between layouts

The suggestion that simulation modeling techniques would be useful in evaluating alternative building designs, on the basis of their relative life safety potential, has been implied throughout the paper. Such applications, however, presuppose that a simulation model (of demonstrated external validity) is in fact capable of distinguishing good from poor building performance. The capabilities of the present model were examined in the illustrative simulation experiment discussed here. The principal issues addressed involve (a) the final status of occupants, (b) the amount of time spent in threat-invaded spatial zones, and (c) the amount of time required by evacuees to reach safety zones.

Final status of occupants: It was hypothesized that more open-office occupants would escape the danger area (and fewer would be consumed) than would occupants of the compartmentized layout. Such an expectation seemed logical, since the open-office design permitted more direct egress routes, more move alternatives, and fewer barriers behind which occupants could become trapped.

A chi-square contingency table was analyzed to evaluate whether simulated occupants' final status at the conclusion of 12 time units was dependent upon the type of design inhabited. The frequencies are given in TABLE 3. The data indicate that final status was not contingent upon design type: chi-square=.09, df=2, n.s.

Time spent in threat-invaded spatial zones: On the basis of hypothetical advantages of open-office designs offered above, it was also expected that occupants of these arrangements would spend fewer time units spatially adjacent to flames, or immersed within smoke, than their compartmentized office counterparts. The mean number of such time units experienced by 30 simulated open-office occupants was 2.40 (s=1.69), while that for 30 compartmentized office occupants was 2.00 (s=1.86).

A t-test yielded -0.872, df=58, n.s. Accordingly, the null hypothesis that there is no difference between occupants of the two designs, was accepted.

Time required by evacuees to reach safety zones: The comparatively barrier-free environment of the open-office spaces was expected (again, hypothetically) to enable evacuees to reach safety zones (i.e. fire stairs) more quickly than evacuees from the compartmented office plan. The mean number of simulated time units required by nine open-office evacuees was 5.70 (s=3.29), as compared with the mean required for ten compartmentized space evacuees, 6.40 (s=3.77).

However, analysis of the data yielded: t=0.405, df=17, n.s. Therefore, the null hypothesis that evacuees from open-space arrangements do not differ from their compartmentized counterparts, was accepted.

4.3 Final remarks

It was found that variations in parameters measured during simulation runs accounted for a rather substantial proportion of the total variance in simulated occupants' final egress status, for each of the design types studied. Consequently, it would appear that other factors not incorporated within the framework of the model are of relatively little importance in predicting behavior in such a simulated building fire system (its external validity notwith-standing). These might include such variables as occupants' anxiety and fear thresholds, predispositions toward stopping to assist injured persons, ability to withstand certain thought-impairing effects of noxious smoke, and so on.

To some extent, the only predictor variables that the architect could be expected to predetermine (or certainly estimate) on the drawing board would be those relating to locations of individuals in the plan, with respect to the locations of proposed work stations, as well as exits, and in connection with the possible location of threat ignition points and migration opportunities (viz. HVAC outlet locations, partition ratings, equipment installations, etc.). The other predictors appear to be those either associated with individual occupant traits, or with individual experiences in a fire situation. Regarding the former, the architect desiring to employ such a model in the evaluation of building designs may be able to apply workable estimates. It may be possible, for example, to develop frequency distributions of relevant traits, for various

building occupancy categories, in various locales, and so on. Indeed, a major objective of research in fire system simulation methods must be the identification of predictor variables which the designer can estimate at the drawing board, and which - at the same time - account for a substantial proportion of the variance in the egress criterion.

The present model is unable to distinguish between two seemingly disparate environmental conditions. Unfortunately, findings which fail to reject null hypotheses are difficult to explain, and shed little light on the question of the model's internal validity. For example, perhaps the hypotheses themselves were incorrect or illogically formulated; perhaps there is in fact little justifacation for expecting open-office arrangements to be superior to others. After all, while the open-plan office designs offer fewer barriers to safe occupant egress, isn't it also possible that the expanding threat - also unimpeded by physical barriers - is counteracting any advantage held by escaping occupants? Analysis of fire-victims' reports should illuminate this issue.

Or perhaps the internal structure of the model is incorrect - concerning its treatment of physical barriers. While it may recognize certain differences between the two designs studied, it may also be so insensitive as to require differences of unrealistically large magnitude. Again, empirical evidence would be useful in refining and sensitizing the model (notwithstanding the difficulties of collecting such evidence).

The difficulty with internal validation seems to lie with the issue of hypothesis selection in large measure, viz. the rationale for the researcher's interests, and their consistency with the model's capabilities. Indeed, the current hypotheses favoring the open-office design were accepted as purely speculative and illustrative, and not as having been clearly derived either from theory or empirical evidence. Accordingly, their value should be considered considered primarily in heuristic, rather than practical terms. The entire issue of distinguishing between alternative designs, however, is quite critical since the ability of a fire system simulation model to guide architects and others in the selection of favorable designs and policies - prior to a buildings construction and use - will be its primary strength.

Author's note: The research reported here was conducted under contract for the National Bureau of Standards, U.S. Department of Commerce, Order Number 512223.

Reference

1. BAER, A.E. A simulation model of multi-directional pedestrian movement within physically bounded environments. Carnegie-Mellon University, Institute of Physical Planning, Pittsburgh, Pa., Report #47, 1974.
2. HOWARD, R.A. Dynamic probabilistic systems, Vol. 2. New York: Wiley, 1971.
3. KEMENY, J.G. and SNELL, J. Mathematical models in the social sciences. Cambridge, Mass.: M.I.T. Press, 1972.
4. LOZAR, R.C. A methodology for the computer simulation of behavior-environment interactions in dining halls. In, Bazjanac, V. (ed.), Man-environment interactions: Part 10: Computers and Architecture. E.D.R.A. 5 Proceedings, 1974, 211-34.
5. MIDLARSKY, E. Aiding under stress: the effects of competence, dependency, visibility and fatalism. J. Personality, 39, 1, 132-49.
6. NEWELL, A. and SIMON, H.A. Human problem solving. Englewood Cliffs, N.J.: Prentice-Hall, 1972.
7. PAULS, J. Fire safety and related man-environment studies. Unpubl. ms. presented at E.D.R.A. 6 Conference, Lawrence, Kansas, April, 1975.
8. RASER, J.R. Simulation and society. Boston: Allyn and Bacon, 1969.
9. RUBIN, A.I. and COHEN, A. Occupant behavior in building fires. Wash., D.C.: National Bureau of Standards, Technical Note #818, February, 1974.
10. SIMON, H.A. Motivational and emotional controls of cognition. Psych. Review, 1967, 74, 1, 29-39.
11. SIMON, H.A. The sciences of the artificial. Cambridge, Mass.: M.I.T. Press, 1969.
12. STUDER, R.G. and HOBSON, R.H. Simulation of human learning in urban movement systems. In, Preiser, W.F.E. (ed.), Environmental design research, Vol. 2. Stroudsburg, Pa.: Dowden, Hutchinson, and Ross, 1973.
13. TURING, A.M. Computing machinery and intelligence. Mind, 1950, 59, 236, 433-60.
14. WOLPERT, R.M. and ZILLMANN, D. The sequential expansion of a decision model in a spatial context. Environment and planning, 1969, 1, 91-104.

TABLE 1: Means for five Simulation Runs, for Two Simulated Environments*

Run No.	Final Status[1]	Dist. to Goal[2]	Dist. from Ignition pt.[2]	Interruption tol. level	No. of inter's. per no. of moves	Total moves in a threat-occ'd. zone.
1	3.67 (4.00)	3.17	1.83	2.17	.41 (.59)	2.00 (1.67)
2	3.00 (2.00)	"	"	"	.57 (.82)	1.00 (2.33)
3	2.67 (3.00)	"	"	"	.60 (.37)	1.67 (2.50)
4	2.67 (1.67)	"	"	"	.60 (.54)	2.17 (3.33)
5	2.33 (3.00)	"	"	"	.31 (.51)	3.17 (2.17)
	2.87 (2.73)				.50 (.57)	2.00 (2.40)

Notes: (1) 1=consumed; 3=trapped; 5=escaped.
(2) distance measured in occupant movement units.

* Values in parentheses are for open-office plan; others are for compartmentized space.

TABLE 2: Correlation Matrix for Two Simulated Environments*

(N=30)	b	c	d	e	f
a. Final occ't status	$-.54^2$ ($-.43^1$)	$.49^2$ ($.36^1$)	$-.26$ ($-.16$)	$-.15$ ($-.34$)	$-.77^2$ ($-.84^2$)
b. Distance to goal		$-.97^2$ ($-.97^2$)	$.72^2$ ($.70^2$)	$.03$ ($.02$)	$.45^1$ ($.66^2$)
c. distance from ignition pt.			$-.70^2$ ($-.69^2$)	$.00$ ($-.08$)	$-.37^1$ ($-.64^2$)
d. interruption tolerance lev.				$-.17$ ($.02$)	$.17$ ($.30$)
e. no. interrupts./ total no. moves					$-.13$ ($.09$)
f. total moves in a threat occ'd zone					

Notes: (1) p less than .05; (2) p less than .01
* Coefficients in parentheses are for open-office design; others are for the compartmented design.

TABLE 3: Frequencies of Occupant Status Outcomes*

	consumed	trapped	escaped	
Compartmentized office design	12 (12.5)	8 (8)	10 (9.5)	30
Open-plan office design	13 (12.5)	8 (8)	9 (9.5)	30

$x^2 = .09$, with 2 d.f., N.S.

* values in parentheses are expected frequencies.

S. start
1. initialize the run
2. advance time
3. threat-move generator
4. look-ahead evaluator
5. interruption prompt
6. inter'n. generator
7. move prob. adjustor
8. move
9. move evaluator
10. consumed or escaped?
E. end

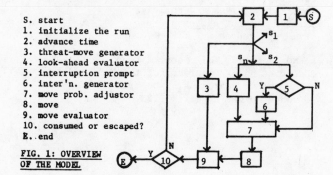

FIG. 1: OVERVIEW OF THE MODEL

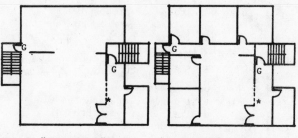

FIG. 2: "OPEN-OFFICE" PLAN   FIG. 3: "COMPARTMENTED" OFFICE PLAN

"G": escape goal; "*": glass partition

THE JOURNEY TO WORK GAME

Howard S. Biel

Program in Urban and Environmental Studies
Case Western Reserve University
Cleveland, Ohio 44106

ABSTRACT

The Journey to Work game is a board game concerned with the daily movement of workers from their residences to workplaces within a metropolitan area. Players (workers) attempt to get to work on time, selecting a particular mode of urban transportation and a specific route from their homes to places of work. Points are accumulated based upon deviations from punctuality and travel times spent getting to work, and players compiling the fewest points during a simulated one-week or two-week playing period are declared winners of the game. The game may be used as a classroom exercise in high school or college level courses, and is capable of accommodating 2-25 students on a single game board. Two particularly worthwhile objectives of the game are (1) revealing the clearly disadvantageous commuting situation of inner-city residents, and (2) estimating modal split consequences of manipulating policy variables such as bus fare, travel time, parking cost, transit accessibility, and surface congestion. In addition, an important behavioral component of the game is noteworthy: players are asked to iteratively identify and discuss the learning process which occurred as they (typically) converged to an habitual mode and route choice pattern.

INTRODUCTION

The Journey to Work game[1] is a board game concerned with the daily movement of workers from their residences to workplaces within a metropolitan area. Players (workers) attempt to get to work on time, selecting a particular mode of urban transportation and a specific route from their homes to places of work. Points are accumulated based upon deviations from punctuality and travel times spent getting to work, and players compiling the fewest points during a simulated one-week or two-week playing period are declared winners of the game. The game may be used as a classroom exercise in high school or college level courses, and is capable of accomodating 2-25 students on a single game

---

[1]Special thanks are due Paul King, Jack Jakubs, and Larry Brown, Departments of Geography, Columbia University, Indiana University, and Ohio State University, respectively, for their numerous and helpful suggestions. The remaining errors are my own.

board.

Journey to Work is decidedly academic in nature, and focus is directed toward several key issues in urban transportation geography and planning. Of particular interest are the following considerations: (1) the spatial mismatch of low income central city residences with peripheral metropolitan employment districts, and the reverse commuter transit problem, (2) trade-offs among various attributes of urban transportation modes influencing journey-to-work vehicular selection, (3) the learning process concerning mode choice, route selection, and human spatial behavior, and (4) characteristics and sensitivities of work trip mass transit demand. The extent to which each of these issues is examined is clearly a function of the expertise of the players and game director (instructor), as well as the amount of time spent playing and analyzing the game.

The reverse commuter transit problem refers to the journey to work of car-less central city residents to decentralized workplace locations in the metropolitan area. Since urban public transportation systems have tended to remain focused upon the Central Business District (CBD), resulting in generally effective "outside-in" transit service, mass transportation from the inner city out to the suburbs as well as between urban districts not located in the downtown city core has usually been inadequate. Increased attention to this problem followed the publication of the McCone Commission Report regarding the 1965 Watts riots in Los Angeles. This report highlighted the relationship existing between transportation and poverty in general, and more particularly, the difficulty and inability of south central Los Angeles residents to fulfill basic needs (getting to employment, educational, shopping, and recreational opportunities) because of costly and inefficient public transport service.

In the Journey to Work game this problem is simulated through the usage of a hypothetical metropolitan area with constituent advantaged and disadvantaged worker residents. Given an existing distribution of employment districts and public transit system, certain players find themselves in a highly desirable position; having access to a private auto, and either being located in close proximity to their workplace or nearby a convenient transport artery which connects their residence to place of work. Other players may be less fortunate; perhaps residing in the central city and working in the urban periphery, without having the opportunity to use private transportation in their journey to work.

Realistic biases have been incorporated within the game structure and disadvantaged players may quickly realize their inability to win or even to do reasonably well against the privileged set of work trippers. To encourage their persistence in playing, therefore, the game permits evaluation of players from several different

perspectives. Players who consistently reduce
their time-in-transit through the simulated game
period, or who reduce their total points
accumulated per game day, are recognized along
with the officially designated winners of the
game (those who minimize total points compiled).

Other key issues receiving attention in the game
are explicitly related to modal split, or the
division of work trips among the available means
of transportation: private auto, rail transit,
bus transit, car pool, taxicab, and walk.
Consideration of trade-offs among modal
attributes influencing journey-to-work vehicular
choice, includes the fundamental question of the
worker's value of time. Implied in the selection
of a particular mode is the player's preference
for work trip speed versus the cost of using
different means of transport. For example, a
player choosing between his private automobile
and one of several forms of mass transit, must in
some manner weigh the advantages of convenience
and speed against such alternative factors as
cost, safety, and reliability. Players select
modes based upon a considerable amount of
information presented before the game begins, in
addition to experience gained through game play,
regarding performance characteristics of each
journey-to-work mode.

The learning process relating to mode and route
choice is simply the summation and extension of
the previously mentioned trade-off consideration.
Players developing a successful strategy early in
the game may rapidly fall into distinctively
routinized behavior, both with respect to their
consistent selection of a means of transport and
specific departure time from home, and also in
terms of a particular route leading from
residence to workplace. Alternatively,
disadvantaged players and players encountering
difficulties during preliminary work trips
generally require many more game "trials" before
any discernible stereo-typical behavior emerges.
Furthermore, some players may experiment quite
extensively with various mode, departure time,
and routing combinations, whereas more conservative players may make only slight alterations in
their successive journey-to-work decisions.

Finally, the fourth issue incorporated within the
Journey to Work game concerns the characteristics
and sensitivities of work trip mass transit
demand. As the game is played, the spatial
pattern of transit usage and reliance changes
to reflect workers' independent decisions of
mode and route choice. Often, these decisions
translate to an expected and relatively stable
profile of mass transit patrons, including a
large proportion of the so-called captive riders
of public transportation -- namely the car-less
players in this simulation -- and a small
percentage of the so-called choice riders of
public transit -- perhaps represented by some
suburban car-owning game players journeying by
bus or rail to workplaces in the CBD.

An increasing imbalance between private and

public transportation system patronage in most
metropolitan areas has resulted from continuous
additions of urban travellers to the "choice
rider" classification, and simultaneously,
fewer choice riders choosing the public transit
option. Conceivably, more choice riders would
utilize some form of mass transit if one or more
critical service variables were changed in a
favorable direction. For example, if buses were
cheaper and faster more patronage might be
realized. Thus, in the Journey to Work game,
sensitivities of travel demand are simulated by
altering certain designated attributes of
particular work trip modes, and identifying
subsequent changes in vehicular usage.

DIRECTOR'S (INSTRUCTOR'S) GUIDELINES

There are two objectives of the Journey to Work
game. The first is to identify and analyze one
major dimension of the urban transportation
problem, namely the reverse commuter transit
problem. The second is to demonstrate the
nature of modal split and route selection in
journey-to-work travel as determined by the
players' cognitive processes of perception,
attitude, and learning.

At the outset of game play, a game director is
selected from among the players, or is external
to the game (class instructor). The director's
purpose concerns the coordination of game play,
the supervision of game rules, and the discussion of worthwhile concepts and problems
generating from the operation of the game. The
individual chosen as director should be qualified
to settle procedural disputes aired by game
participants, and also to incisively direct
examination of key issues and related underlying
processes with which the game is fundamentally
concerned.

Journey to Work proceeds in simulated daily
periods. Focus is directed toward the morning
rush hours, beginning at 7:45 A.M. and
progressing by simulated (game time) 5 minute
intervals until all player workers have arrived
at their proper places of employment. Players
attempt: (1) to get to work by 9:00 A.M. each
morning of a one-week (5 iteration) or two-week
(10 iteration) playing period; (2) to minimize
their expenditures of time and cost in getting
to work; and (3) to leave their residences as
late as possible, so as to minimize opportunity
costs associated with premature departures from
home (for example, the "costs" of not being able
to sleep later, or of having a hurried breakfast).

Though all players would like to reach their
workplaces at exactly 9:00 A.M., circumstances
which occur during the journey to work often
prevent achieving the ideal arrival time.
Whether sub-optimality in arrival time is due
to poor planning on the part of the worker or
unforeseen situations during the work trip,
the player must be assigned a number of arrival
points. A 9:00 arrival time earns (costs)

the player zero points.

Departure points are likewise easily explained and derived. The earlier a player decides to leave his residence, the more departure time points he is assessed. Players departing from home just before 9:00 A.M. will minimize the opportunity costs of a premature start, however increase the chances of arriving late at the workplace, and consequently, of receiving more severe delinquent arrival points.

Minimization of journey-to-work time and cost expenditures is slightly more complicated, with respect to an operational explanation. Optimal (minimum) travel times via the best available mode, or combination of modes, between all residences and all workplaces have been calculated. Players are hence able to compare their efforts concerning travel time with some computed standard. All players are not expected to duplicate their corresponding optimal time -- in fact it may be impossible to do so in some cases where private automobiles are not available. Still, the difference between actual work trip time and hypothetically best time gives an efficiency score upon which travel time point assignment is based. Because of substantial cost differences of alternative means of urban transportation, the efficiency score is then weighted (multiplied by) a cost factor; 1.0, 2.0, or 3.0, depending upon which primary mode of transport was used in getting to work. The resulting product is defined as travel time points.

By summing the three point scores (arrival time, departure time, and travel time) for each player, a daily total point score is directly determined. After the 5 or 10 iteration playing period has terminated, daily total points are summed per player, and the player having the fewest total points is declared the winner.

PLAYERS' INSTRUCTIONS

The following iterative approach (which has deliberately been segmented into discrete steps for discussion purposes) describes the procedure utilized in game play. First, each player selects 1 of 5 residence cards to determine his residential location -- cards are returned to the deck, thus permitting a completely random selection for every participant.

Next, each player selects 1 of 5 workplace cards to determine his workplace location -- and again, cards are returned to the deck. Alternatively, players may be assigned both residential and workplace locations by the game director. In any case, there are 25 possible players on the board at one time (in one game) unless 2 or more players "double-up" (i.e. 2 or more players independently journey to work from the same urban residence to the same workplace). It is suggested that no more than 25 players participate on one board in one game, as the board

becomes excessively cluttered, the time required to play the game increases proportionately, and some players may lose interest if action is too slow. In fact, based upon past experience playing the Journey to Work game, an ideal number of participants ranges between 5 and 15.

Depending upon their residential selection or assignment, players roll the die to determine auto ownership. The chances of having access to a private car correspond to spatially variant percentages of car-less families throughout the metropolitan region.

Players then carefully study the game board and independently evaluate possible routings to their designated workplaces. Obviously, those work trippers owning automobiles have the most flexibility in their routing decisions, however each of the available transport modes and their respective routings, travel times, and costs should be thoroughly investigated. Players with private cars do not have to drive to work. Mode and route selections are quite modifiable, subject to change on succeeding days if found unsatisfactory, while subject to retention if found acceptable.

As mentioned earlier, circumstances encountered during the work trip may negate careful planning with respect to arrival time, departure time, and travel time and cost. These circumstances (both fortunate and unfortunate to the tripper) are governed by the selection of Traffic Condition Cards and Time Adjustment Cards, which will be discussed more fully below. Although the extent of the "fortune" or "misfortune" is not revealed to players before the game begins, probabilities of misfortune have been calculated per mode of travel and per geographic section of the region. The game director may choose to experiment with this information, to see whether advance knowledge of misfortune probabilities (involving journey-to-work time delays) influences modal choice and/or the learning process of players.

Each player decides when to leave his residence every morning (7:45, 7:50, ..., 8:00, ..., etc. -- simulated time) and which of the following modes or combination of modes of urban transportation to use in journeying from residence to workplace: (a) private automobile ... can be used only if the player owns an auto, (b) rail transit ... can be used by any player, (c) bus transit ... can be used by any player, (d) car pool ... can be used by any player owning an auto, as well as any car-less player who rolls a 1, 2, 3, or 4, before play begins (car-less players have only one chance per game to gain the opportunity to use this mode), (e) taxicab ... can be used by any player, or (f) walking ... can be used by any player; but players can only walk within and not between game board zones.

The game director begins actual play by asking

which players are prepared to start their respective work trips at designated time intervals, starting with 7:45 A.M. each day (iteration). Intervals are 5 simulated minutes apart, so the director adjusts the game clock uninterruptedly until at lease one player has started his commuting trip. That is; the game director informs players that it is 7:45 -- if no players wish to depart from their homes until later, the director "moves" the clock to 7:50, ...; and so the process continues until 1 or more players decide to begin their morning journeys.

At each 5 minute interval (again, referring to game minutes and not actual time), each player who has left or who is leaving for his workplace, rolls the die. A roll of 1, 2, 3, or 4 signifies normal journey to work conditions and permits the player to move in a <u>horizontal</u> or <u>vertical</u> fashion toward his proper workplace. The <u>Journey to Work</u> game board represents a major metropolitan area of the United States, and is marked off in a concentric pattern of circles. These circles are spaced farther apart with increasing distance from the center, and are transected by a series of sectors radiating from the middle point. The circles and sectors define individually-labelled urban zones which are much smaller at the center than at the periphery.

Players move their tokens according to a movement schedule which is designed with respect to the relative speeds of the different transportation modes. All movements are made with respect to the underlying grid pattern of the game board. This means that regardless of the mode in question, moving "n" number of zones refers to the zones of the board (labelled with letters and numbers, from A-FF and from 1-21).[2]

After every player who has started, or who is starting his journey to work rolls the die, 5 game minutes elapse on the <u>Journey to Work</u> clock, and the director signals the beginning of a "new" 5 minute interval. For instance, if the director informs players that it is 8:00 (simulated time), all players wanting to start their work trip and all workers in-transit systematically roll the die. Following their corresponding board moves, the director announces the correct time, 8:05, and so on proceeds through the game.

If a player rolls a 5 or a 6 on the die, he must pick a Traffic Condition Card (if 5) or a Time Adjustment Card (if 6). The Traffic Condition Cards apply to the entire playing board, and do not necessarily affect the player drawing the card. Therefore, those players rolling a 5 must move their tokens the same distance which they would normally move, unless they are specifically affected by the traffic condition. "Active"

Traffic Condition Cards (those cards which impose favorable or unfavorable consequences for a designated, continued period of time) should be placed face-up in the lower left hand corner of the game board for the duration of their effectiveness. In addition, accidents, congestion, and other abnormal traffic conditions should be marked in appropriate zones, where possible, using markers or pins.

The Time Adjustment Cards affect only the player who rolls the 6. Due to unusual circumstances, the player rolling a 6 realizes either an acceleration in or impediment to his normal movement behavior. The player must then select from the proper Time Adjustment Cards deck, according to the particular mode of transport being used when the 6 is rolled. Cards are thereupon returned to the bottom of the same stack.

Players thus proceed to their respective workplaces, attempting to consume as little time as possible in their commutation, yet trying to reach their destination very close to the optimal arrival time (9:00). The game director coordinates play throughout the iteration, and after all players have successfully arrived at their places of work, points are totalled for the completed round. The exact same steps outlined above are followed for each iteration (day) of game play, and total points are summed over all iterations to determine the winner(s) of the <u>Journey to Work</u> game.

DISCUSSION AND SIGNIFICANCE OF THE GAME

The <u>Journey to Work</u> game is fundamentally designed to be a learning tool, and its merits rest on its ability to stimulate questions, discussion, and learning. Thus, although participants are encouraged to discuss strategies and decision making problems with each other and with the game director throughout the playing period, without post-game review of "what went on," much of the learning purpose of the game is sacrificed. Subsequent analysis of the game should be supervised by the director, and all players are encouraged to actively participate in the session. Several noteworthy points which will presumably be considered frequently in review periods are now listed and discussed.

Perhaps most obviously, players will notice that the cards have been stacked against workers commuting from central city residential locations. It is nearly impossible to be victorious from the inner-city residence in terms of absolute winners of the game (summing daily <u>total</u> point scores). Additionally, the other residential sites located reasonably close to the Central Business District are not as favorable as the more remote locations with higher probabilities of car ownership. The game board and "hypothetical" city are actually

---

[2]The <u>Journey to Work</u> game board and other special equipment necessary for the gaming/simulation are available upon request from the author.

modelled after Columbus, Ohio, and with the exception of the rail transit line addition, the board fairly represents the metropolitan situation. Players commuting from the most central residence are therefore, correspondingly, black ghetto work trippers.

Employment centers on the board coincide with the 5 major regional shopping districts of the Columbus, Ohio urban area, and given the well-established process of metropolitan decentralization of employment opportunities, central city residential locations are at a decided journey-to-work disadvantage with respect to problems of reverse commutation to peripheral work sites. Probabilities of car ownership per residential location are derived from 1970 census data regarding the matching real world locations, and car-less families are immediately placed in a highly undesirable, negatively biased position. Because however, the game has several options for winning, (including some which have not previously been mentioned -- such as players voting for the "worker" who performed most admirably given his residence/workplace combination, or players evaluating the performance of each game player based upon some other designated criterion), participants drawing or being assigned disadvantaged residence/workplace locations should still be interested in playing. The spatial mismatch of urban workplaces and residences, and related inequities in commuting patterns are fundamental concerns of the Journey to Work game.

A second central topic involves the question of modal split in journey-to-work flows. Players should be asked to reveal (as accurately as possible) their subjective utilities for each of the available transport modes, respective of their particular residence/workplace combination. An attempt may then be made to determine the trade-off between various modal attributes (cost, time, convenience, etc.) so as to shed some light upon the nature and sensitivity of transit demand for work trips in metropolitan areas. Furthermore, if possible, participants should discuss their own specific decision-making processes which were operative in their corresponding play throughout the completed game. By integrating some or all of these considerations, meaningful insight may be gained concerning an entire battery of human spatial behavioral decisions. Recently, urban geographers and transport planners immediately interested in the spatial and temporal dimensions of journey-to-work flows, have increasingly been turning to disaggregate, stochastic, behavioral models of choice (route, mode, and time) to explain movement behavior. Therefore, this second topic appears to have substantial practical significance in addition to contemporary research attention and support, and an extensive amount of participant interaction and discourse is suggested here.

A third noteworthy issue which should repeatedly emerge in post-game discussions is closely related to the previous set of questions regarding the players' decision-making processes. This issue concerns the more specific learning component of the choice process. The Journey to Work game is intended to be a dynamic game, in which choice strategies are learned and relearned via an explicit, multiple feedback mechanism (the daily total point score; arrival time, departure time, and travel time and cost). Players are expected to use a trial-and-error strategy at the beginning of play, and then presumably converge toward some habitual behavioral pattern in terms of modal choice, route choice, and departure time. Certainly the extent and speed of convergence are functions of the length of the game and ability of participants. Hence, an interesting series of considerations regards the variability of convergence (learning) with respect to players, residences, workplaces, modal choices, winners, and number of iterations of game play. Also, do players having prior knowledge of modal time adjustment and traffic condition probabilities develop a stereotyped work trip pattern more rapidly than players not having access to the information? Since Journey to Work is an academic game, focus is upon learning; consequently, learning about the learning process (as it was evidenced during the game) seems to be a very important subject for discussion.

Lastly, there is a wealth of opportunity to experiment with mass transit demand considerations and related elasticities using modifications of the Journey to Work game. Problems of bus transit systems, in particular, throughout metropolitan areas in America have been well-specified and analyzed in recent years by a host of urban students, planners, and policy-makers. Increased car ownership resulting in decreased transit ridership, has led to increased fares and reduced service characteristics, which in turn have been responsible for continued patronage declines.

In the Journey to Work game, the director may investigate transit demand sensitivities with respect to alternative determinants of work trip modal choice. For instance, the director may choose to reduce the bus transit cost factor to .50 or .25 from 1.00, while holding all other "variables" (game conditions) constant. Discussion should then concern changed spatial behavioral patterns and resulting point totals. Additionally, the director may consider travel time improvements in bus transit. A decision may be made to combine both improvements (cost and time) together and record demand adjustments, or to regard each effect separately. A third, but certainly not final possibility would be to permit more complete coverage of the urban area by bus transit. The game director could announce that buses had the same mobility range (in terms of areal extent) as automobiles, thereby again enhancing the desirability of bus transit as a work trip modal option. Careful consideration of play revisions and

outcomes under these new modal attribute
provisions, should follow the extended operation
of the game.

The above mentioned, broad issues are clearly
not an exhaustive set of discussion topics.
Nevertheless, they should be useful in directing
the review session which follows game play.
Many additional arguments and questions may be
brought forward during the review, and each one
should be given proper time and attention.
Originality and interaction in the discussion
period are heartily encouraged.

references

BIEL, H., 1972. "Journey-to-Work Flows from the
Black Ghetto of Columbus, Ohio,"
Discussion Paper 30, Ohio State
University, Department of Geography.

CALIFORNIA, GOVERNOR'S COMMISSION ON THE LOS
ANGELES RIOTS, 1965. Violence in the City:
An End or a Beginning? (McCone Commission
Report).

CURTIN, J., 1968. "Effects of Fares on Transit
Riding," Highway Research Record, Number 213,
8-20.

DAVIES, S., 1970. The Reverse Commuter Transit
Problem in Indianapolis, unpublished Ph.D.
dissertation, Indiana University, Department
of Geography.

FERRERI, M. and W. CHERWONY, 1971. "Choice and
Captive Modal Split Models," Highway
Research Record, Number 360, 80-90.

GREYTAK, D., 1970. "Residential Segregation,
Metropolitan Decentralization, and the
Journey to Work," Occasional Paper 3,
Syracuse University, Urban Transportation
Institute.

GOLOB, T., et. al., 1972. "An Analysis of
Consumer Preferences for a Public Trans-
portation System," Transportation Research,
May, 80-102.

KASOFF, M., 1970. "Socioeconomic Factors
Underlying Public Transit Use in the
Journey to Work," Occasional Paper 1,
Syracuse University, Urban Transportation
Institute.

KEEFER, L., 1962. "Characteristics of Captive
and Choice Transit Riders in the Pittsburgh
Metropolitan Area," Highway Research Board
Bulletin, Number 347, 24-33.

KIBEL, B., 1972. "Simulation of the Urban
Environment," Technical Paper 5,
Association of American Geographers,
Commission on College Geography.

LANSING, J. and G. HENDRICKS, 1967. "How
People Perceive the Cost of the Journey
to Work," Highway Research Record,
Number 197, 44-55.

LAVE, C., 1969. "A Behavioral Approach to
Modal Split Forecasting,"
Transportation Research, V. 3, N.4.

LISCO, T., 1967. The Value of Commuters'
Travel Time: A Study in Urban
Transportation, unpublished Ph.D.
dissertation, Department of Economics,
University of Chicago.

LOWENSTEIN, L., 1971. "An Annotated Biblio-
graphy on Urban Games," Exchange
Bibliography Number 204, Monticello,
Illinois: Council of Planning
Librarians.

McGILLIVRAY, R., 1970. "Demand and Choice
Models of Modal Split," Journal of
Transport Economics and Politics,
192-207.

MEYER, J., 1967. "Urban Transportation," in
J. Wilson (ed.), The Metropolitan
Enigma, Washington, D.C.: U.S. Chamber
of Commerce, 34-55.

MOSES, L., 1963. "Economics of Consumer Choice
in Urban Transportation," Traffic
Engineering, V. 33, July, 26-38.

PAINE, F., A. NASH, and S. HILLE, 1969.
"Consumer Attitudes Toward Auto vs.
Public Transport Alternatives,"
Journal of Applied Psychology,
December, 472-480.

QUARMBY, D., 1967. "Choice of Travel Mode for
the Journey to Work: Some Findings,"
Journey of Transport Economics and
Policy, V. 1, 1-42.

STOPHER, P., 1968. "Predicting Travel Mode
Choice for the Work Journey," Traffic
Engineering and Control, January,
436-439.

TAAFFE, E.,B. GARNER, and M. YEATES, 1965. The
Peripheral Journey to Work: A Geographic
Consideration, Evanston: Northwestern
University Transportation Center.

WABE, J., 1967. "Dispersal of Employment and the
Journey to Work: A Case Study," Journal
of Transport Economics and Policy,
September, 345-361.

WACHS, M. and J. SCHOFER, 1972. "Public Transit
and Job Access in Chicago," Transportation Engineering Journal, May, 351-366.

WOHL, M., 1970. "Users of Urban Transportation
Services and Their Income Circumstances,"
Traffic Quarterly, V. 24, N. 1.

SECTION 4

Design Research and Evaluation

The final test of whether or not we have effectively bridged the applicability gap comes when
designers and behavioural scientists critique
pre-construction design proposals. How should
the design be evaluated? And how should the
results of that evaluation be incorporated into
the design? The fifteen papers in this section
represent efforts to fuse the disparate and
often contradictory viewpoints that result when
deisgners invite such scrutiny by behavioural
scientists.

Four of the papers examine theoretical and systems approaches to design evaluation. The remainder focus on problems within specific design
areas: the design of wards, wings, or buildings
of medical or educational institutions; the
design of neighbourhoods and community facilities;
design for the special needs of the handicapped,
elderly, or other special groups; and the design
of special environments.

The first three papers form a "how-to" primer on
good design research: thinking through the problem, framing alternatives, programming a solution
and assessing the outcome. Campbell discusses

evaluation of the design programme. Walkey,
Carley, Roberts, and Bancroft detail a process
for the development of planning options--speci-
fically for regional correctional services. And
Ostrander and Connell examine post-construction
evaluation, arguing that such work is most
valuable when it provides feedback to actual
decision-makers.

The second group of papers draws on findings of
specific research in special settings. In effect,
these authors are saying: If we closely examine
what people do in a setting, we can find clues
that will lead to more effective and more humane
designs for that type of setting. Kerpen,
Marshall, Whitehead, and Ellison are concerned
with an economical re-design of large, aging
mental hospitals. Pendell and Coray used
behavioural mapping and survey techniques to
compare nursing unit designs in four hospitals.
They then demonstrate how such data can provide
feedback to administrators. Phelps and Baxter
provide revealing data on how academics use
their time and space. They then discuss how their
data can be used in evaluating progress toward
departmental goals and in assessing users'

satisfaction with available facilities. In another study of academic environments, Ochsner examines attitudes and activity patterns in a student dormitory.

The next group of papers is concerned with involving the user more directly in design decidions and their implementation. Brower, Stough, Gray, and Headley report and evaluate a variety of interesting programmes in which inner-city residents are encouraged to initiate and operate various recreational and maintenance programmes in neighbourhood parks. Bender examines how the poor in Bogota, Columbia, create and maintain their own "squatter settlements". And Pressman examines a variety of problems faced by residents of new, small, isolated Canadian communities. He also makes a number of recommendations that could benefit government agencies who are increasingly involved in planning such communities.

A final group of papers examines the needs of special users or users of special environments. From survey research data, Newcomer derives design standards on how far the elderly are able to travel to obtain needed services. Steinfeld, Schroeder, Bishop, Aiello, Andrade, and Buchanan critically review available research on standards for the accessibility of a building to disabled persons, and they promise much-needed new data to help improve these standards. Orleans discusses designs that can help normalize the institutional environment to which the mentally retarded are often subjected. And Culjat reports a study of a new community in the Canadian Arctic where climatic influence is so intensified.

The problems and hypotheses of the applied research discussed in the papers of this section have implications, of course, for designers in EDRA. But, it is also worth pointing out that they have a value to the behavioural scientists in EDRA as well. Practical probelms and the hypotheses developed in doing research on such problems provide a stimulus to basic researchers and, in some cases, even a practical test of some of their favoured notions. In other words, traffic on the bridge over the applicability gap goes in both directions. This collection of papers illustrates the numerous problems encountered by those who attempt to integrate research and application. These papers also illustrate, however, that lines of communication exist and that such communication and interaction between the two emphases can be fruitful to both.

EVALUATION OF THE BUILT ENVIRONMENT:

LESSONS FROM PROGRAM EVALUATION

David E. Campbell

Department of Psychology
University of Kansas
Lawrence, Kansas 66045

ABSTRACT

For some 20 years now, behavioral scientists have been building up a body of knowledge in the area of program evaluation. This knowledge has found application recently in the many federally-funded social action programs--most of which now require some assessment of their success and efficiency. In recent years, evaluation has become a major concern in the area of environmental design. Planners are now concerned with the performance of built environments with respect to the behavioral and cognitive goals of their designs. It would be wise for such design evaluators to ask what advice is available from the program evaluators who have had a number of years of experience in evaluation research. Social action programs and planned environments are both intended to influence behavior in specific ways. The problems of evaluation in assessing the behavioral effects of social action programs and built environments are similar in a number of ways. This paper reviews these similarities. Important questions are raised and some specific advice is given to design evaluators concerning the purposes of evaluation, design goals, data collection plans, measurement techniques, cooperation, and dissemination of findings. This advice should help environmental evaluators to avoid some of the many pitfalls that have plagued program evaluation attempts.

1. INTRODUCTION

Before discussing the lessons to be learned from program evaluators, we should be clear on just what program evaluation is. Program evaluation refers to use of the scientific method in an effort to determine the effects of a treatment or program, especially with respect to the intended effects (Struening & Guttentag, 1975; Suchman, 1967; Weiss, 1972a; Wortman, 1975). The program itself can be any systematic or formal procedure for changing humans in some way. Examples of programs are Head Start (an educational program for lower-socioeconomic children), the American Cancer Association's anti-smoking campaign, the New Jersey Negative Income Tax Experiment (to encourage employment), and the death penalty (to discourage crime). Each of these has specific objectives in changing human behavior. The program

evaluator's task is to determine how well the program is working. This generally involves defining the goals of the program, gathering data according to some plan to ascertain whether the goals are being obtained and why, and communicating the results to the initiating decision-makers. Evaluators use the scientific method as their model in carrying out this task. Unfortunately, the application of experimental controls and scientific measurement techniques is far more difficult when conducting an evaluation in the "field" than when testing a hypothesis in the research laboratory. Program evaluators have encountered a number of problems in the conduct of their work that threaten to discredit the results of their evaluations. Through the years, they have also discovered approaches to their work that can minimize the inherent problems involved (Caro, 1971; Suchman, 1967; Weiss, 1972a,b).

Why should the problems and solutions of program evaluators be of concern to us in design research? Because frequently, we are involved in attempts to evaluate the behavioral impact of built environments. I anticipate that our concern with such behavioral evaluations will increase during the next 10 or 15 years. To a large extent, the evaluation of environmental designs is similar in procedure to the evaluation of social action programs. Not only are the methods similar, but the problems involved are similar. I refer here not to basic research in the design area but to evaluation research--for example, assessment of building performance in terms of user behavior. If we can anticipate the problems that we will encounter in our efforts at design evaluation, then we will have a chance at saving much wasted effort---especially when ways to minimize or circumvent these problems have been demonstrated.

It should be clear at this point that I refer to evaluation of a design's impact on human behavior--on what people actually do. I am far less interested in cognitive processes such as how people perceive their surroundings and how satisfied they feel with where they spend their time. Still, I recognize the value of such internal dimensions in helping to explain why building users behave as they do. It should be clear that this paper does not address evaluations which do not require any assessment of user behavior. Thus assessment studies of structural strength, compatibility of materials, and aesthetic preferences are specifically excluded from this discussion. My concern here with user behavior implies an important assumption--namely, that the design of setting does influence what the setting's inhabitants do. Different possible designs can result in different patterns of user behavior as a direct function of the design itself. Previous research has offered only weak support for this assumption (Gutman, 1966; Michelson, 1970). However, evidence for environmental influence is mounting for such behaviors as accidents and conversation, and for such user groups as the aged and the handicapped. Clearly, this area is far from fully researched.

Discussion of evaluation occurs occasionally in the design literature (Lang, Burnette, Moleski, & Vachon, 1974; Sommer, 1972; Zeisel, 1975) and examples of design evaluations appear from time to time (Heyward, Rothenberg, & Beasley, 1974; Trites, 1969). But there has been virtually no airing of the issues separating successful from unsuccessful evaluation, and the closely related literature on program evaluation has received too little attention in discussions of design evaluation. A major purpose of this paper is to stimulate discussion of the relevant issues from the field of program evaluation. We have much to gain in the way of improved evaluation.

2. WHO NEEDS EVALUATION AND WHY?

One of the first concerns of the evaluator should be to determine who needs evaluation and for what purpose. This is important information simply because the type of evaluation that will be appropriate depends on the level of organization requesting it and the kind of decision involved. One may say that this is a trivial admonition. But reflect for a moment on texts you have encountered giving advice on research methods. You probably encountered information on how to operationalize measures, what methods to use in gathering data, what research plan to follow in timing the data collection, how to choose the sample of subjects, and how to analyze and summarize the resulting data. But you most likely encountered no information on how the conduct of the research depends on who needs it. In evaluation research this information is critical. Failure to attend to this information could result in weeks or months of careful evaluative research producing a report that will never be read by those who asked for it. Suppose a federal agency requests evaluation of the use of open-classroom schools. A report is needed detailing the degree to which the open-school buildings facilitate the activities of the open-education program. The federal agency funding the project may simply need to know the extent to which its objectives are actually being met in using tax money earmarked for schools facilitating a particular type of educational program. Suppose, on the other hand, that the evaluation is requested by the architectural firm that is designing the school building. The firm may be less interested in goal attainment and more interested in information that can be used in the future when a similar project is to be designed. They may be most interested in cumulative information that provides them with information on what design assumptions regarding behavior seem to be valid and which ones should be changed or discarded. Consider a third case. Suppose the evaluation is requested by the school system itself. The school administrators are committed to providing education to the community. If the school design falls short of

planned objectives, the administrators can't shut down the schools and send the designers back to the drawing boards. They have to make the best of the existing situation--good or bad. Consequently, they may require evaluation data that provides them with information on what modifications need to be made to the existing facility or program to result in efficient use of the newly-built school building.

It should be clear here that the form an evaluation should take depends on who needs it and how the results are to be used. We can distinguish here between two types of evaluation: summative and formative (Scriven, 1967). Summative evaluation refers to an overall comparison of the extent to which a program, or in our case a building, is fulfilling its intended goals. Basically, the evaluation consists of a comparison of what is actually occurring with what should be occurring. In the case of formative evaluation, on the other hand, the problem would not be simply to assess how well a building "works". Rather, the problem would be to understand the nature of the fit between building and user so that this fit can be improved by making modifications or adjustments to the building. Formative evaluation would be most appropriate where buildings are purposely made with future adjustments in mind based on evaluative information, or where a few buildings are to be constructed as a pilot project before building others. One example of the former case is the practice of leaving walkways around campus buildings uncompleted until students have indicated where the walkways should be placed by wearing paths in the surrounding grounds.

Identifying the uses of evaluative information in advance can save wasted effort. Usually the results of the evaluation are required for some sort of design decision. The decision may be whether to modify the design for future buildings intended to serve the same function as when a few homes of a housing development are built on a pilot basis. Or the decision may concern whether or not to remodel an existing facility and what specific changes to make. But program evaluators can attest that evaluators are often called into service for entirely different reasons. Sometimes a program administrator needs the evaluators to find evidence justifying the future existence of an ineffective program. The analogous case in the design profession may involve a design firm which wishes to hire evaluators to provide data of a positive nature justifying efficiency of a design in hopes for future federal contracts. In such a case, the design firm may be uninterested in how effective the design actually is; it may just want some scientific-looking evidence that make the design appear affective. Obviously, the design firm would not use or even want a report from the evaluators documenting ways in which the design fell short of its goals concerning inhabitant behavior. It must be stressed here that the evaluators should find out in advance whether negative results are permissible. If not, then the evaluators might be wise to turn down the job. Other reasons for an evaluation include attempts to find fault with a design regardless of its actual value. For example, a political group on seeing inner-city residents relocated as part of an urban redevelopment program might wish to see an evaluation study carried out that will discredit the redevelopment and prevent future relocation of other inner-city residents. Besides attempts to bias evaluation results in a positive or negative direction, occasionally evaluators find that their results are to be ignored altogether. Suchman (1967) has called this "posturing", using evaluation to assume the pose of scientific research and give the appearance of professional sophistication. It is to the evaluator's advantage to spend some time carefully probing the actual reasons for requesting an evaluation before beginning to design the project itself. Generally, this must take the form of frank interviews with individuals involved in the building design and use at several levels.

3. WHAT ARE THE BEHAVIORAL OBJECTIVES OF THE DESIGN?

One of the trickiest problems in the program evaluation area is that of defining the goals of the program. Goal definition must come before any attempt to determine whether the program goals are being met, or even when and how to measure them. The problem is that the individuals who design and administer social action programs often do not have clear and specific objectives in mind. For example, they may have only vague notions of improving the condition of the program's target population in any of a number of ways. It is the task of the evaluator to meet with the program developers and try to get them to specify the program objectives in such a way that measures can be made of how well the program is meeting these objectives. In the case of design evaluation, the situation is little better. Room labels are frequently as close as the designer comes to specifying just what behaviors are expected to occur in a proposed building. Further, there is no set of accepted principles in the design profession making explicit the various structural features that facilitate or impede certain desirable and undesirable behaviors. Instead of a set of known design principles, each designer is left with intuition and previous experiences, different intuitions, and rarely any systematic information to guide them in their decisions concerning the relation of structural features to behavior. As a result, the evaluator is confronted with a challenging task defining the behavioral objectives of a built environment. The problem is further confounded by the frequent use of visual rather than verbal modes of communication in the design profession. Perspective drawings and mat-board models are ineffective in describing the

behavior of building users. When people appear in such visual communication aids, the behavior is all too often passive sitting, standing, or walking--hardly an exhaustive display of the behavioral repetoire intended of users.

It is generally necessary for the evaluator to meet several times with those requesting the evaluation to define the goals in such a way as to make them measureable. To say that a building design should encourage efficient performance by its inhabitants is inadequate. There are too many ways to define efficiency and no indication of what sort of performance the evaluator should examine. Thus, the evaluator's task often involves an effort to get the objectives of a program (or building) redefined in the direction of greater detail and specificity. Often, this means moving toward behavioral definitions. In the case of efficiency as an objective, one must decide what is efficient behavior and how to distinguish it from inefficient behavior.

There is a problem that may develop in working with designers to define the goals of a built environment. Under pressure from the evaluator, the designers may actually be making up the goals on the spot. When the behavioral objectives are decided upon after the design is completed, one can expect less committment to these post hoc goals than would be the case if the goals were foremost in the designer's mind throughout the design phase of the project. If things don't go well during the evaluation--if the environment does not seem to be performing as intended--then it is all too easy for the designers to change the goals to fit the data. They can simply say: "That isn't what we intended. Actually we meant for the users to act just as the evaluator's data show they are acting." Given this possible state of affairs, would it not be better to simply dispense with objectives altogether? Why not just go into the environment-user system after construction is completed and see how the environment is performing? Not only is the problem of goal definition avoided, but the evaluator is free to note unintended effects of the environment as well. For example, the evaluation might focus on variables such as accidents and aggressive behavior as well as more positive behavioral dimensions. Avoiding goals altogether is undesirable because it leaves the evaluator open to the accusation that the evaluation missed all the intended (and often beneficial) effects of the built environment. Also, the lack of objectives leaves the evaluator with an almost infinite array of possible variables to examine in assessing the effects of the environment. Of course, the evaluator can supplement measurement of intended effects by measurement of other variables deemed important based on theory or previous research. For example, one might include in the evaluation of a radial-plan hospital variables such as nurse travel time between nursing station and patients--a variable for which there are intended effects. But in addition, the evaluator might study variables related to general quality of the patient's life such as variety of activities engaged in and number of different settings entered.

4. CHOOSING A PLAN FOR DATA COLLECTION

At first thought, the actual task of collecting data on user behavior seems fairly straight-forward. One need merely observe how an environment is being used, then compare its use with a list of intended uses. Then, the evaluation report is made favorable or unfavorable depending on whether user behavior falls short of or meets the behavioral objectives. Unfortunately, the situation is not quite so simple as this for a number of reasons. The problem is that one needs to know not only what users are doing but why they are doing what they are doing. This brings us into the messy area of causality--what causes people to behave as they do? If the environment is being evaluated, then we need to know whether it is causing people to behave as intended. But when we observe user behavior, we can't tell whether the behavior is caused by certain aspects of the built environment or by other factors, such as the type of people who are users, the users' past experience with other settings, the particular set of rules or program for user behavior, or what. The situation is confounded all the more because we know that behavior often has more than one cause. What we do is influenced not only by where we are, but by who we are with, what we think is expected of us, how we feel, and a number of other factors. All may interact to influence our actions. This state of affairs leads statisticians to speak in terms of the proportion of variance in a given behavior that can be attributed to each of several possible determinants. It leads design evaluators to lie awake at night and ponder why the world can't be simpler. But all is not lost. We do know that sometimes the physical environment has clear effects on human behavior. The construction of stairs can have much to do with the frequence of slips and falls of users. The placement of a church collection box can influence the amount of money contributed by worshippers. The evaluator must plan the schedule for measuring user behavior in a way that will make as clear as possible the role that the physical setting plays in influencing user behavior. Depending on when and how the necessary measurements are made, one can obtain evidence as to how a built environment is influencing user behavior.

We can illustrate this point by reference to the two most frequent evaluation problems, that of evaluating a newly built environment and that of assessing the effects of a remodeling project. The task of evaluating a newly built environment is most difficult. Once people begin using the environment, any data gathered is beset by the already mentioned difficulty of deciding what behavior is influenced by the physical setting and what isn't. One way to handle this problem is to interview users,

simply asking them how the building helps or hinders their attempts to behave as they wish. Sometimes people are accurate at identifying the determinants of their behavior, but only sometimes. Another way to assign causal status to structural features is to locate other environments similar in function and observe how they are used. The comparison of user behavior in the evaluated building with other similar buildings can aid in determining whether users act as they do because of building features or because of other reasons. For example, if a comparison building differs structurally but has a very similar user population (according to variables such as age, education, and socioeconomic status), then it is less likely that differences in building use are due to the type of user. Similarly, if the program, the set of rules by which people know what they are expected to do, is similar in the comparison building, then differences in behavior are less likely a function of the program and more likely a function of the physical setting. Ideally, the evaluator would locate comparison settings that are similar to the evaluated setting in every way except for features of the physical structure. If everything else is the same, then one can ascribe differences in behavior with relatively more confidence to the physical setting itself. Gutman and Westergaard (1974) used this approach in their study of academic research buildings. Assuming similar occupant populations and similar tasks, the different responses to the buildings were more likely actually causally related to the physical features of the buildings. A major task for the evaluator in using this comparison-group research plan is to locate similar environments, obtain permission to gather data in them, and obtain the needed funds from the persons who are paying for the evaluation. The added cost for increased confidence in causal relationships can be considerable.

The second type of research problem involves assessing the impact of a remodeling project. In this situation, one needs to gather data before and after remodeling and see if the changes in behavior meet what was expected. Assuming that the user population does not change appreciably during remodeling and that the behavioral program remains constant, then changes can be considered likely to be caused by the design change. Increased confidence in this assertion can be made if the assessments of building use are made at several times before and after the remodeling. If the behavior changes only at the time of remodeling, one can be even more sure of the effects of the remodeling. Even with this type of research plan, it is best to obtain a comparison group--in this case, a similar setting which did not experience remodeling, or at least not at the same time. Behavioral changes that occur following remodeling in the evaluated setting should not occur at the same time in the comparison settings. Further plans and experimental designs for data-gathering are available in publications by Campbell and Stanley (1963) and by Bechtel

(1974). The need for careful attention to the choice of plan for data-gathering cannot be over-emphasized in design evaluation. With the designers implicit assumption that the physical design does influence its inhabitants, it is all too easy to observe user behavior and glibly ascribe it to the design--ignoring the myriad of other possible causes which can provide competing explanations for user behavior. Unless the design evaluator is willing to argue forcefully for a good research plan, the final evaluation report is in danger of giving a very misleading picture of the behavioral performance of a built environment. Perhaps user behavior will be accurately described, but its ties to the specific design features will be left in serious question.

5. CHOICE OF MEASURES

Choosing the appropriate measuring instruments is especially difficult in design evaluation because this field is so new. However, there are some considerations from the area of program evaluation that should be heeded. One of the most important things to do in program evaluation is to specify the program. Generally the actual program varies considerably from the intended program. Similarly, the final built environment may be quite different from its original design due to a number of factors such as availability of materials and construction costs. Therefore, measures of user behavior should be accompanied by measures of the built environment.

The actual measures made will depend to a large extent on the goals or objectives of the design. But whatever the goals, the measurement phase of the evaluation will probably involve some sort of systematic observation of user behavior. This might take the form of trained observers using the behavior mapping technique (Ittelson, Rivlin, & Proshansky, 1970) and possibly having a sample of the user population fill out activity records of some sort (Michelson & Reed, 1975). One question confronting the evaluator is whether to use direct measures of behavior (like direct observation) or to rely on cognitive measures (satisfaction with an environment). The answer to this question is that both can be useful. One particular role that cognitive measures can play is in helping to explain user behavior. To some extent, we behave as we do because of our intentions and perceptions. Thus the evaluator can learn much by asking inhabitants (by means of interview or questionnaire) about their beliefs and intentions concerning their activities in the setting of interest.

There is a particular danger in the use of cognitive measures. They are relatively easy to use--far easier than direct observation in many cases. Probably one of the easiest ways to gather data is to slap together a questionnaire of items that seem reasonable and pass it out to the user population. Since such cognitive

techniques are so easy, evaluators are likely to dispense with the more difficult behavioral measures. They can obtain data on how people respond to a setting in terms of satisfaction with the environment, then assume that behavioral performance varies directly with satisfaction. The assumption is that satisfied people perform well and dissatisfied people perform poorly. Unfortunately, this relationship rarely holds up when it is checked carefully. In fact, it has been shown that cognitive measures and the behaviors that follow from them frequently appear to be independent dimensions. (Mischel, 1968; Wicker, 1969) For this reason, the evaluator must carefully validate any cognitive measure that is intended to provide indirect data about user behavior. For example, if one wanted to use user estimates of their own activities in a setting (a cognitive dimension), then for at least a sample of users, measures of their behavior must also be made directly (a behavioral dimension). This allows the evaluator to check out the accuracy of user estimates and make sure they provide data on actual user behavior. Potential methods have been summarized by Michelson (1975) and are described in previous EDRA proceedings.

Even when measures are carefully validated in the early stages of an evaluation project, each measure has its shortcomings. Observation sometimes influences the behavior of the observed persons, and questionnaires suffer from all sorts of biases such as central tendency, halo effect, and leniency error--not to mention low reliability. Because of the inherent imperfection of current measures in evaluation projects, the evaluator is well advised to use more than one measure for each dimension where possible. Hence, behavioral mapping can be supplemented by time budgets and interviews to get a more complete and accurate picture of user behavior. Examples of the use of multiple measures can be found in Heyward's study of three playgrounds (Heyward, et al., 1974) and Van der Ryn's study of college dormitories (Van der Ryn & Murray, 1967).

6. COOPERATION

One problem that particularly plagues program evaluators is that of gaining the cooperation of program administrators and staff (Aronson & Sherwood, 1967). It is hard for the academician who does research in laboratories with college-student subjects to appreciate the difficulties that arise in field studies of an evaluative nature. The lack of cooperation shown by program administrators may be partly justified. It is certainly true that evaluation reports frequently report only that social action programs have had no measureable impact despite the thousands of tax-payer dollars that go to support them. Thus the evaluator is seen as a very real threat to the program's continued existence. As design research becomes more commonplace, evaluators may encounter a lack of cooperation with two groups--the designers and the environment users. It is possible that designers would resent the evaluator's presence because the evaluator poses a threat of sorts. After all, the designer believes in the design. The designer's reputation is at stake if the design proves to be a failure--the more so if the design involves expensive construction. The evaluator serves as a reminder that the design may not perform as expected and the evaluator would be just the one to bring any shortcomings to light. This places a burden on both parties to understand the position of the other. Certainly the designer should realize that the evaluator can provide useful information that can be applied to future designs, making them more effective than they would be otherwise. The evaluator needs to have a healthy respect for the somewhat vulnerable position of the designer. The literature on the differing viewpoints of the behavioral scientist and the architect can be of use in helping to sensitize the evaluator and designer to each other's positions (Altman, 1973; Gutman, 1972). It can also be valuable for the evaluator to make sure that the evaluation data is of use to the designer. This may require special effort in gathering data of interest to the designer. Another important way to encourage cooperation is to give the designer as active a role as possible in designing the evaluation plan from the outset.

The other group that may not always be completely sympathetic and helpful to the evaluation project is the design user. Argyris (1968) has discussed some of the ways in which research subjects respond in an undesirable manner to the requests of the researcher. The situation of the design user is similar to that of the research subject. The user can perceive the evaluator's attempts at gathering data as an unpleasant burden from the bothersome task of filling out forms to the invasion of privacy aspect of direct observation. Further, it is easy for the evaluator's intentions to be misread. Industrial studies have shown that people in their jobs may see the evaluator as a lacky of the management, gathering data preliminary to increasing the employees' workload. Design users may show similar suspicion of the evaluation. The best way to gain the cooperation of the users is to involve them in the evaluation project at an early stage. This may take the form of working with representatives of the user population. For example, if one wanted to evaluate the ill-fated Pruitt-Igoe housing project in St. Louis soon after it was built, one might worry about the cooperation of a transient group of lower-socioeconomic inhabitants. It would be wise to recruit some Pruitt-Igoe residents to explain what was needed and to find out how best to contact a sufficiently large sample of residents for the evaluation. Another way to encourage cooperation is to make sure that the residents receive something of value to them for cooperating in the evaluation project. For example, people

could be paid a few dollars for keeping time budgets. If children were to be observed in the play areas, then parents could be given feedback on their children's behavior. It takes some imagination on the evaluator's part to find ways to reward all who give something of their time and effort to provide evaluation data. Yet the return in cooperation and better data for the evaluator and for future projects with the same people makes the effort worthwhile.

7. HANDLING THE RESULTS

In most academic research, handling the results of a study is almost routine. The investigator presents the findings in a paper at the next professional meeting and sends a report in a standard format to the appropriate journal. Handling the results of an evaluation study is not quite so simple. The purpose of an evaluation study is usually to provide data needed in making certain decisions--in the case of design evaluation, decisions about future similar designs. However, evaluation reports frequently find their way onto storage shelves or into files without having any impact on decisions of any kind. An interesting example of how evaluation data can be handled is reported in Weiss (1972c). In 1940, the RAF Bomber Command was using aerial photography to evaluate the effectiveness of bombing raids. Photos were examined for aircraft that had reported their bombs on target. The photographic evidence indicated that only 25% of these "on target" aircraft even got within 5 miles of the target. One officer responded to this evaluation data by refusing to accept the report. Apparently it was less threatening to discredit the evaluation than it was to accommodate some undesirable and upsetting findings. Program evaluators can provide many more examples of rejected evaluation findings. This relates back to the discussion of why the evaluation is being conducted. If only positive results are acceptable, it is best to find this out ahead of time before wasting precious energy on a serious evaluation effort. It cannot be emphasized too strongly in this regard that one must find out at the outset who needs the evaluation results and what they intend to do with them. There are other ways in which the results can be made more acceptable. If it is possible to set up a situation in which several alternative designs are compared simultaneously, then the results may be more palitable. For example, one might design and evaluate several student dormatory arrangements on a pilot basis before embarking on design and construction of the rest of the dormatories that are scheduled to be built. Picking the best of several plans is less threatening to the designer's ego than placing a single design on a spot on a single good--bad continuum.

The actual mode of presenting evaluation reports can influence the impact of a study. The evaluator usually must present the evaluation findings to a group of decision makers who are less knowledgable about research techniques and statistical analyses. Thus the report should not be phrased in terms of research jargon. It is best to present a summary of the findings with charts, graphs, and photographs to illustrate the major points. The details on methods and analysis can be presented in a set of appendices for those who are interested. When presenting to designers, the evaluator must be aware that the design profession is familiar with visual displays as a means of communication. The factor should be made use of by presenting the findings on the designers terms through visual displays. Afterall, the goal in dissemination of results is to communicate effectively, not to achieve satisfaction with an elegant and sophisticated research report. The designers may be impressed by scientific elegance, but they won't use the data.

Another important point in presenting the findings is to draw out the implications of the findings clearly. Researchers are used to maintaining a cautious position with respect to their data. Since one can never be absolutely certain of the generality of one's findings, the researcher is usually reluctant to state the implications of the findings in strong terms. The evaluator, on the other hand, cannot afford the luxury of presenting data and leaving the reader to draw the conclusions. The cost of doing so would probably result in an evaluation without any substantial impact. For this reason, the evaluator should consider the implications of the findings and make very clear recommendations based on the report. The evaluator may even have to become an advocate of the report's findings if the evaluation effort is to have a meaningful impact.

One particularly vexing problem about evaluation data is that evaluation reports too often do not get published--hence, they do not become readily available to others. Since the information does not get out, it is difficult for the results of evaluation to be cumulative. Design evaluation is unlikely to result in a costly change to an already built environment. The value of the information lies in its impact upon future building projects. Thus, it is important that evaluation findings become available to others in the profession. There is no easy solution to this problem. Journal editors are often reluctant to accept the results of evaluation studies on the grounds that they may be of little relevance to theory development and pertinent only to the evaluated setting. Other possible outlets should be explored, including selected bibliographies such as those compiled by the Council of Planning Librarians and computor information storage facilities. (See Sommer, 1972)

8. SUMMARY AND CONCLUSIONS

With the increase in evaluative studies involving built environments as their target, we can anticipate a rediscovery of many of the problems common to program evaluation research in education and sociology. Environmental publications such as the EDRA proceedings have produced a number of discussions of the use of behavioral research methods in design research. However, only a few of these publications have specifically focused on evaluation research in built environments. (e.g., Gutman & Westergaard, 1974; Sommer, 1972; Zeisel, 1975) Only a few of the issues peculiar to evaluation research have been aired thus far. It is hoped that this paper has served to present some of the other considerations that the design evaluator should ponder before embarking on an evaluation project. The importance of finding out who needs the evaluation and why has been stressed. The reasons given include the fact that evaluators are often called into action for reasons other than that someone needs assessment data on a built environment. Sometimes the reasons for the evaluation are clearly political. Formative and summative evaluation were proposed as two possible types of evaluation that may be required. The need for and difficulty of obtaining measurable design goals was discussed since evaluation generally requires some comparison with what occurred and what was intended to occur. Some of the difficulties in choosing a plan for data collection were covered. Comparison or control environments were advocated as an aid in determining what role the physical environment plays in influencing user behavior. The reader was advised to avoid unvalidated cognitive measures when the goal of evaluation is to assess user behavior, not just user satisfaction. Problems of lack of cooperation in evaluation research were presented. Including designers and users in evaluation decisions was advanced as one technique for eliciting cooperation. Finally, the problem of presenting evaluation results in such a way that they will not be ignored was noted along with suggestions for handling this problem; these included attention to presentation format, knowledge of who will use the results, and making clear recommendations that follow from the data.

This paper is not meant to be an exhaustive coverage of all the pertinent issues in program evaluation of which design evaluators should be aware. The author has prepared an annotated bibliography that will serve as a guide to the program evaluation literature for those in the man-environment research (Campbell, 1975). Attention to the already extant literature in program evaluation should have a beneficial impact in making future design evaluation studies of maximum use to environmental researchers and to the design profession.

References

ALTMAN, I. Some perspectives on the study of man-environment phenomena. Representative Research in Social Psychology, 1973, 4, 109-126.

ARGRYIS, C. Some unintended consequences of rigorous research. Psychological Bulletin, 1968, 70, 185-197.

ARONSON, S. H., & SHERWOOD, C. C. Researcher vs. practitioner: Problems in social action research. Social Work, 1967, 12, 89-96.

BECHTEL, R. B. Experimental methods in environmental design research. In J. Lang, C. Burnette, W. Moleski, & D. Vachon (Eds.), Designing for human behavior: Architecture and the behavioral sciences. Stroudsburg, Penn.: Dowden, Hutchinson & Ross, 1974.

CAMPBELL, D. E. Evaluation research in man-environment systems: An annotated bibliography. Unpublished manuscript, 1975.

CAMPBELL, D. T., & STANLEY, J. C. Experimental and quasi-experimental designs for research. Chicago: Rand McNally, 1963.

CARO, F. G. Readings in evaluation research. New York: Russell Sage, 1971.

GUTMAN, R. Site planning and social behavior. Journal of Social Issues, 1966, 4, 103-115.

GUTMAN, R. The questions architects ask. In R. Gutman (Ed.), People and buildings. New York: Basic, 1972.

GUTMAN, R., & WESTERGAARD, B. Building evaluation, user satisfaction, and design. In J. Lang, C. Burnette, W. Moleski, & D. Vachon (Eds.), Designing for human behavior: Architecture and the behavioral sciences. Stroudsburg, Penn.: Dowden, Hutchinson & Ross, 1974.

HEYWARD, D. G., ROTHENBURG, M., & BEASLEY, P. R. Children's play and urban playground environments: A comparison of traditional, contemporary, and adventure playground types. Environment and Behavior, 1974, 6, 131-168.

ITTELSON, W. H., RIVLIN, L. G., & PROSHANSKY, H. M. The use of behavioral maps in environmental psychology. In H. M. Proshansky, W. H. Ittelson, & L. G. Rivlin (Eds.), Environmental psychology: Man and his physical setting. New York: Holt, 1970.

LANG, J., BURNETTE, C., MOLESKI, W., & VACHON, D. (Eds.). Designing for human behavior: Architecture and the behavioral sciences. Stroudsburg, Penn.: Dowden, Hutchinson & Ross, 1974.

MICHELSON, W. Man and his urban environment. Reading, Mass.: Addison-Wesley, 1970.

MICHELSON, W. (Ed.). Behavioral research methods in environmental design. Stroudsburg, Penn.: Dowden, Hutchinson & Ross, 1975.

MICHELSON, W., & REED, P. The time budget. In W. Michelson (Ed.), Behavioral research methods in environmental design. Stroudsburg, Penn.: Dowden, Hutchinson & Ross, 1975.

MISCHEL, W. Personality and assessment. New York: Wiley, 1968.

SCRIVEN, M. The methodology of evaluation. In R. W. Tyler, R. M. Gagne, & M. Scriven (Eds.), Perspectives of curriculum evaluation. AREA Monograph Series on Curriculum Evaluation, No. 1. Chicago: Rand McNally, 1967.

SOMMER, R. Design awareness. Corte Madera, Calif.: Rinehart,Press, 1972.

STRUENING, E. L., & GUTTENTAG, M. (Eds.). Handbook of evaluation research. Beverly Hills, CA: Sage, 1975.

SUCHMAN, E. A. Evaluative research. New York: Russell Sage Foundation, 1967.

TRITES, D. K. Radial nursing units prove best in controlled study. Modern Hospital, 1969, 112, 94-99.

VAN DER RYN, S., & MURRAY, S. Dorms at Berkeley: An environmental analysis. Berkeley, CA: Center for Planning and Development Research, University of California, 1967.

WEISS, C. H. Evaluation research. Englewood Cliffs, N. J.: Prentice-Hall, 1972a.

WEISS, C. H. (Ed.). Evaluating action programs: Readings in social action and education. Boston: Allyn & Bacon, 1972b.

WEISS, C. H. Utilization of evaluation: Toward comparative study. In C. H. Weiss (Ed.), Evaluating action programs: Readings in social action and education. Boston: Allyn & Bacon, 1972c.

WICKER, A. W. Attitudes vs. actions: The relationship of overt and behavioral responses to attitude objects. Journal of Social Issues, 1969, 25, 41-78.

WORTMAN, P. M. Evaluation research: A psychological perspective. American Psychologist, 1975, 30, 562-575.

ZEISEL, J. Sociology and architectural design. New York: Russell Sage, 1975.

A SOCIAL SERVICE DELIVERY MODEL: PLANNING FOR CORRECTIONS

Anna Walkey
Michael Carley
Richard Roberts
Jay Bancroft

Cornerstone Planning Group Limited
22 Creekhouse, Granville Island
Vancouver, B.C.
Canada   V6H 3M5

ABSTRACT

This paper details a process for the development
of planning options for the regional delivery of
corrections services. The impetus for the
design was the desire of a provincial
corrections branch to shift away from traditional
crisis-oriented planning while pursuing their
goals of replacing institutional based services
with community based services.

This process involves the development of a data
base, including an offender profile based on
statistical analysis. The data base is
integrated with current corrections goals and
policies. A service delivery model is
developed, and graphically illustrates the
implications on an existing corrections system
of relocating some offenders from regional
security institutions to local community based
services. By combining previously listed
policy assumptions, present offender counts,
peak load factors, and population projection
indices, the model outlines a framework for
demonstrating the numbers of offenders that will
need to be serviced by a potential range of
program and facility options.

INTRODUCTION - CONTEXT

In December of 1972, following a provincial
election and change in government, a task force
was established by the Attorney-General of
British Columbia. This Task Force on
Correctional Services and Facilities examined
the situation of persons found in conflict with
the law in B.C. and made a series of
recommendations.

The reports of the task force stressed the
inter-relationship of all components of the
justice system and the need for integrated
planning to reflect this. Recommendations for
change were made in a number of areas
including:

1. the role of the police, the courts and
    corrections;
2. the general operation of corrections
    services; and
3. services provided for special offenders

such as drug addicts, women and native
people.

The task force also called for the establishment
of an administrative body responsible for
coordination of justice system planning. The
Justice Development Commission was legislated
into being in early 1974 and charged with this
task. The philosophy behind the commission was
change oriented rather than reactive-adjustment
oriented.

The provincial Corrections Branch of the
Department of the Attorney-General, responsible
for all pretrial custody and for all persons
sentenced to less than two years, supported this
thrust toward change. This was reflected in
A Five Year Plan in Corrections (Corrections
Branch, 1974) which suggested two phases for
revising the services of the Corrections Branch.
The planning and development phase would be
followed by an operational phase during which
there would be changes in the administrative
structure of the Corrections Branch. The
philosophy underlying the Five Year Plan was one
of emphasis on the rational development of
community based programs under regional
administration as alternatives to institutionalization.

A planning division for corrections was
established to provide resources, coordination
and direction in the development of the Five
Year Plan. Of immediate concern was the
development of a planning process for the
coordinated reorganization of the delivery of
corrections services. Specifically, this meant
the eventual phasing down of the inmate
populations in the four large institutions in
B.C.

The authors were retained as consultants in mid
1974 to assist in developing this planning
process. Primary consideration was given to
preparing for the diversion of non-violent and/or
short term, first time offenders from maximum
and medium security facilities.

SERVICE DELIVERY MODEL

Problem Definition

The process seen to be most productive in

implementing the objective was the development of a general model for coordinating the wide range of tasks necessary for any decentralization of services (see Figure 1). The process outlined in the model establishes a data base and develops future projections of service users by employing average numbers, peak factors, percentage distributions and criteria derived from the data base analysis. The possibility of modifying the criteria through subsequent policy input is built into the model. To date, the model has been partially applied in a number of corrections regions in B.C.

In place of specific policy statements needed to constrain and direct the process, assumptions were made from current Corrections Branch philosphy as outlined in A Five Year Plan in Corrections (task 4). These were chosen with respect to their effect on altering the present custody/community based offender population ratios in the planning region. These were "likely" assumptions regarding policy changes; different assumptions could be made, and the results could also be demonstrated through the use of the model. The most important assumptions were:

1. That community alternatives to security custody be developed for first time and/or minor offenders.
2. That offenders who are a threat to society or to themselves be held in a range of small security facilities.
3. That all individuals placed in community

alternatives be located as close as possible to the community in which they reside.
4. That pretrial offenders will be physically and functionally separated from sentenced offenders.
5. That community-based alternatives to pretrial confinement will be developed for those persons who are not a threat to society or themselves.
6. That those persons who are to be transferred to other government departments (i.e. Human Resources, Immigration, etc.) be immediately removed from Corrections Branch supervision, or that some formal arrangement be made for accommodating them within the system.

Part of the problem definition included outlining the data base requirements (task 3). Much of this base would be of educational value for corrections administrators; some parts would be important inputs to the service delivery model.

The data base consisted of four essential components:

1. Regional demographic data.
2. Community issues and available resources.
3. A profile of the users of corrections services in the region during the study period.
4. An international survey of corrections programs appropriate for use within the province.

These components were laid out in a series of four volumes (Cornerstone, 1974-75).

FIGURE 1: SERVICE DELIVERY MODEL - DECENTRALIZING A SERVICE DELIVERY SYSTEM

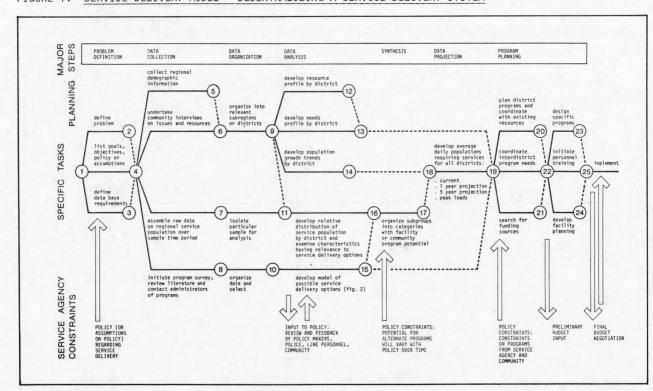

Data Collection and Organization (Tasks 5 through 11)

Regional maps were developed from the assembly of data on existing educational institutions, hospitals, mental health units, employment counselling centres, major industries, and Indian reservations. Social service and justice system facilities were recorded at the community level. Demographic data such as ethnic origin, age, sex, etc. were noted at the community level as well, and included a series of one and five year projections based on Census Canada data and on work done recently at the B.C. Research Council (1974). These data were also mapped to illustrate regional patterns.

Further input on communities was obtained from an interview schedule. Corrections line staff, social workers, police and others interacting with the justice system gave information on issues and local resources then in use.

Another area of the data base concerned an international survey of relevant corrections programs at the community level which was done by a review of existing literature and direct correspondence with program administrators. Primary consideration was given to evaluated programs designed to divert non-violent individuals from custody situations. A notable characteristic of these programs was the effort to restore the relationship between the offender and the conflict situation. Also of importance was the provision of social and medical programs for problem situations no longer considered criminal.

The most important component of the data base was derived from available information on the users of corrections services in the region.

This consisted of information recorded at the time an individual was admitted to, transferred within, or discharged from the system. The variables covered personal data, admissions and offence data, transfer and discharge data. Personal data included age, sex, race, marital status, occupation, last address and educational level. The admissions data included place and date of admission, court location, number of previous adult convictions, and twenty-one "status on admission" codes. The primary groupings for status on admission were pretrial and sentenced. Further codes were recorded as: returned from bail, sentenced in default of fine, sentenced from Adult Court, sentenced from Family Court and others.

The offence data consisted of 115 possible offences from the Criminal Code of Canada grouped in 12 categories, determined in light of the severity of the offence. A first run of the data exposed the eight to ten offences with which the great majority of offenders were charged. Many of these minor offence types, such as drunken driving and theft under $200, were

also those viewed as most suitable for custody alternatives.

Transfer data simply consisted of locations and numbers of transfers within the system. Discharge data included the date of discharge from the corrections system and 23 "status on discharge" codes. The most common discharge status was "sentence completed", but also of note were the individuals admitted to pretrial custody and subsequently released to bail or on their own recognizance (O/R).

After a viewing of univariate information, the total corrections admissions sample was broken down for analysis. The two major subgroups, those admitted to institutions and those admitted to community corrections on probation programs, both required analysis to determine total community program numbers. The probation sample represented persons already involved in community based programs and, in effect, comprised an existing case load that would have to be expanded to accommodate clients redistributed from institutions. It was necessary therefore to develop distributions of average probation admissions from the sample in order to project the future demands they would generate for community programs. To these numbers were added the increased load generated by the candidates for community programs drawn from institutional admissions. The analysis required to produce these figures is described below.

Data Analysis, Synthesis and Projection (Tasks 12 through 19)

An analysis of the demographic and community information led to a description of resources, service needs, and growth trends by district in the region. At the same time, a model of possible service delivery options for the justice system was developed from the data collected in the survey of relevant corrections programs (Figure 2). This model served as a framework for a review of policy assumptions and a guideline for the direction that the service planning might take.

As outlined in Figure 3, the institutional sample, divided into pretrial and sentenced persons, then was examined for characteristics of offence severity and sentence type and length. The relationship between these variables was explored and the outcome revealed that the majority of offenders were under 30 years of age and were admitted to the institution on relatively minor charges for short periods of time. In fact, many were serving time in custody in default of paying a fine levied by the court.

In the analysis, it became apparent that three levels of severity occur in the offence categories. Minor offences, which included over half of the sample, were breaking and entering, theft under $200, most public morals charges, mischief, and motor vehicle related

FIGURE 2: MODEL OF SERVICE DELIVERY OPTIONS FOR
THE JUSTICE SYSTEM

FIGURE 3: THE INSTITUTIONAL SAMPLE

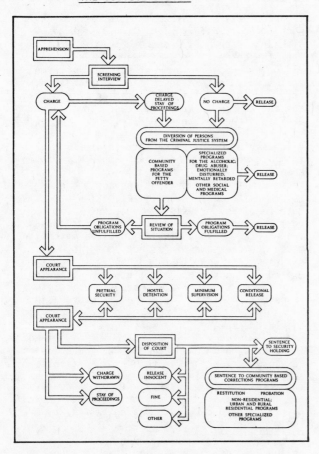

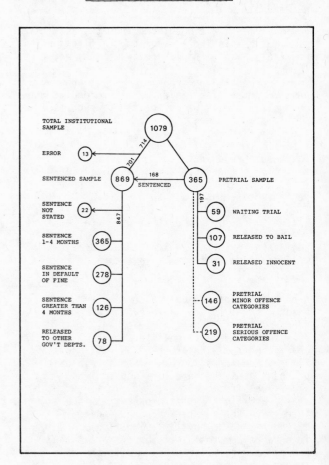

offences. Severe or potentially violent
offences, such as rape, murder, or arson, made
up only about 10%. The remaining offence types
fell between these categories. In this manner,
potential candidates for community alternatives
were identified.

Patterns of daily counts and admissions to the
institution of pretrial and sentenced persons
were examined over the study time period to
develop averages. Maximum figures were
considered as well, to provide peak load
factors.

Leading further toward decentralization and the
placing of persons in community alternatives,
the distribution of the sample was analyzed by
court location and last address. Groupings of
these locations were developed to coincide with
the demographic breakdown of districts in the
region, and population projections for those
districts were applied to the distributions of
average counts.

The map in Figure 4 illustrates the projected
average number of sentenced persons in the
region. Assuming that the crime rate increases
in direct proportion to the increase in
population and that sentencing procedures remain
the same, these figures give an indication of

the daily count of sentenced persons that will
need services or facilities in each local area.

It is estimated, for example, that the major
city in the region, with a population of 60,000,
should provide new services for a count of 64
sentenced persons in 1976, and 68 in 1981. The
projected corrections service delivery needs
for this city are illustrated in Figure 5. A
total daily count of 89 persons is indicated
for 1981, most of them sentenced offenders. The
majority of these probably would be sentenced on
minor charges, such as described earlier, and
could be diverted from custody facilities to
community programs of probation, restitution,
education or work release. Others would
qualify for minimal supervision in residential
settings, perhaps combined with a program
involvement. A relatively small number would
be sentenced on serious offences and custody
facilities may be required for about 10
persons. Also, with the cooperation of other
government departments, it would be possible
to transfer some offenders directly from
court to utilize more appropriate services.

Projected pretrial numbers for this city also
are outlined in Figure 5. The total average
daily count for 1981 would be about 21 persons.
Those persons charged with serious offences

form the greater proportion and security detention would be needed for some with programs of minimal supervision or conditional release for others.

In order to project the maximum number of potential clients for services (task 19), peak load factors were developed for each area distribution from an analysis of peaks experienced over the sample time period studied. In Figure 5, to determine the maximum daily pretrial count expected, the average pretrial numbers would be multiplied by the peak factor of 1.75.

(NOTE: A distribution of the sentenced sample into categories based on sentence length was also considered. The rationale for using this criteria is that short sentences result in net diseconomies to the minor offender and the taxpayer. In the data base analysis wherein this was attempted, the cutoff point for diversion to alternatives was sentences less than or equal to 3 months, including those serving sentence in default of fine. The distribution of offenders in this case paralleled closely the distribution based on offence type for the samples analyzed.)

Program Planning (Tasks 20 through 25)

By combining the projected distributions and groupings of offenders with the resource profiles already developed in the data base, existing programs can be considered for expansion and new programs planned to provide adequately for future service delivery needs. Ideally, the model of service delivery options (Figure 2) is used as a focus for the type and quality of programs to be developed. Interdistrict coordination, funding negotiation and the very important process of responding to and working with community representatives would normally precede the implementation of staff training and facility programming. The confidence exhibited in these negotiations will, in large part, be based on the success with which the overall planning model is used to develop rational and justifiable strategies for service delivery.

UTILITY OF THE PROCESS

As is often the case in political-planning situations, events do not always proceed "rationally". Such is the case in the regions analyzed by the authors. Among other problems, including a change of administration, was a severe downturn in provincial revenues, requiring a curtailment of expansive programs and a concentration on reducing expenditures within the Corrections Branch.

Nevertheless, this planning process seems to have been of value in a number of ways, directly and indirectly. Most significantly and closely in line with its designed intentions, the model

FIGURE 4: PROJECTED AVERAGES OF SENTENCED PERSONS IN THE REGION

has helped corrections decision-makers isolate particular subgroups within the institutional population for planning purposes. This grouping of offenders by offence type, sentence length and actual length of stay, and the attachment of proportional values to the groupings has contributed to a number of policy changes by administrators. Among these changes are special planning for the serious offender, for those serving a sentence in default of fine, and for the drinking driver. Certain facilities within the region were specified as best serving the needs of these subgroups.

FIGURE 5: PROJECTED SERVICE DELIVERY NEEDS

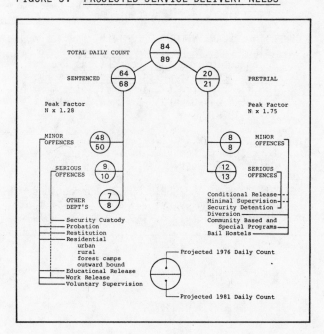

In addition to isolating certain subgroups for specialized planning, the process also served to identify specific community resources which could be utilized by the corrections system. This consisted of a simple regional survey with a record of 26 program variables for each resource, categorized and cross-referenced. By more clearly defining offenders and treatment resources, a matrix of planning options was evolved.

More directly, in the later stages of planning, a number of regional middle-managers became actively involved in the planning process. This was reported to have been of significant value in terms of management integration and in the decentralization of certain decisions.

Most indirectly, but perhaps not least important, the planning process is viewed by some as having established research as a realistic component of corrections activities. Considerable attention is now being given to revising the rather ineffectual corrections data system after it was seen that valuable decision-making inputs could be extracted with some effort.

The authors believe that the planning model has demonstrated its utility sufficiently and when considered in its general form is applicable to the planning process required for the decentralization of most social service delivery systems.

References

ATTORNEY-GENERAL OF BRITISH COLUMBIA, Task Force on Correctional Services and Facilities, 3 vols., February 1973.

BRITISH COLUMBIA RESEARCH COUNCIL, Population Projections 1974-1996, November 1974.

CORNERSTONE PLANNING GROUP LIMITED, The Vancouver Island Justice Region - Demographic and Resource Information, Corrections Program Survey, Community Programs and Opinions, Profile of Corrections Users, Department of the Attorney-General, British Columbia, 1974, 1975.

CORRECTIONS BRANCH, A Five Year Plan in Corrections, Department of the Attorney-General, February 1974.

EKSTEDT, JOHN W. and ROBIN MONTZ, Corrections Planning - An Overview, Department of the Attorney-General, British Columbia, 1974.

MAXIMIZING COST BENEFITS OF POST-CONSTRUCTION

EVALUATION

Edward R. Ostrander, Ph.D.
Bettye Rose Connell, M.S.

Department of Design and
Environmental Analysis
New York State College of Human Ecology
Cornell University
Ithaca, New York

ABSTRACT

Every field has its catch phrases and in terms that are used though the term is ambiguous in meaning. The widespread use of the phrase post-construction evaluation is a current example in the man-environment field. This process is approached here as being most valuable when it is utilized as a means for decision-makers to learn from past experiences. Given the belief that the decision-maker's involvement is a necessary part of post-construction evaluation as applied research, three models are presented and analyzed in terms of their potential to generate beneficial feedback to decision-makers. Suggestions are given for courses of action to bridge the applicability gap.

1. INTRODUCTION

Post-construction evaluation appears to be a form of man-environment research that bridges the applicability gap. This process can best be described as a type of applied research which is an integral part of a larger decision-making process.

This paper addresses two issues. The first argues that the major value of post-construction evaluation is to utilize the research findings as a basis for learning through feedback not as an accountability index. The second is to describe and discuss three evaluation research models that generate feedback of varying degrees of applicability.

2. EVALUATION: LEARNING EXPERIENCE VS

ACCOUNTABILITY

Two opposing philosophies underlie the use of evaluation. It can be used as an accountability index or as a means of learning from past experience. When evaluation is used to determine performance level or to judge quality, it is usually perceived of as a threatening activity. Evaluation in the context of the built environment normally called "post-construction evaluation",

should focus on some aspect of the performance of a building in relation to a set of criteria. Too often evaluation research reports take the form of a catalogue of design mistakes without a clarifying context. Therefore, post-construction evaluation often poses a threat to the architect's and client's professional reputations because of its dollar and cent implications. In this context, it is understandable why so few professionals are interested in having their buildings evaluated. Given that reality, it is not surprising that practitioners view researcher's requests to study their buildings with caution.

If post-construction evaluation research is to be welcomed by practitioners, it must be executed in a non-threatening way and result in a product that is truly of value to the designer and client.

A realistic solution to this problem appears in the notion that Studer (1972) and Brill (1974) advanced when they equated a building with an "experiment". The scientific experiment is a means of creating a controlled situation that reveals to the researcher the relationship between the variables he has manipulated. Each time he carries out an experiment he learns something about the relationship between these variables. Through this cyclical process of alternation and replication, he gains a fuller understanding of the phenomenon under study. A single architectural experiment (or one building) when evaluated, may not tell the architect very much, but a series of experiments (involving a number of buildings) constitutes a learning system that offers both useful feedback and a sense of what direction to take next.

3. PUTTING EVALUATION IN PERSPECTIVE

If one views evaluation as having a definite end which is reached upon completion of judgment, he has rejected the more constructive use of evaluation. Brill (1974) described the two basic aspects of building evaluation to be: 1) gaining information about the usefulness of buildings and 2) using that information in the design and use of new buildings (p. 316). To paraphrase Brill, evaluation is a two-part process which involves making the assessment and transmit the findings from the assessment in a constructive form to decision-makers. An integral aspect of post-construction evaluation is this recycling or feeding back of information from the evaluation activity to the decision-makers so they can use it in future problem-solving. Post-construction evaluation offers a promising means for the design professions to systematically build upon past experience to improve their product.

To develop this perspective of evaluation as a contributor to learning, we must recognize several assumptions that underlie the rationale.

1. For post-construction evaluation to contribute to a learning system the design process is assumed to be open-ended and circular so that past experience in one project will feed into new projects of a similar nature.

2. Post-construction evaluation is an integral part of the design decision-making process, and not an independent activity.

3. For post construction evaluation to produce meaningful and useful feedback, the researcher must: 1) look at the total decision-making process; not just the results of the process and 2) utilize evaluative criteria that reflect issues which served as requirements during decision-making.

Landscape architect, Al Rutledge (1975) has expressed the relationship among these factors as follows.

...design has most often been looked upon as a linear process which expires upon execution of the construction contract. Whereas in reality, the end is not an absolute. It is only a place where the beholder has chosen to put his punctuation mark. Toward enhancing the fit between humans and their built environment, a circular process deserves consideration one without periods, only commas, a continuum of assumptions re-assessed, new assumptions made, ad infinitum. The place of post-construction evaluation in that model is self-evident. (p. 67)

4. MODELS FOR POST-CONSTRUCTION EVALUATION

If post-construction evaluation research is to provide relevant feedback that designers, researchers and clients can learn from, we must closely examine the model that guides the research. The three models presented below vary in their cost benefit potential for providing useful feedback to decision-makers. The models describe representative points on a continuum of post-construction evaluation research studies.

5. MODEL 1: NON-COLLABORATIVE EMPLOYING

A CROSS SECTIONAL USER STUDY

This approach may not constitute a valid case of post-construction evaluation because, though the data is collected at some time after construction in the occupancy life of the building, the researcher uses criteria that are established independent of the design process and they do not focus on concerns that were influential during decision-making. The basic decisions governing the research focus are made by the researcher. It is identified as a cross-sectional study. In research terms this means the study does not encompass the extended period of time that preceded the occupancy of the building. Rather, it cuts across a slice of time to study the current users. This model represents a majority of the user satisfaction building evaluations

that currently exist. It can be characterized as follows.

5.1 Participants

The researcher controls the decisions pertaining to research direction, focus and methods. Designers and clients are not participants in this model. Only the users are approached in the course of evaluating the building.

5.2 Site

The environmental setting or research site is selected solely by the researcher. The choice is frequently dictated by availability, accessibility to users and convenience.

5.3 Time

The cross-sectional research design involves data collection representing conditions at a point in time. This model requires that data is gathered on current user behavior and attitudes. It does not attempt to go back in time to learn what the client's and architect's understanding of user requirements were at the time the building was being designed.

5.4 Evaluation Criteria

The evaluation criteria are based on behavioral issues that the researcher selects to be the focus of the research. These criteria are established independent of the design and/or client decision-making process. They may or may not reflect the critical issues that shaped this process.

5.5 Contextual Constraints

The evaluation usually does not explore the impact of code requirements, financial constraints, client's demands, architect's experience and a host of other "given" factors that influenced the final design. Disciplinary ethnocentrism appears to be a valid criticism of this approach.

A qualitative appraisal of the potential cost benefits this model offers for feedback to designers, researchers and decision makers reveals several points. The evaluation model has very limited potential payoff when viewed in the context of the larger decision-making process that produced the space. It personifies evaluation carried out as an accountability measure. While this kind of feedback might seem useful to those who judge the performance of designers and other decision-makers, it can produce information that is both misleading and biased. It may focus the evaluation and base conclusions on issues and dimensions that were guided by a different set of priorities than the original decision makers used. In addition, it is doubtful that the findings of Model 1 research would be directed to those bodies charged with monitoring accountability unless the researcher was hired for that purpose. Rather, the research reports are likely to be made public only through professional journals and read only by the researcher's peer group.

The researcher will be the only party to benefit directly from this research. Indirectly, the academic research community may be affected through new knowledge on theory and methods. The designers and clients responsible for creating the building are so unlikely to see the research report and any benefit that might accrue to them is so slight that it may as well be discounted altogether.

6. MODEL 2: COLLABORATIVE, EMPLOYING A CROSS-SECTIONAL USER STUDY

This model of post-construction evaluation utilizes two data collection approaches to determine decision-makers' criteria and user reactions. First, discussions with the architect and client are held to identify the major issues, goals and constraints that influenced the design decision-making. Second, a cross-sectional study with users is done to determine how the building is working relative to these decision-makers' concerns. This strategy introduces collaboration and expands the potential value of the research findings as feedback. This model may be characterized as follows.

6.1. Participants

This is a collaborative undertaking. Participation would have to involve at least the architect and the researcher. It would be desirable to also have the client involved.

6.2. Site

The site is selected by mutual agreement between the client, architect and researcher. The cost in time and money will play a role in this decision. The architect and client may select one site over another for reasons of the building's unique design features or because of similar projects they are planning.

6.3. Time

The two phase data collection permits the current users' behavior to be put in context. The approach tries to relate that behavior to the behavioral requirements (as they were understood) that guided the design. This client-designer perspective will help to generate more meaningful questions about current user behavior requirements.

6.4. Evaluative Criteria

In this model, the criteria are necessarily articulated after the decision-making process has been carried out. These criteria, however, reflect issues that were of concern to architect

and client during the decision-making process. The collaborators work out the number and priorities of the issues to be covered.

6.5. Contextual Constraints

In this case the evaluation centers on user behavior in relation to design-relevant issues. The influence of codes, financial considerations, client demands, etc. are clearly taken into consideration.

The cost benefit potential for Model 2 is much greater than for Model 1. Costs in this model revolve around time needed for the participants to produce reliable information about the decisions they made at an earlier date. Experience and planning can reduce the participants' time involvement. An acknowledged weak link in this approach involves the reliability questions introduced by retrieving decision information from memory and old files. There is little that can be done to insure that retrieved information is a realistic representation of the actual decision-making process. Zeisel (1974) has noted that a problem of 'rationalizing' by decision-makers might occur.

This model has a pronounced advantage over Model 1 in that the criteria are based on the decision-makers' concerns. This situation links the evaluation process to the broader decision-making process. In addition, because the evaluative criteria reflect the decision-makers' concerns, the feedback, if presented in a format that decision-makers can understand, should be non-threatening and readily applied.

7. MODEL 3: COLLABORATIVE, EMPLOYING A LONGITUDINAL AND CROSS-SECTIONAL APPROACH

This approach to post-construction evaluation is the most comprehensive and complex. It includes a longitudinal data collecting effort and a close working relationship between the architect, client and research once the decision to build has been made. The researcher becomes a participant observer in the actual design and decision-making process. This model is characterized by:

7.1. Participants

Architect, researcher and client will all be active parties in the early stages. The researcher will be the primary figure during post-occupancy data collecting with the users as in the first two models.

7.2. Site

An appropriate project in which the parties are willing to collaborate will probably dictate the choice of sites. Available funding for the research may be another major determiner of the site choice.

7.3. Time

This approach will require considerable time on the part of the researcher in the pre-construction stages. This longitudinal monitoring can be expected to extend over a number of months as programming, schematic design and design development phases are worked through. The post-occupancy data collecting will follow building occupancy by six to eighteen months. A three to ten year time span may be involved.

7.4. Evaluative Criteria

The evaluative criteria are based on the user behavioral requirements as defined in the program.

7.5. Contextual Constraints

All of the constraints that emerged during the design process, construction and occupancy will be documented for use during the evaluation.

The appraisal of cost benefits for this model will be quite speculative. We do not have even the meager fund of experience to draw on for this "ideal" model that we had for the other two models.

The research effort demanded by Model 3 will extend over a period of years. Therefore, it will be potentially the most expensive approach. The researcher's time involvement necessary to work through this model far exceeds his commitments in the other two models though the periods of maximum intensity are few in number and of limited duration (i.e. programming, schematics design phase and evaluation). The time commitments of other participants would not be proportionately inflated because much of the architect-client exchange would have to be carried out in any case.

Some additional time would be involved as the researcher posed questions to clarify decisions or introduced user issues that otherwise might not have come up.

The benefits would seem to parallel the expanded scope of the research undertaking. Increased understanding of the process of collaboration, programming, and design decision-making would grow out of this effort. It seems not so unrealistic to anticipate increased efficiency in those matters (Ostrander and Groom 1975, Williams and Ostrander 1975). The design relevance of the user feedback should be much greater than would be produced in either of the earlier models. Finally, experience in developing and operating a learning system for design decision-making may be the major return on the application of this model.

7.6 Some Final Thoughts on Cost Benefits

Realistically, the clients and architects who stand to benefit most from systematic post-construction evaluation research as an integral

part of their design decision making fall into identifiable categories. In the case of the architect it is the one who specializes in a building type (i.e. housing, offices, schools) who can feed back information into his new projects from an evaluation of an earlier one. A client that maintains a large, on-going building program (i.e. hotel chain, government agency) has the most to gain from involvement in post-construction evaluation.

At the moment, the question of who supports the research undertaking is one that has not been saitsfactorily answered. With so little tangible evidence in hand that money can be saved by learning from post-construction evaluation, both clients and architects are reluctant financial contributors. Some designers (Ostrander and Groom 1975; Williams and Ostrander 1975; Connell 1975) have found that financial and time commitments to collaborative research have enough payoff to offset the cost. Perhaps these small scale efforts will serve as first steps toward foundation or federal funding to underwrite the research activity on case studies of sufficient size to produce some meaningful conclusions.

8. PROFESSIONAL ACTION TO IMPLEMENT MODELS

Post-construction evaluation has been discussed in this paper as a type of research that holds potential for closing the applicability gap. If we have accurately appraised the current situation, there appears to be several courses of action that might be initiated by researchers, designers and clients who are interested in using research to aid in their decision-making.

8.1. Researchers

1. Develop and test conceptual models which incorporate post-construction evaluation as a learning system.

2. Develop reliable and valid data collecting tools and procedures that enable researchers to provide quick and efficient user feedback.

3. Carry out exploratory case studies at interior space planning and small building scale that allow fast turn around time and require small financial outlays to demonstrate the cost benefit potential of post-construction evaluation. (Williams and Ostrander 1975; Connell 1975).

8.2. Designers

1. Find an opportunity to collaborate with a behavioral researcher on a small scale project.

2. Make presentations describing personal collaboration with researchers to other design professionals reporting your cost benefit experiences.

3. Urge professional organizations to encourage and financially support collaborative research.

8.3. Clients, Owners and Agencies

1. Request designers and researchers to offer alternative design solutions that address user behavior patterns and concerns.

2. Support projects that use collaborative research as a basis for design-decisions.

To bridge the applicability gap it will take more than written and spoken exhortations by academicians and practitioners. The potential collaborators are going to have to seek each other out and accept the risk that working together in order to learn from each other involves. Are there any takers?

Reference

BRILL, MICHAEL. Evaluating Buildings on a Performance Basis. In Jon Lang, Charles Burnette, Walter Moleski, and David Vachon (Eds.), Designing for Human Behavior. Stroudsburg, Pa.: Dowden, Hutchinson and Ross, Inc., 1974. pp. 316-319.

CONNELL, BETTYE ROSE. Research for Design Decision-Making: The Processes of Programming and Evaluation and an Evaluative Case Study of Multi-Family Housing. Unpublished Master's Thesis, Cornell University, Ithaca, New York, August 1975.

OSTRANDER, EDWARD. Behavioral Research for Design Decision-Making: On Making the Myth a Reality. In Basil Honikman (Ed.), Responding to Social Change. Proceedings of the Sixth Annual Environmental Design Research Association Conference. Stroudsburg, Pa.: Dowden, Hutchinson and Ross, Inc., 1975. pp. 133-144.

OSTRANDER, EDWARD AND GROOM, JAMES. The Coolfont Design Process Model: A Finer Grain Look. In Don Conway (Ed.), Social Science and Design, Second Edition. American Institute of Architects, 1975, Section I.

RUTLEDGE, ALBERT, KANA, ARTHUR AND QUALKINBUSH, STEPHEN. First National Bank Plaza, Chicago, Illinois: a pilot study in post-construction evaluation. Urbana-Champaign: University of Illinois, Department of Landscape Architecture, 1975.

STUDER, RAYMOND. The Organization of Spatial Stimuli. In J.F. Wohlwill and D.H. Carson (Ed.), Environment and Social Sciences: Perspectives and Applications. American Psychological Association, Inc., 1972. pp. 279-292.

WILLIAMS, SANDRA AND OSTRANDER, EDWARD. Maximizing Behavioral Inputs and Minimizing Time and Dollar Costs. Paper presented to the Social Science in Architecture Practice Workshop, Environmental Design Research Association Conference, April 22, 1975.

ZEISEL, JOHN. Sociology and Architectural Design. New York: Russell Sage Foundation, 1975.

ZEISEL, JOHN AND GRIFFIN, MARY. Charlesview Housing, A Diagnostic Evaluation. Cambridge: Harvard University, Graduate School of Design, 1975.

AN APPROACH TO THE ANALYSIS AND REDESIGN OF AN OUTDATED PSYCHIATRIC WARD

Stephen Kerpen, David Marshall, Clay Whitehead, and Gail Ellison

People's Housing, Inc.
1424 Old Topanga Canyon Road
Topanga, California 90290

ABSTRACT

The architecture of large, aging mental hospitals often militates against the contemporary therapeutic goals of their users. Since funds are unavailable for construction of new settings, outmoded wards must be redesigned to meet current user needs within tight budgetary constraints. This paper presents a theoretical review and describes a replicable approach and solution to meet this challenge.

The administrators of many large mental hospitals share a problem. Their outdated physical environments often militate against the contemporary therapeutic goals of the psychiatric services which they house, yet many factors have converged in the last few decades to prevent the construction of modern, humanistic facilities.

During the community psychiatry movement of the 1950s and 60s, it appeared that large mental hospitals would be phased out. Indeed, since 1970 no less than twelve psychiatric hospitals have been closed in the United States (Greenblatt, APA Meeting, 1975). Thus the public and its political representatives have been loathe to fund new facilities while supporting a contradictory policy of community-oriented psychiatric care.

However, as the chief of the California Mental Health System observed, the flow of patients from hospitals to the community may have slowed (Cochran). The California experience may well herald developments in other states. Governor Reagan's plan to phase out all of California's state mental hospitals by 1982 encountered strong opposition from the public, mental health administrators, and political adversaries. As a result, in 1974 Reagan's efforts were blocked by the State legislature, which with this move took into its hands the authority to maintain a state mental hospital system (*Los Angeles Times*, January 29, 1974). This dramatic development crystallized the increasing resistance to the flow of patients from state institutions to the community.

The conclusion is inescapable that the treatment of hundreds of thousands of mental patients will continue to be provided in large institutions. Moreover, recent judicial trends (*Wyatt* v. *Stickney* and *Donaldson* v. *O'Connor*) have obliged the states to provide meaningful and active therapy in their deteriorating and outdated environments. The hospital administrator then is faced with rising therapeutic expectations, gradually diminishing per capita budgets, and an implacable decline in the quality of his hospital. His critical question has become: How can an existing hospital be *redesigned* to integrate modern therapeutic concepts, humanistic patient requirements, and pragmatic budgetary limitations?

This paper describes our solution to this dilemma for one psychiatric ward in a large federal hospital operating with a constricted budget and a humanistic treatment philosophy.

Specific Problems in an Aging Hospital

Constructed in the early 1950s, the building we studied is typified by large open dormitories and dayrooms, unsuitable staff areas, long corridors, and poor lighting. The barracks-style dormitories and bleak dayroom which play a major part in the day-to-day life of the patients are unaesthetic spaces that afford little privacy. The dayroom is often little more than an area for listless napping and sedentary television-watching. There has been little development of the multi-purpose potential of the room for recreation, occupational therapy, crafts, socializing, and milieu therapy.

In other areas of the mental health unit, changes in staffing patterns and evolution of the psychiatry service have rendered staff areas unsuitable. Because the ward has become a busy community mental health center for both inpatients and outpatients, there are too few offices and group therapy rooms. Despite philosophical changes on the part of the staff, the nurses' station is glassed off and limits direct patient-staff communication.

The mental health units of the hospital are linked together by seemingly endless tunnels which, like the lengthy corridors within the units, are monotonous expanses of straight lines lacking clear directional orientation.

The floors, walls, and ceilings are covered in monochromatic, glare-reflecting tiles. In addition to the psychological impact of these long corridors, little thought has been given to their evolving function in the integration of inpatient and outpatient services.

To add to the disorienting characteristics of the hospital, the windows are undecorated and frequently do not permit the entry of daylight because of old blackened screens and the use of shades. The light from bare incandescent bulbs is dim and dreary.

Thus, an examination of this mental health unit reveals that utility, efficiency, and ease of maintenance were apparently stressed in the hospital's design, while patient comfort, self-actualization, and safety were given relatively less emphasis.

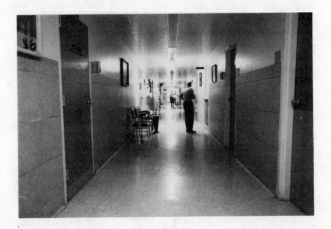

THEORETICAL FOUNDATIONS

We have assumed that there is a dynamic inter-action between the physical environment and behavior. Thus in reconstructing the ward environment the team attempted to simultaneously reflect the needs of patients, staff, and other users of the facility, as well as enhancing the therapeutic processes in which these people were engaged. While the literature on a multidisci-plinary consumer-oriented approach to hospital redesign is markedly limited, much may be learned from a brief review of some of the most valuable contributions in the field of psychi-atric architecture.

The literature describes several trends in con-temporary psychiatry which affect the design of mental hospitals. These trends include changing perceptions of the following therapeutic roles:

1. *The role of the staff.* During one era in the history of mental institutions, the insane were feared, incarcerated, and mistreated. Later they were thought to be in need of regula-tion, "moral treatment", and a strictly ordered life. Both eras contributed to the notion of the staff as overseers whose function was to supervise, protect, observe, and order (Bettelheim).

This responsibility to provide custodial care is now being replaced on many wards by the responsibility to facilitate the functioning of a therapeutic community. Supervision, observa-tion, and authoritarian dicta are less valued than availability, trust, respect of patient needs for privacy, and awareness of patient rights (Baker, Cumming and Cumming, Daniels).

2. *The role of the patient.* A major trend, as Gralnick has observed, is toward viewing a patient as an individual who has a disease rather than treating a disease that happens to reside within a patient. Patients are no longer thought to be "raving, screaming, dirty, and highly fatuous" hoardes who must be herded together for superintendence (Jacobi); the focus is on the patient's assets rather than his pathology. A crucial aspect of this change is that the patient's role is shifting from waiting to be "made well" to taking responsibility for his own growth. Socially acceptable behavior, self-reliance, and participation in decision-making are expected (Gralnick).

3. *The role of the institution.* Recent judicial decisions affirming the nondangerous patient's right to positive treatment, rather than mere custodial care, reflect a changing view of the role of the mental hospital. The goal is not to keep patients away from society, but to get them back into it as quickly as possible. Thus, many hospitals have shifted their concentration from long-term care to a combination of acute care and outpatient services in which the removal of the patient's psychological symptoms is only one area of concern. As Greenblatt has noted, there are also several other areas of rehabilitation: vocational, family, social-recreational, community, and educational. The hospital shares these rehabilitation efforts with a network of diverse settings that include community mental health centers, half-way houses, after-care clinics, and sheltered workshops.

4. *The role of the physical environment.* Due in part to the writings of Ittelson, Proshansky, Osmond, Izumi, Good, Cumming and Cumming, and others, it is now believed by many that the environment *itself* is a therapeutic tool--that **the physical setting can be manipulated to**

change the nature and distribution of behaviors on a psychiatric ward. As Moyer observed, the physical environment can foster activity patterns of new programs, structure relationships between people, and give cues to events taking place. Thus, architecture has taken a place along side treatment theories and administrative decisions as one of the major influences on ward life and patient recovery.

Many theorists are convinced that these four roles *interact* in complex ways that require a differв physical setting from that found in traditional mental hospitals. Some of the architectural changes are straightforward. For example, emphasis on the return of patients to the community necessitates more extensive out-patient facilities: a comfortable waiting area, an easily accessible check-in desk, multiple offices for individual therapy, and meeting places for group and family therapy. Other changes in the physical setting, however, are more subtle and have led to debates around which the literature of psychiatric architecture has focused. These issues are outlined here:

To what extent should the values of observation, protection, and structural security govern ward design?

The traditional view is that patients must be observed at all times and that their security should stem from external protection: locked doors, open toilet cubicles, exterior screens, and glass peepholes. To guard against the occasional violent or suicidal patient, all must surrender their privacy and sometimes their dignity.

Some argue that this fortress approach reduces patient anxiety and its resultant disturbed behavior. The staff also benefits from "reassuring working conditions," and the hospital is less susceptible to criticism or litigation (Hunt in Greenblatt and Baker et al. describe but do not advocate this approach).

Other theorists are now observing, however, that there is risk in planning to allay staff anxiety rather than to meet patient needs. An area that makes a patient feel secure can also lower his self-esteem and make him feel confined, paranoid, and depressed (Good et al., Bettelheim, Howells summarizing Linn). Moreover, as a World Health Organization study observed, with more effective staff training and drugs to control aggression and depression, "prolonged observations and expensive safeguards against suicide or assult" are no longer considered essential (Baker et al., p. 14).

This theoretical change raises a design controversy: Should the nurses' station be open or closed? In the past, most stations were designed to protect the staff and allow them to monitor patients' behavior. The prototypical station is a wired-glass cage with a half-door

through which patients' requests are evaluated.

Many theorists now realize the disadvantages of the closed station:

a) The definition of territories symbolized by the closed station encourages labeling. As one ward chief said: "Now the patients have the dayroom and the staff has the station. Essentially we're saying, 'You're the sick one; you do your thing out there and I'll watch'."

b) The closed station provides the staff with an opportunity to avoid contact with the patients. In one recent study that included VA wards, staff-staff interactions were 125 percent greater than would be expected by chance (McGuire). Some staff members have acknowledged that they spend at least 50 percent of their time doing paperwork in the station.

c) The glass often necessitates nonverbal communication, conveys to the patients the expectation that they are untrustworthy, and increases the number of patient demands on the staff. When the glass was removed in one hospital, staff members spent more time in the dayroom interacting with patients; therefore, 56 percent fewer patients came to the nursing station to have their needs met. Patients reported that they felt less a "bother" and were reassured that the staff was not afraid of them (Edwards and Hults).

A second way this theoretical change affects design is the way possessions are stored on the ward. If the model is authoritarian, with protection and security the predominant values, then patients' belongings are stored in rows of easily supervised lockers or in the nurses' station. Current thinking is that, as a territorial animal, man's security comes in part from being surrounded by his personal possessions in arrangeable, inviolable space (Bayes and Francklin, Hall, Baker et al.).

How pleasant should the environment be?

Although there are few data to confirm a correlation between aesthetics and cure, there exist extensive speculation and controversy around whether a mental hospital should be comfortable and attractive. The disagreement centers around what might be called the grimness/pleasantness dialectic. According to one viewpoint, the hospital should be unpleasant enough to discourage hangers-on, those who would increase the one-third of mental patients who "collect" on the wards. Neo-behaviorism and a puritanical attitude toward comfort are said to lie behind these arguments for a sterile environment: providing decent surroundings would be "rewarding" insanity. Some of these sceptics argue that if you give patients a nice environment, they will probably destroy it (discussed by Sommer, Belknap, Greenblatt, Howells).

Other theorists observe that "human ingenuity can always find a way to destroy things that are physically or spiritually oppressive" (Sommer). Since the reaction to oppressive places is numbness and psychological withdrawal, it is suggested that pleasant surroundings aid therapy (Sommer, Bettelheim). Many writers believe that individuals relate, at either a conscious or unconscious level, to the nonhuman environment as part of the ego, a tendency that is intensified with regression to an earlier stage of development. Thus, a pleasing, life-enhancing environment can provide support that contributes to the rebuilding of failed ego functions (Searles, Bettelheim).

In many ways the current literature returns to the suggestion of Jacobi in 1841:

The whole [building] should bear the stamp of a large lodging-house or hotel at a watering place, so as not to appear by its outward splendour to mock the miseries of its inmates; but yet, in its elegance and simplicity, its cheerfulness and convenience, affording an ample testimonial of the care which has been bestowed to lighten and alleviate the long separation from their friends, to which the process of a tedious cure may subject the unfortunate sufferers (p. 49-50).

What are the therapeutic effects of color?

Perhaps nowhere in the field does confusion reign more solidly than in the domain of color. Research findings vary; their significance is arguable. One researcher finds that blue reduces blood pressure; another reports that green, not blue, has that effect (Bayes reporting the findings of Gerard, Hessey).

Color preference, it is suggested, varies according to the patient's diagnosis. Thus, according to one researcher, schizophrenics like yellow, or, according to another, they do not like green and yellow, which are the colors preferred by anxiety neurotics (Bayes reporting the findings of Mosse, Birren, Deutsch, Warner). The choice of color becomes even more difficult in view of the diversity of diagnoses on most wards.

More important, there is evidence that preferred colors may not be those which are therapeutic. From some studies, for example, a designer might assume that blue would tranquilize agitated patients and red would stimulate the withdrawn. The reverse, however, has been shown to hold: a manic patient is often calmed by a hot, not a cool, color (Bayes, Bayes and Francklin).

How can dehumanization be countered?

For well over a century, observers of behavior have decried the de-individuation that takes place in mental hospitals. The loss of self-esteem, or "mortification of the self," often gives rise to a situational withdrawal that has been labeled "hospitalitis." Its symptoms, described by Sommer, include excessive dependency, loss of the capacity to make decisions, and the absence of spontaneity (Goffman, Vail).

It is now believed that the preventive medicine for hospitalitis is in part architectural. Opportunities to exercise choice, a major component in sustaining autonomy and self-worth, can be designed into the environment. For example, choice may be provided through bedside lamps, windows that can be opened and curtains that can be closed, walls with texture that encourages the display of individual artistic taste, and facilities on the ward for food preparation.

Other writers suggest that the presence of animals and plants can contribute to ego mastery. As Searles points out, adults, like children with toys, use elements of the nonhuman environment as "a kind of practice-ground for the development of a relatedness which can be carried over, later, into relationships with other human beings" (p.85).

Research also suggests that the deviant behavior such as pacing or talking to oneself which characterizes many dehumanized wards might be reduced by increased opportunities for intermingling of staff and patients. One study found that although 75 percent of the time on the wards studied there were only patients in the room, the presence of a staff member had a dramatic effect: social behavior doubled; television-watching dropped; and there was a lower probability of deviant behavior (McGuire).

How do perceptual changes in the mentally ill affect design?

Many researchers have considered the special needs of mental patients. As Foley and Lacy observed, the emotionally disturbed patient is more vulnerable, "and because of this vulnerability his physical environment will have a greater impact on him, either positively or negatively" (p. 1015).

In addition to visual illusions and distortions, mental patients often have acute, exaggerated senses of smell, hearing, and touch. As Osmond has observed, this necessitates the provision of small, manageable spaces, pleasantly textured surfaces, paths for retreat, nonechoic surfaces, and clearly marked rooms. To compensate for changes in the time sense, similar elements should not be repeated. To avoid the diminution of the distinction between body and space that occurs in high rooms, ceilings should be low. To minimize the changes in thinking that sometimes occur, personal items and clothing should be stored near the patient (Osmond, Bayes and Francklin).

One feature of mental institutions over which environmental psychologists have taken issue is long, echoic, glossy corridors which can lead to perceptual distortions of time, speed, distance, and size. As Spivack noted, the schizophrenic tendency to have trouble with size-distance relationships is exacerbated by the reflections, silhouettes, and fuzzy outlines of approaching people who often appear in contrasty backlighting to be headless and footless.

Noise level also affects behavior. It has been suggested that patients are less irritable and excitable and that they exercise more control following the installation of carpeting (J. T. Greco in Griffin et al.). For some patients, however, the stimulant properties of noise may be beneficial. One study showed that a noisy environment increased the motor and verbal performance and improved the perceptual organization and sleep patterns of withdrawn patients, with a resultant decrease in their medication. The withdrawn group in a quiet environment, however, "showed considerable regression with heightened autism, seclusiveness, more conceptual disorganization, and disturbed sleep patterns with increased hallucinations" (Ozerengin and Cowen, p. 241). The reverse held true for the active patients.

How much privacy is desirable?

Research supports the notion that "the growth of interpersonal relationships depends on being able to slip unobtrusively from one to another of three separate zones of sociability--complete privacy, the intimate group, the larger group" (Bayes and Francklin, p. 22; see also Chermayeff and Alexander).

Though common practice favors large open wards and dayrooms, studies show that six to eight persons should be the largest number of patients in a group. If large dorms must be retained, theorists recommend partitioning to provide privacy (Baker et al., Cumming and Cumming). One study found that "in long, open barracks recruits knew the names of more people than they did in partitioned barracks, but they had more friends or 'buddies' in partitioned arrangements" (Blake, Rhead, Wedge, and Mouton in Griffin et al., p. 95).

Some behavior modifiers say that their treatment methods often necessitate single rooms. Most researchers, however, do not recommend the total privacy offered by the single room. In fact, a recent study indicated that the probability of deviance is highest when one person is in the room (McGuire). There are many different opinions about the ideal number of persons per room. Some writers fear that the pressure to interact (often negatively) may be too intense with two persons in a room. Three-per-room creates the problem of alliances of two against one (Baker et al., Bettelheim).

What is the ideal balance between architectural stasis and dynamism?

The contemporary trend in architecture, as Bayes points out, is to erase the articulation between spaces, creating flowing, open areas that merge

without definition and have "spatial continuity." In psychiatric architecture, this direction is one side of a debate between openness and definition, flexibility and ambiguity, fixity and change, and complexity and simplicity.

The new programs require flexible spaces, with "easily crossed barriers" between private and public spaces. On the other hand, spaces that merge without definition can lead to insecurity and confusion. It is argued that because many insane persons are plagued by disturbances in sense perception and "uncertainty about the integrity of the self," mental hospitals must offer consistency, permanence, and solidity. The optimum building, according to adherents of this view, is simple, with a plan posted on the wall to orient patients and signs on every door to define room usage (Baker et al., Good et al., Proshansky et al., Osmond, Bayes and Francklin).

Other writers warn that the attempt to avoid ambiguity may result in insufficient complexity: "The building which takes time to understand, when meaning and association take time to develop and deepen with familiarity, may be more valuable" (Department of Education and Science Bulletin quoted in Bayes, p. 15). A. E. Parr summarizes this view:

A certain level of complexity in the environment is necessary for healthy explorative behaviour. There is a level of monotony beyond which expansion of orbit in search of variety changes to contraction due to insufficient rewards for exploration. When the physical environment ceases to provide the unexpected within a reasonable distance, some seek compensation in the life of the imagination, others. . . either create suspense through delinquent behaviour or succumb to dullness (p. 25, Bayes and Francklin).

METHOD

While refining these theoretical foundations, our group gathered information from three sources. First, we interviewed the users of the ward being studied. In staff meetings, we talked with psychiatrists, social workers, psychologists, occupational therapists, nurses, and aides. Because they tend to elicit candor, private interviews were used to ascertain other genuine needs. Discussions in patient government meetings enabled us to incorporate the patients' points of view and mobilize their support.

Second, the scope, budget, and code constraints of the project were established in meetings with the Assistant Chief of Psychiatry, the Director of the Engineering Service, and the Hospital Director.

Third, we visited twelve diverse psychiatric facilities, including federal, state, county, and private institutions. In addition to providing an opportunity to analyze a range of environmental settings, these visits made possible informal interviews with doctors, nurses, administrators, and other mental health workers whose experiences and viewpoints differed from those found in the subject hospital.

The user needs gathered from these sources were the basis for a large study model of one potential plan for ward modification. Utilization of the model as an adjunct in further meetings with staff and patients allowed those inexperienced with architectural drawings to visualize the effects of the changes on the existing ward space. Their criticisms, based on first-hand experience on the ward, were taken into consideration in revision of the model.

Three schematic plans were developed, each emphasizing slightly different priorities in the use of available space. These were subjected to careful scrutiny by both engineering and health-care administrators and were synthesized into a final form.

Throughout the design conceptualization process, we continually stressed *user needs* and *budgetary limitations*. Because of these limitations, the working drawings were prepared in *phases* for construction, with priorities for implementation based on patient-care benefits and relative construction costs. The phases will be constructed sequentially as additional funds become available.

After the changes are made, researchers from UCLA will return to the ward to conduct follow-up studies, thus providing an unusual opportunity to evaluate the design.

SOLUTIONS

Our approach to the design emphasizes the relationship between human needs and the physical environment. The solution stresses the concept of a mental hospital as approaching a total life-support system for psychiatric patients. During preliminary discussions we grouped the needs of patients, professional staff, maintenance personnel, and hospital administrators into a series of categories which in turn were employed as architectural challenges. Throughout the entire planning and design process, our work was oriented toward the design requirements implied by these need categories. We found that many of the solutions derived for one need category could also be applied to others.

Need Categories

1. *Identity*. Individuality and territoriality are basic human needs. They imply space for the person as well as for his personal possessions. Areas for the expressive display and for the protection of personal property are essential. The distinction between personal and group space should be clear.

2. *Community and social relationships*. The individual requires a community with which to interact and community facilities to meet his needs. Flexibility is essential to promote diversity in a closed environment. Sufficient space must be provided so that relationships do not become disordered.

3. *Work and recreation*. The opportunity for meaningful recreational and occupational activities is a fundamental prerequisite to modern psychotherapeutic ward operation. Patients require an opportunity for personally and socially useful self-expression in work and play.

4. *Rest and relaxation*. Patients need both relaxing diversions and areas designed to promote quiet and rest. Restful areas are also important for staff members.

5. *Aesthetics*. The conscious and creative use of form, space, scale, color, and texture provides a stimulating and interesting environment for patients and staff.

6. *Privacy*. Privacy is essential for both patients and staff. Some degree of visual and acoustical separation is needed between adjacent activities. There is also a need to delimit socially defined realms for the patients and staff.

7. *Security*. The need for security must be met in architectural as well as human responses. Areas for securing personal effects are required by patients and staff. Medical records and medications must be guarded. Occasionally, disturbed patients require secured isolation. Psychological security can be developed by increased patient-staff interaction.

8. *Natural amenities*. The need for satisfactory climate, light, and air conditions must be met. The outdoor environment should be integrated.

9. *Control of disease, accidents, and sensory distortion*. Design concepts must take into account the need for control of communicable disease, the appropriate management of sanitary and safety requirements, and the use of structures and materials which reduce sensory distortion.

Design Constraints

Fiscal and administrative considerations dictated the following design constraints:

a) minimal alteration of basic structural elements and fire separations

b) provision of sleeping facilities for approximately 30 patients

c) provision of office space for two ward psychiatrists, five resident psychiatrists, a psychologist, a social worker, a head nurse, and a ward clerk

d) allowance for three group therapy areas to accommodate 10 to 12 persons

e) meeting of new hospital specifications for toilet facilities and fire-stair access routes

Designing for Flexibility

The concept of *flexible space design* was utilized to meet functional constraints and simultaneously maintain an area adequate for patient needs. For example, moveable, soundproofed partitions (Figure 1) are included to separate group therapy

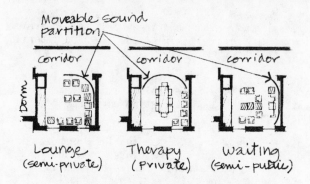

FIGURE 1: FLEXIBLE SPACE DESIGN

rooms from the corridors and provide privacy for therapeutic sessions. When these sessions are not being conducted, the rooms can be converted into outpatient waiting areas or patient lounges which open onto the corridors, allowing natural light to flow into the interior halls. The rooms can be equipped with a television set, a stereo, and groups of chairs to encourage socialization.

Functional flexibility also provided a basis for the approach to the dayroom. A large moveable semi-circular component (Figure 2) serves as a

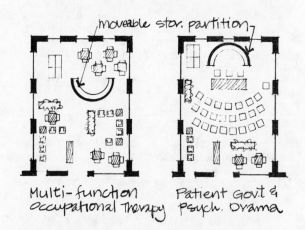

FIGURE 2: DAYROOM FLEXIBILITY

storage area for occupational therapy materials, and, when opened, provides working area for this activity. The divider may be moved to the side to permit large group meetings. In addition,

it can serve as a stage or backdrop for patient-government activities, psychodrama, or other presentations. Furnishings in the dayroom will also be flexible, modular pieces that may be arranged in a wide variety of conformations.

Hierarchy of Spatial Uses

During the process of design, a hierarchy of space utilization ranging from the most private to the most public was developed. The large open dormitories are currently highly public (Figure 3).

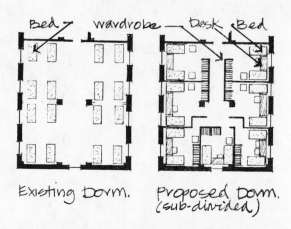

FIGURE 3: DORMITORY SUBDIVISION

Our redesign divides the dormitories into smaller sub-units more closely resembling conventional bedrooms. These areas are semi-private and may be easily identified by the patient as his personal space.

The lounge areas adjacent to each dormitory are in the middle of the hierarchy, providing opportunities for socializing with a small group. When used as semi-private space these areas function like living rooms where users can watch television, read, or work on hobbies. When closed, these areas function as group therapy rooms. When opened, the lounge areas become semi-public and may serve as waiting rooms. This conformation encourages increased patient-staff contact and more casual socializing.

The concept of a hierarchy of spaces ranging from private to public was carried over into the dayroom. The semi-circular divider may be utilized for separating semi-private areas for reading, writing, and card or board games from recreational and occupational activities elsewhere in the room. With the divider moved aside, the dayroom on occasion functions as a meeting room for the entire ward community.

Character of the Public Spaces

The long corridors of the unit represent the most public areas in the hierarchy. In our redesign concept these corridors become community "streets." The semi-private seating alcoves located at intervals along the street represent transition spaces ("porches" or "vestibules") that separate private offices from the passing public. The streets serve as links between all the various ward activities and as routes for travel to the larger community outside the ward. Along the street are located the offices of the professional staff, the medicinal distribution point ("drugstore"), and the patient laundry ("laundromat"). The dayroom is the ward community's library, park, theater, and assembly hall.

The intersection of the crossing corridors is enlarged to accommodate and encourage increased public activity. This focal point ("town square") contains the nurses' station which functions as the center for community services ("city hall," "emergency room," "bank," and "general store"). Across the plaza is an open kitchen and snack bar which functions as the community "cafe." Surrounding the plaza are small seating alcoves where the activity of the area may be observed. Public telephones and toilets increase activity in the area, and a fountain or plants add interest. The nurses' station adjacent to the intersection is almost entirely open in order to encourage communication. This open space underscores the interrelatedness of staff and patients.

The nurses' station also includes lockable work and storage areas for staff members without private offices. Behind this open area is located a semi-private work center where staff may gather for consultation, chart work, or socializing while still maintaining contact with the ward community at large. Next to the semi-private work area, private staff work space has been provided to accommodate work that requires intense concentration such as complicated charting and medication preparation. Finally, the staff also is provided with a private lounge area located away from the focal areas of ward activity.

Other concepts were employed to emphasize the spatial hierarchy in the unit. Corridor widths were altered at selected points to establish a feeling of dynamism and emphasize functional boundaries (Figure 4). Alteration of ceiling heights, variation in surface textures and colors, and changes in the character of lighting serve to delimit functional boundaries.

Graphics play a particularly important part in our redesign. They are used for decoration, emphasis of functional boundaries, and elimination of ambiguity. Graphic design represents a flexible, aesthetically valid, and fiscally conservative adjunct to ward redecoration.

The design concepts employed have been derived from the needs of a ward population in a large institution for the mentally ill. These concepts bring a consumer-oriented and forward-looking humanistic approach into contact with the pragmatic considerations of budgetary limitations and administrative realities. The suggestions set forth here may be easily transferred to other institutions and suggest the possibility

of a vastly improved mental health environment. Such programs have become increasingly crucial for both psychiatric patients and those charged with their care.

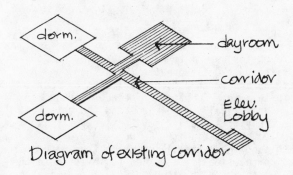

Diagram of existing corridor

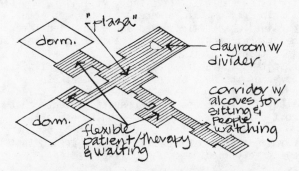

Proposed "street & plaza" system has diversity & activity allowing a progressional series of experiences both spatially & as a potential for human interaction.

FIGURE 4: CORRIDOR ALTERATION

REFERENCES:

References are available from the authors on request.

AN EVALUATION OF NURSING UNIT DESIGN

Sue D. Pendell and Kevin E. Coray

University of Utah

ABSTRACT

Through the use of behavioral mapping and the
Nursing Unit Questionnaire (NUQ), nursing unit
designs and organizational climates of four
hospitals were compared. The NUQ (factor and
item analytically developed) and the data from
the behavioral mapping (chi square analysis) were
studied separately for the unique information
each contained; then information from both sources
was correlationally combined to investigate the
degree to which the 10 questionnaire dimensions
(e.g., operational efficiency, visibility, nursing
station design, etc.) were predictive of actual
nursing behaviors observed and quantified through
behavioral mapping. The results of these analyses
were translated into diagnostic profiles across
hospitals (which indicated the discriminating
power of the NUQ) and provided feedback to
administrators. The methodology used in this
study and the encouraging results indicate that
cost effective longitudinal studies using this
format would result in an understanding of the
climate-design-behavior effects of nursing units
ultimately leading to design implications.

INTRODUCTION

Recently, organizational climate and environment
have become major topics in discussions of the
psychological facets of industry, education, and
public and mental health. An environment exerts
influence and control on the people within that
environment. Some environments impose more
control than others due to their physical and
psychological characteristics. Many environments
have been studied, including psychiatric wards,
organizational-industrial groups, classrooms,
correctional institutions, and university
residence halls. Few of these studies, however,
have considered the effects of the physical
design of the environment, even though this
aspect of the environment forces conformity,
willfully or not. Further, an estimated 20% of
response variance in some groups may be due to
the interaction of individuals and their
environments (Moos & Daniels, 1967). Individuals
with the same job in different settings show
vastly different behavior patterns (Barker,
1963a, 1963b; Ellison, Abe, Fox, & Coray, 1974).

Comparative organizational research has also been
done in many settings. Neuhauser and Anderson
(1972) have reviewed this literature in relation
to hospitals. They have indicated that the
"structural" or organizational features of
hospitals:

> . . . are in part determined by the
> external environment in which the
> hospital operates. Structure in turn
> affects the functioning of the
> hospital service (outcome).

Of the variables in the studies reviewed by
Neuhauser and Anderson, few design variables
were considered.

The present study examined the joint organizational
and design characteristics of a little studied
environment - nursing units. The purpose of the
study was to develop methods which would both
exemplify organizational and design characteristics
and differentiate hospitals in terms of these
characteristics.

METHOD

Many sources were used in the development of the
original item pool for the NUQ. Hospital
architects, hospital administrators, nursing
administrators, and nurses were consulted in an
attempt to isolate problem areas in design.
Observers were placed in nursing units; and
through an automated behavioral mapping technique
(Veneklasen, Taylor, Coray, and Pendell, 1974)
nursing functions within varied nursing station
designs were monitored, analyzed, evaluated, and
design characteristics were isolated. Item from
climate measures were reviewed and four scales
from the Management Audit Survey[1] (IBRIC, 1974)
were adapted.

The Nursing Unit Questionnaire (NUQ) consisted of
52 continuous items and 13 control or demographic
items. This questionnaire was administered to
the fulltime nurses at three hospitals. The
responses on the completed NUQ's (n = 367) on the
52 continuous items were factor analyzed. The
principal components factor analysis, with varimax
rotation, rotated all factors with eigenvalues
greater than or equal to 1.00.

Through investigation of the factors and a series
of item analyses, five factors were eliminated or
absorbed, and ten scores were obtained which were
relatively clean and highly homogeneous. Score
area titles were tentatively assigned to these
factors based on the interfactor item content.

At this point, the administration of the NUQ to
an additional hospital was completed and these
responses were added to the data blank (n = 450).
This additional data produced a 50% return rate
for the fulltime nursing employees across
hospitals (n = 904).

RESULTS

From the final item analysis ten score areas were
developed which identify ten dimensions of
nursing climate or nursing station design. The
score areas, with more than two defining items,

are Operational Efficiency, Workload Balance, Co-Worker Cooperation, Nursing Station Design, Visibility, Patient Care and Room Distance (PCRD), Patient Care and Room Type (PCRT), and Design Characteristics and Patient Condition (DCPT). Contol variables such as shift, title, number of years in present hospital, and number of years in nursing were obtained to assess their relationships with the score areas. The variables and the NUQ scores, along with their N's, means, and standard deviations for the total sample, are presented in Table 1.

The NUQ score intercorrelations indicate that, with the exception of NUQ Operational Efficiency with NUQ Co-Worker Cooperation (r = .61), the score areas were relatively independent.

Table 2 presents the percentile ranks on the NUQ scales across the subsamples using the total sample as the basis of comparison. The score areas differentiated among subgroup samples quite well. Face validity exists in the profiles obtained for each hospital. Hospital age decreases for Hospitals 1 through 4, with Hospital 1 being the oldest, and the percentile ranks generally indicate that the younger a hospital is the better its design features are perceived by the nursing staff. Further, Hospital 4 is very modern with many innovative design features, such as triangular nursing units and single patient rooms throughout the hospital. Hospital 4 ranked highest in 4 out of 5 NUQ score areas dealing specifically with design and above the mean on the 5th score. However, in the same hospital, many personnel changes were occurring in nursing administration. This state of affairs was reflected in terms of Hospital 4 scoring lowest on NUQ Operational Efficiency and NUQ Co-Worker Cooperation and being below the mean on the other three climate scales. Similar types of prescriptive explanations for hospital profiles exist for the other three hospitals.

An abbreviated example of the feedback to administrators for one climate and one design scale follows: 1. NUQ Co-Worker Cooperation - the score may be improved by activities such as: Encourage employee in-put into solution of work problems; hold meetings to obtain their views on work matters; encourage workers to view each other's resources for help in problem solving; make sure that employees are aware of each other's work problems and, where possible, rotate group assignments; occasionally to increase such understanding, review and re-define more clearly the lines of responsibility; avoid favoritism; and restructure jobs and workflow to increase mutual support and reduce conflict. 2. Nursing Station Design - (a) Remodeling considerations to improve score. Redesign patient call light layout such that it can be seen from within the nursing station; adjust the counter space in the nursing station to conform to the volume of paperwork completed therein; and consult the workgroups for human and mechanical noise problems and align policies to adjust the level of human noise and/or

muffle mechanical noise. (b) Workgroup considerations to improve score. Encourage employees to voice complaints concerning the quality of light, heat, air, etc. and attempt to rectify these problems; investigate the possibility of obtaining other space; inform higher level supervisors of the nature of employee complaints; and inform employees in advance of any change in space or equipment. Should suggested actions be unfeasible, see that employees understand why.

On the nurse title sample, Experience and Title & Duties become control scores and demonstrate expected magnitudes and directions (see Tables 1 and 2). Tabulations of the number of percentile ranks above or below the mean on either climate or design scales indicate that nurses with different titles, i.e. different characteristics in terms of education, experience, and job assignment, perceive hospital conditions differently. For example, licensed practical nurses tended to view the hospital design as being generally more well-designed across the design scales than did nurses' aides. Different shifts also perceived the environmental factors of climate and architecture as being different.

DISCUSSION

The results from this study are very encouraging in that an instrument to assess nursing units has been developed which has the necessary psychometric properties to allow its use in a more sophisticated study which collected the needed criterion data (such as cost measures, patient turnover measures, performance measures, etc.) to evaluate the units against the behavioral and architectural scores measured by the NUQ yielding data to imply climate and design changes to benefit all hospital users. Specifically, designing both the organizational climate and the nursing unit itself to meet the deficiencies of existing or as yet unbuilt structures in terms of the particular nursing subgroups (e.g. licensed practical nurses or various shifts) could produce more cohesive work groups which might perceive working conditions as being more satisfactory and hypothetically provide better health care. The sophisticated study mentioned could assess whether or not this was so. Alternately, organizational policies as well as architectural designs of nursing units could have built-in flexibility in order for specific work groups to tailor climate and design to fit their needs. These solutions might be effected for existing structures via remodeling of facilities which limit the health care nurses are capable of giving and revision of traditional administrative policies which are perceived as being out of date.

While the NUQ now exists in a low-cost, easily usable form (the NUQ uses computer scanned answer sheets and computer scoring), the results indicate that some scales might be refined further by adding items or by rewriting existing ones. Also,

TABLE 1

Total Sample

Variables, Keyscores, N's, Means, and Standard Deviations

Var No.		N	Mean	S. D.
	Variables[a]			
1.	Day shift = 1 vs. other = 0	440	.53	.50
2.	Evening shift = 1 vs. other = 0	440	.33	.47
3.	Night shift = 1 vs. other = 0	440	.14	.35
4.	Registered Nurse (RN) = 1 vs. other = 0	394	.54	.50
5.	Licensed Practical Nurse (LPN) = 1 vs. other = 0	394	.25	.43
6.	Nurses' Aide (NA) = 1 vs. other = 0	394	.21	.41
7.	No. of years of present hospital	442	2.23	1.51
8.	No. of years in nursing	442	3.05	1.61
	NUQ Scores[b]			
9.	NUQ Operational Efficiency	450	99.72	2.39
10.	Nursing Station Design	450	100.70	2.74
11.	Visibility	450	99.66	1.85
12.	Patient Care & Room Distance (PCRD)	450	99.60	1.99
13.	Patient Care & Room Type (PCRT)	450	100.18	2.14
14.	Experience	450	99.82	1.63
15.	Design Characteristics & Patient Condition (DCPC)	450	99.35	1.59
16.	NUQ Workload Balance	450	100.37	1.91
17.	Title & Duties	450	99.78	1.26
18.	NUQ Co-Worker Cooperation	450	99.61	2.97

[a]Variables 1 through 6 are dichotomous, thus the mean is equal to the proportion of the total sample endorsing the alternative coded 1.0, e.g. on Variable 1, 52% (binary mean = .52) of the total sample answering this question answered that they were on dayshift.

[b]A constant of 100 is added to each individual's score to eliminate negatives.

TABLE 2

Percentile Ranks on NUQ Score Areas Across Samples

Score Areas	Hospital				Title[a]			Shift[a]		
	1	2	3	4	RN	LPN	NA	Day	Eve.	Night
1. NUQ Operational Efficiency	49	51	61	40	51	55	44	51	51	45
2. Nursing Station Design	44	46	44	76	48	51	37	50	52	50
3. Visibility	53	39	51	67	55	43	52	49	52	48
4. Patient Care & Room Distance	35	66	51	52	45	57	56	48	50	59
5. Patient Care & Room Type	37	60	40	72	51	54	46	50	51	49
6. Experience	44	52	56	48	52	59	47	51	48	50
7. Design Characteristics & Patient Condition	56	35	54	67	48	48	50	46	51	63
8. NUQ Workload Balance	54	48	48	49	47	51	53	48	54	67
9. Title & Duties	57	53	37	42	23	61	91	50	52	48
10. NUQ Co-Worker Cooperation	44	56	60	39	51	52	50	50	50	51

[a]RN = Registered Nurses; LPN = Licensed Practical Nurses; NA = Nurse's Aides;

Day = day shift; Eve. = evening shift; Night = night shift

Page 258

the original factor structure of the NUQ was such that other scales could be developed which would yield scores on dimensions not yet fully isolated. Further, composite scores for the climate and design scales might add to the general utility of the instrument.

Finally the stability of climate dimensions across organizations, as demonstrated by the characteristics of the MAS and NUQ climate scales, lead to implications for future research concerning the set of climate dimensions which are common to all organizations, as well as those that are specific to particular classes or organizations. While this study indicates interesting relationships among climate and design dimensions, further research is necessary to assign causation either through the use of criteria or analyses across time. Should such investigations yield encouraging results, classifying organizations in terms of their climate and design correlates might lead to future theoretical developments.

NOTES

1. The Management Audit Survey (MAS) was developed by the Institute for Behavioral Research in Creativity and has been administered to over 20,000 employees of the U. S. Department of Labor. 19 subscales concerning organizational climate and an automated feedback system to all levels of management on the 19 scales are available.
2. Part of this research was funded by a private grant from Kaplan & McLaughlin, Architects/Planners to whom the authors wish to express their appreciation. Further, the authors wish to thank Dr. Calvin W. Taylor for his guidance, Dr. Robert L. Ellison for his review of the item pool, David G. Fox for his data processing help, Stuart Burgh and Joyanna Geisler for their coordinating efforts and observations, and the aministration and staffs of the St. Marks, the University Medical Center, the Holy Cross, and the Latter Day Saints Hospitals.

REFERENCES

BARKER, R. G. On the nature of the environment. Journal of Social Issues, 1963, 19, 17-28 (a).

BARKER, R. G. (Ed.) The stream of behavior. New York: Appleton-Century Crofts, 1963 (b).

ELLISON, R. L., FOX, D.G., ABE, C., CORAY, K.E., and TAYLOR, C.W. The Management Audit Survey of Organizational Climate. Paper presented at the meeting of the American Psychological Association, Chicago, 1975.

MOOS, R.H., and DANIELS, D.N. The differential effects of ward settings on psychiatric staff. Archives of General Psychiatry, 1967, 17, 75-82.

NEUHAUSER, D., and ANDERSON, R. Structural comparative studies of hospitals. In B.S. Georopoulos (Ed.), Organizational research on health institutions. University of Michigan, Ann Arbor, Michigan, 1974. pp. 85-126.

VENEKLASEN, W.D., TAYLOR, C.W., CORAY, K.E., and PENDELL, S.D. Results of three hospital studies. Paper presented at Engineering Foundation Conferences, Asilomar, Calif., November, 1974.

THE UTILIZATION OF SPACE IN AN ACADEMIC ENVIRONMENT

(title underlined in source)

Randy Phelps

Texas Research Institute of Mental Sciences
1300 Moursund
Houston, Texas 77025

James C. Baxter

Department of Psychology
University of Houston
Houston, Texas 77004

ABSTRACT

The utilization of space in a large university
academic department was assessed through a multi-
variable, multi-method information generating
system. Due to the complexity of the interaction
between an organization and the physical environment which supports it, data on the organizational
goals, user attitudes and needs, and existing
behavior patterns were gathered in three phases:
1) structured interview, 2) questionnaire survey,
and 3) behavioral observation.

Results provided information concerning departmental goals which might have implications for
space utilization, allowed the assessment of user
satisfaction levels with available facilities,
and permitted the description of ongoing behavior
patterns supported by the physical system. Considering the three bodies of data as a whole
afforded some evaluation of progress toward
departmental goals. Further refinement and use
of the model for assessing subsequent changes in
the physical and social system of the department
was encouraged.

1. INTRODUCTION

Like a majority of man-environment studies, the
main thrust of the present research is its practical, problem-solving orientation. Broadly,
the purpose of the research was to provide an
assessment of current space utilization within
a large university psychology department, from
which some guidelines and suggestions might be
generated for future space programming in the
setting. As a result, the study attempted to
relate ongoing behavior patterns to the institutional setting in which they occur.

A number of assumptions guided the research.
First, any physical environment is embedded in
and is inextricably related to a social system
(Ittelson, Proshansky, Rivlin, & Winkel, 1974).
Therefore, the research needed to be holistic in
approach, providing data on the physical system,
the human components of the environment, and the
interaction of the two. Second, the complexity
of studying the department as a man-environment
entity would necessitate a multi-variable,
multi-method data generating system. Third,
only after assessments of the organization's
goals, user needs and attitudes, and actual
ongoing patterns of behavior were conducted
might the goal of presenting guidelines for
future space programming be realized.

A comprehensive data-collection system was
generated, consisting of structured interviews,
behavioral observations, and user questionnaires, as suggested by Moleski (1973). By
effectively utilizing each method to obtain
the most appropriate data it would elicit, the
inherent weaknesses of employing any single
method were to some degree offset. And, though
the information generated by each system was of
a different nature, each provided some internal
checks on the consistency of data from the
other methods.

Structured interviews with executive and
management level personnel provided useful
information on the social context of the
environment and organizational goals of the
department. However, since management personnel
often tend to be poor judges of employee's
attitudes and environmental needs (Moleski,
1973), user questionnaires to assess these
needs and attitudes constituted an integral
part of the research. And, since self-report
data such as interviews and questionnaires are
subject to a number of weaknesses (Webb,
Campbell, Schwartz, & Sechrest, 1966), structured
observation was deemed necessary to provide data
on the actual behavior patterns occurring within
the environment. Observations themselves are
subject to a number of weaknesses, namely, the
lack of explanation of the purpose and meaning
of observed behavior and the probability that
behavior patterns are affected as a result of the
participants being observed (Ittelson, et al.,
1974). However, naturalistic observations are of
value since organizations do locate ongoing activity systems spatially as well as temporally.

Specifically, then, the goals of the present
study were as follows. First, to provide a

descriptive analysis of the organizational goals, user satisfaction and spatial needs, and actual existing behavior patterns of the environment. Second, to evaluate the various forms of data in relation to each other. Trends, as well as disparities evident across the data would provide useful information for future programming. For example, if the standing patterns of behavior identified in a particular subsetting were discrepant with respect to the organizational goals or perceived purpose of that setting, these findings might have important implications for change leading to more efficient utilization of the setting.

Finally, the research was addressed to a broader goal in addition to providing meaningful data on a particular environmental system. In this respect, the research would provide a useful model of data-collection techniques and data analysis systems for the future study of similar academic environments. Such further applications of the model might provide data which could be statistically compared to the present data to advance knowledge in this aspect of environmental research and possibly contribute to a broader theoretical framework.

2. METHOD

2.1. The Setting

The focus of the present investigation was the Department of Psychology of the University of Houston. At the time of the study the department was physically located in the Science and Research Building, a large, seven-story structure housing a number of other academic departments. Functionally the department consists of office, research, general purpose, classroom, and storage space occupying portions of the second, fifth, and seventh floors of the building and all of the sixth floor, representing a total of 28,671 square feet of space.

For purposes of the present study allied or satellite facilities not housed in the building, yet functionally under the jurisdiction of the psychology department were omitted for practical reasons. Additionally, most of the general classrooms were not included as the majority of them are located outside the department.

The personnel comprising the department may be differentiated by the various roles which they serve within the organization. The department consists of 32 full-time faculty members serving in teaching and/or administrative positions, three of whom are adjunct faculty members housed in another campus location; a business administrator; ten full-time secretarial staff members and a number of part-time clerical staff members; 173 graduate students, some of whom were on internships at the time of the study; and approximately 1,300 undergraduate majors.

At an organizational level, the department may be viewed as a number of subsystems differing along functional dimensions yet highly interrelated in the pursuit of the organization's goals. The various subsystems consist of administrative, support, academic/training, and research components. These components may be further subdivided according to specialty or primary area of concern. For example, the subdivisions include the biopsychology, clinical, developmental, social, educational, industrial-organizational, and cognitive programs. Each of these programs provide training at the undergraduate, graduate, and, to a small degree, at the post-doctoral level. Additionally there exists an applied psychology program providing training at the M.A. level only, and three special training areas consisting of a small number of students at the doctoral level whose interests overlap formal training areas.

2.2. Interviews

The initial phase of the investigation consisted of a series of structured interviews with key faculty members representing the various organizational components within the department. The purpose of the interviews was two-fold. First, information was needed concerning the organizational structure and immediately foreseeable goals of the components which might have implications for space utilization. Second, the interviews were to identify problem areas and generate the initial research questions to guide future phases of the research.

A total of ten faculty members serving in administrative capacities were interviewed. Through the interviews, information concerning existing activity systems, spatial needs, and areas of satisfaction and dissatisfaction for each program area and the department as a whole was gathered. Also, future trends which might affect the group's functioning, structure and spatial needs were noted. The duration of the interviews was approximately thirty to forty-five minutes.

2.3. Structured Observation

Phase two consisted of structured observations of the department modelled after Ittelson, Rivlin, and Proshansky's (1970) behavioral mapping technique. The behavioral maps provided descriptions of the ongoing activities and participants throughout the department, as well as relating behavior to its physical locus.

2.3.1. Coding Categories

The initial step in developing the coding form was to determine the behaviors to be considered. After postulating a number of observable activities, the experimenter spent considerable time cataloguing specific examples of individual and group behavior observed while walking through the department. Only molar activities such as typing or reading were recorded.

Molecular behaviors such as moving a limb, or shifting position were not included.

Eleven observational categories were developed from the resulting inventory of behaviors, by combining them into groups on the basis of homogeneity and observability. That is, the categories represented sets of behaviors which could be readily described for observers and easily identified by them. A description of the coding categories and examples of behaviors subsumed under each may be found in Table 1.

2.3.2. Observers

The data were collected by three observers: the senior author, another graduate student and a senior psychology student. Descriptions of the various behaviors constituting each of the observational categories were supplied the observers. In addition, training sessions were employed in which the senior author accompanied the observer on the pre-determined route, clarifying questions concerning the use of the form and the behaviors recorded as problems arose.

2.3.3. Observations

The entire department was observed a total of 80 times by the three observers over a three-week period from the latter half of March to the second week in April, a period when the departmental workload is normally at a peak. The duration of each observation varied from twenty to thirty-five minutes, depending on the time required to walk the specified route. Observations were conducted randomly throughout the day from 8:00 A.M. to 6:00 P.M., five days per week, as the observers' schedules permitted.

The physical settings observed on the route consisted of each location displaying a numerical address and all the major traffic and hall areas. The hall areas themselves were assigned addresses according to their physical location. For example, a waiting area adjacent to the fifth floor elevators was designated location "500 E". A total of 177 addressed locations were observed on each pass.

On a single observation the observer initially entered the date, day, start time, and his name on the coding form. Then he began walking the prescribed route recording information in the following manner. Before entering the specific setting, the address was noted. Upon entry, the observer scanned the setting to determine the ongoing action and persons involved. To facilitate recording and reduce confusion, observers were instructed to take a "mental photograph" of the scene as it was first encountered, disregarding subsequent changes of activity or persons in the setting. After leaving the setting, the observer coded the behavior pattern by placing the number of persons observed under the observational category or categories which best described the activity

pattern in the setting. The participants themselves were also identified in terms of their university status: faculty member, staff member, graduate student, undergraduate student, or unknown. Additionally, the coding form allowed observers to record instances where a particular location was unobservable as well as when a location was observable but uninhabited.

Observers were instructed to enter only those settings with open doors or having "public hours" posted to avoid invasions of privacy. Also, the observers were to remain as unobtrusive as possible to avoid disrupting the ongoing behavior sequences in a setting.

2.3.4. Interobserver Reliability

To assess interobserver agreement, reliability checks were obtained by having two observers independently code the same physical locations at the same time for the entire department. A total of four reliability checks were obtained.

TABLE 1: DESCRIPTION OF CODING CATEGORIES

1. Information Storage & Retrieval
Clerical activities which involve manipulating paperwork and supplies. Includes: filing; manipulating books, journals, papers; delivering, sorting and retrieving mail; inventorying supplies; posting notices in halls, bulletin boards.
2. Use of Office Machines
Use and maintenance of office machinery. Includes: typing; using ditto, mimeo, and photocopy machines; collating and stapling; dictating; transcribing dictation; routine operator maintenance.
3. Reading
All reading activities regardless of the nature of the material. Includes: technical reading--books, journals, papers; recreational reading--newspapers, magazines; reading graphs, charts, tables, computer printouts; reading bulletin boards, notices.
4. Writing
All writing activities with pens, pencils, chalk, markers. Includes: note-taking; grading papers; writing on blackboards; technical writing; flowcharting; signing up for experiments.
5. Data Processing
Involves use of computer or calculator hardware. Includes: keypunches; teletypes; computer terminals; calculators; pocket calculators.
6. Telephoning
Any use of telephone for business or recreation.
7. Equipment Monitoring and Maintenance
Involves the use of audio/visual equipment and aids as well as monitoring and repairing research equipment. Includes: coding from video playbacks; watching films and slide presentations; setting up equipment; shop repair and maintenance; monitoring electronic equipment.
8. Personal Maintenance
Involves maintenance of bodily functioning.

Page 262

TABLE 1 (Cont.)

Includes: resting; sleeping; grooming and
hygiene; eating meals and snacks; drinking.
9. Task Group
Involves direct social communication between
groups of two or more persons which is task-
oriented in nature. Includes: teacher-student
conferences; administrative discussions; work
supervision; colloquia; continuing education
activities; seminars; committee meetings;
academic discussions; class discussion; test
taking; lecture; discussing research; routing
inquiries.
10. Socialization and Recreation
All direct social communication between two or
more persons which is clearly recreational in
nature.
11. Travelling
All travel including entering, departing,
waiting for elevators and using stairs.

2.4. Questionnaire

The final phase of data-collection consisted of
a questionnaire which was distributed to departmental faculty, staff, and graduate students
through departmental mailboxes, the postal system,
and in person. The purpose of the questionnaire
was to assess user attitudes and perceived needs
concerning the various types of physical space
and facilities available in the department.

Specifically, users were requested to provide
ratings of each of seven attributes: size,
location, visual privacy, auditory privacy,
comfort, adaptability/flexibility, and availability for those types of space the person was
currently using. The attributes selected for
inclusion had been previously mentioned by one
or more persons in the faculty interviews as
areas of satisfaction or dissatisfaction regarding various types of space. The types of
space to be rated were derived from a departmental
space inventory and included office space,
research space, conference/meeting rooms, storage
space, duplicating facilities, data processing
facilities, shop facilities, a reading room, and
lounges. Users provided ratings by placing an
"S" indicating satisfaction, "D" indicating
dissatisfaction, or "N" indicating not important
or not applicable, under each of the seven
attributes for each category rated.

The questionnaire was designed to permit users
to record responses with ease and in a short
period of time in a structured format. Care was
also taken to provide opportunities for further
user input if desired. Space was provided on
the form for additional comments concerning
needs and explanations of ratings.

3. RESULTS

3.1. Interviews

The faculty interview data was summarized by

listing the immediately foreseeable goals which
might have space implications for the program
areas and the department as a whole. Particularly noteworthy was the emphasis placed upon
research activities in the various areas. A
trend toward research in the field was apparent,
though continued labortory research was also
projected. These findings were consistent with
general departmental goals emphasizing the in-
tensification of basic laboratory research and
increased involvement in applied and field
setting research. The space implications of
these goals seemed to be primarily a need for
a) general and academic support space, such as
offices and conference rooms and b) specialized
space with audio/visual monitoring capabilities.

To further assess the importance of various types
of space/facilities in the department, the notes
from the interviews were content analyzed
(cf. Holsti, 1969). The categories selected for
the analysis were based on the existing types
of space available in the department. The
frequency of comments concerning both projected
and existing space usage for each type of
facility provided a general indication of importance of the space for the individuals interviewed. The analysis revealed that the number of
responses concerning both existing and projected
space utilization was greatest for research,
conference and meeting rooms, and storage space.

3.2. Structured Observation

The data in Table 2 represent a hypothetically
"average" observation of the department, in the
sense that the figures represent the mean number
of persons observed over 80 observations.
Examination of the table reveals a great degree
of variability in the number of persons engaged
in the various activities. Task groups constitute the greatest amount of activity, followed
by socializing, reading, and travel. Data
processing was the least observed activity,
constituting only 1.16 percent of the total
number of persons observed.

TABLE 2: DISTRIBUTION OF BEHAVIOR IN THE
DEPARTMENT: AN AVERAGE OBSERVATION

ACTIVITY	f	%
Information Storage and Retrieval	4.15[a]	5.93
Office Machine Use	4.20	6.00
Reading	7.89	11.27
Writing	3.79	5.41
Data Processing	0.81	1.16
Telephoning	2.50	3.57
Equipment Monitoring/ Maintenance	1.25	1.79
Personal Maintenance	3.21	4.59
Task Group	24.73	35.33
Social/Recreational	9.95	14.21
Travel	7.49	10.70
Total	69.97	100.00

[a]Figures are $\bar{X}$ number of persons observed in the
activity over 80 observations.

Page 4

That only approximately 70 persons were observed on an average observation seems surprising in view of the large number of potential users of the department. Inspection of Table 3, in which the mean number of active, inactive, and unobservable locations is reported, sheds light on this situation. On a typical observation, approximately two out of three locations were unobservable. Further, of the remaining locations only about half were inhabited; the remainder were observable but empty. Apparently, the 70 people observed were utilizing about 30 locations, representing only 17.03 percent of the observed sites.

While the actual number of persons engaged in various activities is open to speculation, it is probably much greater than 70 people. Nevertheless, the very high number of unobservable locations is itself particularly noteworthy, especially in view of the fact that a number of the locations surveyed were corridors and hallways. Apparently the department consists, to some degree, of a collection of closed doors.

TABLE 3: OBSERVABILITY OF LOCATIONS: AN AVERAGE OBSERVATION

LOCATIONS	f	%
Inactive	27.95[a]	15.79
Active	30.13	17.03
Unobservable	118.91	67.18
Total	177.00	100.00

[a]$\bar{x}$ number of locations over 80 observations.

Clearly this information is of use only if the data are reliable. Since a number of observers were used in collecting the data, four checks of observer agreement were made in which different pairs of observers independently coded the activities in the entire department at the same time. For each check, the percentage of agreement was calculated by dividing the number of agreements by the number of agreements plus disagreements. The mean percentage of agreement for the four reliability checks was 81.75 percent. This is quite high given that the figures represent both observers agreeing on the number and activity of persons utilizing the specific location.

That standing patterns of behavior exist in a given setting over time regardless of the specific individuals involved, was one of the initial assumptions of the research. To assess the stability of activity patterns and the degree to which they were identified by the observational system, the distribution of activities from the first 40 observations were compared with those of the second 40 observations. The percentage of people observed in the eleven activity categories in each half of the observations differed by a mean of only 1.33 percent, with a range from 0.21 to 6.34 percent, revealing that the patterns in the distribution of activity are indeed relatively stable over the time period examined.

For purposes of further analysis the 177 observed locations were grouped into twelve categories. The activity site concept as proposed by Moleski (1973) served as a useful model for the groupings.

An activity site is a physical area within organizational boundaries, in which prescribed activities directed toward the achievement of organizational goals regularly occur. The various locations may themselves be grouped on the basis of functional similarity toward the achievement of the organization's objectives. Therefore, three types of office space were identified as distinct activity sites, including faculty offices, graduate student offices, and staff offices. Four types of academic support sites, research facilities, conference/seminar rooms, the department reading room, and an undergraduate office were also identified. In addition, three categories of general support sites emerged: storage facilities, duplicating facilities, and data processing facilities. For purposes of the present report, however, the results of only four of the groupings, the three types of office sites and research sites, will be discussed.

The data presented in Table 4 emphasize the problem of the different degrees of observability of activity sites. In the table, the percentage of observations in which an average location was observable versus unobservable is reported for each type of activity site. As may be noted, there exists wide variability in the observability of different activity sites. For example, the average faculty and graduate student offices were unobservable 70.97 and 77.73 percent of the time, respectively. Research space was unobservable 73.49 percent of the time. In contrast, the average staff office was open to view all but 25.63 percent of the time.

TABLE 4: OBSERVABILITY OF ACTIVITY SITES

ACTIVITY SITE	OBSERVABLE			UNOBSERVABLE	TOTAL
	Active	Inactive	Sub-Total		
Faculty Office	12.21[a]	16.81	29.02	70.97	100.00
Graduate Office	10.65	10.70	21.35	77.73	100.00
Staff Office	55.94	18.44	74.38	25.63	100.00
Research Office	7.09	19.42	26.51	73.49	100.00

[a]Figures reported are percentages of total number of times the average activity site was surveyed.

These differences in observability become important in further analysis and comparison of activity sites. In comparing office sites, for example, greater confidence may be placed in the nature of the distributions of activities and persons observed in the more public secretarial areas than in faculty or graduate student offices.

TABLE 5: DISTRIBUTION OF ACTIVITES BY ACTIVITY SITES

ACTIVITY	Faculty Office (N = 31)		Graduate Office (N = 47)		Staff Office (N = 16)		Research Space (N = 45)	
	f	%	f	%	f	%	f	%
Information Storage	42[a]	9.33[b]	52	9.17	170	12.81	22	4.74
Office Machines	8	1.78	17	3.00	254	19.14	10	2.16
Reading	64	14.22	149	26.28	106	7.99	31	6.68
Writing	24	5.33	60	10.58	83	6.25	52	11.21
Data Processing	1	0.22	3	0.53	7	0.53	9	1.94
Telephoning	40	8.89	1	0.18	125	9.42	7	1.51
Equipment Monitoring	3	0.67	0	0.00	4	0.30	64	13.79
Personal Maintenance	29	6.44	33	5.82	87	6.56	23	4.96
Social/ Recreational	23	5.11	139	24.51	209	15.75	54	11.54
Task Group	205	45.56	105	18.52	226	17.03	173	37.68
Travel	11	2.44	8	1.41	56	4.22	19	4.09
Total	405	100.00	567	100.00	1,327	100.00	464	100.00

[a]Total number of persons observed in the activity over 80 observations.

[b]Percent of total number of persons observed in the location type over 80 observations.

The distribution of activities observed in the various activity sites is reported in Table 5. The actual number of persons engaged in a particular activity over all observations is reported for each activity site, providing an index of the intensity of the activities supported by the site. For purposes of comparing sites, the percentage of the total number of persons observed in the sites engaged in a given activity is also reported.

Inspection of this table reveals a number of characteristic differences in the activities observed in various sites. For example, in faculty offices the most frequent activity was task group discussions. Regarding individual activities, reading, information storage, and telephoning were most often observed. In graduate student offices, the primary observed activity was reading, followed by socializing and task-oriented discussions. The use of office machines was highest in staff offices, as might be expected, followed by task group discussions, socializing, and information handling.

In research sites the greatest amount of activity was devoted to task groups followed by equipment monitoring and maintenance, socialization, and writing.

While the general occupancy patterns in office sites are generally what might be predicted, some additional observations are suggested. First, office sites are predominantly interpersonal settings with a great emphasis on communication. This is probably as one would expect, given the conditions of observation. That is, coding occurred only when the particular sites were open. This might tend to distort the data concerning solitary activities such as reading, writing, or telephoning, which often require the privacy of closed doors. In this respect, though, it is interesting that the graduate students' primary activity was reading despite the fact that it was observed in open offices.

Second, though the visibility factor precludes the total assessment of activities, the observational system nevertheless revealed characteristic topographies of behavior across sites. For example, in comparing sites of approximately equal visibility, both differences and similarities in behavior patterns are readily apparent. Research sites and faculty offices maintain high levels of task group activity, while much higher levels of reading and socializing were apparent in graduate student offices than in the other two types of activity sites. Likewise, a predominant usage of research sites for the monitoring and maintenance of equipment is in contrast to very low levels in graduate and faculty offices. On the other hand, all three sites share some common features. Data processing was observed at very low levels in all sites. This may suggest that this activity goes on behind closed doors, or very possibly that other departmental sites maintain such activity. Similarly, the use of office machines is low in these locations as might be expected. And, in all three site the occurence of personal maintenance behaviors falls at almost equal levels.

3.3. Questionaire

A total of fifty-eight questionaires were

returned by faculty, graduate students, and
staff personnel. Approximately 55 percent of
the faculty, 20 percent of graduate students,
and 60 percent of the staff members surveyed
responded to the questionaire.

In the construction of the questionaire, seven
attributes mentioned in faulty interviews concerning space were included. These served as
the categories on which each type of activity
site was rated. For purposes of analysis, however, some of these categories were omitted for
certain activity sites. Attributes which were
rated as "not important" by 50 percent or more
of all three respondent groups were considered
irrelevant for the particular site and were
thus deleted. For example, more than 50 percent
of all groups rated visual privacy as an unimportant feature of data processing facilities,
so ratings of this attribute were not considered
in further analyses.

Total satisfaction ratings for each type of
activity site were determined by computing the
mean ratings of attributes applicable to the
site. The mean satisfaction ratings of each
group was generally high for all activity sites.
However, some differences were apparent across
groups, particularly in ratings of dissatisfaction in certain areas. Faculty members were
most dissatisfied with research and storage
space, which seems consistent with the results
of the faculty interviews, and with data processing facilities. Graduate students were
most dissatisfied with offices, duplicating
facilities and lounges, while staff personnel
rated storage and duplicating sites unsatisfactory.

Examination of respondents' ratings of relevant
attributes for the various activity sites supports the conclusion that users are, as a rule,
satisfied with most aspects of the facilities
available. Probably the most noteworthy area
of dissatisfaction concerned levels of noise
from adjacent areas as a major nuisance factor
in offices. Also the availablity of particular
types of space was a prime concern of many users.
On the whole, the data suggested a need for
greater accessibility to space for research-
related activities, including more generalized
space, storage space, and data processing
facilities, which seems consistent with the
needs expressed in the faculty interview data.
And, regarding academic support space, some need
for more graduate student offices and for greater
accessibility to duplicating facilities was
evident.

4. DISCUSSION

An important assumption guiding the research
was that any assessment of a physical system
must be considered within the context of the
broader social system to which it is bound.
Since the bodies of data from the three phases
of the reserach are related along a common
dimension, that of physical space,

a more holistic approach is suggested. By viewing the data as an integrated, though to some
degree overlapping body of information, a broader
view of the social system itself is afforded.

That such a holistic approach is not only valid,
but necessary, becomes evident in attempting to
evaluate departmental activities and associated
space needs at a specific level. For example,
the behavioral mapping provides little information on the existing research activities of the
department, let alone the implications of these
activities for space utilization, due to the
low visibility of research sites. However,
research appears to be an integral part of the
organization's functioning, as reflected in
the emphasis placed on research in the goals of
the various training areas and the department as
a whole. That increased field-setting research
as well as intensified laboratory research may
hold implications for space utilization was
evident in the faculty interviews and satisfaction questionaires. Apparently more generalized multi-purpose space and special-function
space are needed to maintain both field and
departmentally-housed research.

Nevertheless, since the low visibility of research sites precluded the identification of
actual existing patterns of research, the
evaluation of the organization's progress toward
its research-oriented goals is difficult. At
best, the assumption may be made that research
activities are occurring in the field or behind
closed doors.

In a similar respect, the assessment of other
academic pursuits is also obscured by lack of
visibility of some of the sites in which they
may occur. For example, that individual
scholarly pursuits such as reading and writing
are undoubtably occurring in meaningful patterns
is suggested by both the mapping data and the
finding that noise levels are a nuisance for
many office occupants in performing their duties.
However, the actual incidence of these activities
is difficult to assess, probably as a result of
the inherently private nature of many of these
tasks. These findings seem to corroborate
those of Jenkins, Nadler, Lawler, and Camman
(1975) who concluded that the characteristics of
some jobs in an organization are less amenable
to measurement through structured observation
techniques than others. In the present study,
the activities of secretaries, whose offices
were much more accessible to view than those of
graduate students or faculty members, were more
readily apparent than those of other staff members. Apparently, a great deal of the difficulty
encountered in the behavioral assessment of job
characteristics is environmentally determined.

Despite the limitations encountered, the present
study demonstrates that a multi-method, multi-
variable assessment model can provide valuable
information for space programming in an academic
setting. On the basis the data gathered, it
became possible to suggest a number of guidelines

for future programming based on the spatial redistribution of existing activity systems or through possible changes in the physical characteristics of particular settings to affect behavior patterns.

Whether these changes occur through administrative planning or simply evolve to accomodate the needs of the social system, the fact is that over time, changes in both the physical and social system of the department will occur. Perhaps, this is where the greater value of the present research lies. Through subsequent applications of the present model, these changes may be assessed by comparing the resultant data against that of the present investigation. And, besides providing data on the progress in a particular environmental setting, future research with the model could be addressed toward a broader goal, that of contributing to the identification of a general topography of behaviors common to similar academic environments.

In the future, however, additional efforts should be made toward refining the data collection techniques to provide more information on actual behavior patterns. Undoubtably, a complete description of all behavior will prove difficult given the nature of roles and tasks of the organization's personnel. Nevertheless, a refinement of the model might include some means of increasing the visibility of activity sites.

A number of alternatives are possible. From a research design standpoint, the use of electronic surveillance equipment might be preferred, though the cost and availability of such equipment presents severe limitations. Other self-report forms of the data collection such as diaries could be used to supplement behavioral observation data, though this would require the time and cooperation of many of the organization's personnel.

Perhaps, in line with the emphasis in the current research toward feasibility and simplicity of design in data collection, it might prove fruitful to knock on a selected sample of the closed doors encountered during an observation, recording whether there was an acknowledgement from within. Though this would not allow description of the activities occurring behind closed doors, it might at least afford a clearer assessment of the extent to which some of the less observable locations were actually maintaining activity at a given time. Obviously, the incorporation of such a method would require the cooperation of the organization's members, but would minimize the invasions of privacy and disruption of ongoing activities which would result from entering closed settings.

Reference:

HOLSTI, O. R. Content analysis for the social sciences and humanities. London: Addison-Wesley, 1969.

ITTELSON, W. H., PROSHANSKY, H. M., RIVLIN, L. G., AND WINKEL, G. H. An introduction to environmental psychology. New York: Holt, Rinehart & Winston, 1974.

ITTELSON, W. H., RIVLIN, L. G., AND PROSHANSKY, H. M. The use of behavioral maps in environmental psychology. In H. M. Proshansky, W. H. Ittelson, and L. G. Rivlin (Eds.), Environmental psychology: Man and his physical setting. New York: Holt, Rinehart, and Winston, 1970.

JENKINS, G. D., NADLER, D. A., LAWLER, E., AND CAMMANN, C. Standardized observations: An approach to measuring the nature of jobs. Journal of Applied Psychology, 1975, 60, 171-181.

MOLESKI, W. H. Behavioral analysis and environmental programming for offices. In J. Lang, C. Bornette, W. H. Moleski, and D. Vachon (Eds.), Designing for human behavior. Stroudsburg, Penn.: Dowden, Hutchinson, and Ross, 1974.

WEBB, E., CAMPBELL, D. T., SCHWARTZ, R. D., AND SECHREST, L. Unobtrusive measures: Non-reactive research in the social sciences. Chicago: Rand McNally, 1966.

The authors would like to express their appreciation to Neil Mann and Paul Bartlett for assistance in collecting the behavioral mapping data.

LEARNING BY DOING: APPLYING THE TECHNIQUES OF BEHAVIORAL SCIENCE TO THE ANALYSIS OF CONSTRUCTED BUILDINGS

Jeffrey Karl Ochsner

Graduate Student
Rice University School of Architecture
Houston, Texas 77001

ABSTRACT

This paper presents a study of attitudes and activity patterns of residents of one floor of a girls' dormitory at Rice University. It represents an attempt at identifying certain characteristics of the physical planning and design of the floor as affectors of the residents' behavior.

While such applied research has validity in its own right, this paper is presented as a demonstration of the kind of work that students of architecture can be expected to do in "learning by doing" in the context of a course in the Behavioral Impacts of Design. It is suggested that architects trained in this way will have a better understanding of the potential of the behavioral sciences and will be better equipped to apply the results of behavioral research in actual building design.

1. INTRODUCTION

1.1. The Context

This project, conducted within the framework of an academic course in the Rice University School of Architecture, was designed to demonstrate the applicability of the techniques of behavioral science to the study of built environments.

Within the academic curriculum of the Rice University School of Architecture a course is offered at both the undergraduate and graduate levels to provide an overview of research, theory and practice of relating building design and community development to individual and collective behavioral responses. The course is presented in three segments: concepts, theories and methods in man-environment; the future of social policy planning; and practical application of man-environment research. In this context each student is required to design and implement an original research project. Obviously, in the few months available to students, it is not possible to do research projects of considerable depth. However, such projects can engender an understanding and appreciation for the methods of behavioral science and their potential for environmental design.

The following project, then, represents the kind of work an architecture student with no previous background in behavioral science can carry out in such a course.

1.2. The Study Concept

Research concerning the environmental and social impact of college residency has concentrated largely on issues of student attitudes and prejudices. Undergraduate student populations have long served for experimentation and the study of attitude changes due to environmental and peer pressures, but rarely have the impacts of the specific architectural designs of college buildings been considered as a major factor in such studies.

However, a few studies have been suggestive of the kinds of impacts architectural design may have. In Defensible Space (1972), Oscar Newman reported a comparative study of two Sara Lawrence College dormitories, one a new slab structure with long internal double-loaded corridors and the other composed of three separate "houses" each with its own small internal corridors and stairs. The social activities and individual attitudes of the two groups of residents were markedly different.

This study and similar ones leave unquestioned the level at which architectural design begins to play a role as an important factor determining activities and attitudes. The study reported here is a small scale attempt to identify the attitudes, concerns and living patterns of students living in one college residence on the Rice University campus. It was organized as a pilot study using an interview and structured questionnaire technique. Because the type of questionnaire used allowed open responses, the results are of only limited statistical significance. Nonetheless, they are also very suggestive.

2. STUDY DESIGN

2.1. Location

The third floor of Jones College South was selected for study. This floor was selected because its organization as a double-loaded corridor structure broken by a central lobby and circulation core area created a "natural experiment". The central core breaks the floor into two distinct areas, which, as a result of their differeing plans, it was thought, would show significantly different activity patterns and attitudes on the part of the residents. Comparison of these differing attitudes and activities could begin to indicate the kinds of influence that architectural planning might have on users. (Further, it must be admitted that the author already had some familiarity with the floor residents and the floor layout. It was, therefore, easier to interview the study subjects than might otherwise have been true.)

2.2. Plan of Third Floor (See FIGURE 1)

The third floor of Jones College South is organized along a double-loaded corridor running roughly east and west. On the north side of this corridor are 8 rooms (7 singles and 1 two-person suite with bathroom); on the south side of the corridor are 12 rooms (all doubles). The two fire stairs at eith end of the floor are located on the north side of the corridor.

The center section of the floor is planned with a large communal bathroom, an elevator and stair core and a lobby and communal kitchen. The effect of this core is to intrude on the corridor space so that it is impossible to see from one end of the floor to the other.

The major environmental differences between the two ends of the floor are the number of rooms and the length of the corridors. SHORT END, to the west, has 8 rooms (5 doubles, 2 singles, 1 two-person suite); LONG END, to the east, has 12 rooms (7 doubles, 5 singles). The main lobby is actually closer to LONG END. The kitchen is slightly closer to SHORT END. The communal bathroom is organized to serve both ends. LONG END hall is about 85 feet long; SHORT END hall is about 60 feet long.

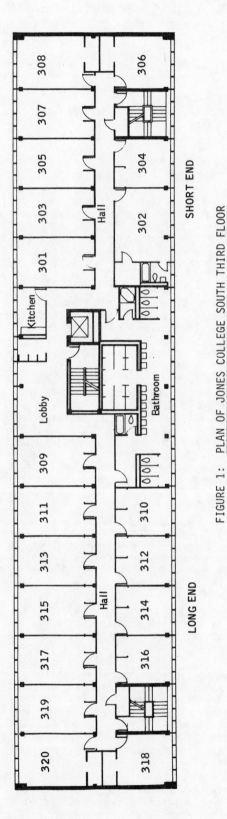

FIGURE 1: PLAN OF JONES COLLEGE SOUTH THIRD FLOOR

2.3. Population

At the time of this study, the floor housed 30 undergraduate girls, from freshmen through seniors (FIGURE 2).

SHORT END		LONG END	
Fr	5	Fr	6
So	4	So	5
Jr	2	Jr	4
Sr	2	Sr	2
	13		17

FIGURE 2: POPULATION

(When the survey was conducted two girls were in the process of moving on to the floor, but had not yet done so. They were not included. One LONG END junior girl could not be located for survey and was not included. The survey population numbered 29.)

No concentration of majors was found on the floor, nor was there any correlation between majors and location. There were no architecture majors; the population split between academic and science-engineering students. Five students listed biology as a major (or part of a double-major), but this was not regarded as significant.

At the time of the survey, many floor members had outside activities. Five were active in the Jones College government. Seven held part-time jobs either on or off campus. Fourteen members listed some extra-curricular activities; most of these were in intramural or intercollegiate athletics. No floor members were currently active in either of the two women's literary societies (Rice equivalent of sororities), though three had once been active for a single semester. (Participation in the literary societies must be regarded as being below the Rice average, since these organizations do exist and function. However, they are apparently irrelevant to members of third floor, Jones South.)

2.4. Hypothesis

It was expected that there would be significant differences in the living situations of the residents of LONG END and SHORT END. Since SHORT END was smaller, it was expected that this would be a more intimate environment, probably encouraging more friendships and a greater sense of community. It was though that overall, LONG END residents would be more dissatisfied with their environment due to the greater number of people which would mean more noise and less privacy.

A second hypothesis was that the floor would be strongly separated into two groups of residents following the division of the floor into the two ends. Friendships within each end, it was thought, would outnumber those between ends. It was expected that the central core would be a strong

barrier on an interpersonal as well as a physical level.

2.5. Study Method

Each floor resident was requested to fill out an eight page questionnaire in an interview situation. It was thought that the use of a structured questionnaire might help to eliminate subjective interpretations by the interviewer of subject responses. However, the interviewer was present at all times while subjects filled out the questionnaire in order to answer questions and clarify confusing issues. These interviews were conducted either in the subject's room, the third floor lobby or the first floor lobby. The average time to complete the questionnaire was about thirty minutes, although some subjects took up to an hour.

All of the interviews were conducted between March 3 and March 10, 1975. Each subject was asked not to discuss the questionnaire with any other floor member until the study was completed in order to avoid any pre-knowledge of the questions.

The eight pages of the questionnaire were organized as follows:

Page 1: Introductory comments about the nature and confidentiality of the study.

Page 2: General information: Each subject was asked to give name, room number, major and classification, and to answer several short questions about part-time work, extra-curriculars, and so on.

Page 3: Plan of Jones College South third floor with rooms numbered. In blanks provided next to each room, the subject was to give the names of the residents of that room.

Page 4: Third floor plan. Subjects were asked to describe as many room interiors as possible, giving decor, major colors, furniture positions, and so on.

Page 5: Third floor plan. Subjects were asked to list how many times each week they visited each room on the floor other than their own.

Page 6: A list of all residents of third floor. Subjects were asked to identify each resident as close friend, friend, acquaintance or unknown using a numerical scale (3, 2, 1, 0).

Pages 7, 8: A 30 item questionnaire (multiple choice) to ascertain the attitudes and concerns of floor residents.

The design of this study was primarily organized to detect differences in the knowlege and concerns of residents of the two ends of the floor. The residents were not told the study was seeking to discover the effects of the division of the floor into two ends.

The three plan pages were designed to distinguish knowledge and movement patterns to determine the influence of the plan on the level of individual awareness of the floor.

The residents listing was designed to detect the relationship of friendship patterns to the architectural planning.

The thirty item question set was organized by two major categories:

1. Stress, noise: concerns with door-locking, unescorted males, dissatisfaction with noise by time of day, point of origin and perceived impact;

2. Social interaction: degree of perceived community, privacy, meeting place locations, commonality of values, responses to intrusion, extent of sensed personal territory.

Each of the questions related to one of these categories, although some may be considered to have related to both. The questions were multiple choice with a three point scale such as "often", "sometimes", "rarely" or "most", "some", "few". Subjects were invited to add comments or qualify or clarify their answers. Some of these added comments proved highly illuminating.

By the end of the interview process, it was evident that some questions which should have been asked had been missed. As a result, some factors which might have proved significant were omitted, and this study was not as conclusive as it might have been.

3. RESULTS

3.1. Names

The first task was to fill in the names of the residents of each room next to that room on a plan of the floor. (Unfortunately, it was not made clear that both first and last names were desired. Some subjects listed only first names. This resulted in a loss of significance for this task.)

SHORT END   13 subjects   25.2 names (ave.)
LONG END   16 subjects   28.7 names (ave.)

FIGURE 3: NAME IDENTIFICATIONS

(Statistical correlations by class showed little variation, although more juniors and seniors than freshman and sophomores were able to list all thirty names.)

3.2. Room Descriptions

These data proved very inconsistent and therefore difficult to analyze. Some individuals gave long descriptions of each room, while others gave very sparse descriptions. It was not easy to determine what actually constituted knowlege of a room interior. However, the following analysis is reasonably accurate.

SHORT END   13 subjects
    ave.:   7.6 rooms total   38% of all rooms
             4.2 short end rooms 52%
             3.4 long end rooms 28%

LONG END   16 subjects
    ave.:   9.3 rooms total   46% of all rooms
             2.4 short end rooms 30%
             6.9 long end rooms 57%

FIGURE 4:   CORRECT DESCRIPTIONS OF INTERIORS

Notably, LONG END residents knew about the same number of SHORT END rooms as SHORT END residents knew of LONG END rooms. (Indeed, the difference in overall percentages can be accounted for by the fact that the average SHORT END resident passes by 4 rooms on the way to her own, while the average LONG END resident passes by 6 rooms on the way to her own! Thus, other than showing that residents do have a slightly higher knowlege of neighboring rooms, the data have no statistical significance.)

3.3. Room Visiting Patterns

Each subject estimated her number of visits per week to every other room on the floor. The total number of weekly visits listed was 772, divided as follows.

To:		LONG END	SHORT END
		465 visits	307 visits
From:		39 visits/ room	38 visits/ room
LONG END	478 visits	301 visits	177 visits
	30 visits/ person	1.36 visits/ room/person	1.30 visits/ room/person
SHORT END	294 visits	164 visits	130 visits
	23 visits/ person	1.57 visits/ room/person	1.25 visits/ room/person

FIGURE 5:   THIRD FLOOR VISITING PATTERNS

These data suggest that residents of LONG END do slightly more visiting each week, and that most of this visiting is within LONG END. Further, a greater percentage of SHORT END residents' visits are also to LONG END rooms.

However, these data must be highly suspect. Checks with certain floor members show that the number of visits that may have actually been received is considerably below the totals of visits estimated by all other floor members. This could suggest a problem in interpreting the word "visit". Some subjects thought actually entering a room constituted a visit, while others said afterwards that they thought intent was sufficient and that a visit could be counted even if they knocked and no one answered.

3.4. Friendship Patterns

Each subject rated her friendships with every other floor member using the scale: 0-unknown, 1-acquaintance, 2-friend, 3-close friend. This produced the matrix shown below when tabulated (FIGURE 6). It should be noted that this matrix is not symmetrical—some subjects regarding a relationship on one level, while the other participant in the relationship saw it on a higher or lower level.

```
                  1 1 1 1 | 1 1 1 1 1 2 2 2 2 2 2 2 2 2
      1 2 3 4 5 6 7 8 9 0 1 2 3 | 4 5 6 7 8 9 0 1 2 3 4 5 6 7 8 9
   1|   ③ 2 3 2 1 1 1 1 2 2 ③ 2 | 1 1 1 1 1 2 2 2 2 2 2 2 1 2 ③ ③
   2| ③   2 2 1 0 1 1 1 1 1 2 2 | 0 1 1 1 1 2 2 1 2 1 2 1 1 1 2 2
   3| 2 2   ③ 1 1 1 1 1 1 1 2 2 | 1 1 2 1 1 ③ 3 3 1 1 2 2 1 2 ③ 2
   4| 2 1 ③   1 1 1 1 1 1 1 2 2 | 1 1 1 1 1 ③ 3 ③ 1 1 2 2 1 1 ③ 2
   5| 2 2 2 2   1 1 1 1 2 2 2 2 | 1 1 2 1 1 2 2 2 0 2 2 1 2 ③ 2 2
   6| 1 1 2 1 0   0 1 0 1 0 2 2 | 0 0 2 0 0 1 1 1 0 0 0 0 1 2 1 1
   7| 1 1 1 1 0 0   2 1 2 2 1 0 | 1 1 1 1 1 1 1 1 1 1 1 0 0 1 1 1     SHORT
   8| 2 2 2 2 1 0 3   1 2 2 1 1 | 1 1 1 ③ ③ 1 2 2 1 1 1 1 1 1 1 1     END
   9| 1 1 1 1 1 1 1 1   1 1 1 1 | 1 1 1 1 1 1 1 1 1 1 1 1 1 ③ 1 1
  10| 2 2 2 2 2 0 2 2 2   ③ 2 2 | 2 2 2 2 2 2 2 1 1 0 2 0 2 2 2
  11| 2 2 2 2 2 1 2 2 1 ③   2 2 | 2 2 1 2 2 1 2 2 1 1 1 1 1 2 1 1
  12| ③ 3 3 3 1 2 1 1 1 1 1   ③ | 1 1 2 1 2 2 2 2 1 2 1 1 2 2 ③ ③
  13| 2 2 2 2 0 2 1 1 1 1 1 ③   | 1 0 2 0 0 2 2 2 2 1 1 1 2 1 3 2
  --+-----------------------------+--------------------------------
  14| 1 1 1 2 1 1 1 1 1 2 1 1 2 |   ③ 1 1 1 2 2 2 2 2 2 1 1 2 2 2
  15| 1 1 2 2 0 0 1 1 1 1 2 1 0 | ③   2 1 1 3 ③ ③ 2 2 2 1 1 2 2 3
  16| 1 1 2 2 1 0 0 0 1 0 1 2 2 | 1 1   1 1 2 1 0 1 1 2 2 1 1 2 2
  17| 1 1 1 1 0 0 2 ③ 1 2 2 1 0 | 1 1 1   ③ 1 2 2 1 1 1 1 1 1 1 1
  18| 1 0 2 2 0 0 2 ③ 1 2 2 1 1 | 2 1 1 ③   2 2 2 2 2 1 1 1 1 2 1
  19| 2 2 ③ ③ 1 1 1 1 1 1 1 2 2 | 1 1 2 1 1   2 2 1 1 2 1 1 1 2 2
  20| 2 1 2 2 1 0 1 2 1 2 2 2 2 | 2 ③ 2 2 2 2   ③ 1 2 1 1 1 2 ③ 2
  21| 2 2 2 ③ 1 1 1 2 1 2 2 2 2 | 2 ③ 1 3 2 2 ③   2 2 1 1 1 2 2 2     LONG
  22| 3 2 2 2 1 0 0 1 1 1 1 2 2 | 2 2 2 1 1 2 2 2   ③ 2 1 1 1 2 3     END
  23| 2 1 1 1 1 0 1 1 1 1 1 1 1 | 2 2 1 1 1 1 1 1 ③   2 0 1 1 2 2
  24| 3 2 2 2 1 1 1 1 1 1 1 2 2 | 2 2 2 1 1 2 2 2 2 2   2 2 2 ③ ③
  25| 2 1 3 2 0 1 0 1 2 1 0 2 2 | 1 1 2 1 1 2 1 1 0 0 2   1 2 2 2
  26| 1 1 1 1 1 1 1 1 ③ 1 1 1 2 | 1 1 2 1 1 2 2 2 1 1 2 2   1 1 1
  27| 3 1 3 3 ③ 1 1 1 1 2 2 3 3 | 2 2 1 2 1 3 3 3 2 2 3 3 2   3 3
  28| ③ 3 ③ ③ 1 1 1 1 1 1 1 ③ 2 | 1 2 2 1 1 3 ③ 3 2 2 ③ 2 1 2   ③
  29| ③ 2 2 3 1 1 0 1 1 1 1 ③ 2 | 1 1 2 1 1 2 2 2 2 1 ③ 2 2 2 ③

          SHORT END                    LONG END
```

FIGURE 6: PERCEIVED FRIENDSHIPS ON THIRD FLOOR

0 - unknown
1 - acquaintance
2 - friend
3 - close friend

This matrix can be evaluated by dividing it into four quadrants according to location on the floor: SHORT END resident relationships with other SHORT END residents, SHORT END resident relationships with LONG END residents, LONG END resident relationships with SHORT END residents, and LONG END resident relationships with other LONG END residents. (See FIGURE 6 above and FIGURE 7 below.)

QUADRANT 1			QUADRANT 2		
SHORT END-SHORT END			SHORT END-LONG END		
3 -	15	9.6%	3 -	17	8.2%
2 -	61	39.1%	2 -	68	32.7%
1 -	69	44.2%	1 -	106	50.9%
0 -	11	7.1%	0 -	17	8.2%
	156	100.0		208	100.0

QUADRANT 3			QUADRANT 4		
LONG END-SHORT END			LONG END-LONG END		
3 -	23	11.1%	3 -	32	13.3%
2 -	61	29.3%	2 -	107	45.6%
1 -	103	59.4%	1 -	97	40.4%
0 -	21	10.1%	0 -	4	1.7%
	208	100.0		240	100.0

TOTALS:		
3 -	87	10.7%
2 -	297	36.6%
1 -	375	46.2%
0 -	53	6.5%
	812	100.0

FIGURE 7: THIRD FLOOR FRIENDSHIPS BY LOCATION

3 - close friend
2 - friend
1 - acquaintance
0 - unknown

On the whole, residents of LONG END seem to feel they have a slightly greater number of friends within LONG END on a percentage basis than seems to be found among SHORT END residents. (But, even these data are subject to question. Some subjects may have interpreted the term "close friend" to mean only very close friends, while some others may have interpreted it to mean closest friends on the floor.)

To clarify this issue, a comparison can be made by isolating symmetrical friendships--those cases in which the two subjects agreed on the level of their friendship--particularly with respect to close friends. (See FIGURE 6 and FIGURE 8.)

Interestingly, more symmetrical close friendships seem to exist between LONG END and SHORT END than exist within either one alone. However, the percentage of close friendships of this type

is also very slightly higher in LONG END than in SHORT END.

QUADRANT 1:	SHORT END-SHORT END	
	5	3.2%
QUADRANT 2,3:	SHORT END-LONG END, LONG END-SHORT END	
	13	6.3%
QUADRANT 4:	LONG END-LONG END	
	10	4.2%

FIGURE 8: SYMMETRICAL CLOSE FRIENDSHIPS BY LOCATION

3.5. Response to Questions

3.5.1. Safety

The three items on the question set which dealt with the relative "safety" of LONG END and SHORT END showed no significant differences. The amount of door locking and relative numbers of unescorted males seen on the two ends were about equal. Several subjects suggested that the amount of door locking was higher than normal because of a rash of thefts which had occurred on the floor earlier in the year.

3.5.2. Privacy, Noise

Some differences appeared between the two ends on the question of noise.

People make too much noise and intrude on my privacy:

	sometimes		rarely	
SHORT END	6	46%	7	54%
LONG END	9	56%	7	44%

The hall is noisy in the morning:

	sometimes		rarely	
SHORT END	5	38%	7	62%
LONG END	2	12%	14	88%

The hall is too noisy between 11 p.m. and 2 a.m. to sleep:

	sometimes		rarely	
SHORT END	7	54%	6	46%
LONG END	5	31%	11	69%

Most of the noise comes:

	from hall		thru walls		other	
SHORT END	3	23%	8	61%	2	16%
LONG END	9	56%	4	25%	3	19%

These answers suggest that although SHORT END has fewer residents, it actually tends to be perceived as being noisier throughout the day. However, the first set of answers seem to indicate that LONG END residents see noise as a greater intrusion on their privacy.

3.5.3. Social Interaction

Only a few of the social interaction questions showed any significant differences between the two ends.

Each person has a responsibility to help make the hall a better place for all to live:

	agree		agree/disagree		disagree	
SHORT END	10	76%	3	24%		
LONG END	9	63%	5	31%	1	6%

Which people generally live up to this responsibility:

	most		some		few	
SHORT END	4	30%	9	70%		
LONG END	8	50%	7	44%	1	6%

Have a lot in common with how many others on the floor?

	most		some		few	
SHORT END			6	46%	7	54%
LONG END	2	12%	8	50%	6	38%

Apparently, SHORT END residents feel that not all their neighbors are helping to improve the quality of life on the floor. Also, there seem to be significantly fewer perceived common ties among SHORT END residents.

The numbers of people who indicated different levels of friendliness toward other floor residents matched exactly on both ends of the floor. About half the residents said they were friendly toward most others.

The hall itself proved to be the most common meeting place on both ends. However, more LONG END residents claimed to use the lobby and the kitchen.

I meet people in the lobby:

	sometimes		rarely	
SHORT END	8	61%	5	39%
LONG END	14	88%	2	12%

Few people tried to study in the lobby. All agreed that the kitchen is usually filthy, but many use it regularly, nonetheless.

On each of the two ends, residents split in half on the issue of community. Half said it was just right and half said it was not enough. (On LONG END several subjects added that there was really very little community, but that they found this acceptable.)

Eight residents on LONG END wanted more privacy (50%), but only three residents on SHORT END wanted more (23%). The two ends differed sharply on the issue of respect.

People on the hall generally respect each other's wishes:

	most of the time		sometimes	
SHORT END	10	77%	3	23%
LONG END	7	44%	9	56%

The question which sought to have residents define the part of the floor in which they felt comfortable and secure showed that most residents claimed to be comfortable anywhere on the floor (about 55%).

4. ANALYSIS

4.1. Discussion

These results proved rather surprising. As stated earlier, it was expected that there would be significant differences between LONG END and SHORT END. It was thought that SHORT END might show greater intimacy and more community due to its smaller size. Also, it was expected that the physical division between LONG END and SHORT END would be a major impediment to friendships and visiting patterns. Even a cursory glance at the results shows these hypotheses generally false.

The first conclusion reached was that a much higher degree of familiarity existed on the floor than had been expected. It had been guessed that the average floor resident would be able to properly name and locate only 15 to 20 other floor residents. Instead, the average was closer to 26 names out of the possible 30 (See FIGURE 3.). This immediately suggests that the division of the floor may not be significant in effect.

The numbers of rooms which the average floor member knew well enought to describe accurately were somewhat lower, but these did not vary significantly over the floor (See FIGURE 4.). The one slight variance can be accounted for merely in the difference in length of the two ends of the floor. Unfortunately, statistical analysis of this simplified type tends to mask the extremes. Several residents were able to describe only one or two rooms while several others could describe almost every room on the floor.

As was noted, the visiting pattern data must be highly suspect. The fact that so many floor residents seemed to overestimate their visits by

so much indicates a possible desire to appear
more sociable than they really are. (According
to one floor resident, to whom the estimated
visits per week totalled 28 or 4 per day, she
rarely received more than 4 per week!)

The differences in visiting patterns of LONG END
residents who claim to visit most in LONG END and
SHORT END residents who claim to visit most
outside SHORT END, also in LONG END, has been
pointed out. While the statistical tabulations
mask the exact nature of such visits, the
original visits patterns noted by SHORT END
residents seem to follow more structured lines
than those by LONG END residents.

The friendship pattern data suggested that there
exist several friendship groupings on the floor.
None of these groupings appear at all limited
by the LONG END-SHORT END division. Indeed, all
the major friendship groupings include members
from both floor ends.

The 30 item question set gave even further proof
of the relative homogeneity of the floor and the
relative insignificance of the physical division
as an activity determinant. (Those differences
which did appear are not as large as those
hypothesized.) One high effect which permeated
the entire floor was the number of people who
seem to feel they have a lot in common with only
a few other floor members. This suggests an
unexpected degree of alienation on the floor.

LONG END residents twice indicated a desire for
greater privacy: once by saying that noise often
intruded and later by suggesting that privacy was
needed. In contrast, SHORT END residents said the
degree of privacy was adequate, but that more
community spirit was needed. Noise from others
appears to be a major problem for SHORT END
residents. On the whole, the divisions which
exist on the floor appear to be strongest within
SHORT END.

4.2. Conclusions

The physical design of the floor does not appear
to be a significant factor insofar as there do
not exist major divisions or differences in the
activities and attitudes of the residents of the
third floor, Jones College South, which correlate
with the physical separation of the floor into
two ends. Indeed, the overall level of
familiarity with the floor is relatively high.
The determining factors for attitudes and
activities are not found in the planning at this
level. Activity patterns transcend the division
of the floor into two ends. SHORT END proved no
more intimate or communal than LONG END. The
differences that can be discovered are minor, and
can probably be attributed directly to the
individual attitudes and desires of floor
residents independent of the physical plan of the
floor itself.

Several extraneous issues did appear which should
be considered. First, several residents noted

the role of the communal bathroom as a meeting
place. (This had not been included in the 30
item question set.) Since the one large bathroom
does serve the entire floor (See FIGURE 1.), it
may serve as a device to create a high level of
familiarity where otherwise the LONG END-SHORT
END division might be stronger.

One resident suggested that her attitudes toward
the floor had changed significantly over the
three years she had lived there. She suggested
that as a freshman she had known every room on the
floor, but now knew only a few. Further, she
stated that there had been a higher level of
community one or two years previous, recalling
that in previous years almost all floor residents
had kept their doors open whenever they were in
their rooms. Now this policy has disappeared.
Doors are kept closed all the time. (This might
be a response to the liberalization of the rules
which now allow men on the floor any time of day
or night.)

Another influence which may have caused a major
change in the past few years was the exodus of a
large number of girls from Jones when two Rice
residences which had had all male populations
were made co-ed. This resulted in a major break
and may have caused the disappearance of a number
of traditions. This, of course, is only
speculation, unsupported by data of any kind.
However, it does suggest that the experience of
upperclasswomen on the floor and that which new
residents can expect may be very different.

4.3. Further Study

As s pilot study this work should, at least in
theory, lead to further explorations along these
lines. One very necessary step would be
clarification of the questionnaire by a much
more specific description of the tasks required.
However, since the initial hypothesis seems to have
been disproved, there may be little reason for
going further with studies of this type.

Perhaps the next level of study should be the
comparison of the experiences of students in
various types or residences to determine their
effects. One might, for example, choose to study
the different impacts of the different designs of
the various men's residences at Rice. This would
be a comparative study of two or more residences,
rather than just within a single one.

5. RESEARCH IN ARCHITECTURAL EDUCATION

The problem of communication between architects
and behavioral scientists has plagued the field
of man-environment for years. While the problem
may never be entirey solved, a large part of the
gap between the two groups can be bridged if
architects are given some background in the
behavioral sciences. Projects of the kind
reported here, carried out by architecture students
as part of their training, are probably the best
method to foster this kind of development.

THE DESIGN OF OPEN SPACE FOR RESIDENT MANAGEMENT

Sidney Brower

Baltimore City Department of Planning
222 East Saratoga Street
Baltimore, Maryland 21202

Roger Stough

Center for Metropolitan Planning and Research
The Johns Hopkins University
Baltimore, Maryland 21218

LaVerne Gray
Bernard Headley

Baltimore City Department of Planning
222 East Saratoga Street
Baltimore, Maryland 21202

ABSTRACT

The man-environment approach is being used to evaluate the open spaces in an inner city residential area, and to initiate and evaluate improvements. The paper deals with inner-block parks that are underutilized, vandalized, littered, and otherwise misused. In an attempt to improve management, local residents were encouraged to initiate and operate a variety of recreational and maintenance programs in the parks. Some of these programs succeeded, others failed; all were observed and evaluated. The information was used to develop recommendations for design features that would facilitate resident management. Recommendations are not limited to physical changes, but include also changes in the rules governing the use of spaces, and in the attitudes and perceptions of users.

This study was supported by the Center for Studies of Metropolitan Problems, National Institute of Mental Health, under Research Grant # 1RO1 MH24047.

1. WHAT THIS PAPER IS ABOUT: THE DESIGN OF INNER-BLOCK PARKS

This paper deals with small inner-block parks constructed during the past fifteen years in Baltimore, and with the way that residents perceive them and use them. The parks studied were all in the inner city, in low income, black neighborhoods. The overall purpose of the study was to address the questions: have the inner-block parks led to the improvement of living conditions; and can design have a significant effect upon their usefulness?

1.1 What Is An Inner-Block Park?

An inner-block park is a small public recreational open space in the center of a residential block surrounded by the rear yards of surrounding houses and with alley connections to the streets. The special interest in these parks stems from the fact that during the past fifteen years, about thirty-five inner-block parks have been built in the City of Baltimore, and present plans call for the construction of twenty-five more.

Both residents and city agencies see them as a convenient way to introduce recreation space into dense inner city areas with a minimum of disruption and dislocation.

1.2 How Do We Define Design?

The design professions today would probably accept that design is purposeful action directed toward the physical environment with the intention of influencing human behavior. But human behavior in a man-environment system is influenced not only by changes in the physical environment, but also by changes in the way environment is used and perceived. In this paper we recognize all three areas as the legitimate concern of design, and we present a case study in which, we feel, there is need for a balanced mix of: (1) change in the physical environment (for example, by planting trees, providing paving and play equipment); (2) change in the rules that govern the way the physical environment is used (for example, by providing recreation leaders, restricting ball playing); and (3) change in people's attitudes and expectations with respect to the physical environment (for example, by providing rewards and education).

We suggest, then, design intervention at three points in the man-environment system.

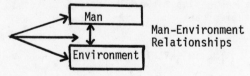

Man-Environment Relationships

2. CONTEXT OF THE STUDY: WHAT ELSE IS BEING DONE AND WHAT WENT BEFORE

The work reported on in this paper is part of a larger study of the use of outdoor space in urban residential areas.

The study had its origin in the work begun in 1971 by the Baltimore City Department of Planning as part of the Community Renewal Program. In 1973 the original study area was enlarged to include an adjacent community, known as Harlem Park, which contained twenty-nine inner-block parks.

In 1974 the present study was initiated, and detailed space-use information is being collected in nine individual blocks. This paper is a report of a special intervention strategy initiated in three of these blocks.

Data collection methods included a walking census, resident diaries to record individual out-door use, interviews to identify attitudes and neighboring patterns, perceptual tests to find the symbolic value of objects and spaces, doll-play with elementary-age children to discover the location and nature of play spaces, and systematic observation and evaluation of the use and condition of various open spaces.

These methods and some of the findings of the early studies have been reported on elsewhere (Brower, 1973; Stough, 1973; Brower, 1974; Brower and Williamson, 1974). The findings may be summarized as follows. Most people out-of-doors were engaged in recreational activities, and playing and sitting-and-talking were the most popular of these activities. While the inner-block parks were used, they were used well below capacity, and most recreators of all age-sex groups were on the streetfront. The parks did, however, have the effect of reducing the number of children playing on the street-front. Children and teenage boys were the groups best represented in the parks and the concentration of teenage boys in the parks increased during late afternoon. Neighboring activity focused heavily upon the streetfront; the existence of an inner-block park did, however, lead to some increase in cross-block neighboring. There were many complaints about the inner-block parks because of the accumulation of trash and the lack of security. Many residents would not let their children play there; troublesome and anti-social elements were felt to collect there. In spite of these complaints, however, residents had a positive attitude toward the parks.

We concluded that an inner-block park, with adequate supervision, can be of clear benefit to a neighborhood. If, however, residents have to depend entirely upon the City for supervision, then the inner-block is a poor location for a public park.

3. THE INTERVENTION STRATEGY

3.1 Purpose

While an unsupervised inner-block location may be inappropriate for a public park, the facts are that Baltimore already has a great many such parks and is committed to build more of them. Given the existence of inner-block parks and their problems, we wanted to know whether they could be improved through design.

In looking at the design of existing inner-block parks in Harlem Park, we recognized that the details and placement of play equipment leave much to be desired. We felt, however, that physical improvements in these areas would have, at best, a marginal effect because the problems could not be explained as responses to unsuitable or insensitively designed play elements. The basic problems related to social behavior, and we did not see how they could be resolved without some form of human intervention in the space. As the City does not have the resources to provide paid managers for each of the parks, management responsibilities, if they are to be assumed at all, will have to be assumed by local residents. The general question then became: could the parks be designed so that they foster the development of resident management?

There were several specific questions that we felt our study should address. Does the need for resident management have any implications for the physical layout and furnishing of the parks; are there particular uses that are most suitable for resident management; are there particular conditions under which residents will be more willing (or less reluctant) to assume management? We considered all of these to be appropriate design questions.

3.2 Method

We departed from our previous approach of simply observing and recording on-going behavior and began to work directly with residents in three of our study blocks, encouraging and helping them to manage activities in the parks. We studied the programs that succeeded and those that failed, and the circumstances surrounding success and failure. This intervention strategy began in the winter of 1974 and continued through the summer of 1975. This paper is a discussion of our findings and conclusions during that time period.

Before initiating any intervention procedures, we obtained the approval and support of local community groups and of the affected city agencies. We developed the following guidelines for ourselves.
1. We would encourage residents to initiate and run their own programs in the parks. We would try to increase communication among block residents in order to identify communities of interest within the block.
2. We would provide direct assistance to residents and would help them take advantage of resources available through the city agencies; we would act as in-house spokesmen for the release of these resources where necessary. We would not, however, support the introduction of any special city-operated programs in the parks.
3. We would not run any of the programs. An exception could be made where a new activity is introduced, but our leadership would last only if residents demonstrated an interest in taking over after an introductory period.
4. We would not dictate what programs should and should not be introduced in the parks. This was up to the residents, but they had to develop the necessary agreement and support among themselves. There was one exception to this rule: we would in all cases encourage residents to undertake regular clean-up programs.

These guidelines were motivated by several considerations. We recognized that our study was not a continuing activity and that no lasting benefits could accrue that depended upon the continuing influence or talents of the project staff. We also wanted to develop an approach that could be introduced in all inner-block parks: this meant that we could not demand an unfair share of total available resources.

3.3 Description of Study Blocks

Of the three blocks selected for the intervention strategy, two were in Harlem Park and they contained fully developed playgrounds. The other block was in the adjacent Upton area and contained a grassy open space, with no equipment.

Harlem Park is an urban renewal project that was begun in 1959 and was closed out in 1969. It involved the rehabilitation of about 1,760 buildings, mainly three-story row houses, the construction of a centrally-located school and recreation center, and twenty-nine inner-block parks. Residents were, and continue to be, low income black families. Most of the parks were between one-half to three-quarters of an acre in size. They were each designed in conjunction with a committee of local residents so that they vary one from another, but in general each was predominantly hard-surfaced, with fixed metal or concrete play equipment, sometimes with benches and tables, and trees. Spatial definition within the parks was handled with level changes, walls, and railings. The private rear yards that surrounded the parks were fenced, with gates leading out into the park or into an alley that surrounded most of the parks. The alleys connected to the streets at several points, and provided public access to the park as well as access for sanitation, oil delivery, and emergency vehicles.

Most of the houses were divided into apartments. All ground floor units, but not all upper floor units, had direct access to the rear yard and hence to the park. All units had their front doors on the streetfront. Home ownership rate was less than thirty percent, and average family size was 3.2 people.

The selection of the two Harlem Park study blocks was based upon the findings of the 1973 study. One block was on the east side, and we call it the East block. It had been the subject of a number of complaints from residents, but, because it was pleasant looking and well-equipped, we felt that it stood a better chance than most of succeeding (Figure 1). The second block was on the west side and more intensively used. It was chosen because there seemed to be so much against it succeeding; it was barren, vandalized, and constantly strewn with litter and broken glass. We called this the West block (Figure 2).

The third study block was in the Upton area, immediately to the east of Harlem Park. Upton is an ongoing renewal project. It is similar to Harlem Park in both social and physical composition. The study block was of triangular shape with a triangular patch of open land, about one-tenth of an acre in size, in the center. The open space was created in 1972. We call this the Triangular block (Figure 3).

FIGURE 1: EAST BLOCK

Aerial View

Ground View

FIGURE 2: WEST BLOCK

Aerial View

FIGURE 2 (continued)

Ground View

FIGURE 3: TRIANGULAR BLOCK

Aerial View

Ground View

3.4 Intervention Programs

The following is an overview of the intervention programs. We will briefly describe the
history of each of the programs and then discuss
some of the more significant issues that have
emerged. From these we will derive some implications for the design of inner-block parks.

3.4.1 Environmental Manager

A job description was developed for a new Civil
Service position. We called this position
Environmental Manager (E.M.). The E.M. was a
city employee who would work directly with residents in his or her own community, to assist,
encourage, and advise them in solving problems
associated with the use of neighborhood open
spaces. Normal Civil Service procedures of job
listing and testing were followed and a Harlem
Park resident was added to the project staff as
E.M. in Octover 1974. A working relationship
was established with city agencies and bureaus,
primarily Health, Sanitation, and Recreation and
Parks, who had responsibilities for servicing
and maintaining the public open spaces, and contact was made with individual householders
living around the study blocks and with local
religious and community groups in the area. The
position was seen not only as helpful in conducting the intervention experiment, but also as
an experiment to see if a useful role existed
for this kind of person in City government.

3.4.2 Block Newspaper

One of the first jobs of the E.M. was to help
produce a biweekly newspaper in the East block.
The purpose of this newspaper was to increase
communication among residents and to lead to a
greater sense of community. The paper was
initiated and produced by project staff, and
distributed door-to-door by the E.M., who also
solicited contributions - stories, opinions,
personal histories, notices, advertisements -
from residents. As the circulation was limited
to residents of the East block, we tried to get
material that addressed local issues and invited resolution by local residents, rather than
material related, say, to the larger issues of
vacant housing or of racial discrimination.
Submissions could be written, dictated, or
taped. Contributors' names were printed in the
paper. The newspaper continued for six issues.
Contributions became scarcer and more repetitive.
There was no indication that residents were able
to take over the production of the paper, and so,
in accordance with our guidelines, it was discontinued.

3.4.3 Youth Workers

In one of the papers we ran an advertisement
for two youth workers to serve as assistants to
the E.M. This was another project initiated by
the staff. Two girls were appointed. They came
in for immediate criticism from local residents
who had been working with the E.M., sweeping the
park and painting the equipment, and who felt
that it was unfair that the youth workers should

get paid for work that they themselves did for nothing. To resolve this issue, it was decided that the girls would not be used to do anything for which residents were volunteering their time. Residents were invited, again through the block newspaper, to apply to the E. M. for help with any house-related jobs, such as sweeping the yard, cleaning the steps, doing the food shopping. The youth workers would be available for these jobs, and an hourly rate was set that was substantially below that at which the girls were being paid. All of the money contributed by residents was to go into a special community fund to be used for special programs. We thought that the workers would help to foster a spirit of helping among residents, and that residents were more likely to appreciate a service that they got at a bargain price than one that they got for nothing. After three weeks and no takers, the program was withdrawn, and the two girls assigned to assist at a local home for the elderly.

3.4.4 Planting

The open space in the Triangular block was bounded along its northern edge by a raised planting box. Because many of the surrounding yards were remarkable for their well-tended flowers, project staff felt that a local planting program in the park was likely to succeed and to produce visible evidence of a communal presence. Several residents were approached. They feared that plants in the planting box would be trampled by the children. We then approached a resident who had an excellent rapport with children in the block. The result was that the children, with adult supervision, agreed to plant the flowerbed. The Bureau of Parks prepared the ground and provided residents with bulbs. They also divided the long planter into seven equal plots, and it was suggested that the plots be assigned and identified with name tags. The bulbs were planted during the early winter months, but the name tags never did materialize. There was an uneven showing in the spring and no further planting activity occurred during the spring or summer.

3.4.5 Ball Games

A resident of the Triangular block initiated a program of summer activities in the interior space. He was joined by a neighbor and later by two friends, and they organized a regular baseball game three evenings a week. They also arranged a volleyball game once a week, and planned an ambitious program that included a fashion show, a cookout, and arts-and-crafts classes. The games were spirited and well-attended. A team was formed and a match with the adjoining public housing residents was arranged. Adults and teenagers joined in the activity.

There was an outcry from some of the older residents. They objected to the noise and to the ball going into their yards, and insisted that the ballplaying be stopped immediately. Feelings on both sides ran high, and a meeting was called, mediated by the director of the Upton Planning Committee, the local citizen action group. At the meeting it was concluded that the ballplaying be moved to an adjacent school playfield, but that the other scheduled activities in the open space should proceed. Arrangements for the school playground came to naught, however, because it was fully scheduled for Recreation Center programs, and so all organized ballplaying stopped. By this time the residents who had been responsible for the organization were discouraged and the other scheduled programs never materialized. The organized ballplaying had lasted for about three weeks.

3.4.6 Children's Play

A number of box games, such as checkers, snakes-and-ladders, etc., were acquired from the Bureau of Recreation and placed in the custody of a resident of the East block who would, from time to time, bring the games out to the park and supervise their use. This developed into a regular program of supervised play for young children that met in the park for four weeks, three times a week between the hours of 2:00 and 4:00 p.m.

3.4.7 Clean-up

A regular clean-up was one of the first activities undertaken by residents in the Triangular block. This was a part of their program of activities. Brooms and cans were obtained from the Bureau of Parks, and trash collections were coordinated with the clean-up program. The clean-up continued while the ballplaying was permitted. When the ballplaying stopped the clean-up stopped too, and the open space acquired the usual accumulation of trash and glass.

This issue was brought before the Upton Planning Committee by a group of concerned residents. In the interest of having the clean-up continue, a subcommittee was appointed to negotiate with the ballplaying and no-ballplaying elements in the community, and to come up with an acceptable compromise. This was the situation at the end of the summer.

In the West block, a number of young men who habitually hung around in the park asked that a basketball court be constructed. A poll of residents who lived around the park showed that there was little opposition to this idea. The men who wanted the court were encouraged to start a clean-up program to establish themselves as a prime user group. At a meeting held in conjunction with the Harlem Park Neighborhood Council, residents in the study block paired up with those in the block immediately to the north (also with an inner-block park) and elected a slate of young residents as leaders for the twin blocks. As in the case of the Triangular block, brooms and trash cans were provided, and trash collections were coordinated with clean-up days. Officials from

Recreation and Parks visited the parks, complimented the residents on their activity, and agreed to construct a basketball court in the West block. Since then, the activity in the twin blocks has diffused to two adjacent blocks. They too have elected a slate of young officers and are carrying on their own clean-up program.

3.4.8 Paint-up

At their request, residents in the East block were provided with paint brushes to redecorate the benches and tables in the park.

Residents of the West block also requested paint and brushes. They not only painted the equipment but also painted a series of colorful cartoons on the paving. The cartoons were very carefully reproduced from comic books: each character had a "balloon" urging that the park be kept clean. Similar messages were painted elsewhere on the paving and around the equipment. On the day that project staff were first invited to see the paintings, there were between six and eight people busy sweeping the park.

3.4.9 Arts and Crafts Classes

A resident indicated that she was willing to run an arts and crafts class for young children in the East park. A local church offered to solicit its members for contributions: a flyer was distributed to local residents informing them of the program and asking them to save such items as cardboard boxes, plastic bottles, and egg cartons for use in the class; most of the materials, however, were obtained from the Bureau of Recreation. The classes were scheduled on weekdays from noon to 2:00 p.m. and, except for interruptions due to illness and inclement weather, they continued throughout the summer. They made use of the fixed benches and tables and the shelter that are permanent features of this park. An exhibition of finished items was arranged at the Recreation Center and in the church hall.

3.4.10 Movies

A resident of the Triangular block came up with the idea of having movies in the park one evening a week. The Planning Department had a movie projector and a screen, and a staff person could act as projectionist. Several residents were taken to the public library to register for library cards and to select and reserve films. (These are available to the public at no charge.) Flyers advertising the film show were distributed door-to-door in the block.

The first film was attended by more than seventy people. Chairs were brought out from the houses and people sat on the grass and on the curb. It appeared, however, that residents saw this as a program of the project staff. At the second film showing, there were about one hundred people. At our suggestion, one of the block leaders made a short speech in which she commended the residents responsible for the

film shows for programming activities in the park. She presented them with a personal donation toward the cost of future programs. The film was disrupted toward the end when several small boys began throwing stones and many of the adults left. The third week residents had become divided over the ballplaying issue. Audience for the film was about thirty people. A makeshift game of basketball that had been in progress continued throughout the showing, creating a disturbance. There appeared to be no initiative on the part of residents to take over the film series, and so, in accordance with our guidelines, the program was terminated.

4. DISCUSSION

4.1. Why Are Residents Reluctant to Manage Inner-Block Parks?

Most residents agreed about the problems in the parks, and felt that these problems were serious and that something needed to be done about them. While most people interviewed felt that local residents should determine what may and may not happen in the park, they indicated that they were more likely to call for the police in case of trouble than intervene themselves. So that residents, while recognizing problems in the parks, were reluctant to take an active role in the management of the inner-block parks.

4.1.1 Fear

Fear was a prevalent theme among all residents in all the blocks studied. They were fearful for themselves and their family and for their property and possessions. Some residents were suspicious of getting together with strangers unless in the presence of a reputable mediating agency, such as the church, or the neighborhood council, or a city agency. For many, the best strategy was to keep to oneself; to make oneself too conspicuous was to present a clear target; to take sides on a public issue was to invite reprisals. This was one of the reasons why it was so difficult to get contributions to the newspaper. One of the reasons that there was no demand for the services of the youth workers was that residents did not want to let strangers into their homes; the girls might have stolen, or acted as scouts for their boyfriends. Some residents saw balls flying into their yard as a deliberate trick to see whether there was anyone at home.

As a group, teenagers invited the greatest fear. They were felt to be disrespectful and rowdy, and prone to violence and crime. The reason why many parks were designed as tot lots was that residents wanted it clearly established that the park was not for use by teenagers. Nevertheless, as the census shows, teenagers tended to collect in the parks, especially in the evenings. There was nothing "legitimate" for them to do there, and their presence made residents extremely restless. Many residents would not move from their homes at night, even to watch the movies in the park. Home was a haven.

4.1.2 Conflict

Although all low income and all black, the population of each block differed greatly with respect to the age, lifestyle, and social values of the residents. At the one end of the scale there might be an elderly retired schoolteacher or tradesman with fixed ideas about proper work habits, child rearing, and property care, who owned his home, had been in the area a long time, and had seen a better "class" of people in the neighborhood. At the other end of the scale there might be a young woman on welfare, with several small children, a pile of unpaid bills, and an unsympathetic landlord. In such a situation it was not easy to reach a consensus as to the proper purposes and programs for a shared facility, and social issues became easily confused with personality conflicts. The activities in the Triangular block accentuated these problems. One faction wanted active intensive use of the park and in return were prepared to organize games and take responsibility for maintaining the cleanliness of the area. The other faction wanted quiet activities such as storytelling or arts and crafts classes, but would not lead them and felt that the park should not need special maintenance; it was all the fault of certain people, who had to be "taught" not to litter and to clean up after themselves.

4.1.3 Lack of Reward

Residents who led or arranged activities in the park must have had to struggle with the feeling that this was a lot of trouble and not much satisfaction. If they could not count on the approval of their neighbors, what was to be their reward? When ballplaying became an issue in the Triangular block, the resident who had been responsible for organizing the games proclaimed that he would only continue if residents who were opposing the program paid him to run it. His strange logic suggested that if he could not win social approval, then he was going to have to be rewarded in some other way. When we established as our guideline that we would assist residents but not run any programs ourselves, we had intended that project staff work primarily behind the scenes, leaving the limelight for resident leaders. This was, however, not the role that residents had in mind for us, and we soon began to realize that our presence was expected at all meetings and activities, not necessarily to help, but simply to see what was being done. Our encouragement and approval were powerful reinforcers. It became clear that any design for continuing resident management had to include the provision of some form of gratification for program leaders.

4.2. Implications for the Design of Inner-Block Parks

The reasons for residents not becoming involved in management of the inner-block parks are powerful ones. One might even question whether resident management is possible under prevailing social and economic conditions. We feel that it may be overly optimistic, even in the long range, to expect effective resident management in all of the inner-block parks, or to expect that resident management is the solution to all problems. We are convinced, however, that it is possible to achieve a far greater degree of resident management than we found in the parks, that this can be influenced by the way the spaces are designed, and that it can lead to a significant increase in residents' satisfaction.

There are several areas in which design can contribute toward resident management of inner-block parks.

4.2.1 Make The Inner-Block Spaces Easier To Defend

Residents regard the inner-block parks as a high security risk. Some residents never venture into them at all, and many are afraid to go into them at night. Removed from the active life of the streetfront and hidden from the view of passersby, the inner spaces are ideal for undercover activities. Multiple entrances and low illumination levels at night make it difficult to detect and apprehend offenders. These factors contribute to the ineffectiveness of resident surveillance in the inner-block spaces.

Residents have shown great concern over the presence of "outsiders" in the inner-block spaces. There are two approaches to the solution of this problem. The first is to increase the intensity of use of the park; the second is to close the park to outsiders. In an ongoing urban renewal project in Baltimore, one in which the Triangular study block is located, the design concept for the inner-block parks is one of a network of linked spaces that extends through the community. The idea is to generate movement and activity in the back spaces of the kind that is found on the streetfront: a busy streetfront is felt, by residents and designers, to be safer than an inaccessible unsupervised interior space.

We suspect, however, that residents associate safety not with the presence of passersby, who are seen as a source of trouble, but rather with the visible presence of other residents, people whom they know, who have a social investment in the area, and who are likely to help one in case of need. At present, adult residents recreate on the streetfront. The possibility for pedestrian movement through the rear spaces, by itself, is unlikely to change this pattern of space use, especially as many of the units have no direct access to the rear, and all have their front entrances on the streetfront. The opportunity for "outsiders" to pass through the interior block spaces is not likely to increase their sense of security; it may in fact have the opposite effect, unless abutting residents can be persuaded to take a proprietary interest in the space in the same way that they currently take a proprietary interest in the strip of sidewalk in front of their houses.

An alternative approach is to restrict the use of the space. Eliminating direct street access entirely, and so effectively restricting use to surrounding residents and their guests, is perhaps the most direct way of placing the space under the control of residents. Unfortunately, there are problems in the way of implementing such a design. Access to the rear of the houses is needed occasionally in the case of fire trucks and routinely in the case of trash collection and oil delivery trucks. Some of the upper-level units surrounding the inner-block spaces have no direct access to the rear. There are also legal questions as to whether access to a public park can be restricted in this way. Restrictions that are enforced only at certain times, for example by closing the park at night, would be more reasonable from a legal standpoint, but they are difficult to enforce. Who, for example, would evict users at dusk and lock the gates, and then open them again each morning?

While there are problems in restricting access to the inner-block parks, there are other design features that could be introduced to make the spaces less sheltered: the number of access points could be reduced, windows could be introduced in the blank end-walls of the houses that line the entrances to the park, equipment and site work that provide hiding places could be removed, lighting levels could be increased, and benches and equipment that provide attractive gathering places at night could be eliminated. Further suggestions for making a space more defensible are described by Oscar Newman in his book Defensible Space (The Macmillan Co., New York, 1972).

Some of these measures, while making the spaces more defensible, would however also make them less suitable for recreational use. Modifications aimed at making the spaces defensible must therefore be considered in relation to the major purposes to be served by the space.

4.2.2 Assign Spaces To Existing Groups

In trying to identify residents who were willing to work together to improve neighborhood conditions, we found that our best chance for success lay with the existing social networks. Social interaction was strongly influenced by the neighboring pattern. In ten years the inner-block parks in the East and West study blocks have had little effect on changing the traditional pattern of neighboring activities being focused on the streetfront. Inner-block parks are, then, located at a boundary between four social groups, and at the place where each group has least control. One possible design response to this situation would be to divide the interior space into several areas, each clearly related to a particular streetfront. The areas could be separated from one another with an alley, or a wall, or through landscape treatment and the placement of equipment. Responsibility for management of the interior space could then be divided among several social groups, groups that are more likely to develop and be self-sustaining than groups that repre-

sent all the residents who live around a park.

4.2.3 Design Facilities So That Management Enhances the Play Experience

Most play equipment is designed to eliminate the need for a leader; the kind of play that they cater to needs no assistance or organization. Perhaps the best example of an equipment-playground in Baltimore is a school playground with a sand base and an elaborate and handsome series of heavy wood frames and masonry structures suitable for climbing, crawling, swinging, jumping, sliding, and sitting. Teachers at the school who take their classes down to the playground have complained that there is no room for them to organize any activity; the children are dispersed on the equipment and the teacher is left with the passive and thankless job of watching, cautioning, and reprimanding.

If we plan to increase resident management of activities in inner-block parks, it is necessary to design the facility in such a way that there is a role for the resident manager. He should not only be necessary to facilitate certain play activities, but his presence should contribute to, rather than inhibit, the quality of the play experience.

The arts and crafts program in the East block depended on resident management. The ball games in the Triangular block depended on adult residents for organization, leadership, and participation. There was a sprinkler in the East block which was not officially in operation during the summer; one of the residents had found a way of switching it on and off, and she initiated regular water-play sessions with young children. Here the children were entirely dependent upon her for the play opportunity. The park provided the opportunity for her to "create" the equipment and to "remove" it when she left. One could think of other possibilities: lights for nighttime activities that could be controlled by resident managers; moveable seating that could be stored in residents' houses and brought out only when required (as residents brought out seats for the movie show in the Triangular block); nets, balls, and baskets in charge of local residents that could be installed at scheduled times and removed at other times.

Playground elements can be designed so that their functions are less narrowly defined, leaving it up to residents to determine what play they will and will not tolerate. The arts and crafts classes could not have been held had there been no shelter and no benches and tables in the East park, but we observed these same facilities used for crab feasts, checkers games, children's play, and simply sitting around. In the same way, a high wall could be used for a game of strike-out, or it could be used for murals or graffiti, or to climb over, or to project a movie onto. Steps can be used for coin-pitching games, for playing step ball, or for sitting on. A low railing can be used to separate one space from another or it can serve as a "net" in a game of volleyball and so join two spaces; it can be used as a seat, or for balancing games. A hardtop surface can be used for a variety of court games, or for riding cycles; if it is on an incline that makes it better for wheeled toys and roller skating. An area of dirt can be used for planting or for digging. A pole can be used for scaling or for fixing a basketball net. Spaces can be designed so that each subarea and piece of equipment is suitable not simply for a single designated use, but for a number of contingencies, including adult activities such as carwashing and community meetings, leaving it to residents to settle on those that are most desirable (or least objectionable).

4.2.4 Make Management A Play Activity

It would be helpful if residents were invited to participate in park management, not as fulfillment of their public responsibilities, because this has never worked, but rather as volunteers. If they are to be volunteers, then the work must be made rewarding to them. At present, participation in park management is more likely to be aversive. An involved resident will have to face opposition from some residents, and even the possibility of reprisals. There is no feeling of completion, no clear measure of achievement. One may feel that one has done one's civic duty, but the problems have not gone away and, as some residents said, "Let someone else do it now."

We believe that one of the goals of playground design should be to build a system of immediate rewards for managers, and that one of the most obvious rewards can be the enjoyment of play. All of the programs that succeeded during the intervention period were those that the managers participated in and enjoyed. The clean-up, usually an unpleasant task, succeeded as an aspect of a program of play. The paint-up succeeded when it assumed the aspect of a fun activity rather than a maintenance job.

Johan Huizinga, in his book Homo Ludens (Beacon Press, Boston, Chapter 1), defines some of the characteristics of play. 1) Play is a voluntary activity, not required, not a task, done at leisure during "free time"; 2) play is a stepping out of "real," "ordinary," life; an activity that is outside the immediate satisfaction of wants and appetites; 3) play takes place within certain limits of time and place, and is repeated at any time or at fixed intervals; 4) play has rules, also an element of uncertainty, a chance to succeed, to achieve something difficult.

In an attempt to emphasize some of the play aspects of management we are at present working on the design of a competition. There will be several entry categories and resident groups will be invited to compete for the most attractive park, the most unusual park, the best recreational program, and so on. The competition will have specified time periods and clearly defined rules, and prizes will be offered. The nature of these prizes is still to be determined. They may take the form of cash, of city services, or of social recognition. The competition format is not new in Baltimore: the Afro-American newspaper has run a clean-block competition each summer for the past forty years and the response in the inner city has been quite dramatic.

This kind of competition would have implications for the physical design of the parks. Heavy, naturally finished timber climbing equipment and sonte mounds are good-looking and fun to climb on, but they do not look much different for being cleaned. In contrast, the effect of painting the old metal pipe equipment is, if not long-lasting, immediate and dramatic. Flowerbeds can provide similar satisfaction for their managers. The parks should be designed so that there is clear visible response to the kinds of improvement efforts that residents are capable of making.

4.2.5 Provide Residents With Support And Advice

Even with strong motivation, residents need help and advice if they are to assume a management role. To keep the parks clean they need brooms and trashcans and they need to coordinate their efforts with the collection services. They need mowers and clippers if they are to trim the grass and shrubbery. If they are to plant the flowerbeds they need bulbs and seedlings, and mulch, and to decorate the equipment they need paint and brushes. They need supplies if they are to lead an arts and crafts program, a projector if they are to show movies, and so on. Residents need to know what help they can expect to get from city agencies, and city agencies need to know what demands they will be subjected to if resident management comes about. We see the role of Environmental Manager as one of liaison between the resident groups and the various city agencies that are able to help and advise them. During the coming year, the Environmental Manager will work more closely with the Department of Recreation and Parks, the City Health Department, and with the Harlem Park Neighborhood Council so that a set of guidelines for city aid and residents' responsibility can be designed, and so that an assessment can be made as to whether the position of Environmental Manager should be continued once this study is ended.

4.2.6 Educate Residents Involved In The Design Process

Residents participate in the design of the inner-block parks. They tend to see the facility under design as a physical product separate from any social outcomes.

It was not uncommon for a resident in the interview to say that they did not like their children to play in the park behind their house, and never went out there themselves, and then to say, later in the interview, that they thought inner-block parks were good because they provided a place for children to play, for people to sit. We think that they were implying that if the equipment were there, people would use them if the neighborhood were better. This attitude, that one recognizes desirable rather than present conditions, influenced design decisions. Benches were requested because they were seen as pleasant places for elderly people to sit, despite the knowledge that elderly people seldom ventured into the parks, let alone sat in them. Space was allocated to one particular age group or another depending on what the land was felt to be "suitable" for or according to the group that was felt to be least objectionable (generally young children). Responsibility for maintaining this spatial distribution of activities was entrusted entirely to equipment and posted signs. People who did not conform must be taught, or they must be required to conform by city agencies.

An educational program is needed for residents involved in the design process to help them evaluate alternative proposals not simply on visual or symbolic qualities, but on a realistic assessment of their social consequences in terms of use and of demands on management. To assist in the development of such an educational program we are in the process of developing a series of movies and video films that present the findings of this study in a way that is understandable to local residents and that presents some of the attitudes, activities, and problems that should be recognized as inputs in the design process.

5. CONCLUSIONS

We are conscious of the fact that some of our recommendations may seem regressive to some playground designers, because we argue against playground equipment despite the revolutionary changes in playground design in recent years that have resulted in more handsome and delightful equipment-playgrounds. We do not make the argument that equipment-playgrounds are bad, but in an area such as Harlem Park, where open space is at a premium and where various conflicting groups vie with one another for its use, the many problems associated with the playground will not be decided through equipment but through resident management of the facility. The equipment-playground does not offer enough incentive nor sufficient reward to develop management skills among residents, nor does it provide a management group with sufficient flexibility to negotiate with potential user groups.

The kind of playground we are recommending can best be compared to the stage of a theater which has no fixed set, but which is far more than bare boards; it is equipped to facilitate the production of plays as different as Hamlet and Hair. It may in itself be visually ambiguous, but it can be tailored to suit a wide range of contingencies.

There is of course the risk that resident management will fail to materialize. What then of a facility that is designed to be so dependent on management? At worst it will be little different from one of the Harlem Park inner-block parks; less festive-looking, perhaps, than a Harlem Park playground when it is new, but similarly underutilized, vandalized, and littered. It will be full of unrealized opportunities. At best the community will seize upon these opportunities to create a facility that satisfies them far more than the traditional park is capable of doing.

Reference

BROWER, SIDNEY, "Recreational Uses of Space: An Inner City Case Study," in Richard H. Chase (ed.), Social Ecology, EDRA-5, Section 7 (Environmental Design Research Associates, 1974):153-167.

BROWER, SIDNEY, "Streetfront and Sidewalk," Landscape Architecture, Volume 63, #4 (July, 1973).

BROWER, SIDNEY AND PENELOPE WILLIAMSON, "Outdoor Recreation As a Function of the Urban Housing Environment," Environment and Behavior, Volume 6, No. 3 (September, 1974).

NEWMAN, OSCAR, Defensible Space. (New York: Macmillan, 1973).

STOUGH, ROGER, "The Effect of Inner City Open Space on the Lives of Residents." A report of the Baltimore Urban Observatory, 1973.

CREATION & MAINTENANCE OF PHYSICAL ENVIRONMENTS:
EVOLUTIONARY SETTLEMENT DEVELOPMENT

Stephen O. Bender

RICENTRO Program Director
Rice Center for Community Design + Research
1929 Allen Parkway, Office Suite 400
Houston, Texas 77019

ABSTRACT

Traditional views of Latin American squatter
settlement development, those built outside of
accepted legal parameters, have been seen as
blighted areas that must be removed and replaced
by institutional means; and later, as homogeneous
settlements marginal to the rapid growth of
urban areas, but significant in their internal
organization, spontaneous creation and development, and potential impact on the city's economic and political life. Only recently has the
importance of squatter settlements been identified - that of viable, adaptive physical environments which allow their occupants to participate in and benefit from development.

Moreover, the growth and change which takes
place in these settlements, that of transforming aggregations of dwelling units (however
rudimentary in nature) into a mature urban
community with a full range of public and private
services, is duplicated in government sponsored
settlements for similar income groups. This
evolution is brought about by investment and
construction under the control of the dwellers
themselves. Their housing costs are kept as
low as possible and real economic gains are made
from provision of housing and commercial services to the settlements's inhabitants, which
improves income distribution.

This phenomenon as it occurs in Bogotá, Colombia,
is influenced by the availability of land, construction materials, key public services, and
the decision of the settlement dwellers to
exercise control over the creation and/or maintenance of their physical environment. All of
these are dynamic factors whose modification
could bring about reduction or cessation of
settlement development.

I. INTRODUCTION

Patrick Geddes wrote in 1918, "I have to remind
all concerned: 1) that the essential need of a
house and family is room, and 2) that the
essential improvement of a house and family is
more room."[1] While written for another place,
the statement is still timely if we are to
examine in some detail the growth and development of low income settlements in Latin American
urban settings. The traditional analysis of the
growth of such settlements, usually in socio-
political and economic terms, has left us with
an array of classifications by which to understand one of the most significant occurances in
the history of man's urbanization. Such analysis has allowed us to describe in some detail
the extent to which low income families, often
migrant in origin, have sought to resolve their
housing needs outside accepted norms, and to
scrutinize the efforts of the public sector to
aid in (if not to control) the housing of these
poor. The preceeding type of anlaysis has
brought into focus the dissimilarities between
housing built and maintained by its inhabitants
and housing provided through government intervention.

Critical to the understanding of settlements,
however, is an analysis of the commonalities
of low income housing development and, more
specifically, the physical characteristics
which over time make settlements of various
legal origins indistinguishable from one another.
"That the mass of people demand no more than
they can economically support is the existence
of the squatter settlement"[2] is not only applicable to clandestine developments, but also
appropriate to all low income housing development. Low income families continually match
available resources with existing needs and over
a period of time change simple shelters into a
community with a full complement of services.

The role this housing development plays and some
of the economic opportunities it presents are
examined in this paper. In summary, traditional
views of squatter settlement development, those
built outside of accepted legal parameters, have
been seen as blighted areas that must be removed
and replaced by institutional means, and later,
as homogeneous settlements marginal to the rapid
growth of urban areas, but significant in their
internal organization, spontaneous creation and
development, and potential impact on the city's
economic and political life. Only recently has
the importance of squatter settlements been
identified as that of viable, adaptive physical
environments which allow their occupants to participate in and benefit from development.

Moreover, the growth and change which takes
place in these settlements, transforming aggregations of dwelling units (however rudimentary
in nature) into a mature urban community with a
full range of public and private services, is
duplicated in government-sponsored settlements
for similar income groups. This evolution is
brought about by investment and construction
under the control of the dwellers themselves.
Their housing costs are kept as low as possible
and real economic gains are made from the

1. Patrick Geddes, Town Planning Towards City
Development, a report prepared for the Durbar of
Indore, India (1918), I, p. 85.

2. John C. Turner, "A New View of the
Housing Deficit," San Juan Seminar Paper (April
1966).

provision of housing and commercial services to the settlements' inhabitants, which affects income distribution.

The phenomenon as it occurs in Bogotá, Colombia, is influenced by the availability of land, construction materials, and key public services, and by the decision of the settlement dwellers to exercise control over the creation and/or maintenance of their physical environment. All of these are dynamic factors whose modification could bring about reduction or cessation of settlement development.

Section II of the paper deals with squatter settlements and their role as traditionally understood in resolving urban housing and development issues. The dynamics of these settlements are explored to better understand the settlements' participation in the low income housing sector. Section III discusses housing and community, describing how income settlements, regardless of origin, take part in common development processes. In Section IV, some specific characteristics of low income family settlements and sources of income that are derived from investment in building space are examined. Finally, in Section V, some summary observations are made concerning the future development of these settlements.

II. OBSERVATIONS CONCERNING SQUATTER SETTLEMENTS IN AN URBAN GROWTH AND CHANGE CONTEXT

Squatter settlements have been the dominant force in shaping the large urbanized areas in Latin America. Their formation and growth have brought into focus the problems of rapid in-migration of peasants from rural and semi-rural areas. Housing becomes the immediate and most pressing need of these migrants, a need which they are both able and accustomed to provide for themselves.

The formation of such settlements on the edges of urban areas has traditionally been seen in varying ways. These views have developed out of the realization by governments, planners, and academicians that tremendous growth was taking place in urban areas after the Second World War. The postwar era produced a development boom in most Latin America countries. Urban places expanded as the countries began to industrialize. Rising incomes brought about a rapid in-migration to urban areas ports, industrialized agricultural and mineral extraction centers of rural peasants seeking employment, education, health care and the other services urbanized areas could offer. Colonial towns became cities and colonial cities grew rapidly, their character changing from a meeting place between a primarily agricultural-based society and its produce exchange for imported consumer goods, to one of a center for the production and consumption of goods.

The inner core of the expanding urban areas had been developed during colonial times as residential centers by and for those who controlled both the agricultural production and the commercial arenas. Imported advances in transportation and communication, and massive public works projects now allowed those inhabitants to establish residential enclaves on the perimeter of the urban areas, leaving the colonial cores as their business centers. The vacated colonial dwellings were quickly converted into dense low cost rental units and were rapidly occupied by the peasant influx.

This housing stock being consumed, the migrants were then forced to seek housing solutions through other means. Housing institutions, both the private and the newly established public agencies that supplied dwellings units to the middle and upper economic classes, did not respond adequately to the needs of the lower economic class. Alternatives had to be sought outside the existing social, legal, and physical order, generally taking the form of provisional shelters, rudimentary in nature, illegally built on publicly or privately held land in a clandestine manner by migrant families acting individually or in large groups, often numbering in the thousands. Land could also be attained from private entrepreneurs who, capable of withstanding social and political pressure, would sell parcels illegally.[3] These areas grew quickly as cities doubled in size every twenty years, with low income families approaching 50% of the urban population.

Seen on the one hand, the growth of invasion and "illegal" housing settlements was condoned, perhaps even secretly supported, by governmental agencies and political parties if only to gain the political support of the migrants, silence their demand for housing, and avert facing the major problems of urban development directly.[4] This was accompanied by official political and professional positions declaring such settlements as festering sores rings of poverty, filth, and political radicalism that encircled and threatened the peaceful and orderly social, economic, and physical operation of cities. Settlements were decried as illegal, unplanned, dangerous growths that blighted the environment

---

3. This form of development, called *piratas* in Colombia, is especially prevalent in that country, accounting for 41% of all dwelling units in Bogotá; invasion settlement dwellings account for only one percent of the total dwelling units. See Jaime Valenzuela and George Vernez, *Actividad Constructora Popular: Analisis General y Elementos Para Una Politica de Apoyo* (DNP, April 1972), p. 68.

4. See David Collier, "The Politics of Squatter Settlement Formation in Peru," February 1973 (Mimeograph).

and whose only solution was eradication.[5] At the same time national and international development interests recognized the potential promise and danger of a rapidly urbanizing Latin America and sought to create standards and master plans to guide and control growth and development.[6]

During the 1960s, the study of the origins and organizations of these settlements began. It became apparent that while their development was outside the framework of traditional, overt powers and controls, the settlements had mass political potential and (in and among themselves) possessed a high degree of planning and organization. The view of squatter settlements changed to one of marginality - a group of homogeneous developments characterized by illegal land tenure and owner-built housing, with a migrant base, but necessarily outside the mainstream of urban life. Studies emphasized the internal organization of the settlements and their roles in the urbanization of peasants as the last step of the rural to urban, colonial core to fringe settlement migration pattern.[7] It was recognized that the settlement dweller's objective in coming to the city to seek opportunities was fulfilled to the greatest extent through acquisition of housing. The social and physical redeeming graces of squatter settlements and their part in providing housing were explained.

The "festering sore" view of squatter settlement development demanded overt control of urban growth by traditional means, assuming that settlements could be forcefully removed and replaced by institutionalized housing solutions. The "marginality" view suggested that the settlement phenomenon was separate from its larger urban context, particularly physically, and established a characterization of homogeneous micro-organizations residual to urban growth as a whole. Neither view is adequate.

Squatter settlements are diverse in their characteristics. Their formation takes place in a variety of patterns that respond to social and political organization, leadership availability, economic status, and ability to operate effectively in the larger urban environment.

Migration may take place directly to the settlement from rural or semi-rural areas without participation in the inner city urbanization process.[8] Although their adult population is still predominantly migrant, squatter settlement population will soon be composed largely of first generation urban dwellers.

Land tenure is more complex than was originally presumed. Invasions and illegal formation of settlements form the basic land acquisition methods, later complemented by organized, complex systems of buying, selling, and renting land parcels. The development potential of squatter settlements, which gives an opportunity for capital formation through land acquisition and building, not only has been recognized by the dwellers themselves, but also has been discovered by the more traditional and institutional land development interests, who have sought entrance into the market.[9]

Self-help housing (autoconstruccion), the term usually applied to owner-built dwelling units, has generally characterized the housing development, but the term should be understood to include owner-contracted housing, built by a variety of subcontractors for fees or in-kind services by the owner. The volume of such construction approaches conventional housing construction in quantity and represents a substantial part of total consumption of construction materials.[10]

Most importantly, squatter settlements have shaped the urban areas. Their development responds to locational factors in much the same fashion as other sectors of the private housing market. Because of their magnitude, they have dramatically altered the growth patterns of many cities, forming away from and beyond the existing infrastructure of the city, thus dictating where future transportation and other services must be located. Substantially altering master plans, their growth demands a review of existing construction standards, zoning and building ordinances, and housing policies and programs. Squatter settlements are the most dynamic, adaptive physical environment in the urban

5. See William Mangin, "Latin American Squatter Settlements: A Problem and a Solution," Latin American Research Review 1, no. 3 (Summer 1967); pp. 65-98.

6. This parallels policy and planning thinking in most western, industrialized nations, particularly in the United States, laying the groundwork for vast urban renewal projects in deteriorated urban areas, and massive public expenditures to house the urban poor.

7. John C. Turner, "Housing Priorities, Settlement Patterns, and Urban Development in Modernizing Countries," American Institute of Planners Journal 34, no. 6 (November 1968): pp. 354-363.

8. Albert Berry, Algunos Caracteristicas del Sector de Auto Construccion de Viviedas: Proyecciones de Su Importancia Relativa El Futuro (DNP, 1972), p. 16; hereafter cited as Berry.

9. Research is underway to examine the legal aspects of pirata land sales and settlement development in Botota (FEDESARROLLO).

10. Valenzuela and Vernez, Actividad Constructora Popular, p. 13.

setting, reflecting a determination and ability to grow and change.[11]

III. HOUSING: SHELTER AND COMMUNITY

Much of the study of squatter settlements stems from the view that these communities have one function to perform - that of shelter. Their formation and development are seen as evolving from fulfillment of this need.

Squatter settlements certainly have as their basis the provision of shelter. Because of the inability of settlement dwellers to gain substantial control over the provision for other needs they possess - employment, education, health services, transportation, clothing, food- they find shelter the only necessity of their daily lives over which they can exact overt control. Whether inside or outside the existing social, economic, and political standards, shelter is obtained.

Governments and institutions, in the face of rapidly increasing urban population, seek to provide housing alternatives for low income families. The objective is to house as many families as economically and efficiently as possible. Minimum space standards become maximum accommodations. The production of dwelling units (shelter) through a variety of projects - self help, sweat equity (investment in housing through manual labor), sites and services, core units, etc. - often becomes the short, medium, and long-range goals of the housing programs.

At the outset, then, squatter settlements and public sector housing begin at the same level: shelter. And just as shelter reflects only one need, aggregations of housing units at their conception represent only the static beginning to a dynamic process of creating a community. Growth and change occurs. Communities mature; commercial uses are immediately introduced; infrastructure elements are upgraded or established if not already present. A transformation takes place which allows for integration into the larger urban context.

The growth and change which takes place in the settlements provides for security of ownership, protection from the elements, investment in housing as formation of capital, supplementing family income with home-based business, and the need to establish and identify the dwelling as a personal possession.[12]

For Bogota, it would appear that the issue should not be the share of production of low income housing the public and private sectors must assume, but whether these sectors will be able to continue to deliver the opportunity for evolutionary development of housing at the same rate that it has been delivered in the past. Autoconstruccion (housing through private sector initiative and government housing programs) has accounted for approximately 50% of the housing unit starts in Bogotá in recent years.[13] These settlements have been instrumental in providing shelter to low income families, as well as opportunities for formation of capital, immediate utilization of available disposable income, reduction of housing costs, and sources of income through renting or creation of nonresidential uses.

There are advantages, however, to the government's taking a more dominant role in the development of urban areas, particularly with regard to the development of low income housing. Because of the explosion of squatter settlement development over the last three decades, the ability of the government in most cases to determine growth patterns has been minimal. The principal advantages of planning for further growth, however, do not lie so much in the more efficient development of the dwelling unit itself,[14] as in the guiding of the growth of the city as a whole and, most importantly, in the adequate provision of necessary transportation, utilities, health, education, and social services.

IV. INCOME AND LOW INCOME HOUSING DEVELOPMENT

Because the preponderance of low income families find housing solutions through self-contracted, self-help means in the invasion, pirata, and government sectors of the housing market, it is necessary to examine the income characteristics of those families and the importance the dwelling unit as a source of income. DANE estimates that 50% of all Bogotá households earn less than 2,500 pesos (1970) per month.[15]

---

11. See DESAL, Marginalidad en America Latina, I and II (Santiago, Chile, 1967). For a critical analysis of this concept, see Jose Nun, "La Marginalidad en America Latina," Revista Latinoamerica de Sociologia 2 (July 1969).

12. Turner, "Housing Priorities", pp. 354-363.

13. Berry, p. 7.

14. It seems doubtful that more controlled construction practices in the development of low income housing, although eliminating some of the inefficiency incurred through phased construction, can offset hidden costs in administration, under-utilization of resources (time, money, exchange of services, etc.), and general loss of control of the owner over the building process.

15. DANE, Encuesta de Hogares (E-H2) (unpubliched tables); see DAPD, Mercadeo de Tierras en Barrios Clandestinos de Bogota (April 1973), p. 10.

According to Valenzuela and Vernez, family income categories are distributed across the housing submarket groups as shown in Table 1.

TABLE 1: FAMILY INCOME BY HOUSING SUBMARKETS, BOGOTA

Income/Month (1970 pesos)	Invasion	Pirata	Government	Commercial	Total units	Percent
0-500	653	9,392	1,930	21,530	33,505	7.4
501-1250	2,863	87,897	8,673	21,850	121,283	26.9
1251-2500	1,333	85,143	21,419	13,431	121,326	26.9
2501-4000	104	21,847	10,295	61,382	93,628	20.8
4001+	--	--	6,426	74,934	91,360	18.0
Total	4,955	204,182	48,740	193,124	451,102	100.0
%	1.1	45.3	10.8	42.8	100.0	

Source: Valenzuela and Vernez, La Actividad Constructora Popular: Analysis General Y Elementos Para Una Politica de Apoyo (DNP, April, 1972), page 27.

Since the dwelling units these families occupy are primarily single family attached units built over an extended period (excluding the commercial submarket), it can be assumed that 79.4 percent (from tables 1 & 2) of families with monthly incomes of 2,500 pesos or less are finding their housing solution as owners, renters, or roomers in self-contracted units.[16] Examining the housing tenure status of these families brings into focus the importance of accumulation of capital through the housing development process. In tenure status, owners represent the majority in all housing submarkets except the commercial (see Table 2).[17] Renters occupy the majority of commercial submarket units and approximately one-fifth of the priata units, but are not found in the government submarket (government housing for this income category offers ownership rather than rental programs). For the pirata and government submarkets, roomers account for a significant portion of the households and most likely re-

present the portion above unity (.2 to .3) of the ratio of the number of households per dwelling unit (1.2 to 1.3).[18]

TABLE 2: HOUSEHOLD DISTRIBUTION BY HOUSING SUBMARKET AND HOUSING TENURE

Housing submarket	Tenure owners	Renters	Roomers	Total %
Pirata	52.9	19.7	27.4	100.0
Invasion	61.8	0.0	38.2	100.0
Government	85.7	0.0	14.3	100.0
Commercial	34.7	65.3		100.0

Source: Valenzuela and Vernez, Actividad Constructora Popular: Analisis General Y Elementos Para Una Politica de Apoyo (DNP, April, 1972), page 30.

Previous studies of housing expenditures indicate that for the pirata settlements, 51% of the households pay nothing for housing services,[19] a figure approximately equal to the 52.9% of the households who are owners in this housing submarket. In invasion settlements, an even higher percentage pays nothing for housing services.

For those households in this low income category (2,500 pesos or less per month) that do pay for housing services, the cost is generally 20-25% of monthly incomes.[20] Actual payments seldom exceed 500 pesos and are seldom less than 150 pesos[21] with a median cost of 200 to 250 pesos.[22]

If the fraction of households per dwelling unit over unity (.2 to .3) can be attributed to roomers in owner occupied or rented dwelling units, it can be estimated that for approximately 25% of the families who rent to roomers, the income derived is 26% of total monetary income (median rent paid divided by median total income).[23] This figure, no doubt, varies greatly from household to household.

A study limited to three distinct settlements - invasion, pirata, and government - at different levels of development and distinct locations in the city, indicates a similar occurrence of roomers and income generated. The percentage of dwelling units with roomers varies between 38% and 22% for the government and pirata settlements, respectively (both settlements more than

---

16. Roomers include the "inquilinatos" or those who rent rooms from a household, sharing common sanitary facilities. As will be discussed later, the government housing solutions offered in this income category are of a self-contracted nature, with the family making modifications and/or additions to the units they build or buy through the government programs. See Valenzuela and Vernez, Actividad Constructora Popular, pp. 27 and 30.

17. Invasion settlements are eliminated from the discussion because of their minor role (1.8% of total families) in housing this income category (see table 1).

Renters and roomers represent 65.3% of the families in the commercial submarket. Moreover, this submarket houses the poorest segment of the population--76.0% of the families in the submarket have household incomes of 1,250 pesos or less.

---

18. See DAPD, Mercadeo de Tierras, p. 78.

19. Berry, p. 8.

20. DAPD, Mercadeo de Tierras, p. 25.

21. ICT, Normas Minimas.

22. DAPD, Mercadeo de Tierras, p. 48.

23. Berry, p. 12.

85% developed into permanent structures).[24] The percentage of total monthly income represented by income from dwelling units with roomers is 24.1% for the government settlement and 21.5% for the pirata.[25] The study indicates that the roomers occupied 1.6 rooms per dwelling or 27.2% of the total rooms in the unit (excluding baths, patios, and storage areas). Although more detailed study of the phenomenon is necessary, these figures may serve to indicate the importance of renting as an income source to a primary occupant of a dwelling unit who has the ability to develop and expand his unit to other uses over a period of time.

Current migration patterns reinforce the importance of offering housing services to low income migrant families. Vernez estimates that between 50% and 80% of the immigrants to arrive in Bogotá became roomers in pirata and invasion settlements. Only 7% to 27% of the immigrants arriving go first to the city's center, their traditional destination,[26] the remaining migrants going directly to low income settlement areas. Migrants pay a portion of their income as rent to families who are investing that income in developing housing services. Self-contracted housing, then, includes self-financing. Low income families provide housing solutions for families with income characteristics similar to theirs, substantially aiding in the resolution of the housing shortage in Bogotá, and, at the same time, increase their ownership of capital.

A second important source of revenue for low income families is utilization of the dwelling unit for nonresidential purposes. There has been little study done of the importance of nonwage income as part of the total earnings of low income families. Given that underemployment or occasional employment is prevalent among low income families, the opportunities to supplement fixed income with rental of dwelling unit space for nonresidential uses or the use of space by the family for business or commercial concerns deserves attention. Berry states that when small shops in the dwelling provide the principal income source for the family, incomes from these businesses surpass wages from labor or salaried employment. Moreover, a small sample study in Bogotá and Cali indicates that

goods-producing shops represent the principal income for 14-25% of the families.[27]

A land use inventory done in 1973 of the three previously mentioned settlements plus an additional pirata and invasion settlement (both more than 75% developed into permanent construction) by the author shows that 21-29% of all dwelling units quarter some type of nonresidential use.[28] The percentage of different types of nonresidential use is shown in Table 3.

TABLE 3: NONRESIDENTIAL USES IN FIVE LOW INCOME SETTLEMENTS (BOGOTA)

Settlement	Small food store %	Small production Shop (goods) %	Small retail Shop (goods & ser.) %	Restaurant %	Office %	Total # Units %
Pirata	30.3	21.4	22.3	16.5	9.5	100.0
Invasion	38.0	27.5	19.7	11.3	3.5	100.0
Government	25.2	18.9	30.8	9.4	15.7	100.0

Source: Bender Settlement Land Use Inventory Land Use Inventory, 1973-74.

The most prevalent activities found are those which provide commercial goods and services to the community (small food stores, small retail shops, and restaurants). These are probably operated by someone other than the head of the household - the women and children in the family - who can operate the businesses while carrying on the functions of the family. The two remaining activities (small production shops and offices) most likely are activities carried on by the heads of households, and they perhaps offer employment to other persons.[29] Although no detailed information concerning income from these activities is available, the study by Bender and Gauhan may provide some insight. For the first group of activities - conducted by nonheads of households - the incomes from these represented 15.9, 21.7, and 25.5% per total income in priata, invasion, and government settlements, respectively. For those activities conducted by heads of households, the percentages were 19.5, 24.9, and 13.4% respectively. The lower percentage in the government settlement for the second group is probably due to the income requirements of the government housing programs which tend to accept heads of households with

---

24. 1974 study of three settlements by Stephen Bender and Timothy Gauhan, Program of Development Studies, Rice University, Houston, Texas.

25. The invasion settlement was less than 30% developed into permanent housing, was situated 350 meters above the city in the hills to the southeast of the central business district, and was a 35-minute bus ride away.

26. Berry, p. 16.

27. Ibid., p. 5.

28. The invasion settlement mentioned earlier (see note 25) showed only 7% of the dwelling units having some type of nonresidential use. This would appear to be due to the recent establishment of the settlement (1967), the still provisional condition of most of the construction present, the small size of the dwellings, the hilly characteristics of the terrain, and the lack of clearly defined streets.

29. Berry, p. 5

stable employment. In addition, the reduced size of rooms and lots in the government programs make space allocations to nonresidential uses difficult.

Of the nonresidential uses identified in the three-settlement study, less than 13% occur in rooms identified as rented space, indicating that these activities are carried on by the primary occupants of the dwelling unit. Comparing the percentage of total income that these business activities represent and the rental value of the space they occupy, it appears that the return is approximately the same. Moreover, as Berry points out, these shops often provide the family with goods at wholesale prices, thus increasing the value of having a business in the dwelling unit.[30] There would also appear to be more family satisfaction in operating a business, in that it gives the appearance (if not the income) that the family is progressing and economically active. Also, business activities may interfere less with family life than the presence of roomers who must share sanitary facilities.

Less than two percent of those dwelling units with roomers indicated that they also rented space for nonresidential uses. Unfortunately, specific data is not available as to whether or not roomers are also present in those dwelling units with businesses operated by dwelling owners or renter families. From the above, it would seem that it is improbable. Since dwellings in these settlements tend to have 5.77 rooms and 7 persons per unit, it can be assumed that no more than 1 to 1.6 rooms per dwelling would be devoted to nonfamily use (the family occupying a living area, kitchen, and two sleeping areas).

Summing the percentages of dwelling units with nonresidential uses and those with roomers, 10% to 57% of the dwelling units surveyed utilize dwelling unit space as an income producing source representing 15% to 25% of the total monthly family income. While further study is needed in this area, the Bender-Gauhan study indicates the importance of the dwelling unit as an income source to the families during the development of the settlement.

Almost all income producing use of dwelling unit space takes place in units which are of permanent construction. Rental of space to roomers is most commonly found in smaller units and is associated with households with lower incomes. Nonresidential activities are likewise most generally found in dwelling units of permanent construction, and total monthly incomes of the households who own the units are usually higher than those who rent space.

TABLE 4: INCOME PRODUCING USES IN LOW INCOME DWELLING UNITS (BOGOTA)

	Settlement		
	Pirata	Invasion[*]	Government
% Nonresidential	21	7	19
% Boarders	22	3	38
% Total	43	10	57

[*]The low percentage of income producing uses in the invasion settlement is due to its state of development and location rather than to its condition of being an invasion settlement.

Source: Bender Land Use Survey in Five Bogotá Settlements, 1973-74; Bender and Gauhan Settlement Study, 1973-74.

In summary, the income derived from utilization of dwelling unit space can be matched with perceived opportunities for investment by the dwelling unit owner. Needs can be closely matched to resources at any given moment, providing a flexibility that is not offered by other investment opportunities. It is doubtful that the available funds and labor of low income families can be invested in other sectors so effectively and efficiently.

A third important source of income to the settlement families is the housing expenditure relief that possession of dwelling unit (with or without legal title) represents. As noted earlier, it is estimated that half of the low income families in the pirata settlements pay nothing for housing services.

The amount that this housing expenditure relief represents as a percentage of total income calls for comment. Since most units average from 4.5 (invasion) to 6.6 (pirata) rooms per dwelling,[31] it can be assumed that for dwelling units without rental space, the value of monthly housing services consumed is from 1,125 to 1,650 pesos (250 pesos per room for units without rental space, and from 750 to 1,125 pesos for units with rented space.[32] Table 5 presents the inputed value of housing services as a percentage of total monthly family income.

TABLE 5: IMPUTED VALUE OF HOUSING SERVICES AS A PERCENTAGE OF TOTAL MONTHLY FAMILY INCOME[*]

		Monetary Family Income Level (pesos)		
		1,250	2,500	4,000
Pirata unit	w/rental space	47.4%	31.0%	22.0%
	w/o rental space	61.1%	39.8%	29.2%
Invasion unit	w/rental space	37.5%	23.1%	15.6%
	w/o rental space	47.4%	31.0%	22.0%

[*]Based on (1) 4.5 rooms/dwelling unit in invasion settlements and 6.5 rooms/dwelling unit in pirata settlements, (2) 250 pesos per room per month rent, and (3) 1.5 rooms rented.

_____

30. Ibid.

31. Bender and Gauhan Survey. These figures correspond to 31 m[2] (invasion) and 58 m[2] (pirata) as described by Valenzuela and Vernez, Actividad Constructora Popular, p. 78.

32. Bender and Gauhan Settlement Study, 1973, 1974. Also see DAPD, Mercadeo de Tierras, p. 67.

Although only approximate in nature, the percentage of total income represented by the consumption of housing services is significant, particularly in the lower income categories. Clearly, if families who possess dwelling units in these settlements were forced to seek housing on the rental market, it would be extremely difficult for them to duplicate the services that they are now consuming. They, like the families to whom they rent, would be forced to locate in fewer rooms, lose the income resource the dwelling unit represents, and pay a significant portion of their real income for rent.

V. SOME SUMMARY REMARKS

The income generated through rents and home-based businesses, and the reduction of housing costs through home ownership, are significant when compared with the total incomes for low income families. The opportunity for these families to continue to better their economic situation through this type of housing development is changed, however, by several key issues. Access to land, availability of construction materials, provision of public services, and the decision to create, develop and maintain one's own dwelling are priority issues to be dealt with if the process is to continue.

The issue of access to land is critical. Clearly land costs will be a determining factor in determining the composition of the housing market in Bogotá in the future, the locational characteristics low income family settlements will have, and the type and density of dwelling units that will be developed. Undeveloped land will have to be made available to low income families at affordable prices. If ownership of capital (land and its improvements) is now seen as the most effective way of redistributing income while achieving growth, housing may prove to be the most accessible capital to be acquired by the poor.

Regarding provision of public services, low income housing settlements are often established before there is adequate provision of water and sewerage systems, paved streets, public transportation, education and health facilities, telephones, etc. This is particularly true in the case of invasion and pirata settlements. A long process through legal, political, and administrative channels then ensues to bring these services to the community, unless the settlements themselves attempt to provide them. Major development loan commitments of international and national agencies for provision of such services reflects the high priority given them by local governments and dwellers, although few studies have been conducted examining settlement origin, development patterns, and the impact these services have on the ability of the settlements to develop. Given the limited amount of resources available for utility provision, priorities must be established which will enhance development

capabilities. It is clear, however, that continued growth and development of low income housing settlements is dependent on their inclusion into the urban network of services.

The issue of availability of construction materials is similar to that of land accessibility. Limited quantities of basic construction materials are available. Settlement dwellers must purchase these materials on the open market, competing with the demands created by the institutionalized housing industry, and the transportation, commercial and manufacturing sectors. Unavailability of construction materials because of price or production severely limits the ability of the settlements to grow and expand, thus reducing the amount of housing and commercial services offered through settlement development.

In summary, access to land and construction materials at affordable prices, and provision of public services, are necessary to permit continuing low income settlement development. These issues are, by and large, controlled by forces external to the settlements themselves. The benefits derived from the growth and change that take place enable many of the settlements' inhabitants to survive and prosper in the city.

It is important to remember, however, that a clear decision is made on the part of the low income settlement dweller to assume direct responsibility for the creation and maintenance of his dwelling unit as part of a settlement development process. He not only provides shelter for his family, but also maximizes the opportunity offered by investment in land and improvements made with the income gained through provision of housing and other goods and services.

At present, this decision comes from a lack of alternatives. There is no assurance, however, that future generations will accept direct participation in housing development. Instead, they may demand more traditional alternatives, realizable or not. There is also no guarantee that housing policies and programs will provide the resources necessary for continued settlement development by the dwellers themselves. It cannot be simply assumed that settlement development will continue.

SOCIO-PSYCHOLOGICAL PREREQUISITES FOR NEW AND

EXPANDED COMMUNITY PLANNING AND DESIGN

Norman E. P. Pressman

School of Urban and Regional Planning
University of Waterloo
Waterloo, Ontario, Canada

ABSTRACT

Throughout Canada there is increasing activity
and interest in the expansion of small
communities and the creation of new ones. This
interest has been stimulated by several factors.
These include the need to create settlements
which ensure an improved quality of life, the
need to accommodate limited growth, the need to
contribute to the stabilization of regions which
are on the verge of stagnation and the need to
ensure that families moving to resource towns
have a suitable environment in which to make
their homes. The need for knowledge on new and
expanded communities has become particularly
crucial because there are indications that, in
spite of a higher quality of physical environment, the residents of such communities are
still suffering from acute degrees of tension,
stress and unhappiness. With a growing awareness of these problems, a need has arisen to
develop an understanding of the nature of this
malaise, how it may be treated and what might
be done to prevent its reoccurrence in planning
for community expansion.

This paper represents a fundamental initial step
towards resolving such problems. It is an
investigation which focuses upon the identification and description of psychological and social
problems likely to occur in small communities
experiencing growth as well as in new communities
and the prescriptions being developed to prevent
these problems in planning for the future.

The information found herein is based upon a
comprehensive study recently completed by the
author, for the Ministry of State for Urban
Affairs - Canada, entitled "Social Planning
Prerequisites for New and Expanded Communities"
which focuses on these problems for future
Canadian urban community development.

1. THE PROBLEMS

1.1. The Pre-Schooler

Two trends in Canadian society are important in
meeting the needs of pre-schoolers in rapidly
growing communities. The first is that a
disproportionate number of the dependent
children will be preschoolers. The second is
that more and more women in Canada are desirous
of finding employment outside the home. The net
result of these trends is that the community
must provide an alternative to the traditional
"mother-raising-child" syndrome that exists in
many established communities. Most communities
have taken some action on this problem but it has
been, at best, on an ad hoc basis. In Canada,
national and provincial assistance programs have
been developed which are designed to stimulate
the creation of daycare, nursery and kindergarten
programs. Still, these programs have been
mainly brought to the community at the initiative
of local groups which have had a particular need
for them. They have not been a part of the
formal planning and are often privately operated.
They have been too centralized, too far from the
homes of the potential users, too expensive and
too rudimentary. Because of the cost and
distance factors these facilities are often
beyond the budget and time limits of lower income
families. Two questions must be focused upon:
How does the child-care time sequence match the
employment sequence? And, what happens to the
child in the remaining waking hours? In a
resource community setting there will be little
problem in handling time sequences, for most
people will work at the same time in the same
general area. Therefore, child-care facilities
can be co-ordinated with relative ease. But in
a community which has a diversified work force
the problem is much more critical. In this case
both the community and the employers must work
together in order to see that a satisfactory
solution can be found.

Regarding children, parents perceive for them
(in an advocate sense) the assets that will be
gained by moving. These include safe play spaces,
monitored play areas and high quality schools.
Many have substantially "satisfied" this requirement in a physical sense but not in a social
sense.

Canadian society has obtained a degree of
intimacy and community from the extended family,
the neighbourhood group and children's play
group. The extended family often does not exist
and the neighbourhood group is slowly being
replaced by "communities of common interest".
Yet the child's play group is as strong as ever
and is a necessary part of daily living.
Regardless of the characteristics of the
residents, providing they have children, then
they will most likely interrelate with their

neighbour's children.

Because of low density and the "separateness" of neighbourhoods, there has arisen a need for the creation of the small neighbourhood playground. It is typically both small in scale and small in land area. The key reason for the creation of these small play areas is quite simply that the typical two, three or four year old cannot walk very far. In terms of demand, the number of children in a neighbourhood within this age group is not large. The placing of these facilities is of strategic importance.

With the change in child raising habits, the arrival of "women's liberation", and the desire of more and more women to enter the work force, the responsibility of the community toward child raising must increase. Particular attention must be directed to family controlled play areas which call for virtually no direct supervision; tot lots which, with decreasing family sizes, provide children the opportunity to socialize, and child care facilities and programs which allow mothers the freedom to work.

1.2. The Teenager

The teenager, like the elderly person, is treated as a social minority in many planned communities. He is there because of the decision of his parents and is dependent upon them. Thus, the teenager is not living in the community out of choice and has little or no say in its governance or operation.

In small communities undergoing rapid growth and in new towns there are typically few teenagers. Those families that do move to such communities in Canada are usually quite young and, consequently, have few children if any at all.

The lack of members in their peer group is a major contribution to the feeling of isolation among teenagers. It is also compounded by the typical low density living arrangements of these communities. There are many real "perils" that afflict Canadian teenagers particularly in resource towns:
Being accepted as young adults; they have a terrible burden to overcome, that of being a teenager or young punk. We, as adults, cannot accept them for what they are.
Too many outside activities to distract young people from their studies.
Indiscriminate use of alcoholic beverage perhaps due to easy access to money.
Youth's reluctance to accept personal responsibilities in all phases of community life, leading to trouble areas such as delinquent attitudes in community and highway traffic laws.
Problem of developing a practical philosophy on life; set high standards and objectives for themselves, have to realize that these can seldom be reached, but this should not discourage them or diminish their efforts.
Failure to get the much needed schooling because of family needs in some cases, and in

others, the desire for the "fast buck".
The problems of a materialistic world put pressure on youth to accept a wrong set of values - material gain above service.
Choosing between furthering one's education or leaving school for what seem attractive wages while still young.
Predominance of low-skilled jobs in the community encourage school dropouts. Inducement of "big summer money" encourages teenagers to drop out of school.[5]

There is a tendency among planners to recommend the building of teen centers in the hope that they will mitigate against teenage dissatisfaction. The answer cannot be found so simply. This is a positive contribution in the sense that it stimulates the intermingling of teenagers. However such an approach is divisive. This is particularly true in the sense of teenagers being placed in a special category and in a special area. While few can argue with the desirability of such a facility it should not be the sole measure used. The facility should be one part of a social program which enables teenagers to contribute to the sustenance and growth of the community.

There is also a tendency for planners to group teenagers as one monolithic group. Yet there are few cases where differentiations within the teen groups have been made. There is need for a wide range of facilities and activities. These include recreation fields, bowling alleys, movie theatres and public meeting places.

Planners should also look at the teenager as a potentially employable resource. The typical teenager is desirous of finding local employment and has a large amount of time on hand. As teenagers view the environment, the quality and amount of recreation facilities and the presence of friends as the three most critical factors in terms of urban living, it is important to pay careful attention to them.

1.3. The Elderly

The problems of the elderly have generally received little attention, yet there is a great need to understand the unique needs of this group. This point is reinforced in the research of Rex Lucas (See Rex Lucas, Minetown, Milltown, Railtown, Toronto, University of Toronto Press, 1971) who has found that in the maturation phase of rapid growth communities there will be a large number of elderly people on pension or retirement incomes. These people will have different needs from those provided by the developer when the community was first created.

Foremost among the problems concerning the elderly is the lack of persons of that age group (over the age of 65). These people have a great desire to relate to other people within their own age group. Further, because they are on pension or are living with their children they are of dependent status. They are less mobile than other age groups in the community but, by and large, have a high degree of intellectual independence. Their role as potential participants in community decision making is usually ignored. Some will require special personal needs (e.g., "meals on wheels", ramps, improved health care, bannistered walkways, easy-open doors) while others will be highly desirous of collective facilities which bring them together. Some will desire "senior citizen" or "golden age" clubs while others will avoid them like the plague. In all cases it is essential that these problems be recognized before planning begins for the harmful results can ultimately cause a great degree of social disharmony. In Canada these problems will be particularly severe in resource towns unless they are recognized and are resolved during the initial planning stages.

The more these people are treated as useful active members of the community the less a sense of social isolation will occur. They are too valuable a resource to ignore.

Studies by Rosow[11] and Lawton[4] have shown that social class, sex and marital status are factors which greatly influence the feelings of belonging and acceptance. The individual personality of the elderly person will often be the key element in determining how he settles into a newly changing community. Rosow has constructed a chart which relates personality and neighbourhood preferences of older people[12]. This chart reflects the same personality types that one could expect to find moving to rapidly expanded communities (albeit at a low rate). The break-out is as follows:

Character Type and Description
1. Cosmopolitan: little contact with neighbors, no desire for more friends, most friends live outside this person's neighborhood.
2. Phlegmatic: Socially inactive, prefer little outside contact.
3. Isolated: Wish for more contact with neighbors; presently have few friends.
4. Sociables: Satisfied with their present level of contact.
5. Insatiables: High level of contact, but wish for still more.

Suggested Age Composition of Neighbourhood (Refer to above numbers of 'Character Type and Description')
1. Might like to move closer to the reference group (regardless of age composition) if mobility were restricted. At present, age composition of the neighborhood doesn't seem important.
2. Need minimal social support from the environment; can be satisfied in normally-found age concentrations.
3. Neighborhoods with a predominance of elderly.
4. Neighborhoods with a predominance of elderly; although they might be satisfied anywhere.
5. Neighborhoods with a predominance of elderly.

From these five character types it appears that the key to successfully meeting the requirements is to have as great a knowledge as possible of the people who are moving into the community. The British experience in this regard has been quite notable. When interest is expressed or application to move into an expanded community is made, the party doing so is visited by the community social development officer[1]. This person then ascertains the needs of the party, explains what is available and, perhaps more importantly, what is not available. After this screening, the more extreme cases are discouraged from moving and those who do move have a realistic sense of what will be available to them in terms of facilities and what to expect in terms of community age composition and configuration.

There are several implications which have become increasingly clear concerning the role of the elderly in community planning and upon which planners must focus attention. These include the following:
1. The morale of the elderly is affected by such factors as religion, race, socio-economic status, education, health, intelligence and personality. This is no different than the typical family condition upon moving.
2. There are indications that morale is influenced by the community environment. However, the degree of influence is a function of the relationship between the personality of the resident and the type of change.
3. The age composition of a neighbourhood is a variable which has a potential major impact upon the sense of community.
4. There are no clear findings as to the desires of the elderly with respect to the type of community that best fits their needs.
The most rational approach would be to provide a range of options.

1.4. Women

During the past decade great strides have been taken in the area of understanding women's special needs and requirements. In many sectors of society there is still a sense of recalcitrance in accepting a changed view of women. Older people, schools, religious organizations, peers, and the media still see women cast in their traditional roles. The net result of the views and behavioural approaches of these groups is forcing women into a social confinement which is often manifested in marital conflict, guilt feelings concerning childcare and familial relations, alcoholism, insomnia, drug abuse, depression, frustration, a lost sense of confidence and a lack of self esteem.

There is also the question of expectations. Communities in rapid transition frequently create an image around them which says "Here is the new future". In terms of homes, amenities, facilities and architecture this image is often accurate. There are low-maintenance houses, day-care centers, a wide range of recreation facilities, strongly defined neighbourhoods with local shops and somewhat of a homogenizing effect on social class. However, these improvements have contributed to the isolation and frustration of women from two viewpoints. The first is that the new improvements have made their chores and duties less time-consuming with the result of providing more free time. The second is that, while there is a new physical environment, the same traditional views toward women are carried into the community. The opportunities and facilities are there but their use requires women to recognize that any changes in their role will only result from their own initiative. The role of the planner here can be critical. For example, if as a result of his work, a recognition of women as part of the labour force is noted then one potential problem will be mitigated. If, through social development programs, the free-time resources are channeled into productive ends then, again, another potential problem will be eliminated. In essence it is a problem which centres upon the availability of equal opportunity, freedom of choice and the channeling of highly motivated "person power". To ignore these issues will be to continue to expand communities without building better communities.

In Canadian resource communities the problem of integrating women into the community is particularly severe. The paternalistic obligations of the company or resource new community to absorb other members of the family into the mainstream of work hardly appear to exist. Sons, daughters and wives all have difficulty finding work. As Lucas writes:
The daughters have even greater difficulties because the work force is basically male. The few clerical jobs and service occupations cannot possibly provide jobs for all the girls. The major alternatives are marrying within the community or finding work outside. There is a shortage of marriageable females because there is no work for them to any extent. They leave town. [5]

If there is no work for the single women, given their flexibility and maneuverability, then it is certainly understandable that there would not be any work for wives and mothers. This situation will be intolerable in the future. Women are desirous of working outside the home and, in many cases, are finding it a necessity in order to maintain a comfortable standard of living.

However, the traditional role of women as the housekeeper and child raiser is rapidly changing. Benjamin Schlesinger recently has written a book entitled "Families - A Canadian Perspective" in which he focuses upon how the Canadian family roles will change and what the impact will be. By examining each of the movements that are predicted one can note that there will have to be many changes in the future planning of communities. These movements include the following: [8]
The family will spend less time in child-rearing; more day care centres will look after children.

Canadians will marry later and have fewer children.
The family will have more years of freedom from child-rearing, i.e. childless.
The family will have a longer time in empty-nest stage.
That is, husbands and wives will spend more time together after the children have left home.
Canada will have more working women.
We will have more active family planning -- resources, clinics, etc.
We will have more aged people living in Canada.
We will have more day care services -- for all social classes -- including industry day care services.
We will have more living in urban areas in apartments and family complexes.
We will have more divorces and remarriages.
Divorce will be available from Family Court.
We will have "Family Bureau" as part of the Department of Health and Welfare.
We will have travel and transportation changes -- more children away from home.
There will be more togetherness, and more apartness.
We will have a change in the way family members view each other -- not in terms of power relationships, i.e. head of household, etc.
Women will refuse to be subservient to men.
Mothers will be working more to "fulfill themselves", rather than for "extra income".

1.5. Entry Problems

Leaving an established community constitutes a major crisis. To some people it is a move to a better style of life while to others it is a step backward. The loss of friends, the separation from family and the removal from familiar places can be quite depressing. In fact, quite often as one prepares to leave, there is a sense of overwhelming nostalgia for the "old place". The move itself can be distressing for one has to overcome all the problems of "settling in". A new dwelling has to be found and furnished, children have to be enrolled in schools, new professional contacts have to be established and an adjustment to the social climate made.

The majority of people move to expanded towns largely for two reasons: the availability of employment and the availability of better quality living environments. The need to go where the jobs are can be called a pull factor while the desire to improve the living environment can be viewed as a push reason. There are a series of push and pull factors which can be stated as follows:
PULL REASONS
1. We wanted better job-opportunity.
2. We wanted to be nearer work.
3. We wanted to better ourselves and our family.
4. We wanted to be nearer (or more distant) from friends and relatives.
5. We had no choice, we had to follow the company's orders.
PUSH REASONS
1. We wanted a nicer, safer, cleaner area in

which to live.
2. We wanted a different sized house (or apartment).
3. We wanted a house not an apartment.
4. Our present home was unfit to live in.
5. Better accommodation was available.[2]

Since the majority of families are young, it follows that they are less financially stable than older more established families. Thus, the purchase of a home, often times the proverbial dream come true, can be nightmarishly burdensome. This appears to be particularly true when the purchase is made at the same time that the "entry" problems are being overcome.

Those who encounter social adjustment problems are in the minority. Many of those who have encountered such problems can have them simply removed or prevented by ensuring that the incoming resident is full cognizant of the "state of the community" and that the basic needs of shelter, heat, access and security are met. This is particularly important because most of the residents will be coming from suburbanized or urbanized areas with relatively high standards of service. In fact if the following basic conditions are met then the chances of a traumatic entry into the newly found community will be drastically mitigated:
1. The new dwelling is complete and operational.
2. There is a range of employment opportunities for working mothers.
3. Shopping facilities and schools are within walking distance.
4. Local transit is available.
5. The new resident is of a compatible economic class with that of his neighbours.
6. Immediate contact is made and maintained with the community's officials.
7. An information service is provided.

1.6. Community Integration

As people move to new expanding regions in Canada, planners will be faced with two major problems. The first centers upon whether the communities should be integrated by economic and social class. The second, and perhaps more realistic, is whether integration can be achieved.

Canada has encouraged the evolution of a multi-cultural mosaic[10] This has resulted in the development of strong ethnic communities scattered throughout the nation. It also means that "Canadianization", or the amalgamation of diverse cultures into one, evolves over a longer period of time. The creation of these pockets of ethnic culture has been particularly marked in long established large urban centres where ethnic roots have existed for decades or longer.

There are indications that cultural homogeneity, desirable as it may be in terms of forging an amorphous and monolithic society, will not occur in many Canadian communities. This is due to the desirability of many social sub-groups to maintain a separate identity. Through this ideology of separation these sub-groups seek to utilize new forms of social, economic and political pressures in order to gain a greater share of society's goods and services and to influence the decisions which affect their lives. It is also desirable in their opinion from a protective-security viewpoint. Not being totally accepted by other segments of society they see great value in banding together to gain mutual support and assistance. The wishes of such sub-groups have been generally supported by Canadian government policy. With the exception of economic stability, the issue of heterogeneous versus homogeneous neighborhoods is the most crucial issue that planners must encounter in terms of psychological and social problems. This point was recognized by the Plantown Group for North Pickering where the range of options were reviewed in terms of the individual, social and community alternatives . Included were the following:[9]

Individual
Wide range of choice vs Limited choice; Stimulation vs Stress; Freedom vs Security; Privacy vs Community.

Social
Mixed population (heterogeneity) vs Uniform population (homogeneity); Wide range of values vs Shared valued; Priority to social goals vs Priority to economic goals; "Man-Centred" community vs Man viewed as part of total natural ecology.

Community
Priority to desires of the community's residents vs Priority to regional goals; Goals of community vs Needs of society at large; Public housing as part of community vs Private housing exclusively; Desires of current residents vs Desires of future residents.

Human Development Services
Comprehensive services system vs Specialized system; Privately offered services vs Public services; Integrated services vs Opportunity for choice; Centralized uniform services vs Decentralized local orientation; Build-on current services vs Design new service system.

Planning
Certain facilities and services in place vs Determination of services and facilities by residents; Comprehensive planning vs Focalized issues of interest groups; Long range planning vs Flexibility and meeting of needs as required.

Depending upon the manner in which the costs of services in a community are passed on to the resident, there is a great potential for supporting low income groups. One of the most immediate effects would be to eliminate the sense of stigma which is often associated with the place where these people live. That is, that each community provide for lower income housing in such a way that the social balance would not be upset so as to create a typically "we-they" defensive relationship.

The key to successful integration of the lower

economic classes rests with the quality and availability of jobs. If there are employment opportunities for the lower income workers and a supply of affordable housing then there is reason to believe that they will move there.

Much has been written on economic, ethnic and social integration in expanded communities but no clear approach to the problem has evolved to date. There are those who argue for homogeneity on the grounds that similar people desire to live together while there are others who argue that integration and heterogeneity are essential on the grounds that they are socially equitable concepts. The only answer for policy-makers is to provide for the opportunity of choice.

1.7. Isolation

The lack of community, the mobility syndrome, the trend towards communities of interest, and the widening gap between the two generation family and extended family are all phenomena which are characteristic of rapidly growing and new communities. While these facotrs may all have positive connotations, they also have negative side effects. This is particularly notable in terms of isolation.
Social and Physical Isolation
Social isolation is the inability to get along with neighbours, to find compatible friends and to participate meaningfully in the dominant community life activities. The problem affects some people more than others and is especially prevalent among married women, racial minorities, ethnic minorities and working class people.

Racial minorities feel isolated in two ways. The first is that their exterior image is often different from the people around them. This difference is either due to attire or to skin coloration. Thus there is a continuous and constant visual reminder to themselves and to others that they are different from their neighbours. There is also the fact that most of the personal values held by minorities remain intact after they have moved to another community. Thus, since most people appear to be reticent about inter-acting socially with minorities it is likely that the values held by these new residents would remain.

Members of ethnic enclaves find it particularly difficult to break away from a "Little Italy", "Little Portugal" or "Little Greece". One reason is that they have had to depend upon each other for support as they acclimatize themselves to Canadian society. This dependence and need is a major contributor to the sense of community that is so often lacking. Included among these are strong extended family influences, a common language base easing social compatibility and the availability of jobs for unskilled or semi-skilled workers which is often quite high.

Isolation in expanding communities can be both "real" or "perceived". It is real when the physical design of the community creates conditions which hinder or prohibit the positive interaction of neighbours. It is perceived when, due to several inter-related psychological variables there is an inability of the resident to find a "place" in the community which is comfortable for him. Studies have resulted in some improvements but not to the extent that isolation as a problem has ceased to exist. The problems are manageable, in most cases, providing there is proper staffing and attention.

On a broad base these problems must be met at four levels:
1. in the planning stage by the development administration,
2. through the attention of the growing community's administration,
3. through the development of a realistic and flexible social development program, and
4. by providing an adequate economic base.

Extensive financial disparities among the residents of established neighbourhoods and newly expanding sectors can contribute to feelings of social disparity. It has been suggested that a screening of potential residents be undertaken in order to eliminate or discourage those who may find the life-style difficult to maintain.

In the case of the growth pole variety of expanded community there is a potential added problem: the role and participation of the residents of the established community upon which the new community will be grafted. There is often a physical separation between the old and the new and most often considerable differences in the range and quality of the facilities and services. The residents in the new area are young people with small families who have not maximized their earning power. They are usually more willing to spend money on capital improvements for the future and more willing to expand services than residents in the established community. Only through a carefully planned effort involving communication between the old and the new communities can problems be mitigated.

Social isolation, both real and perceived, can be overcome by advance planning. If people have knowledge as to what is happening around them and if provisions are made to ease their way into the growing community then much of the stress can be mitigated.

While the above problems are perceived by the various groups through their interaction with other people there are also similar problems which emerge as a result of physical isolation. This can be particularly noted in resource towns. These problems, center on boredom and on "being stuck". Several reasons can be found which contribute to this feeling. First is that the move to a new town is a major move, usually outside of the commuting range of the former place of residence. This means that ties with friends cannot be maintained with the same degree of involvement and that familial exchanges become diminished. For those who rely on the camaraderie of friends and strong family ties the new community will indeed be a place where they are "stuck". This feeling may be reinforced if the mother does not drive or has no adequate and efficient transportation. In essence, the physical sense of isolation is closely tied to the mobility of the resident and one can loosely hypothesize that the greater the ease of mobility the less of a sense of isolation will occur.

1.8. The Sense of Community

In terms of site planning and mental health the major research focus has been upon the problems of identification with a community and personal integration into the social mainstream. Despite this orientation there have been no clear findings on the relationship between devotion to "place", the need and desirability of "roots", the "sense of belonging" and "personal integration". Some researchers including Whellis[14] and Goffman[3] have found that there is a strong relationship while there are others such as Webber[13] and Meier[7] who stress the fact that technological advances have antiquated the need for such relationships.

Clearly, in all of the above areas, more research is necessary before the impact of site planning as a cause or cure of social disharmony can be ascertained. This research should focus upon the following:
1. The effects caused by differing sites on differing behaviour patterns.
2. The impact of technological and communication factors upon community life.
3. The impact of density on behaviour in expanded communities.
4. The impact of the lack of "roots" upon community behaviour.
Perhaps by focusing on the above a clearer understanding of site planning and community behaviour will emerge. However, the following generalized statements can reveal important insights:
A. Whether there will be community homogeneity or heterogeneity is dependent upon several factors. Foremost is government policy. Without government sanctions, inducements, or rewards, communities will become divided according to economic status, ethnicity or housing type.
B. While separate neighbourhoods can serve as stimuli for the creation of a strong sense of neighbourhood spirit, they can also be counter productive in terms of developing a strong community spirit. As time passes neighbourhoods tend to become economically homogeneous, that is they reflect the "ability to pay" of the resident. This results in a social class separation.
C. "Propinquity" is becoming less important as a requirement in the development of a spirit of community. It appears that, in the future, "communities of interest" will become more important in the development of a sense of belonging.
D. Planners should be aware that the need to

socialize in expanding communities does not necessarily mean that residents are willing to sacrifice fundamental personal desires for the collective good.
E. The location of the school is an important element in the creation of a positive sense of community. Neighbourhood schools are more desirable than centralized facilities which require busing.
F. It is desirable that each neighbourhood has a "corner store" which serves as an informal meeting and communication focal point.
G. The age composition of a neighbourhood is a variable which has a potential major impact upon the sense of community. The younger the resident, the less the possibility a strong sense of community will emerge.
H. In spite of the changing social milieu and the attention being paid to "communities of interest", the neighbourhood is still the most important settlement form in terms of alleviating psychological and social problems.
I. Extensive financial disparities among the residents can contribute to feelings of social disparity. It has been suggested that a screening of incoming residents be undertaken in order to eliminate or discourage those who will find the life style difficult to maintain. This would assist in creating stronger community bonds.
J. Community facilities by themselves will not alleviate the problems of isolation and alienation. Rather, they must be associated with various social programs before the problems can be overcome.

2. RECOMMENDATIONS: ON THE ROLE OF GOVERNMENT

It appears that the Federal Government of Canada will, in all likelihood, become an active participant in a national community building effort in the future. If such action is undertaken then there are several recommendations which would be of benefit. This is particularly evident in terms of the new development and expansion of resource communities. They are the following:
- Emphasis should be placed on a relatively stable population base, rather than a shifting population. Thus in building the town, construction workers might be recruited according to their willingness to settle in the town upon its completion, and perhaps to undergo retraining to fit their skills to the occupational needs of the town. If the town is constructed in the Native hinterland, natives should be encouraged to participate as full and equal partners, without being segregated in neighbourhoods, schools, and other facilities. This should hold also even if only a small portion of the native population is prepared to accept an "urban" life style. This will probably require extensive state subvention but will enhance immensely the viability of the town's population, while beginning to break down casta-like structures into a more open and mobile class structure, in which ethnicity will not discriminate between

population categories, while these categories will be able to maintain major cultural foci which they value.
- The above would require a careful screening of all prospective population elements, especially in the early phases of the town, to ensure a population composed of persons who are prepared to co-operate closely for the good of the town. If located in the ethnic hinterland, considerable resources should be invested in re-training persons for as many positions as possible, along the full range of the occupational ladder.
- All persons recruited to the town should be prepared to live there as permanent residents, rather than doing a tour of duty, in order to develop their attachment and commitment to the community. Again, considerable inducements, presumably state-subventioned, may have to be provided. This will enable a full and stable range of professional and service facilities to be provided.
- Effort should be expended in developing a diverse industrial/occupational base - in order to provide persons with some occupational choice, rather than being locked completely into a particular occupational slot; and because economic diversity can buffer the shock of economic crisis better than a single-industry town.
- The expectation will be that the core of "prime settlers will demand high standards of health, education, shopping, recreation, etc., which should then be shared with all population elements of the community. The assumption then is that aspirations and standards of community upkeep and viability will be spread throughout the community, enhancing commitment and viability.

In the five points mentioned above the key to success rests upon the willingness of the national, territorial and/or provincial governments to actively participate at all levels of the community development from inception to implementation. Governments will have to develop sets of sanctions and inducements in order to see that the desired scenarios are carried out. Based upon present laws and policies such scenarios are not likely to be made easily operational. Even with a massive governmental assistance program, problems of racism, bi-culturalism, and economic disparity will continue to exist. However, because these problems are complex and time consuming, does not mean that action should not be undertaken. To allow for the continuation of conditions as they presently exist is to build more new and larger communities without building better communities. Indeed, there would be little improvement in the quality of life.

References

1. See RICHARD BERTHOUD and ROGER JOWELL, Creating a Community: A Study of Runcorn New Town. London: Social and Community Planning Research Institute, 1973, p. 22.

2. BERTHOUD and JOWELL, op. cit., p. 19

3. See E. GOFFMAN, The Presentation of Self in Everyday Life. Garden City: Doubleday, 1959.

4. M.P. LAWTON, "Ecology and Aging". L.A. Pastalan and D.H. Carson, editors, Spatial Behaviour of Older People. Ann Arbor: University of Michigan, 1970, pp. 40-67.

5. REX LUCAS, Minetown, Milltown, Railtown. Toronto: University of Toronto Press, 1971, page 291.

6. LUCAS, op. cit., p. 95

7. See R. MEIER, A Communications Theory of Urban Growth, Cambridge: The MIT Press, 1962.

8. As quoted in PLANTOWN CONSULTANTS, Social Development Background Paper Number One: Initial Observations on The Changing Nature of Urban Man and Approaches to Human Development Services, Toronto, 1973, p. C-15. (North Pickering Project)

9. Plantown, op. cit., p. C-27

10. See J. PORTER, The Vertical Mosaic. Toronto: University of Toronto Press, 1965.

11. See IRVING ROSOW, "Housing and Local Ties of the Aged: Patterns of Living and Housing of Middle-Aged and Older Persons". Proceedings of the Department of Health, Education and Welfare Conference on the Aged, Washington D.C., 1965, pp. 47-57

12. Summarized from ROSOW, op cit., pp. 48-57. As found in L. H. Snyder, The Environmental Challenge and the Aging Individual. Urbana: Council of Planning Librarians. Exchange Bibliography, No. 254, January, 1972.

13. See M. WEBBER, "Order in Diversity: Community Without Propinquity", in L. Wingo, editor, Cities and Space, Baltimore: John Hopkins University Press, 1963.

14. See A. WHELLIS, The Quest for Identity. New York: Norton, 1958.

AN EVALUATION OF NEIGHBORHOOD SERVICE CONVENIENCE FOR ELDERLY HOUSING PROJECT RESIDENTS

Robert J. Newcomer, Ph.D

Human Resources Agency
Office of Senior Citizens' Affairs
1955 Fourth Avenue
San Diego, California 92101
Phone (714) 236-4621

ABSTRACT

Site, neighborhood and tenant characteristics of elderly housing projects are examined from a national probability sample. The distance and other circumstances which define service convenience and predict the frequency of use are identified. Service distance recommendations are proposed.

1. INTRODUCTION

One aspect of urban form which has been both revered and studied by city planners is the concept of a neighborhood. Axiomatic in this concept are a number of household locational requirements such as that: living areas should be in convenient proximity to work and leisure times areas and within easy walking distance to convenience community facilities (i.e., grocery stores, elementary schools) (Chapin, 1965). The standards of which land-uses go into a neighborhood, and the time-distance measures of convenience, proximity and mode of travel are generally based on an implicit assumption of households with children (A.P.H.A., 1960). Much of America's residential settings have been shaped by these notions. Since 1956, when the first public housing project designed specifically for older people opened, planners, designers and administrators have been confronted with the difficulty of matching these group housing projects to the neighborhood needs of project tenants. Consequently, expanded notions of neighborhoods - specifically neighborhoods for the elderly have had to be generated. The past 20 years of building experience in housing for the elderly has been essentially an experiment into dynamic relationships between buildings, their environs, and residents. Enough variety now exists to begin a systematic evaluation and prescription for design which may help alleviate the problems confronting these and future projects, and their residents.

This paper has at its task, the development of site performance standards from the standpoint of access to needed goods and services. These standards are derived from the empirical investigation of the question: *"At what distance from a given service is there a significant adverse effect on service use?"*

2. METHODOLOGY

2.1. Sample Selection

The group housing residents examined in this study (n=575) were drawn from a national probability sample of 104 public housing and 50 section 202 housing for the elderly projects built before 1968 and a random sample of 4000 tenants. A subsample of 1000 residents were given extended interviews. This subsample in addition received follow-up mail out/back questionnaires in the fall of 1972. The study design links together survey data both from 1971 interviews and the mail questionnaires, but includes only those S_s who completed the mail questionnaire. The completion rate was 57.5% after three follow-up attempts. An additional 199 questionnaires were returned because the subject was physically or mentally unable to complete it, they had moved, or were deceased. Subjects accounted for other than rejections thus totaled 77.4%. The 1971 National Survey of Housing for the Elderly provided the subjects for this paper. Dr. M. Powell Lawton of the Philadelphia Geriatric Center is the Principal Investigator for the National Survey. It was funded under contract number 93-P7506413 from the Social Rehabilitation Service, Administration on Aging. The encouragement and assistance of Dr. Lawton and his staff in making this paper possible is gratefully acknowledged.

2.2 Defining Environment

Critical to the study design is a working definition of environment, knowledge of the tolerable limits of stress, and a model of the interactive effects of physical and social environments on the individual. M. Powell Lawton's (1970) environmental taxonomy consisting of five components: the individual, interpersonal relationships, suprapersonal relationships, social norms and the physical setting has been used to define environment. A Man-Environment Transaction model postulated by Lawton and Lucille Nahemow (1973) has been used as the conceptual framework for relating predictor, control and outcome variables. Figure 1 provides a diagrammatic presentation of the behavioral and effective outcomes of this model.

The Lawton - Nahemow model's applicability to the present study can be best seen in a practical example. The study's major outcome variable is the frequency of service use. Distance to services in combination with various individual capabilities such as the ability to walk six blocks are representative of the adaptive range. Needed services outside the adaptive range would be unusable.

This study's analysis seeks to identify those attributes both individual and environmental influencing the adaptive range parameters. In other words, we are attempting to discover service distances which minimize non-use of service.

FIGURE 1: MAN-ENVIRONMENT TRANSACTION MODEL

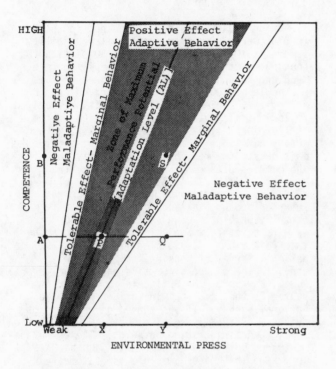

Source: Lawton and Nahemow, 1973

The transactive relationship is illustrated by the following example. Consider an individual of competence (B) receiving environmental press of magnitude (Y). This individual would be operating at (S) which is in the range of satisfactory adaption. High ability is matched by high press. The individual is able to maximize his independence or satisfaction. If ability declines to point (A) such as from illness or chronic physical decrements, environmental press must decrease to level (X) in order for the individual to remain functioning within his adaptive range. Functioning at this new level would also maximize environmental competence. If environmental press was not correspondingly decreased for this individual, the individual would be overstressed by the demands made by his setting as shown by point (Q) which lies just outside the zone of adaptive behavior.

2.3 Measuring Influences on Service Use

The reasonably extensive literature regarding environmental influences on older people (as it applies to the present study) has been summarized in Figure 2. For a full discussion of this literature see Robert Newcomer (1975).

FIGURE 2: PREDICTORS OF SERVICE USE

$$SU_i = S + NF + AD + FD (PS + SD_i) T_i + AF + SR_j$$

Where

SU_i = Frequency of service use for service i; i = 1 to 23 representing 23 service types.

S = Socio-economic status of respondent as measured by the Hollingshead Index for Social Position (1957).

NF = Number of friends reported to be living on project site.

AD = The level of age density in the housing project defined by the percentage of elderly to total residents as was done by Irving Rosow (1967).

FD = The level of female density among elderly housing project residents measured by the percentage of elderly females to the total population

PS = Respondent subjectively perceived safety in neighborhood.

SD_i = Distance to service from project site; i = 1 to 23 representing each of 23 services.

T_i = Transportation availability to selected services; i = 1 to 18.

SR_j = Service richness of project neighborhood; j = 1 to 4 representing the cumulative services available within each of the four service types: convenience needs, luxury needs, medical facility needs, and social recreational needs.

AF = Familiarity with project neighborhood measured by length of project residence.

This equation implicitly presents the hypothesis that service use is a positive additive function of service proximity, area familiarity and on-site services richness. Familiarity is thought to produce the confidence and awareness needed to be actively involved in the residential neighborhood. On-site activity richness is thought to either attract a more active tenant population or to develop a group norm which encourages a variety of activity. Substantial intervening effects from the other variables are not expected. For a discussion of the excluded variables and greater elaboration on the operational characteristics of those variables used see Robert Newcomer (1975).

The 23 services and facilities measured as the service use variables consist of:

| small grocery | physician | public library |
| supermarket | eye doctor | post office |

butcher shop   foot doctor   church/
department store dentist   synagogue
cleaner   luncheonette/   bank
beauty parlor   snack bar   laundromat
barber   movie (commercial)   senior center
bar   outdoor space   center (all ages)

Respondents were asked to indicate the frequency
with which they used each service: several times
a week, once a week, several times a month,
several times a year or not at all.

The measures of distance from project sites to
each of the several service locations were
obtained by asking project administrators to
describe the approximate distance. These
distances were coded: on-site, 1-3 blocks, 4-10
blocks, 11 or more blocks and not available.

2.4 Data Analysis

A two step analytic process has been used in
order to establish critical distance measures.

The first involves the use of forced order stepwise multiple regression to identify variables
having significant influence on service use
patterns.

As shown in Figure 2, control variables were
entered first to maximize their variance explaining ability. This partial correlation procedure
relying as it does on the criterion of contribution to R^2, permitted a conservative test of the
predictor variables. This procedure is adapted
here in conformance with a common practice in
man-environment research. (It should be recognized that disciplines such as economics strongly
argue that the criterion should be the regression
co-efficient rather than contribution to R^2. In
such a case, order of entry is insignificant in
the ultimate establishment of unbiased regression
coefficients.) The area familiarity and service
richness variables were entered after service
distance to test their service enhancing affects
(independent of distance). Transportation was
the only variable thought to have an interactive

FIGURE 3: MULTIPLE REGRESSION TEST OF NEIGHBORHOOD SERVICE USE

Neighborhood Services	Service Use	R	R^2	F Ratio
Physician	No test performed (a)			
Eye doctor	No test performed (a)			
Foot doctor	No test performed (a)			
Dentist	No test performed (a)			
Beauty/Barber shop	+.269 distance - .072 yrs res + 3.808	.302	.091	*
Snack bar	No test performed (a)			
Laundromat	+1.787 distance - .097 yrs res + .152 soc act + 2.378	.552	.305	**
Cleaners	+.116 distance + .198 shop a + .033 soc act + 4.384	.276	.076	**
Small grocery	+.357 distance + .103 soc act + 3.344	.239	.057	**
Supermarket	+.392 distance - .074 yrs res + .108 soc act + 2.574	.310	.096	**
Butcher shop	+.868 transp - .153 distance + .113 soc act + 4.799	.262	.069	**
Department store	+.263 distance - .073 yrs res + .121 soc act + .121	.270	.073	**
Commercial movies	No test performed (a)			
Public library	No test performed (a)			
Post office	+ .423 distance - .130 yrs res + .111 soc act + 2.37	.353	.124	**
Church, synagogue	No test performed(a)			
Bank	.297 distance + .183 soc act + 3.629	.272	.074	**
Public transit	No test performed (b)			
Bar	No test performed (a)			
Outdoor space	No test performed (b)			
Senior center	.237 soc act + 4.501	-.230	.053	*
Center (for all ages)	No test performed (a)			

Note. * significant at .05 level
       ** significant at .01 level

(a) Too few cases used service to establish meaningful variance across variable categories.

(b) Practically all sites provided this service, therefore there is little variance across
     variable categories.

effect. The assumption underlying this was that transportation would have an affect only when there was perceived neighborhood danger or when distance was great.

The multiple regression yields a holistic assessment of the influences on service use and also identifies those variables with the greatest effect on use patterns. As the associations between use and the other variables is not entirely linear, this process does not pinpoint the specific thresholds at which service use patterns change.

Simple crosstabulations, the second step in the analytic design, are more effective for this purpose. Distance to service and frequency of service use are the variable crosstabulations reported here. These variables were chosen for this analysis because of their intuitive importance in site selection and because distance emerged, in the multiple regression analysis, as the strongest and most consistent influence on use patterns. (On-site activity richness and length of project residence two other variables having important influence on use patterns have not been singularly analyzed. The former variable has been shown to enhance service use within the critical distance parameters rather than by compensating for longer distances. Length of residence is a policy variable outside the control of the body regulating site selection, the functional ability decrements associated with length of residence moreover are controlled by tenant screening criteria.)

3. FINDINGS

3.1 Multiple Regressions Analysis

Figure 3 lists the results of the multiple regression analysis. Equations are given for only those variables having sufficient variance to warrant analysis. Regression coefficients are given only when standard error for the regression coefficient has $p < .15$. All regression coefficients shown, however, are based on equations where the full complement of control variables were included with the calculation.

Service distance predicted service use in all but one of the significant equations. Transportation availability significantly entered only one equation. Years in residence was significant in five of the ten equations. Age segregation and number of friends between them produced no significant correlations. A third group of variables concerned project or neighborhood richness. Social recreational richness of the project site had a consistent pattern of emergence (nine equations) to the exclusion of the other richness variables. In virtually all these equations either distance or social recreational richness dominated the variance. As such, these results sustain the hypothesis that service use is a positive function of proximity and, that the pattern of activity is enhanced by the service richness of the site.

The third component of the hypothesis - area familiarity - here represented as years in

FIGURE 4:   NEIGHBORHOOD SERVICE CRITICAL DISTANCE RECOMMENDATIONS

Service	Critical Distance	Maximum Recommended Distance
Bus stop	on-site to 3 blocks	1 block
Outdoor area	on-site to 3 blocks	3 blocks
Laundromat	on-site	on-site
Grocery store	1-10 blocks	6 blocks
Supermarket	1-10 blocks	6 blocks
Bank	1-10 blocks	6 blocks
Post office	1-3 blocks	3 blocks
Department store	1-3 blocks	3 blocks
Cleaners	1-11 blocks	6 blocks
Senior center	on-site	on-site
Beauty/barber	on-site to 10 blocks	10 blocks
Physician	1-10 blocks	10 blocks
Butcher shop	1-10 blocks	6 blocks
Snack bar	1-10 blocks	10 blocks
Public library	on-site to 10 blocks	10 blocks
Dentist	1-10 blocks	10 blocks
Eye doctor	1-10 blocks	10 blocks
Foot doctor	indeterminate	10 blocks
Center (for all ages)	used as a senior center	on-site
Movie	indeterminate	10 blocks
Church/synagogue	indeterminate	indeterminate[a]
Bar	no importance	no inportance

[a]Indeterminate critical distance due to high percentage of persons who do not use, and only small number who do use.

residence, yielded a rather surprising result. It produced negative correlations. In other words, length of residence was associated with a decrease in activity rather than an increase. This finding confirms what many administrators have said about the declining ability of their tenants with age. At the same time, it argues against the positive enhancement that familiarity is supposed to bring to perceptual decrements. Further work is needed here to identify the turning points with length of residents and adjustments.

Age density and number of friends had little predictive influence, which was expected due to tenant homogeneity among these attributes. Transportation, the remaining control variable, too did not produce its anticipated interactive affects.

This is perhaps a consequence that tenants generally had such a high level of perceived safety and were familiar with their neighborhoods. In such cases, transportation was of little importance for short trips. Trip purposes beyond walking distance were infrequent regardless of transportation availability.

While the hypothesis predicting service use is basically sustained, note should be directed to the low correlations and multiple R^2 produced by these variables. With the exception of laundromats, the amount of variance explained for neighborhood services ranges from only 7 to 12.4%. This figure is not a real encouragement to those trying to improve the quality of life for project tenants with better site suitability criteria. Nevertheless, as most of the service uses examined here are activities demanding minimum levels of routine attendance, any improvement is worth achieving.

3.2 Neighborhood Services and Distance

The analysis of the crosstabulations in terms of critical distances and recommended distances are summarized in Figure 4. Copies of the cross-tabulation tables are available upon request from the author.

The services shown include commercial establishments, health, and religious facilities. In all 23 services and activities are listed. They are ranked by the percentage of persons who use these facilities when they are provided within the critical distance. Location within this distance produces positive neighborhood service use. It can be observed that on-site locations are needed for two services: laundromats and senior centers. A one block radius is suggested for public transportation and a three block radius for outdoor areas such as parks. Convenience goods such as grocery stores, supermarkets, banks, post office, department stores, cleaners, barber/beauty shops and butcher shops are all recommended to have maximum distances of from three to six blocks. Obviously food stuffs will be obtained even if people must go further, but the likelihood of

at least weekly trips is maximized at this distance. For the remaining convenience goods, especially department stores and post offices, proximity appears to have an important trip generative affect on services that typically tend to be infrequently used. Proximity to bars appears to have no importance whatsoever.

The other services physician, eye and foot doctors, dentists, public library, snack bar, churches, and movies appear to have no neighborhood orientation. These services are so infrequently used that distances of 10 blocks or greater seem to have little affect on use patterns.

The ranking and recommended distances shown, for the most part, substantiate the service distance recommendations made in the Niebanck and Pope study (1965) while simultaneously answering the original question underlying this study. Niebanck and Pope investigated only 12 facilities: grocery store, bus stop, church, drug store, clinic/hospital, bank, social center, library, news-cigar store, restaurant, movie house and bar. The present study examined all of these but drug store, news-cigar store and hospital/clinic.

Additionally, these findings correspond to the service travel values and cognitive neighborhood radius reported in recent work which show the average walking distance to be less than 10 blocks and of 15 minutes duration for convenience goods and up to 30 minutes for social, recreational, and medical purposes (Nahemow & Kogan, 1971; Regnier, 1973; and Eribes, 1973).

4. DISCUSSION AND CONCLUSIONS

4.1 Summary

Principal among the concerns voiced at the outset of this investigation was that national housing policy for the elderly as exemplified by public housing and Section 202 housing programs may have been produced with too little sensitivity to the special needs of older people. In particular it was noted that there were few guidelines regarding site selection and service accessibility.

This investigation in responding to these concerns sought to link the study of man-environment relations to these design issues and to develop site suitability criteria for elderly housing.

Service distance recommendations for 23 neighborhood services were developed to answer the question "At what distance from a given service is there a significant adverse effect on service use." A variety of intervening variables such as age, sex, income, socio-economic status, the presence of on-site friends, area familiarity, age density, perceived safety, service richness and transportation availability were examined for their differential influence on the site suitability criteria. Distance emerged as the single most important predictor of use. On-site activity frequency had augmenting service use influences within the recommended distances.

The distance recommendations, although emphasizing proximity for many services, appear to be achievable. Locations near supermarkets very likely assures proximity to many commercial and other services. This is a reality of urban service aggregation. Services not strongly influenced by the supermarket forces are churches and medical facilities - neither of which evidenced a strong neighborhood orientation nor frequent use. An orientation of housing projects to natural clusters of services will require adjustments to the currently used per unit building cost, and land density constraints of federal housing legislation. Simply stated, desireable sites for elderly housing often may have to compete against bids from the "higher and better" uses of commercial establishments. More funds will be needed to do this.

In light of the cost implications of these recommendations, the limitations to the generalizability of the study's findings must be emphasized. This discussion will also highlight issues of theoretical and methodological concern for future work.

4.2 Environmental Adaptation

By far the most surprising outcome of the study was the negative relationship between service use and length of project residences. This tendency is contrary to the presumed expansive effects of neighborhood familiarity. Has the housing now in place been designed and located such that it is exciting for new residents, but becomes unchallenging with length of residence? Although this question is basic to the policy orientation of the study's recommendations, its answer is not possible from available data. Future work is needed which isolates the new in-mover and her adjustment behavior patterns, particularly as these relate to neighborhood expansion. The pattern of activity over time also requires investigation. At what points does it peak and why? How fast is the decline? And, at what point in this cycle does the tenant begin looking for alternative living arrangements?

These unknowns should not be used to paralyze construction. Stated another way, if the concern in designing for the elderly is a possible erosion of their "competence" or interest in life as expressed by their activity levels then the decision choices narrow to these: (1) should interest be maintained by demanding more in daily activities; or (2) by supporting daily activities with the expectation that adventure seekers would look outside the residential setting for stimulation? Though this issue is not resolved by the present findings, I support the notion of guaranteed levels of service access for all new housing sites with the expectation that there will be a monitoring process to learn from what has been done.

4.3 Environmental Self-Selection

The ability to differentiate critical differences between environments or individuals is partially preconditioned on the variance within the sample used. A profile of this study's Section 202 and public housing tenants confirms these settings are rather homogeneous in their social attributes. Tenants seemingly have selected environments matched to their needs. White (71%) women (76%) who live alone (82%) and who are somewhat less active than community samples of elderly (Lawton and Cohen, 1974) predominate. All tenants are further screened on threshold income and functional ability values during the admission process. The housing design, which features small units contributes to the natural attraction of single person households. Older people who meet these criteria are currently women rather than men, white rather than minority. As long as the screening criteria and unit size patterns remain constant there is a high probability that housing projects such as these will continue to attract a similar population. The findings reached in this study are therefore limited in their applicability to projects meeting these criteria rather than being universal. Retirement communities, mobile home parks, community residents and boarding homes are examples of alternative living environments which attract unique populations and which may need their own site suitability criteria and other guidelines.

4.4 Future Model Sample Proposals

To date, research efforts in man-environment relations (such as the present study) have tended to concentrate on single environments at any one time, on residents living within those projects, and on a random (at best) or haphazard (at worse) selection of sites. The evidence found here strongly suggest a new approach along all three dimensions.

Project selection within a class of similar projects yielded a selection of subjects who were attracted to that environment. Without an attempt to examine a cross-section of environments as well as a cross-section of the population a generalized prescription of critical distances (or other adaptive limit) cannot be determined. Such determination is important if one desires to modify an environmental setting so as to broaden or limit its attractiveness. Would the provision of more recreational resources in public housing be a service to those now living there? Would it bring in a different type of resident? Such questions cannot be adequately answered without generalized guidelines.

Unit size mix in a building predetermines many attributes of the tenant population. So do many other physical and policy actions. These need to be studied in order to establish their relationship to the population selected. In turn, varied population mixes such as in functional ability, age, sex, SES, and race are needed in order to evaluate the efficacy of campus facilities, mixing low income elderly into all housing projects, and other likely design applications. Irving Rosow (1967) has provided some information on the ranges of age density, but as a whole, the subject of contextual congruence is virtually unexplored. This research was not able to really examine this question because the selection processes had already operated to exclude the deviant. All this again underscores the importance of sample selection. As an initial step to improving the sampling process it is essential that a range of varied facilities be examined with the same instruments and methods. Further, it seems reasonable that in selecting projects greater attention should be given to the deviant rather than to the common. In other words, the very bad and the very good should be sought out for study. This likely will maximize heterogeneity in individual as well as environmental attributes.

Finally, as "self-selection" is so predominant a concern, and adjustment so expected within such a setting, more attention has to be given to the disatisfied within a setting. This includes the in-mover and the person who has given notice of leaving. It also includes an examination of the antecedent environments from which the tenants come, and why they left.

4.5 Closing Comments

The product of this research as reflected in site suitability guidelines for Section 202 and public housing is timely. National housing policy has placed much responsibility for new housing on local governments. Further, they have placed an explicit priority on elderly housing. Enough information has been provided here to produce specific guidelines for projects intended to house white females who live alone. The rather limited spatial demands reflected by these guidelines offer some hope of their transferability to other household sizes and cultural groups. Further study however is needed before comprehensive guidelines for alternative housing types will be possible. Adherence to the proposed sample selection process will greatly enhance this work.

References

AMERICAN PUBLIC HEALTH ASSOCIATION (A.P.H.A.), Chicago, 1960, Planning the Neighborhood.

CHAPIN, F., University of Illinois Press, Urbana, Illinois, 1965. Urban Land Use Planning (2nd edition).

ERIBES, R., Unpublished Master of Architecture Thesis, University of Southern California, 1973. The Spatio-Temporal Aspects of Service Delivery: A Case Study.

HOLLINGSHEAD, A.B., 1965 Yale Station, New Haven, Connecticut, 1957. Two-Factor Index of Social Position.

LAWTON, M.P., University of Michigan Press, Ann Arbor, Michigan, 1970. Ecology and Aging. In Pastalan, L., & Carson, D. (Eds), Spatial Behavior of Older People.

LAWTON, M.P., & COHEN, J. Journal of Gerontology, 1974, 29, 194-204. The Generality of Housing Impact on the Elderly.

LAWTON, M.P., & NAHEMOW, L., American Psychology Association, Washington, D.C., 1973. Ecology and The Aging Process. In Eisdorfer, C., & Lawton, M.P. (Eds), The Psychology of Adult Development.

NAHEMOW, L., & KOGAN, L, New York Mayor's Office for the Aging, New York, 1971. Reduced Fare for the Elderly.

NEWCOMER, R., Unpublished Doctoral Dissertation, University of Southern California, Los Angeles, 1975. Group Housing for the Elderly: Defining Neighborhood Service Convenience for Public Housing and Section 202 Residents.

NIEBANCK, P., & POPE J., Institute for Environmental Studies, University of Pennsylvania, Philadelphia, Pennsylvania, 1965. The Elderly in Older Urban Areas.

REGNIER, V. Unpublished Master of Architecture Thesis, University of Southern California, 1973. Neighborhood Cognition and Older People: A Comparison of Public Housing Environments in San Francisco.

ROSOW, I. Free Press, New York, 1967. Social Integration of the Aged.

HUMAN FACTORS RESEARCH ON BUILDING STANDARDS
FOR ACCESSIBILITY TO DISABLED PEOPLE

Edward Steinfeld, Steven Schroeder, Marilyn
Bishop, James Aiello, Stephen Andrade, Richard
Buchanan

Syracuse University
School of Architecture
Research Office
118 Clarendon Street
Syracuse, NY 13210
Phone: (315) 423-3212

ABSTRACT

Existing empirical research concerned with
accessibility of buildings for people with
disabilities is reviewed and problems with
validity are identified. Research in progress
is described that will generate data for
revising a concensus standard now used throughout the U.S.

1. INTRODUCTION

This report describes human factors research
now underway at Syracuse University's School
of Architecture and Gerontology Center. As
part of a two-year contract with the U.S.
Department of Housing and Urban Development,
we are generating information needed for revising and augmenting the present ANSI
Standard, A117.1, "Making Buildings and
Facilities Accessible To and Useable By the
Physically Handicapped".

Presently, this voluntary building standard
is used as a basis or has been adopted in
whole or in part by many Federal agencies
and 50 states for use in design of public
buildings (with varying definitions). Since
the standard was first approved in 1961, it
has become apparent that many inadequacies
exist in it, particularly the lack of
criteria for the design of housing units for
people with disabilities. Furthermore, these
inadequacies, coupled with the lack of hard
research data for many concerns of accessibility, have resulted in a profusion of
different and unvalidated recommendations
from many sources. The secretariat of the
committee responsible for the ANSI A117.1
Standard consists of HUD, The Easter Seals
Society and The President's Committee for
Employment of the Handicapped. Realizing
that this situation seriously hampers the
effectiveness of ANSI A117.1, they gave us a
mandate to propose new standards based on
comprehensive objective data.

We completed a state-of-the-art survey that
identified the scope of accessibility concerns
and knowledge gaps. We then developed research
methods and built a testing laboratory and
recently began data gathering activities.

2. SCOPE

When determining the scope of the research,
three major questions were: 1. Who is the
population of concern? 2. What buildings are
to be covered? and 3. What parts of a building
will be covered? The existing ANSI Standard
focuses on six disability groups: 1. confinement to wheelchairs, 2. semi-ambulant
disabilities, 3. sight disabilities, 4. hearing
disabilities, 5. incoordination, 6. manifestations of the aging process. We expanded this
list to encompass those disability concerns
represented in Figure 1. While the existing
ANSI Standard was developed primarily for
application to publicy used buildings built
with public funds, we will propose expanding
the scope to include application to all
publicly used buildings, including commercial
facilities and housing of all types. This
extension of scope is consistent with the
current emphasis on normalization of life for
people with disabilities since it would
provide access to all normal community facilities.

The existing ANSI Standard has sections concerning Site Development and Buildings. The
new proposals will give much more detailed
attention to sites and also to the selection
of building products, including signage.
The proposed standards are also to be perfor-
mance-based. That is, they will not prescribe
specific design solutions but will present
criteria that can be met in a variety of ways.

The building, its site and products within it,
can be conceived as a task environment for
access. Figure 2 shows all the human tasks
involved in obtaining access and information
needs for design of an environment to
facilitate these tasks. This set of information needs was used as the basis for the
research design.

3. PREVIOUS RESEARCH

Empirical studies related to accessibility were reviewed and compared to the set of information needs in Figure 2. They were also evaluated for external generalization and internal validity. From this comparison, we established what research would have to be done. Previous empirical research on accessibility for disabled people has taken place in the United States, United Kingdom and Sweden. These are the major studies with satisfactory documentation of methods and results:

1. Charles Dixon, U. of Illinois, Division of Rehabilitation-Education Services, Champaign-Urbana, Ill., "A Study to Determine the Specifications of Wheelchair Ramps", 1957.
2. Helen E. McCullough, et.al., U. of Illinois College of Agriculture Extension Service, Champaign-Urbana, Ill., "Space and Design Requirements for Wheelchair Kitchens", 1960.
3. W.F. Floyd, et.al., National Spinal Injuries Centre, Stoke Mandeville, U.K., "A Study of the Space Requirements of Wheelchair Users", 1966.
4. Felix Walter, Disabled Living Foundation, London, U.K., "Four Architectural Movement Studies for the Wheelchair and Ambulant Disabled", 1971.
5. P.M. Howie, Disabled Living Foundation, London, U.K., "A Pilot Study of Disabled Housewives in their Kitchens", 1968.
6. Sven-Olaf Brattgard, et.al., Department of Handicap Research, University of Goteborg, Sweden, "Maneuver Space for Indoor Wheelchairs", 1974.
7. P.J.R. Nichols, Nuffield Orthopaedic Centre, Oxford, U.K., "Door Handles for the Disabled".
8. A. Ownsworth, Institute for Consumer Ergonomics, Leichestershire, U.K., "An Ergonomic Study of the Space Requirements of Wheelchair Users for Doorways and Corridors", 1973.
9. American Telephone & Telegraph Co., Research Section/Marketing Department, "Universal Public Telephone Height for Handicapped and Able-Bodied Users", 1975.

In addition to the above, the Department of Handicap Research at Goteborg has completed two additional research studies for bathrooms and for kitchens with people in wheelchairs, but only design recommendations are presently available in English. Also, the University of Illinois, Division of Rehabilitation-Education Services, under the direction of Timothy Nugent, completed numerous useful, but informal, investigations leading to the development of ANSI A117.1. There has been some empirical work on the use of the built environment by the blind, but it has focused on developing technical aids for the person, i.e. maps, rather than design criteria (Leonard, 1972 and Kidwell and Greer, 1973).

Most of the empirical research focuses on the needs of people confined to a wheelchair. Thus, most design recommendations are limited to that group, yet they represent only a small proportion of the population with disabilities. The argument for such an approach is that, if the needs of the person in a wheelchair are satisfied, everyone else's needs are also. This is true to an extent, but it overlooks a major characteristic of the disabled population--their great diversity and the resulting individual styles of adaptation to the physical environment. It also results in a focus on orthopedic impairments to the neglect of sensory and stamina problems.

The scope of design features investigated has been limited. Although turning spaces, doorways, ramps and kitchens have all been studied, bathrooms, telephones and door hardware have only been subjects of one study each. Moreover, some design features have been neglected entirely, e.g. grab bars, windows and elevators. Studies of some features have only examined one particular variable, e.g. ramp slope, rather than the slope/length relationship.

Several methodological criticisms of previous research limit its usefulness. Ownsworth's study used mostly able-bodied people in wheelchairs, introducing considerable bias from functional ability, attitudinal and adaptation differences. Walter's study used a relatively large number of people who were institutionalized. Attitudinal factors related to institutionalization may lower human performance levels. Some studies use the person's own wheelchair, others supplied a wheelchair. Some chairs provided require more space for manipulation than others (Brattgard, 1974). Howie's study was done in actual dwelling units and the A.T. and T. study was done in naturalistic settings, whereas all other studies were done in laboratory settings.

There is a lack of standardization in the methods used to identify the functional limitations of individuals within their medically determined disability categories. The samples of subjects were too specialized for generalization. There were also differences in age-makeup and in cultural background. The actual procedures and laboratory test facilities differ significantly and may have major built-in bias. For example, Walter assumed a continuous turn for a U-turn and Brattgard allowed two 90 degree turns, in Walter's study, partitions were used to make confined spaces for turns, while in Brattgard's work, turns were completed in an open space which reduced the judgmental component of the task. Finally, data analysis in some cases was questionable; for example, Walter used parametric statistics with a sample that was unlikely to be at all representative of a normal distribution (Brattgard, 1974). Design guides, such as in Goldsmith's Designing for the Disabled, and Dreyfus Associates' Human-scale 1,2,3, rely on the work of selected empirical research and interpolations of anthropometric data. Such data, particularly when it is of able-bodied subjects, is of questionable value.

A review of the research available demonstrates a need for comprehensive, empirical research on accessibility that can overcome the limitations in generalizability to the U.S. scene and the methodological problems with existing empirical work.

Previous research has, however, allowed us to limit our task in various ways. The work of Brattgard and his associates in Goteborg has been particularly useful as a starting point since their approach has not been biased by poor sample selection and methodological weaknesses. We are building on their studies of turning radius by introducing the constraint of immovable walls. Our door research is limited to testing only two standard-size American doors, slightly smaller and larger than the metric size recommended by the Goteborg team, rather than a wide range of doors. Also, our experiments with kitchen and bathroom fixture heights assume a wide range of need as found by the Swedish researchers and include simulations of use as in their work. The work of Howie, Brattgard, et.al. and McCullough et.al., as well as several kitchen studies with able-bodied users, provide much useful and verifiable data on kitchen layouts. The work of Dixon and Walter with ramps has allowed us to develop a more sophisticated approach to ramp research than previous work. Nichol's study on door handles was sufficient to omit that concern from our work and utilize his recommended opener in our doorway experiments. The A.T. and T. study was done only with able-bodied people and wheelchair users. We are repeating it with people having other disabilities as well.

The first part of the research now underway includes laboratory studies of: 1. wheelchair turning radius, 2. oven work center, 3. sink work center, 4. mixing/food preparation work center, 5. range work center, 6. doorways, 7. elevator, 8. bathtub/shower arrangement, 9. toilet arrangement, 10. lavatory height, 11. push and pull forces for windows and doors, 12. ramp slope and length, 13. public telephone height, 14. public mail box use, 15. anthropometric and wheelchair measurements, and 16. apartment layouts. These studies are concerned with the use of buildings by people with orthopedic disabilities, limitations of stamina and balance. Ambulant, semi-ambulant and non-ambulant people are participating.

We are also doing field research on mobility in buildings with people having severe visual problems. This includes studies of: 1. direction finding, 2. use of environmental cues, 3. aids to environmental cognition, and 4. safety issues. This part of the research is taking place in a campus building with both people who are totally blind and those who have partial vision.

In both laboratory and field studies, we will test able-bodied people as well for comparison purposes.

A third part of the research, not yet underway, will gather technical data on wheelchairs, frequency levels for alarm systems and other information not requiring the involvement of consumers.

4. LABORATORY TESTING METHODS

4.1. Subjects

The selection of subjects is a particularly important concern for this type of research. Our goal is to provide standards that will make the built environment accessible to any-one who can use it independently without elaborate changes in construction technology. Some people with the same orthopedic disability can overcome more physical obstacles than others due to differences in stamina, attitudes, rehabilitation training and styles of adaptation. Orthopedic, balance and stamina disabilities can vary considerably in themselves, and they can be multiple in nature. We developed a method to screen participants in a way that would give us representation of individuals at all functional ability levels within a particular disability concern. This "diagnostic method" utilized a self-report interview about tasks of daily living. Some example questions are shown in Figure 3. Self-report data is used for screening and then verified by observation of actual tasks in the laboratory. Carefully defined limits were established to eliminate those people below a minimal level of independent functioning and to eliminate those people who were not disabled enough to have difficulties in negotiating the environment.

Arbitrary numbers of subjects were assigned to each category (either 10 or 5) yielding a total number of 260. Since statistics are not available giving a breakdown of individuals in the total disabled population into functional categories, we could not develop a proportionate sample. Moreover, it is not necessary that this be done since our goal is to make the environment accessible to anyone who can function independently in it without elaborate techno-logical changes. Our diagnostic method allows us to determine which people, but not how many, will be considered by the proposed standard.

Subjects are being located by an elderly consumer advocate organization but they are not limited to older people. Only non-institutionalized individuals qualify. All subjects are provided with transportation to the laboratory and are paid for their participation.

4.2. Kitchen Counter Work Centers and Lavatory Procedures

All of these units have adjustable counter and shelf heights and can be used with a closed or open front. Counter heights adjust from 24 in.to 36 in. Shelf heights, from 40 in. to 72 in. The mix center has a feature that allows us to test reach to a corner cupboard.

Testing procedures at each unit include two fitting trials for comfortable counter heights (Jones, 1969) and maximum and comfortable reach trials to the shelf. Trials are conducted using simulated tasks common to each unit, e.g. scrubbing a pot, washing one's face. At the mix center, users repeat the procedures with a closed counter front, reach to low shelves and laterally as well. All reaching tasks utilize a two pound cylindrical cannister that can be grasped easily with one hand.

4.3. Toilet and Bathtub

Both of these units have multiple sets of grab bars, any of which can be chosen by the user. The lateral bars start at 27 in. and increase in height by 3 in. intervals to 37 in. Reach measurements are taken for placement of controls and other items. The toilet unit has an adjustable height from 14 in. to 20 in. and moveable walls that can move from within twelve inches o.c. with the bowl to 48 in. away. Chairs are available at the bathtub for placement inside or outside the tub. Users select the grab bar height they think is best. Initial trials determine minimal conditions of use and adjustments are made for optimal conditions. Since grab bars are available at most conceivable locations, actual spots on the bars used are recorded as well as which bars are used.

4.4. Doorways

Two doorways are being tested—a 32 in. door and a 34 in. door. Moving walls are used to determine minimum hallway widths. All door openers are the single-lever type. The user tests the door using their least favored hand (a left-handed person tests a door that favors a righty) in three opening approach patterns—direct forward, from the latch side and from the hinge side. Several trials of each are run to determine minimal size door and corridor width. Space requirements are noted. Criteria for successful use are not bumping walls, jambs and doors and the ability to complete the trial without undue adjustments and time delays. A second phase of research will examine the effect of door closers on

performance.

4.5. Elevator

Testing includes the time required to reach the elevator from a point 18 ft. from the door (maximum distance likely from floor button), the space needed inside the cab and the height and location of call buttons. The testing unit is a simulated elevator of adjustable size. We are testing the smallest sizes currently available for 2,000 pound and 2,500 pound elevators. People in wheelchairs test both front and backward entry maneuvers.

4.6. Oven

A simulated oven can be set up in six different configurations of height, door type and accessible space under a side counter. Users simulate using and cleaning ovens. Success in all tasks with one oven configuration, constitutes a successful trial.

4.7. Push-Pull Forces

The device used to measure forces simulates the method required to open sliding and double-hung windows and to push and pull side-hung doors. Maximum effort registered with a force gauge is recorded for each trial.

4.8. Ramp Slope and Length

A 40 ft. ramp at 1:12 slope is being tested. Length and time of travel are recorded as well as a measure of energy expenditure, based on heart beat rate. Selected people with unsuccessful and successful trials will return to test the ramp at steeper and less steep slopes until we can determine the needs of people at all ability levels.

4.9. Public Telephone and Mailbox

Standard units were obtained for testing. Both are tested for use under normal conditions. The telephone is mounted on an adjustable unit with a coin slot height ranging from 61 in. to 23 in. Starting at a 54 in. coin slot height, the telephone is lowered until it can be used.

4.10. Wheelchair Turning Radius

People in wheelchairs are asked to do a 180 degree turn, in whatever way they find most efficient within a three-walled space. One wall and their starting position are adjusted until the minimum space is found. A 36 in. high counter is set in place at one side and its effect on turning radius partially underneath is noted.

4.11. Anthropometric and Wheelchair Measurements

A complete set of body and wheelchair data is obtained by reading off measurements of individuals as they stand and sit next to a wall grid. Vertical reach and forward reach are included. Toe clearance data for wheelchair users is obtained with an adjustable device simulating toe clearances under counter cabinets.

4.12. Apartment Layouts

In a second phase of testing, selected individuals will be invited back for simulated use of various kitchen layouts and apartment unit plans. The former tests will be done in an adjustable, simulated kitchen. The latter will take place primarily to measure clearances, alignments and energy utilization with layouts plotted with tape on a gymnasium floor.

4.13. Opinion/Adaptation Interview

All participants in the laboratory testing are administered a 30-45 minute interview. This interview assesses the adaptations they have made to their own living environment and their preferences regarding alternative design features. The interview focuses on kitchens and bathrooms, but also has questions on features common to public buildings.

5. FIELD TESTING METHODS

5.1. Subjects

As with orthopedic disabilities, the functional ability of people with impaired vision is affected, not only by the condition itself, but also by attitudinal and experiential variables. Since no empirical research had been done previously in blind and partially sighted mobility in buildings, we decided to utilize a small group of people, doing extensive testing with each individual.

Participants include risk and rote travelers. Risk travelers are people who go to unfamiliar places on their own. Rote travelers have to be escorted to a place before they will go by themselves. Most participants use long canes and some use dogs. We hope to involve 30 people in the testing.

There is no readily useable and objective technique to measure the functional ability of blind and partially sighted individuals, thus, we are measuring ability levels as we identify problems. All participants have had some formal mobility instruction and are independent in mobility at least in their home environment.

5.2. Experimental Setting

With the help of a local mobility instructor, Dan McGlaughlin, a route was identified in a campus building that presents many types of problems to the visually impaired user and also many types of orientation cues. The

route includes these environmental features: 1. maze-like corridors, 2. large, undefined open space, 3. obstacles of many kinds, 4. several different acoustical cues and properties, 5. olfactory and thermal cues, 6. changes in floor textures, 7. various types of doors and openings, 8. a ramp and a stairway, 9. crowded and uncrowded areas, and 10. several types of intersections. It takes about 10 minutes to walk through and we have divided it into 5 segments.

5.3. Problem Identification

Each participant is given directions before each segment. They proceed through the route and are timed and observed using a standardized checklist to note difficulties. Afterwards, a debriefing interview ascertains their cognition of the route and identifies problems as well as methods used to negotiate it. Each person, during the debriefing, constructs a tactile map of the route.

Background interviews are also conducted to ascertain attitudes of risk taking and self-esteem and to identify their actual disability.

Analysis of data will identify the major difficulties with the route and those features that aid mobility. Also, we will have a record of individual performance in a standardized environment and task.

5.4. Route Modification

From the initial testing results, two groups of about 5 users each will be matched for performance, attitudes and disability. Both groups will negotiate the route a second time to verify our matching procedure. One group will go through the route a third time and then help us to determine the non-structural changes that could be made in the building. The other group will negotiate the route a third time with modifications in place. This experimental design will allow us to measure the effect of modifications while controlling for experience with the route.

6. CONCLUSION

In the past, design guides and standards concerned with accessibility of buildings for people with disabilities have been based on research with many weaknesses in external and internal validity. Previous research has focused on the wheelchair user and has particularly neglected the needs of people with stamina and sensory disabilities. The research described above seeks to establish a more generalizeable data base than exists presently--one which will help to end confusion and ommission in contemporary design practice and environmental policy.

The weaknesses of past research are not difficult to understand. They may be traced to inadequate funding, researchers who are unfamiliar with the actual use of buildings, to lack of international communication and discussion regarding accessibility issues, to regionalization of research applications and to lack of standardization in methods and equipment. It is hoped that the present study will form a foundation for eliminating many of these problems. That is not to say that future research will be unnecessary. Due to the immediate need for concensus standards, the present work cannot study long-term adaptation issues, for example. Another area for future study is the influence on attitudes of individuals on performance. A third area is in methods of socio-physical intervention for improving independence of the individual and the responsiveness of society.

It is hoped that accessibility research will now begin to give attention to cognitive and social variables which may, in fact, provide even more useful data for implementing an environment that treats all people as normal.

FIGURE 1:   **THE ENABLER**

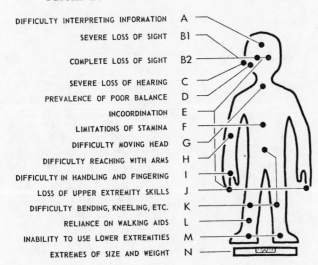

DIFFICULTY INTERPRETING INFORMATION — A
SEVERE LOSS OF SIGHT — B1
COMPLETE LOSS OF SIGHT — B2
SEVERE LOSS OF HEARING — C
PREVALENCE OF POOR BALANCE — D
INCOORDINATION — E
LIMITATIONS OF STAMINA — F
DIFFICULTY MOVING HEAD — G
DIFFICULTY REACHING WITH ARMS — H
DIFFICULTY IN HANDLING AND FINGERING — I
LOSS OF UPPER EXTREMITY SKILLS — J
DIFFICULTY BENDING, KNEELING, ETC. — K
RELIANCE ON WALKING AIDS — L
INABILITY TO USE LOWER EXTREMITIES — M
EXTREMES OF SIZE AND WEIGHT — N

THE ENABLER IS AN IDEOGRAM REPRESENTING A PERSON'S ABILITIES AS A BASIS FOR DESIGN. THE ENABLER ILLUSTRATES THE DIFFERENT AREAS OF DISABILITY CONCERN IN A LOGICAL ORDER FROM TOP TO BOTTOM: MENTAL FUNCTIONING, THE SENSES, AND MOTION IMPAIRMENT. THE ENABLER SHOULD HELP DESIGNERS VISUALIZE THE VARIOUS DISABILITY CONCERNS AND THEREBY ENABLE DISABLED PERSONS TO USE THEIR DESIGNS.

FIGURE 2:

TASK	INFORMATION NEEDS
1. passing through openings	a. height of openings b. width of openings c. shape of openings d. approach configuration e. number of openings needed
2. operating electronic and mechanical controls	a. configuration of control b. location vis-a-vis reach c. force activation d. type of activation motion e. speed of activation f. relationship to other controls g. number of controls h. type of feedback
3. movement along route of travel	a. characteristics of surface b. friction between user and surface c. length of routes d. configuration of route e. exposure along route (to climate) f. overall pattern of circulation
4. negotiating changes in level	a. degree of slope for ramp incline b. configuration of stair nosing c. height of stair raiser d. width of step e. length of run for incline of stairs f. location of movement assists g. configuration of movement assists h. configuration of stairways and ramps i. configuration and size of landings
5. transferring from one body posture to another	a. number and type of assists needed for transfer b. configuration of assists c. location of assists d. strength of assists e. size of zone f. configuration of transfer zone g. size and configuration of built-in elements that are transfer points (e.g. toilet) h. location of transfer points in relationship to each other & other building elements
6. searching for direction-finding information	a. type of coding method for awareness b. location of display c. exposure of display d. where information is needed e. content of information needed f. number of displays needed
7. interpreting information displays	a. type of coding method for interpretation b. complexity of information transmitted c. symbolic content of information d. where information is needed e. content of information f. exposure of display g. location of display h. number of displays needed
8. negotiating a series of movements in a confined space	a. size and configuration of dynamic space b. layout of elements in a space c. proximity of elements to each other d. number of space types needed
9. negotiating human and vehicular traffic	a. constraints on traffic flow b. controls on flow rate and direction c. separation of human and vehicular traffic
10. use of fixtures, storage and work surfaces	a. height of placement b. clearances to approach c. configuration of fixtures d. type of surfaces
11. avoiding hazards in the path of access	a. definition of hazards that should be avoided b. configuration of hazard-free zone c. size of hazard-free zone d. guards against exposure to hazards

FIGURE 3:

3A. Do you ever have difficulty OPENING A MILK CARTON, POURING MILK INTO A GLASS AND DRINKING WITHOUT SPILLING IT?

( ) yes ( ) sometimes ( ) no

                                    YES NO

B. Can you fasten your clothing within a reasonable time period?   B. ( ) ( )

C. Can you cut your meat with a knife and fork?   C. ( ) ( )

D. Can you handle a bar of soap yourself?   D. ( ) ( )

E. Can you fasten buttons?   E. ( ) ( )

F. What is the condition that causes any difficulties you may have?_____

G. Do you have a hook prothesis or hand splint?

( ) yes ( ) no

                                    YES NO

H. Are you able to bathe( ), dress( ),and feed( ) yourself?   H. ( ) ( )

I. Do you need to rely on another person to help you bathe( ), dress( ) and eat( )? I. ( ) ( )

COMMENTS:_____

4A. Do you ever have difficulty REACHING WITH EITHER ARM?

( ) yes ( ) sometimes ( ) no

B. Can you raise your arms in front of you   YES NO
and out to the side of your body?
    1. without holding anything   B1. ( ) ( )
    2. while holding a one pound can   B2. ( ) ( )

C. Can you raise your arms straight out
in front of you at shoulder level and
out to the side of your body?
    1. without holding anything   C1. ( ) ( )
    2. while holding a one pound can   C2. ( ) ( )

D. Can you raise your arms in front of
you up past shoulder level?
    1. without holding anything   D1. ( ) ( )
    2. while holding a one pound can   D2. ( ) ( )

E. What is the condition that causes these difficulties?_____.

COMMENTS:_____

5A. Do you ever have difficulty MOVING YOUR HEAD?

( ) yes ( ) sometimes ( ) no

B. Can you bend or turn your head part of   YES NO
the way without moving your body?   B. ( ) ( )

C. Can you look to the side, up to the
ceiling or down to your feet without
moving your body?   C. ( ) ( )

D. Can you bend your head to the ceiling
or turn it all the way to both sides
without moving your body?   D. ( ) ( )

E. Are these movements difficult for you?   E. ( ) ( )

F. What is the condition that causes these difficulties?_____

COMMENTS:_____

reference

AMERICAN TELEPHONE and TELEGRAPH COMPANY. Universal public telephone height for handicapped and able-bodied users. New York: Research Section/Marketing Department, American Telephone and Telegraph, 1975

ANSI A117.1 Making buildings accessible and useable by the physically handicapped. New York: American National Standards Institute 1971.

BIRREN, JAMES E. Psychology of aging. Englewood Cliffs, New Jersey; Prentice Hall, 1964.

BRATTGARD, SVEN OLAF. Unpublished research at the University of Goteborg, Sweden, 1967-1974.

DIFFRIENT, NIELS, TILLEY, ALVIN R. and BARDAGJY, JOAN C. Human-scale 1/2/3. Cambridge, Maine: MIT Press, 1974.

DIXON, CHARLES E. A study to determine the specifications of wheelchair ramps. PhD dissertation. University of Illinois, 1957.

FLOYD, W.F., GUTTMEN, L., NOBLE, W., PARKES, K.R. and WARD, J. A study of the space requirements of wheelchair users. Paraplegia, 4, pp 24-37, May, 1966.

GOLDSMITH, SELWYN Designing for the disabled. New York: McGraw-Hill, 1967.

GRANDJEAN, ETIENE. Ergonomics of the home. London: Taylor and Francis, and New York: Halstead Press (a division of John Wiley and Sons), 1973.

HARRIGAN, JOHN E. Human factors information taxonomy: Fundamental human factors applications for architectural programs, Human factors, 16:4, pp 432-440, 1974.

HOWIE, P.M. A pilot study of disabled housewives in their kitchens. London: Disabled Living Foundation, 1972.

JONES, J. CHRISTOPHER. Methods and results of seating research, Sitting Posture Grandjean, E. (ED.). London: Taylor and Francis, 1969.

KIDWELL, ANN MIDDLETON and GREER, PETER SWARTZ. Sites perception and the non-visual experience. New York: American Foundation for the Blind, 1973.

LEONARD, J.A. Studies in blind mobility, Applied Ergonomics. March, 1972, pp37-46.

McCORMICK, ERNEST J. Human factors engineering. New York: McGraw-Hill, 1970.

McCULLOUGH, HELEN E. and FARNHAM, MARY B. Kitchens for women in wheelchairs. Urbana, Illinois: College of Agriculture Extension Service, Circular 841, 1961

McCULLOUGH, HELEN E. and FARNHAM, MARY B. Space and design requirments for wheelchair kitchens. Urbana, Illinois: College of Agriculture Extension Service, Bulletin Number 661, 1960.

MURRELL, K.F.H. Ergonomics. London: Chapman and Hall, 1965.

NICHOLS, P.J.R. Door handles for the disabled. Oxford, United Kingdom: Nuffield Orthopedic Centre

OWNSWORTH, A. An ergonomic study of the space requirements of wheelchair users for doorways and corridors. Leicestershire, United Kingdom; Institute for Consumer Ergonomics, 1973.

PARSONS, HENRY M. Why human factors research in environmental design? Man environment transactions (EDRA 5), Carson, D.H. (ed). Milwaukee: Environmental Design Research Association, 1974.

POULTON, E.C. Bias in ergonomic experiments, Applied ergonomics, 4:1, pp 17-18, 1973

STEIDL, ROSE E. and BRATTON, ESTHER C. Work in the home. New York; Wiley, 1968.

STEIDL, ROSE E. Difficulty factors in homemaking tasks: Implications for environmental design Human factors, 1972, 14(5), pp 471-482, 1972.

TEMPLER, JOHN A. Stair Shape and human movement. Unpublished doctoral dissertation. New York: Columbia University, 1974.

THIBERG, SVEN and WESTER, PER-OLOF. Anatomy for planners. Stockholm: National Institute for Building Research, Reports 20: 1965 and R12: 1970.

WALTER, FELIX. Four architectural movement studies for the wheelchair and ambulant disabled. London: Disabled Living Foundation, 1971.

WEBB, EUGENE J., CAMPBELL, DONALD T., SCHWARTZ, RICHARD D. and SECHREST, LEE. Unobtrusive measures. Chicago: Rand McNally, 1966.

DESIGN FOR NORMALIZATION IN AN INSTITUTION FOR THE MENTALLY RETARDED

Peter Orleans

228 Dexter Street
Denver, Colorado 80220

ABSTRACT

This paper presents the rationale for the architectural modification of a State facility housing severely and profoundly retarded people.

Architectural patterns, based on the concept of normalization, are developed to guide and evaluate design decisions, examples of some of these patterns, adopted as part of the architectual program are offered.

Much of the current concern about the institutionalized retarded in America centers upon the recently acknowledged importance of changing patterns in residential services for these people. (Helsel: 1971) Professionals in the field seem increasingly to agree that the de-institutionalization of as many of the retarded as possible should be accomplished as soon as possible. This view appears to be bolstered by an abhorance of the inhumane conditions that seem inevitably to characterize institutional custodial care for the retardate (Blatt: 1969) and by the conviction that habilitation of the retardate can best be accomplished through a process of normalization. (Nirje: 1969; Kushlick: 1975)

In its essentials this process of normalization, patterned on the Scandinavian model, entails the de-institutionalization of the mentally retarded. I say this because normalization seems to require changes in the daily lives of the retarded that are so drastic and so comprehensive as to be possible only in non-institutional settings.

However, the reality of the situation is that in all probability the only candidates for normalization, insofar as it involves de-institutionalization, are persons capable of functioning in and being accepted by the larger community, persons now classified as borderline or mildly retarded, some twenty-eight percent of an institutionalized population of 200,000 people. (Butterfield: 1969) Even if moderately retarded individuals, comprising an additional twenty-two percent, were to be included, this would still leave half of the institutionalized population behind, namely those who are either severly or profoundly retarded.

If normalization for these 100,000 individuals is not to be accomplished through de-institutionalization, what is to become of them?

The scope of the problem is almost beyond comprehension, for what we are considering is that segment of the mentally retarded population that is seen to be most in need of intensive attention and which at the same time is thought to be least likely to be responsive to such attention. It is composed of those individuals who most closely approximate the classic stereotype of the retardate as a subhuman organism. (Wolfensberger: 1969)

It is this population that is the focus of attention in the design project described in the following pages. They are the client, or at least the 214 residents of six units, the upper rounds, of the State Home and Training School in Wheatridge, Colorado, are the clients. All of them are classified as either severely or profoundly retarded. And, all of them will probably live their entire lives within the confines of that institution.

The design problem is simply stated: Suggest architectural modifications that can be made to the physical facilities in the upper rounds at the State Home and Training School that will personalize this institutional environment. But, that simple statement belies a complex set of interrelated questions: a) What is the intended effect?--Is it normalization? b) Can the intended effect be achieved through architectural means alone? c) How does the facility design relate to (support) existing and projected institutional programs and functions?

A review of the relevant literature, observation in the setting itself, and interviews with the unit supervisor, all suggest that the more down-to-earth, nitty-gritty, questions have to do with money, staff, and institutional program considerations, and just how they relate to the design of the facility and the lives of its inmates.

Superficially, the State Home and Training School appears to stand in sharp contrast to its counterpart institutions elsewhere--it is not a snake pit. Actually, against considerable odds, including the oppressive architecture of the upper rounds, it has managed to provide more than adequate care for the resident retardates. But, if the institution is now to shift its emphasis from an essentially custodial mode to a developmental program, which is what is implied by the idea of normalization, more than architectural modification is required.

This point is an important one. There is ample evidence that the original design of the upper rounds, intentionally or not, was based on a custodial model. What is so dehumanizing about the upper rounds at Ridge is precisely what has been designed into it to facilitate the ease of custodial care---that it is abuse-resistant, that inmate activity is under complete and constant surveillance, that inmate access to control of the environment has been minimized, that "keepers" are physically separated from the "kept," that environmental stimuli and ammenities are kept to a minimum, and the like (Wolfensberger: 1969).

Each unit is circular in physical form, with a glass enclosed nurse's station at the center. As indicated in the schematic diagram (Figure 1) the unit is partitioned into day room, ward room, service and toileting areas. All exposed surfaces are made of structural ceramic tile, light switches are keyed, and the floor is radiant heated with a supplemental perimeter heating system.

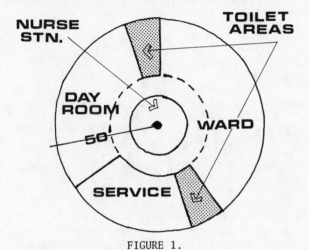

FIGURE 1.

Alter <u>any</u> of these conditions and the problem of custodial care is immediately and significantly complicated. So, appropriate institutional programmatic change must accompany architectural modification. Better yet, institutional programmatic changes should, ideally, precede, anticipate, and subsequently require supportive architectural alteration. If this is not the case, then it must inevitably follow that the condition under which custodial care occurs will become more difficult, the level of care itself will decline, and the retardate-- that is to say, the client--will suffer.

DESIGN STRATEGY

There are two aspects to the strategy employed in this design project. Initially our concern is with the sheer comfort of the client. Once that comfort is insured our concern is with the client as a developing person. In typical architectural terms, then, the first aspect is concerned with architectural barriers. The second aspect simply related to programmed design where the architectural program is fashioned around the principal of normalization.

It is difficult, if not impossible, to separate out these two aspects from each other, even for

analytical purposes. I say this because, if stereotypic behavior (discussed in a subsequent section) so characteristic of institutionalized retardates, is in fact an outcome of their lack of control of their environment, then normalization of the environment (including institutional programmatic modifications regarding daily living patterns) should have the consequence, as a side effect, of reducing such stereotypic behavior.

Because what is at issue here is the ticklish matter of environmental determinism, some clarifying remarks are in order. Although the recent architectural literature is rife with suggestions that environments can have a significant impact on behavior---for example, the discussions of "hard architecture" (Sommer: 1974), of the "soft cop" aspects of architecture (Goodman: 1971), and of the possibilities of "indeterminate architecture" as a means of accomodating to institutional change (Weeks: ND)---sophisticated writers typically have stopped short of concluding that environments can <u>control</u> behavior (Gans: 1962; Newman: 1972). Most observers are content to suggest that environments can play a significant role in expanding or limiting the repertoire of behavioral options.

It is, however, my contention here that the matter of the incarceration of the mentally retarded represents an extreme situation, though perhaps it is illustrative of a generic type applicable to any population involved in a total institution (Goffman: 1961). In any case, because institutional architecture for the retarded in the past has been based upon the perception of the retardate as non-human (Wolfensberger: 1969), it intentionally sets out to control inmate behavior by denying behavioral options. Some of the design features typically involved include:

(a) Switches controlling the lights in resident areas such as dayrooms, sleeping quarters, toilets, etc., are made inaccessible to residents by placement in staff control areas such as nursing stations, placement in locked cabinets, or keying (i.e., a key is required to turn a light on or off).

(b) Water temperature in lavatories, showers, etc., is controlled by thermostats. The water flow itself may be controlled by caretakers by means of removable portable handles.

(c) Temperature, humidity, and air movement controls are locked or keyed.

(Wolfensberger: 1969)

The inclusion of such design features denies to the inmate the possibility (legitimacy) of choice---that is it denies the essence of <u>normal</u> human behavior, behavior that is deemed socially appropriate.

Learning opportunities are provided by turning on individual light switches for different parts of the building, instead of having florescent lighting switched on by a master switch; by choosing the component parts of a meal instead of having to accept plated meal service centrally cooked; by selecting among a small choice of clothes the correct style according to weather and occasion; by deciding where one likes to sit rather than having to limit oneself to the day-room area; by going to the kitchenette to cook a snack; by managing a small personal cash allowance and being able to choose things other than sweets and cigarettes--such opportunities are countless in normal life, but the sub-normal is starved of them in his protected life.

The story of Rosie, a middle-aged, severely subnormal woman, illustrates well the pernicious effect of institutional dormitory life and habitual disregard of the person's social competence. In the course of a social education programme Rosie was taken by staff to a department store to buy her foundation garments; a satisfactory choice was made and paid for. Having successfully supervised this novel transaction, the accompanying member of staff became interested in some clothing, and left Rosie for a short while to her own devices. Her attention was sharply recalled to her charge when she sensed public commotion. To her consternation she discovered Rosie in the act of embarking on a striptease in her desire to try on her newly bought garments. Quite oblivious of the need for privacy, to which she had never been accustomed in ward life, Rosie had simply transferred her abnormal way of living, imposed by institutional disregard for some degree of personal dignity, to the normal environment. She had practised what she had been taught, directly or indirectly, but was blamed for her abnormal behavior.

(Gunzburg and Gunzburg: 1973)

The denial of appropriate choice behavior in the institutional setting contributes to inappropriate behavior which, in turn, simply confirms, as a self-fulfilling prophesy, the retardates status as an abnormal being.

STEREOTYPIC BEHAVIOR & ARCHITECTURAL BARRIERS

The idea of architectural barriers is relatively recent and it has been applied almost exclusively to environmental restraints as these affect the physically handicapped. Typical of the concern with architectural barriers is the effort to make buildings accessible to the physically handicapped by providing ramps, handrails, elevators, and the like. ASLA and HUD: 1975) While it is the case that many retardates, and especially the most severely and profoundly retarded persons, also suffer from physical handicaps and would benefit from barrier-free architecture, our concern here is

somewhat different. Aside from their physical impairment, mentally retarded persons suffer from impairments which have to do with their ability to apprehend and respond to the environment. This particular disability is evidenced in stereotyped behavior.

The individual engages in various rhythmic and repetitive movements, examples of which are rocking, swaying, posturing, head-banging, body-banging, eye-poking, and peculiar hand-waving. Some of these involve striking the head or other parts of the body and have been variously referred to as self-mutilation, or self-injurious behavior. Stereotyped behavior of the noninjurious form is commonplace; it is seen in about two-thirds of institutionalized SMR (Severely Mentally Retarded) persons.

(Baroff: 1974)

The most common explanations of stereotyped behavior "relate it to elevated tension states and/or to self stimulation in the service of organismic 'activity' needs. Studies have shown that the frequency of stereotyped behavior tends to increase (worsen) under a variety of conditions most of which seem to reflect heightened stress or reduced stimulation. ...In general, a reciprocal relationship appears to exist between stereotyping and responsiveness to external stimuli. ...In order to maintain some level of sensory input, the person who is either cognitively and/or sensorily deprived will depend on those sense that do not require external stimulation but can be evoked through his own body. Thus, rocking can reflect self-kinesthetic stimulation while head- or body-banging can generate self-tactual as well as kinesthetic stimulation." (Baroff: 1974) In short, one can conceptualize the individual who engages in stereotyped behavior as being in a kind of state of "sensory deprivation."

Inasmuch as stereotyped behavior appears to be exaggerated in institutionalized persons, it would appear that institutional environments, typically devoid of stimulus-type ammenities, constitute a peculiar kind of architectural barrier for their inmates. Therefore, following the lead and recommendations of two architects who have reviewed environmental barriers to children with learning disabilities (Bednar and Haviland: 1969), a survey of architectural barriers will be undertaken. Barriers in the upper rounds at Ridge, thought to influence stereotyped behavior, will be assessed, and specific design (redesign) recommendations will be made based on the results of this survey.

NORMALIZATION AND PROGRAMMING

If the design strategy is to be one of normalizing the environment, that is to say, providing an environment within which normal behavior can occur and can therefore be learned through experience (through repetition and a little bit at a time under the aegis of a supportive institutional staff and program), one must consider: What is normal? What is the community standard that is to be approximated? What are the special environmental requirements of the retardate that must be satisfied if normalization is to be accomplished?

Gunzburg and Gunzburg (1973), in the only extensive and comprehensive discussion of retardation and the environment, go to great lengths to explore the nature of the special environmental requirements of the retardate. Where the retardate is concerned provision of a "normal" environment does not automatically result in "normal" behavior because the retardate is apparently constitutionally incapable of such behavior independently. It is not as though the abnormal behavior is itself a product of environmental deprivation (though such deprivation undoubtedly exaggerates the problem), and that therefore it can be modified simply through environmental enrichment.

A normal person lacking the opportunity to modify his environment---for example, an office worker who cannot control the lighting and ventilation in his office---if given the opportunity to do so will do so. Given a desk lamp, he can switch it on or off, or given an operable window he is capable of opening and closing it. The retardate, however, lacking the opportunity to alter his environment in an institutional setting, when given that opportunity must first learn the mechanics involved in such manipulation (how to switch a light, how to operate a window) as well as its consequences, its costs and benefits with respect to his comfort---which is to say he must also learn the motivation necessary to consider such manipulation worth the effort.

In other words, the retardate must be socialized to appropriate normal behavior and this socialization ought to occur within a supportive context---with sympathetic attendant assistance, and---within a physical environment so constructed as to maximize opportunities for learning, not only to manipulate the environment, but the mechanics that make it possible for him to do so.

This brings us back to the first question: In the principle of normalization what is to be the referent for "normal?"

When talking about normalizing an existing environment or planning a new normal one, people concerned usually interpret normalizing as that which they find agreeable and desirable for themselves. This seems justified to them because they maintain that "normal" relates to the mainstream of society. Although Nirje (1970) states quite clearly that "the normalization principle means making available to the mentally subnormal patterns and conditions of everyday life, which are as close as possible to the norms and patterns of the mainstream of society," the qualification of "as close as possible" is usually overlooked and is certainly not investigated. This qualification should be considered as a realistic appreciation of actual needs, because otherwise pursuance of the principle will lead to a thoughtless aping of "normal life" practices with little benefit to the mentally handicapped and often harmful and disturbing (consequences) for him.

(Gunzburg and Gunzburg: 1973)

What this suggests is that an architectural program based on replicating what we know to be normal, even if it were possible to write one, would neither be adequate nor appropriate for the mentally retarded client (or the institutional staff attendent either for that matter). What we call a "normal" environment, experienced daily by "normal" people varies a great deal. A place of eating for a normal person may be a dining room, a kitchen, a corner of a living room, or occasionally a bedroom from a portable tray. Bathrooms do and do not have showers and tubs, may include or exclude toilets. Living rooms may be fully used by all members of a family each day, or may be reserved as "parlors" for a few adults on Sundays and holidays. The social life of a family may occur in the kitchen. "Obviously discussion of what is normal would be never-ending if they were for the purpose of deciding on one type of environment which would represent the particular requirements of the 'main stream.'" (Gunzburg and Gunzburg: 1973)

If then there is a commitment to making life for the mentally retarded as normal as possible, the definition of a normal way of life must be relevant to and supportive of the client, with due consideration being given to his handicap. A normal way of life must be constructed with attention to the benefits, the positive effects it might have on the retardate. The architecture of most ordinary houses, with some exceptions, does not force a standard of living on their occupants. People introduce the standard with their choices and arrangements of furniture, their interests and their activity preferences. Although some adaptation inevitably occurs, by and large it is people who make the dwelling fit their needs, and not the other way around. Mentally retarded people are not often in a position to do this, and it is even more important therefore to create a residential environment for them which suggests, stimulates, and encourages a way of life which is of benefit to them. Ultimately such an environment will benefit the institutional staff attendent as well.

This leads to the conclusion that the environment for the subnormal must contain a wealth of elements to help to meet his emotional and physical needs and to support the aim of socialization. But in order to achieve this the environment must be on a plane which can be understood by him enough to encourage him to manipulate the environment.

There seem to be three demand areas for which the right elements, the right combination of elements, the right application and the right character of elements have to be found:

a. For supporting the creation of a feeling of physical comfort, a sense of security and personal relationship to the surroundings.

b. For inducing normal stimulation, awareness, normal action, simple normal reaction, normal choice and normal routine, thus making the person accessible to teaching and training.

c. For teaching and training relevant to eventually leading a satisfying and useful life.

(Gunzburg and Gunzburg: 1973)

It follows then that an architectural program, based on the principle of normalization, should derive its design directives from the requirements enummerated above.

PATTERNS FOR DESIGN

In recent years many architects, following the lead of Christopher Alexander (1968), have adopted the method of developing a pattern language in which information about a design problem is collated, evaluated, and arranged so that it is useful to the design process. The information, once organized, highlights specific design consequences to the solution of specific design problems. This is one method (among many) of architectural programming. The appeal of this method is that it facilitates open-ended programming, and that is why it is being employed here.

The open-ended programming involved in this design implies the following: First, facts are evaluated as they are gathered.

Values are placed on the data and precepts are formed based on the facts the programmer has at (a given) point in his gathering process. This approach assumes that in any design problem there are facts that are "prime organizers" for synthesis and that the sooner these are identified the sooner the synthesis process can begin. (White: 1972)

Second, fact gathering is integrated with design synthesis. The assumption here is that

conceptual design decisions require only "overview" data and that specific information need not be gathered until those decisions are being made. (White: 1972)

Third, an "atomistic" approach may be taken to design synthesis in which an attempt is made

to find optimal solutions to sub-problems (the elements or "atoms" of the larger problem) as these are uncovered in the fact gathering process. In other words the organization and evaluation of facts suggests designs. Designs then may suggest other facts, which are then expressed in new and other designs. There is an interplay between the problem "facts" and the developing design. Afterwards an attempt is made to combine these sub-solutions (interim and partial designs) into a coherent whole (the final design) without compromising them. Thus, it is assumed that

the whole is no more than the sum of the parts and that if all of the specific aspects of the building are successful, the "whole" by definition will be successful. (White: 1972)

The design synthesis is evident when the specific elements of the problem and the design are integrated and responsive to one another.

In Christopher Alexander's work patterns take the form of statements:

IF: X THEN: Z / GIVEN PROBLEM: Y

where X defines a set of conditions; Y defines a problem liable to occur under conditions X; and Z defines some architectural response under conditions X to resolve problem Y. In short, if conditions X occur, then we should do Z to resolve problem Y.

In the present instance a somewhat looser format has been adopted (although for the most part the statement IF: X THEN: Z / GIVEN PROBLEM: Y underlies each of the patterns). Additionally, the traditional formulation in which patterns include only design responses to stated problems has been expanded to include three distinct kinds of information. The first set of patterns concerned with BACKGROUND and FACTS includes:

Institutional Models (IM)
Design and Programming (DP)
Individual/Group Planning (IG)
Retardate Capabilities (RC)
Architectural Barriers (AB)
Resident Mix (RM)
Staffing Pattern (SP)
Existing Facility Constraints (EF)

The second set of patterns refering to NEEDS and REQUIREMENTS includes:

Surveillance Visibility (SV)
Service Access (SA)
Normal Routing (NR)
Appropriate Scale (AS)
Small Groupings (SG)
Knowable Environs (KE)
Inside/Outside (IO)
Places to Pause (PP)
Elements Supporting Training (EST)
Relevant/Diverse Stimuli (RDS)

And, the third set of patterns dealing with ELEMENTS and ACTIVITIES includes:

Personal Space & Possessions (PSP)
Individualized Lighting (IL)
Indoor Activity Areas (IAA)
Floor As Furniture (FF)
Outdoor Activity (OA)
Kitchen & Food Preparation (KFP)
Toilet Area (TA)
Staff & Parent Lounge (SPL)

Examples of three of the patterns follow.

PATTERN NR: NORMAL ROUTINE

A normal routine can hardly be created or insured by modification of the physical design of the upper rounds. Ultimately a normal routine is a matter of institutional policy and program (pattern DP). Edgerton's description of "The Everyday Life of Institutionalized 'Idiots'" hardly suggests a normal routine. This is because institutions designed for custodial care, based on models of the retardate as either sick or subhuman (pattern IM), are not conducive to such a routine. The spaces designed into them do not facilitate it because they have not been designed for individuals (pattern IG). Nevertheless, there is much to be said for establishing a daily routine in which the residents can participate in some of the activities involved in "running a household"--- the sorting of the linen delivered from the laundry, the possibility of going to the kitchen to get a snack (pattern KFP), and especially engaging in a series of daily routines, many of which already exist, but routines that involve movement through activity spaces (patterns IA and OA) in conjunction with the passage of time (pattern EST). The adjacencies of such spaces can be planned so that the architecture supports a normal routine, and the spaces themselves might be differentiated with respect to sensory elements (pattern RDS) such as lighting, color, texture, scale, and the like.

PATTERN AS: APPROPRIATE SCALE

Intensive care type institutional settings, which is to say environments for the profoundly retarded, such as those found in the upper rounds, lend themselves to a ward-like, rather than a home-like, atmosphere. To the extent that this is due to group-oriented planning (pattern IG), or to out-dated institutional models (pattern IM), it can be rectified to some extent through design modification. However, some institutional exigencies, such as staffing patterns (pattern SP), and some institutional requirements, such as continuous moniters of the residents by staff (pattern SV), impose real limits on design alternatives.

Some design "solutions" that will contribute to appropriate scale involve designing for the

individual (pattern IG), as well as designing for a normal routine (pattern NR). Especially important is the need to approximate a residential scale with respect to room dimensions and layout.

Additional considerations, taken up in the discussions of specific patterns, are providing for privatization in the toilet area (pattern TA), enabling a connection between inside and outside (pattern IO), and planning for the appropriate arrangement of activity spaces (pattern IA) to support a household, or normal, routine (pattern NR). Finally, it is thought that an approximation of a residential scale might also be achieved through the incorporation of individualized lighting (pattern IL).

PATTERN EST: ELEMENTS SUPPORTING TRAINING

Each mentally subnormal person, as indeed each normal person, is capable of manipulating (the environment) only up to a degree, depending on his individual handicaps. A certain number of people are not able to manipulate (the environment) at all without intensive training for it. Training may take different forms; there is direct training, for instance when a person is trained to manipulate stairs by actually using stairs, whereas with indirect training a person might be sent to the gymnasium to train by means of apparatus the movements necessary for manipulating steps.

When we look at the physical environment from the point of view of how many opportunities there are for manipulation, we have to bear in mind not only that it is a question of providing for those occasions which a person might utilize by himself if the opportunities are given, but also to speculate what further manipulation he could achieve with appropriate training.

(Gunzburg and Gunzburg: 1973)

Both the Gunzburgs, in the quote above, and Wolfensberger in his discussion of institutional models (pattern IM), stress the importance of the manipulability of institutional environments by the residents. And, both strongly suggest that the architecture---the physical design--- of the environment can play an important role in making this possible. Wolfensberger suggests that this might be accomplished simply through the process of "refitting" of fixtures, hardware, and switches, thereby giving the residents access to environmental controls. The Gunzburgs', while in apparent agreement on this point, further stress that the designer take cognizance of the residents' potential for further environmental manipulation---that he not be deceived by the residents' present state of incapacity. Bednar and Haviland, in considering the role of the physical environment in the education of children with learning disabilities, suggest yet another dimension of the concern that the environment consist of elements supporting training. (Bednar and Haviland: 1969) Their concern is much more akin to matters already discussed in the context of knowable environs (pattern KE). It is their contention that the environment is useable to the extent that it is understandable, and they comment on several aspects and therefore its useability. Particularly appropriate in this context are their comments regarding:

Space-Time Identity

To know where you are, where you have been, and where you are going is important in evolving one's activities in space. The poorly designed environment can do a great deal to reinforce an already distorted sense of space-time; e.g., moving through identical spaces or amongst identical buildings gives one the impression of standing still---the feet are moving but the scene isn't. It would seem that the environment could be used to help establish space-time identity.

The possibilities enumerated by Bednar and Haviland include:

--using calendars with seasonal pictures, clocks with colored discs, and growing plants to make time more real

--considering the sequence of physical environments the child passes through in his daily routine, providing not only variety but also definite "breaks" and "punctuations" to help indicate that he has passed through space over time. (This could also help combat perseveration).

--ordering architectural space on the basis of space-time interdependence rather than functional grouping, that is, making activities which are adjacent in time also adjacent in space.

Ambiguity

There is almost universal agreement on the necessity to avoid ambuguity in buildings for emotionally disturbed and mentally subnormal children. Sometimes architects create ambiguity consciously, and at other times they do it unconsciously. Ambiguity can be avoided by expressing environmental cues directly.

The possibilities enumerated by Bednar and Haviland include:

--disclosing all light sources, natural and artificial (thus avoiding the "where does it come from" problem of indirect lighting).

--using matte rather than polished surfaces; for instance, people seem to "float" when walking on highly polished floors.

--avoiding highly rhythmic patterns which may confuse the senses; a floor with alternating black and white tiles seems to "pulsate".

--showing a simple transfer of load in the building's structural system, avoiding supports, cantilevers, and overhangs which seem to defy the forces of gravity.

Decisions and Alternatives

This has to do with the decisions which the user of an environment must make simply to exist within it. There are two extremes which (according to Bednar and Haviland) must be avoided:

--no alternatives may result in frustration. For example, a person wants to leave the room and sees an exit which he cannot use (a large window, a firedoor, etc.) or cannot get to.

--too many alternatives (or undemarcated alternatives) may also result in frustration. For example, a person sees many identical rooms with identical doors and cannot figure out where he should be; or, he sees many activities proceeding simultaneously in a space and cannot decide which to join.

Consistency

While variety and punctuation are necessary and important aspects of the environment, particularly in dealing with perceptual disabilities, one cannot (according to Bednar and Haviland) overlook the fact that the built environment must also provide a degree of consistency. Among other things (the resident) is learning to manipulate his surround, and it should provide him with successful experiences in doing this. The lack of consistency in his behavior must be compensated by consistency in the environment.

Examples of how this might be accomplished include:

--doors which generally swing the same way.

--hardware on doors, windows, cabinets, and even toilet partitions which is not only simple to operate, but which is consistent throughout.

--avoiding seemingly meaningless differences in colors, textures, lighting patterns, and surfacing materials.

--careful consideration of changes in the environment such as furniture rearrangement, paint color changes, space use alteration, and shifts in lighting level and quality.

BIBLIOGRAPHY

ALEXANDER, CHRISTOPHER, et. al, A Pattern Language Which Generates Multi-Service Centers (Berkeley: Center for Environmental Structure, 1968)

AMERICAN SOCIETY OF LANDSCAPE ARCHITECTS AND
    U.S. DEPARTMENT OF HOUSING AND URBAN
    DEVELOPMENT OFFICE OF POLICY AND DEVELOPMENT
    AND RESEARCH, Barrier Free Site Design
    (Washington: U.S. Government Printing
    Office, 1975).

BAROFF, GEORGE, Mental Retardation: Nature,
    Cause and Management (Washington:
    Hemisphere Publishing Corporation, 1974)
    especially Chapter 9: "The Institution:
    With Special Reference to Services to
    Severely and Profoundly Retarded Persons".

BEDNAR, MICHAEL J., and DAVID S. HAVILAND, The
    Role of the Physical Environment in the
    Educating of Children with Learning
    Disabilities A position paper developed
    for Educational Facilities Laboratory by
    the Center for Architectural Research,
    Rensselaer Polytechnic Institute, Troy,
    New York. March, 1969.

BLATT, BURTON, "Purgatory" in Kugel, Robert B.,
    and Wolf Wolfensberger (Eds.) Changing
    Patterns in Residential Services for the
    Mentally Retarded (Washington: The
    President's Committee on Mental Retardation,
    1969.

BUTTERFIELD, EARL C., "Basic Facts About Public
    Residential Facilities for the Mentally
    Retarded" in Kugel, Robert B., and Wolf
    Wolfensberger (Eds.) Changing Patterns in
    Residential Services for the Mentally
    Retarded (Washington: The President's
    Committee on Mental Retardation, 1969.

GANS, HERBERT, "City Planning and Urban
    Realities," Commentary XXXIII (1962).

GOFFMAN, ERVING, Asylums: Essays on the Social
    Situation of Mental Patients and Other
    Inmates (New York: Doubleday and Company,
    Inc., 1961) especially Chapter 1: "On the
    Characteristics of Total Institutions".

GOODMAN, ROBERT, After the Planners (New York:
    Simon and Schuster, 1971) especially
    Chapter 4: "The Architecture of Repression".

GUNZBURG, H.C., and ANNA L. GUNZBURG, Mental
    Handicap and Physical Environment: The
    Application of an Operational Philosophy
    to Planning (London: Bailliere Tindall,
    1973).

HELSEL, ELSIE D., "Residential Services," in
    Mental Retardation: An Annual Review,
    Joseph Wortis (Ed.) III (1971).

KUGEL, ROBERT B., and WOLF WOLFENSBERGER (Eds.)
    Changing Patterns in Residential Services
    for the Mentally Retarded (Washington: The
    President's Committee on Mental Retardation,
    1969).

KUSHLICK, ALBERT, "The Rehabilitation of
    Habilitation of Severely or Profoundly
    Retarded People," Bulletin of the New York
    Academy of Medicine, 51 (1975).

LINDHEIM, ROSLYN, GLASER, HELEN, AND CHRISTIE
    COFFIN, Changing Hospital Environments for
    Children (Cambridge: Harvard University
    Press, 1972).

MACANDREW, CRAIG, and ROBERT B. EDGERTON, "The
    Everyday Life of Institutionalized 'Idiots,'"
    Human Organiztion, 23 (1964).

NEWMAN, OSCAR, Defensible Space: Crime Prevention
    Through Urban Design (New York: The
    Macmillan Company, 1972).

NIRJE, BENGT, "The Normalization Principle and
    Its Human Management Implications" in
    KUGEL, ROBERT B., and WOLF WOLFENSBERGER
    (Eds.) Changing Patterns in Residential
    Services for the Mentally Retarded
    (Washington: The President's Committee on
    Mental Regardation, 1969).

OSMON, FRED LINN, Patterns for Designing
    Childrens Centers (New York: Educational
    Facilities Laboratories, Inc., 1971).

SOMMER, ROBERT, Tight Spaces: Hard Architecture
    and How to Humanize It (Englewood Cliffs:
    Prentice-Hall, 1974).

STATE OF COLORADO, These Truths Are Evident:
    A Plan for the Mentally Retarded of
    Colorado (Denver: Department of
    Institutions, Division of Mental Retardation,
    1965).

WEEKS, JOHN, "Indeterminate Architecture,"
    London: Llewelyn-Davies, Weeks, Forestier-
    Walker, and Born, n.d..

WHITE, EDWARD T., Introduction to Architectural
    Programming (Tucson: Architectural Media,
    1972).

WOLFENSBERGER, WOLF, "The Origin and Nature of
    Our Institutional Models," in KUGEL, ROBERT
    B., and WOLF WOLFENSBERGER (Eds.) Changing
    Patterns in Residential Services for the
    Mentally Retarded (Washington: The
    President's Committee on Mental Retardation,
    1969).

CLIMATE AS THE MODIFIER OF MAN-ENVIRONMENT INTERACTION

Boris Culjat (B. Arch., Tekn. Dr.)

This paper is a short description of one part
of a study done at the Royal Institute of Technology, School of Architecture, in Stockholm,
under the title "Climate and the Built Environment in the North". The case study, a project
in progress at the office of architect/planner
Ralph Erskine, and now under construction, is
a new community at Resolute Bay, Cornwallis Is.
in the canadian arctic.

The case study is characterized by an extremely high degree of climatic pressure, and
is in that respect not typical of the "normal"
northern situation. It is a test-tube condition where all the aspects of climatic influence
are intensified.

The problem

The most obvious pressures, those that are readily quantifiable and can be related to some
known limits of the human organism (e.g. the
physiological limits) are usually responded to
first. The stronger the pressure, the higher
the cost of maintaining the safety and comfort
levels, and consequently this aspect of the
parameter receives a higher priority. A conflict can thus occur between the most tangible
aspects of climatic influence (e.g. satisfaction
of physiological requirements) and the less
tangible ones (e.g. phychological well-being,
information input, execution and form of different activities, etc.). This is precisely the
danger of the "energy panic" we are about to
experience. Having realized that the conventional energy sources are in fact finite, we are
going to give energy saving the absolute priority.

It becomes, therefore, vital to look at
things in a more comprehensive way, and try to
predict some of the possible consequences.

I propose to do this by looking at how
climate influences what could be called the
"perceivable existence", i.e. the aspect of
human existence that is manifested through
Man's interaction with his environment - a
kind of an ecological model, or rather a modest
beginning of one.

The model for parameter analysis

In the proposed model, the human environment consists of three sub-environments: the
natural, the artificial, and the social.

The eco-system according to the above definition looks then as shown in Fig 1., where
the interactional process between Man and the
three elements of his environment is completed
with interactional processes between the environmental elements themselves.

In terms of this model, the built environment, being the spatial/material manifestation
of Man's existence, has the ultimate existential goal of facilitating the interactional

process between Man and his environment.

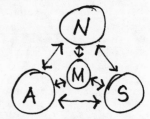

M = Man
N = Natural
    environment
A = Artificial
    environment
S = Social
    environment

Fig 1.

Climate can influence the satisfaction of these
"existential requirements" in two principle
ways: directly and indirectly. The influence
is termed direct when an aspect of the Man-environment interaction is changed or eliminated
by the direct action of the meteorological elements; it is termed indirect when characteristics of the built environment are changed by
the climate, which in turn causes an altered
behavioral pattern. An alternative to the latter case is when the climatic pressure generates an architecural solution that by the virtue
of its specific physical and symbolic characteristics changes the premises for the Man-environment interaction process.

The evidence material presented here, derived from literature, from own field observations and from the case study, is for the most
part qualitative, the aim at this stage, being
to illustrate the tendencies.

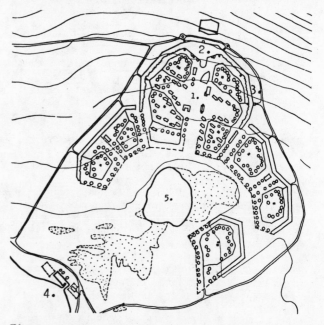

Fig 2. Site plan

1. Single-fam. housing 2. Town centre
3. Continuous 2,3 storey bldg.: apts., hotel,
town housing 4. Town harbour 5. Town lake.

Climate's influence on Man's interaction with the natural environment

In terms of need satisfaction, Man's relationship with the natural environment means: firstly, satisfaction of physiological needs of breething, eating, etc, secondly, satisfaction of psychological needs of experiencing nature in its different elements, and thirdly, individual's consciousness of "relatedness" of man to nature.(1)

If the harmonious relationship to the natural environment is important for Man's wellbeing, even his existance, it becomes even more critical in a situation where a high degree of segregation between Man and nature is a necessary response to ensure survival.

A somewhat paradoxical situation occurs, where the interactional possibilities have to be created, at the same time as a separation from the natural environment is necessary for survival.

Being outdoors

Individual's involvement with the natural environment can be manifested as experience (e.g. visual), as well as in terms of direct interaction. Being outdoors is a major prerequisite for both the interactional and experiential levels, and it is here that the cold climate exerts one of its major restrictions.

A Norwegian study defines the concept of the "outdoor season" as that period of the year when it is comfortable to be outdoors without heavy clothing. The study establishes that the acceptable comfort level minimum in the Oslo area is about +11°C in the fall and +9°C in the spring (with avr. humidity and rate of air movement). Lower temperatures are normally accepted after a long winter than at the end of the summer, depending partly on body's adaptability and partly on attitude.(2)

A Swedish study (3) and a Danish one (5) register 2-3 times as many people outdoors during a test period April—June, as during a Jan—Feb period.

However, a study done in Stockholm of children's winter-time outdoor activities shows that the amount of time spent oudoors by children decreases somwhat during the winter, but not nearly as much as that of adults. The amount of outdoor play was affected differently for different age groups. The smaller children were affected most by the change. Parents, who usually accompany them were very seldom seen outside, and this meant that the children either stayed indoors as well, or if they were allowed out, they were forced to stay in sight of the parents, who watched them from the windows. This limited moving radius meant that these children were often not able to take advantage of the new opportunities.(4)

Amount of outdoor activity is not determined by temperature alone. Fig 3. shows numbers of people outdoors at different times of the day during different weather conditions.

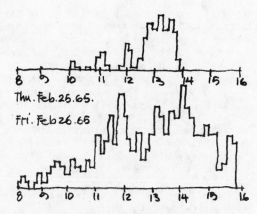

Thu. Feb.26.65.

Fri. Feb 26.65

Fig 3.

The Norwegian study shows that this desirable outdoor season can be extended up to six weeks during the marginal seasons with proper micro-climatic planning. In the Oslo area this meant an extension of 30%, mostly during spring when lower temperatures are accepted, and when being outdoors is most desirable.

Separation from the natural environment

Architectural solutions, when responding to climatic pressure, can increase the separation from the natural environment. Great building bulk with a minimum of openings is the most effective way to conserve energy, but small buildings, environmental control at a local level, exposure and easy access to the outdoors, provide better possibilities for a meaningful contact with nature. At the smaller scale, it also becomes possible to use natural elements directly in creating the micro-climate: tree belts and land formations for wind shelter, trees for shade, etc., thus extending the realm of the Man-Nature relationship. This relationship is reinforced if the environmental control systems (the buildings) are responsive to climatic variation, rather than if they only exclude the climate.

Size and location of openings can significantly influence the possibility for visual contact with the natural element. Small area of glass is essential if heat losses are to be minimized, and the feeling of protection and enclosure is often psychologically important in hostile environmental conditions. However, there are other considerations. Erskine talks of the miners in northern Sweden, who after working all day underground often want exposure, light, sun, and the view of the landscape — not enclosure and protection. But large glass areas are not necessarily a pre-requisite for a good visual relationship with the natural environment. Placement, orientation and form of windows related to different aspects of the surrounding topography and vegetation can be as effective, and may at the same time give the opportunity to create a feeling of protection and shelter if that is found desirable.

Reference to case study

The native population, the Eskimos, have a

tradition of intimate relationship with nature
Living outdoors in the almost impossible arctic
climate has always been part of everyday life.
In spite of the employment at the airbase, hunting and fishing are still important to many families as a secondary economy. Easy access to
the shore and to the surrounding landscape is
still a necessity. Most of the Eskimos live in
extended family groups and are presently housed
in detached dwellings. Some of the existing
dwellings are retained with extensions and improvements, others are replaced with new houses, but the pattern of detached dwellings is
kept.

Compared to the fishing and hunting Eskimos, being outdoors is not as much a functional
necessity for the southern colonizers as it is
a psychological and physiological one, created
by the fact that the greatest majority of their
time is spent indoors, in the artificial environment. Although some users stressed the convenience factor of the indoor environment, the
need to be outdoors, even in the extreme climate
of the polar night, was emphasized time and
time again in discussions with people that have
experience of living in the arctic, and proposals for indoor circulation and too many unnecessary indoor spaces were received with scept-
icism. The desire to come outdoors was expressed and it was   pointed out
that proper arctic clothing made the outdoor
activities possible at almost any part of the
year, and during almost any kind of weather.
The different attitude to the natural environment exhibited by the two ethnic groups is exemplified by the discussions about the planning
principles for the new community. The Eskimos
were unanimously more interested in reducing the
snow clearing problems (i.e. allowing the wind
to penetrate the development); "Wind is part of
arctic life". The southerners were, on the
other hand, very eager to get wind shelter, even
if it meant removing the snow with heavy machine equipment.

The physical design of the town tries to
foster and encourage the use of the outdoors.
The town is compact, i.e. the overall area is
kept as small as possible, one of the reasons
being to shorten the distances between the
dwellings and different service facilities and
thereby encourage outdoor pedestrian circulation. Apartment buildings have their entrances oriented toward the centre, and the main
pedestrian circulation path follows the inside
of the perimeter building. This path is partially sheltered from snow and wind, but is not
enclosed. An indoor link is provided on the
outside of the perimeter building, and consists
of a series of semi-private corridor spaces
around which groups of apartments are organized. This corridor system can be used during
poor weather, but is not as conveniently available and as public as the outdoor ones. Different possibilities are provided, but the degree of use of each alternative is finally left
to the choice of the users.

Outdoor play and recreational areas located in
the most advantageous position micro-climatica-
lly, are in direct contact with the public functions, such as the school and the town centre,
and are planned and equipped for winter use.
Concentration of direct and reflected solar radiation in this area, and protection from the
chilling wind, along with the enrichment of the
existing soil by the organic matter produced by
the town's sewage treatment plant, should improve conditions sufficiently to support the growth
of creepers, smaller bu hes and some vegetables,
i.e. a sub-arctic rather than arctic flora.

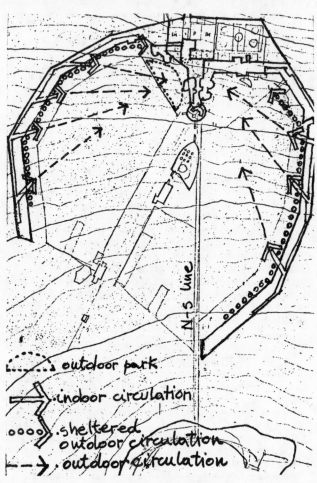

Fig 4.

Provision of visual contact with the surrounding natural environment is attempted at
several levels. The view of the few available
landscape features, such as the bay and the
shoreline, the river delta, and the surrounding
hills, is maximized by orientation of the dwelling units and the communal activity spaces.
Penetration of light and sunshine are maximized
with the help of reflectors, skylights, and
southern orientation of windows, and generally,
the positive aspects of the natural environment
are exposed whenever possible. Even though the
use of the outdoors and the direct interaction

with the natural environment are encouraged, the
possibilities are limited and the Man–nature
interaction should be supported at other more
indirect and symbolic levels. Experience of
the southern flora: trees, bushes, flowers and
vegetables, in a climatically controlled indoor environment can be beneficial to the southerners who are used to it, as well as to the
Eskimos for whom it can provide a new exotic
experience. The central part of the town centre complex, directly adjacent to the school,
consists of a green house – an indoor park –
which can be an important part of the school's
activity, as well as providing possibility for
individual families to grow own flowers and vegetables, either on a "rent-a-garden patch"
system or in "vegetable clubs".

Climate's influence on Man's interaction with the artificial environment

Man's interaction with the artificial environment isrealized in two principle ways:
a) actual physical change of the artificial environment
b) use of the arificial environment
     As it was illustrated in thesection on
Man-nature interaction, theharsh, cold climate
has to be modified in order to make it congenial
to human life: a separation from the natural environment becomes necessary. In other words,
a high degree of environmental pressure requires a high degree of sheltering capacity by the
built environment, i.e. a high material and
equipment input.
     Most northern societies are also affluent
societies, highly developed economically and
technologically. The cost and the technical
nature of the environmental control systems,
the high quality expectations, the cost of labour, etc, have all contributed to the development of the factory-made shelter. As Feuerstein
says, thedwelling is completed to the last bolt
when it comes out of the factory. The high
equipment input and thegeneral sophisitication
and "completness" of the product make it impossible for the individual dweller to partake in
any meaningful way in the forming (or even understanding) of his own physical environment.
This fact gains in importance as the dependence
on the artificial increases with the increase
of climatic pressure.
     The dilemma: harsh climate makes a larger
artificial input necessary, which in turn increases the control that the environment exerts
on the individual. How to build "more", i.e.
satisfy the requirements for high degree of environmental control, and still produce a soft,
responsive artificial environment – one that
invites and supports individual's participation?
     An example of this would be the case where
a mechanical system (e.g. air conditioning),
which is installed as a direct response to the
prevailing climatic conditions, does not allow
even the slightest alterations of the artificial
environment by the user, such as opening a
window.

Usability of the artificial environment

Meteorological elements typical for the cold
climate, such as wind, low air temperatures,
snow, etc, can change the physical characteristics of different elements of the artificial environment and thereby change the way these artifacts are used. In the oudoor situation, climate
can influence these aspects of interaction both
positively and negatively, i.e. it can either
inhibit the possibilities to use the artifacts
(a wet bench, an icy stair, etc), or it can introduce new uses and new possibilities for personal interpretation (recreational activities).

Fig 5. Climate can inhibit or facilitate use
of the artificial environment

     The Stockholm study mentioned above (4)
shows that the major influence of climate on
children's winter activites was that they
used the area differently and that they sometimes used different areas then they didin the
summer. Their games changed according to different opportunities given by ice and snow, and
by the fact that most of summer-type play equipment had either been removed or had become
useless. The older children's outdoor activities seemed to be affected according to whether
or not there were any good facilities for winter sports like hockey or skiing. But the
marginal early spring season is a problem. Ti-
red of winter games they look for summer equipment, dry and sunny places to play with dolls
etc. Thisis often frustrated by poor micro-
climatic planning.
     Climatically controlled environment is not
influenced by precipitation, wind, etc, and has
therefore the capacity for supporting uses that
might otherwise be difficult or impossible.
But at the same time some of the positive

aspects of winter are excluded as well.

The most notable characteristic of the cold-climate areas is the great range of temperatures and weather conditionsover the span of the year. This means that the artificial environment has to respond to a variety of conditions: warm, green summers - cold, dark winters, etc. This can mean that the same spaces/objects have to be usable under different conditions, or that different spaces/objects are available for different conditions.

Reference to case study

Extreme arctic climatic conditions restrict in some ways the possibility of actual physical change that the users can effect on their dwellings. This is evident in the case of the detached houses where problems associated with wind and snow drifting determine the smooth, aerodynamic form of the building. Projections and irregularities are minimized, and any additions or alterationsto the building's form create the risk of unwanted snow drifts against the entrances and windows, the road, or other neighbouring structures. It is also these dwellings that, because of the varying makeup and size of families, may actually have the greatest need for additions or alterations.

The communal town centre, provides features that invite the involvemnt of the users: walls for painting, changeable "furniture" that can respond to different activities, etc. The present inhabitants are also going to be involved in the building of the town.

The outdoor space south of the centre can be used both summer and winter. The southern slope and the terraces that are during the summer used for summer-type play and gardening, are used for tobogganing and snow play during the winter. The space is sheltered from wind and oriented toward south and south-west, providing inproved micro-climatic conditions all year round. This means that the summer equipment is usable longer, and the winter facilities are more usable because of the more comfortable conditions.

However, flexibility of spaces/objects, i.e. their usability under different climatic conditionsis more difficult in such an extreme situation, since flexible solutions can seldom be optimal for all conditions, in the way that specialized solutions can. Great seasonal variation of climatic conditions as well as the daily variations during the critical marginal seasons, require absolute maximization of the limited environmental resources. The environment has to be tailored perfectly to the characteristics of each particular condition, i.e. different plades/objects for different conditions.

This principle is applied, for example, on the circulation system where different circulation paths are available for different conditions, from completely exposed to completely controlled. The same is true of the communal play and recreational areas, where both outdoor

and indoor spaces are provided for different seasons: an outdoor park and playground south of the centre, and the climatically controlled alternative inside the centre complex.

Certain aspects of the arctic climate can create environmental conditions of extreme stimulus poverty even in the natural environment. Continuous darkness and low solar altitude make the visual field ore homogeneous and there is a lack of scale and colour variation in the summer as well as in the winter landscape. A specific aspect of thisis the "white out" (combination of snow and wind) which creates a completely even and homogeneous visual field removing all detail and irregularity in the surrounding landscape. The relative stimulus poverty of the nautural environment and the fact that most of the time is spent indoors, increase the requirement for rich and varied stimulus input by the artificial environment.

Climate's influence on Man's interaction with the social environment

As shown in the part on Man-Nature interaction, the cold climate can drastically reduce the outdoor season - uncomfortable conditions limit outdoor activities and thereby the social interaction related to these activities. Another aspect of climate's direct influence is the effect it has on the physical characteristics of the built environment, as when snow or ice become actual elements in the physical setting, and consequently influence the social activities related to this physical setting.

Indirect influence of climate is the influence that architectural solutions, created in response to some climatic pressure, exert on Man's social interaction by virtue of their specific physical and symbolic characteristics.

Influence of climate on "necessary" and "optional" activities

Gehl defines two distinct groups or types of activities: necessary activities which take place in any case (work, goal-oriented movement) and optional activities which only take place if the external conditions are favourable.(6) Gehl mentiones observations done at the pedestrian Strøget in Copenhagen - a place with a very high activity level in the summer. Not only is the number of people lower in the winter, the nature of their activity completely changes. Activities like standing and looking, talking, or sitting and eating and drinking, exhibitions, demonstrations, music, etc, all disappear, as shown in Fig 6.

Fig 6.

"Necessary" activities, those activities that have to be carried out regardless of environmental conditions are not eliminated by the negative aspects of the cold climate in the same way as the "optional" ones, but their pattern may be changed. Fig7.

Fig 7. Same bus stop summer and winter

Influence of climate on the nature of "physical settings"

Appart from the specific characteristics that the physical settings have by the virtue of their form and content, their effect on the social interaction also depends on the external influences like climate. By changing the physical characteristics of the physical setting, climate can influence the social occassions anchored to these settings.

As already illustrated above, the number of activities isreduced during the cold season, spontaneous activities being the first to go. However, even organized forms of recreation, entertainment, and commerce, such as the outdoor theatre, the market, or the park ice-cream stand, are shut down completely or reduced to minimum. Fig 8.

Climate's influence can very clearly be observed during the marginal season, i.e. spring and fall, when outdoor temperatures are such that good micro-climate can be achieved locally during dry conditions, with exposure to solar radiation, and protection from wind. During these marginal seasons, the optional activities that do exist are clearly concentrated to those parts of the physical environment that have better climatic conditions.

Fig 8.

Influence of climate on social interaction via architectural solutions

As shown above, the cold climate influences Man's interaction with his sodial environmant by limiting or eliminating activities, and by changing the characteristics of the physical environment (settings) to which different kinds of social activities are anchored.

Man's reaction to this influence can be manifested in different ways. Either the social patterns are altered or the activities given up in accordance with the nature of the climatic pressure, or the cause of the disturbance is removed, i.e, the climate is modified to suit the activities. The particular architectural means used to modify the climatic pressure, can by virtue of their own, specific physical characteristics and their congruence with activities in question, alter the form of the interactional process.

An example of thisgiven by Parr, is the influence that central heating had on the use of a family dwelling. Central heating eliminated the necessity of concentrating the activities in the dwelling around the source of heat, which was usually a stove or a furnace in the main space. In a centrally heated dwelling, the members of the household can, for better or for worse, dispearse throughout the dwelling according the the functional requirements of their activities.

In the public realm, climatic control of
a space implies often that other kinds of controls exist as well. The amount of resources
necessary for modification of the cold climate
means that emphasis is placed on accommodation
of some primary or necessary activity or function such as commerce or transportation. But
since these spaces are still considered as public places, there is always the possibility that
other activities may take place and cause a
conflict of interests between the necessary and
optional activities.

Erskines Luleå shopping centre in northern
Sweden is an example. An attempt was made here
to combine the primary commercial functions with
purely social optional activities. The centre
was open late at night and its varies physical
form and free areas facilitated a variety of
spontaneous activities that would be normal in
an outdoor public place: sitting about, talking,
meeting, etc. It was conceived as an indoor
extension of the street. However, it seems that
behavioural patterns that are acceptable outdoors are not acceptable inside a building.
This was also the only indoor public place of
this kind in the community, and certain groups
got to dominate it, i.e. teenagers and "bums",
which created a conflict with the store owners
who depended on the economically stronger groups.
The building is now, after 20 years, rebuilt.
All the open, "unused" space has been turned
into store floor area, and there is no allowance left for any kind of optional social
activity. The place closes at 7p.m..

Fig 9 shows two indoor public spces in
Stockholm with entirely different premises for
optional activites. The upper picture is an
entrance hall at a subway station where only
the primar y activity of transportation is
allowed. The lower picture is from the rail-
way station where a mix of functions and facilities create possibilities for all kinds of
optional activities.

Fig 9.

The consequence of this sort of situation is
that some activities and some forms of social
interaction disappear during the cold portion
of the year, and are sometimes replaced by
others. When the summer type of activities become impossible, people stay at home in their
private domains, or spend more time on organized
activities such as school, work, indoor sports,
theatre, etc. In other words, there is a functioning pattern in the urban life of cold climate
areas, with an emphasis on specific types of
activities during different periods of the year.
The northern people have developed this way of
life partly because of the climatic conditions,
and it cannot be wright to try to introduce the
"Italian" way of life.

But at the same time it does not follow
that the optional type of activity which is so
easy during the summer has to be abandoned during the winter. In some cases the cold season
is much too long for that. The need for this
kind of activity isdemonstrated by the fact that
people do use the climatically controlled environments where such are made available. And the
escape "down south" during the worst part of
the winter is not only a response to physiological needs.

The point must be that the outdoor spaces
have to be located, designed, andequipped to
facilitate all kinds of interaction during even
the cold parts of the year, even if not necessarily with the same intensity or in the same
way. These outdoor spaces that respond to
different climatic conditions can then be com-
lemented with indoor spaces, knowing that it
is impossible to duplicate the nature of the
outdoor environment and that it is impossible
to duplicate exactly the form of social interaction generated by the outdoor environment.

Reference to case study

Because of the small size of the community, most
of the common functions have been concentrated
in one location in order to maximize the social
interaction potential by both increasing the
number of activities in one location, and by
bringing together different categories of users
(children, adults, natives, colonizers, etc.).

The indoor town centre combines shopping
facilities, administration, health service, library, auditorium, school, recreational facilities, restaurants, service facilities of different kinds, and the indoor park with its green
houses. The hotel and apartment units are immediately adjacent to the centre. Note that
the school, shown adjacent to the centre in
Fig 10, has now been completely integrated, and
is located in the complex in place ot the pool.
Integration of the school into the centre, will
help to expose the activities of adults to the
children, as well as introducing the adults to
the often foreign educational environment.

It must be realized, at the same time, that
too great a concentration of people and activities can be experienced negatively. When such
effort is made to create possibilities for

contact and interaction, it is vital to provide the opposite condition, i.e. the possibility for withdrawal and privacy. Not only should private space be available for individuals and groups, but the public space should be such that direct contact and interaction are not forced upon the individual. It should be possible to step over to the other side of the "street" and avoid confrontation in much the same way that this is possible in the "normal" outdoor situation. Since some groups tend to congregate more easily, the activities should be geared to attract the groups that may otherwise opt out.

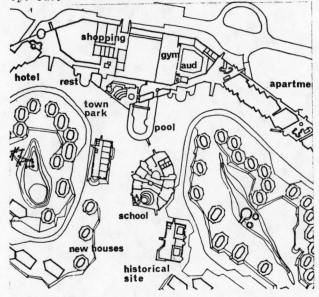

Fig 10. Typical town segment

Fig 11. North-South section through centre

Because of the extreme climatic conditions, the usability of the outdoor environment is extremely limited. This is especially true in the case of optional activities that require favourable external conditions in order to develop. For this reason the common functions have been organized around an interior, climatically controlled public space. The outdoor public places are used mostly for recreation and circulation during the cold season, but have direct contact with the indoor areas, so that most of the activities can move outside

as soon as the weather permits, in the usual arctic manner.

The feeling of togetherness and nearness to other people is important in the desert situation where the nonhuman environment is so overpowering. The built environment expresses human presence. The community is introverted and compact, the individual is visually aware of the other human beings around him — he does not have to be alone unless he makes that choice himself.

(1) Searls, H.F.:
The Nonhuman Environment,
International Universities Press, 1o60.

(2) Bjørkto, R.:
Atriumhus i Norsk Klima,
Norges Bygforskningsinstitut,
Oslo, 1965.

(3) Carlestam, G.:
Metod för studium av aktiviteter med mekanisk data insamling,
Grindtorp i Täby Köping,
KTH, Stockholm, 1966.

(4) Follin, V. & Larsson,K.:
Barn och lek vintertid i våra bostadsområden,
Att Bo, 1964.

(5) Gehl, J.:
Mennesker till fods,
Arkitektur (Danish) 1968, no.20.

(6) Gehl, J.:
Livet mellem husene,
Kunstakademiets Arkitktskole,
Copenhagen, 1971.

PART 2

Invited Events and Participation Sessions

EDRA-7 will include, in addition to discussion of the refereed papers, three other program elements. Three Distinguished Speakers will give presentations to plenary sessions of the conference. Four Invited Theme Symposia will discuss aspects of the conference theme, and a synthesis of issues raised at EDRA-7. More than thirty participation sessions will develop specific aspects of the conference theme, or continue discussion and work on other elements within EDRA's broad field of interest. Some of these participation sessions will be tightly planned, with formal papers assembled by the convening group, and presented or discussed within a formal schedule. Some are how-to sessions, in which persons interested in a particular activity will meet to exchange experiences, ideas, and techniques. Some, such as Childhood City, consist of a whole series of related sessions, occurring in sequence in a single meeting room that has been booked for every period of the entire conference. A few are scheduled for ten or more hours, in several sessions over two or three days. Most are planned to last only a few hours in a single session. And some spaces have been set aside for events not yet scheduled.

The co-chairmen of EDRA-7, and the EDRA-7 planning committee, reviewed the proposals for participation sessions, and the nominations for Distinguished Speakers and Invited Theme Symposia, selecting a broad spectrum for formal scheduling and inclusion in the conference publications. Summaries of talks by the Distinguished Speakers and of the Invited Theme Symposia are given on the following pages, together with summaries of all the accepted participation sessions for which suitable material had been received at date of publication, (mid-February.)

Book Two of the EDRA-7 publications is scheduled to contain the full text of the talks by the Distinguished Speakers; edited and summarized texts of the Invited Theme Symposia; and summaries or synthesis statements from all the participation sessions for which suitable material for publication is provided to EDRA-7. Full listings of participants, with addresses, are anticipated, again subject to the effectiveness of the session convenors in providing the information.

The following pages therefore contain only a partial preview of EDRA-7 conference activity.

Distinguished Speakers

DANIEL E. BERLYNE

Psychology Department
University of Toronto
Toronto, Ontario, Canada M5S 1A1

Former President of the Canadian Psychological
Association, President of the International
Association of Empirical Aesthetics, a Fellow
at the Center for Advanced Study in the Beha-
vioral Sciences, and at the Centre International
d'Epistémologie Génétique, he is author of
Conflict, Arousal and Curiosity, Aesthetics and
Psychobiology, and editor of Studies in the New
Experimental Aesthetics.

THE NEW EXPERIMENTAL AESTHETICS AND ENVIRONMENTAL
PSYCHOLOGY (Tuesday, May 25, 1976)

There is clearly an overlap between environmental
psychology and psychological aesthetics. In investigating reactions to aesthetic aspects of environments, environmental psychologists have
shown the influence of recent psychological aesthetics, taking over both research techniques
and theoretical ideas.

Nevertheless, there seems to be a tendency for
environmental psychologists to repeat some of the
errors that long held up progress in experimental
aesthetics.

First, there is the error of excessive reliance
on verbal judgments. Secondly there is the error of using arbitrarily selected verbal measures
without checking their importance. Various reasons for studying verbal expressions of aesthetic preference will be discussed and evaluated.
Consideration will also be given to problems
involved in choosing appropriate measures of
non-verbal reactions to aesthetic properties of
patterns and those involved in the choice of
scales and other devices for recording verbal
judgments.

Recently, new techniques have come into use that
offer prospects of overcoming these problems.
They will be illustrated with brief reviews of
research recently carried out at the University
of Toronto.

N. JOHN HABRAKEN

Department of Architecture
Massachusetts Institute of Technology
Cambridge, Massachusetts 02139

One of the most frequently referred to but least
understood figures in architecture today. He is
the author of Supports: An Alternative to Mass
Housing, which is the exemplary effort to combine
research and design. Presently Head of the
Department of Architecture at MIT, he was founder
and Research Director of the Netherland's S.A.R.
(Stichting Architekten Research), a housing research organization financed, interestingly, by
architects.

SOME BASIC CONCEPTS IN ARCHITECTURAL DESIGN AND
THEIR IMPLICATIONS ON DESIGN METHODS
(Thursday, May 27, 76)

Architecture - no matter how we may define it -
can only be properly understood if we first
understand the nature of the built environment
at large.

Architectural theories - and therefore their
offspring: design methods - must have their
roots in a more general theory that explains
the existence of the built environment.

Such a more comprehensive undertaking may serve
to evaluate the role of specific groups -
professional and otherwise - in the process of
cultivization of the built environment. It may
help such groups to develop adequate methods as
tools to effectively fulfill their role.

A number of concepts that are generally accepted
and understood in everyday communication are examined as "keys" to an understanding of the
built environment.

First of all there is the concept of "site".
There is always a larger physical context given:
human action changes the environment by adding
or subtracting or replacing within that context.
Therefore "change", representing the dimension
of time, is an inherent aspect of the built
environment. This change is the result of
"powers" that act upon the environment. At any
given time this environment can be seen as representing the balance - or lack of balance - of
such powers. Each power recognizes the environment as composed of "elements". The identification of elements and their coordination into a
system is essential for the effective manipulation of the environment. Through the identification of elements the environment can be understood as a complex of systems by those who act.

"Site" and "element" therefore represent the physical world - in fact the built environment as such. "Powers" and "change" represent the continuous interaction between the physical environment and human beings.

These four concepts could be formalized in a theoretical construct. Closer examination will reveal that certain hierarchies can be distinguished. Physical systems operate on different levels and there must be a symmetry with the powers that control them. If therefore we observe how: "the site is changed by the manipulation of elements by specific powers", the concept of "Level" can be introduced to formalize the hierarchical interaction of powers and physical systems. This fifth concept - as it encompasses the four previous ones - offers us a context in which methodical approaches to design problems can be developed successfully. Two such methods - operating on different levels - that have been effectively tested in practice in the Netherlands are offered as illustrations.

JOHN PLATT

Mental Health Research Institute
University of Michigan
Ann Arbor, Michigan

His power to synthesize, summarize and distill the essentials of the kinds of knotty problems that face EDRA are revealed in recent articles including, in Science, "What We Must Do" (1969) and "Conditions Favoring Major Advances in Social Science" (with Deutsch and Senghaas, 1971). His article, "Social Traps" (American Psychologist, 1973) formalizes the kinds of difficulties we face in delivering design solutions that benefit from the behavioral sciences.

John Platt will address the following topic:

TOWARDS A SUSTAINABLE SOCIETY IN A SUSTAINABLE ENVIRONMENT. (Friday, May 28, 76)

Invited Theme Symposia

THEORETICAL ISSUES IN RESEARCH ON ENVIRONMENT AND BEHAVIOR

Irwin Altman

Department of Psychology
University of Utah
Salt Lake City, Utah 84112

This session will involve a panel discussion of central theoretical issues in the environment and behavior field. The format of the session will not be of the paper-presentation type, but will involve a relatively spontaneous discussion among panelists.

Panelists will respond in a round robin fashion to a series of prearranged questions about theoretical issues in the field, making short comments on each question, followed by a discussion on each other's comments, as appropriate. Questions to be addressed will have been agreed upon prior to the session, and panelists will have individually prepared to deal with each question. In addition, the audience will be invited to submit questions to the panelists during the session proper, and these will be extemporaneously commented upon by one or more panelists. A summary of the final list of questions, replies and discussion will be prepared for later publication in the EDRA proceedings.

Questions will deal with a range of issues related to theoretical developments in the environment and behavior field including the current state of theory, needed directions of theoretical progress, levels of theory presently appropriate to the environment and behavior field, examples of promising and not-so-promising approaches, theory vs application, projections for the future, the responsibilities of the theorist to the practitioner and vice versa, and the like.

Panel Participants

Irwin Altman
University of Utah

Donald Appleyard
University of California - Berkeley

Harold Proshansky
City University of New York

Raymond Studer
Pennsylvania State University

BRIDGING

Gerald Davis, Symposium Chairman
c/o TEAG - The Environmental Analysis Group
2001 - 2075 Comox Street
Vancouver, B.C., Canada
V6G 1S2

The participants will discuss bridging between theory and research on the one hand, and designers, users, managers and builders on the other. They will suggest to the theoreticians and researchers the issues which they could most fruitfully address. They will suggest to designers, builders, users, managers and others how they might more effectively draw on the theoretical structures and research data that is becoming available. They will describe how the applicability gap between theory and research, and design and use, can and is being bridged, with examples of successes and failures.

Douglas Shadbolt, Director of the School of Architecture at Carleton University, Ottawa, will discuss the need for "briefing", to bridge between the needs of user and designer, for publicly developed buildings. He will review the client's responsibility in helping the consultant architect to learn and use those elements of theory and research directly applicable to the project at hand. Prof. Shadbolt taught the first course in Canada on building programming, at Halifax in 1961.

Jack Bibby, Director of construction for the British Columbia Medical Centre, is a professional project manager, and former head of a major building construction firm. He has also been active in labor relations in the construction field. He will discuss the problems for builder and client when "bridging" has been inadequate.

Norman Fletcher will deal with the interrelationship between the physical environment at work, and the organization that occupies it. There is almost no overlap between the literature and work of environmental psychologists, and those who practice organizational development. Fletcher is Director of Personnel for Bell-Northern Research, the research arm of the Bell system in Canada, at Ottawa.

Gerald Davis will summarize current work in bridging from theory and research into design, and will cite examples from the application of work by panelists in the previous session. He will describe problems in application, and will suggest areas where theory and research could make immediate contributions.

Depending on the conference scheduling, two additional panelists may join the symposium, broadening the discussion to include bridging problems and successes in industrialized and complex building projects.

Page 338

THE DESIGN PRACTITIONER AND HIS
RESEARCH NEEDS

John W. Wade, Session Chairman
Department of Architecture
University of Wisconsin - Milwaukee
Milwaukee, Wisconsin 53201
Phone: (414) 963-4014

SCENARIO

A group of practitioners who represent
various national practice organizations
from the U.S. and Canada, or who have an
active interest in design research, will
present short (three minute) position
papers in response to a theme paper
previously sent them by the session
chairman. They will then engage in a
discussion of the design practitioner
and his characteristics, the challenges
that he faces, and his research needs.

ABSTRACT OF THEME PAPER

The design practitioner is described in
a paradigmatic way (perhaps even in a
cartoon manner) in order to evoke
pertinent and elaborating comments from
session participants. The description is
based in comparisons between the design
practitioner and: (1) the design user,
(2) the design client, and (3) the design
researcher.

PERTINENCE OF THIS SESSION

Few researchers have a very strong
sense of what information the design
practitioner needs. Very few researchers
know what level of information is
required in design practice. If the
designer has been unable to tell the
researcher what his needs are, it is
because he has approached the acquisition
of information in a different manner from
the manner of the researcher. The
designer has been unable to communicate
his needs to the researcher because he
has not known what the researcher's
capabilities are, and he has not known
what the researcher didn't know about
design.

By describing the designer and his needs,
it may be possible to improve the level
of understanding between designer and
researcher. It may be possible to improve
the quality of design information; it may
be possible to increase the market demand
for design research.

SYNTHESIS

Colin Davidson, Chairman and Rapporteur

Editor, Industrialization Forum
and Professor,
Faculte d'Amenagement
Universite de Montreal
P.O. Box 6128
Montreal 101, Quebec
Canada

Professor Davidson will attend each of the Theme
Symposia as Rapporteur, and will chair the sessions at which the Distinguished Speakers will
make their presentations.

On the last morning of the Conference, Davidson
will present a brief synthesis of these talks
and symposia, pointing up those areas on which
agreement appears to exist, and crystallizing
the issues which appear significant.

He will then ask the Distinguished Speakers, and
some members of the panels from the Theme Symposia,
to join him in a focussed discussion of these
issues.

Where do we go from here, what should we do?
In the context of the research papers and work-
shops, the panel will link towards the talk by
John Platt.

Davidson will also pose to the panelists questions raised by conference registrants. These
questions should be passed to Davidson in writing
before or during the session. He will draw
related questions together, so as to cover a
wide range of issues during the discussion
period.

THE DESIGN PRACTITIONER AND HIS

RESEARCH NEEDS

John W. Wade, Session Chairman
Department of Architecture
University of Wisconsin - Milwaukee
Milwaukee, Wisconsin 53201
Phone: (414) 963-4014

ABSTRACT

This paper is intended to describe the design practitioner in a manner that will evoke pertinent and elaborating comment from the session participants. The description is based in comparisons between the design practitioner and: (1) the design user, (2) the design client, and (3) the design researcher.

1. INTRODUCTION

Very few researchers have any very strong sense of what information the design practitioner needs. Very few researchers know what level of information is required in design practice. If the designer has been unable to tell the researcher what his needs are, it has been because his approach to the acquisition of information has been from a very different basis from that of organized research. The designer has not been very able to communicate his needs to the researcher because he has not known what the researcher didn't know about design.

By describing the design practitioner and his information needs, it may be possible to improve the level of understanding between the researcher and the practitioner. It may be possible to increase the usefulness of information for design; it may be possible to increase the market demand for design research.

2. THE DESCRIPTION PROCESS

There is great difficulty in description when the group of persons being described has the degree of variety that design practitioners have. Rather than attempt an accurate description in this limited space, it will be better to develop a paradigm of what the designer is. It will be better to risk a cartoon (and the exaggerations that a cartoon implies) of the designer in order to make the description a vivid one.

I will attempt to make the description vivid by contrasting the designer with three other kinds of persons. The designer is very different from each of these persons, but he is different from each kind of person in a very specific way. I will compare the designer with the design user, i.e., the architectural designer with the building user; I will compare him with the design client; I will compare him with the design researcher.

The designer is different from the design user in his attitude toward the actualization of the designed environment. He is different from the design client in his perception and decision processes. He is different from the researcher in his attitude toward information and the factuality of information.

3. THE DESIGNER AND THE DESIGN USER

While the designer deals with a potential environment, the design user deals with an actualized environment. Things could not be otherwise.

The designer's work provides a framework and a background for the persons who will later use the environment that he designs. Since the designer typically does not know exactly who the occupants of the environment will be, he must design for the anonymous user.

One of the designer's difficulties is in identifying as closely as possible who the design users will be. Will they be identifiable by some geographic range, by some age range, by some family size, by an ethnic grouping, or by some other identifying characteristic. But even when the designer is able to identify his user population very closely, he knows that such a user population can change. The designer must deal with the problem that if he designs an environment to fit a specific user group very well (as some user-oriented designers have urged) then he might have designed to fit a successor user group very badly indeed.

By contrast with the designer, design users know completely what their needs are. While they might not always be able to describe those needs articulatly in words, they express those needs by the manner in which they interact with their environment. By occupying and using their environment, they "actualize" it. They furnish the designed environment with their possessions, they attach things to its walls, they place things on its floors, they modify it both purposefully and accidentally.

By contrast with the designer, design users experience the environment with all of their senses. They hear, smell, feel, taste, and see their environment. Ordinarily, the designer has only "seen" the environment in his imagination. The design user has so strongly experienced the environment, that it becomes part of his memory structure, and to some degree thereafter, modifies his behavior.

Because the designer has become accustomed to dealing with potential environments, he is more comfortable with an environment that is in process of be-coming. He might well be bored with an environment that has already become. By contrast, the typical design user is probably just the reverse. He ordinarily prefers an environment that has already become rather than an environment that is in process of becoming.

4. THE DESIGNER AND THE DESIGN CLIENT

The design fields are in sharp need of a sustaining theory and of carefully developed information. This is so because the design profession has been under increasing attack because of the "soft" nature of its decision process. The architecture profession has been challenged in its criteria for the accreditation of its schools, in the criteria that its schools set for graduation, and in the qualifications that it uses for licensing practitioners. In an earlier time when the architect held similar values with his client there

was seldom a need to justify a decision; today when he evidently does not share values with all of his clients, he must regularly face demands that he justify his decisions and that he make his decision process explicit.

The decision process that designers have used has been acquired through experience. Because design typically involves the integration of many different elements into a whole proposal, the designer has emphasized, the integrative, holistic nature of his process. He has understood his work as being strongly aesthetic in nature, and has therefore expected that it depended on a trained artistic sensibility; he has believed that much of his decision process was subjective in nature and not susceptible of clear explanation.

By contrast, the design client has come to expect, more and more, explanations for the proposals that the designer has made. In all other phases of the typical institutional client's experience he has learned to expect, analytic analyses in direct terms. He has learned to expect a display of the costs and benefits that will be associated with any particular course of action, as modified by the probability of occurrence of different related events.

By contrast with the designer whose trained sensibility is able to deal in the abstract with shapes and ordered relationships of form, the design client's untrained sensibilities read directly through forms to their meanings.

Although the design process uses a considerable amount of analysis, the designer has deemphasized this analysis in favor of an emphasis on synthesis; he has in this manner neglected to develop a ready means of articulating the processes by which design decisions are made.

5. THE DESIGNER AND THE DESIGN RESEARCHER

While the designer deals with action problems, the research scientist deals with non-action research problems. Although the applied research scientist (and presumeably, the design researcher) is somewhere between these extremes, he is often more research-concerned than he is action-concerned.

These different concerns have an immediate impact upon the form of information with which the designer and the design researcher are concerned. While the design researcher tends to seek _defensible truth_ (which tends toward complexity of statement), the designer tends to seek _actionable truth_ (which tends toward simplicity of statement).

The designer needs actionable truth. He works within a very complex environment. There are multiple influences on his decisions; he must deal with costs, his client's preferences, the requirements of enforcement agencies, the effect of taxes, and so on. However "exact" some piece of researched information might be, it might not be any more helpful than comparatively crude "inexact" information. Since not any design decision is based on a single fact, the most careful researched fact might be outweighed by some peripheral and casual rumor. A carefully researched fact might be placed out of possible considseration by the existence of some arbitrary and illogical building code requirement.

In addition to these influences on the use of information, the designer's process is time constrained. He cannot usually wait long for the information that he needs. Because this has been his circumstance for many years, the designer has learned to make decisions based not so much on exact _positive_ information, as on inexact _non-negative_ information. It is possible for the designer to make such decisions (based partly in typological information) because he knows that the persons who use his building are far more adaptable to his building, than his building could ever be to those persons.

By contrast, the researcher's attitude toward information is that it is valuable in itself. The research discipline has caused the researcher to value the explicit empirical development of information about an existing situation. His discipline has also caused him to be very careful in what he reports. He is careful not to believe what he sees unless other researchers have seen the same thing. If he is attempting to develop information from a sample, he is careful to state the mathematical probability that the information drawn from the sample can be applied to the entire population from which the sample was drawn.

The researcher is handicapped in assisting the designer, when he does not have available techniques for extrapolating from the information that he has obtained. If he cannot use his empirical infor-

mation as a base, in order to project the implications of that information onto some other situation that is to some degree different, then his information might not be helpful to the designer.

6. SUMMARY

It is clear that the designer needs great amounts of information that he does not presently have. It is possible that design research can supply that need. The designer needs more information about his clients, about the differences between his approach to the potential environment and the user's approach to the actualized environment. The designer also needs more information about the ways in which his values are different from the values of his different clients. He needs information about his own decision process and ways in which that process can be made more explicit. Finally, the designer needs "actionable" information that is useful within his decision context. "Crude" information is needed, but that information must be accompanied by some indication of the probable range over which that information is approximately accurate. Such an indication is undoubtedly more important than an indication of the probable accuracy of information collection process.

Participation Sessions

BEHAVIORAL SCIENCE INPUT TO ENVIRONMENTAL POLICY

Organizers:

John Archea, National Bureau of Standards
Thomas O. Byerts, Gerontological Society
Don Conway, American Institute of Architects
R. Stirling Ferguson, National Research Council
Charles Gordon, Carleton University
Don Henning, National Research Council
Stephen T. Margulis, National Bureau of Standards
Tad Ogrodnik, Department of National Health & Welfare
Jake Pauls, National Research Council
Willo P. White, American Psychological Association

Over the past ten years there has been a continuing accumulation of research on the relationships between the organization of the built environment and patterns of individual and collective behavior. Although much of this work has been directed to questions posed by the behavioral science and design segments of the academic community, similar questions are beginning to arise in conjunction with the establishment of public policy. In recent years legislative bodies, regulatory and enforcement agencies, and the courts have shown and increasing concern for 1) the environmental aspects of crime, consumer safety, imprisonment, and aging and 2) the behavioral aspects of fire protection, energy, land-use, and housing. One of the most fully developed examples is the Crime Prevention Through Environmental Design (CPTED) program that the Law Enforcement Assistance Administration (LEAA) has built around the concept of defensible space.

On the surface, it is clear that there ought to be a working dialogue between members of the research and policy communities on matters relating human behavior to environmental design. In practice, it is becoming apparent that the development of such a dialogue is confounded by basic differences in the procedures by which the two communities operate and the priorities to which each responds.

The long range intent of these four sessions is to identify and encourage the effective use of various mechanisms for linking research on environment and behavior to the establishment of building regulations, environmental legislation, and court decisions that affect such relationships. The more immediate objective is to bring key representatives of the research, design, and policy communities together to confront the scientific and political realities of critical environment-behavior issues that are of mutual concern. The four sessions will cover the following topics:

1. THE STANDING OF RESEARCH IN ESTABLISHING PUBLIC POLICY (Chair: John Eberhard)

This session will explore the generic issues, prototypical examples, and fundamental strategies confronting the research and policy communities

as they attempt to interact. As an introduction to the remaining three sessions it will address the distinctions between empirical, pragmatic, consensual, and adversary approaches to establishing the credibility of evidence on the part of researchers, politicians, regulatory officials, and attorneys, respectively. Although the overall concern of these sessions is the policy implication of research on environment and behavior, the main focus of this particular session will be the proper utilization of research per se within the policy-making process.

The major speaker will be Daniel DeSimone, Deputy Director of the Office of Technology Assessment (OTA), which was established in 1973 to advise the United States Congress on the scientific and technological ramifications of pending legislation. Among the current OTA assessment programs of direct relevance to the concerns of EDRA members are evaluations of rural telecommunications, alternative energy sources, and public transportation. DeSimone will draw upon his current work at OTA and his previous experience in advancing scientific and technological innovation for the National Bureau of Standards, the U.S. Treasury, and the White House in addressing the kind of "applicability gap" that has become the theme of this year's conference.

Discussants from both the behavioral science and environmental design segments of the EDRA community will assess the relevance of the OTA model and other models to the current development of the field of environmental design research. Specific emphasis will be placed upon the researchers' concern about the utilization of findings in policy decisions and the physical designers' concern about assuming responsibility for the consequences of someone else's research findings.

2. RESEARCH ON ENVIRONMENT AND BEHAVIOR AS A BASIS FOR LEGISLATION (Chair: Don Conway)

Although most researchers tend to view their own discipline as an outgrowth of theoretical imperatives that stem from the cumulative growth of scientific findings, their ability to pursue these issues often requires the commitment of resources that are independent of the research process itself. In documenting the enormous growth of environment-behavior research in the United States during the 1960s, it must be noted that financial support for a very large proportion of this work came from federal funds appropriated to the National Institute of Mental Health (NIMH) under the provisions of the Mental Retardation and Community Mental Health Facilities Construction Act of 1963 (PL 88-164). It is also clear that much of the more recent funding in the field is indirectly attributable to the impetus provided by the National Environmental Policy Act of 1969 (PL 91-190). Increasingly, the mandate to support new research on environmental quality, architectural barriers, low-cost housing, and health care facilities is coming directly from legislation at the national, provincial, and state levels.

The position of legislation in the development of the field of environmental design research is central since public laws can either follow from acceptable research findings in an area related to the public need or, in the absence of such findings, can direct that appropriate research programs be initiated.

The purpose of this session is to illustrate, through the portrayal of actual cases, the direct and indirect processes by which research findings and needs are made known to legislative decision-makers and are accepted by them. The general focus will be on housing programs for the elderly with a special emphasis on the fatal consequences of forced relocation. The sometimes fortuitous and sometimes fragile link between 1) research on this problem by Dr. Leon Pastalan and others, 2) guidelines issued by the Pennsylvania Department of Public Welfare and then by the U.S. Administration on Aging, and 3) legislation introduced by Senator Percy (S. 1275) which guarantees institutionalized older persons the right to a program preparing them for relocation, will be presented in considerable detail. The relevance of these case histories to other legislation affecting the design and management of facilities for the elderly and other vulnerable populations will also be presented.

3. APPLICATIONS OF BEHAVIORAL RESEARCH TO BUILDING REGULATIONS (Chair: R. Stirling Ferguson)

The decisions that architects and other designers make about how a building will serve human needs are invariably constrained by the rule systems within which the designer, client, or building must operate. These rules, in the form of building codes, enforcement policies, and programmatic guidelines issued by public agencies and underwriting institutions, are often as critical to the provision of habitable environments as the decisions made by the designer. In some respects, the benefits and impact of directing research findings toward the appropriate regulatory body may be greater than trying to influence the design profession directly.

While the regulatory authority of government is

generally restricted to matters of life safety and health, a number of voluntary standards organizations like the American National Standards Institute (ANSI) and the American Society for Testing and Materials (ASTM) develop a much wider range of standards and guidelines that directly affect the manner in which products and environments are delivered to the marketplace. The focus of this session will be a comparison between the manner in which behavioral research is applied to the preparation and enforcement of building code requirements in the United States and Canada. The general issue of pedestrian safety and access to facilities in and around buildings will be developed through presentations of ongoing case studies involving 1) the direct collaboration between researchers at the National Research Council of Canada and building officials in the City of Calgary on the design and evaluation of experimental exitways and washrooms for a large public grandstand, 2) the HUD-sponsored revision of the ANSI Standard for Making Buildings and Facilities Accessible to the Handicapped (A117.1) being conducted by Dr. Edward Steinfeld, and 3) the recent work by Dr. John Templer and researchers at the National Bureau of Standards on the development of new stairway safety requirements for the U.S. Consumer Product Safety Commission.

While it is becoming increasingly necessary to relate behavioral research to specific regulatory issues, this relevancy is often not sufficient to insure that even well documented findings will outweigh the numerous protective arguments and special commitments that other interest groups frequently contribute to the preparation and application of building regulations. It is precisely this impasse with which participants having experience and expertise on both sides of the applicability gap will contend during this session.

4. THE ENVIRONMENT-BEHAVIOR RESEARCHER AS THE EXPERT WITNESS IN COURT (Chair: Willo White)

In many respects, the ultimate accountability for providing environments that are suitable for human occupancy is being resolved in the courts. In many instances, the final decision rests upon the research-based opinions of expert witnesses. In Frye v. U.S. (293 Federal, 1013, D.C. Cir., 1923), an important case bearing on the introduction of expert witnesses, the court states that "...expert testimony deduced from a well recognized principle or discovery, the thing from which the deduction is made must be sufficiently established to have gained general acceptance in the particular field in which it belongs". The assumption is that the special knowledge, training, or experience allows the expert to form a better opinion on the basis of a set of facts than could be presented to a jury through the testimony of ordinary persons.

Court cases bearing on the relationships between environment and behavior are becoming increasingly common. Everything from injunctions seeking curb-cuts for wheelchairs to dismissals of unsupported code requirements to the liability of architects for the accident-producing behaviors of building occupants are being adjudicated. One issue that is particularly relevant to the concerns of many social scientists is the widespread finding that solitary confinement and crowding in prisons constitutes cruel and unusual punishment. Recent decisions in North Carolina, Alabama, two boroughs of New York City, Washington, D.C., and British Columbia have led to the closing of facilities, the reassignment of inmates, and the development of major new construction programs. Since the issues of density, crowding, and confinement are among the central concerns of many EDRA researchers, the issue of crowding in prisons has been selected as the focus of this session.

The format will be a mock trial in which the decisive testimony from at least one of these recent cases will be reenacted by researchers who have previously served as expert witnesses in such cases. Direct and cross examination by attorneys for the plaintiff and the defense will be used to elicit this testimony and to illustrate the differences between the scientific and adversary methods of establishing facts. In addition to simulating and explaining courtroom procedures, this session will begin to assess the credibility and acceptance of environment-behavior research by the courts.

The following researchers, public officials, and designers have agreed to participate in these sessions. Those marked with an asterisk are tentatively committed.

John Archea, Architectural Research Section, National Bureau of Standards

James R. Bartley, Head, Codes Enforcement and Rehabilitation Division, City of Jacksonville, Florida

Michael Brill, President, Buffalo Organization for Scientific and Technological Innovation*

David Canter, Director, MSc Program in Environmental Psychology, University of Surrey*

Don Conway, Director of Research Programs, The American Institute of Architects

Daniel DeSimone, Deputy Director, Office of Technology Assessment, U.S. Congress

John Eberhard, President, AIA Research Corporation

R. Stirling Ferguson, Building Design & Use Section, National Research Council of Canada

George Fleming, President, Canadian Building Officials Association*

Nicole Gara, Director of Congressional Liaison, The American Institute of Architects

Margaret Goglia, AIA Research Corporation

Charles Gordon, Department of Sociology, Carleton University

Don Henning, Building Design & Use Section, National Research Council of Canada

Kiyoshi Izumi, School of Urban and Regional Planning, University of Waterloo

Henry Lagorio, Advanced Environmental Research & Technology, National Science Foundation

Pai Lin Li, Coordinator of Building Regulations, City of Calgary, Alberta

Peter Mill, Faculty of Environmental Design, University of Calgary

Leon A. Pastalan, Director of Research, Institute of Gerontology, University of Michigan

Jake Pauls, Building Design & Use Section, National Research Council of Canada

Edward Steinfeld, School of Architecture, Syracuse University

Daniel Stokols, Department of Psychology, University of California at Irvine

John Templer, School of Architecture, Georgia Institute of Technology

Francis Ventre, Institute for Applied Technology, National Bureau of Standards.

Willo P. White, Office of Scientific Affairs, American Psychological Association

URBAN HOUSING, SOCIAL VALUES AND IMPLICATIONS FOR DESIGN.

Gilles Barbey

I.R.E.C.
Institute for Research on the Built Environment
14, avenue de l'Eglise-Anglaise
1006 Lausanne, Switzerland

1. Introduction

While assessing the quality of housing types and dwelling units, one should bear in mind the following considerations:
There is a general tendency to exaggerate the influence of architecture on behavior and overlook such major aspects as the social factors. Buildings are inhabited and used by their tenants according to accepted social values, whose identification may be important in the design process. There are considerable differences between the expected and the effective use of the dwelling units by their inhabitants. Such differences should be analyzed. Also, some social effects of housing will only appear in the long term and be revealed by a longitudinal study of the building and its changing population. On the other hand, the evolution of life styles over time is reflected in the changes occurring in the housing types.

2. Research Area

Following aspects of urban housing should be explored:
How different housing types either favor or inhibit various life styles. For example, it is useful to have some expectation of the preferred furniture displays, while studying alternative layouts of apartments. Also, the relative meaning of concepts is important, especially when the same physical arrangement has differing meanings for various social groups. Symbolism and class values play a significant role in the relationship between social considerations and physical requirements in housing.

3. Purpose of the Participation Session

It is proposed to illustrate different types of urban housing and discuss some of the social values evident from these examples. The Participation Session will facilitate the comparison between different housing experiences from differing cultural contexts. It will also explore the possibility of parallelling social values with the physical attributes of the environment, thus offering a new instrument for the assessment of housing quality. For example, the concepts of social dignity and respectability tend to be expressed in terms of monumentality, massivity and style.

4. Conclusion

The common dimensions to such studies are twofold: identify the links between social values and the corresponding attributes of the physical environment, and determine the major implications of different life styles on housing types.

PRACTICAL APPLICATIONS OF ECOLOGICAL PSYCHOLOGY METHODS

Robert B. Betchel

Environmental Research & Development Foundation
Kansas City, Missouri

Often in the past research findings in ecological psychology have been praised but sometimes not understood. Recent advances in the methodology provide a wider range of techniques for applications to design and organizational problems. Three speakers will illustrate the use of three different methods in the application of ecological research to design and organizational problems. After each presentation a problem or set of problems will be presented to the audience to be solved by the methods illustrated. The workshop will then be opened up to discussion of the problem, introduction of new problems from the audience, and the answering of any questions about ecological psychology.

Burgess Ledbetter will show how the K-21 scale, one technique of ecological psychology, has been used to diagnose boundary problems in an office space and provide new design solutions. K-21 scales will be passed out to the audience so they can participate in their own design solutions to the problems. A question and answer period on K-21 techniques will follow.

Rajendra Srivastava will describe how under-manning theory, a theory and method of ecological psychology, was applied to an organization that specializes in care for the multiply handicapped. Before and after data will be shown on the reeducation and upgrading of personnel and the creation of new settings while keeping essentially the same space. A hypothetical problem in undermanning will then be presented to the audience for its own solutions. Following this, a question and answer period will take up questions on undermanning theory and its applications.

Robert Bechtel will present data on families from three societies, a military base in Alaska, urban families in Teheran, and American expatriates living in Saudi Arabia. The data will illustrate use of the activity patterns rating scales, another technique of ecological psychology.

Since these scales have been reduced to a questionnaire, members of the audience will be given data from questionnaire answers to convert into activity patterns. Suggested design solutions from the life style profiles will be shared among the audience. A question and answer period will follow in which new problems can be introduced to the panel of three speakers. Other techniques of ecological psychology, such as focal points and general richness index, will be discussed at audience request.

Conference participants who wish to bring their own problems for diagnosis by ecological methods are urged to do so. Information on number of people, their age and sex, the amount of time spent in the area of concern, the measurements of areas, and the characteristic behavior should accompany the problem when it is presented at the workshop.

Participants:

Robert B. Bechtel, Ph.D., President
Environmental Research & Development Foundation
P.O. Box 7208
Kansas City, Missouri 64113

C. Burgess Ledbetter, Research Architect
Construction Engineering
Research Branch
Department of the Army
U.S. Army Cold Regions Research & Engineering Laboratory
Hanover, New Hampshire 03755

Rajendra K. Srivastava, Ph.D.
Senior Research Associate
Environmental Research & Development Foundation
P.O. Box 7208
Kansas City, Missouri 64113

THE ROLE OF ENVIRONMENTAL PSYCHOLOGY IN BASIC DESIGN EDUCATION

Charles Burnette, Ph.D. Chairman

The School of Architecture
The University of Texas at Austin
Austin, Texas 78712
Phone (512) 471-1922

ABSTRACT

This participation session will meet May 28 in two sessions (5 hours). Invited presentations will begin in the morning session chaired by Charles Burnette and lead into a synthesis session to be chaired by Donlyn Lyndon. The intent is to share educational philosophies, theoretical foundations and pedagogical practices as they relate to the studio teaching of man-environment relations at the introductory level of design. An exhibit of student work is anticipated and an outline of implications for architectural education will be attempted.

1. INTRODUCTION

The fundamental intent of this session is to examine the manner by which current knowledge of environmental psychology and concern for the building user is being-or might be-introduced into the basic design education offered by schools of Architecture. Those who will make presentations have been invited to do so because their work directly addresses the theoretical issues of basic design education from a perspective based in Man-Environment Relations or because they have already introduced a related approach in the courses on Basic Design which they teach.

While the issues which surround the academic teaching and conduct of research in man-environment relations is of interest the primary focus of this session will be on the introduction of the concerns of environmental psychology into the process of designing as taught in the studio and in the philosophy and theory of basic design education. The intent is to reformulate the foundations of basic design education left by the Bauhaus in order to reflect more up to date theories of perception, cognition and spatial behavior, a deeper commitment to the self-expression and accommodation of the building user, and to the findings of educational psychology and other disciplines.

2. PROGRAM CONTEXT

The following outline reflects the probable order and focus of the 15-20 minute presentations to be given by each individual. The entries below are not titles and the focus may change at the participants discretion.

1) Jon Lang - The implications of an information processing theory of perception for design education.
2) Michael Benedikt - Understanding vestibular knowledge of the environment.
3) Kent Bloomer - Body image theory and its implications in the teaching of design.
4) Ray Lifchez - Developing self-awareness and knowledge of environmental values through design.
5) Michael Ertel - The uses of scenarios from literature as a humanistic basis for design projects.
6) Jay Farbstein - The uses of direct experience of environments to develop awareness and analytic skill.
7) Jerry Finrow - The implications of the pattern language for basic design education.
8) Charles Burnette - A comparative evaluation of a behavior based approach to the teaching of design.
9) Archie Mackenzie - The role of form giving principles in relationship to intentions in design.
10) Mike Martin - Integrating the concerns of environmental psychology into the basic design curriculum.
11) Gary Moore - The issues of creative behavior, group processes and cognitive development in design education.
12) Philip Thiel - The goals of design education.
13) Donlyn Lyndon - Discussion (1.5 hours) Where are we? Going?

3. PARTICIPANTS

Michael Benedikt
School of Architecture
The University of Texas
Austin, Texas 78712
512-471-1922

Kent Bloomer
School of Architecture
Yale University
New Haven, Connecticut
P. O. Box 1605   06520
203-436-0550

Michael Ertel
The Boston Architectural Center
School of Architecture
Boston, Massachusetts 02115
617-536-3170

Jay Farbstein
California Polytechnic State University
School of Architecture & Environmental Design
San Luis Obispo, California 93401
805-546-2010

Jerry Finrow
Center for Environmental Research
School of Architecture & Allied Arts
University of Oregon
Eugene, Oregon 97403
503-686-3650

Jon Lang
Graduate School of Fine Arts
The University of Pennsylvania
Philadelphia, Pennsylvania 19104
215-594-8321

Ray Lifchez
College of Environmental Design
University of California
Berkeley, California
415-642-4942

Donlyn Lyndon
Massachusetts Institute of Technology
School of Architecture & Planning
Cambridge, Massachusetts 02139
617-253-7791

Archie Mackenzie
College of Architecture, Art & Planning
Cornell University
Ithaca, New York 14850

Michael Martin
Kansas State University
College of Architecture & Design
Manhattan, Kansas 66506
913-532-5953

Gary Moore
School of Architecture
University of Wisconsin
Milwaukee, Wisconsin 53201
414-963-5964

Philip Thiel
College of Architecture & Planning
University of Washington
Seattle, Washington 98195
206-543-4180

EVALUATION RESEARCH IN ENVIRONMENTS AND AGING

Organizers:
Thomas O. Byerts, M Arch
Gerontological Society
Washington, DC

Paul G. Windley, D Arch
Department of Architecture
Kansas State University
Manhattan, KS

1. INTRODUCTION

Growth in environments and aging has been part
of EDRA almost from the beginning. At first,
diverse examples of elderly housing research/
design were presented. These were followed
later by a more cohesive emphasis on methodology, collected data and experience contributing both to the growing body of Man-
Environment knowledge and to techniques of
research application. Due to the growing
backlog of experience, those involved in environments and aging are anxious to share
their concerns and findings with the EDRA
community for comment and criticism. The
conference theme, "Beyond the Applicability
Gap" is a welcome opportunity to focus this
effort.

2. BACKGROUND

One of the most significant reasons for the
rapid growth and apparent success of work in
environments and aging is the sense of mission
which subsumes most scientists, applied researchers, design specialists, consumer groups,
and funding agencies in this area. Elderly
individuals are found to be particularly sensitive to physical environmental factors. Thus,
a mismatch resulting from their changing or
decreasing abilities encountered in an inappro-
priate/non-adaptive environment is now relatively easy to identify. Proposals for remedial action can then be structured. The need
for an appropriate comprehensive response is
almost immediate since even minor environmental
constraints can dictate over institutionalization, morbidity and even mortality for some
older people. On the other hand, caution must
be exercised since disruption caused by environmental modification and the stress of relocation (to a better environment) can have dramatic negative effects.

Behavior based design criteria and approaches
are ready now for testing in elderly housing,
institutional building design, senior centers,
transportation and planning. Clearly, the
practitioners' cry for applicable research is

being addressed, though results are far from
definitive enough. The essential next step is
broad full scale implementation and evaluation
to see whether such criteria and approaches are
valid and will remain so over time.

Post-construction evaluation and follow up
occupant survey/observation are not a widespread practice. They are a logical and rather
straightforward activity, but philosophical,
methodical and pragmatic barriers face both
practitioners, researchers and consumers alike.

The purpose of this workshop then is to narrow
the applicability gap by not only clarifying
what the problems are but also suggesting some
solutions. The organizers encourage full EDRA
participation due to the implication of this
work not only for this country's 22 million
elderly and other millions of environmentally
vulnerable people, but as an approach toward
improving the quality of the built environment
for everyone. This is in everyone's best interest for we are the elderly of tomorrow!

3. THE PROGRAM

A summary of the agenda including listing participants and reactors and summaries follows:

3.1 Methodologies of Evaluation in Environ-
     ments and Aging - M. Powell Lawton, PhD,
     Philadelphia Geriatric Center, Philadelphia

Standard behavioral science research methods and
procedures that gain useful finding from adult
samples are seldom valid instruments when applied exclusively to the elderly. Furthermore,
the resultant data generally lacks clear design
relevance and often requires major translation
effort (due to language problems and levels of
abstraction). Weaknesses of key research methodologies contrasted against aging and design
oriented models will be traced and examined
suggesting fruitful areas for further work.

3.2 The Empathic Model: A Research Tool for
     Designers - Leon Pastalan, PhD, Institute
     of Gerontology, University of Michigan,
     Ann Arbor

Researchers and designers view the same problem
from different perspectives. A tool that helps
to overcome this is the "Empathic Model." It
is a series of devices that simulate normal age
related sensory loss. Wearing them over time,
the designer actually becomes an older subject,
thus building a body of reproducable observational findings and a strong sense of concern
for vulnerable populations.

3.3 Utilization of Evaluation Research in Environments and Aging - John Archea, National Bureau of Standards, Washington

Results of completed evaluation studies tend not to be fed into subsequent design decisions. Recurring misfits between the evaluators' often academic conceptualization of the physical environment and time-consuming methods versus the designers' more pragmatic notions and timetables are shown to present formidable obstacles to the utilization of evaluation findings in design. Questions surrounding assessment of ongoing building programs matched against one-shot project evaluations plus the relative benefits of directing findings toward the building regulatory process instead of the more fragmented design community are also discussed. While systematic assessments of the behavioral consequences of prior design decisions could ultimately contribute to improved environment for the elderly, such promises will remain unfulfilled until the numerous extra-scientific roadblocks are overcome.

3.4 Case Studies

3.4.1 Post Construction Evaluation: A Case Study of Elderly Housing - Sandra C. Howell, PhD, and Gayle Epp, MCP, Department of Architecture, MIT, Boston

The development of evaluation methodology is described as part of the restudy of a national sample of elderly residing in federally subsidized housing. Emphasis is placed upon initial use of the survey interview and photography as predominantly content validation and heuristic devices helping to focus the evaluation protocols and hypotheses generation. The paucity of design detail in public reporting documents is noted along with its effects on the development of the building typology necessary to advance environment-behavior research to a predictive state.

3.4.2 Collaboration in Architectural Design Lucille Nahemow, PhD, Psychologist, New York City and Greg Downs, AIA, The Architects Collaborative, Boston

When user needs are septemmatically analyzed and the findings actually applied to the programming and design of a building, the participating disciplines must work together under a clear framework of mutual expectations. As the work on the design for the new Oxford Home for the Aged progressed from concept development to working drawings, tasks and responsibilities performed by each professional changed. An inductive process model of program planning recognizing these changing roll definitions was developed and will be highlighted here along with observations on this collaborative effort.

3.4.3 An Evaluation of Neighborhood Source Convenience for Elderly Housing Residents Robert Newcomer, PhD, San Diego Office of Senior Citizens' Affairs, San Diego

Data on site, neighborhood and tenant characteristics of elderly housing projects are examined from a national sample. The distance and other circumstances which define service convenience and predict frequency of use are identified. Service distance recommendations leading toward development of performance standards are proposed. A systematic evaluation of these recommendations when implemented is called for here.

3.5 Reactors

Behavioral Scientist - Irv Altman, PhD
Department of Psychology, University of Utah, Salt Lake City

Design Educator - Michael Bednar, M Arch
School of Architecture, University of Virginia, Charlottesville

Architect - Pamela Cluff, MRIAC, FRIBA
Cluff and Cluff, Architects, Toronto

Research Facilitator - Don Conway, AIA
Director of AIA Research Programs, Washington

HUD Representative - Pam Dinkle, MLA
Program Analyst, HUD Policy Development and Research, Washington

CMHC Representative - Sylvia Goldblatt, MSW, Social Development Officer, Central Mortgage and Housing Corporation, Ottawa

TWO DESIGN PROBLEMS IN SEARCH OF A SOLUTION

Marvin J. Dainoff,
Richard Sherman, and
Daniel Miskie

Departments of
Psychology and Architecture
Miami University
Oxford, Ohio 45056

The goal of this workshop is to improve
the effectiveness with which designers and
behavioral scientists interact in approaching
common problems. In particular, it is hoped
that through the workshop experience architects and designers will discover the kinds of
information which behavioral researchers can
provide, and that the behavioral researchers
will discover the kinds of questions which are
most important in the design process. In
order to provide a realistic context for the
interaction between these two groups, actual
problems involving a nursing home and a
university infirmary/counseling center will
be the focus of discussion.

The workshop will be conducted in two
phases. During the first, design features
will be the major concern, while in the second,
aspects of evaluation will be addreseed. A
number of behavioral researchers and architects who have been prepared in advance will
be present to provide the basic framework for
the discussion, though audience participation throughout the workshop will be given
priority. It should be stressed that the
objective of the workshop is to increase the
awareness of all parties of the ways in
which effective interaction can be achieved.

FEATURES OF WORKSHOP FORMAT

1. Two Phases---design interaction phase and
    evaluation interaction phases.

2. Minimum of two architect/designers and
    two behavioral researchers will be
    assigned prior responsibility for inter-
    acting with respect to the problems posed.

THE S.A.R. (STICHTING ARCHITEKTEN RESEARCH) AND HABRAKEN'S STUDIES OF URBAN TISSUES APPLIED TO PROBLEMS OF HOUSING

Eric Dluhosch, Ph.D.

Research Associate
Department of Architecture
Massachusetts Institute of Technology
Cambridge, Massachusetts

ABSTRACT

The S.A.R. method is the result of a decade of research and actual development carried out under the leadership of Professor N.J. Habraken in Holland and other countries in Europe.

With the establishment of an institutional base for such research at M.I.T., the opportunity now exists to apply and extend the work of this man in the American context and test the power of his approach by applying it to the many issues surrounding the problem of housing, including the influence of energy conservation on policy-planning, design, and realization of housing projects on all levels of the decision implementation hierarchy.

What is the core of the S.A.R. method? Basically it provides a convenient and structured means by which to deal with housing environments both relative to participatory decision-making and in terms of its technical aspects as far as explicit normative strategies for implementation are concerned. Conceptually, decision making in housing is assumed to operate in two spheres: The individual-private sphere and the communal-public sphere. Decisions in the former affect those elements of housing which are defined as "detach-ables" while the latter refer to the "supports" (the superstructure). The one has implications on short term decisions made by individual consumers, while the other defines planning policy affecting the whole community and pertaining to long term decisions.

On the larger, urban scale, housing is generally characterized by certain morphological patterns, which are the spatial manifestation of the positioning of material according to implicit or explicit norms, rule systems, or other standard conventions. These patterns exist as urban tissues (somewhat similar to organic tissues in the human body), subject to global and/or local constraints (social, technical, political, etc.). Urban tissues are developed over time as the result of societal "agreements" which are made technically explicit by accepted (or imposed) rule systems governing the disposition of both prototypical or "thematic elements and special or "non-thematic" elements (often referred to as "monuments" by architects).

THE STUDY OF URBAN TISSUES IS AN EXTENSION OF THE S.A.R. METHOD IN THAT IT LOOKS AT THE PHYSICAL WORLD AS A SYSTEM OF HIERARCHICALLY STRUCTURED LEVELS OF DECISION-MAKING WHICH BECOME INSTRU-MENTALLY EFFECTIVE BY MEANS OF MUTUALLY AGREED UPON RULE SYSTEMS, STANDARDS, AND NORMS. THE METHODOLOGY IS DESIGNED TO MAKE EXPLICIT THE LINKS BETWEEN THE VARIOUS LEVELS AND THE EFFECT OF THE PROCESS OF NEGOTIATION ON INTERACTION BE-TWEEN POLICY, PLANNING, AND DESIGN IMPLEMENTA-TION IN THE NORMATIVE SENSE, WITHOUT SPECIFICALLY PRESCRIBING OR PROSCRIBING VARIATIONS TAKING PLACE WITHIN THE OVERALL CONTEXT OF AGREED UPON CONSTRAINTS.

The diagram below represents a graphic represen-tation of the hierarchical interrelationship be-tween the conceptual aspects of the methodology and the various levels of decision making in the real world.

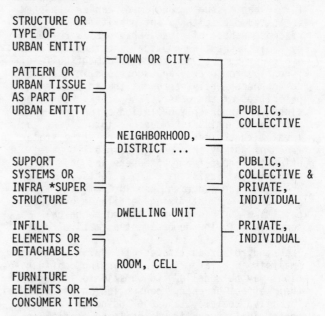

Unlike conventional methodologies in the social or physical sciences, which tend to separate conceptually "software" from "hardware" the S.A.R. method provides a convenient took for both "soft" analysis and "hard" technical implementation by providing a means for translating societal agree-ments in terms of design usable standards into clearly stated and technically comprehensible norms (or performance measures). This is done by means of zoning, sector analysis, the elaboration of alternative plan variants, modular coordina-tion, etc.

In that sense the methodology can be used 1) as a tool for analysis, 2) as a modeling device, and 3) as an instrument of policy implementation. Most important, by making explicit both the role of the various actors in the decision making hierarchy and the effects and implications of their decisions on technical and spatial rule systems, each party is enabled to find it easier to adapt to changing conditions based on enlightened self-interest, while at the same time being more aware of the consequences of decisions made at each level and the ensuing relationship between policy making and physical implementation.

The emergence of energy conservation as one of the crucial elements affecting decision making in the built environment requires -- by definition -- a deep understanding of the cause-effect relationship between behavior and its effects on the physical environment. Careful allocation on diminishing resources and substitution of new energy sources for conventional ones will inevitably affect existing life-styles and their physical setting. In order to render the process of change orderly and in order to provide for maximum flexibility and freedom of choice within clearly defined parameters of mutually agreed upon socio-technical goals, methods have to be developed which allow for connecting purposeful behavior with corresponding patterns of physical form. Aside from that, the modeling of alternative urban tissue morphologies can be expected to foster explicitness and permit the estimation of consequences of given behaviors as reflected by their respective physical settings. For example, producers view the environment quite differently from users, and decisions in one category do not necessarily represent the interests and priorities of the other. The S.A.R. method provides for an orderly evolution of an open-ended and non-deterministic model by interfacing each level with the next, and by translating statements of policy into design usable language, using the input from both users and producers to simulate and investigate the effects of either group's value judgements in instrumental technical terms, without fixing details beyond the necessity of providing spatial and technical compatibility in the broadest normative sense.

The study of urban tissues allows for a similar analysis on a larger scale. Varying configurations may be modelled and questioned in terms of their effect on energy consuption on the communal (or city) scale. Standards and norms can be tested against configurational and spatial combinations of varying material characteristics and use functions. Inadequacies pertaining to dysfunctions in the decision-making process can be made explicit by matching them with opportunities offerred by the normative matrix of a given tissue. Conversely, rule systems can be brought into balance by looking at the behavioral dynamics of a given context or situation. Inadequacies of the system can be resolved by negotiation rather than coercion, by being based on the recognition of legitimate self-interest, rather than abstract notions as to what behavior ideally

should be or how a given technical solution might work in isolation. Such a model obviates legislative fiat by allowing an orderly transformation of obsolete or impracticable normative structures by using a dialectic developmental approach, which recognizes the need for establishing a clearly defined set of freely negotiated agreements on overall policy while at the same time providing the opportunity for maximum choice within the limits set by such a policy.

The need for effective energy conserving strategies is both urgent and crucial to the preservation of the productive capacity of our society and is necessary for the maintenance of the high living standards and the expectations of a population which has come to expect present standards as "normal". Contrary to some alarmist views, it is not a foregone conclusion that energy conservation must inevitably lead to the impoverishment of life.

However, strategies must first be tested and implemented which will make the necessary changes (and possibly some sacrifices) comprehensible not only in terms of technical and behavioral adjustments to a new situation, but also clarify the interrelationship between decisions made both in the public and private realms and their deliberated consequences on the physical setting and its technical components. This can only be accomplished by developing means by which the process of decision-making is linked explicitly to policies of implementation and technical compatibility. In other words, the worlds of the user and the producer need to be made compatible by providing conceptual and technical tools for both to coordinate technical expertise and behavioral knowhow in an atmosphere of mutual advantage and trust, rather than solving problems in an atmosphere of distrust and antagonism. The only way to achieve such a goal is to allow for testing and trying out any method which bridges the current gap between the "hard" and "soft" sciences and which contains within its corpus the means by which to make effective both.

The workshop session will deal with the instrumental aspects of the S.A.R. methodology and the "tissue studies". Application of the various S.A.R. principles and methodology to housing will be presented, along with and a discussion of the underlying philosophy will be encouraged.

PHYSICAL DESIGN AND THE OPEN CLASSROOM

Chairperson: Dr. Gary W. Evans

Program in Social Ecology
University of California, Irvine
Irvine, California 92717

OVERVIEW

The purpose of the proposed workshop session
is to bring together persons from various perspectives to discuss the problem of physical
design and the open classroom. The format
will be a brief video segment presentation of
an open classroom in operation. A limited
set of questions derived from earlier discussions and viewings of the tape by the participants will be circulated and discussed by the
panel members and the audience. Open discussion will follow. We are taking a problem
oriented approach - 'What design and program
interventions can one make in an open classroom to improve the learning experience?'

PARTICIPANTS

Mr. John Tritipaut
Blurock and Associates
2300 Newport Blvd.
Newport Beach, California

Dr. Daniel Stokols
Program in Social Ecology
University of California, Irvine
Irvine, California

Dr. Kathy C. Pezdek
Department of Psychology
California State University, San Bernardino
San Bernardino, California

Dr. Rudolf Moos
Social Ecology Research Center
Stanford University
Palo Alto, California

Dr. David Campbell
Department of Psychology
University of Kansas
Lawrence, Kansas

Ms. Barbara Lovell
1242 W. Ocean Front
Newport Beach, California

TEACHING AND LEARNING A LINK: ENVIRONMENTAL

PROGRAMMING AND DESIGN

Jay Farbstein, Ph.D.

School of Architecture and Environmental Design
California Polytechnic State University
San Luis Obispo
California 93401

ABSTRACT

A discussion session for teachers and students
to explore issues around the teaching and learning of behavioral science applications to
design, especially environmental programming
and evaluation.

1. INTRODUCTION

This participation session is intended as an
opportunity for teachers and students to
share experiences and concerns about the
application of behavioral science approaches
to environmental design: programming, design
process and evaluation.

The purpose of the session is to discuss and
compare present practices and outline possible
future directions for the teaching and learning
of environmental design as an expression and
realization of developments in person-environment relations.

Environmental programming is viewed as the
direct input to design of data developed in
research and evaluation studies. Thus, the
teaching of programming will take the major
emphasis in this session.

2. FORMAT

The format will consist of a single session.
It will be introduced by a small number of
brief contributions in the form of position
papers, polemics, or descriptions of current
activities. The majority of the session will
be devoted to responses and free discussion.

3. ISSUES

Issues which will be addressed include, in
part:

1) The integration (or lack of it) of programming into the design curriculum and with
design activity.
2) Conceptual and methodological problems
of programming which carry over to teaching.
3) Evaluation of design in terms of program

precepts.
4) Degree of student competence aimed for;
level at which taught.
5) Subject matter covered and manner of
presentation.
6) "Live" programming exercises: arrangement,
commitment, success.
7) Lack of textbook material, etc.

4. PARTICIPANTS

It is hoped that 25 to 30 teachers and students
will take part. So far, the following persons
have agreed to submit brief position papers:

Jay Farbstein, Ph.D.
School of Architecture and Environmental Design
California Polytechnic State University
San Luis Obispo, CA 93407

Robert Hershberger, Ph.D., AIA
Faculty of Environmental Design
Arizona State University
Tempe, AZ 85281

Peter Manning, Head
School of Architecture
Nova Scotia Technical College
Halifax, Nova Scotia, Canada

Pleasantine Mills
Faculty of Environmental Design
University of Calgary
Calgary, Alberta, Canada

Other teachers and students are invited.
Position papers, course outlines and lecture
notes are solicited for advance duplication
and distribution. Examples of student work
can be exhibited at the session.

PARTICIPATION SESSION:
VIDEO AND FILM APPLICATIONS IN ENVIRONMENTAL
DESIGN RESEARCH

Lawrence P. Friedberg

Department of Architecture
Kansas State University
Manhattan, Kansas   66506

ABSTRACT

Although the potential of videotape and film
for gathering and communicating information
about person/environment relations is
recognized by many, use of these media has been
limited for many reasons. One prime factor in
their limited use has been the lack of
opportunity for researchers to communicate
first hand about their experiences. The
intention of this participation session is to
provide a forum in which those interested in
videotape and film technologies can view work
in these media and generate discussion
regarding their application to environment/
behavior research. Issues to be explored
include: (1) reduction of data into manageable
form, (2) time and cost of videotape vs. return
for effort, (3) eomplementarity of film data to
data gathered using other procedures, (4)
analysis and interpretation of film and video
data, (5) studio processing of "raw tape" for
presentation purposes, (6) technical advantages and disadvantages of video and film use.

1.1 Comparison of Film and Videotape Validity in Environmental Simulation

Donald Appleyard and Kenneth Craik
University of California
Berkeley, California

Extensive footage of film and videotape of the
same environment were shown to subjects and
investigations of responses to the media were
compared. (Further information not available
at publication deadline. L.P.F.)

1.2 Videotape Analysis of Stair Accidents

John Archea, Larry Steel, and Amon Young
Architectural Research Section
National Bureau of Standards
Washington, D.C.   20234

About 50 hours of videotape was recorded with
the intent of determining causes of stair
accidents. Micro-analysis (counting of scan
lines and tracing falls in precise time) of
individual subjects using our scoring
technique suggested that there were patterns
of head, eye and foot orientations associated
with the approach, descent and exit of stairs.

1.3 Behavioral Observation Using Videotape

Asher Derman
University of Tennessee
Knoxville, Tennessee

Asher Derman utilized videotape to observe
children in novel environments and on stair-
ways. He will discuss primarily the
technical problems involved with use of the
equipment and problems of analysis of the
information gathered. (Further information
not available at publication deadline. L.P.F.)

1.4 Using Data from Visual Observations

Guido Francescato and Sue Weidemann
Housing Research and Development Program
University of Illinois
Urbana, Illinois   61801

We propose to use a cinematographic procedure
for recording observed behavior in housing
areas as an illustration of the potential, as
well as the limitations, of this type of data
collecting method. More specifically, we are
interested in discussing questions of content
(i.e., appropriateness of the technique to
the substantive issues under study), questions
of complementarity with other data gathering
procedures (i.e., relationships with self-
reports, records, etc.) and data analysis
(including interpretation).

1.5 A Video "Walk Around the Block": An Investigation of Person/Environment Relationships

Lawrence P. Friedberg
Department of Architecture
Kansas State University
Manhattan, Kansas   66506

This tape demonstrates various capabilities of videotape to produce and communicate information related to design issues and human behavior. Interview segments are juxtaposed to provide comparison of viewpoints of users in a manner similar to television journalism. Observations of subjects and supplemental scenes are edited in to provide specific visual information related to inter- view responses. A character generator is used to emphasize issues brought up by subjects and as a means of applying a layer of analysis to the tape. Black and white tape is used to indicate less obtrusive observation of subjects and color tape used to indicate direct confrontation of subject by interviewer and camera. Questions of the effectiveness, and validity of these manipulations appropriateness, will be considered.

1.6 Unobtrusive Videotaped Recordings of Pedestrian Movement and Stationary Behavior in the Columbia, Maryland Shopping Mall

Wolfgang F. E. Preiser
Department of Architecture
University of Illinois
Urbana, Illinois   61801

Some of the issues related to the topics indicated in the title are: For movement behavior, the problem of standardization of velocity measurement units, the problem of accounting for changing human environmental conditions, e.g., different traffic densities, the problem of subject identification and categorization for analysis purposes. Further, for stationary behavior, the problem of time lines and tracking of subjects and that of reducing the overwhelming amount of informa- tion contained on tape into manageable form, e.g., through use of event recorders, etc. Last, the problem of time, cost and effort to be invested in recording and analysing videotaped behavior recordings, as compared to the value of resulting data.

HOSPITAL TRANSPORT PLANNING

Phil Gusack
Pat Schilling

Stone, Marraccini and Patterson
Architects/Planners
455 Beach Street
San Francisco CA 94133

ABSTRACT

THIS PAPER SUMMARIZES THE APPROACH AND METHODOLOGY
FOR THE ANALYSIS AND PLANNING OF CIRCULATION
ROUTES AND MATERIELS HANDLING INSTALLATIONS IN
HEALTH FACILITIES.   THE PURPOSE OF THIS RESEARCH
WAS THE DEVELOPMENT OF PROCEDURES FOR SYSTEMATIC
TRANSPORT PLANNING CLOSELY INTEGRATED WITH THE
DESIGN PROCESS.

In the last 25 years the development of mechanical
equipment for the movement of people and materiels
has had an emormous influence on hospital design.
The bed tower on a podium, which typified American
hospital design for two decades and is still influential, followed the notion that vertical movement was invariably the best solution to hospital
design problems. Today, however, when the emphasis is on planning for growth and change, the
state-of-the-art is represented by "horizontal"
hospitals; that is, hospitals which generally
are three or four stories high and planned with
expansion in mind, in which the building and
services subsystems are organized to facilitate
future change.

In response to this trend, and the search for
greater operating efficiency, a wide range of
automated materiels handling equipment has been
developed for hospital use. This has had both
good and bad results. On the plus side the design palette has been extended, and it has been
possible to bring a new lease of life to some
older facilities and cut down on staff costs in
others. On the minus side there are many cases
where expensive equipment has been installed
in hospitals which were badly planned from the
outset. Perhaps the most significant problem
to date is that hospital transport planning has
been confined to specific materiels handling
issues and has been delegated to consultants and
manufacturers who have not been able to consider
the impact of their preferred solutions on total
building design in cost or performance terms.
In this sense the designer has been at the mercy
of diffused and dependent specialists

Our work has had one goal -- the development of a
methodology for systematic transport planning which
can be performed simultaneous with hospital design.
It is based on an important premise: better transport planning without better hospital design will

not necessarily solve critical problems, and similarly, better hospital design without better
transport planning is self-defeating. In attempting to integrate transport planning within the
general scope of building design we identified one
element which is essential for quality assurance
in hospitals design. We initiated this work in
1971, and were awarded a contract by the
Veterans Administration in 1972 to determine user
needs for the movement of people, goods and
written information and to develop a procedure for
cost-benefit analysis of transport systems. At
the time of writing we have been engaged in
transport planning for projects representing
close to $100 million in construction.

TRANSPORT PLANNING IN THE DESIGN PROCESS

Figure One, a generic facility design process,
indicates the parallel development of planning,
operational and physical concepts, and their
delineation as systems for successful integration,
cost analysis and design development. Because
hospital traffic is dependent upon the operational
policies of each department it follows that
transport planning will be a major activity in
the development of operational concepts.

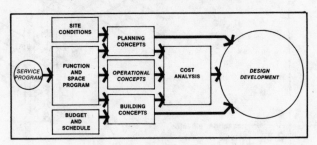

FIGURE 1: A GENERIC DESIGN PROCESS

TRANSPORT PLANNING METHODOLOGY

Figure Two, the methodology for transport planning, indicates the relationships between the compilation of traffic data and its subsequent analysis. Because traffic is generated by the functional demands of hospital services it is possible to start the compilation of the traffic data once the functional program is established. Flow analysis provides computer output which describes the traffic patterns inherent in a given functional program. This is intended for use by the design team in the development of block plans; that is, scale plans which must indicate departmental layout but do not need to show room layouts. The location of departments and vertical transportation is key input to the block plan analysis procedure. Materiels are categorized as payloads which can be transported by transport modes - individual materiels handling installations - and the complete hospital network of all circulation routes and all transport modes constitute a transport system. The methodology is intended to be performed with increasing detail in repeated cycles.

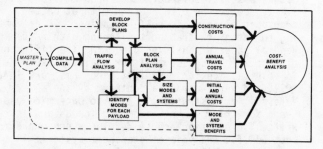

FIGURE 2: THE TRANSPORT PLANNING METHODOLOGY

CAPABILITIES

Block plan analysis uses the subroutine ELSEV of the program JUGGL2 to compute elevator traffic for the identification of potential bottlenecks, the calculation of average waiting times and thereby the number of elevators needed in each bank. The subroutine COREV computes traffic for the identification of bottlenecks in corridors and the evaluation of circulation in floor plans. The annual travel costs computed by JUGGL2 and performance benefit scores assigned to transport modes and systems are both incorporated in a life-cycle cost-benefit analysis procedure.

We can therefore determine the cost-impact of alternative department and elevator locations, and the reduction in elevator and corridor traffic affected by the installation of materiels handling equipment. These quantitative analyses form the basis of the preparation of generic specifications for transport systems and the coordination of contract documents, against which manufacturers can bid competitively in terms of established life-cycle cost and performance criteria.

APPLICATIONS

In the 500-bed hospital illustrated in Figure 3 the installation of an automatic-cart network was found to be economically and functionally desireable. Our studies indicated that surgery and radiology locations could be switched, that a radiology satellite was needed, and the canteen could be separated from the warehouse, each improving planning with no increase in travel time or cost.

FIGURE 3: TRANSPORT SYSTEM ROUTES IN A 500-BED HOSPITAL (below)

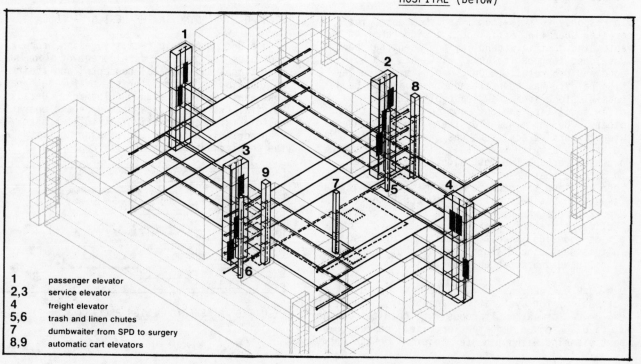

1	passenger elevator
2,3	service elevator
4	freight elevator
5,6	trash and linen chutes
7	dumbwaiter from SPD to surgery
8,9	automatic cart elevators

CHILDREN AND YOUTH AS PLANNERS AND DESIGNERS

Roger Hart
Environmental Psychology Program
The City University of New York Graduate Center
33 West 42 Street
New York, New York 10036

For many years now a growing number of people scattered throughout North America and Europe have been quietly exploring and experimenting with approaches for involving children and youth in the process of planning and designing. Most of the people have been members of the design and planning professions, disenchanted by the undirectional flow of design and planning ideas, but also to be included are a few educators and environmental psychologists.

While this workshop will focus on children and youth, its concern for public participation in design and planning is of general applicability to all age groups, as are many of the approaches and techniques that will be discussed. The emphasis on children and youth in this workshop however, is not without a rationale. Children are the largest easily identifiable group having no influence on their environment. Also, because this is the age group in which formal education is emphasized in this society, they offer an ideal opportunity to encourage an open and flexible attitude to the environment. In fact, children are rarely taught to look at the environment in terms of change, and almost never encouraged to contemplate their own role in the transformation of environments.

In this workshop those who have worked in the area will share their experiences with each other and hopefully, encourage others to develop approaches to these two important and, were we honest, inseparable areas of participatory design/planning and environmental education.

In order to maximize the breadth of discussion, the afternoon will be broken up into two halves. The first half will deal with children's spontaneous design activities, and with the various methods which have been and might be used to encourage and develop it. The second half will emphasize approaches to working with children in the planning process, and will include discussion on the development and improvement of techniques for involving children in research.

The following is a resource list of persons who have worked in this area of interest. The rather arbitrary-looking division into five categories was adopted because of the very different positions these persons occupy along the continuum from basic research to application on this issue of children as designers/planners. Most of these people truly span more than one category. However, due to space limitations, I have chosen to list them under the category to which I believe they have contributed most at the present

time. Because so little has been published, this list is undoubtedly not comprehensive. Very little research has been done on the subject of the first category, children's spontaneous design activities, but it is a logical starting point to this workshop. The second category is constituted of those persons who have attempted to develop methods and materials to encourage children in the development of their design ideas. The emphasis has been educational. The third category, children's participation in the planning process, emphasizes approaches with more direct applicability to the planning process. The fourth includes just a partial listing of those who have developed methods for evaluating children's environmental design and planning preferences. Finally, the fifth category lists one or two of the gallant North American brigade who have attempted to develop Adventure Playgrounds. This movement recognizes that children's desires to transform the environment should be a central concept in the planning of children's environments.

There will be an opportunity to encounter the particular experiences and approaches of the workshop participants, as well as of those individuals who cannot be present, via film, slide and video presentations during the two evenings preceeding the workshop. Thus, the session will be free to devote itself entirely to the cross-fertilization and mutual growth of these approaches through discussion.

* confirmed participants at press time

(1) CHILDREN'S FREE BUILDING ACTIVITIES

Jean Boris and Genevieve Hirschler, Paris, France.
*Roger Hart, Environmental Psychology Program, City University of New York Graduate Center.
Jose Muntanola-Thornberg, University of California, Berkeley.
Charles Zerner, School of Architecture, University of Oregon.

(2) METHODS FOR REVEALING AND ENCOURAGING CHILDREN'S DESIGN ABILITIES

Lowery Burgess, Center for Advanced Visual Studies, Massachusetts Institute of Technology.
Yona Friedman, Paris, France.
Doreen Nelson, Los Angeles, California.
*Deborah Snow, Hoboken, New Jersey.
*Don Wall, School of Architecture, New Jersey Institute of Technology.
Richard Wurman, Group for Environmental Education, Philadelphia, Pennsylvania.

(3) <u>WORKING WITH CHILDREN AND COMMUNITIES IN THE PLANNING PROCESS</u>

Stephen Carr and Jim Zion, "Arrowstreet, Inc.," Cambridge, Massachusetts.
Dr. Stephen Cohen, Department of Psychology, University of Vermont.
Jerome Durlak, Urban Studies Program, York University, Toronto, Canada.
*Mark Francis and Raymond Lorenzo, Cambridge, Massachusetts.
*Stanley King, Vancouver, B.C., Canada.
*Florence Ladd and Elaine Ostroff, Graduate School of Design, Harvard University.
*Robin Moore, Department of Landscape Architecture, University of California, Berkeley.
Kevin Lynch, Department of City Planning, Massachusetts Institute of Technology, Cambridge, Massachusetts.
*Simon Nicholson, The Open University, England.
*Cornelia Oberlander, Vancouver, B.C., Canada.
John and Lorraine Van Dusen, Toronto, Canada.
*Leanne G. Rivlin, *Marilyn Rothenberg and Fred Wheeler, Environmental Psychology Program, City University of New York Graduate Center.

(4) <u>METHODS FOR EVALUATING CHILDREN'S ENVIRONMENTAL DESIGN AND PLANNING PREFERENCES</u>

*John C. Baird and Jill N. Nagy, Department of Psychology, Dartmouth College, Hanover, N.H.
*Sidney Brower and Penny Williamson, Baltimore City Planning Department.

(5) <u>ADVENTURE PLAYGROUNDS: THE STATE OF THE ART IN NORTH AMERICA</u>

<u>In Canada</u>

*Poly Hill, Director, Children's Environmental Advisory Service, Central Mortgage and Housing Corporation, Ottawa, Canada.
*Bill Rock, Department of Landscape Architecture, University of Toronto, Canada.

<u>In the United States</u>

Paul Hogan, Playground Clearing House Philadelphia, Pennsylvania.

*Robin Moore, Department of Landscape Architecture, University of California, Berkeley.

A WORKSHOP: THE USE OF FILMS FOR ENVIRONMENTAL EDUCATION AND RESEARCH

Rob Hollister
Assistant Professor

Department of Urban Studies and Planning
Massachusetts Institute of Technology
Cambridge, Massachusetts 02139

Alcira Kreimer
Assistant Professor

Department of Urban Studies and Planning and
Department of Architecture
Massachusetts Institute of Technology
Cambridge, Massachusetts 02139

Documentary and feature films are currently being used for a variety of purposes in environmental education and research. However, there are enormous film resources which are almost unused--what is probably one of the most complete reservoirs of knowledge, experience, and images concerning the environment of this century lies untapped. How can we improve our access to, and use of, documentary and feature films for environmental education and research? What are the obstacles to more effective use of these resources (costs, copyrights, lack of systematic information, etc.)? How can these obstacles be overcome?

The goal of this workshop is to allow persons active in this area to exchange their experience and ideas and to jointly address a series of issues dealing with improving the use of films. The workshop will explore the following topics:

1. The use of films for teaching environmental design and related courses.

2. The use of films in environmental research.

3. The use of films as simulation media in planning and design processes.

We urge participants to bring films that are examples of their own work or films they use in their practice. In addition to the two sessions devoted to the discussion of these topics, separate sessions for screening films will be scheduled.

Rob Hollister
Assistant Professor

Department of Urban Studies and Planning
Massachusetts Institute of Technology
Cambridge, Massachusetts 02139

Rob Hollister is director of the undergraduate Urban Studies Program at the M.I.T. Department of Urban Studies and Planning. In addition to working with films, he teaches and studies fiction about cities and is interested in how various media convey and popularize urban images and attitudes. He has a B.A. from Antioch College, an M.C.P. from the Harvard Graduate School of Design, and a Ph.D. from M.I.T.

Alcira Kreimer
Assistant Professor

Department of Urban Studies and Planning and
Department of Architecture
Massachusetts Institute of Technology
Cambridge, Massachusetts 02139

Alcira Kreimer is currently teaching in the Environmental Design Group at M.I.T. She teaches and has done research on environmental communication and in the uses of media for environmental education. She is interested in the evolution of human consciousness of the city. She is an architect (School of Architecture and Planning, University of Buenos Aires) and is finishing her Ph.D. in Environmental Planning, University of California at Berkeley. She taught at Stanford University, Program on Urban Studies.

FANTASY AND PHYSICAL FORM

Convener:
Joseph B. Juhasz

College of Environmental Design
University of Colorado
Boulder, Colorado 80309 USA

Participants:
Roland Fischer
Maryland Psychiatric Research Center
Baltimore, Maryland USA

Stephen Friedman
Psychology Department
Montclair State College
Upper Montclair, New Jersey 07043 USA

John Fritz
Board of Studies in Anthropology
Fellow of College Five
University of California
Santa Cruz, California 95064 USA

Phillip Winter
Department of Fine Arts
Montclair State College
Upper Montclair, New Jersey 07043 USA

ABSTRACT

The purpose of this workshop is to clarify issues
regarding fantasy and physical form from the
theoretical and practical viewpoint. The physical environment stimulates fantasy on the one
side and is a target for it on the other. Specifically, the natural environment is the point
of origin of the transformations which yield the
made forms. The principal issue confronting us
is to relate, compare, and contrast natural with
made forms. This process of relating can then
be the source of inferences about the intermediary
between the natural and made forms: fantasy.

In attempting to relate fantasy and physical
form, mind is then seen as an intermediary, a
"kitchen" between the order of natural objects
and made forms. The natural objects are the
"raw food" while the made forms are "edible"
as objects of admiration or utilitarian use, or
both.

It is rare to encounter what is truly needed to
account for the facts: a theory of fantasy that
encompasses both the paradoxicating and unequivo-
cating tendencies of mind. In our theoretical
efforts we shall address ourselves, from our
various disciplines to the question of the structure, functions, and possible form of such a
theory of mind and fantasy.

Aesthetic tendencies of built form similarly
strive for hegemony either for a built environment that is redundant and immediately knowable
or an environment that is complex, contradictory,
and uncertainty increasing. Should we build
signposts (a knowable environment) or labyrinths
(mysterious pregnant meaningful space)? Theories of fantasy that allow for the complicating
as well as simplifying tendency of mind will see
the need for both kinds of built form. In our
efforts to speak in practical terms we shall try
to begin to discuss the question of the relative
utilities of functionalist and symbolist form
according to place, time, and purpose. At least
we can begin to ask the much postponed question
about the role of symbolist and functionalist
(romantic or classicist) form in regard to the
courses of living: which is suited for main
dish and which for desert, in order to create
the greatest harmony between ourselves and our
surroundings (natural and made).

The current open dissatisfaction with the aesthetic sterility of much of contemporary design
parallels the rediscovery of imagining in its
many names in contemporary psychology. From an
exclusive concern with functionalism in architecture and design and with learning and problem
solving in psychology, we are progressing to an
appreciation of a need for an understanding and
acceptance of ourselves as the complete beings
that we are, and of an environment that accepts
our chaotic as well as our rationalist longings.

Roland Fischer, a cartographer of inner space,
has done considerable work in psychopharmacology
particularly the relation between eating various
substances and levels of vision (hallucination).
He has recently developed an interest in relating
inner and outer cartography.

Stephen Friedman brings to the discussion a background in cognitive psychology and its relation
to community psychology, with a particular interest in knowable environments.

John Fritz is an archeologist who has done extensive research in the Southwest particularly
on prehistoric Kivas. His interest is in external architectural form and ceremonialism; particularly highly structured ceremonial/architec-
tural form.

Phillip Winter is an artist who has designed
play environments for children using available
materials. He is interested in fueling the
fantasies of others as well as the externaliza-
tion of his own dreams.

Joseph Juhasz, the convener, teaches societal
science and design studio in a College of Environmental Design, University of Colorado. He
has done research in the psychology of imagining
with particular reference to the generating of
physical forms that are inaccessible to linguis-
tic coding. He is currently at work on a project
relating fantasy and physical form.

NOBODY WANTS TO LIVE NEXT TO A GAS STATION

Environmental Characteristics Planning

Jacob Kaminsky

Regional Planning Council
701 St. Paul Street
Baltimore, Maryland 21202

Behavior and attitude are closely linked with knowledge and experience. The public's negative attitude towards nonresidential uses and higher density residential development grows out of its experience with the existing quality of such uses. Despite the fact gas stations, shopping centers, etc., are functional, people prefer to see such uses separated as much as possible from their communities. More and more community associations are opposing certain uses from being built in their communities; proposals by developers and planners are constantly being fought by citizens. The reason for such dissatisfaction is understandable. Current development has been and is still occuring on the basis of use segregation, which results in a melange of character types. There is usually little compatibility between residential and commercial use. It is due to this incompatibility that people continue to hold on to their negative attitude towards the integration of commercial uses with their communities. This is also a reflection of dissatisfaction with the existing development character of higher intensity uses.

In order to improve the quality of overall development and change people's attitude towards diversified land use in their communities, the development character of these various uses must change to ensure compatibility with the community character. There are a few examples, in which the development of nonresidential uses is compatible with the adjacent residential character.

The proposal which will be discussed during the session is that planning practices change from a use segregation system to a development characteristics type system.

Communities or areas would be divided into districts, with each district having a designated Development Character Type. Each Development Character Type would have its own set of development standards to insure the compatibility of development among the different uses.

To set up standards for a development character type requires an understanding of the factors which define character and of the development of measurements which quantify character. This understanding of measuring and quantifying is an important key to the concept of development characteristics types.

Change in behavior and attitude requires change in experience. If we continue to develop under the existing concepts of land use segregation we will not provide the required modifications needed to overcome the public's dissatisfaction with the environment of higher intensity and nonresidential uses. It is important to educate the public (citizens and developers) as to how to evaluate development character. This will enable concerned citizen groups to intelligently evaluate development proposals concerning their communities.

For such a change to occur, however, is ultimately up to the willingness and ability of urban designers and planners to change their perceptions and practices.

The session on Environmental Characteristics Planning will be divided into two sections:

1.) Presentation with slides
The main concepts of the Development Characteristics Type system will be discussed. This presentation will be illustrated with slides.

2.) Discussion
A group discussion concerning the concepts and applications of Development Characteristics Type planning will follow the presentation.

CHILDREN'S - ENVIRONMENTS EVALUATION - RESEARCH:
THE STATE OF THE ART AND - WHERE DO WE GO FROM
HERE?

Clare Cooper Marcus

University of California, Berkeley

Leanne Rivlin

City University of New York

ABSTRACT

The time is right for a pause in the on-rush of
research and anlaysis, to consider what has been
done in the field of children's environment
research, to what extent research-findings have
been translated into policy and what gaps exist
in this research.

The impetus for this workshop was an open
discussion session at Childhood City, EDRA 5
(Milwaukee, 1974) in which we debated the "state
of the art" in children's environment research.
As an "assignment" to complete in the following
year, Clare Cooper Marcus and Nanine Clay
undertook to survey Childhood City participants
as to their views on current research gaps,
reasons for the lack of effect of existing
research on policy and decision-making, etc.
About 20% of the mailed questionnaires were
returned, and the responses were summarized and
distributed at EDRA 6 (Lawrence Kansas, 1975).

In an attempt to further this important area of
discussion, Clare Cooper Marcus and Robin Moore
co-authored a working paper entitled "Children's-
Environment Evaluation-Research: 1955-75", an
abridged version of which appeared in the
Spring 1976 issue of the Journal of Architectural
Education edited by Ellen Perry Berkeley. Since
this paper only attempted to cover outdoor
environments (both natural and man-made), a group
of researchers at City University of New York
(Environmental Psychology Program) was invited
to prepare a similar working paper covering
indoor environments used largely or exclusively
by children. This paper, entitled "Evaluations
of Built-Environments for Children: 1955-75" is
co-authored by Leanne Rivlin, Maxine Wolfe,
Marion Beyda Golan, Betty Mackintosh, and
Marilyn Rothenberg.

A third paper prompted by the current debate on
research findings and applicability is one by
Roger Hart, who in his on-going naturalistic
research on children's use of the total landscape in Wilmington, Vermont, has pioneered an
approach totally opposite to earlier controlled,
laboratory experiments. His paper entitled
"Prospectus for the Ecological Investigation of
Children's Use of the Outdoor Environment" will
also be discussed at this workshop session.

The purposes of the workshop are four-fold. First,
to present a summary of major work to date in
evaluating children's environments. Second, to
present an opportunity for panelists and audience
seriously to debate the question - why are the
results of child-environment research often
ignored by public officials and designers? Third,
to discuss ways in which we can facilitate the
communication and implementation of research
findings so as to ultimately improve the quality
of children's environments. And fourth, to
discuss what gaps currently exist in children's-
environment evaluation-research.

The format for the workshop will be as follows:

1. Major events in children's-environment
research and significant gaps in knowledge.
Leanne Rivlin: Built Environments
Clare Cooper Marcus: Outdoor Environments
Roger Hart: An Ecological Approach

2. Why are the results of children's-environ-
ment-research often ignored by public officials
and designers? Open discussion between Roger
Hart, Clare Cooper Marcus, Robin Moore, Ann-Marie
Pollowy, Leanne Rivlin and participants.

3. In what ways can we facilitate the communication and implementations of research findings so
as to ultimately improve the quality of children's
environments? Continuation of open discussion
between panelists and participants.

Our intent is to summarize and circulate widely
the results of this workshop as a concerted
effort by concerned children's environment
researchers to really improve the quality of
environments used by children. We are not
content merely to sit in our Ivory Towers
computing statistics! We have a responsibility
to the coming generation of children...we intend
to make good that responsibility.

USER-ORIENTED PROGRAMMING OF FACILITIES:

WORKSHOP PROSPECTUS

Wolfgang F.E. Preiser
Visiting Associate Research Professor
Department of Architecture
University of Illinois
Urbana, Illinois 61801

1. INTRODUCTION

Institutions, government, and large corporations control an ever increasing share of building activity, resulting in communication problems between clients, designers and users and frequent misinterpretations of user requirements. Buildings are assumed to serve established and well-known functions and activities. The truth is that the changing environmental and technological conditions as well as growing organizational units require innovative communication devices and programming process facilitators in order to improve the quality and habitability of designed environments. The emerging new professional consulting role of the functional programmer and process facilitator will be the focal point of the workshop discussions which will relate to the process, methods, concepts and experiences of programming user-oriented facilities, based upon data from man-environment research.

2. PURPOSE AND STRUCTURE

The purpose of this workshop is to provide a selective overview of current, user-oriented programming methods within the field of environmental design. Further, to describe procedures and information content of innovative approaches used by leading programming experts in the private and institutional sectors. The focus will be on increased livability or habitability of environments from the user's point of view. Emphasis in presentations will be on three aspects: (1) Description of the programming process, including establishment and differentiation of goals and objectives of user groups and/or organizations, resolution of conflicts and analysis of context variables; (2) Description of the human requirement content of programming through the presentation of a case study involving major input of user-related information. Categories of issues to be included may be addressed at three levels of human requirements in facilities (environments):

   a. Health and safety requirements:
       Preventing fire, disease,
       vandalism, accidents, etc.

   b. Functional use requirements:
       Providing conditions conducive
       to the performance of a job,
       for the proper functioning of
       living environments, including
       public places, etc.

   c. Psychological comfort and
       satisfaction requirements:
       Providing conditions conducive
       to aspects like sensory stimu-
       lation, territorial integrity,
       speech and visual privacy,
       proximity to valued resources,
       status, expression of indivi-
       duality, etc.

3. SYNTHESIS AND EVALUATION

The presented case studies will be analyzed in terms of various criteria of "success." Some of the following relevant questions in this context may be asked. Did a more satisfactory solution (from the user's point of view) result from the programming effort with particular emphasis on human requirements? Did the input of human requirement information (and perhaps social science consultants) add to the professional satisfaction and expertise of those involved in the programming effort? What was the estimated added cost in time and dollars associated with programming for human requirements?

4. CONTENT AND FORMAT

Following the structure outlined above, topics of presentations will vary with the programming requirements and complexity of the building type each author has chosen for his case study. Such case studies are envisioned to cover programming for various scales of environments, from downtown redevelopment to large institutional settings, health care facilities, offices, etc.

This workshop is intended to demonstrate the applicability of man-environment concepts and research results to programming of facilities. Some of the invited contributors are programming consultants or specialists, while others are academically or research oriented. The workshop is scheduled to last five hours, broken up into two sessions. During the morning session four 30-minute presentations of programming methodology and case study applications will be made, followed by a panel discussion. The same procedure will be followed in the afternoon session which will have 3-4 scheduled presentations. Preferred attendance at the workshop sessions is no more than 30 participants who can break up into discussion groups after the formal illustrated presentations.

Dependent upon participant interest, it is expected that the workshop will stay in session beyond the five officially scheduled hours. The list of workshop contributors was not finalized at press time.

DESIGNING RESEARCH FOR ENVIRONMENTAL CHANGE IN

CHILDREN'S SETTINGS

Workshop Leaders
Marilyn Rothenberg - Moderator
Leanne Rivlin
Penny Williamson
Linda LeResche
Robert J. Boese
Gary Moore

This workshop provides the opportunity to
discuss research in which the application of
findings was an important initial consideration. The major participants have worked in a
variety of settings--playgrounds, hospitals
and schools and have used varied approaches
with differing emphasis on the research and
design components. In addition, a diversity
of research methods have been used including
observation, interview, video-tape and workshop. What unites these diverse approaches is
the basic assumption that behavior is best
understood when considered in light of the
physical and programmatic contexts of specific
settings.

The workshop format was chosen to enable the
participants to address a number of issues
relevant to bridging the applicability gap
through a discussion of their current research.
The topics to be discussed will consider the
process as an important aspect of the
researcher's intentions and findings. Among
the questions to be addressed are:

   How and why did you enter the specific
   setting?

   What were your goals in terms of research
   and applicability?

   To what extent did these goals overlap?
   conflict?

   How did you attempt to meet your goals?

   How did you perceive the goals of the
   people, both children and adults, using
   the setting?

   How did the research design consider the
   nature of the relationship between
   researchers and the users of the setting?
   Was the process of benefit to the research?
   To the user?

   What was the nature of the findings? Were
   they useful within the setting? Can they
   be generalized to other settings?

   How can you best communicate your findings?

   How well were your goals met? How would
   you design future research? What parts
   of the process would you include or omit?

Towards Better <u>Person</u>-Environment Relations: The Changing <u>Relationships</u> of Women and Men to the Environment.

This group of three concurrent, small workshops grows out of the enthusiastic interest in and large response to the <u>EDRA</u> VI workshop on Women and the Environment. Last year over sixty people crammed into the workshop room full of questions about sex roles and environmental planning ranging from the desire to organize designers to address the needs of changing sex-role definitions and duties to concerns about the development of sex stereotyping in children's interactions with their environments. The large size of the group and the heterogeneity of their interests made the actual exchange of ideas difficult. Some twenty of the heartier participants reconvened in the evening to continue the discussion and make plans for ongoing communication.

Since last year, the network of people involved in this topic has expanded: books and articles have been written; architectual exhibits have been put together; conferences have been held and university courses have been taught. These three workshops described below are intended to raise basic questions in each area, suggest answers and methods of proceeding that those leading the workshops have been evolving and, most of all, provide a forum for exchange among designers and researchers. In each session, the workshop leaders will give brief introductory overviews of issues and problems in their area, then the floor will be opened to discussion. One page descriptions from other participants of their research and other projects are being solicited and will be available in each workshop. Brief descriptions of each workshop are given below:

<u>Changing Sex-Roles and Residential Environments</u>
Moderator: Susan Saegert

The major topics to be considered in this workshop revolve around the relationships among the physical forms of residential environments, sex-role stereotyping of activities and self-definition, and personal identity.

Gwendolyn Wright, an architect from the University of California at Berkeley, will begin by giving an historical overview of the interrelations between changes in domestic architecture and the technology of homemaking and the definitions of women's roles, focusing primarily on American developments. Drawing on historical sources, she will trace the development of the application of scientific management to domestic duties and its architectural and technological concomitants as well as its effects on women's activities and identities, particularly as manifested in obsessive standards of cleanliness and concern with consuming accompanied by actual increases in the time devoted maintenance chores. Issues will be raised concerning current design practices and ideas

which perpetuate division of labor by sex. The architecture of communes in which such division has been avoided will be briefly described, using examples covering a time span from 1790 to 1975.

Susan Saegert and Carol Sullivan, of the Environmental Psychology Program of the City University of New York Graduate Center will describe an ongoing research project that addresses the relationships among (a) sex-role definitions and divisions of activity, (b) the functional and symbolic qualities of the home and neighborhood and (c) the values and self-definitions of women and men in these various settings. Respondents, all professional and relatively well-educated, are drawn from two geographic areas: an urban residential area and a suburban one. The first phase of the study involves the administration of a questionnaire survey on the three topics described above to 240 households in each location. Data are being analyzed to suggest general patterns of residential characteristics and lifestyle and to serve as a basis for selecting participants in an in-depth interview study with a smaller group of couples. Three groups of households will be selected in each area: couples classified as traditional in sex-role definition, those categorized as ambivalent and those considered non-traditional. The conceptual framework of the study will be described, preliminary data analysis will be presented and implications for the design of residential environments and the symbolic and functional place of the home in people's lives will be discussed. Problems of methodology and ethical responsibility in such work can also be discussed, if interest and time permit.

Judy Rodin, Professor of Psychology at Yale University, will consider the effects on female undergraduates residing in dormitories built explicitly for males, and more generally, the problems women encounter living in a male-defined context. Her discussion will be based both on her experiences teaching women at Yale and on her ongoing research. Issues of environmental segregation of men and women (i.e., separate dorms, separate colleges etc.,) will be discussed in light of their possible negative and positive effects and the planning implications for truly unsegregated environments.

After discussion of the specific remarks of each speaker, Susan Saegert will summarize the common points made by the various workshop leaders and raise questions for discussion.

<u>Women as Creators of Environments</u>
Moderator: Susan Niculescu

The purpose of this workshop will be to discuss both the contributions and problems of women designers and the needs and contributions of non-professional women in creating environments that really facilitate women and men's changing lives.

Susan Niculescu will introduce the workshop leaders. As an architect and research associate in the Environmental Psychology Program of the City University of New York Graduate Center, she will discuss the problems and contribution of women architects, drawing on a recent research report from a women's task force within the A.I.A. She will briefly describe the contributions and plights of women architects which are increasingly coming to light (e.g., the 1975 A.I.A. exhibition of the work of women architects and the Brooklyn Museum show on Women and Architecture by Susan Torre and Associates planned for Spring, 1976). These topics will be related to the stereotype of women's roles and needs on which many design decisions are based and possible alternatives to this situation.

Gerda Wekerle, an urban sociologist, and Rebecca Peterson, an environmental psychologist, both on the faculty of Environmental Studies at York University, will provide discussion of a broad range of issues related to the ways women's needs are not being met by current environmental options. Various aspects of the social and physical context in which women have created special environments to respond to their changing roles will be discussed; these environments include crisis centers, housing for sole-support mothers, day care centers and women's cultural centers. Problems of transportation and restrictive territorial norms in urban environments will be raised also. Speculations about the design and planning implications of these issues will be set forth for group discussion.

Sharon Davidoff, of the Design and Environmental Analysis Program at Cornell University, will relate the issues that have been raised to participatory design as a strategy for human liberation. She will discuss (1) types of participatory design techniques, (2) why women should be interested in participatory design, (3) participatory design and its implications for design as a "profession" and environmental psychology as a "profession" and (4) the use and misuse of power in a participatory design process.

Developmental Sex Differences in Learning Environments

Moderators: Marilyn Rothenberg, an environmental psychologist, and Roger Hart, a geographer, both with the Environmental Psychology Program of the City University of New York Graduate Center.

Attempts to equalize educational opportunities for girls and boys have focused on the rights to attend school, take similar courses and go on to higher education. The direction to equalize course content and skill opportunities are obviously necessary, but important questions remain as to whether skill competence is sufficient to enable constructive action.

What we hope to do in this workshop is to focus on a range of these early environments to discuss child/environment interactions with a view towards understanding how physical and social interactions may lead to very different perceptions and behavior for girls and boys. Starting with some recent empirical work in a number of areas and discussing related personal experiences from childhood, and as adults providing for children will enable consideration of the differences in cultural expectations for girls and boys.

Important differences have been recorded in opportunities afforded children on the large-scale environment. Cross cultural studies have shown that home range, that is the distance traveled from home are generally greater for boys than girls (Munroe & Munroe, 1971; Nerlove, et al., 1971; Saegert & Hart, in press). Not only does the opportunity to travel and explore the landscape enable a view of the world and oneself through a variety of perspectives, but the opportunity for a range of social and environmental experiences are enhanced. It has also been shown that behaviors which frequently characterize the sexes are related to particular contexts, for example, nurturant behavior is associated with social opportunities in the home (Ember, 1973; Whiting & Whiting, 1975).

On the micro-indoor scale also, environmental provisions and social opportunities differentiate between the sexes. An index of parents' behavior has been demonstrated in the decoration and equipping of boys' and girls' bedrooms (Rheingold & Cook, 1975). Preschool boys were provided with more vehicles, educational-art materials, sports equipment, depots and machines, whereas preschool girls were provided with more dolls and domestic toys. Animal motifs were more likely in boys' rooms and floral motifs, fringes and lace in girls' rooms.

In institutional settings such as preschools and elementary schools similar differences have been found. It has been repeatedly documented and it is no surprise to find that boys play more with transportation toys and blocks, girls more with dolls.

Although it is likely that these experiences lead to diverse skills, some hypothesized to be important to cognitive ability, such as spatial ability relating to block building, the emphasis in the workshop will be on the spatial and social opportunities that accompany these actions. That is, boys' activities are generally associated with more space, greater freedom of movement, and more peer and less adult interaction that girls' activities.

To be considered is how these experiences lead to constraints on the behaviors and expectations of each of us and the possible means by which the pervasiveness of these patterns can be influenced.

ARCHITECTURAL JOURNALISM AND EDRA RESEARCH
(Convener: Nancy Starnes
             National Bureau of Standards
             Architectural Research Section
             Washington, D.C. 20234
             (301-921-3595

In line with the conference's applied research
theme, architectural journalists, who are well-
established in their field, will attend EDRA
sessions on May 25, 26, and 27 to examine or
"cover" EDRA research from the point of view of
the media. On Friday, May 28, they will meet
in a panel discussion with several EDRA members.
A participating journalist, Forrest Wilson,
ex-editor of Progressive Architecture and
presently Dean of Catholic University's
Architectural and Planning Department, described
the purpose of the panel as follows:

Part of applicability is being published before
the right audience. This does not appear to be
the case for the majority of EDRA members.
Architectural journalists can give immediate
feedback to EDRA members and help them express
themselves. "We will try to get a mutual
formulation of objectives out of the discussion,"
Dean Wilson said, expecting some of the questions
touched on would be: Is it newsworthy? If not,
why not? Does the fault lie with the reporting
of journalists, the nature of the material, or
the way researchers present their findings?
Dean Wilson said journalists believe it would
be a mistake on researchers' part not to seek
to put their research into journalistic form
since "it is the only means they have of
getting their material out and before the
public, Congress, the building community, and
consumer groups."

The two groups--journalists and EDRA researchers--
will also explore such questions as to what
ends a broader audience; if EDRA seeks a wider
audience will members be encouraged to
"popularize" their research to its detriment.
The panel, conceived of as a two-way street
(not only EDRA members gathering information
from the media), will also serve to introduce
journalists to the widening scope of the EDRA
social science research. Comment is also
expected to touch on such special EDRA communication problems as the language barriers
involved in interdisciplinary research.

CROWDING RESEARCH AS A BASIS FOR HIGH-DENSITY

DESIGN

Chairperson: Daniel Stokols

Program in Social Ecology
University of California, Irvine
Irvine, California 92717

1. OVERVIEW

This session will consider implications of
recent research on crowding for the design of
high-density environments. The design relevance
of crowding research is likely to be reflected
in the form of two major contributions: (1) the
delineation of basic behavioral principles and
psychological processes which mediate the relationship between high physical density, perceived
crowding, and stress; an understanding of these
principles and processes should suggest a set of
general architectural strategies for minimizing
density-related problems (e.g., excessive stimulation, behavioral constraint, resource scarci-
ties) within a variety of settings; and (2) the
development of situation-specific analyses which
offer a basis for matching the unique needs and
activities of different user groups with the
functional and physical attributes of particular
settings (e.g., residential, transportation, work,
and recreational environments); such analyses
should suggest differential design strategies for
avoiding crowding stress depending upon the
situational context in which high density occurs.

All of the papers in this session review current
theoretical perspectives on crowding and critically
assess the potential relevance of research in this
area to the development of design criteria. The
first two papers explore the implications of general behavioral concepts, such as personal control,
stimulus overload, personal space, and territoriality, for the design of high-density settings.
The remaining papers examine a variety of methodologies for assessing the impact of crowding in
both micro- and macro-environments, and offer
theoretical frameworks for predicting the differential effects of crowding in relation to the
functional dimensions of environments. Finally,
the presentations by three environmental designers
explore "implicit theories" and assumptions about
density and behavior from the perspective of the
practitioner, and assess the potential utility
of behavioral research to the design process in
light of economic and political constraints,
as well as the difficulties involved in translating psychological theories into design criteria.

2. PARTICIPANTS

Density, Personal Control, and Design

Drury R. Sherrod and Sheldon Cohen
Department of Psychology
University of Oregon
Eugene, Oregon 97403

Theorists have observed that density can restrict
freedom of choice, create stimulus overload, and
negatively affect human performance and social
behavior. Several lines of research have shown
that a perception of personal control can ameliorate the negative effects of restricted freedom
and stimulus overload. Such perceptions of personal control over density may be enhanced through
the design process. A number of suggested design
techniques are considered in light of theory and
research on personal control.

Design Implications of Personal Space Research

Gary W. Evans
Program in Social Ecology
University of California, Irvine
Irvine, California 92717

The theoretical linkages between crowding and
personal space are considered and recent research
in these areas is reviewed. The relevance of
this theoretical and empirical work to the
development of design criteria is discussed.

Amelioration of Crowding Through Design Decisions

Allen Schiffenbauer
Department of Psychology
Virginia Polytechnic Institute and State
University
Blacksburg, Virginia 24061

Several case studies involving the construction
of high-density housing are examined to illustrate the various ways in which psychological
analyses and behavioral data might be utilized
in the design process to reduce crowding stress
among setting occupants.

An Applied Research Perspective on Crowding

Yakov M. Epstein, John Aiello, and Robert Karlin
Department of Psychology
University College
Rutgers University
New Brunswick, New Jersey 08903

An analysis of crowding and its effects on users
in different types of environments is presented.
This analysis is utilized as a basis for developing design strategies to alleviate crowding
in residential, transportation, work, and
recreational settings.

Determinants of Perceived Crowding and Pleasantness in Public Settings

Lou McClelland and Nathan Auslander
Department of Psychology
University of Colorado
Boulder, Colorado 80302

68 subjects viewed 144 slides of public settings
(restaurants, stores, sports events, airports,
libraries, etc.) in the Denver area, and rated
each slide on crowdedness and pleasantness.
The slides varied on several dimensions thought
to be important in determining perceptions of
crowding: number of people, amount of space,
lighting, type of activity, social factors, and
others. These dimensions were used to predict
the crowding and pleasantness ratings in stepwise multiple regression. Scenes are rated
as more crowded if they picture more people in
less space with smaller interpersonal distances,
if the scene is more complex and disorderly
with fewer visual escapes, and if the people
are working rather than playing. The correlation between crowding and pleasantness is
negative except for settings in which the
presence and observation of others is an integral
part of the activity (a professional basketball
game, for example).

Urban Crowding: Theoretical Approaches And Implications for Design

Donald E. Schmidt
Department of Psychology
University of Washington
Seattle, Washington 98195

The results of a field study conducted in a
two-community area of Southern California are
reported in an attempt to test the primary
theoretical propositions that have been
advanced concerning the individual's perception
of crowding. Separate analyses were conducted
for the residential, neighborhood, and city
levels to determine what urban factors were
important and which overriding theoretical frameworks seemed most viable. The results indicated
that the conceptualization of crowding as a
condition related to reduced freedom and control
for the individual was the best general explanation. In addition, it was found that physical
density is important when it has a direct impact upon the individual, however, unimportant
as one moved to less immediate interation spheres
at the neighborhood and city levels.

Translating Psychological Research Into Design Criteria: The Practitioner's Perspective

Michael Brill
Buffalo Organization for Social and Technological
Innovation
812 Kenmore Avenue
Buffalo, New York 14216

Gerald Davis, President
TEAG - The Environmental Analysis Group
2001-2075 Comox St.
Vancouver, B.C., Canada
V6G 1S2

Edward Ostrander
Department of Design and Environmental Analysis
Martha Van Rensselaer Hall
Cornell University
Ithaca, New York 14853

GAME DEMONSTRATION WORKSHOP

Luis H. Summers

Department of Architectural Engineering
101 Engineering Unit "A"
The Pennsylvania State University
University Park, Pennsylvania 16802

ABSTRACT

This session will detail the state of the art in
operational games in land use planning, participatory design, social organization and behavior,
and the pretest of new behavioral ecology. The
first part of the session will present overviews
of each topic, the second part will present
simulated play of a prototypical game detailing
each of the four topics.

1. DESCRIPTION

This session has been designed for the individual
wishing to obtain a quick overview of the role of
operational gaming in environmental design and
research. Although economic, managerial, war and
elementary education gaming are highly developed
and rich fields, this session will not cover them
and will concentrate on those branches of gaming
concerned with some design aspect of the environment. Specifically this session will discuss and
illustrate the use of games for analysis, and
design in: land use planning (urban and regional),
participatory design (neighborhood), social
organization and behavior, and the pretest of new
behavioral ecology.

2. ORGANIZATION

The first part of this session will consist of
brief overview presentations on the use of gaming
in each of the above mentioned fields. At the
conclusion of this part participants will issue
resource material about each topic. The second
part of this session will consist of demonstrations
of prototypical games used in each of the fields.
Audience participants will select the topic they
are most interested in, and will proceed to meet
with individual gamesters for the remaining of
the session. Although game play is not possible
because of time limitations, the demonstration
workshops will present the audience with a
simulated play of one prototypical game. If the
audience and the gamesters are willing, they can
schedule time slots for actual game play.

3. SECTIONS AND PARTICIPANTS

3.1. Land Use Planning - Urban and Regional

Sidney Cohn

Division of Man Environment Relations
S-126 Human Development
The Pennsylvania State University
University Park, Pennsylvania 16802

Regional and urban games have proliferated
during the last fifteen years. The basic
structure of the many games in the field can be
traced to those initial games, POGE, CLUG, and
METROPOLIS. These games and their offshoots
METRO, APEX, CITY, RIVER BASIN, Urban Dynamics-
Urbandyne, New Town, Polis, etc. will be
discussed. A prototypical land-use planning
and economics game will be demonstrated at the
conclusion of this section.

3.2. Participatory Design-Neighborhood

Eugene Bazan

Division of Man Environment Relations
S-126 Human Development
The Pennsylvania State University
University Park, Pennsylvania 16802

In recent times a number of games have been used
in planning as a means of obtaining citizen
participation in the design of their environment.
Games such as TRUAX-HOUSING, Site Planning,
ARC-ARC, SIMU SCHOOL, U-DIG, INHABS, etc. have
been used in order to bring the user into the
decision process which shapes his environment.

The H-BURG PLAYGROUND DESIGN SIMULATION brings
together children, adults, professionals, school
officials, and politicians to work out issues in
the redesign of decrepit city playgrounds. This
simulation will be demonstrated as a prototype
for participatory design games.

3.3. Social Organization and Behavior

Luis H. Summers

Department of Architectural Engineering
101 Engineering Unit "A"
The Pennsylvania State University
University Park, Pennsylvania 16802

This section will discuss the context in which
these games are played and the description of
those games which have proven most successful.
Some of the games to be discussed are: Star
Power, SIMSOC, They Shoot Marbles Don't They,
The End of the Line, Bafa Bafa, Baldicer, etc.

BALDICER - a game about world hunger and
population growth will be demonstrated or played
during the second part of the session.

3.4. Use of Simulation to Pretest New Behavioral Ecology

Raymond Studer

Division of Man Environment Relations
S-126 Human Development
The Pennsylvania State University
University Park, Pennsylvania 16802

The game STIR (Simulation of the Total Inmate
Response) - which simulates both the behavioral
environment of a medium security prison, and the
social and economic environment that the paroled
convict faces outside the community - will be
demonstrated as a prototype of the use of games
to pretest social behavior.

PROGRAMMING AND ENVIRONMENTAL ANALYSIS IN
PRACTICE

Françoise Szigeti
2001 - 2075 Comox Street
Vancouver, B.C. Canada V6G 1S2

Jacqueline Vischer
3661 West 8th Avenue
Vancouver, B.C. Canada

Barry Herring
2631 Fernwood Road
Victoria, B.C. Canada V8T 3A1

1. FOCUS

How does this bridging function actually occur
in practice.

To what constraints is it subjected.

What are its accomplishments.

2. QUESTIONS TO BE RAISED

2.1 The Gap

Is the gap where we think it is, or is it somewhere else.

What are the alternate routes used in practice
to incorporate new demands and perceived needs.

2.2 Bridging

How to attack the problem on a particular project; how to decide where the emphasis should
be.

How to present what information, in what format, at what depth, at what time and to whom.

How does the process of sharing information
complement documentation and vice-versa.

What kinds of work and study can be specifically
defined as falling into the bridging function.

How does the bridging function happen when it
is:

- an independent function;

- subsummed into the design function

- a client in-house function.

2.3 Inter-professional relationships

How to deal with the blurring of traditional
professional boundaries.

How to use the project team approach to overcome limiting professional boundaries.

How to deal with the emergence of new roles
and tasks.

How to deal with potential role conflicts.

How to delineate responsibilities.

How to redefine project leadership, depending
on the client in-house capacities, the project
complexity, the design approach and the relationships between the professionals involved.

2.4 Skills, experience and knowledge

What basic knowledge and skills are required to
perform the bridging role successfully.

How to acquire the necessary multidisciplinary
background needed.

How to avoid specialization, without being
superficial.

How to acquire the necessary experience and
judgement.

3. WORKING METHOD FOR THE WORKSHOP

The conveneers have contacted resource persons
in the Vancouver area to act as catalysts. A
preparatory work session will be held in Vancouver prior to EDRA-7. This session will be
summarized by the conveneers. The summary will
be circulated to the resource persons for further response. A synthesis will then be prepared for distribution at EDRA-7.

PRODUCTION OF NEW MANPOWER IN ARCHITECTURAL/
ENVIRONMENTAL PSYCHOLOGY

Calvin W. Taylor, Session Chairman

Architectural Psychology Program
University of Utah
Salt Lake City, Utah 84112

Most of the graduate Architectural/Environmental
Psychology programs that have produced new manpower will have a representative to report on
the nature of their program. The program director's report may be supplemented by reports from
one or more of the graduates now working in the
field. The four main themes of the EDRA-7 conference will be kept in mind as the reports are
prepared. These themes are (1) research, methodology, and theory in environmental design research; (2) bridging the gap between design research and design itself; (3) applications to
design, architecture, and planning; and (4)
synthesis.

In particular the panelists will give some indications of the relations between the nature of
their program and the nature of the work into
which their graduates have become employed for
their careers. The issue is: what kinds of jobs
their graduates have moved into and to what degree have they been adequately prepared for such
jobs? On this last question they will comment
especially on three points. First, it would be
good to know what academic training they had
which was irrelevant and has proved to be of
little or no use -- or even handicapping to them.
Secondly, what training proved to be relevant,
including what was of most value. And thirdly,
what training they lacked or even sorely lacked
as they tried to learn to fill their new jobs
and function effectively therein. The latter
point could include any in-service training they
were given or that they greatly needed and what
experiences on the job were most valuable as
they learned to become more efficient in their
work.

A few other programs may be included. It is
also hoped that a listing of all such graduate
training programs now known to exist will be
presented, perhaps with brief descriptions or
handouts of some programs.

Current List of Participants

Donald Appleyard
Department of Landscape Architecture
University of California
Berkeley, California 94720

David Canter's representative
Environmental Psychology Program
University of Surrey
Guildford, Surrey, England GU2 5XH

Sidney Cohn, Director
Man-Environment Relations
College of Human Development
Pennsylvania State University
University Park, Pennsylvania 16802

George Rand
School of Architecture & Urban Planning
UCLA
Los Angeles, California 90024

Edward K. Sadalla
Department of Psychology
Arizona State University
Tempe, Arizona 85281

One or two other names and programs may be added
later.

Architectural Discussant

Robert G. Hershberger
Faculty of Environmental Design
College of Architecture
Arizona State University
Tempe, Arizona 85281

UWGB-MIT-PENN STATE-COLO: FOUR TEACHING PROGRAMS.

UWGB Environmental Design Program
(Dr. Per K. Johnsen)
University of Wisconsin-Green Bay
Green Bay, Wisconsin, 54302.

ABSTRACT

The workshop will consist of a student designed
presentation of four undergraduate programs in
Environmental Design. Each program will be
presented by its students who will outline the
program's intent, methods, and output in terms
of student work. The workshop will conclude
with a session to evaluate undergraduate Environmental Design teaching as presented.

This workshop focuses on the teaching of people/
environment relations and the design process.
Representatives of undergraduate Environmental
Design programs at UWGB, MIT, Penn State, and
Colorado will present a student designed workshop communicating the nature of their programs
and the manner in which each deals with the
theme of the conference, "Beyond the Applicability Gap". Each participating program will
present a half day workshop session. Each workshop session will consist of a description of
the program in terms of the following: 1) its
definition of Environmental Design and the
"philosophical underpinnings" of the program,
2) teaching methods used in the program, 3)
presentations of students' own work, and 4) an
open discussion of the program. Each of the
sessions in the workshop is the result of student response to a design problem statement
distributed to the participants in January of
this year. Thus, each workshop session is an
example of the design work in the participating
programs.

A fifth workshop session will be held early in
the evening of the second day. This final session will begin with four panel discussions
focusing on the critical evaluation of the
teaching programs presented and the development
of recommendations for each. Each panel will
be organized to include representatives from
each of the four participating programs. At
the close of the panel discussions, there will
be an informal meeting of Environmental Design
students to consider future participation in
EDRA meetings and to investigate the development
of a student organization within EDRA. The session will conclude with an informal social
sponsored by the UWGB Environmental Design
Program.

As an adjunct to the five sessions described,
students from programs not included in the workshop will be provided with the opportunity to
display and informally discuss their work.

APPLICATIONS OF DECISION THEORY TO ENVIRONMENTAL DESIGN

Session Convener: Dr. James A. Wise

Department of Architecture
Gould Hall JO-20
University of Washington
Seattle, Washington 98195

This workshop session involves participants in gaining experience with various decision theoretic methods especially applicable to design decision making.

The first part of the session is an illustrated introduction to the various ways in which certain techniques have been previously utilized. This includes a sampling of structuring via decision trees, representing and communicating risk and uncertainty, and the measurement of subjective utilities.

After this overview, participants will have the opportunity to engage in two extensive exercises using some recent theoretical models that show the most promise for handling complex design decisions. These are multi-attribute utility theory and hierarchical utility theory. Each of these relies on a different structuring or "breakdown" of the decision makers "world view", but each is capable of quantitatively representing subjective preferences and involving these with subjective uncertainty to direct decisions demanding complex considerations.

Multi-attribute utility theory (MAUT) models are a means of evaluating design alternatives with multiple value relevant characteristics. In these procedures, relevant dimensions of value are identified and rated in terms of their importance ratios. Then the location of each alternative on each dimension is measured, and utilities are calculated for each alternative by multiplicatively combining the normalized importance weights with the dimensional values. An aggregate utility is usually computed via a linear combination rule across the evaluated dimensions.

In the workshop, participants will use the MAUT procedure as members of a hypothetical architectural jury and will evaluate some prepared projects. The workshop discussion will compare the type of feedback information the MAUT procedure provides with that traditionally given in the jury process.

Hierarchical utility theory is similar to MAUT in that it reduces the complexity of an overall decision evaluation through an analytical process that subdivides the problem into manageable chunks. But it does so by focusing on the larger set of concrete outcomes that may accrue from a design decision, and then dividing this set into classes of similar outcomes. The classes are successively combined into higher order classes until a hierarchy results that is organized under a universal class that is the entire area of interest. Then importance ratings that are normalized to sum to 1.00 are attached to the constituents of each class at the various hierarchical levels. Finally, these evaluative measures may be multiplied down the "branches" of the hierarchy to generate utilities for each of the resultants. Subjective probabilities may also be assessed, and the subjective expected utilities across the bottom level classes may be computed for the various decision alternatives.

This procedure is particularly applicable when there are strong social or subjective elements to be considered, and the decision maker has difficulty in sorting out and keeping track of the complex value considerations.

At the workshop, participants will acquire practice in the construction of their own value hierarchies for some specially prepared problems, as well as learning some assessment techniques associated with the method.

SOCIAL IMPACT ASSESSMENT IN CROSS-CULTURAL

PERSPECTIVE

C. P. Wolf

Office of Technology Assessment
Congress of the United States
Washington, DC 20510

Within the past few years significant advances have been made in the social impact assessment of environmental modifications. Much less attention has been given to determining social impact on populations different from the core North American population, such as North American Indians and third world populations. In such situations, not only is the data base generally available in North America often lacking, but the human ecology, social organization and cultural values are often quite different. The purpose of this workshop is to bring together researchers with experience in social impact assessment in different cultures to compare models and methods which they have used successfully. The objective will be to identify problems confronting the assessor in a cross-cultural situation and alternative strategies for determining potential social impact, evaluating its human consequences, and mitigating adverse effects through culturally sensitive development planning and environmental design.

Generally speaking, then, the purpose of the workshop is to develop criteria and procedures for insuring the proper consideration of peoples and cultures in development planning. This is an abiding concern among anthropologists and other professionals; what is novel is the context in which such concerns may now be expressed. That context is a natural and logical extension of environmental impact assessment as mandated under the National Environmental Policy Act of 1969 (NEPA), with emphasis placed on the distinctively human environment. For much of the world, much of the time, that environment is a "built environment." Hence problems of urban rehousing, civic amenities, mass transportation and the like are of paramount concern. At the same time, these must be viewed in the larger contexts of rural depopulation, urban scatteration and resource scarcity--among many others--and those in turn as they impinge on natural habitats (e.g. the disruption of watersheds and wetlands, the destruction of natural ecological diversity through the practice of monocultures). Thus the workshop will focus on the set of cultural variables present in impact situations and their interrelations with other environmental, social and economic factors.

The "work" of the workshop will be devoted to the preparation of research proposals for investigating these relations in situations

where widespread impacts have occurred or are anticipated as a consequence of major engineering works. The Aswan High Dam is one conspicuous example, but many others spring quickly to mind: the Trans-Amazon highway, the Alaska pipeline, energy development in the Northern Great Plains, the Garrison Diversion, etc., etc. A first order of business then will be the identification of such widely impacted areas and an inventory of their cultural resources, previous adjustments and probable responses. In this process a number of leading questions arise:

o How ethnocentric is social impact assessment? How might it be adapted to specific cultural contexts?

o Is social impact assessment manipulative? What code of professional ethics should regulate its conduct?

o How is it possible to reconcile the very short deadlines for study completion typical of social impact assessment with the far more lengthy period of research normally involved in field studies?

o How viable are small-scale alternatives (e.g. "intermediate technology") to large-scale engineering approaches?

o How can the professional reward system be restructured so as to direct professional attention towards the performance and review of social impact assessments in cross-cultural settings?

o Who are the prospective users of social impact assessments and what are the contexts in which they may fruitfully apply its methods and results?

Since adequate preparation of research proposals entails a literature search of pertinent studies, part of the effort will be directed towards compiling and codifying a resource inventory of existing research in community development, applied anthropology and related fields. Multidisciplinary foci for structuring this search may be by geographic region (e.g. Great Plains), ecologic type (e.g. tropical rain forest), societal development (e.g. tribal), functional area (e.g. water resources development) or some others. A propositional inventory of research findings will be one product of this search. A review of appropriate methodologies for their verification will likewise be undertaken. Criteria for the preparation and review of research proposals, e.g. timeliness, will be formulated. The workshop should emerge with a research agenda covering major areas and impacts of large-scale engineering works, one that will lend itself to further refinements and lead directly to consideration by funding sources and early implementation in field studies. A summary position paper consolidating these proposals and discussions will be prepared for further review and updating.

PRIVACY: CURRENT THEORY AND RESEARCH

Maxine Wolfe, Chairperson

City University of New York Graduate School
Environmental Psychology Program
33 West 42nd Street
New York City, New York 10036

1. DESCRIPTION OF WORKSHOP

The goal of this workshop is to bring together
people who are interested in the topic of
privacy with the specific purpose of sharing
current research finding and discussing
theoretical, methodological and application
issues.

While there will be no formal papers read, the
first half of the session will involve the
informal presentation of some current research
and theory. The purpose of this part of the
workshop is to present specific research findings as a stimulus for further discussions.
Maxine Wolfe (City University of New York)
will present data from a study of the development of concepts of privacy, focussing on the
physical and social descriptors of "private
places"; the extent to which place references
occur in descriptions of other aspects of
privacy, i.e. invasions of privacy; descriptions of private times; and differences in
place references as a function of age and
environmental experiences (number of rooms in
house, number of occupants per room).
Francine Justa and Marian Beyda Golan (City
University of New York) will describe research
on privacy in office settings, focussing on
the role of expectations in experiences of
privacy, role-definitions and privacy needs,
privacy as a "with-others" situation, and
physical vs. social environmental means of
achieving privacy. Charles Holahan (University
of Texas) will discuss research findings on
invasion of privacy and self disclosure in an
interview situation, focussing on the role of
physical (spatial dividers) and interpersonal
(intensity of interaction) variables in
creating a sense of privacy and intimacy.
Marian Beyda Golan and Maxine Wolfe (City
University of New York) will describe a study
of privacy in a children's psychiatric
facility which focuses on ways in which a
given socio/physical context can affect
concepts of privacy.

The second half of the session will be devoted
entirely to an open discussion of methodological and theoretical issues, applications and
future areas of research.

2. WORKSHOP PARTICIPANTS

We invite all interested people to come and
participate in the workshop discussion. If you
are currently doing research on the topic of
privacy and have some specific data to report,
please contact me and we can arrange time for
it during the session. So far, four individuals who are currently doing research on the
topic of privacy will give informal presentations during the first half of the session.
They are:

Maxine Wolfe
Environmental Psychology Program
City University of New York Graduate School
33 West 42nd Street
New York City, New York 10036

Charles Holahan
Department of Psychology
University of Texas at Austin
Mezes Hall 330
Austin, Texas 78712

Francine Justa
Environmental Psychology Program
City University of New York Graduate School
33 West 42nd Street
New York City, New York 10036

Marian Beyda Golan
Environmental Psychology Program
City University of New York Graduate School
33 West 42nd Street
New York City, New York 10036